God and Business

Christianity's Case for Capitalism

Robert R. Richards

PRESS

God and Business
by Robert R. Richards

Printed in the United States of America

Library of Congress Control Number: 2002100824
ISBN 1-931232-27-X

Unless otherwise indicated, Bible quotations are taken from the New International Version, copyright © 1984 by the International Bible Society; published by Zondervan Publishing House.

Xulon Press
11350 Random Hills Road
Suite 800
Fairfax, VA 22030
(703) 279-6511
XulonPress.com

To the memory of two great Scotsmen who, separated by two centuries, made enormous contributions to the reformation of religion and economics:

John Knox, disciple of Calvin and Luther, who faithfully, courageously transformed a nation

"I will once again proclaim the gospel from that great church."
"Great God, give me Scotland, or I die."

Adam Smith, the moral philosopher who identified the mechanism for corralling sinful humans

"By pursuing his own interest he... is led by an invisible hand to promote .... [the interest] of the society."

Contents

Foreword

Capitalism, the business enterprise and the marketplace have all received a bad press in recent years.

When is the last time you saw a movie in which a top business executive was portrayed in a positive manner? Have you heard a college professor who is not a member of the business faculty or the president say anything positive about the benefits of private enterprise recently? Has your pastor ever noted the blessings of business in a sermon or explicitly commended business people in the congregation for their faithful service for the Lord in the marketplace?

The popular (mis)conception of business is that of cut-throat competition, the survival of the fittest, a dog-eat-dog world, or the like. Business is obsessed with the pursuit of 'filthy lucre,' the worship of 'Mammon,' the accumulation of wealth for its own sake, with little thought for the common good (not to mention the poor and starving people in the world). Worse, business corporations are seen as the cause of world poverty, the source of ecological degradation, and, in short, most of what is wrong with the world.

The essence of business as portrayed in much of the popular and academic press is characterized by greed, avarice, rapacity, unfair competition, exploitation, economic survival of the fittest, domination of the privileged and powerful over the weak and disadvantaged, self-serving self-interest, selling people what they neither want nor need, pursuit of the proverbial bottom line, whatever the cost. The positive benefits of business, of which all of us are daily recipients, are rarely noted.

In spite of the bad press that capitalism has had, it is a fact that it has been, and continues to be, a great blessing to humankind.

For a start, the economic growth engendered by the capitalist enterprise has created the greatest social benefits in human history. If we take the long view, the life of humankind until very recently has been characterized by poverty. A small handful of families in a variety of societies in the past have possessed the economic wealth at the level that middle class Americans, Europeans, and, increasingly, citizens of some Asian countries take for granted today, but most people have lived lives of grinding poverty. Only within the past two centuries have more than a small percentage of any people experienced economic prosperity in any meaningful sense. Today, while there are still pockets of poverty in even the most highly developed countries, the move is steadily toward affluence and away from famine and hunger, disease and a very low life expectancy, and the subsistence level existence and concern for mere survival that has marked our ancestors.

All of us are dependent, either directly or indirectly, upon the capitalist enterprise for our livelihoods. Of Americans employed today, roughly 80% work in the for-profit business sector. Some 15 percent work for the government, and about 5 percent work in the so-called 'Third (non-profit) Sector' (including the church). It is obvious that the 80% who are employed in the so-called private or business sector are dependent on the market for our daily bread, but the same is true of people who work in government (which is supported by taxation on businesses and individuals) and the non-profit sector (which is largely supported by gifts from businesses and individuals). Those who work in schools, museums, libraries, churches, and soup kitchens are all supported by either taxes upon or the voluntary support of men and women whose wealth is dependent upon the capitalist enterprise. Without the business sector, the wealth dedicated to support the other two sectors would mostly disappear.

The Bible teaches that all are called to be 'ministers' (servants), not in the sense of called to serve the church or the temple but rather to serve the world. Therefore, not merely of necessity but by divine principle, most of us are called to work in business and the professions rather to serve as clergy and religious workers. And yet many believers who work in the economic marketplace tend to feel guilty about spending their days in business. Rather than see business as a calling, they regard it as a necessary evil. If they really had the courage to follow their convictions, they would be following the example of Mother Teresa.

Sir John Templeton, the financier, wanted to be a missionary. He deliberately sought out the company of missionaries. Eventually, he came to the conclusion that he did not have the gifts to be a missionary, but that God had given him different gifts, gifts that have been demonstrated in the world of finance. He would probably have been a failure as a missionary. But as an investor he has been a great success, and hundreds of thousands of people who have invested in the various Templeton funds or who have been touched by the many philanthropies in which he has been engaged have been the beneficiaries of his faithfulness to his true calling.

Each of us has been given different gifts to fulfill our different callings. The real question is: what are my gifts? what has God created me to do? Saint Paul had a sense that he was called from his mother's womb to be a missionary to the Gentiles. The reality of this calling was demonstrated in history. But if God has called us to work in business, we ought not to hanker after something else. Business is as worthy a calling as preaching, social work, healing, teaching, or any of the caring professions.

What is the essence of business? Is it competition? Or perhaps the accumulation of wealth? Some years ago it dawned on me that *cooperation* rather than competition was the essence of the modern business enterprise. It was just after Christmas, and I was in a New York hotel room, sick with the flu. I was amazed as I thought of all the people who had been involved in making it possible for me to have orange juice, aspirin, a warm room, a comfortable bed, and, as I grew healthier, a well balanced meal. Hundreds of people were involved in the process of bringing each of these items to me, some of them thousands of miles away, all of them unknown to me personally, but bringing all of these things to me via the private marketplace.

In his marvelous little book, *Business as Calling* (1996), Michael Novak, winner of the 1994 Templeton Prize for Progress in Religion, suggests that the three cardinal virtues of business are: creativity, community and realism. All three of these virtues can be found in the first three chapters of Genesis, the story of the creation and the fall. Our ancestors, Adam and Eve, were created 'in the image of God' (Gn.1:26): to represent God in the world, to do his work, and to demonstrate his character 'in community.'

Humankind is called to stewardship and cooperation. God is the great Artist. He made the world and saw that it was good. And He has called us to be co-creators with Him, in keeping with the special gifts He has given each one of us. God is also the great Friend. He created humanity for fellowship, for walking and talking in the garden in the cool of the day. We are called, therefore, to community, to cooperation, to friendship. The most successful business people I have known have also been among the most creative people I have known. They have also been great friends. Creativity is essential to entrepreneurship, and friendship is essential to doing business.

The story of the fall in Genesis chapter 3 lays the foundation for the third fundamental to the business enterprise, namely, realism. All humans are sinners! Thus, we do not expect the world of business, any more than the world of the church, to be made up of 'saints' who never make mistakes. Rather, we learn to deal with the world as it is, even though we may be guided by the values of a new world that is coming.

What is the purpose of business? Some would say, quickly, "To make a profit!" Profit is a scorecard to indicate how you're doing and whether you'll be able to stay in business. If you do not create wealth, end up with a surplus, you will not be able to sustain the enterprise. The business will fold. But the purpose of business is not profit. The real purpose of business is *service* (which is another word for ministry). The business of business, as Peter Drucker has often said, is people!

In business, we are called to serve society (by offering a product), to serve workers (by providing a means of livelihood and significance), and to serve God (by fulfilling his creation mandate). We serve God and our fellows by joining hands with one another in the enterprise of business, and the result is we also serve ourselves and our families.

Bob Richards is a man who has spent most of his adult life in the world of business. Early in his career he served as a professor, teaching economics in a highly respected liberal arts college. But he soon sensed a call to banking, and in this vocation achieved a high level of success. A few years ago he was able to step out of the business world and devote himself to studying the faith that he had professed since his youth, in an attempt to bring his experience of faith and life together. This book represents the fruit of this new endeavor.

Having read, debated with its author, and re-read each chapter, I commend this work not only as a helpful discussion that seeks to give both laity and clergy a more positive view of the commonalties of capitalism and Christianity and to dispel the false caricatures of the business enterprise, but, more importantly, as a model of the sort of integration of faith and vocation that every serious man or woman of faith should attempt. Too long have we separated Sunday from Monday, faith from employment in the marketplace, religious and secular professions.

Bob Richards has given us a foundation for thinking about the economic order in the 21st century.

—W. Ward Gasque

Chapter I

Introduction

L et me acknowledge in the very first sentence that the message of Scripture overwhelms the relatively trivial matter of the appropriateness of worldly systems. Throughout the Bible we are called upon to live a life of faith, simply enduring the particular social, political and economic systems. The faith advocated in Scripture does not guarantee a life of satisfaction. It is a "tough faith," a consistent imperative to hang on and trust in God regardless of the social, political or economic environment.

Nevertheless, as a professional economist and a lay Christian, for many years I have been intrigued with the question of the relationship between capitalism and Christianity. To what extent is capitalism in accord or not in accord with Christianity? Further, the Bible is a manual for living in this world. Scripture does not regard faith as passive; rather, it is an active term. God expects us to act in accordance with our faith. What, then, is the relationship between faith-filled action in this world and the economic system of capitalism? I am not alone in posing these questions. Today there is widespread interest in the relationship between economic activity and the Truth of Christianity.

Searching for the answers to these questions, I have devoted the past three years to the study of the Bible and related writings of theologians and have studied under some impressively able and inspiringly faith-filled scholars at Fuller Theological Seminary's facility in Seattle as well as received insightful and loving instruction from my two marvelous pastors at Mercer Island Presbyterian Church, Dale Sewall and Jeff Holland. This book represents the results of my research, analysis and quiet prayerful contemplation toward the end of a reconciliation of capitalism with Christianity.

My first discovery was that there is no explicit Scriptural basis for either the advocation or the condemnation of capitalism nor, for that matter, of any other worldly economic, political or social system. The absence of Scriptural advocations of worldly systems notwithstanding, my systematic study of Christianity has led to the general conclusion that within the doctrines of Christianity a compelling case can be made for capitalism. Further, as I will show later, of the world's two dominant economic systems, capitalism and socialism, only capitalism is in accord with the tenets of Christianity.

Important Distinction

Note that the subtitle of this book is not *Jesus Christ's Case For Capitalism*. Jesus made no such case. Indeed, Jesus' message transcended any social/political/economic agenda. Jesus Christ's message was profoundly simple:

> "You shall love the Lord your God with all your heart, and with all your soul, and with all your mind, and with all your strength." (Mt. 22:37; Mk. 12:30; Lk. 10:26)

> "You shall love your neighbor as yourself." (Mt. 22:39; Mk. 12:31; Lk. 10:27)

Such love as prescribed by God through Jesus can be extended in the context of *any* human system of society, politics or economics. Throughout this book the term "love" is principally used in the same way that the apostle Paul most commonly used it, as *agape*, which according to James R. Edwards, Professor of Religion at Whitworth College, is "love which commits itself to the good of the other regardless of cost to self.... Christian love is shaped neither by the standards of the world nor by the promptings of self, but by the power of the Holy Spirit bearing witness within believers to the character of God."[1] As defined by the *Westminster Dictionary of Theological Terms*, love, *agape* as distinguished from *eros* and *philia*, "is a primary characteristic of God's nature (1 John 4:8,16) and the supreme expression of Christian faith and action. See also Romans 12:9-21, 1 Corinthians 13, Galatians 5:14, Ephesians 5:2 and 1 John 4:7-21."[2]

If humans achieved perfection in extending such love, everything else would take care of itself.

> "all things are possible with God." (Mt. 19:26; Mk. 10:27; Lk. 18:27)

> "Lord, when did we see thee hungry and feed thee, or thirsty and give thee drink...see thee a stranger and welcome thee or naked and clothe thee?.... as you did it to one of the least..., you did it to me...and the righteous will go into eternal life." (Mt. 25:37)

To Jesus worldly, human-created institutions such as governments and commercial enterprises lacked importance. "For whoever would save his life will lose it, and whoever loses his life for my sake will find it. For what does it profit a man, if he gains the whole world and forfeits his life?" (Mt. 16:25-6; Mk. 8:35-7; Lk. 9:24-5, 17:33) "Do not labor for food which perishes, but for the good which endures to eternal life." (Jn. 6:27) No, to Jesus the question of the relative appropriateness of alternative systems of society, politics and economics was irrelevant to the question of one's relationship to God and to others.

As noted by Jaroslav Pelikan, Sterling Professor of History Emeritus at Yale University, "In expounding in his sermons of 1530-32, Luther attacked those 'who have failed to distinguish properly between the secular and the spiritual, between the kingdom of Christ and the kingdom of the world.' Jesus here 'is not tampering with the responsibility and authority of the government, but teaching his individual Christians how to live personally,...' [T]he Christian was not to attempt to use the teachings of Jesus or the laws of the Bible to govern the state.... The Gospels did not, as such, provide any special insight into the specifics of what it meant to rule justly. Therefore, politically involved though he and his

Reformation undoubtedly were, Luther did not evolve a 'Christian politics,' for that was not why Jesus Christ had come to earth."[3] And I humbly add, neither did Jesus infer any sort of "Christian economics."

Lord Brian Griffiths, former Dean, City University Business School in London, director of the Bank of England, and economic adviser to Prime Minister Margaret Thatcher, explains, "In this teaching [on wealth] Jesus was concerned with enunciating principles, not policies. He was not concerned directly with the creation of wealth or the removal of poverty. He did not examine in any detail the causes of either wealth or poverty..... He did not explore at all the relationships which might have existed between the inequality of wealth and poverty..., and it is significant that he did not.... [B]ecause of the nature of the Kingdom he had come to establish, it is inconceivable that he would have concerned himself with issues such as these."[4]

Similarly, the early followers of Jesus did not advocate any particular agenda regarding the social, political or economic order in which they lived. In fact, they seemed to exhibit a strong disposition toward maintaining the status quo. Many practices which today are regarded as abhorrent—slavery, dictatorship, subordination of women—were condoned. While Nero viciously tortures, Peter exhorts us to "Submit yourselves...to every authority instituted among men;..." (1 Pt. 2:13) And later, in the same letter, "Slaves, submit yourselves to your masters with all respect....Wives, in the same way be submissive to your husbands,..." (1 Pt. 2:18; 3:1) Jesus and Paul issued similar directives on many occasions. Also, reverse exhortations were made: masters to be compassionate to slaves, husbands to be loving toward wives and rulers to be just, fair and generous to subjects.

Each and every one of us, regardless of our station, is to express love in all directions. Clearly, in the early church order, peace and stability were matters of high priority. Because the message of Christianity transcends the social, political and economic order, it is understandable that the early church was not more outspoken and a leader in social, political or economic reform. The Head of the Church was not. His agenda transcended such issues. His agenda was considerably more revolutionary.

Faith demonstrated through love is the message of Christianity.

Human systems are subordinate. L. Ann Jervis, Associate Professor of New Testament at Wycliffe College, makes this point eloquently in her commentary on Galatians, "Further, spending time studying Paul is a summons to be less attuned to the pressures and pleasures of our social context and more aware of the presence of Christ in our midst. Paul's attempt to put into words the fundamental importance of the profound and all-encompassing knowledge of being 'in Christ' speaks to the possibility of living by faith, not achievement, in our time. Paul invites us to be molded not by inner needs or external circumstances, but to know freedom—the freedom of being 'in Christ."[5] Nevertheless, Professor Ward Gasque, Biblical scholar widely recognized as an expert on the apostle Paul, expands, "While Paul was not concerned with the direct transformation of society, he was concerned with the transformation of values which eventually would lead to the transformation of society."[6] For example, Constantine eventually outlawed the branding of slaves on the basis that they too were made in the image and likeness of God. Indeed, the teachings, practices and challenges of Jesus Christ, his disciples and the Christian church have sewn the seeds of social, political and economic change. Danker in his commentary on Luke states it more strongly, "Luke presupposes for Christian existence a revolution of the mind that prepares one to be a catalyst for change in the creative enterprise of exploring the needs of one's fellow human beings.... Jesus as the Son of God... refused to bow down before the alter of status quo. He found his own ethical unity in obedience to his heavenly Parent's purpose, defined as creative awareness and response to the possibilities of mercy."[7]

Nevertheless, its title notwithstanding, this book does not pretend to relate a human system such as economics to salvation. Indeed, to imply that somehow a "noble" or "righteous" economic system is a vehicle to attain salvation is presumptuous and reflects a misunderstanding of humanity's relationship with God. As Martin Luther, who discovered Paul's declaration, "For in the gospel a righteousness from God is revealed, a righteousness that is by faith from first to last, just as it is written: 'The righteous will live by faith." (Rom. 1:17), in turn pronounced to us, salvation does not come about by good works; salvation comes only from God's grace. And when humans achieve righteousness, possess the faith that translates into complete obedience of and trust in God, the particular economic system in place will be immaterial. One of the conditions that gives rise to this book is that humans have not yet achieved righteousness. The utopians do not understand this. Ronald Nash, professor of philosophy and religion at Western Kentucky University, with a solid understanding of economics, instructs, "No economic system or political system that assumes the essential goodness of human nature or holds out the dream of a perfect earthly society can possibly be consistent with the Biblical world view."[8] Similarly, F.F. Bruce warns, "When the Christian message is so thoroughly accommodated to the prevalent climate of opinion that it becomes one more expression of that climate of opinion, it is no longer the Christian message. The Christian message must address itself in judgement and mercy to the prevalent climate of opinion, and can do so only when it is distinct from it."[9]

In summary, the question being explored here is not, are there various economics imperatives in Scripture? There are not, although there certainly are values and principles put forth which have significant implications regarding economic systems. Jesus Christ makes no case for capitalism; the early Christians make no case for capitalism. Indeed, nowhere in the Bible is the case made for capitalism. The Oxford Declaration, the consensus report of the Conference on Christian Faith and Economics, Oxford, England, January 4-9, 1990 attended by over one hundred theologians and economists, affirms, "We recognize that no particular economic system is directly prescribed by Scripture."[10] Nash puts it this way, "There is no such thing as revealed economics."[11] Nash adds, "The gospel message must not be subordinated to a political agenda."[12] Nash then offers an example of proper exegesis, using Luke 4:16-19, "Jesus… read from Isaiah 61:1,2—'The Spirit of the Lord is on me, because he has anointed me to preach good news to the poor. He has sent me to proclaim freedom for the prisoners and recovery of sight for the blind, to release the oppressed, to proclaim the year of the Lord's favor.' But,… the poverty … is *spiritual* poverty. Every member of the human race is poor in the sense of being spiritually bankrupt. None of us has any righteousness of our own. All of us are too blind spiritually to see the nature of our problem or the way of deliverance. All of us are oppressed by the chains of sin. Jesus came to deliver us from the power and penalty of sin. He came to give us spiritual sight and to end our spiritual poverty by making available the righteousness that God demands and that only God can provide…. Jesus' basic message dealt with such things as human sin and independence from God, the human need for deliverance from sin, and the establishment of his Father's Kingdom. It was not a blueprint for changing society economically or politically."[13]

Clearly, I reject the illusions of liberation theology and its false notion of an earthly kingdom. The title of this book refers to the case that I, the author, am making for capitalism in the context of my understanding of Christian tenets. That is, this book explores the question: given Christianity, to what extent is capitalism in accord with its tenets, compatible with its attitude and behavior principles, and conducive to the unfolding of a future which Christianity desires for humanity?

What this book is not

It is important to keep in mind while reading this book that there are two things that it is *not*. It is not primarily a comparative analysis of capitalism with other economic systems, nor is it an historical account of the development of capitalism.

First, this book is not principally a comparative analysis. While considerable comparative material is presented, its primary purpose is to emphasize a point being made about capitalism. I am not endeavoring to prove that capitalism is the only economic system that is compatible with Christianity. A testimony to Christianity's divine nature is its having flourished in the context of the full array of political, social and economic systems. I am not in any way suggesting that Christianity needs capitalism—nor any human system. Christianity has God. As English historian Edward Gibbon observes, "the triumph of Christianity…was owing to the convincing evidence of the doctrine itself, and to the ruling providence of its great Author."[14] Further, neither directly, nor indirectly by inference, am I suggesting that Christianity is the religious system that is most compatible with capitalism. Judaism, for example, has proven to be a religious system that is conducive to capitalism, and it could very well be that other religions could be equal or superior to Christianity in terms of a satisfactory religious environment for capitalism. I have arbitrarily limited my discussion to the relationship of economics to Christianity, simply because I am a Christian and this is the subject that interests me. I in no way want to imply that the observations and conclusions that follow apply solely to Christianity. Indeed, they could very well apply to many religions and, in fact, could very well apply more so to other religions than to Christianity. Furthermore, I am not asserting that Christianity does not have a case for economic systems other than capitalism. It may very well have; however, as will be shown, Christianity presents a much better case for capitalism than for socialism. I am simply saying that Christianity (though not necessarily exclusively among religions) has an immense case to be made for capitalism (though not necessarily exclusively among economic systems).

Second, this book is not an *historical* account of the relationship of Christianity to its various economic contexts over the past two thousand years. Such a subject of the relationship of the development of the church to the various economies in which it has existed is a fascinating subject which has been addressed by myriad theologians and scholars (Aquinas, Luther, Calvin, Niebuhr, Weber, Tawney.....to name just a few). While the historical development of capitalism is interesting, this book nevertheless limits its scope to the *current* relationship between Christianity and capitalism. It is strictly a *contemporary,* rather than an historical, analysis. This is a critically important point to keep in mind while reading this book. We are talking about capitalism and capitalists *today.* Equating business people today with some of those at the time of Scripture and their attendant greed and oppression is akin to equating today's clergy with some of the priests at the time of Scripture and their attendant hypocrisy and false prophesy. Indeed, today's professional business practitioners are as different from those in Biblical times as today's clergy are from their Old and New Testament predecessors. Further, if one is going to throw out capitalism on the basis of the abominable pollution and working conditions of the Industrial Revolution, then one must throw out Christianity on the basis of the horrible persecution and wars of the Middle Ages. In this book we are talking about contemporary capitalism and Christianity.

Contemporary capitalism is an economic system wherein the means of production and distribution are privately owned and operated for profit in the context of a free market limited by statutes and regulations adopted through a political democracy. That is, the economic system considered in this analysis is referred to by some as "modified capitalism" or "democratic capitalism." Capitalism, as used in this discussion, does not assume laissez faire; i.e. unfettered behavior. Rather, it assumes a free market with competitive alternatives operating within regulations adopted by a democratic political system. This should be clearly understood, and therefore I elaborate with a quotation from Michael Novak, Resident Scholar in Philosophy, Religion and Public Policy at the American Enterprise Institute in Washington, D.C., "Oddly, many scholars have missed the fact that capitalism… is embedded in a pluralistic structure in which it is designed to be checked by a political system and a moral-cultural system…. Democratic capitalism is not a 'free enterprise system' alone."[15] That is, in this book "capitalism" refers to Novak's tripartite system: (1) private enterprise / market economy, (2) democracy / limited government regulation and (3) Judeo-Christian cultural values. This political environment of capitalism is further enunciated by Fareed Zakaria, managing editor of Foreign Affairs and fellow at the Hoover Institution at Stanford University, "The United States, the world's greatest democracy, has always kept its own popular pressures on a leash. Its court system is free from public oversight, its Bill of Rights is designed to thwart majority rule, and its regulatory apparatus keeps tabs on rogue traders and large corporations. Indeed, one could argue that the American way is so successful because both capitalism and democracy are tightly regulated by the rule of law."[16] In addition to its role as a regulator, the government plays other important roles in capitalism; for example, as a participant, buying and selling goods and services, and, perhaps most noteworthy, as an implementer of monetary and fiscal policy, affecting aggregate performance of the economy. To paraphrase Novak, *capitalism* as used in this book implies private enterprise operating in a free market within a democratic political system, a respected legal system, and a moral ethical system. Further implied is significant regulation of the private sector by the government to prevent abuses and to protect the benefits of a free market as well as meaningful transfer payments by government to provide a certain level of social welfare. To enable the reader to visualize the economic system being addressed here, I am discussing capitalism as it exists today in the United States, within that country's constitutional and legal framework and with all of the attendant political and cultural characteristics. Often, such a political / economic / cultural system and values have been defined as a *mixed economy*. This is the way in which I am using the term *capitalism* in this book.

Methodology

This book is a highly personal document; it is my own prayerful interpretation and application of economics to Scripture. It presents my understanding of Christianity's case for capitalism, realizing that I, and all humans, bring to any subject a set of predispositions. Accordingly, the exercise of writing this book involved prayer as much as research—prayer that I might be unshackled from preconceptions and therefore open to seek, recognize and embrace the Truth.

The translation of the Bible which I have used is the New International Version. All Scripture quotations are taken from *The Holy Bible, New International Version* (North American Edition), copyright 1984 by the International Bible Society; published by Zondervan Publishing House, Grand Rapids, Michigan. I accept the theological tenet of Christianity that the Bible is holy scripture, "the self-revelation of God wherein the biblical writers and editors communicate what God wished to communicate."[17] Further, I regard the Bible as a theological etiological document, rather than an historical discourse. Theology, rather than chronology, is the sole perspective with which the Bible has been used for this treatise. Finally, I regard the Bible as a manual for living one's life, related to both spiritual and physical realms.

Understanding and interpreting the Bible is an extremely difficult—and precarious—exercise. When one commences a thoughtful study of the Bible, utilizing scholarly reference works, one becomes dramatically aware of the multitude of differences in interpretation of Scripture among theologians and Biblical scholars. Virtually every verse in the Bible has been the subject of substantial interpretation debate, reflecting considerable disagreement among equally highly reputed scholars.

A major obstacle to accurate Biblical interpretation for this particular book related to economics is that the economic, political and social systems and structures of Biblical times were entirely different than those of today. Accordingly, one must not fall into the trap of assuming the social, political, or economic structural frameworks and institutions of Scripture in one's contemporary analysis. For example, oppression of the poor—an economic issue given immense attention by Scripture—was manifest in many ways including selling into slavery, onerous taxation, land expropriation, etc., none of which occur in the same way today. The major recipients of lashing criticism by the prophets in the Old Testament and by Jesus and his disciples in the New Testament are (1) priests and other religious leaders for their hypocrisy and (2) political and military leaders for their greed and lust for power. At the time of Jesus the political and economic systems were intertwined, with most people working on the land controlled by the political leaders. The economies throughout the periods covered by the Bible were principally agrarian. The peasant masses served virtually as indentured servants to the landowning aristocracies, who with military and political leaders made up a tiny elite. There was no broad middle class. A client-patron system existed embodying all sorts of relationships with implications for debtors and creditors, servants and masters, buyers and sellers, etc. Numerous tomes have been written on the various economies and societies as well as political structures and practices existing throughout the various epochs of the Bible. Suffice it to note here that those structures, conditions, practices, relationships, assumptions, mores, morals and even terminology are so dramatically different than those of today, that interpreting various passages of the Bible and applying the Biblical message to economic matters today is, at best, difficult and, at worst, dangerous.

Further adding to the difficulty of interpreting Scripture in the context of economic issues is the use of the same terms to refer sometimes to material concepts and conditions and sometimes to spiritual concepts and conditions. Often in Jesus' teaching and throughout the Old and New Testaments, the reference to being poor refers to a state of *spiritual* poverty. Accordingly, care must be taken not to impute in all such references that Jesus was necessarily addressing material poverty. Jesus clearly asserts that true riches are spiritual riches and the poverty with which He is principally concerned is spiritual poverty. Similarly, as noted by Holland, "the epistles of Paul most often are addressing spiritual rather than secular matters, as Paul was seeking to create a whole new culture based on a new understanding of life."[18] Further complicating interpretation, Bruce points out, "Paul's letters are all 'occasional' documents in the sense that each of them was addressed to a particular situation. None of them was written primarily as a systematic exposition of doctrine...."[19]

To endeavor avoiding misinterpretation and misapplication of the Bible, I have identified and considered the major, universal points being made rather than fall into the trap of latching onto specific passages that relate to my interest. It is the eternal truths of Scripture, not the historical conditions and relationships, which must be applied to current and future economic, political and social issues. That is what I have given attention to in this book. As a second guard against misinterpretation and misapplication, the *entire* Bible must be included in one's study. The Bible, a divinely inspired document revealed by God, is intended to be considered in its entirety. Indeed, the two testaments and each book and each verse relates to all of the others, and understanding one requires understanding the other. I have attempted to follow the lead of Jack L. Stotts, President, Austin Presbyterian Theological Seminary, "to write more in terms of biblical understandings, biblical themes, and biblical perspectives, more than being engaged with specific passages."[20]

While many passages of Scripture are cited in this book, I have endeavored to avoid "proof-texting," the practice of claiming validity or truthfulness of a particular assertion or idea merely by an apparent agreement with it by a passage quoted from Scripture, often lifted from its Biblical context. All types of evil human activity have been justified by ignorant or perverted "proof-texting." Nevertheless, a considerable number of passages are cited to identify the origination of or exemplify a particular point being made. Indeed, Jesus and Paul were frequent quoters of the Old Testament. How often do we read in the Gospels, "It is said...." or "to fulfill what had been spoken...?" Regarding Paul's use of over ninety quotations, Biblical scholars William LaSor, David Hubbard and Frederic Bush note, "Both his dominant theological themes and his means of argument are drawn from the Jewish Scriptures. Paul bowed to the authority of Scripture; he used it to clinch his cases. He respected its verdicts; he revered its holiness."[21]

Additionally, the *order* of analysis is of critical importance. I have endeavored to refrain from applying Scripture to my understanding of economics but, rather, first to study Scripture openly, prayerfully and receptively and, then, second, to rethink my understanding of economics. As indicated previously, I understand clearly that God's message, as revealed in Scripture and as enunciated by Jesus Christ, transcends economics (and all worldly social and political systems). It is not the responsibility of Scripture to fit one's view of economics; it is the responsibility of one's view of economics to fit Scripture.

I have been guided in my own interpretation by the six steps of the contextualization process outlined in the *Dictionary of Paul and His Letters* which are intended to help overcome the distance problem, the historical-cultural gap between the biblical world and contemporary society. "First, determine the surface message via historical-grammatical exegesis.... Second, study the underlying theological... message via... theological exegesis.... Third, ... study the situation (giving rise to the points in the text).... Fourth, seek the parallel situation in the modern world.... Finally,... decide whether to contextualize the passage generally at the level of principle or specifically."[22] It is interesting to note that this contextualization dilemma existed from the very beginning of the church. "Paul consciously contextualized the Jewish-Christian gospel of the primitive church for his Gentile mission.... The gospel content was inviolate, but the form that it took in Gentile circles varied."[23]

One could spend a lifetime only researching, becoming increasingly confused and distraught, never coming to a conclusion regarding the message of the Bible. Eventually, the responsible Christian who intends to apply Scripture to one's life and analysis of the human condition must at least periodically adjourn from the research and draw some conclusions. In the context of broad scholarly disagreement one can only humbly and hopefully apply one's own personal prayerful and thoughtful exegesis in the best way one can. Indeed, I have heeded the kind, loving constant warning of Ward Gasque to avoid being a manifestation of the old, well-known lament of Biblical scholars,

Wonderful things in the Bible I see.
Some put there by God; some, by me.

In this process I endeavored to take to heart the instruction of Bruce Milne, pastor of the First Baptist Church in Vancouver, Canada, "God makes his truth available only to the humble. As we come in utter dependence, acknowledging our sinful ignorance and blindness and our constant need of His divine illumination, He stoops to us in grace and grants us again the gift of his truth."[24]

This book reflects my own personal exploration through Scripture with an eye toward the relationship between Christianity and capitalism. In the interest of conciseness, quotations from Scripture in this book are brief and, of course, lifted from their contexts. Hopefully, however, the analyses of such passages were sufficiently made within the context of total Scripture as I have endeavored conscientiously to seek the Truth.

Nevertheless, throughout this book you will find yourself immersed in innumerable quotations from the Bible. While this may slow the pace of your reading, I purposefully have included all of the relevant passages in order that you may experience as closely as possible my measured walk through Scripture. I considered using just a few, representative passages, but that would have diminished the experience for you. Only through a total immersion into Scripture can one commence to comprehend and internalize God's Truth. Join me, then, in my three-year walk through Scripture, searching for, then discovering, the answer to the question of the relationship between capitalism and Christianity.

The approach which I have taken can be summarized in the following diagram.

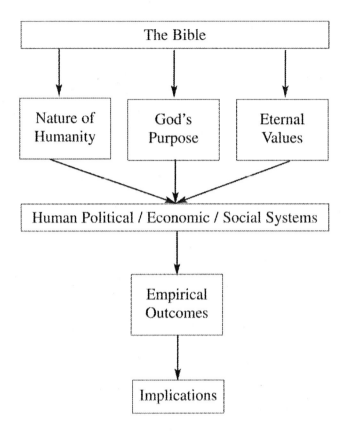

A prayerful study of Scripture will lead to insights regarding (1) *the dual nature of humanity*: a creation of God and a sinner, (2) *God's purposes* such as love, generosity, stewardship, calling and peace as reflected in the four dimensions of worldly possessions and wealth: their source, legitimacy, role and attitudes toward, and (3) *eternal values and principles* such as faith, justice, liberty and trust. These three elements in turn suggest the appropriateness of alternative human systems, which then can be evaluated in terms of their empirical outcomes. Finally, all of this has profound implications for us humans functioning within and influencing the structure of these systems.

Chapters two and three of this book deal with the nature of humanity and the implications for economic systems, particularly capitalism. Chapters four through seven deal with God's purposes, discussing the source, legitimacy, attitudes toward and role of material possessions and wealth, focusing on stewardship, work, calling, generosity, and attitudes which impede and those which coincide with God's purposes. Capitalism is further evaluated in this context. Chapters eight and nine deal with eternal values such as love, faith, hope, egalitarianism, trust, and liberty and their relationship to capitalism. Chapters ten through twelve deal with the empirical outcomes of capitalism in the context of Christianity. Chapter thirteen deals with the implications for two groups: capitalists and clergy. Chapter fourteen attempts to reconcile the entire discussion, relating capitalism back to the message of Scripture. In summary, this book explores the question: given Christianity, to what extent is capitalism in accord with its tenets, compatible with its attitude and behavior principles, and conducive to the unfolding of a future which Christianity desires for humanity?

Finally, however, all of the foregoing notwithstanding, I acknowledge the lesson of Job and agree with the respected theologian Shirley Guthrie, Professor of Systematic Theology at Columbia Theological Seminary, that "we never 'arrive' in our understanding of the depths of the truth of God."[25] A full understanding of *any* matter related to God will not be ours until we find it in heaven.

Chapter II

God's Creations

"In the beginning God" (Gn. 1:1)

In the very first sentence of the Bible we are presented with truth that has profound implications for economic systems. Every assertion in this entire book rests on the acceptance of God as the Supreme Being, the divine ultimate sovereign over all matter, the Alpha and Omega, omnipotent, omniscient, omnipresent, eternal, holy, infinite, life, love, intelligence, truth, perfection, who always was, is, and always will be—to name just a few of God's characteristics which are beyond my capability and that of any mortal to fully know and understand.

Moses tried, "Before the mountains were born or you brought forth the earth and the world, from everlasting to everlasting you are God." (Ps. 90:2) Isaiah declared, "This is what the LORD says:.... 'I am the first and I am the last; apart from me there is no God." (Is. 44:6) and "I am God, and there is no other; I am God, and there is none like me." (Is. 46:9) and "I am the first and I am the last." (Is. 48:12)

My favorite enunciation of God's nature in Scripture is Hannah's prayer, "There is no one holy like the LORD; there is no one besides you; there is no Rock like our God.... For the foundations of the earth are the LORD's; upon them he has set the world." (1 Sm. 2:2,8)

And God's eternal nature is reflected in Jesus' beautiful prayer, "And now, Father, glorify me in your presence with the glory I had with you before the world began…. the glory you have given me because you loved me before the creation of the world." (Jn. 17:5,24)

And from the Scots Confession, "We confess and acknowledge one God alone,… eternal, infinite, immeasurable, incomprehensible, omnipotent, invisible; one in substance and yet distinct in three persons: the Father, the Son, and the Holy Ghost. By whom we confess and believe all things in heaven and earth, visible and invisible, to have been created, to be retained in their being, and to be ruled and guided by his inscrutable providence for such end as his eternal wisdom, goodness, and justice have appointed, and to the manifestation of his own glory."[26]

THE NATURE OF THE MATERIAL WORLD

God as the creator of the material world is affirmed throughout Scripture.

Old Testament

"In the beginning God created the heavens…earth… light,…water,…sky,…land,…vegetation,… stars,… animals (in the sky, sea and on land),…day,… night,…seasons." (Gn. 1:1-25)

"Thus the heavens and earth were completed in all their vast array." (Gn. 2:1)

All matter is created by God. God is the source of everything. God is the source of the very concept of a universe. The divine nature of creation is further illumined by use of the Hebrew word, *bara,* in Genesis. Elsewhere in the Bible another Hebrew word is used for the verb, *create* applied generally, e.g., an artisan creating a work of art. LaSor explains, "This word (*bara*) is a key word,… This word has God as its only subject in the Old Testament, and no mention is made of the material out of which an object is created. It describes a way of acting that has no human analogy. Only God creates,…."[27] Finally, the momentous nature of the creation act by God is revealed in God's declaring a command, "Let there be…"

Creation is not simply an interesting story told in the third person; God speaks, declares, commands to bring things into being.

God reaffirms God as the creator with the rhetorical question posed to Job: "Where were you when I laid the earth's foundation?" (Jb. 38:4)

How God created matter, how long it took, the continuing process of creation, and other such questions are irrelevant to this discussion. While these are fascinating questions, answering them is not necessary to proceeding with the subject of this book. (In the context of the foregoing notions of God and the essence of life and the essence of matter, the "Darwin debate" is nonsensical. "Evolution" is simply the word that describes the God-directed process of adaptation by the species. "Evolution" is another term for "re-creation." Creation is an on-going process. God was the Creator, is the Creator and will be the Creator. Accordingly, God is responsible for evolution. Additionally, the current alleged science/religion schism is senseless. Indeed, the mathematical elegance of matter and motion is a manifestation of Intelligent Design and testimony to the perfection of God's creation! As Thomas Mann, Minister of the Parkway United Church of Christ in Winston-Salem, North Carolina, who has taught at Converse College and Princeton Theological Seminary, observes in his book, *The Book of the Torah*, "The orderly structure of *his* work reflects the orderly design of the cosmos: every part of the world appears before us in perfect balance and symmetry, majestic and wondrous."[28] Further, Guthrie notes, "The Christian doctrine of creation and the scientific description of the origin of the world answer different kinds of questions. They are not alternative truths, but different kinds of truth."[29] Finally, the reader is directed to the 1998 encyclical of John Paul II, *Faith and Reason*.)

Because of the sovereign nature of God, creation was a voluntary act. God did it because God wanted to do it. God also did it with care and protectiveness: "...the Spirit of God was hovering over..." (Gn. 1:2) Further, because of the nature of God, it can be assumed that God did it lovingly. This leads us to the next declaration of Scripture:

"And God saw that it was good." (Gn. 1:4,10,12,18,21,25)
"God saw all that he had made, and it was very good." (Gn. 1:31)

God—the definition of goodness—makes this observation of the goodness of His creation seven times, each in the context of relating His different types of creations. Indeed, all matter, *everything* is intrinsically good. Everything has a role within God's overall purpose. Accordingly, therefore, the notion held by some that matter and materiality—the physical realm—is intrinsically bad is not correct. It flies in the face of God's own declaration. Material—physicality—is good. It is *materialism*—the idolatry of material—which is bad. We will return to that later.

Of course nowhere in the Bible are thoughts more beautifully expressed than in the Psalms, and in them many references are made to God as Creator of all. "O LORD,...your heavens, the work of your fingers, the moon and the stars, which you have set in place,..." (Ps. 8:1-3) "The heavens declare the glory of God; the skies proclaim the work of his hands." (Ps. 19:1) "By the word of the LORD were the heavens made,... Let all the earth fear the LORD;... For he spoke, and it came to be; he commanded, and it stood firm." (Ps. 33:6-9) "The heavens are yours, and yours also the earth; you founded the world and all that is in it." (Ps. 89:11) "Your hands made me and formed me;... you established the earth and it endures." (Ps. 119:73,90) "My help comes from the LORD, the Maker of heaven and earth." (Ps. 121:2) "Give thanks to the LORD, ...who by his understanding made the heavens, who spread out the earth upon the waters, who made the great lights—the sun to govern the day, the moon and stars to govern the night:..." (Ps. 136:1-9) "... the LORD his God, the Maker of heaven and earth, the sea, and everything in them" (Ps. 146:5,6) "Let them praise the name of the LORD, for he commanded and they were created." (Ps. 148:5)

The entire Psalm 104 is a beautiful declaration of God as creator and description of the nature of God's creations. I call it "The Economist's Psalm" because it eloquently relates some of God's creations to their economic meaning. The magnificence of this Psalm must be experienced in its entirety, so I have included it as Appendix A, although here I will state one verse, "How many are your works, O LORD! In wisdom you made them all; the earth is full of your creatures." (Ps. 104:24)

The wise King Solomon, son of King David, notes that wisdom was present at the creation and, therefore, wisdom is part of the nature of the Creator, God. "By wisdom the LORD laid the earth's foundations, by understanding he set the heavens in place: by his knowledge the deeps were divided, and the clouds let drop the dew." (Prv. 3:19,20) "The LORD brought me [wisdom] forth as the first of his works, before his deeds of old; I was appointed from eternity, from the beginning, before the world began...., I was given birth, before he made the earth..... I was there when he set the heavens in place, when he marked out the horizon...., when he established the clouds above.... when he gave the sea its boundary...., and when he marked out the foundations of the earth.... I was filled with delight...., rejoicing in his whole world." (Prv. 8:22-31) Note that in the first verse above cited from Proverbs reference is made to both earth and heavens about which Roland Murphy, Carmelite priest and former professor at Duke University, observes in his commentary, "Earth and heavens are a merismus, or two representative components, standing for the totality of the world."[30] This "oneness" of heaven and earth is an important concept which relates to the goodness conveyed on matter by God and which emerges later in the discussion of the legitimacy of the material realm.

Hezekiah prays, "O LORD, God of Israel,... You have made heaven and earth." (2 Kgs. 19:15) Jonah declares, "I worship the LORD, the God of heaven, who made the sea and the land." (Jon. 1:9) Isaiah tells us, "This is what the LORD says: 'Heaven is my throne, and the earth is my footstool.... Has not my hand made all these things, and so they came into being?" (Is. 66:1) The basic goodness of matter is implied in Isaiah's exclamation, "Holy, holy, holy is the LORD Almighty: the whole earth is full of his glory." (Is.6:3) "To whom will you compare me? Or who is my equal?' says the Holy One. Lift your eyes and look to the heavens: Who created these?" (Is. 40:25,26) "This is what God the LORD says—he who created the heavens... who spread out the earth and all that comes out of it, who gives breath to its people, and life to those who walk on it: 'I, the LORD, have called you in righteousness; I will take hold of your hand." (Is. 42:5,6) The foregoing verse suggests that God not only created matter and humans, but he also guides us. We will return to this later. "It is I who made the earth and created mankind upon it.... For this is what the LORD says—he who created the heavens, he is God; he who fashioned and made the earth, he founded it" (Is. 45:12,18) "I who set the heavens in place and laid the foundations of the earth." (Is. 51:16) Jeremiah proclaims the same creation message, "This is what the LORD God almighty, the God of Israel, says:…'I made the earth and its people and the animals that are on it, and I give it to anyone I please." (Jer. 27:5) "This is what the LORD says, he who made the earth, the LORD who formed it and established it." (Jer. 33:2) He made the earth by his power; he founded the world by his wisdom and stretched out the heavens by his understanding." (Jer. 51:15) Finally, the postexilic prophet Zechariah, "The LORD, who stretches out the heavens, who lays the foundation of the earth, and who forms the spirit of man within him." (Zec. 12:1)

New Testament

God as the Creator of matter and the intrinsic goodness of matter are reaffirmed in the New Testament.

The apostle John states, "In the beginning was the Word, and the Word was with God, and the Word was God…. Through him all things were made;…" (Jn. 1:1) Upon their release from prison, Peter and John along with the other believers reaffirm God's sovereignty, "Sovereign Lord,… you made the heaven and the earth and the sea, and everything in them." (Acts 4:24)

Paul declares, "… the living God, who made heaven and earth and sea and everything in them." (Acts 14:15) "The God who made the world and everything in it is the Lord of heaven and earth." (Acts 17:24) "The earth is the Lord's, and everything in it." (1 Cor. 10:26) "He [Christ] is the image of the invisible God,…. For by him all things were created: things in heaven and things on earth, visible and invisible,…and in him all things hold together." (Col. 1:15-17) "For everything God created is good,…" (1 Tm. 4:4) And the book of Hebrews asserts "…God is the builder of everything" (Heb. 3:4) and "By faith we understand that the universe was formed at God's command, so that what is seen was not made out of what was visible." (Heb. 11:3) "…by God's word the heavens existed and the earth was formed…." (2 Pt. 3:5) From Paul's utterances we learn, according to biblical scholar David Williams, "The world was not a thing of chance, but the work of God….God is not detached from the creation…. God is greater than the creation."[31]

Finally, we discover in Revelation that not only does the Bible commence with the material realm—its creation and the goodness thereof—it ends with the material realm. "You are worthy, our Lord and God, to receive glory and honor and power, for you created all things, and by your will they were created and have their being." (Rev. 4:11) "Fear God and give him glory,....Worship him who made the heavens, the earth, the sea and the springs of water." (Rev. 14:7) Indeed, physicality is quite relevant to the whole Bible's story of alienation and restoration. "Then I saw a new heaven and a new earth,... 'Now the dwelling of God is with men,'..." (Rev 21:1,3)

Conclusion

God as the creator of all is reaffirmed in the Apostles' Creed, the Nicene Creed, and in various denominational confessions. Creation and the nature of matter have been effectively summarized by Dr. Bryan Burton, senior pastor of John Knox Presbyterian Church in the Seattle area, "God has created, continues to create and will continue to create. God creates the universe by an act of freedom (not obligation) as a sovereign God.... an act of love (agape) as a loving God....God creates the universe out of *nothing*...God is distinct but not separate from creation....God relates to both the spiritual and physical realities of creation....God is the LORD over creation, yet provides for human stewardship within creation. Because God created the creation, the GOODNESS of creation is understood and appreciated."[32]

Matter is intrinsically good—declared so by God. Matter is purposeful—not just passively allowed to come into existence, but commanded into existence by its Creator. Milne sums up in the following manner. "The world is not to be denied. It is God's world, having come from him.... 'God likes matter; he invented it' (C.S. Lewis). The world is not to be idolized. It has come from God but it is not itself God."[33]

Further, Christian doctrine holds that creation was not a one-time thing; it is an on-going process. Guthrie observes, "The Bible says not only that God *was* but that God *is* and *will be* the Creator.... God is *continuously* making new beginnings, opening up new possibilities, initiating new events."[34] Note the passage quoted previously from the hymn in Paul's epistle, "in him all things hold together." (Col. 1:17) gives rise to the notion that there is a structure and a logic and a system to the universe and to all materiality.

Arthur Patzia, Fuller Theological Seminary scholar, interprets this passage as, "Thus the Lord who creates the universe also sustains it."[35] Pelikan expands, "The concept of harmony in the universe expressed in the Greek word *systema* also hovered over one of the most powerful of the New Testament statements about the Cosmic Christ..... Because the Logos incarnate in Jesus was the Reason of God, it was also possible to see the Logos as the very *Structure of the universe....*"[36] We will return later to this concept of structure, order and re-creation.

Clearly, then, Scripture is dealing, not with some supernatural or exclusively spiritual realm, but indeed, with the material realm. Further, its Creator declares the material realm as intrinsically good. Accordingly, therefore, economics, the discipline which deals with the functioning of the material realm—resource management and allocation—is dealing with goodness.

THE NATURE OF HUMANITY

A study of Scripture leads to the discovery that humanity has two essential characteristics. We are created in the image of God, and we are sinners. Both of these characteristics have important implications for the appropriateness of economic systems.

Humans as Creations of God

Old Testament

"Then God said, 'Let us make man in our image, in our likeness, and let them rule over the fish of the sea and the birds of the air, over the livestock, over all the earth, and over all the creatures that move along the ground.'

"So God created man in his own image,
in the image of God he created him;
male and female he created them.

"God blessed them and said to them, 'Be fruitful and increase in number; fill the earth and subdue it. Rule over the fish of the sea and the birds of the air and over every living creature that moves on the ground.' Then God said, 'I give you every seed-bearing plant on the face of the whole earth and every tree that has fruit with seed in it. They will be yours for food. And to all the beasts of the earth and all the birds of the air and all the creatures that move on the ground—everything that has the breath of life in it—I give every green plant for food.' And it was so." (Gn. 1:26-30)

Creation and the nature of humanity is related again in the second chapter of Genesis. "...the LORD God formed the man...and breathed into his nostrils the breath of life, and the man became a living being....The LORD God took the man and put him in the Garden of Eden to work it and take care of it....Now The LORD God had formed out of the ground all the beasts of the field and all the birds of the air. He brought them to the man to see what he would name them;...." (Gn. 2:7,15,19)

God's creation of humanity is affirmed a third time in Genesis: "When God created man, he made him in the likeness of God. He created them male and female and blessed them." (Gn. 5:1,2)

That humans are creations of God is further affirmed in Exodus. "The LORD said to him, 'Who gave man his mouth? Who made him deaf or mute? Who gives him sight or makes him blind? Is it not I,...? Now go, I will help you speak and will teach you what to say." (Ex. 4:11,12) God's creation of all is further mentioned in the Ten Commandments, "...the LORD made the heavens and the earth, the sea, and all that is in them,..." (Ex 20:11)

This also is proclaimed by a psalmist, "Know that the LORD is God. It is he who made us, and we are his;..." (Ps. 100:3) and by the prophet Isaiah, "Yet, O LORD, you are our Father. We are the clay, you are the potter; we are all the work of your hand." (Is. 64:8) "the people I formed for myself that they may proclaim my praise." (Is. 43:21)

When commencing to relate economic systems to Christianity four extremely important characteristics of humans are observed in the very first two chapters of Scripture.

First, God created humans in His image and likeness. While this does not mean that God duplicated Himself, it does mean that humans are a reflection of God. Pamela Scalise, Professor of Old Testament, Fuller Theological Seminary, explains that humans are created "like," but not identical to, God.[37] The English word "image" is a translation of Hebrew terms suggesting "according to a similar but not identical representation."[38] Therefore, according to Randy Rowland, pastor of the Presbyterian Church at the Center in Seattle, "humans are not God and we are not to try to be."[39] Nevertheless, humans do, by God's intention, have the capacity to be creative and to express love through kindness, compassion, and forgiveness. Each human is a special being. Each human has a divine character underlying an intrinsic self-worth and therefore a potential for and purpose of self-actualization and fulfillment.

Note that human worth is intrinsic—by virtue of being created by God—it is not based on physical characteristics, intellect, wealth, talents, achievement, possessions, rank, position or the like. It is based solely on the fact that God intentionally, with love and purpose, created us. Interestingly, even after the fall, God reaffirms humans having been made in the image and likeness of God. In the "re-creation" story, God says to Noah and his sons, "...for in the image of God has God made man." (Gn. 9:6) A manifestation of humans having been created in the image of God is humans' ability to create. Humans' creativity is a reflection of the Holy Spirit within. The form which any particular individual's creativity takes is a reflection of that person's God-given talents. It is in our creative expression that we reflect the glory of God.

Second, God is referring to humankind—all humans. The notion that *all* humans are creations of God is implied in the creation story and explicitly asserted in Genesis through God's call to Abraham, "and all peoples on earth will be blessed through you." (Gn. 12:3) Accordingly, if we are all creations of God, we all are brothers and sisters, members of the same family. Each of us is equal. Each of us is here for a purpose, a role within the family. Therefore, each of us possesses a dignity worthy of respect by the other. This combined with our capacity and purpose to love implies our responsibility to maintaining a loving attitude and behavior toward each other. Being created in God's image means to be in loving relationship with each other.

Third, God explicitly places humans superior to and with dominion over all other of His creations. Twice he directs us to "rule" over them. (Gn. 1:26,28) He goes even further commanding us to "...fill the earth and subdue it." (Gn. 1:28) But not only are we superior to all plants and animals, we indeed *own* them. Three times he declares them as our possessions: "I give you..." "They will be yours..." "I give every..." (Gn. 1:29,30) Finally, Genesis declares, "And it was so." (Gn. 1:30) No question, no doubt, humans are superior to all other matter. Notably, Professor Scalise points out that humans are the only creation to whom God speaks directly.[40] Milne affirms, "At creation humankind was invested by God with a special dignity, appointed ruler of the world under God, summoned to possess and subdue it and to rule the other creatures."[41]

This superiority of humans over other creatures is reaffirmed when God tells Noah "...all the beasts of the earth and all the birds of the air,...every creature that moves along the ground, and...all the fish of the sea; they are given into your hands. Everything that lives and moves will be food for you. Just as I gave you the green plants, I now give you everything." (Gn. 9:1-3) This attribute of humankind is also beautifully affirmed by David in Psalm 8, "what is man that you are mindful of him,...? You made him ruler over the works of your hands; you put everything under his feet:..." (Ps. 8:4-6)

Thomas Mann sums up the foregoing three characteristics in his comment, "Unlike any other part of creation, human beings reflect something of the divine nature, namely, God's sovereignty. Humanity is, as it were, the vice-regent of God on earth,.... Of course, this in no way questions the ultimate sovereignty of God. The very fact that human beings are...created by God...enforces their utter dependence. Nevertheless, ...humankind's power and control over the earth is unquestioned...."[42]

Of course, ownership conveyed to humans by God implies a huge responsibility for caring stewardship, just like parents who have total authority over young children have a commensurate ultimate responsibility for the nurturing, loving care of those children. "Should not shepherds take care of the flock?" (Ez. 34:2) This concept of stewardship is discussed later.

A fourth characteristic of humanity is that its purpose is to work. "....and there was no man to work the ground,....The LORD God took the man and put him in the Garden of Eden to work it and take care of it....The LORD God said, 'it is not good for the man to be alone. I will make a *helper*'...." (Gn. 2:5,15,18) (italics mine); "....By the sweat of your brow...." (Gn. 3:19) "As long as the earth endures, seedtime and harvest,..." (Gn. 8:22) The nobility of work is suggested in the passage, "By the seventh day God had finished the work he had been doing; so on the seventh day he rested from all his work." (Gn. 2:2)

Mann points out the connection between characteristics numbers three and four above, noting that ownership of the world's resources is not passive, but active: "...indeed, it (dominion over all other creatures) clearly requires some human effort. The pronouncement...is phrased in the imperative mood: be fertile, increase, fill, subdue, rule.... (God) 'charges' the recipient with a task and a responsibility."[43]

New Testament

The importance of humans to God, the intrinsic worth of humans and our unique role as God's creations is emphatically pronounced in God taking the ultimate step toward fellowship with us by God joining us in human form as Jesus Christ. "All this took place to fulfill what the Lord had said..., 'and they will call him Immanuel'—which means 'God with us." (Mt. 1:22) "In the beginning was the Word,...and the Word was God....The Word became flesh and made his dwelling among us." (Jn. 1:1,14) Professor Laurel Gasque notes, "God incarnate as Jesus is God's affirmation that the earthly is good; that God's interest is with what is in the world."[44]

Further, Jesus affirms humankind's superiority to God's other creations, "How much more valuable is a man than a sheep!" (Mt. 12:12) "The One who cares for the birds...will certainly care for His children for they are more valuable than the birds." (Mt. 6:26, Lk. 12:24)

And Paul further asserts, "God.... himself gives all men life and breath.... God did this so that men would seek him and perhaps reach out for him and find him, though he is not far from each one of us. 'For in him we live and move and have our being.'... 'We are his offspring." (Acts 17:27,28) "Don't you know that you yourselves are God's temple and that God's Spirit lives in you?....you are of Christ, and Christ is of God." (1Cor. 3:16,22) "For we are God's workmanship, created in Christ Jesus to do good works, which God prepared in advance for us to do." (Eph. 2:10) That Christians are children of God is affirmed in the New Testament no more resoundingly than the following, "How great is the love the Father has lavished on us, that we should be called children of God! And that is what we are!" (1 Jn. 3:1)

Finally, believers as God's special children for whom our Father cares and will continue to care and grants us His grace is reaffirmed in Revelation, "Now the dwelling of God is with men, and he will live with them. They will be his people, and God himself will be with them and be their God...." (Rev. 21:3) "Whoever is thirsty, let him come, and whoever wishes, let him take the free gift of the water of life." (Rev. 22:17)

In summary, Dr. Darryl Amundsen, Affiliate Professor of Medical History and Ethics at the University of Washington School of Medicine, observes, "all human beings are categorically distinguished from the rest of creation."[45] God...Christ...humans—no intermediary nor any mortal, worldly thing superceding the individual human being. God created humanity, and therefore there is a direct relationship between humans and God. Between each of us and God there is no intermediary—not monarch, nor priest, nor government.

Gregory Gronbacher, Director of the Center for Economic Personalism at the Acton Institute, drawing from George Williams' *The Mind of John Paul II: Origins of His Thought and Action*, expands, "Jesus is *the* revelation of what humanity now is—a unique refraction of the divine image.... The assertion that people are of immense dignity has profound significance.... It speaks of the human being's God-given greatness... The value of the person is not derived from an individual's contributions, talents, or achievements but has to do with the ineffable ontological significance of their being."[46]

So throughout Scripture it is declared that God, the creator of all things, is the parent of humankind. It follows, therefore,

- each human possesses an intrinsic dignity;
- we all are brothers and sisters in one family who are to love one another;
- humans are given dominion over and therefore stewardship responsibility for all other creations;
- effort, work, is expected from humans to fulfill their role; and
- God has created us in His own image and endowed each of us with all that we need to realize our potential if we live faithfully.

Given the characteristic of humanity as a creation of God, what economic system is most compatible with Christians living out their role as children of God? Before addressing this question, let us examine the second major characteristic of humans.

Humans as Sinners

Old Testament

In the third chapter of Genesis we discover another characteristic of humans, and perhaps humanity's most important characteristic in terms of implications for economic and political systems: our sinfulness, our alienation from God. The symbolic act of the fall to sinfulness, of course, was Adam and Eve, representing all humankind, eating the forbidden fruit and in so doing disobeying God, as related in Genesis 2:16,17 and 3:1-19. The sinful pride and arrogance of humans caused them to want to elevate themselves to God, knowing good and evil. They thereby alienated humanity from God.

Sinfulness is intrinsic to the nature of humans. Sinfulness pervades humanity. God provides humans with free will, and humans have made their own decision to ignore God. Stories in the book of Genesis provide compelling evidence of the sinful nature of humanity: Cain's jealous murder of his brother Abel, Lamech's vengeful murder of a man, the flood in response to "man's wicked- ness" (Gn. 6:5), confusing the language and scattering the people in response to human's prideful, egocentric "...build[ing] a city [Babel], with a tower that reaches to the heavens." (Gn. 11:4) The chief manifestations of this sinfulness are pride, egoism and hedo- nism which translate into idolatry and exhaltation of self over others.

King David affirms this nature of humankind, "Surely I was sinful at birth...." (Ps. 51:5) and later, "there is no one who does good, not even one." (Ps. 53:3) And as Solomon, with his God- given wisdom, observes in his prayer to God "...for there is no one who does not sin...." (1 Kgs. 8:46 and 2 Chr. 6:36) and as he notes elsewhere, "Who can say, 'I have kept my heart pure; I am clean and without sin'?" (Prv. 20:9) The sinful nature of humanity is also affirmed in Ecclesiastes, "The hearts of men, moreover, are full of

evil…." (Eccl. 9:3) Micah also makes reference to universal sinfulness manifest in corruption-ridden Judah, "The godly have been
swept from the land; not one upright man remains…… Both hands
are skilled at doing evil;… a man's enemies are the members of his
own household." (Mi. 7:2-6)

As summarized by Rev. Bryan Burton, "we have chosen to turn
away from God's original intention for us and have sought to live
according to our own ways and purposes, [reflecting] the denial of
our relatedness to God and our need for God's grace, the tendency
towards domination, pride and destruction, [and our] denial of a
human destiny appointed and purposed by God."[47] As a result of
our turning away from God, separating and alienating ourselves
from God, we face a reality of pain, suffering, evil and death.

New Testament

The sinfulness of humans, originally related in Genesis, is reaffirmed at length by Paul, devoting a major portion of his letter to the
Romans to it. Statements of Paul include, "…the godlessness and
wickedness of men…" (Rom. 1:18) "Jews and Gentiles alike are all
under sin." (Rom. 3:9) "…all have sinned and fall short of the glory
of God." (Rom. 3:23) "…just as sin entered the world through one
man, and death through sin, and in this way death came to all men,
because all sinned…." (Rom. 5:12) "…as the result of one trespass
was the condemnation for all men;…. Through the disobedience of
the one man the many were made sinners…." (Rom. 5:18,19) Paul
also notes in his letter to the Galatians "But the Scripture declares
that the whole world is a prisoner of sin,…" (Gal 3:22)

Much of Paul's discussion of sin cited above was in the context
of the juxtaposition of Adam, the corporate head of sin, with Christ,
the corporate head of grace and redemption. "For if many died by
the trespass of the one man, how much more did God's grace and
the gift of the one man, Jesus Christ, overflow to the many!…. the
gift followed many trespasses and brought justification. For if, by
the trespass of the one man, death reigned through that one man,
how much more will those who receive God's abundant provision
of grace and of the gift of righteousness reign in life through the
one man, Jesus Christ." (Rom. 5:15-17)

Mann explains further, "But sin remains an active force, even though we are now under grace rather than under the Law, and Rom. 6:12-23 warns against being enslaved by Sin."[48] The entire chapter twelve of Romans is Paul's exhortation to embrace the freedom of righteousness. Indeed, this is the ongoing charge to humankind, as we all are players in this Biblical drama of alienation (Gn. 1-3) and restoration (Rev. 21,22) as now we live in the times between the resurrection and Parousia. Sin is humans' abandonment of God manifest most commonly in disobedience, lack of a loving heart or pride. Guthrie makes a critically important distinction: "...we do not just *do* sinful things, we *are* sinners."[49] Edwards agrees, "Paul regarded sin not solely as bad acts, but as brokenness, fallenness, and spiritual lostness.... All humans share a solidarity of impoverishment with one another in God's sight"[50]

The Doctrine of Sin is a complex theological concept which I do not pretend to fully understand. Nevertheless, for our purposes in this discussion, given the sinful nature of humanity, what economic system best counteracts this nature and turns humans' sinful behavior to the general good?

Summary

We have observed the contrasting duality of the nature of humanity. We are divine creations with a God-given purpose and we are sinners, having alienated ourselves from God and possessed by pride and egoism. What economic system accommodates both of these characteristics?

Herein lies the genius of capitalism.

Chapter III

The Genius of Capitalism

A lready, in the first chapter of the first book of the Bible we are provided with insights that have profound implications regarding political and economic systems. Christianity's case for capitalism not only starts to emerge at the outset of Scripture, but, indeed, certain basic considerations leap off the very first page of the Bible.

We learn in Genesis that the material realm is good. We also learn that humanity has two essential elements to our nature: we are God's creations and we are sinners. Scalise refers to "the human predicament," humankind created in the image of God, yet with mortal weaknesses and imperfections."[51] This same observation is made by Amundsen, "Humanity is the crown of creation, made in the image and likeness of God and given charge of the earth. Humanity, however, is fallen, utterly lost, and…. Dead in trespasses and sins."[52] *The genius of capitalism is that it is the only economic system that satisfactorily accommodates both of these characteristics.*

Humans as Creations of God

God created humans in His own image. God also gave humans dominion over, indeed ownership of, all other creations. After God, humankind is the end. This is intrinsic to humanity. It is in our very nature. Accordingly, it cannot be usurped.

The creation story suggests that a political/economic model that would be consistent with the Christian concept of the nature of humanity and matter would look something like the following.

CONSISTENT MODEL

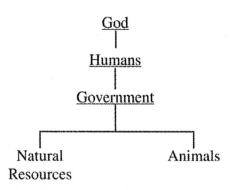

The model above tends to resemble more the political/economic framework of a democratic, capitalistic society such as the United States. "We hold these truths to be self evident, that all men are created equal, that they are endowed by their Creator with certain unalienable Rights, that among these are Life, Liberty and the pursuit of Happiness....That to secure these rights, Governments are instituted among Men, deriving their just powers from the consent of the governed,... with a firm reliance on the protection of Divine Providence." Bastiat, the 19th Century French champion of economic freedom, notes in his famous treatise, *The Law*, "It is not because men have passed laws that personality, liberty, and property exist,... On the contrary, it is because personality, liberty, and property already exist that men make laws.... Each of us certainly gets from Nature, from God, the right to defend his person, his liberty, and property."[53]

Capitalism is an economic system which recognizes and respects the direct link between humans and God. It does not inject an intermediary, such as government, between the two. In fact, the United States, one of the world's major capitalistic countries, was founded on this premise. This is not to say that capitalism does not accept the legitimate limitations which humans place on themselves through democratically enacted government statutes and regulations. Recall from the discussion in the "Introduction" that we are discussing democratic capitalism, not some sort of unconstrained laissez faire capitalism.

Further in this regard, capitalism, which is primarily occupied with production, unlike socialism which is primarily occupied with distribution, unleashes the creative powers of economic humanity. In the previous discussion of the Nature of Humanity, we observed that God *mandated* humans continue the creation process. The Oxford Declaration notes, "Production is not only necessary to sustain life and make it enjoyable; it also provides an opportunity for human beings to express their creativity in the service to other."[54] The ultimate economic expression of creation is entrepreneurialism, bringing into being a commercial enterprise. In this process capitalism rewards discovery and innovation.

Indeed, whether one is an artist, musician, business person, or whatever, our viewing ourselves as creations of God stimulates us to a general full actualization of our God-given talents. Further, can it not be asserted that it is sinful *not* to use one's talents to their maximum potential? The Parable of the Talents (Mt. 25:14-30; Lk. 19:11-27) can be interpreted that God has endowed each of us with certain attributes and resources and one's purpose in life is to utilize these God-given resources with which one has been endowed to their maximum potential toward fulfillment of God's purpose and to the glory of God. The role of one's physical, intellectual and spiritual resources is to achieve one's potential in such a manner that the glory of God is served and God's kingdom is furthered. (See later discussion of "Calling" in Chapter V, "Legitimacy of Material Possessions and Wealth.") Theologian Mounce notes, "The point of the parable is crystal clear. The servants of Christ, as they await his Parousia, have been entrusted with the responsibility of utilizing the gifts they have been given by the Master. To fail in this critical obligation is to be excluded from the kingdom when Christ returns."[55]

The Bible is a manual for living. All of its terms are active. We are not simply to receive God's love passively. Rather, God's love demands a response that we love others—a love demonstrated in compassion, generosity and responsible stewardship of all of God's creations. Faith is not passive; it implies works. Hope is not passive; it implies works. Capitalism is active; the focus is on creating. On the other hand, socialism is passive; the focus is on receiving. Capitalism is a positive sum game, focusing on production toward fulfilling needs; socialism is a zero sum game focusing on distribution. The driving forces of socialism are covetousness and envy; the driving forces of capitalism are creativity and innovation. The behavior mechanism of socialism is coercion; that of capitalism is voluntarism and cooperation. The focus of socialism is the present; that of capitalism, the future. Indeed, socialism, which in some models places humans subordinate to government, is a coercion-dependent economic system that is not consistent with Christianity's view of humans as created in God's image. This has been affirmed in many Christian writings, including John Paul II's encyclical *Laborem Exercens* (1981).

George Gilder, the highly respected editor of Gilder Technology Report and a fellow at the Discovery Institute in Seattle, expresses it eloquently, "The wealth of America is not an inventory of goods; it is an organic, living entity, a fragile pulsing fabric of ideas, expectations, loyalties, moral commitments, visions. To vivisect it for redistribution would eventually kill it. As President Mitterand's French technocrats discovered in the 1980's, the proud new socialist owners of complex systems of wealth soon learned that they are administering an industrial corpse rather than a growing corporation."[56]

It would be not just simplistic but incorrect to view the human solely as pecuniary. The most wealthy entrepreneur or employee can be motivated by a variety of objectives other than wealth accumulation. Commencing with Maslow's hierarchy of needs, there have been literally thousands of empirical studies which unequivocally demonstrate that, particularly after reaching a certain basic level of income, individuals are motivated more by non-financial rewards than money, including the motivation to contribute to improving the well-being of one's fellow human.

This was being demonstrated abundantly as the 20th Century came to a close and we entered the third millennium. The burgeoning of multitudes of high tech companies in the 1990's was fueled largely by the geometrically cumulative effect of "the fire of invention," to use Michael Novak's phrase. Rev. Robert A. Sirico, a Roman Catholic priest and President of the Acton Institute for the Study of Religion and Liberty and perhaps the most prominent champion of economic personalism, continues with this theme, "In stoking this fire we reflect God's creative character and display that part of us created in His image….the entrepreneur is often driven, not by a rational calculus of costs and benefits, but by an imaginative passion for the task at hand."[57] Indeed, Bill Gates leads a long list of immensely wealthy entrepreneurs who are simply caught up in an imaginative, creative passion, the vehicle for expression of which is the relatively small, independent, non-bureaucratic, highly flexible entity called the business firm.

Humans as Sinners

The second half of the genius of capitalism is its design to function with humankind as we are: sinners. It makes a realistic, rather than a utopian, assumption regarding the nature of humankind. Because humankind is sinful, all human systems and institutions—capitalism, socialism, communism, democracy, business firms, governments, even the church—are sinful. A. M. C. Waterman, professor of economics at the University of Manitoba notes David Hume's observation, "Each person loves himself more than any other person,…[and] avarice or the desire of gain… is an universal passion, which operates at all times, in all places, and upon all persons."[58]

As enunciated by Dr. Burton, "We have chosen to turn away from God's original intention for us and have sought to live according to our own ways and purposes."[59] First and foremost we are self-interested. While to the capitalist this tends to lead to pursuit of wealth, to the socialist this tends to lead to position and power. Even if it is not money that is one's interest, as seems to be the case with many of the high tech entrepreneurs, it nevertheless is other forms of self-interest: ego in being the first, ego in beating the competition, ego in changing the world, the fun of discovery, the psychic return from creativity and innovation, etc. The fact is that we humans are sinners. We humans are selfish and greedy and have a lust for power and material comfort. The question is, which economic system most readily turns our sinful nature into socially responsive behavior?

As observed by Adam Smith, the great Scottish moral philosopher, in his classic, *Inquiry into the Nature and Causes of the Wealth of Nations*, published on March 9, 1776, capitalism takes the self-interest of the sinner and converts it into the socially responsible outcome of the saint. "As every individual,...by directing that industry in such a manner as its produce may be of the greatest value, he intends only his own gain, and he is in this,...led by an invisible hand [the profit motive] to promote an end which was no part of his intention.... By pursuing his own interest he frequently promotes that of the society more effectually than when he really intends to promote it. I have never known much good done by those who affected to trade for the public good."[60]

Novak expands, "A system designed as closely as possible to fit human character, Smith argued, is best designed to unleash human creativity. The key to the wealth of nations lies in human creativity more than in any other source.... Smith gave many examples in which he judged ... political intervention useful and commendable. There can be no doubt, however, about the main thrust of Smith's argument: that markets as free as possible from governmental and religious command best serve the common good. Such a system frees the intelligence, imagination, and enterprise of individuals to explore the possibilities inherent in world process,..."[61] Nash observes, "the mechanism of the market actually neutralizes greed as individuals are forced to find ways of serving the needs of those with whom they wish to exchange.... [G]reed must be channeled into the discovery of products or services for which people are willing to trade. Every person in a market economy has to be other-directed. The market is one area of life where concern for the other person is required."[62] This, Smith asserts, rather than the extent to which it is endowed with natural resources, is what causes the wealth level of one nation to be different from the wealth level of another nation. I wonder how many clergy have ever been interested in the question, why is there more poverty in Brazil than in Japan when the former has many-fold more resources than the latter?

The elements of capitalism which make it work so incredibly effectively are the profit motive and the price system. But before turning to an examination of these two elements, let us listen to Novak and his distinction that it is humans, not systems, which are sinful, "Finally, democratic socialism trades upon the imagery according to which all things private—like businesses and markets—are selfish, greedy, and corrupt, while it neglects even to study the historical record of the selfishness, greed and corruption of bureaucracies (whether of church or of state) which in the past and the present have claimed to speak for the public."[63] Indeed, Smith saw oppression of individuals by rulers, whether by the state or the church, as the major constraint to any particular society's advance. Conversely, the way to achieve peace and prosperity is to unshackle humans. "Dugald Stewart, a student of Smith's, reported that in a lecture... Smith declared, 'Little else is required to carry a state to the highest degree of affluence from the lowest barbarism but peace, easy taxes, and a tolerable administration of justice; all the rest being brought about by the natural course of things. All governments which thwart this natural course,.... Are obliged to be oppressive and tyrannical."[64] Let us now turn our attention to that "natural course of things."

Profit Motive

The market system and its profit motive have been described as the eighth wonder of the world. Indeed, the profit motive is probably the most under-appreciated element of contemporary society.

Every morning each person in the United States wakes up and has not the slightest concern whether or not sufficient supplies of toothpaste, lettuce, shoes or haircuts are going to be available to him or her. Yet nowhere is there any public official sending out memos to various people directing them to send lettuce to Manhattan or shoes to Sioux Falls or toothpaste to Denver or provide haircuts in Atlanta. It just happens—a miracle in itself.

But that's not all. It happens in an incredibly efficient and effective manner. This is because businesses maximize profits in one of three ways. First, by selling a higher volume of products, second by reducing the cost of providing the product or third by introducing new products. In my thirty years in business every day was spent devoted to either making my customers more satisfied or controlling my expenses of doing business. Every effective business person in the world maintains the same focus. Further, large corporations pour hundreds of billions of dollars into research and development toward developing new products and more efficiently producing existing products.

In the United States and most capitalistic countries the quality and the quantity of goods and services "automatically" outpours in such an overwhelming abundance that the average consumer is overflowing with a cornucopia of good and services. Alaska Natives in Unalakleet are going hunting on snowmachines with all of the fuel that they need; retirees in Coral Gables are sitting in their air-conditioned homes enjoying their favorite television program, changing channels and volume at the mere flick of a finger; grade-schoolers in Wyoming are riding on safer buses; people suffering from illness are presented with new pharmaceuticals to cure or alle-viate their pain; churches are better furnished, including special sound systems for the hard of hearing; ambulances responding to emergencies are better equipped; grandparents and grandchildren send e-mail back and forth; the average cost of printing and distributing a Bible has fallen lower and lower, etc. etc. etc. etc. etc. etc. etc.—all because of the same mechanism, first identified by Adam Smith: the "invisible hand," the profit motive. No, first iden-tified by, as you can imagine, Solomon, "The laborer's appetite works for him; his hunger drives him on." (Prv. 16:26)

Bastiat expresses it eloquently, "Here are a million human beings who would all die in a few days if supplies of all sort did not flow into [Paris]… It staggers the imagination to try to comprehend the vast multiplicity of objects that must pass through its gates tomor-row, if its inhabitants are to be preserved from the horrors of famine, insurrection, and pillage. And yet all are sleeping peace-fully,… without being disturbed for a single instant by the idea of so frightful a prospect…. What, then, is the resourceful and secret power that governs the amazing regularity of such complicated movements?… That power is an *absolute principle*, the principle of free exchange. We put our faith in that inner light which Providence has placed in the hearts of all men, and to which has been intrusted the preservation and the unlimited improvement of our species, a light we term *self-interest*…."[65]

Friedrich August von Hayek, the Austrian economist and Nobel laureate, in his famous *The Road to Serfdom*, "laid out the funda-mental advantage of the free market: by allowing millions of deci-sion makers to respond individually to freely determined prices, it allocates resources—labor, capital, and human ingenuity—in a manner that can't be mimicked by a central plan, however brilliant the central planner."[66] Hayek's assertions were clearly vindicated by the Soviet Union experiment which resulted in a dismal failure in resource allocation and income distribution.

Interestingly, all of the obvious benefits to consumers emanating from private ownership and the profit motive have been achieved at an incredibly low cost. It is fascinating to observe that, after all of this considerable effort to create and build better products, risking their investment capital, the entrepreneur and the shareholder, of all groups in our society, come away with the smallest piece of the pie. When we examine national income statistics for the United States in the decade of the 1990's, we see that workers, the hired employees who take little or no risk, get two-thirds of the pie! Corporate profits and proprietors' income account for 19% of national income. Recognizing that proprietors are mostly family businesses, and breaking out the portion going to corporate profits, we discover that in the 1990's corporate profits accounted for a modest 11% of national income.[67] Fascinating. All those hundreds of billions of dollars and all of that creative brainpower spent on product research and development to serve the consumer, and the only return that those organizations get for it is 11% of the pie. Wages and salaries to employees account for 65%. (In fact, it has been asserted by some champions of capitalism that this enormous entrepreneurial energy and corporate resources expended for a mere 11% of the share represents an exploitation of corporations by the rest of us, not the other way around!)

Clearly, we consumers have come out beautifully. All of this preoccupation on the part of some people in our society with the "evil of obscene corporate profits" is simply misplaced in that it results from ignorance of the facts. Looking at profits from another perspective, over the past decade the average annual return on stockholders' equity of the 500 largest U.S. industrial corporations has been about 12%[68]—certainly not "obscene" by any criteria.

In light of the virtual self-evidence of the immense economic and social benefits of the profit motive, it is baffling to me that it is so maligned. It is tragic that in some circles the word "profit" has a bad connotation. Profit is a neutral term, neither intrinsically good nor bad. Profit is simply an economic term for the return to a factor of production. Profit is the payment to the business entity for taking the entrepreneurial risk of bringing a product to market. The following are the economic terms for the payments to the various factors of production:

Term for Payment	Factor of Production
Wage / Salary	Employee / Manager
Rent	Real Estate / Property
Interest	Capital
Profit	Owner / Entrepreneur

Each of the factors of production plays an important role in the economic process. Without payment, the factor of production does not function. The return to the worker is wage or salary; to real estate, rent; to capital, interest; to the entrepreneur, profit. Without payment—profit—the entrepreneurial factor of production does not function.

Further, in any given business enterprise, profit is a residual. The other three factors of production get paid first. Profit occurs only if the revenue generated by the business operations are sufficient to cover all of the costs. So profit involves a high degree of risk, which would tend to justify a higher rate of return. But, as has been shown, relative to aggregate returns to the other factors, profits have been relatively modest in the United States.

The result of the effective functioning of the factors of production in developed capitalistic countries has been an incredibly high level of efficiency and innovation. Paul M. Romer, Professor of Economics at the Graduate School of Business of Stanford University, Senior Research Fellow at Stanford University's Hoover Institution and father of the New Growth Theory, has completed considerable study which leads him to conclude, "In basic discoveries and applications alike, it is the incentives created by the market that profoundly affect the pace and direction of economic progress.... basic science follows practical opportunities, not the other way around. The transistor caused the development of the field of solid-state physics. The steam engine led to the development of thermodynamics ....we make progress in almost any area we put our minds to [as incented by the market]....Take overnight delivery at FedEx, just-in-time inventory management at Toyota, and discount retailing at Kmart and Wal-mart. These may not seem glamorous, but in the aggregate, discoveries of this type probably account for the bulk of the increase in the standards of living we enjoy."[69]

To borrow a mundane example from the late Paul Heyne, a

marvelous faith-filled economist and one of the most popular professors at the University of Washington, that makes the point in its eloquent simplicity: the profit motive is "why we *expect* long lines at the post office but not at the grocery store."[70]

To anyone doubled over in gales of laughter at the assertion that capitalism brings forth saintful outcomes out of sinners' behavior, quickly pointing to environmental degradation, exploitation of workers, etc., let me note again for emphasis that we are not talking about laissez faire capitalism. Rather, we are talking about regulated capitalism wherein businesses face a multitude of statutory and regulatory constraints on their behavior. Today over 40,000 regulations over commerce are included in the U.S. *Federal Register*. Further, we are talking about 21st Century enlightened capitalism, not the past era of the robber barons. Additionally, it must be noted that, when it comes to social costs such as pollution, shoddy output, poor working conditions, etc., government has a worse record than private enterprise. While we are taking this brief historical aside, it is appropriate to acknowledge one of the unsung heroes in the capitalistic system: labor unions. Unlike many of their brethren abroad who were intent on overthrowing their respective capitalistic systems, American labor unions focused on issues such as wages and working conditions. Rather than radically changing the pie, they were concerned with enlarging their members' piece of the pie. As a result, workers' incomes rose, their consumption rose, business profits rose, and, most importantly, a broad middle class emerged, contributing to a stable, constructive political environment which has pervaded the United States, enabling capitalism and its participants, businesses, workers and consumers, to flourish.

The drive for profits creates a powerful force to increase production efficiency and improve product quality. This is a phenomenon that eludes the understanding of many people. As suggested above, the profit motive is the least understood and appreciated concept of modern civilization. It is tragic that this is so, because no human mechanism has done more for the improvement—in all respects—of God's children than the profit motive. That is a bold statement, but it will become clearer when I expand upon this assertion later in Chapter X, "The Brilliant Outcomes of Capitalism."

Most business people understand that profits are not the end. Profits are simply the fuel of the economic engine. Profits, when reinvested into the system, fuel its expansion and improvement, enabling it to accomplish its real end: advancing the standard of living of humanity—God's creations. Two things are accomplished. First, the poor, through the creation of jobs and on-the-job training are given the opportunity to become unpoor. Second, through relatively high wages and relatively low costs, consumers' needs and wants are satisfied. The *end* is the standard of living of the individual creation of God.

This distinction regarding the role of profits was eloquently stated by Dennis Bakke, CEO of AES Corporation, a global energy producer and distributor: "Where do profits fit? Profits…are not any corporation's main goal. Profits are to a corporation much like breathing is to life. Breathing is not the goal of life, but without breath, life ends. Similarly, without turning a profit, a corporation, too, will cease to exist."[71] It is the aggregate reinvestment of profits—the business owners foregoing dividends and instead reinvesting in research, product development, and plant expansions and improvement that is the key element in causing the standard of living, health, education level and virtually all elements of the quality of life of humans to be as high as it is in capitalistic nations.

Another analogy conveying the real role of profits is that business is simply a game and profits are the score. As the teams compete vigorously in the games on the field, the winners are two groups: first, the players who share in the exhilaration and return to them of their objective of playing the game; i.e. the workers who receive jobs and incomes as well as psychic return from their jobs; and, second, the spectators who are entertained; i.e., the consumers who receive goods and services generated by the game of business.

Further, when discussing profits, we must look at the receivers of profits. Today the huge corporations, to which so many misinformed take pleasure in attributing virtually all of society's ills, are owned, not by black-cloaked, gaunt, mean-spirited men conspiring in dark rooms, but by workers covered by pension plans, retired folks enjoying the fruits of their working years, young people saving for college via mutual funds, the responsible breadwinner owning life insurance, churches, hospitals, colleges and, yes, even environmental organizations paying their staffs with the earnings from their endowment funds—the broad spectrum reaching every corner of our society. Nearly three-fourths of the households in the

United States own stock in corporations directly or indirectly through pension funds. Novak sums it up this way, "The plaints and wails of poets and preachers about the sins and errors of the market system screech through intellectual history, while friendly voices are few. Yet no other form of economy has resulted in so many books being published, schools founded, churches built, philanthropies undertaken, and intellectual and religious liberties maintained."[72]

Finally, I will discuss later how today private and public interests are not only not incompatible, they are quite compatible. I am asserting that the profit motive leads to as many public benefits as private benefits. Indeed, although it has been said, and I agree, that money can't buy happiness, money via the profit motive certainly buys courtesy, friendliness and helpfulness as Nordstrom, Inc. and its myriad emulators have demonstrated. Many a successful business person can give an account of a situation wherein the profit motive induced her / him to be civil in an otherwise uncivil situation. The profit motive even induces improvement and protection of the environment as I will discuss later under "Stewardship" in Chapter IV, "Source of Material Possessions and Wealth." And it certainly has contributed to promulgation of the Gospel.

Concluding this discussion of profits, I draw on comments from John Paul II, "The Church acknowledges the legitimate role of profit as an indication that a business is functioning well. When a firm makes a profit, this means that productive factors have been properly employed and corresponding human needs have been duly satisfied."[73]

The Mechanics that Make Capitalism Work:
the Miraculous Price System: Free Markets

The profit motive daily brings forth a response to our every desire. And the mechanism for signaling our desires is the price system.

Prices signal to suppliers what consumer want. Every second of every day the multitude of consumers, digesting the vast array of information available, "vote" for what goods and services each wants. They each vote by placing down money for a particular good or service. Those items "voted" for get produced; those items not "voted" for don't get produced; the more the "votes," the more is produced, the less "votes," the less is produced. Further, as von Mises, the famous Austrian economist who emigrated to the United States in 1940, observes, unlike the political system where the minority votes do not result in effecting decisions (majority rules), in the economic system, "...no vote is cast in vain. Every penny spent has the power to work on the production process. The publishers cater not only to the majority by publishing detective stories, but also to the minority reading lyrical poetry and philosophical tracts. The bakeries bake bread not only for healthy people, but also for the sick on special diets...."[74]

Not only is the system incredibly efficient, it is incredibly neutral in terms of extraneous noneconomic considerations. Note that nothing has been said about the nationality or political party or relatives or race or religion or any other characteristic of the consumer. The number of votes (amount of money) any consumer has is determined solely by his or her *economic* value; i.e. his or her income—not whom he or she knows or can bribe or any other personal characteristic. The system is neutral. This is not to suggest that the humans who function within the system are neutral. But the system itself is neutral and this is one of its most distinguishing characteristics, differentiating it from a planned or controlled economy such as socialism which is not neutral.

The *price system*, which reflects the law of supply and demand, is one of the most miraculous innovations in the history of humankind. Here's how it works.

Every good and service faces a demand curve which is the schedule of the various quantities of a good or service that are demanded at various different prices. Generally, the lower the price, the higher the quantity demanded. This is because, with a lower price, a consumer can afford more at the same level of income. It is also because, at a lower price relative to other substitutable goods and services, more of this particular product will be substituted for other goods.

Hence, the Demand Curve:

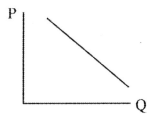

Also, every good and service faces a supply curve which is the schedule of the various quantities of a good or service that are supplied at various different prices. The higher the price, the higher the quantity supplied. This is because, with a higher price, a producer can afford to produce more. It is also because, at a higher price relative to other goods or services, more producers will be attracted into supplying this particular product.

Hence, the Supply Curve:

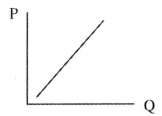

Note that the Demand Curve is determined by the voluntary free acts of all of the consumers and that the Supply Curve is determined by the voluntary free acts of all of the suppliers and potential suppliers.

The quantity of any particular good or service that actually gets produced and purchased is determined by the intersection of the supply and demand curves as depicted below.

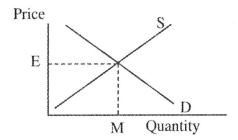

M quantity of the good or service will be produced and sold/bought at E price. It is as simple as that. It is easiest to show why E (for "equilibrium") and M (for "market") will be the prevailing price and quantity by showing that any other level will *not* occur. For example, at a higher price, a higher quantity would be supplied than demanded, and the price would fall; at a lower price, a higher quantity would be demanded than supplied, and the price would rise. Hence, E is the equilibrium price, and M is the equilibrium quantity.

The foregoing relationship—*the Law of Supply and Demand*—is irrefutable. Further, it is not some theoretical construct that differs from reality. It explains reality. It explains how the prices of *all* goods and services are determined. It explains why the price of plywood in the United States soared after Hurricane Andrew in the early 1990's. It explains why college professors salaries rose more than average following World War II. It explains why the wages of everyone in Alaska went up when the oil companies moved into Alaska to develop the North Slope. It explains the price of everything. There are no exceptions. When I taught Principles of Economics to college freshman and sophomores, I issued the challenge that anyone who could refute the Law of Supply and Demand would receive an automatic "A" in the course. No one was ever able to do it, although many tried. Most attempts were actual confirmations of the law. They were just showing different types of curves. For example, although the demand for air is huge (all living things need it), the price of air is zero because the supply is infinite at price zero. Another interesting example are certain luxury items with high "snob" appeal which actually face an upward sloping demand curve; that is, as the price rises the demand *rises*. It could be argued, for example, that if the price of caviar were 1/10 of what it is, it would not be viewed as such a "delicacy" and therefore not as much would be demanded. Similarly, a lower price for a Mercedes automobile within some range might actually decrease the demand.

But there it is in all of its simple elegance. That is precisely how a free market economy determines how much of each type of good or service is produced. Novak summarizes, "Market systems are not, then, as anarchic as intuition may lead one to suppose. Buyers may have motives of limitless variety and may intend quite personal consequences. Sellers may have an equally broad array of motives and intentions. Yet this vast array of purposes somehow results in orderly kinds of behavior which reduce many economic activities to rather dull routines."[75]

What is so baffling and tragic in terms of bungled public policy is how many people either (1) don't understand the Law of Supply and Demand or (2) think they can ignore or repeal it. But repealing it cannot be done. The Law of Supply and Demand is as irrefutable as the law of gravity. Yet, it is amazing to me how many public officials don't understand this.

The classic example is rent control. If it is determined by someone that the natural market price for apartments is "too high," and therefore a city council places an upper limit on rental rates, one of two things is going to occur, either the supply of apartments is going to decline or the upkeep and maintenance of apartments is going to decline to permit the supply curve to shift. Both outcomes are indicated below.

Natural market situation:

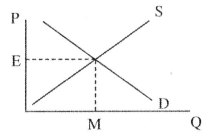

The two possible results after rent controls are enacted are displayed in the charts below.

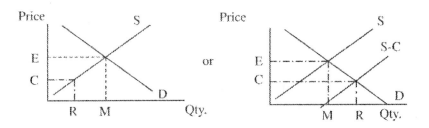

Under rent control which establishes a maximum rental rate of, say, "C" (for "control") which is lower than the natural market rental rate of E (for "equilibrium"), the city will find that fewer apartments are built and made available as in the left hand example above and/or, in order to accommodate the lower rental income, the apartment owners spend less on upkeep, in effect shifting out the supply curve as in the right hand example above. Either way, the people whom rent control was intended to help are hurt. Either there are fewer apartments available, or the condition of the apartments deteriorates, or some combination of the two. There is nothing theoretical about this. This is what actually occurs (as can be readily observed by a drive through New York City), and presented above are simply the economic principles explaining why. (The outcome of the market system relative to housing costs is exacerbated further in the market system because of the relatively low elasticity of supply and demand for housing. For a specific, more technical discussion of this phenomenon see Appendix B. Also, a second example of how well-intended public policy can have the opposite effect—minimum wage laws—is presented in Appendix C.)

To paraphrase Professor Heyne, blaming high prices for scarcity is like blaming the thermometer for low temperatures and attempting to warm up the house on a cold day by holding a candle under the furnace thermostat.[76] Scarcity cannot be eliminated by price controls; in fact, just the opposite occurs as shown above.

And to return to these amazing principles. They translate into an impressively efficient economic system that rapidly finds out and responds to what people want. The Law of Supply and Demand and the Profit Motive explain why the average American consumer is awash with a lavish amount of goods and services.

To give an example, look what happened after Hewlett Packard came out with the HP 35, the very first popular hand-held calculator. Seeing the huge demand, a multitude of other suppliers were induced to produce hand-held computers, coming up with ways to reduce the cost of manufacture, causing the supply curve to shift, and the price has plummeted—all to the benefit of the consumer!

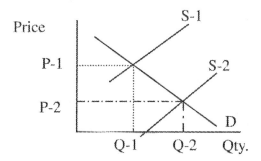

This dynamic process is occurring every second of every day as free consumers go around voting with their dollars and creative, profit-motivated producers innovate to achiever higher productivity to lower costs and to introduce better products. The winner: the consumer.

The general term applied to the foregoing phenomenon is the *efficient allocation of resources*. This refers to the notion that as products and services are demanded, producers, seeking profit allocate resources to those products and services. The major productive resource allocated is labor; hence, workers are drawn to do that which has high economic value and therefore capable of generating high wages. At the same time, producers, in order to increase profit also organize their operations and apply technological advancements in equipment to the production process, increasing output per worker, in turn raising the amount which the producer is able to pay workers. *This efficient allocation of resources* is a well-known concept in economics which all economists agree, as a general outcome of the free market, accrues to the benefit of all of us in the following ways:

- Consumers get what they demand.
- Workers are paid relatively high wages.
- Job opportunities arise permitting the poor to become unpoor.
- Profits accrue to investors in return for risking capital.
- Abundant public goods and services are produced from taxes on profits and wages.
- The poor, the arts, and others not directly in the market system or disenfranchised from the social system

receive voluntary philanthropic contributions from workers' wages and companies' profits.
• This entire process grows and improves through the reinvestment of profits.

Everyone wins. This is not just some theoretical meandering on my part. The empirical demonstration of this is profusely evident around us. Indeed, it also is evident as the cargo Boeing 747 touches down on the airstrip in Mozambique loaded with food, clothing, medical supplies, fuel and the like to provide to our flood-stricken brothers and sisters—fellow creations of God.

The brilliant outcome of the market system is not only its miraculous efficiency and effectiveness, but additionally, it is completely impersonal; it is absolutely unbiased. Note that only three things count: characteristics of the particular product or service, the demand curve and the supply curve. We have no knowledge regarding nor do we care in the slightest what the characteristics of the suppliers and demanders are. Their race, sex, color, religion, nationality, sexual orientation, income, education, family, neighborhood, etc. are totally irrelevant to the marketplace doing its thing. Note, however, that this neutrality of the marketplace can translate into some huge disparities. The Law of Supply and Demand explains why Dennis Rodman got paid a thousand-fold times my minister. This is why a society, rightly so, makes qualitative adjustments to the outcome of the market system through various government regulations, taxes and social programs. It is not the exclusive role of economics to determine what those adjustments ought to be. It is the role of all disciplines and of all the considerations of human beings. It *is* the expected role of economics to identify, measure and point out the economic costs of those adjustments. Regretfully, these costs, more often then not, tend to be ignored by the populace in general. For example, refer back to the discussion of the social costs of rent control: fewer or less well maintained apartments. (We will return to the subject of income disparities later.)

In addition to income disparities, another problem accompanying the free enterprise system is the strong tendency toward materialism. This is a result of the immense role played by advertising as individual firms attempt to push out the demand curves for their products. Indeed, consumer demand for some products has been *induced* by producers contriving demand for their products through inordinately heavy advertising. Much advertising contributes to many social costs, none the least of which is a pervasive sexual preoccupation. However, it should be acknowledged that advertising appeals to the instincts already existing within humans. These instincts were not placed within humanity by the system. Further, it should be acknowledged that advertising also makes available at no cost many benefits to consumers, including entertainment, news and information. Were it not for advertising, the wonderful magazine "Christianity Today"—and myriad others—would not be published. The materialism flowing from advertising is discussed thoroughly in Chapter VI, "Attitudes Toward Material Possessions and Wealth."

These imperfections notwithstanding, the price system is elegant in its efficiency and effectiveness. As eloquently enunciated by Hayek in "Economics and Knowledge," published in 1937 and "The Use of Knowledge in Society" published in 1945, "free markets and free prices are a means of conveying and exploiting information. In any society, the central economic problem is how to best organize production and employ available resources in order to satisfy the needs and desires of millions of different people.... Centralized systems may look attractive on paper,... but they suffered from a basic and incurable ailment: the 'division of knowledge' problem. In order to know where resources should be directed, the central planner needs to know both what goods people want to buy and how they can most cheaply be produced. But this knowledge is held in the minds of individual consumers and businesspeople, not in the filing cabinets (or, later, computers) of a government planning agency.... 'We must look at the price system as such a mechanism for communicating information.'.... In a market system, people simply go out and buy the things they like, leaving unwanted goods on the shelves. If they want more of something—say, heating oil—it becomes scarce and its price rises, thereby prompting oil companies to increase production and consumers to economize. If people decide to use less oil, say, because natural gas has become cheaper, the price of oil will fall, and its production will be scaled back—all this taking place without any orders being issued by a government agency. [Hayek concludes] 'I am convinced that, if it were the result of deliberate human design,… and people understood,… this mechanism would have been acclaimed as one of the greatest triumphs of the human mind."[77]

One of the reasons for so much misunderstanding of economic systems and the debate over socialism and capitalism is that the outcome of each is so counter-intuitive. That is, socialism, which relies on centralized planning and directives so often results in bureaucratic snafus, breakdowns, reversals and therefore shortages, poor quality, etc—chaos of outcomes; while capitalism, which relies on chaotic inputs—separate decisions by thousands of individual producers and consumers—results in efficiency, timeliness and elegant order in outcomes.

It is tragic that the price system is not better understood and is so maligned when, in fact, the profit motive and the price system have saved more lives, brought more people out of poverty, cured more illnesses, educated more people, and assured the political freedom of more people than all of the churches in the world combined. If more clergy had a better understanding of economics, they would enthusiastically embrace their natural ally.

When it comes to evaluating capitalism's market system in terms of its *social* impact, the worst that can be said is that it is neutral. There is sin in the world not because of a sinful system. There is sin in the world because of sinful humans. I recall a statement made forty years ago to this young college sophomore by Professor Henry Buechel, one of the legendary teachers of Principles of Economics at the University of Washington, that "under capitalism, sinful, self-interested humans seek money; under socialism sinful, self-interested humans seek power." He was paraphrasing John Maynard Keynes, "[D]angerous human proclivities can be canalized into comparatively harmless channels by the existence of opportunities for money-making and private wealth, which if they cannot be satisfied in this way, may find their outlet in cruelty, the reckless pursuit of personal power and authority and other forms of self-aggrandizement. It is better that a man should tyrannize over his bank balance than over his fellow citizen."[78] It is interesting also to listen to a comment made by Dr. Blaine Charette, Associate Professor of New Testament, Northwest College, that "the opposite of love is not hate, but power. The pursuit of power is what gives rise to all of the characteristics that get in the way of love."[79] This concern gives rise to the warning by Donald Hay, Fellow and Tutor in Economics, Jesus College, Oxford, "The danger [of intervention by government authorities] is always that they will exceed their God-given responsibilities, and use their powers for their own ends.... But given that governments are corruptible, just as much as businessmen, we are right to be skeptical about too great reliance on government to right the wrongs in a capitalist economy."[80]

Finally, concluding this section of capitalism accommodating humanity's sinful nature, let me refer to Novak, "Democratic capitalism, then rests on a complex theory of sin. While recognizing ineradicable sinful tendencies in every human, it does not count humans depraved. While recognizing that no system of political economy can escape the ravages of human sinfulness, it has attempted to set in place a system which renders sinful tendencies as productive of good as possible."[81] Niebuhr admits, "It (socialism) completely failed to appreciate the possibility of corruption through self-interest in any structure of society."[82] Gilder puts it this way, "Under a system of forced redistribution, the rich, aggressive, and ambitious gain their inevitable advantages not by giving but by taking; they earn money and power only at the expense of others, but pursuing the zero-sum maneuvers of excessive government, financial finagling, sclerotic bureaucracy and legal pettifoggery, or by retreating into the invisible arms of an overgrown system of public sumps and subsidies. It is capitalism that best combines the desire and ability to do good and create value with the resource to accomplish these goals. This process, however, is not well understood. For some the problem begins with a misreading of scripture: confusing the creation and investing of wealth with the seizing and hoarding of it. For most, the problem is a misunderstanding of the nature and role of giving in human society."[83]

Summary

Indeed, humans are (1) created in the image of God and (2) sinners. Of all the economic systems, capitalism best accommodates this dual nature. This is the genius of capitalism in the context of Christianity.

First, capitalism accommodates humans as created in the image of God by acknowledging the individual as the center. God's creations as workers and consumers are the end, the raison d'être, of the system. Further, humanity's God-given mandate to create is unleashed and motivated by capitalism. Finally, capitalism provides the opportunity for genuine expression of love, as we will explore later.

Second, capitalism forces the sin of humanity's avarice to serve the public good a la Adam Smith's observation of the "invisible hand." Profits are maximized by providing consumers with what they want, creating better and/or less expensive goods and services. Incomes are generated by people being hired to produce these goods and services. Productive resources are allocated to their most valuable use. The result: higher standard of living. And all of this is done with incredible efficiency.

An academic colleague recently remarked to me that "I agree that humans need the discipline of the marketplace, but, if humans were saints rather than sinners, socialism would be the economic system of choice." Such a false notion reflects an ignorance of how economies work, particularly the critical social role played by free markets, prices and profits. When prices are set in a free market, then profits measure (1) how much of a particularly product is desired by consumers and (2) how efficiently a particular supplier is producing the product. Profits also determine how many funds are going to be retained by this producer to enable it to (a) expand to satisfy growing demand by consumers, (b) improve the product to give consumers greater value, and/or (c) improve operations to reduce prices and/or increase wages. As Adam Smith notes, it is the retaining, rather than distributing, of profits that underlie the growth of the wealth of a nation. Interestingly, it was in Smith's earlier treatise, *The Theory of Moral Sentiments,* that he first identified the role of capital accumulation and related it to the moral virtue of prudence, foregoing present consumption in favor of future consumption.

For either saints or sinners capitalism's free market is glorious! It empowers consumers—they, rather than producers or bureaucrats, decide what is produced. It assures maximum efficiency in the allocation of resources causing lowest possible prices to consumers and highest possible wages to workers. And it creates a base for future wealth generation. Even if all humans were saints, we would want the benefits of free prices and profits serving as important communication mechanisms of how well the economic system is serving consumers and creating opportunities for workers. This is a critically important point and therefore is expanded upon in the following pages.

An Ingenious System for Both Saints and Sinners

Let me emphasize the genius of capitalism by summarizing its elegant outcomes whether or not humankind is comprised of saints or sinners. This has been effectively conveyed by the late Paul Heyne whose analysis benefits from his rare background as both an ordained Lutheran (M.Div. Concordia Seminary) and Ph.D. in Economics (University of Chicago). His insights are presented in his critique of the *First Draft of the U.S. Bishops' Pastoral Letter on Catholic Social Teaching and the U.S. Economy.* "The principal virtue that most economists find in the so-called market system is its effective management of information problems. A modern economy is an extraordinarily complex system in which innumerable decisions have to be continuously coordinated if food, clothing, shelter, heat, light, transportation, medical care and a multitude of other goods are to be regularly and dependably made available to those who want them on terms that they are willing and able to meet. It is neither an accident nor a fact of nature that the quantity of milk New Yorkers want to consume each day, for example, consistently makes its way from distant dairy farms to waiting glasses, cereal bowls, and coffee cups. On the contrary, it is the product of a vast system of social cooperation that is continuously coordinated through the information that relative prices supply.

"These information problems would still exist in essentially unchanged form in a nation of saints. The human deficiency that relative prices overcome is not so much selfishness as ignorance. The higher relative price attached to a particular good is first of all *evidence*—evidence that the good has become more scarce. In the absence of such concrete and readily available evidence regarding the relative scarcities of countless inputs and outputs, modern economic life simply could not go on.

"... the *Letter* talks about the responsible management of economic resources by business and financial institutions without once recognizing the role that relative prices play in promoting good (or poor) stewardship. The use of land and other natural resources 'must be governed by the need to preserve the fertility of farmland and the integrity of the environment,' the bishops say. Owners, managers, and financiers are urged to be accountable to their employees and their local communities in making investment decisions....

"But the bishops do not see that relative prices reflecting relative scarcities, both current and prospective, are essential information for those who want to manage resources responsibly rather than arbitrarily.... The pursuit of profit—an activity always viewed with suspicion when mentioned in the *Letter*—is also required, because pursuing profit means paying attention to relative prices. And relative prices are ordinarily the best available social indicators of what good stewardship requires concretely....

"Those who fail to recognize the role of prices as coordinating signals almost always fail to notice that markets are mechanisms of social coordination..... It's time to retire the claim that a market economy is an 'unplanned' economy. The *Letter* reveals no understanding at all of what effective economic planning requires or of how the U.S. economy is in fact coordinated.

"This point was first made famous... by Adam Smith in *The Wealth of Nations*. In the realm of economic activity, people promote the public interest not by aiming at it directly but by aiming at their own private interest. It is not from the benevolence of the butcher, brewer, or baker, Smith says, but from their self-love, their regard to their own advantage, that we expect our dinner. Smith's point is missed, however, if we suppose he was contrasting benevolence with selfishness and regard for the public interest with attention to selfish interests. He was not.

"Smith had a high regard for benevolence, as his *Theory of Moral Sentiments* abundantly demonstrates. But he knew that benevolence was a virtue too vague and uncertain to guide and coordinate the cooperative activities of a society that depended extensively upon the division of labor. Benevolence doesn't tell people what they ought to do if they want to promote the common good; but people must know *exactly* what to do if the economic system is to function.....

"Despite the central emphasis of the *Letter* upon justice, its authors have not reflected concretely enough to supply any coherent sketch of what they are aiming at. It is clear enough that they consider current inequalities of income and wealth, within the United States but especially in the world, morally unacceptable. But that isn't the issue. The important questions are why these inequalities exist and what can and should be done to change them. If the bishops provide any guidance at all on these questions, it is toward solutions that have already been tried and found wanting....

"Within the United States, the *Letter* recommends more generous welfare benefits offered to more people and with fewer conditions such as work requirements. The impression given repeatedly by the sections on welfare reform is that the bishops are standing resolutely in the year 1964, urging that we begin a War on Poverty..... One wonders what would remain of the bishops' proposals if each member of the committee sat down and read Charles Murray's *Losing Ground: American Social Policy, 1950-1980.*

"The problem runs deeper, however, than the bishops' inability to provide defensible suggestions for alleviating poverty. It goes back to their failure to provide a coherent statement of what they mean by economic justice. The reason for this failure is that they are looking in the wrong direction. The justice or injustice of a social system will not be found in the pattern of outcomes it yields—its end-states—but in the procedures through which those outcomes emerge. This is simply the only kind of justice of which social systems are capable.....

"The next step is the deduction that 'government economic policies must ensure that the poor have their basic needs met before less basic desires of others are satisfied.' This is perilously close to demagoguery. Is the government supposed to call a halt to all skiing (surely a luxury) until everyone in the society is receiving a sound education? If is doesn't mean something like this, what *does* it mean to assert that 'the needs of the poor take priority over the desires of the rich'? And if it doesn't really mean anything, why is such a statement made?....

"But such a system... tailored to the peculiar circumstance of each individual, would be tantamount to the minutely detailed system of central planning and control that the bishops explicitly repudiate. If the bishops don't see this contradiction in what they are proposing, it must be because they are assuming that poor people consume nothing but necessities and that the luxuries of the rich can be unambiguously identified.....

"The bishops' criteria for income distribution, even if they could be made consistent, would be useful only to someone who was omniscient, and they could be enforced only by someone who combined omniscience with omnipotence. *Economic [free market] systems have come into existence, however, precisely because of limitations on individual knowledge* and that most fortunate corollary, limitations on individual power."[84] (Italics mine.)

Nash concurs with Heynes, "The market system is spontaneous in the sense that no one invented it.... Without help from any group of central planners, the impersonal market system does a remarkable job of supplying the countless wants of countless numbers of people It does this by supplying information about people's ever-changing wants and preferences through changes in prices."[85] von Mises concludes that "socialism can never work because it is an economic system that makes economic calculation impossible. Rational economic activity is impossible without certain kinds of information. But that information is supplied only by attending to changing prices in a free market system."[86] That is, in a centrally planned economy determining people's wants is an impossible task because that depends on prices, and prices depend upon voluntary exchange in the market.

The market system is a marvelous communication mechanism of great benefit to even a society of saints, if one ever happened to exist. Only through the functioning of the price system does a society communicate the information enabling the multitude of individual decisions necessary in order for a society to achieve the most efficient allocation of productive resources and thereby achieve maximum return to the factors of production such as labor.

Again, I must assert that the foregoing is not some vague theoretical construct. The foregoing is empirically proven in the world today. If you have any doubt, get on a plane, travel to centrally planned economies and have the comparison demonstrated for you.

Further, in addition to the structural advantages of the free market system, it is fascinating to read Heyne's foregoing remarks in the context of now having had the experience and the empirical observation that the major inroads in solving the poverty and welfare problem, reducing crime and achieving other social objectives in the United States in the 1990's occurred as a direct result of the extremely strong economic advance during this period, combined with welfare reform focused on work requirements. It did not result from social programs.

Before closing this section, it must be re-emphasized that the profit motive and the law of supply and demand are as fundamental and important to our lives as the law of gravity or a multitude of other physical laws. Further, however, not only are these economic laws of fundamental importance to humankind, they are, tragically, among the most mis-understood and under-appreciated mechanisms of humankind today.

As related in Scripture, God understands the market system quite well and used prices as determined by the Law of Supply and Demand three thousand years ago to make important points. A dramatic example is Samaria's facing a severe famine in response to the Israelites lack of faith and the manifestation was a drying up of supply causing a skyrocketing of prices for agricultural products. "… the siege lasted so long that a donkey's head sold for eighty shekels of silver, and a quarter of a cab of seed pods for five shekels." (2 Kgs. 6:25) Later, to demonstrate God's power, "Elisha said, 'Hear the word of the LORD. This is what the LORD says: About this time tomorrow, a seah of flour will sell for a shekel and two seahs of barley for a shekel at the gate of Samaria." (2 Kgs.7:1) Soaring prices followed by collapsing prices, responding to changes in supply and demand via the market system are God's mechanism for dealing with the Israelites!

There are other examples in Scripture where God uses value as reflected in prices to drive home a point. When David insists on paying Araunah for land and oxen which Araunah offered to freely contribute for a location for an alter and burnt offerings to God, "No, I insist on paying you for it. I will not sacrifice to the LORD my God burnt offerings that cost me nothing." (2 Sm. 24:24) The lowliness to which Israel, as symbolized by Hosea's wife Gomer, had fallen was dramatized by her worthlessness as reflected in the pitifully low price that God needed to pay to get her back. "So I bought her for fifteen shekels of silver and about a homer and lethek of barley." (Hos. 3:2) Another case in which God uses the price system to drive home a point was when the shepherd was paid an insulting 30 pieces of silver, signifying the worthlessness of the shepherd in the people's eyes, symbolizing a rejection of the Messiah. "So they paid me thirty pieces of silver. And the LORD said to me, 'Throw it to the potter."

(Zec. 11:12,13) Potters were in the lowest social class.

This theme utilizing a low price to make a point is carried over into the New Testament with the contemptible severity of Judas' betrayal of Jesus dramatized by his doing so for a very low price: a paltry 30 silver coins (Mt. 26:15), equal to the compensation paid to an owner for a slave gored by an ox. (Ex. 21:32) Interestingly, to further emphasize the insult, when Judas, who eventually became filled with remorse, returned the thirty silver coins to the temple, the priests used them to buy a potter's field. (Mt. 27:3-7) Finally, Matthew summarizes and connects these two critical incidents utilizing the price system to underscore the point of how lowly the people would regard the Messiah, "Then what was spoken by Jeremiah the prophet was fulfilled: they took the thirty silver coins, the price set on him by the people of Israel, and they used them to buy the potter's field." (Mt. 27:9,10) Jesus himself uses prices to make a point, "Are not five sparrows sold for two pennies? Yet not one of them is forgotten by God.... Don't be afraid; you are worth more than many sparrows." (Lk. 12:6,7; Mt. 29-31)

Utilization of the price system to make a point continues with Paul. In Ephesus, "Many of those who believed now came and openly confessed their evil deeds. A number who had practiced sorcery brought their scrolls together and burned them publicly. When they calculated the value of the scrolls, the total came to fifty thousand drachmas. In this way the word of the Lord spread widely and grew in power." (Acts 19:18-20) Paul gives emphasis to his message by noting the very high value of these scrolls.

Reconciliation of Humanity's Two Sides

As noted by William Gibson of the Center for Religion, Ethics, and Social Policy at Cornell University, "The Reformed tradition thus understands the economic order as necessary for life, though sin permeates every actual order."[87] Before leaving this discussion of capitalism and the nature of humanity, let us take a look at the challenge of humankind to deal with its dual nature.

In Leviticus we are presented with a way in which these two sides of humanity (creation of God and sinner) can commence to be reconciled. Mann explains, "...Leviticus offers not only a way in which righteousness may be followed, but also a way by which *un*righteousness may be remedied. It holds before Israel the command, 'you must be holy' (Lv. 11:45), but also the promise, 'atonement shall be made for you' (Lv. 16:30). The new way of righteousness now includes a way out of sin."[88]

Further, Leviticus, with its lengthy detailed descriptions of sacrifice and purification procedures and regulations, conveys the general conceptual point that we humans have a *responsibility* to our God not only in return for the blessings which God confers on us but also simply in return for being God's people. "I am the LORD your God; consecrate yourselves and be holy, because I am holy." (Lv. 11:44,45) Recognizing the definition of "holy" as "set apart for God's sake" or "spiritually whole," the present day application seems to be that we Christians are expected to strive to be spiritually separate from sin.

And God's own declaration through Isaiah,

> "You heavens above, rain down righteousness;
>   let the clouds shower it down.
> Let the earth open wide,
>   Let salvation spring up,
> Let righteousness grow with it;
>   I, the LORD, have created it." (Is. 45:8)

LaSor notes, "This is one reason for the greatness of the prophecy of Isaiah: it stands astride two worlds. It speaks to the sinners who face an angry God and also to the remnant who are to receive salvation from the same God, revealed for them as Father and Redeemer. From this perspective, Isaiah's prophecy speaks with authority to every person of every age."[89]

The entire message of the New Testament is the reconciliation of God and God's creations through Jesus Christ. The Christian Doctrine of Atonement provides that the quest of God and humanity is the achievement of a reconciliation between God and humans. There is hope, and that hope comes through Jesus Christ, "I am the way, the truth and the life." (Jn. 14:6) The apostle Paul summarizes, "Therefore, no one will be declared righteous in his sight by observing the law; rather, through the law we become conscious of sin. But now a righteousness from God, apart from the law, has been made known,...This righteousness from God comes through faith in Jesus Christ to all who believe." (Rom. 3:20-22) Edwards interprets, "Righteousness has now been manifested in the once-for-all redemptive act of God in Jesus Christ.... [B]ecause Jesus is the personal manifestation of God's righteousness, righteousness must be received through a relationship of faith in God's Son.... Grace is the intersection where unconditional love meets human unworthiness."[90] Interestingly, Edwards notes that "Paul by his own admission was 'the chief of sinners' (1 Tim. 1:12-17), but he was also a 'chosen instrument' of God (acts 9:15-16). These two statements reveal the paradox of grace."[91]

There is great hope for humanity. Righteousness comes by faith, and faith is a voluntary act. That is the message of the Gospels. "So in everything, do to others what you would have them do to you, for this sums up the Law...." (Mt. 7:12) And later Peter declares, "...We must obey God rather than men!" (Acts 5:29) Paul then proclaims, "...love is the fulfillment of the law." (Rom. 14:10) Gary Thomas, founder of the Center for Evangelical Spirituality, observes, "The essence of the Christian life is a love relationship with God..... Holy holiness results from a tranquil reliance on God for the care of our souls. Holy holiness depends on grace, not self-effort, and it cooperates with God rather than tries to replace God.... Holy holiness is a relational holiness—it is God's overwhelming presence in my life, causing me to do what He wills as He give me the strength to do it.... The essence of holy holiness is loving God."[92]

Capitalism, which I suggest assumes a direct line between God and humans without government between and with its reliance on individual initiative rather than on legalism and coercion, is an economic system conducive to pursuing Thomas' notion. Further, capitalism, to work, requires the very virtues that are in concert with those associated with righteousness: faith, trust, generosity, cooperation, justice, honesty, creativity, egalitarianism and hope. As the people of the former Soviet Union countries dramatically discovered in the late 1990's, in the absence of such human virtues and societal norms, capitalism does not work as a viable economic system. Capitalism presents the opportunity for the economic expression of Luther's "priesthood of all believers."

Dr. John West, who has done so much ground-breaking work on political science and religion at the Discovery Institute in Seattle, expresses this notion eloquently, "The problem with making unlimited government our savior, according to (C.S.) Lewis, is that it undermines human dignity and ignores human depravity. It undermines human dignity because it does not take seriously the connection between freedom and human excellence. Government can make humans behave, but ultimately it cannot make them good. That is because virtue presupposes free choice. The society where all good acts are compelled is a society where no act can be virtuous. It is a society without Mother Teresa, Martin Luther King, or George Washington.... Lewis granted that the freedom required for virtue to flourish also 'makes evil possible,' but this is the price that must be paid, he said, for 'any love or goodness or joy worth having."[93] West continues, "If unlimited government undermines the dignity of human nature, it likewise fails to come to grips with human depravity.... In the words of Lewis, 'Mankind is so fallen, that no man can be trusted with unchecked power over his fellows. Aristotle said that some people were only fit to be slaves. I do not contradict him. But I reject slavery because I see no men fit to be masters."[94]

And finally, the ultimate reconciling genius of capitalism. Christianity is a religion of community. It deals with humans in relationship with each other as suggested in the first two commandments. Our love of God is to be demonstrated by our active love of each other. Similarly, capitalism is an economic system of community in at least two ways.

First, note the very title of Adam Smith's famous treatise, the "bible" of capitalism: *An Inquiry into the Nature and Causes of the Wealth of Nations.*" Note that the title refers to the wealth of *nations,* not the wealth of *individuals.* Smith's study and evaluation of capitalism as an economic system was within the criterion of its effect on the aggregate wealth of the nation, not on the personal wealth of individuals. It was within this *community* criterion that Smith found the great contribution of capitalism. As sinful individuals pursued their self-interest, the saintful outcome of community well-being was maximized. This first point coincides with Biblical and classical morality as enunciated by Arthur Lovejoy, "men never act from disinterested and rational motives, but... it is possible, nonetheless, to fashion a good whole, a happy and harmonious state, by skillfully mixing and counterbalancing these refractory and separately antagonistic parts."[95]

Second, in order to function, capitalism requires cooperative interaction among the various members of the community: producers, consumers, workers, employers, suppliers, regulators, owners, customers, competitors (within industry associations), educators, etc. embodying such saintful behavior and attitudinal characteristics as trust and love.

The foregoing is strikingly compatible with the discussion of the triune nature of God as the Father, the Son and the Holy Spirit by Jurgen Moltmann, Professor of Systematic Theology at the University of Tubingen in Germany. "The three divine Persons have everything in common, except for their personal characteristics. So the Trinity corresponds to a community in which people are defined through their relations with one another and in their significance for one another,... The Christian doctrine of the Trinity provides the intellectual means whereby to harmonize personality and sociality in the community of men and women, without sacrificing the one to the other."[96] Is not capitalism, as identified by Smith, an exemplification of such: "By pursuing his own interest he... is led by an invisible hand to promote .... (the interest) of the society"[97] and, I add, by fully cooperating with the other members of society.

All of these matters associated with a reconciliation of humanity's two natures in the context of capitalism and Christianity are revisited in later chapters and are woven throughout this book.

Perhaps the following table relating capitalism to socialism will shed further light on the characteristics of capitalism which cause it to be more compatible with the dual nature of humans.

	Socialism	Capitalism
View of economics:	Zero sum game	Positive sum game
Occupied with:	Income distribution	Income generation
Principal activity:	Consumption	Production
Attitudes:	Envy, covetousness	Innovation, creativity
Property ownership:	Collective	Private
Mechanism:	Coercion	Voluntarism; cooperation
Societal value:	Compliance	Trust
Scope:	National	Global
Decisions:	Centralized	Decentralized
Focus:	Present	Future
Upward mobility:	Political obedience	Creativity, risk-taking

Living standard reflects:	Political perquisites	Economic contribution
Dominant outcome:	Static	Dynamic
Implementation first step:	Measuring equal shares	Identifying needs
"Score"	Hierarchical status	Earnings
"Winning"	Power from political prowess	Profits from fulfilling needs

These differences will be clearly understood as they are addressed in discussions which follow.

Chapter IV

Source of Material Possessions and Wealth

================================

D ale Sewall, my minister, observed, "In our church every time there is a need, there is a response—sometimes pedestrian, sometimes stunning—provided by God to meet that need."[98] A glorious aspect of being a Christian is the privilege of participating in God's inexhaustibly providing what we humans need.

The Old Testament

In the earlier discussion of the nature of Matter, we observed that God is the source of everything. "In the beginning God created the heavens...earth...light,...water,...sky,...land,...vegetation,... stars,...animals (in the sky, sea and on land),...day,... night,...seasons." (Gn. 1:1-25) Now we focus on God as the source of material possessions and wealth.

Early in Scripture we see the affirmation that God is God of all humanity and the source of humanity's possessions. "The LORD said to Abram.... All the land that you see I will give to you and your offspring forever. I will make your offspring like dust of the earth, so that if anyone could count the dust, then your offspring could be counted. Go, walk through the length and breadth of the land, for I am giving it to you." (Gn. 13:14-17)

God, himself, declares that he is the provider of material possessions, the satisfier of all human needs. "The LORD said, 'I have indeed seen the misery of my people in Egypt..., and I am concerned about their suffering. So I have come down to rescue them from the hand of the Egyptians and to bring them up out of that land into a good and spacious land, a land flowing with milk and honey....'" (Ex. 3:8) "....I have promised to bring you ...into... a land flowing with milk and honey." (Ex. 3:17) "When the LORD brings you into the land...flowing with milk and honey...." (Ex. 13:5) Indeed, it is not just any land, not just beautiful land, it is productive land.

Further, in the context of the foregoing statements made by God in a discussion with Moses, the whole tenor of which is God as protector and provider, God reaffirms, "I will be with you."—a condition as true today as then. This is quickly followed by God revealing to Moses his divine nature, his eternal, omnipotent, omniscient and omnipresent nature: "I AM." (Ex. 3:14,15) Included in the all-encompassing name must be the role of provider, and the name itself implies that God's identity can only be understood by God's unfolding story as father of humanity.

Then in the Desert of Sin, "the LORD said to Moses, 'I will rain down bread from heaven for you." (Ex. 16:4) Later Moses says to the people, "You will know that it was the LORD when he gives you meat to eat in the evening and all the bread you want in the morning,..." (Ex. 16:8) "And then, God said, 'At twilight you will eat meat, and in the morning you will be filled with bread. Then you will know that I am the LORD your God' That evening quail came and covered the camp, and in the morning there was....'the bread the LORD has given you to eat." (Ex. 16:11-15). Later, "I will stand there before you by the rock at Horeb. Strike the rock, and water will come out of it for the people to drink." (Ex. 17:6) "The wilderness period was a constant demonstration of the Lord's provision for the people's needs. [The book of] Numbers highlights this care in ... the stories of guidance, protection and material supplies (10:11-14:45; chs. 16-17; 20-25; 27:12-23; 31:1-33:49)."[99]

In Deuteronomy Moses reminds the Israelites before they cross the River Jordan into the Promised Land, "The LORD your God has blessed you in all the work of your hands..... These forty years the LORD your God has been with you, and you have not lacked for anything." (Dt. 2:7) "The LORD your God has given you this land to take possession of it." (Dt. 3:18) "When you have eaten and are satisfied, praise the LORD your God for the good land he has given you.... He brought you water out of hard rock." (Dt. 8:10,15) "When you have entered the land the LORD your God is giving you,..." (Dt. 26:1) From the Song of Moses, "The LORD alone led him;... and fed him with the fruit of the fields. He nourished him with honey from the rock, and with oil from the flinty crag, with curds and milk from the heard and flock and with fattened lambs and goats, with choice rams of Bashan and the finest kernels of wheat. You drank the foaming blood of the grape." (Dt. 32:12-14)

Joshua reaffirms God as the source, "... this good land, which the LORD your God has given you." (Jos. 23:13) Note, not only land, but *good* land. Throughout the Old Testament land is a key element in God's covenant relationship with God's people. Hannah, in her prayer of thanks to God for giving her a son, Samuel, acknowledges God as the source of everything, including, "The LORD sends poverty and wealth; he humbles and he exalts." (1 Sm. 2:7) The prophet Nathan is instructed by God to tell David, "The LORD declares to you that the LORD himself will establish a house for you." (2 Sm. 7:11)

But God providing for us requires at least two conditions: first, unequivocal *faith* on our part that God will provide; second, our consistent, continuous *obedience* to God. An example of the presence of both of these conditions is Elijah's interceding for the widow at Zarephath in asking God to provide food and to restore life to her son. "As surely as the LORD your God lives,' ... 'I don't have any bread....' She went away and did as Elijah had told her. For the jar of flour was not used up and jug of oil did not run dry, in keeping with the word of the LORD spoken by Elijah.... 'Now I know that you are a man of God and that the word of the LORD from your mouth is the truth." (1 Kgs. 12-24) Elisha performs similar miracles to demonstrate God as the source in response to faith and obedience. "... she kept pouring. When all the jars were full,.... she went and told the man of God, and he said, 'Go, sell the oil and pay your debts. You and your sons can live on what is left." (2 Kgs. 4:1-7) "A man came from Baal Shalishah, bringing the man of God twenty loaves of barley bread.... 'Give it to the people to eat,' Elisha said. 'How can I set this before a hundred men?' his servant asked. But Elisha answered, 'Give it to the people to eat. For this is what the LORD says: 'They will eat and have some left over.'' Then he set it before them, and they ate and had some left over, according to the word of the LORD." (2 Kgs. 4:42-44)

Later King David, after everyone had made huge donations of their personal wealth to building the temple in Jerusalem, acknowledges God as the source of all. "Wealth and honor come from you; you are the ruler of all things.... Everything comes from you, and we have given you only what comes from your hand....O LORD our God, as for all this abundance that we have provided for building you a temple for your Holy Name, it comes from your hand, and all of it belongs to you." (1 Chr. 29:12-16) Finally, in one of David's psalms, "The earth is the LORD's, and everything in it." (Ps. 24:1) Later we will return to the concept of giving to God that which is already God's. King Solomon, David's son, continues the affirmation, "for the LORD his God was with him and made him exceedingly great.... ask for whatever you want me to give you. " (2 Chr. 1:1,7) "Praise be to the LORD,...who made heaven and earth!" LaSor takes this notion further, asserting that God is the source of the Israelites' kings' very kingship. "The choices are based not on the laws of authority or inheritance but on God's sovereign will and power. Consequently the mighty accomplishments of these persons are not their own. God is their source."[100]

God as the source is affirmed again in Nehemiah as the Levites reminded the Israelites, "You alone are the LORD.... In their hunger you gave them bread from heaven and in their thirst you brought them water from the rock; you alone told them to go in and take possession of the land.... For forty years you sustained them in the desert; they lacked nothing,...They captured fortified cities and fertile land;... They ate to the full and were well-nourished; they reveled in your great goodness." (Neh. 9:15,21-25) God is the source of all because God is the owner of all as affirmed in the book of Job, "Everything under heaven belongs to me." (Job 41:11) and again in Psalms, "The earth is the LORD's, and everything in it, the world, and all who live in it;" (Ps. 24:1)

Again, as with so many subjects addressed in Scripture, this subject of God as the source is most beautifully expressed in the Psalms. "LORD, you have assigned me my portion and my cup; you have made my lot secure." (Ps. 16:5) "Fear the LORD,..., for those who fear him lack nothing." (Ps. 34:9) "You care for the land and water it; ...The streams of God are filled with water to provide the people with grain,.... You crown the year with your bounty,..." (Ps. 65:9-13) "The LORD will indeed give what is good, and our land will yield its harvest." (Ps. 85:12) "He brought out Israel,.... He brought them quail and satisfied them with the bread of heaven. He opened a rock, and water gushed out;" (Ps. 105:37-41) "Let them give thanks to the LORD for his unfailing love and his wonderful deeds for men, for he satisfies the thirsty and fills the hungry with good things." (Ps. 107:8,9) "He provides food for those who fear him;" (Ps. 111:5) "...the LORD, the Maker of heaven and earth,..." (Ps. 134:3) "... and who gives food to every creature." (Ps. 136:25) "You open your hand and satisfy the desires of every living thing." (Ps. 145:16) "...he supplies the earth with rain and makes grass grow on the hills, He provides food for the cattle.... And satisfies you with the finest of wheat." (Ps. 147: 8,9,14) Finally, as we did when discussing creation previously, we now, when viewing God as the source of everything, should go back and again experience the magnificence of the entire Psalm 104, "The Economist's Psalm" ".... These all look to you...." (Ps. 104:27) See Appendix A.

"A man can do nothing better than to eat and drink and find satisfaction in his work. This too, I see, is from the hand of God, for without him, who can eat or find enjoyment?" (Eccl. 2:24,25) In Ecclesiastes we find a marvelous passage which, for purposes of this book, I have given the following title:

THE ENTREPRENEUR'S AND VENTURE CAPITALIST'S CREED

Cast your bread upon the waters,
   for after many days you will find it again....

As you do not know the path of the wind,...
So you cannot understand the work of God,
   the Maker of all things.

Sow your seed in the morning,
   and at evening let not your hands be idle,
for you do not know which will succeed,

whether this or that,
or whether both will do equally well." (Eccl.
11:1,5,6)

But, while God is the source of material possessions and wealth,
there is a critically important qualification. "God gives man wealth,
possessions and honor, so that he lacks nothing his heart desires,
but God does not enable him to enjoy them,…" (Eccl. 6:2) We will
come back later to this major point.

The prophets proclaimed that God is the source of material
possessions and wealth. Some expressed it in the negative; that is,
without God, destruction is the outcome. "For the day of the LORD
is near, it will come like destruction from the Almighty. Has not the
food been cut off….? The seeds are shriveled…. The storehouses
are in ruins, the granaries have been broken down, for the grain has
dried up. How the cattle moan!…. even the flocks of sheep are
suffering…." (Joel 1:15-19) Then, when God turns to forgiveness
and blessing, "The LORD will reply to them: 'I am sending you
grain, new wine and oil, enough to satisfy you fully;'… Surely the
LORD has done great things….the open pastures are becoming
green. The trees are bearing their fruit; the fig tree and the vine
yield their riches…. The threshing floors will be filled with grain;
the vats will overflow with new wine and oil…. You will have
plenty…. Then you will know that I am in Israel, that I am the LORD
your God, and that there is no other." (Jl. 2:18-27) Hosea, in equating Israel to an adulteress, states "She has not acknowledged that I
was the one who gave her the grain, the new wine and oil, who
lavished on her the silver and gold—which they used for Baal.
Therefore I will take away my grain when it ripens, and my new
wine when it is ready. I will take back my wool and my linen,… "
(Hos. 2:8,9) Indeed, if God is the source, then God has the power to
withhold.

Isaiah declares, "He will also send you rain for the seed you
sow…, and the food that comes from the land will be rich and plentiful. (Is. 30:23) "I will make the rivers flow…. I turn the desert into
pools of water,…. I will put in the desert the cedar and the acacia,
the myrtle and the olive, I will set pines in the wasteland, the fir and
the cypress together, so that people may see and know,… that the
hand of the LORD has done this," (Is. 41:26) "The LORD will guide

you always; he will satisfy your needs.... You will be like a well-watered garden, like a spring whose waters never fail." (Is. 58:11) "...to the honor of the LORD your God, the Holy One of Israel, for he has endowed you with splendor." (Is. 60:9) Isaiah quotes God, "I form the light and create darkness, I bring prosperity and create disaster; I, the LORD, do all these things." (Is. 45:7) Also, stated negatively, "...the Lord, the LORD Almighty, is about to take from Jerusalem and Judah both supply and support:..." (Is. 3:1)

The prophet Jeremiah makes similar declarations, "Blessed is the man who trusts in the LORD, whose confidence is in him. He will be like a tree planted by the water that sends out its roots by the stream. It does not fear when heat comes; its leaves are always green...and never fails to bear fruit." (Jer. 17:7,8) "Do not I fill heaven and earth?' declares the LORD." (Jer. 23:24) "This is what the LORD God almighty, the God of Israel, says:...'I made the earth and its people and the animals that are on it, and I give it to anyone I please." (Is.27:5)

God, as Creator, also affirms ownership when he declares to Job, "Everything under heaven belongs to me." (Jb. 41:11) and later, through Asaph, "I am God, your God.... Every animal of the forest is mine, and the cattle on a thousand hills.... And the creatures of the field are mine...., for the world is mine, and all that is in it." (Ps. 50:7-12) and later, through Jeremiah, "The God of Israel, says:... 'With my great power and outstretched arm I made the earth and its people and the animals that are on it,..." (Jer. 27:4,5)

The prophet Ezekial presents considerable testimony of God as divine sovereign and therefore with ultimate control of everything, including material possessions and wealth. "I will cut off the supply of food in Jerusalem,... food and water will be scarce." (Ez. 4:16,17) "I will bring more and more famine upon you and cut off your supply of food." (Ez. 5:16) "for their land will be stripped of everything.... Then you will know that I am the LORD." (Ez. 12:19,20) "I clothed you....adorned you with fine jewelry.... Your food was fine flour, honey and olive oil. You became very beautiful and rose to be a queen.... The splendor I had given you made your beauty perfect, declares the Sovereign LORD." (Ez. 16:10-14) "For this is what the Sovereign LORD says: I myself will search for my sheep and look after them.... They will feed in a rich pasture...." (Ez. 34:11-14)

God as the source of prosperity is beautifully conveyed in the passages wherein Ezekiel is describing the restored Israel in his message of hope to the exiles, "The water was coming down from under the south side of the temple,.... I saw a great number of trees on each side of the river..... Swarms of living creatures will live wherever the river flows. There will be large numbers of fish,.... there will be places for spreading nets.... Fruit trees of all kinds will grow on both banks of the river. Their leaves will not wither, nor will their fruit fail. (Ez. 47:2) The message: all of our needs will be supplied from the abundant flow from God, as represented by the temple.

Then later, when rebuilding the temple after the exile, Haggai reminds the people, "The silver is mine and the gold is mine,' declares the LORD." (Hg. 2:8) Zechariah reminds them, "The seed will grow well, the vine will yield its fruit, the ground will produce its crops, and the heavens will drop their dew. I will give all these things as an inheritance to the remnant of this people.... It is the LORD who makes the storm clouds. He gives showers of rain to men, and plants of the field to everyone." (Zec. 8:12; 10:1)

New Testament

Jesus continues the affirmation of God as the source of all material possessions and the satisfier of all needs. This is perhaps most directly enunciated in the Lord's Prayer, "Give us today our daily bread." (Mt. 6:11) Jesus is acknowledging that, on a daily basis for our most mundane needs, God is our provider and sustainer. Accordingly, we need not—and should not—look elsewhere.

In looking to God as the source of all that we need, Jesus also introduces, however, a very important condition. "Therefore I tell you do not be anxious about your life, what you eat...drink.... wear....your heavenly Father knows that you need them all. But seek first his kingdom and his righteousness, and all these things shall be yours.... Therefore, do not be anxious about tomorrow,..." (Mt. 6:25-34; Lk. 12:22) Indeed, worry tends to take our minds off focusing on God and weakens our faith in God as the source of all of our needs for sustenance and fulfillment.

Later Jesus continues, "Ask, and it will be given you; seek, and you will find; knock, and it will be opened to you. For every one who asks receives, and he who seeks finds, and to him who knocks it will be opened. What father among you, if his son asks for a fish, will instead give him a serpent; or if he asks for an egg, will give him a scorpion? If you then, who are evil, know how to give good gifts to your children, how much more will the heavenly Father give the Holy Spirit to those who ask him!" (Mt. 7:7-11) While Jesus was talking about the importance of persistent prayer and spiritual sustenance, nevertheless in so doing he emphasized the parent/child relationship between God and humanity, as noted by Mounce, "drawing a comparison between parents' natural acts of kindness toward their children and the perfection of God's generosity toward those who seek his favor."[101]

A miracle reflecting God as the source occurs in a passage of Scripture dealing with Jesus teaching his disciples to pay the temple tax, although they believed that members of God's kingdom were not obligated to do so. When the tax collectors of Capernaum ask Peter for payment, Jesus says, "Go to the sea and cast a hook, and take the first fish that comes up, and when you open its mouth you will find a shekel; take that and give it to them...." (Mt. 17:24) Nowhere in the Gospels is this notion demonstrated more clearly than in the feeding of the five thousand and the four thousand (Mt. 14:15; Mt. 15:32; Mk. 6:35; Mk. 8:1; Lk. 9:12; Jn. 6:5.) Jesus turns to God; in Matthew, Mark and Luke, he "looked up to heaven and blessed;" and in John "he had given thanks." Then enough bread and fish were distributed of *such great abundance* that not only had everyone eaten all that they wanted, but there was a considerable amount left over. The miracle is dramatic. In the face of apparent insurmountable obstacles—a meager supply of food and money—a multitude is fed. While this and all of the Gospel miracles have been subject to a broad array of widely differing interpretations, I agree with that of Mounce that these were actual events teaching our "utter dependence on God."[102] Similarly, in John's Gospel the resurrected Jesus says to the disciples, "Cast the net on the right side,...so they cast it, and now they were not able to haul it in, for the quantity of fish." (Jn. 21:6) Each of these stories has as a greater meaning the metaphorical demonstration of Jesus as the source of the spiritually abundant life.

Earlier in the Gospel of John, Jesus is even more forceful: "Ask, and you will receive, that your joy may be full....Whatever you ask in my name, I will do it, that the father may be glorified in the Son;…. If you abide in me, and my words abide in you, ask whatever you will, and it shall be done for you." Wheeler raises the question: is the attractiveness of all of this simply enlightened self-interest? Then she answers the question, "But the tension remains….the appeals are eschatological, and there is a disparity:…the necessity of bearing true witness to Christ, and….a situation of persecution to which no deliverance is promised….These exhortations amount to a call to follow Jesus."[103]

The conclusion is clear. The top priority of humans should be God. Any dilution of putting God first impedes the process of His taking care of us and of our entering the kingdom of God. Complete, genuine faith is what one needs. "If you have faith as a grain of mustard seed, you will say to the mountain, 'move from here to there,' and it will move; and nothing will be impossible to you…..whoever has faith and does not doubt…, but believes that what he says will come to pass, it will be done…." (Mt. 17:6; Mt. 21:21; Mk. 11:22; Lk. 17:6). *Faith* is the key. "…if you have faith and never doubt,…if you say to this mountain, 'be taken up and cast into the sea,' it will be done. And whatever you ask in prayer, you will receive, if you have faith." (Mt. 21:21) "…whatever you ask in prayer, believe that you have received it, and it will be yours." (Mk. 11:23) "If you ask anything in my name, I will do it." (Jn. 14:13)

Note, however, there are two caveats: (1) the request must be "in my name" and (2) the passages in the books of Matthew and Mark continue right on, as if part of the process above, with the directive, *forgive*. All motivations must be honorable; that is, pursuit of anything must be done genuinely in God's name—for the good of all of God's kingdom—and accompanied by complete forgiveness of others.

The foregoing passages are mostly from the farewell discourses of Jesus wherein he is comforting his disciples by reassuring them that God is the only source upon which they need rely. God will supply all of their needs. The key ingredient to all of this is faith. As emphasized by Wheeler, "Faith is absolutely central to the reality perspective on which this passage—Luke 12:22-34—relies….faith in God…and faith in Jesus' proclamation of the kingdom as the proper point of orientation for a human life."[104]

An interesting conclusion to this matter of the relationship between the material and the spiritual is presented by Dietrich Bonhoeffer as quoted by Fuller and Rice, "Let us reverse the words of Jesus (in Matthew 6:21) and our question is answered: 'Where thy heart is, there shall thy treasure be also.'"[105] Wheeler elaborates on this thought and ultimately provides the answer to the dilemma (reliance on the material or the spiritual) suggesting that one take the exhortations above quite seriously and with absolute faith; then, "In Luke, Jesus offers the kingdom as the only goal worthy of human pursuit. He *promises* that it will be given on the single condition that it is sought above all other things."[106] Interestingly, no moral stance is taken on possessions per se, other than they clearly are not the end.

Wheeler continues, the exhortations above are based on "a comprehensive account of reality that makes it intelligible, even entirely rational, to heed such a call. The paradox of such a summons is that viewed from the other side, …it is equally a gift. It is 'wise counsel,' which if followed would enable one to accomplish the ends he desires, to secure his life in fact in the only way it can be secured.…The liberating character of …Jesus' confidence frees those who shared it from fear…and such freedom would create new possibilities of joy."[107] This joyous faithful obedience will be manifest in worldly material possessions and wealth as well as acceptance into the kingdom. Wheeler concludes: "Looking for God's kingdom is the only business worth the serious attention of a human being.…Beyond the assurance that God will provide what God's children need, there is the claim that what they need is not finally the things that all pursue, but God's own reign, to which all these are added almost incidentally."[108] In Jesus' interpretation of the Parable of the Sower he makes the critically important distinction that pursuit of God's kingdom comes first. Then only secondarily are our worldly needs accommodated. "The one who received the seed that fell among the thorns is the man who hears the word, but the worries of this life and the deceitfulness of wealth choke it, making it unfruitful. But the one who received the seed that fell on good soil is the man who hears the word and understands it. He produces a crop, yielding a hundred, sixty or thirty times what was sown." (Mt. 13:23; Mk. 4:20; Lk. 8:15) The harvest, however, is not necessarily material possessions, as Jesus in this parable was teaching about the kingdom of God.

This message is continued by the apostles, "We are bringing you the good news, telling you to turn to the living God, who...provides you with plenty of food and fills your hearts with joy." (Acts 14:15,17). Paul, in many of his letters affirms the truth that God is the source of all wealth. "God is able to make all grace abound to you, so that in all things at all times, having all that you need, you will abound in every good work....Now he who supplies seed to the sower and bread for food will also supply and increase your store of seed and will enlarge the harvest of your righteousness. You will be made rich in every way so that you can be generous on every occasion,...Thanks be to God for his indescribable gift." (2 Cor. 9:8,10,15) "Do not be anxious about anything, but in everything, by prayer and petition, with thanksgiving, present your requests to God....Finally, whatever is true, whatever is noble, whatever is right, whatever is pure, whatever is lovely, whatever is admirable— if anything is excellent or praiseworthy—think about such things. Whatever you have learned or received or heard from me, or seen in me—put it into practice. And the God of peace will be with you." (Phil. 4:6-9) Note also all of the strings attached! Finally, Paul states, "And my God will meet all your needs according to his glorious riches in Christ Jesus." (Phil. 4:19) Note that Paul often refers to "needs," as distinguished from "wants," suggesting moderation and sufficiency as distinguished from opulence. As we will discuss in Chapter VII, "Role of Material Possessions and Wealth," generously sharing with others is a Divine imperative.

Elsewhere in Scripture we read, "Every good and perfect gift is from above,..." (Jas. 1:17) New Testament scholar Peter Davids suggests that the gift being spoken of here is believed to be wisdom, but God is acknowledged as the source of all perfect gifts.[109] "Again he prayed, and the heavens gave rain, and the earth produced its crops." (Jas. 5:18) "His divine power has given us everything we need for life..." (2 Pt. 1:3) "This is the confidence we have in approaching God: that if we ask anything according to his will, he hears us." (1 Jn. 5:14) Note two very important modifiers in the previous two passages. First, God gives us everything we *need* for life—not necessarily everything we want. Clearly there is an implication of necessities only. Furthermore, the meaning of the passage turns on the definition of *life*—the Christian life, a life built around Christ, or the pagan, hedonistic life? Peter was referring to the former which means a life not centered on material wellbeing. Secondly, if we ask anything *according to his will*, he hears us. God is the source of all that is in accord with his will. Accordingly, our requests must coincide with what God wants for us; prayer is a searching communication not a demanding communication.

Private Property

   While acknowledging God as the source of all worldly goods, Scripture nevertheless makes provision for private ownership. This is an important concept in economics because private property underlies the notion of economic incentives related to sinners' self-interest as well as underlies the notion of political liberty. The latter—political liberty / democracy—is a condition required for the existence of capitalism. It is private property which protects one against political oppression because, when the state owns all property, dissent and the protection of minorities is impossible.

   The concepts of private ownership and commercial transactions are introduced very early in the Bible. Abraham obtaining a place to bury his deceased wife, Sarah, involved him in negotiating with Ephron in a well-established bargaining process which culminated in "...Ephron's field...the cave in it, and all the trees within the borders of the field...deeded to Abraham as his property..." (Gn. 23:3-20) As Mann notes, "The point of the story...is that Abraham holds legal title to a piece of the land of Canaan. Indeed, the purchase of the burial plot is narrated as the report of a legal transaction....The action takes place in the city gate, which served as the courtroom in ancient Israel, and includes repeated references to the presence of formal witnesses. In the lively bartering between Abraham and Ephron, Abraham insists on *buying* the land...the author concludes the chapter with a deliberately redundant summary reemphasizing Abraham's title."[110] It should be noted that Abraham's posture in the negotiating was steadfastly one of fairness and equity to the other party, a reflection of his righteousness.

   Later Jacob bought land in Canaan. "For a hundred pieces of silver, he bought...the plot of ground where he pitched his tent..." (Gn. 33:19), and Hamor offers him more land, "...the land is open to you. Live in it, trade in it, and acquire property in it." (Gn. 34:10) The concept of private ownership is extended further to include the notion of inheritance when, upon his death, "Abraham left everything he owned to Isaac." (Gn. 25:5) Later, Rachael and Leah, Laban's daughters, refer to "the inheritance of our father's estate." (Gn. 31:14)

It is clear in Scripture that land has an economic purpose associated with private ownership. Rather than simply being a symbol of identity for the Israelites, land's utility results from its supporting subsistence and commerce. Livestock, crops, minerals, clay and other economic resources were related to the land. In the famines in Egypt and Canaan, people bought food. (See Gn. 47:13-24)

In Leviticus private property is referred to as a legitimate concept. "...each one of you is to return to his family property..... everyone is to return to his own property. If you sell land,....If one of your countrymen becomes poor and sells some of this property,...If a man sells a house,..." (Lv. 25:10, 13,14,25,29) Although there is no evidence later in the Bible of the Year of Jubilee ever having been celebrated[111] and possessions returned to original owners and debts cancelled, the notion of private ownership is clearly reflected in the Year of Jubilee instructions (Lv. 25:8-55). They also expressed the ideal that every Israelite family should possess land as a source of self-sufficiency in that agrarian society. That general point relating private ownership to the responsibility of self-sufficiency can be applied today. The Year of Jubilee instructions regarding the forgiveness of debts and the return of land to the original family ownership also reflected the attitude of God that material possessions not become ends in themselves; materialism and greed were to be avoided through viewing our possessions "on loan" from God and to be shared with the poor. These concerns will be discussed later in Chapters VI and VII, "Attitudes Toward Material Possessions and Wealth" and "Role of Material Possessions and Wealth."

The concept of private property is further noted in the book of Numbers, "and the LORD said.... You must certainly give them property as an inheritance among their father's relatives and turn their father's inheritance over to them." (Nm. 27:6,7) Additionally, in the Ten Commandments the concept of private ownership appears. "You shall not steal." (Ex. 20:15, Dt. 5:19) "You shall not set desire on your neighbor's house or land,...his ox or donkey, or anything that belongs to your neighbor." (Ex. 20:17, Dt. 5:21) Later in Deuteronomy, "Do not move your neighbor's boundary stone...." (Dt. 19:14) "Cursed is the man who moves his neighbor's boundary stone." (Dt. 27:17) Then in the book of Judges, "After Joshua had dismissed the Israelites, they went to take possession of the land, each to his own inheritance." (Jgs. 2:6) As Lindsel notes, "commandment set up that no one was to.... steal land which belonged to his neighbor.... Each family held title to the land. Each family was responsible for creating wealth from the land. All had equal opportunity. But no guarantee was given that all would produce equal results."[112]

In the book of Ruth God uses a real estate transaction for God's purpose as Boaz cleverly acquires property owned by Naomi and Ruth, opening up the opportunity for Boaz to marry Ruth and continue the lineage which eventually would lead to the Messiah. Private property is mentioned also when David says to Mephibosheth, "I will restore to you all the land that belonged to your grandfather Saul,..." (2 Sm. 9:7) and to Araunah, "let me have the site of your threshing floor so I can build an altar to the LORD,.... Sell it to me at the full price." (1Chr. 21:22) "So David bought the threshing floor and the oxen and paid fifty shekels of silver for them. David built an altar to the LORD there..." (2 Sm. 24:24,25) The temple in Jerusalem is built on private property! Similarly, Samaria, the capital of Israel, the Northern Kingdom, was built on private property. "He [King Omri] bought the hill of Samaria from Shemer for two talents of silver and built a city on the hill, calling it Samaria, after Shemer, the name of the former owner of the hill." (1 Kgs. 16:24) The concept of private property emerges later in the context of the returnees from exile in Babylon who "...resettle on their own property..." (1 Chr. 9:2)

The legitimacy of private property is reflected in an exchange between King Ahab of Samaria and Naboth. "Ahab said to Naboth, 'Let me have your vineyard.... since it is close to my palace. In exchange I will give you a better vineyard or, if your prefer, I will pay you whatever it is worth.' But Naboth replied, 'The LORD forbid that I should give you the inheritance of my fathers." (1 Kgs 21:2,3) In response to a trick conjured up by Ahab's wife Jezebel, who some regard as the most evil person in the Bible, Elijah intercedes on behalf of God's attitude toward property.

Not only is the legitimacy of private property affirmed in Scripture, but the legitimacy of an economic return to property is affirmed as well. "Now Elisha had said to the [faithfilled] woman whose son he had restored to life, 'Go away with your family and stay…, because the LORD has decreed a famine in the land that will last seven years…. At the end of seven years she came back… and went to the king…. The king said, 'Give back everything that belonged to her, including all the income from her land from the day she left the country until now." (2 Kgs. 8:1-6)

King Solomon also implies the validity of private property and economic return thereto in his warning, "My son, pay attention to my wisdom,… lest strangers feast on your wealth and your toil enrich another man's house." (Prv. 5:1,10) King Lemuel similarly suggests that private property is valid. "A wife of a noble character…. She considers a field and buys it; out of her earnings she plants a vineyard." (Prv. 31:10,16)

The prophets also affirmed the validity of private property. Micah refers to in the negative, "Woe to those who plan iniquity, to those who plot evil on their beds!…. They covet fields and seize them, and houses, and take them. They defraud a man of his home, a fellowman of his inheritance." (Mi. 2:1,2) LaSor observes, "these actions have denied the sacred right of land tenure that celebrated God's gift to the people."[113] Old Testament scholar Elizabeth Achtemeier agrees, noting in her commentary that by being defrauded of their landholdings, "probably by foreclosing on loans or by corrupt dealings in the courts,… they were deprived of their rights and security and life."[114] Indeed, property ownership was a key element in the protection of individual freedom and sufficiency—a similarity between the Biblical times and today. The notion of private property—even in the eschaton—is also implied in Micah 4:4, "Every man will sit under his own vine and under his own fig tree,…"

Jeremiah is personally involved in a fascinating real estate deal, the viability of which depends entirely upon Jeremiah's trust in God. Jeremiah is instructed by God to buy land outside of Jerusalem immediately prior to Judah's defeat by the Babylonians—lousy timing. Jeremiah's faith is vindicated when God eventually brings about the return of the exiles. "I knew that this was the word of the LORD, so I bought the field….and weighed out for him seventeen shekels of silver. I signed and sealed the deed…. I gave Baruch these instructions:…'Take these documents, both sealed and unsealed copies of the deed of purchase, and put them in a clay jar so they will last long time." (All similar to real estate transaction practice today.) "For this is what the LORD Almighty, the God of Israel, says: 'Houses, fields and vineyards will again be bought in this land…. So I will give them all the prosperity I have promised them…. Fields will be bought for silver, and deeds will be signed, sealed and witnessed…. because I will restore their fortunes." (Jer. 32:8-15,42-44)

Ezekiel proclaims, "The prince must not take any of the inheritance of the people, driving them off their property…. None of my people will be separated from his property." (Ez. 45:18)

In the New Testament Jesus uses several parables involving private ownership, including the parable of the workers paid equally, "like a landowner…. The owner of the vineyard…" (Mt. 20:1-16), the parable of the wicked tenants, "There was a landowner…. owner of the vineyard…." (Mt. 21:33-44; Mk. 12:1-11; Lk. 20:9-18), and the parable of the lost son, "divided his property between them…. Everything I have is yours." (Lk. 15:11-31) While private ownership is only incidental to the message of these parables, nevertheless the way in which it is used reflects Jesus' regarding it as legitimate. In the story of the rich young man, Jesus' directive, "Go, sell everything you have and give to the poor,…." (Mk. 10:21) is not the advocation of communism, but is stated by Jesus in the context of responding to the man's inquiry regarding what it takes to gain eternal life. Jesus was emphasizing the immense magnitude of the commitment required to becoming a follower of Jesus, far beyond simply keeping the commandments. Nash points out, "Jesus' teaching stresses human obligations that cannot be fulfilled unless one first has certain financial resources. For example, passages that oblige believers to use their resources for God's purposes presuppose the legitimacy of private ownership. Jesus taught that children have an obligation to care for their parents (Mt. 15:3-9) and that his followers ought to be generous in their support of worthy causes (Mt. 6:2-4). It is rather difficult to fulfill such obligations unless one has certain financial resources."[115]

Similarly, throughout Acts and the letters of Paul the continuous exhortation by Paul to be generous implies the ownership of possessions and wealth with which to be generous. "There was no needy persons among them. For from time to time those who owned lands or houses sold them, brought the money from the sales and put it at the apostles feet,..." (Acts 4:34) Presumably, then, there was a buyer.

Private property is a fundamental condition within capitalism. It is what permits capitalism to work. This is true for three reasons.

First private property, by protecting the rights of minorities and protecting the ability to dissent, undergirds democracy which is necessary for a free market to work. Yes, there are other political/ economic systems involving private ownership, fascism and "crony (phony) capitalism" (capitalism in a nondemocratic society) found in some Southeast Asia countries today, for example. But only bona-fide capitalism facing the rigors of the marketplace and limited by relevant government regulations to insure competition and socially responsible behavior is what I am talking about in this book. Accordingly, capitalism and democracy are necessary for each other, and the connecting link is private property. Heyne observes, "People will not invest for the future, organize useful projects, or initiate any other costly undertakings in the absence of reasonably secure property rights."[116]

Second, private property permits the emergence of the profit motive which functions like an "invisible hand" to achieve public ends from private property. This was discussed thoroughly in the previous chapter. No other type of incentive has been found to be as powerful, efficient and effective in utilizing the world's resources to the general benefit of humanity.

Third, private property creates a direct vested interest in economic activity which in turn keeps everyone intently interested in what is going on, carefully overseeing economic activity and creatively coming up with better ways of doing things. As clearly demonstrated in those societies which have experimented with collective ownership of property, the problem with such a system, given humans' sinful nature, is that when everyone owns some- thing, no one owns it. This was a concept even Aquinas enunci- ated in his advocating private property.[117] The small, private farms in the Soviet Union were intently managed while the collec- tive farms were tragically neglected. Absenteeism was a way of life in socialist factories. Robert Conquest, a fellow at Stanford University's Hoover Institution quotes the Soviet sociologist Tatyana Zaslavskaya, "The primary reasons for the need for *pere-*

stroika were… an underlying mass alienation of working people from significant social goals and values. This social alienation is rooted in the economic system…, which made state property, run by a vast bureaucratic apparatus, the dominant form of owner-ship…. For 50 years it was said that this was public property and belonged to everyone, but no way was ever found to make workers feel they were the co-owners…."[118] Jennifer Roback Morse, economist at the Hoover Institution, notes, "Collapse of the Soviet Union has shown that collective ownership and centralized control cannot work. Few economists need that collapse as a demonstra-tion; they have known for a long time that collective ownership tends to diffuse responsibility. People under-invest in maintaining a collectively owned resource because they correctly perceive that they will reap only a fraction of the rewards for their efforts."[119]

Finally, although the term "private property" is used, reflecting those assets to which a person holds title, it must be acknowledged that all property belongs to God who simply "loans" us the assets which we possess. While virtually all of the laws of the Pentateuch relate to the social customs and mores of that time, the generaliza-tion can be drawn here that everything within the world is God's creation and therefore belongs to God. While today private owner-ship is the common custom, we are to treat our possessions as belonging to God and as if we are merely caretakers, husbanding them and sharing them with the poor. This brings us to the concepts of stewardship and generosity. The former is discussed below. The latter is discussed in Chapter VII, "Role of Material Possessions and Wealth."

Stewardship

The foregoing discussion has expanded upon the notion intro-duced at the beginning of Scripture that God is the source of every-thing. "In the beginning God created the heavens…earth… light, …water,…sky,…land,…vegetation,… stars,…animals (in the sky, sea and on land),…day,… night,…seasons." (Gn. 1:1-25) And this notion is reaffirmed throughout Scripture. In the Gospels John takes us back to Genesis, "In the beginning was…God….all things were made through him." (Jn. 1.1-2) Also earlier in this book we acknowledged that God explicitly places humans superior to and with dominion over all other of His creations. Twice he directs us to "rule" over them. (Gn. 1:26,28) He goes even further commanding us to "...fill the earth and subdue it." (Gn. 1:28) But not only are we superior to all plants and animals, we indeed own them. Three times he declares them as our possessions: "I give you..." "They will be yours..." "I give every..." (Gn. 1:29,30)

Therefore, humans have responsibility for stewardship of all of God's creations for two reasons. First, they are *gifts* from God. Like any responsible recipient of any gift, we demonstrate our gratitude for the gift by remaining sensitive to and honoring the wishes of the giver. The Giver being God, it is clear that loving care of His creations is expected. Further, as suggested above, it is argued by some that our material possessions are not gifts, but are on *loan* from God. Nowhere is a perspective on material possessions more emphatically suggested than by God's assertion that "The land must not be sold permanently, because the land is mine and you are but aliens and my tenants." (Lv. 25:23) Therefore, it is implied that we "tenants" have a stewardship responsibility to the landlord. Regardless, whether gifts or loans, it follows that we who use these possessions have a responsibility to the Provider for their care. Walter Owensby, Associate Director of the Public Policy Office of the Presbyterian Church (U.S.A.) in Washington, D.C., put it this way, "Biblical faith acknowledges individual property rights but only within the context of a stewardship ethic that regards the whole of creation as God's capital on loan... to meet the needs of all God's people.... God lays a prior claim upon all of the resources of the earth and upon all human systems in order to achieve an envisioned world of plenty shared in justice and in peace."[120]

Second, our being given authority over all matter implies a responsibility for matter. The relationship between humans and animals, plants and all other creations is akin to a parent—child relationship. While the parent has unlimited authority, the parent also has unlimited responsibility for the interests of the child. Accordingly, it is the *responsibility* of humans to be conscientious stewards of all of that which God has created for us. This responsibility for stewardship of all of God's creations—everything in the world, human, animal, physical...everything—is a tremendous responsibility.

Finally, it is important to note that we humans ourselves are the ultimate possession—the possession of God "The Israelites belong to me as servants. They are my servant, who I brought out of Egypt. I am the LORD your God." (Lv. 25:55) It follows, then, as servants of God, we are meant to carry out his wishes of stewardship.

As summarized by Gasque, "Here we hark back to the early chapter of Genesis where man is made in the image of God, where the created order is good, and where man (as male and female) is placed in the world to be a steward, to represent God, to tend for the created order. All possessions, including this earth, are possessed temporarily. Ultimately, God is the owner and man is simply the steward, His vice-regent to look after God's property. Therefore, the biblically oriented Christian sees private property as something held in trust, something that a person has been entrusted with by God. The Christian thus has a responsibility before God to use private property for His glory and to thus share it with others."[121] Nash adds, "Human beings are only stewards of their possessions.... Whatever possessions a human being may acquire, he holds them temporarily as a steward of God and is ultimately accountable to God for how he uses them as well as for how he acquires them."[122]

Stewardship takes many forms. The concept of conservation arises early in the Bible story as God directs humans to practice moderation in the use of resources. In the manna miracle, while in the Desert of Sin, Moses instructs the Israelites, "This is what the LORD has commanded: "Each one is to gather as much [bread] as he needs....' He who gathered much did not have too much, and he who gathered little did not have too little." (Ex. 16:16-18) Another form of stewardship found in Scripture is protection against pollution. God instructs the Israelites through Moses prior to their entering Canaan, "Do not pollute the land....Do not defile the land where you live and where I dwell, for I, the LORD, dwell among the Israelites." (Nm. 35:33,34)

Solomon notes the importance of refraining from waste, conserving resources and using resources in moderation. "The lazy man does not roast his game, but the diligent man prizes his possessions." (Prv. 12:27) "In the house of the wise are stores of choice food and oil, but a foolish man devours all he has." (Prv. 21:20) "If you find honey, eat just enough –" (Prv. 25:16) "Be sure you know the condition of your flocks, give careful attention to your herds;

for riches do not endure forever, and a crown is not secure for all generations." (Prv. 27:23,24)

The prophets who chastised people for our multitude of sins, included the absence of stewardship among them. "The earth dries up and withers,.... The earth is defiled by its people." (Is. 24:4,5)

While addressing stewardship responsibilities of church leaders to their followers, nevertheless Ezekiel's analogy conveys a valid general message, "Is it not enough for you to feed on the good pasture? Must you also trample the rest of your pasture with your feet? Is it not enough for you to drink clear water? Must you also muddy the rest with your feet?" (Ez. 34:18)

Interestingly, in the feeding of the five thousand and of the four thousand, each of the Evangelists observe that the disciples gathered up the leftovers. (Mt. 14:20; Mt. 15:37; Mk. 6:43; Mk. 8:10; Lk. 9:17; Jn. 6:12) John adds the phrase "that nothing may be lost," driving home the point that even the largesse of God should be neither taken for granted nor wasted. (This phrase has also been interpreted to mean that "none of those who believe in Jesus will be 'lost,' left alone to wander from his saving care."[123]) In the Parable of the Unjust Steward, although the parable principally deals with another lesson, it is noteworthy that the steward was fired for wasting goods. "A steward was...in charge of all supplies. His duty was to manage the working force, measure out the rations...."[124]

In the same way that capitalism ingenuously accommodates the dual nature of humanity, capitalism also displays a genius in its role in the stewardship of God's creations. In this arena of stewardship capitalism is not only conceptually compatible with the tenets of Christianity, but, indeed, has established a stellar empirical record of accomplishment. Three structural components of capitalism lead to enlightened stewardship of God's resources.

First, the central component of the capitalistic system is the business firm, which can take the form of proprietorship, partnership or corporation. Interestingly, corporations, which are established in perpetuity, is the economics equivalent of the spiritual notion of eternal life! A corporation, unless explicitly terminated, will live forever. And contrary to popular myth, most corporations are managed as if they expect to <u>continue forever.</u> While there are many exceptions, the mind-set of most corporate executives is one of perpetuity, eternity if you will. (Despite the proclivity of many workers to check the quarterly performance of their pension funds and the commensurate pressure on mutual fund managers and investment advisors to generate quarterly stellar results, most business leaders operate their businesses for the long run and, as stated by many, "let the price of the stock do what it may.") There are a multitude of examples of this all around us. Interestingly, it was private timber companies, not the government, that introduced the concept of sustained yield management to ensure adequate forest resources in perpetuity. In a mature, wealthy economy most participants in renewable resource industries, timber and fish, for example, adhere to resource management practices which ensure a sustained livelihood through continued abundance of the resource. This will be expanded upon in Chapter X, "The Brilliant Outcomes of Capitalism." This is not to say that there are not myriad conflicting owners and users of natural resources, necessitating government mechanisms for reaching compromises and accommodations for the various counter-interests.

A second component of capitalism that undergirds an impressive stewardship record is the profit motive which in turn stimulates a drive for productivity increases which in turn induces technological advance. Nothing beats vested interest for ensuring genuine conservation of resources. As previously stated, an intrinsic problem of socialism is, when everyone collectively owns everything, no-one owns anything. This in turn leads to inefficient use and waste of God's resources. There are a multitude of testimonies to this. Why, for example, was the output per acre from the former USSR communal farms so far below that of the small pieces of land carved out for the individual Soviet farmers' own personal output? Indeed, the required acreage of natural land and timber that must be cultivated for crops and timber per person in the Soviet Union far, far exceeds that of the United States and capitalistic Europe. It is widely recognized that the American farmer generates enough food from his land to feed not only the United States but a large portion of the world. At the same time, considerably too much land is devoted to generating an insufficient amount of food in countries that ought to be considered resource-rich. The American farmer, out of his interest in maximizing productivity, has created an immense benefit for humankind all over the world. The American farmer, chemical companies developing and producing fertilizers and insecticides, equipment manufacturers, transportation companies, wholesale distributors, etc. (yes, as well as the agricultural research activities of universities funded by grants from and taxes on private companies and the extension services of the U.S. Department of Agriculture, similarly funded by taxes on private entities), through a profit-driven largess, have done more to alleviate starvation around the world than all of the churches and government agencies combined.

The foregoing generalization applies not only to the American farmer, but to the American and other capitalistic producers in general. Capitalistic firms supply the bulk of humanity with most of the goods and services it needs for sustenance. In its vigorous pursuit of productivity, efficiency and maximum value, the capitalist producer has contributed to the most efficient allocation of the world's—God's—resources.

The third component of capitalism underlying conservation of God's resources is the price system of the free market. This is very simple. When a resource becomes relatively scarce—in less supply—the price is bid up, and less of the product is consumed and substitutes are brought forth. While this happens imperceptibly, gradually over time, occasionally there are dramatic short-run occurrences that exemplify the point. One very clear example was the oil shortage in the 1970's when the major oil producing countries held back output, causing prices to sky-rocket. The reaction of consumers was immediate and radical—car-pooling; buying smaller, more fuel-efficient cars; less discretionary travel; increased sales of diesel-fueled vehicles; etc. As indicated, daily in small increments the price system, responding to increased scarcity of particular products, induces behavior changes in consumers worldwide.

The foregoing discussion is not just some theoretical musing on my part. It is an accurate description of reality. Contrary to the machinations of the Club of Rome and the naïve utterances of "Chicken Littles," Malthus' *An Essay on the Principle of Population* (1798, rev. ed. 1803) which held that "population has a constant tendency to increase beyond the means of subsistence," has been fully discredited by empirical data. Indeed, the supply of the world's economic resources has not been outrun by demand. Malthus', and later Marx's, essential flaw was their viewing humans as primarily consumers, while Smith and capitalism's other champions correctly view humans as primarily creators.

In summary, these three components of capitalism: business firms organized in perpetuity, the profit motive stimulating high productivity and the price system inducing substitutes for scare commodities, underlie a record of stewardship of God's resources that can only be defined as phenomenal, stupendous, and awesome—never, ever imagined by anyone in Malthus' time.

However, there is an element of capitalism that is detrimental to good stewardship of God's resources. It is the problem of externalities; that is, the costs of individual private actions which are born by no one, or rather, more accurately, by everyone. Perhaps the best examples include an industrial plant discharging effluent into a river or lake or discharging contaminates into the air, or a family driving in its car discharging exhaust or adding to the psychological cost of heavy congestion, or an airplane taking off, contributing to noise pollution. Interestingly, private property, to the extent that it causes costs to be internal rather than external, is a mechanism for governing such costs. The existence of external costs are a bona fide reason for government action to either limit the activity which causes the external cost or require the source of the cost to pay such cost. In this regard the wealth of a nation, the capacity of a nation to deal with such costs, has a critical effect on whether or not a populace commits itself to such action. This will be revisited in Chapter X when discussing the actual outcomes of capitalism in the context of Christianity.

One final word on stewardship. "Protection" of the animal species, defined as freezing the current species mix status quo, for some peculiar reason has become considered "politically correct." However, lest we make a naïve error, it is imperative that we step back and rethink this matter. It must be acknowledged that the characteristics and mix of earth's life forms (God's creations) has been evolving for billions of years, and it can be presumed that, unless encumbered, this evolutionary process will continue for billions of years into the future. It seems to me that it is perhaps somewhat arrogant to declare that in this minuscule flicker of time during which I happen to be alive, we're going to declare the characteristics and mix of the animal species to be perfect and therefore freeze them in the present state for the remainder of eternity. Alas, no more progress! No more extinction and replacement by superior, more purposeful, more appropriate species. When the U.S. Congress passed the Endangered Species Act, I wonder if Darwin rolled over in his grave? What might the human condition be today had Neanderthals made the same arrogant decision? Nevertheless, despite my passing off this subject rather briefly, admittedly huge questions exist regarding the role of biodiversity and whether or not we in the 20th Century have a blind spot on this subject similar to the lack of thought given environmental pollution in the 19th Century.

It seems to me that there is nothing intrinsic about animals and natural resources that warrant protection from extinction. In fact, humans have been given the explicit, unequivocal directive by God to the contrary. Clearly, without any doubt, God made humans superior to and with authority over, in fact, gave us ownership of, His other creations with further instructions to tend them. (Gn. 1:26–30) There is no argument anywhere in Scripture for treating natural resources and animals as equal to humans. There is, however, the implicit responsibility for thoughtful, enlightened management of God's creations for the long run purpose of humanity.

In this context of recognizing the nature of humanity and distinguishing between God's relationship with humans and God's relationship with other of God creations, it is interesting to keep in mind Amundsen's assertion that "the deification of nature is as repugnant as the abuse of nature."[125] C. S. Lewis, in *The Abolition of Man*, has much to say about the nature of humanity, particularly humans' differentiation from all of God's other creations. He warns against the ill-founded tendency of social engineers to treat humans as just another form of raw material.[126]

Perhaps the most enlightened statement on stewardship is *The Cornwall Declaration on Environmental Stewardship* which emanated from a conference conducted by the Acton Institute and agreed to on February 1, 2000 by a group of clergy, theologians, economists, environmental scientists and policy experts and which subsequently has been endorsed by hundreds of the United States' religious leaders. The Declaration, which lays out concerns, beliefs and aspirations regarding environmental stewardship says, in part, "the increasing realization… of humans… as bearers of God's image, to add to the earth's abundance…. has enabled people in societies blessed with an advanced economy not only to reduce pollution, while producing more of the goods and services responsible for the great improvements in the human condition, but also to alleviate the negative effects of much past pollution. A clean environment is a costly good; consequently, growing affluence, technological innovation, and the application of human and material capital are integral to environmental improvement. The tendency among some to oppose economic progress in the name of environmental stewardship is often sadly self-defeating.... Sound environmental stewardship must attend both to the demands of human well-being and to a divine call for human beings to exercise caring dominion over the earth. It affirms that human well-being and the integrity of creation are not only compatible but also dynamically interdependent realities.... We aspire to a world in which advancements in agriculture, industry, and commerce not only minimize pollution and transform most waste products into efficiently used resources but also improve the material conditions of life for people everywhere."[127]

All of the foregoing discussion notwithstanding, it is acknowledged that all of God's creations are important to God. Gibson points out, "biblical writers by no means confine the significance of the earth to its usefulness to human beings. They assume and express God's high valuation of, and delight in, the nonhuman creation, for its own sake as well as its sustenance of human life. 'The Lord is good to all, and his compassion is over all that he has made.' (Ps. 145:9) Similar passages are found throughout the scriptures." [128] The Oxford Declaration asserts, "Biblical life and world view is not centered on humanity. It is God-centered. Non-human creation was not made exclusively for human beings.... Though only human beings have been made in the image of God, non-human creation too has a dignity of its own."[129] Indeed, the issue is not to let the pendulum swing too far in either direction. Neither desecration nor deification of nature, but a balanced co-existence of human and nonhuman creation is the objective.

Opportunity Cost

The science of economics assumes that at any given moment in time resources are limited. In fact the definition of economics is "the study of the allocation of scarce resources among alternative ends." *Opportunity Cost* refers to the economic relationship that the real cost of any action is the value of the opportunity that must be sacrificed in order to take that action.

Economists often comment, "There's no such thing as a free lunch." This refers to the reality that *everything* we do has a cost; that's right, *everything*, because the cost of doing any particular thing is the value of what was foregone in order to do that particular thing. When we go to a movie, two costs are involved, the direct cost of the money required for the ticket *plus* the foregone benefit of doing something else. Opportunity costs can be measured in terms of both actual monetary costs or psychic costs; e.g., when we go to a movie, we forego enjoying the symphony. And, of course, the psychic opportunity cost must be weighed against the psychic opportunity benefit received from what we did do.

The concept of opportunity cost is an extremely important tool particularly related to public policy regarding stewardship of God's creations. Regretfully, opportunity costs are often ignored when considering stewardship issues, specifically the benefits of environmental protection. A dramatic example is the recently adopted program to protect salmon under the Endangered Species Act. While the protection of salmon is noble and the rules established by the National Marine Fisheries Service making killing protected fish a crime were applauded, it must be recognized that a meaningful direct cost of protecting fish in Washington state is the loss of farming—both its economic benefit and its life style benefit—in eastern Washington as a result of inadequate volumes of water available for critically important irrigation. Regulations by the federal government requiring buffer zones along streams, taking acreage out of production, was the straw that broke the camel's back, putting some marginal farms out of business. The issue in this context is not whether or not fish or farming is preferable, but that adequate analysis of issues such as saving fish requires a full measurement of the opportunity cost of reduced farming.

It is the discipline of including both direct and opportunity costs in resource allocation that contributes to the incredibly efficient allocation of resources that occurs in capitalistic countries. This reveals another social role of profits. When deciding whether of not to pursue a particular investment opportunity, the evaluation criteria used by most business firms is relative profitability as measured by return on investment, ROI. If the ROI of a considered investment alternative exceeds the established "hurdle ROI," the firm's opportunity cost, then the investment will be pursued. In this way, the most efficient allocation of God's resources is achieved.

Regretfully, many people either don't see or ignore opportunity costs and therefore end up taking some inconsistent positions on public issues. For example, an opportunity cost of devoting land to parks, greenbelts and other open space uses, is the cost of not having that land available for residential use. As we observed in the earlier discussion of the price system, as a lower supply of land is available for residential use, the result will be a higher price for land. In this example we can measure opportunity cost precisely; it is a portion of the higher cost of land that a homeowner must pay when buying a house. Suppose further that your church decided to sponsor a rally tomorrow morning advocating more land for parks and open space and a rally tomorrow afternoon advocating lower housing costs. Well, one could choose to attend the morning rally and carry banners and chant slogans about more parks and open space *or* one could choose to attend the afternoon rally and carry banners and chant slogans about lower cost housing, but to attend *both* rallies is irrational, and, at least to an economist who understands opportunity costs, one would look silly. Nevertheless, it is utterly amazing to me how many people attend both rallies. (Now, there *is* a way in which attending both rallies would be rational, not silly, and that is if one attends a *third* rally on the following day, a rally devoted to slowing down economic growth in order to reduce the growth in *demand* for housing. Of course, if you attend that rally, then you can't logically serve on the capital campaign for the new church nor can you complain that the church doesn't have a better sound system for the older members to more readily hear the sermons nor can you attend the rally for more teaching materials in the Sunday School. *Everything* has an opportunity cost!)

Perhaps one of most dramatic recent examples of opportunity cost and the law of supply and demand is the recent energy "crisis" in California. In the past Californians through their elected public officials decided that, because of a high value which they placed on protecting fish, protecting forests and other open land and avoiding the trauma of living in the vicinity of a nuclear power plant, decided to prohibit the construction of dams, natural gas pipelines and nuclear power plants. Hence, the energy supply curve in California is somewhat inelastic, represented by the graph below.

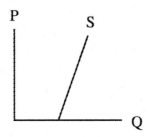

That is, regardless of the price, the supply of energy was relatively fixed, except for minor expansions or improvements to existing facilities, because of the various prohibitions against adding additional dams, pipelines and plants.

Now let us add the demand curves for energy, showing the demand curve that might have existed in 1980 (D1) and, after considerable population growth and economic expansion, the demand curve that might have existing in 2000 (D2) as follows:

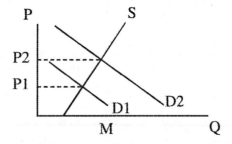

Under normal circumstances, while demand for energy grew from 1980 to 2000, represented by demand curves D1 and D2 respectively, the price would have risen from P1 to P2. Part of the rise in price would have been due to the rise in demand, but the major part of the rise in price would have been due to the fairly vertical (inelastic) supply curve, reflecting the prohibitions against adding energy facilities. This added rise in the price as a result of limiting the supply is the "opportunity cost" of receiving the benefits of protecting fish, protecting forests and other open land and avoiding the trauma of living in the vicinity of a nuclear power plant. Hence, the *law* in economics that there is no such thing as a free lunch.

However, economic laws have never stopped politicians, particularly either ignorant or intellectually dishonest politicians. So, of course, on the six-o'clock news we see a self-serving politician standing in front of the home of a poor and, to add fuel to the fire, minority family expressing outrage at the greedy, profit-lusting electrical utilities who are oppressing these poor folks. The politician is overwhelmingly elected and eventually adopts a price ceiling at, I suppose, whatever level feels good, say, PP (for politically set price). Now let's see what happens.

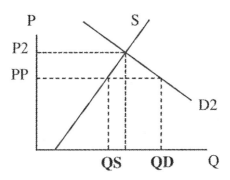

At the artificially low price, PP, the quantity of energy demanded is QD, while only QS quantity of energy is supplied, leaving a "crisis" shortfall of QD—QS, and everyone is up in arms! As I asserted earlier when explaining the law of supply and demand, trying to circumvent the law of supply and demand or ignore the concept of opportunity costs is akin to trying to circumvent or ignore the law of gravity. Yet, particularly with issues related to the stewardship of God's resources, many, particularly self-serving politicians, endeavor to do it every day—with catastrophic outcomes, none the least of which was the recent, logical, easily explained and totally unnecessary California energy "crisis." With supply being limited in the face of growing demand, with retail prices being held below natural market equilibrium level, the only thing surprising about the recent California energy crisis is that it is surprising to anyone; the only thing confusing about this crisis is that it is confusing to anyone. Thomas Sowell, the brilliant Stanford economics professor, elaborates, "The very notion of making things affordable misses the key point of a market economy. An economy exists to make trade-offs, and a market economy makes the terms of those trade-offs plain with price tags representing the relative costs of producing different things. To have politicians arbitrarily change the price tags, so that price no longer represents the real costs, is to defeat the whole purpose. Reality doesn't change when the government changes price tags.... Less supply, poorer quality and longer waits have been the consequences of price controls for all sorts of goods and services, in all sorts of societies, and for thousands of years of human history."[130]

Opportunity cost also explains why it is better for some people with high incomes to donate money rather than their time to their church. Take, for example, the case of a wealthy attorney or stockbroker in a church congregation. Is the church better off by that person donating her/his time or is the church better off for that person working at her/his vocation earning money during the time spent at that vocation and donating a portion of those earnings? Of course, this is to set aside the even more important question of whether the *soul* of that attorney or stockbroker is better off. However, the economic relationship remains, as explained by the concept of "opportunity cost:" the church is very likely better off by that person working at her/his high value vocation and donating all or a portion of those funds earned to the church. Because resources are limited, the cost of doing one thing is the value of the other thing foregone.

The concept of opportunity cost has many applications in explaining economic phenomena. Professor Heyne presents a marvelous example of opportunity cost and efficiency. "Why in the last 50 years, has the cost of getting a haircut gone up so much more than the cost of goods generally? It is because people who want barbers to cut their hair must be willing to pay them enough to keep them in the trade. If productivity in haircutting had kept pace over the last 50 years with productivity in manufacturing, barbers would have been able to maintain their incomes by trimming more heads per hour. But with productivity virtually unchanged, only a higher price per head could keep them working in the barber shop. We who want our hair cut by professionals have bid up the price of haircuts to meet the rising opportunity cost to barbers of working at a job in which productivity increases very slowly, if at all."[131] There is another point that flows from this example. We see the benefits that accrue from productivity in the sense of keeping costs down and therefore standards of living up, generating increases in quantities demanded, expanding job opportunities, reducing the numbers of poor.

Indeed, one of the factors contributing to the efficient use of God's resources is the economics concept of "opportunity cost." Finally, the concept of opportunity cost is not applicable solely to economics. It is applicable to life. A wise proverb says, "Judge your success by what you had to give up in order to get it."

Summary

We have observed that God is the source of all matter and therefore all material possessions and wealth, and Scripture places material possessions in their appropriate perspective as not ends in themselves but as almost incidental to an unwavering focus on and faith in God. "Fear the LORD….those who fear him lack nothing." (Ps. 34:9) "Seek first his kingdom and his righteousness, and all these things shall be yours…" (Mt. 6:25; Lk 12:22)

While all material possessions are gifts or loans from God, the concept of private property is validated within Scripture. Not until we each come forward with our own possessions can we have a true expression of love through community and generosity. This relationship between private property and love will be expanded upon in Chapters V and VII discussing the legitimacy and role of material possessions and wealth.

Possession of God's creations by humans is accompanied by an enormous responsibility for stewardship of God's creations by humans. Capitalism is conducive to enlightened stewardship of God's creations for three reasons: (1) business firms are organized for and operated in perpetuity, (2) the profit motive induces severe pressure for productivity, minimizing the quantity of input per quantity of output and (3) the price system signals and induces substituting more plentiful resources for scarce resources.

The concept of opportunity costs, applicable to a fallen world wherein resources are limited, leads to including all of the direct and indirect costs in economic decision-making and therefore to more rational public policies. However, the words of the late Paul Heyne, economist-theologian, are appropriate to consider: "The earth was created by a just and loving God, so that its resources are not going to run out before their Creator intends."[132]

Nash provides a concise summary, "Instead of condemning wealth, Jesus' teaching offered an important perspective on how people living in materialistic surroundings should view the material world.... Every Christian, rich or poor, needs to recognize that whatever he or she possesses is theirs temporarily as a steward under God."[133] Finally, if God is the source of all that we have, then there are considerable implications particularly regarding the attitudes which we hold toward our possessions and the use to which we put our possessions. Each of these is discussed later.

Chapter V

Legitimacy of Material Possessions and Wealth

One of the first, startling surprises of the Bible is discovering God's attitude toward prosperity. Throughout Scripture God explicitly and directly declares prosperity as good. However, it should be acknowledged that the Scriptural definition of prosperity includes more than a wealthy financial condition. It includes abundance of the other elements of a good life: honor, good health, wisdom, peace, contentment, happiness, intelligence, knowledge, artistic talents, a favorable disposition, physical attractiveness, physical strength, a happy family, etc. Surprisingly, God often raises the notion of prosperity to the level of a reward, a blessing. God's blessings refer to both the spiritual and the material. God's most common definition of blessing is prosperity. Clearly, God wants His children to be prosperous, enjoying a good life.

However, as often with God, there is a limiting modifier. Prosperity as a blessing assumes prosperity righteously gained. Further, an important line must not be crossed. Prosperity is not the end. Material goods are fine. Materialism is not. Materialism, in that it represents a form of idolatry, is clearly and unequivocally sinful. Both of these notions, the goodness of material and the sinfulness of materialism will be expanded upon further. The goodness, or legitimacy, of material possessions and wealth is addressed in this chapter. The sinfulness of idolatry of wealth is discussed in the next chapter, "Attitude Toward Material Possessions and Wealth."

Old Testament

Despite our sinfulness, God loves us and intends for humanity to be blessed as revealed by His first covenant with Abraham, "I will make you into a great nation and I will bless you....and all people on earth will be blessed through you." (Gn. 12:2,3), and later by the Abrahamic covenant: "I have made you a father of many nations.... I will establish...an everlasting covenant...for generations to come, to be your God and the God of your descendants.... The whole land of Canaan,..., I will give as an everlasting possession...." (Gn. 17:5-8) Later, God reaffirms this with Isaac, Abraham's son, "...through your offspring all nations on earth will be blessed,..." (Gn. 26:4) and then again with Jacob, Issac's son, "All peoples on earth will be blessed through you and your offspring..." (Gn. 28:14; see also Gn. 48:3,4,15-22) As summarized by LaSor "the salvation promised Abraham will ultimately embrace all humankind. God has not dismissed the human family in wrath forever, but now acts to mend the breach that sin placed between him and his world. This promise stands as a key to understanding all of Scripture."[134]

Throughout Genesis "God's blessings" are defined in terms of material prosperity. Scripture explicitly regards the accumulation and enjoyment of possessions as an outcome of receiving God's blessings. As noted by Mann, "the themes...of the Ancestral Saga...: the relationships between divine will and human responsibility, humanity and the earth,.... Abraham's success and affluence are a sign of blessing"[135] Riches are clearly viewed as good by God who often refers to wealth as a reward. Abraham, Isaac, Jacob and Joseph each became wealthy. Reflecting his faithful relationship with God, "Abraham had become very wealthy in livestock and in silver and gold." (Gn. 13:2; see also Gn. 12:5, 7, 16, 20; 15:7,14,18; 20:14-16; 24:35,53) "Isaac planted crops in that land and the same year reaped a hundredfold, because the Lord blessed him. The man became rich, and his wealth continued to grow until he became very wealthy." (Gn. 26:12,13; see also Gn. 27:27-29, 36,37; 28:4) Jacob's comment to Laban, "The little you had before I came has increased greatly, and the Lord has blessed you wherever I have been." (Gn. 30:30) Later, regarding Jacob, "...the man grew exceedingly prosperous..." Jacob to Rachel regarding Laban's cheating, (Gn. 30:43) "So God has taken away your father's livestock and has given them to me." (Gn. 31:9-13) When Jacob is saved from harm by Laban, he states, "But God has seen my hardship and the toil of my hands and last night he rebuked you." (Gn. 31:42) Later, Jacob states, "God has been gracious to me and I have all that I need." (Gn. 33:11) Finally, "The Lord was with Joseph and he prospered." (Gn. 39:2) In prison "the Lord was with Joseph and gave him success in whatever he did." (Gn. 39:23; see also 39:5) Mann observes, "As often elsewhere, 'success' or 'prosperity' is a manifestation of divine blessing. Everything that Joseph touches turns to gold."[136] Then later as a further manifestation of God's blessings, Jacob and his sons are given land and jobs by Pharaoh (Gn. 47:5,6,11,12). At the end of the Joseph story, which is the end of the Ancestral Saga of Genesis, the story of Israel as God's chosen people is stated in material terms, "Now the Israelites settled in Egypt in the region of Goshen. They acquired property ("possessions" in RSV) there and were fruitful and increased greatly in number." (Gn. 47:27) "God Almighty... blessed me and said to me....I will give you this land as an everlasting possession...." (Gn. 48:3,4)

The stories of Abraham, Isaac, Jacob and Joseph are more than stories of God's love. The other equally important lesson from these stories is God's requirement of faith. Each of the patriarchs remained steadfast in their *genuine* obedience to and trust of God. "Abraham believed the Lord, and he credited it to him as righteousness" (Gn. 15:6) and, of course, the ultimate demonstration of obedience to God, "He bound his son Isaac and laid him on the altar,..." (Gn. 22:1-14) The connection between faithful obedience and reward is quite explicitly made by God. "...because you have done this, ...I will surely bless you....Your descendants will take possession of the cities of their enemies and through your offspring all nations on earth will be blessed, because you have obeyed me. (Gn. 22:16-18; see also Gn. 12:7; 13:4,18; 14:22-24; 17:1). "Isaac prayed to the Lord..... Isaac built an altar there and called on the name of the Lord" (Gn. 25:21; 26:25; see also Gn. 26:28,29; 28:3,4) Jacob, after seeing and hearing God speak to him in a dream, "...made a vow...'if God will be with me...and give me food...and clothes...., then the Lord will be my God..." (Gn. 28:20-22; see also Gn. 28:10-19; 31:5-8) Later, however, Jacob returns to Canaan on the basis of God saying to him in a dream, "I am the God of Bethel, where you anointed a pillar and where you made a vow to me. Now leave this land at once and go back to your native land." (Gn. 31:13) And Jacob followed God's instructions. (See also Gn. 32:9-12, 24-30; 33:5,11) Again, at Bethel Jacob reaffirms his faith in God, "...I will build an alter to God,...who has been with me wherever I have gone." (Gn. 35:3; see also Gn. 35:9-15;49:22-26) Finally, when near death and blessing Joseph's sons, Jacob reaffirms, "the God who has been my shepherd all my life to this day." (Gn. 48:15) Joseph refuses the advances of Potiphar's wife in order not to "sin against God." (Gn. 39:9) Later, "I cannot do it,' Joseph replied to Pharaoh, 'but God will give Pharaoh the answer he desires." (Gn. 41:16. See also Gn. 41:25,28,32,37,39,51,52) To his brothers Joseph states, "...it was not you who sent me here, but God." (Gn. 45:8. See also Gn. 45:5-9; 48:9; 50:19,20) And finally, Joseph acknowledges his understanding of the story of Israel, "...But God will surely come to your aid and take you up out of this land to the land he promised on oath to Abraham, Isaac and Jacob." (Gn. 50:24) Mann observes further, "This is the first and only time Joseph refers to the divine promises. They are promises he has never heard from God. Thus his trust in these promises—and in the God who stands behind them—is perhaps the most exemplary in the entire Ancestral Saga, for in order to trust in God, Joseph must also trust in the 'witness' to God."[137] Is nothing more asked of us today?

The stories of Abraham, Isaac, Jacob and Joseph are stories of faith and reliance upon God's grace—but not passive faith, blind to the earthly challenges around us. No, what is required is active faith, using one's mortal mental and physical capacities received from God. The general conclusions drawn from these stories (Gn. 12-50) is that humans' relationship with God is not some supernatural phenomenon, but is very much an earthly, material phenomenon, requiring the use of intelligence, cunning, decisiveness, courage, physical strength and dexterity—the whole array of one's humanness as well as involving the production and accumulation of material wealth and the utilization of that wealth in *accordance with unequivocal faith in and reliance upon God.* The italicized phrase is the key. While God is very much with us mortal humans, and God intends for our happiness and fulfillment on earth, what is required from humanity in return is total unwavering faith and reliance upon God. Further, if humans ever achieve this state, then, do not material possessions take on a whole new meaning?

In Exodus we observe that the requirement of financial wherewithal for living was recognized by God in this discussion with Moses regarding the Israelites leaving Egypt, "…when you leave, you will not go empty-handed. Every woman is to ask her neighbor…for articles of silver and gold and for clothing,…" (Ex. 3:21,22) "Tell the people that men and women alike are to ask their neighbors for articles of silver and gold." (Ex. 11:2) "The Israelites did as Moses instructed and asked the Egyptians for articles of silver and gold and for clothing. The LORD had made the Egyptians favorably disposed toward the people, and they gave them what they asked for;…" (Ex. 12:35,36)

Later in Exodus, God reaffirms to Moses, "And I will bring you to the land…. I will give it to you as a possession." (Ex. 6:8) Then, in the course of the plagues all of the Egyptian's livestock die, but none of the Israelites', reflecting the utility of livestock. (Ex. 9:6) Further, the very value of the Israelites to Pharaoh was as free labor for the construction of cities. This is what gave rise to Pharaoh's "hardened heart" and in turn enables the dramatic illustration of God's power through the deliverance story.

In Leviticus God reaffirms "You will possess their land; I will give it to you as an inheritance, a land flowing with milk and honey." (Lv. 20:24) Again God conveys the notion that prosperity is a blessing, but it is a blessing from God, not our own efforts. "Follow my decrees….Then the land will yield its fruit, and you will eat your fill and live there in safety….I will send you such a blessing in the sixth year that the land will yield enough for three years" (Lv. 25:18-22)

Again in Leviticus prosperity is presented as a blessing; a reward for obeying God. "If you …obey my commands, I will send you rain in its season, and the ground will yield it crops and the trees of the field their fruit abundantly…. I will look on you with favor….You will be eating last year's harvest when you will have to move it out to make room for the new." (Lv. 26:3-5, 10)) And again in Numbers prosperity and material well-being are viewed by God as not only good, but, indeed, as a reward for maintaining faith in God. "They gave Moses this account: 'We went into the land to which you sent us, and it does flow with milk and honey!'" (Nm. 13:27) The key of course is to keep first things first; one is to obey God because of one's relationship with God, not in order to become prosperous.

In Deuteronomy prosperity is again viewed positively by God, as reflected in Moses' comment to the Israelites just prior to their crossing the Jordan River into Canaan, "Walk in all the way that the LORD your God has commanded you, so that you may live and prosper and prolong your days in the land that you will possess." (Dt. 5:33) Shortly later, "Hear, O Israel, and be careful to obey so that it may go well with you and that you may increase greatly in a land *flowing with milk and honey,* just as the LORD,..., promised you." (Dt. 6:3) (Italics mine; this phrase is used many times in Scripture to describe the Promised Land.) "The LORD commanded us to obey...and to fear the LORD our God, so that we might always prosper...." (Dt. 6:24) "He will...bless..., the crops of your land—your grain, new wine and oil—the calves of your herds and the lambs of your flocks..." (Dt. 7:13) "For the LORD your God is bringing you into a good land—a land...with wheat and barley, vines and fig trees, pomegranates, olive oil and honey; a land where bread will not be scarce and you will lack nothing; a land where the rocks are iron and you can dig copper out of the hills." (Dt. 8:7-9) "The LORD will grant you abundant prosperity.... The LORD will....bless all the work of your hands." (Dt. 28:11,12) "You will again obey the LORD.... Then the LORD your God will make you most prosperous in all the work of your hands and in..., the young of your livestock and the crops of your land." (Dt. 30:8,9) "See, I set before you today life and prosperity.... But, if your heart turns away and you are not obedient,..." (Dt. 30:15) While the principal message of the foregoing passages was the importance of faithfully obeying God, nevertheless, the result of such obedience was declared by God to be material prosperity.

Scripture is quite clear and consistent; beyond simply viewing wealth favorably, God's intent is that humans be prosperous *as long as humans recognize God as the source and listen to and obey God accordingly.* "When the LORD your God brings you into the land he swore to your father,..., to give you—a land with... houses filled with all kinds of good things,...wells,... and vineyards and olive groves...—then when you eat and are satisfied, be careful that you do not forget the LORD,..." (Dt. 6:10-12) God seemed to anticipate the affect that prosperity can have on humans, when later he issued a similar warning. "When you have eaten and are satisfied, praise the LORD your God for the good land he has given you. Be careful that you do not forget the LORD your God, failing to observe his commands,... Otherwise, when you eat and are satisfied, when you build fine houses and settle down, and when your herd and flocks grow large and your silver and gold increase and all you have is multiplied, then your heart will become proud and you will forget the LORD your God,..." (Dt. 8:10-14) Moses repeats this message, "...the LORD your God ...will send rain,...so that you may gather in your grain, new wine and oil.... Will provide grass in the fields for your cattle, and you will eat and be satisfied. Be careful, or you will be enticed to turn away and worship other gods and bow down to them." (Dt. 11:14-16) Finally, Moses goes further, predicting "When I have brought them into the land flowing with milk and honey,... and when they eat their fill and thrive, they will turn to other gods and worship them, rejecting me and breaking my covenant." (Dt. 31:20) This continues as an enormous problem, characteristic of humanity today, and will be expanded upon later in the next chapter, "Attitudes Toward Material Possessions and Wealth."

Finally, a positive view of material prosperity is expressed by Moses in the various blessings he pronounced just prior to his death. "About Joseph he said: 'May the LORD bless his land...with the best the sun brings forth...; with the choicest gifts of the ancient mountains and the fruitfulness of the everlasting hills; with the best gifts of the earth...' About Zebulun he said: '...will feast on the abundance of the seas, on the treasures hidden in the sand.' About Gad he said: 'He chose the best land for himself;...' About Asher he said: '...let him bathe his feet in oil. The bolts of your gates will be iron and bronze,...' Jacob's spring is secure in a land of grain and new wine,..." (Dt. 33:13-28)

A main theme of the story of the Israelites is obedience to God, and one of God's explicit, stated rewards for this obedience is prosperity. God says to Joshua, "Do not let this Book of the Law depart from your mouth; meditate on it day and night, so that you may be careful to do everything written in it. Then you will be prosperous..." (Jos. 1:8) "Then Joshua... said to them, 'You have done all that Moses the servant of the LORD commanded, and have....

carried out the mission the LORD your God gave you'…. When Joshua sent them home, he blessed them, saying, 'Return to your homes with your great wealth…." (Jos. 22:2,3,7,8)

Throughout the Old Testament prosperity—wealth—is given a positive connotation by God. Ruth, as a result of her faithfulness eventually marries Boaz, a wealthy farmer, and, of course, they continue the family line leading to the Messiah. Not only is wealth treated as favorable, but God also uses cleverness and cunning in a commercial transaction to achieve God's purpose, as Boaz outwits another relative and gain's Naomi's land and Ruth as his wife.

Perhaps the ultimate statement of prosperity as viewed as a blessing by God is in the description of David's and Solomon's immense—overwhelming—wealth. In fact, the familiar childhood Bible story of David and Goliath notes that "The king will give great wealth to the man who kills him [Goliath, the Philistine]. He will also give him his daughter in marriage and will exempt his father's family from taxes in Israel." (1 Sm. 17:25) And regarding Solomon, "King Solomon was greater in riches and wisdom than all the other kings of the earth." (1 Kgs. 10:23) To get the full impact, one should read in their entirety 2 Samuel and 1 Chronicles concerning David and 1 Kings and 2 Chronicles concerning Solomon. Reading about David causes one to understand that the legitimacy of material possessions and wealth which we are discussing in this chapter flows from the fact that the source of material possessions and wealth is God. "King David dedicated these articles to the LORD, as he had done with the silver and gold he had taken from all… nations…." (1 Chr. 18:11) "And I will also give you wealth, riches and honor,…" (2 Chr. 1:12) However, despite the faithfulness and wisdom of David and Solomon, in both cases wealth, to the extent that it gave rise to feelings of self-sufficiency and pride, was a contributing factor to their sinful behavior—a concept we will return to later in the discussion of "Attitudes Toward Material Possessions and Wealth." "David said to God, 'Was it not I who ordered the fighting men to be counted? I am the one who has sinned and done wrong." (1Chr. 21:17) And on his death bed David reveals that he understands cause and effect as he charges his son Solomon, "…. Observe what the LORD your God requires: Walk in his ways,…., so that you may prosper…." (1 Kgs. 2:3)

Clearly, material prosperity is viewed favorably by God and lack of prosperity is viewed unfavorably by God. "This is what God says: 'Why do you disobey the LORD's commands? You will not prosper." (2 Chr. 24:20) "..., he sought his God and worked whole-heartedly. And so he prospered." (2 Chr. 31:21)

Even in the book of Job, which is exceedingly complex and perplexing (see discussion under "Pride" in the next chapter), nevertheless prosperity is clearly implied as favorable. "After Job had prayed for his friends, the LORD made him prosperous again.... The LORD blessed the latter part of Job's life more than the first. He had fourteen thousand sheep, six thousand camels, a thousand yoke of oxen and a thousand donkeys." (Jb. 42:10,12) Similarly, in Job poverty is viewed as unfavorable. "...I rescued the poor.... I was father to the needy." (Jb. 29:12,16)

The association of prosperity with God's goodness is also beauti-fully expressed in several Psalms. "But his delight is in the law of the LORD,... Whatever he does prospers." (Ps. 1:2,3) "Who, then, is the man that fears the LORD? He will instruct him in the way chosen for him. He will spend his days in prosperity, and his descendants will inherit the land." (Ps. 25:12,13) "You love righteousness...therefore your God.... All your robes are fragrant with myrrh and aloes and cassia; from palaces adorned with ivory...." (Ps. 45:7,8) "In his days the righteous will flourish; prosperity will abound.... Let grain abound... Let its fruit flourish.... All nations will be blessed through him. " (Ps. 72:7,16,17) "If my people would but listen to me, ...But you would be fed with the finest of wheat; with honey from the rock I would satisfy you." (Ps. 81:13-16) "Remember me, O LORD,..., that I may enjoy the property of your chosen ones,: (Ps. 106:4,5) "Blessed is the man who fears the LORD,... Wealth and riches are in his house," (Ps. 112:1,3) "For the sake of the house of the LORD our God, I will seek your prosperity." (Ps. 122:9) "Blessed are all who fear the LORD,...; blessings and prosperity will be yours." (Ps. 128:1,2) "Our barns will be filled... Our sheep will increase...; our oxen will draw heavy loads...; blessed are the people whose God is the LORD." (Ps. 144:13-15) Even in the well-known Twenty-third Psalm: "The LORD is my shepherd,... You anoint my head with oil; my cup over-flows...." (Ps. 23:1-5) Conversely, "But the needy will not always be forgotten, nor the hope of the afflicted ever perish." (Ps. 9:18) "...the groaning of the needy," (Ps. 12:5) "He will take pity on the weak and the needy..." (Ps. 72:13) "Rescue the weak and needy;" (Ps. 82:4)

"He raises the poor from the dust and lifts the needy from the ash heap;" (Ps. 113:7; also in Hannah's prayer, 1 Sm. 2:8)

King Solomon, the wise son of King David, made many observations directly and indirectly implying the legitimacy of material possessions and wealth. "My son, do not forget my teaching, but keep my commandments in your heart, for they will prolong your life many years and bring you prosperity." (Prv. 3:2) "My son, pay attention to my wisdom,… lest strangers feast on your wealth and your toil enrich another man's house.…" (Prv. 5:1,10) "I [Wisdom] love those who love me, and those who seek me find me. With me are riches and honor, enduring wealth and prosperity." (Prv. 8:17,18) "The blessing of the LORD brings wealth,…" (Prv. 10:22) "prosperity is the reward of the righteous." (Prv. 13:21) "The wealth of the wise is their crown," (Prv. 14:24) (Note, NSRV uses "wisdom" rather than "wealth") "he who cherishes understanding prospers." (Prv. 19:8) "The plans of the diligent lead to profit as surely as haste leads to poverty." (Prv. 21:5) "He who pursues righteousness and love finds life, prosperity and honor." (Prv. 21:21) (Note, many modern versions eliminate "prosperity" which is also lacking in the Greek.)[138] Finally, King Lemuel suggests the legitimacy of manufacturing and commercial transactions, "A wife of noble character.… She sees that her trading is profitable,… She makes linen garments and sells them, and supplies merchants with sashes." (Prv. 31:18,24) While focusing on the wisdom of Solomon applied to the subject of wealth, it is interesting to note that we are blessed with the words of Solomon partially because of his immense wealth that contributed to his obtaining and recording his insights. LaSor observes, "… fresh light on the splendors of Solomon's reign have brought renewed appreciation for his role as patron of Israel's wisdom movement. He enjoyed intimate contacts with the Egyptian court, access to foreign learning afforded by a far-flung empire,…. and his fabulous wealth could support companies of scribes and recorders on a scale impossible for his heirs."[139] However, it should be noted that Solomon obtained his wealth by onerous taxation and confiscation of other people's property! Nevertheless, throughout the wisdom passages of Proverbs there is a strong positive connotation to wealth, linking it to such favorable traits as industriousness, diligence, care, conscientiousness, responsibility, foresight, and deliberation.

However, there is a huge caveat. While throughout Scripture material abundance is viewed by God as favorable and poverty is viewed by God as unfavorable and worthy of sympathetic aid, material abundance is *not the end*. The end is loving God and God's creations. "Unless the LORD builds the house, its builders labor in vain. Unless the LORD watches over the city, the watchmen stand guard in vain. In vain you rise early and stay up late, toiling for food to eat..." (Ps. 127:1,2) The wise Solomon asserts this strongly. "Blessed is the man who finds wisdom, the man who gains understanding, for she is more profitable than silver and yields better returns than gold. She is more precious than rubies;" (Prv. 3:13-15) "My [Wisdom's] fruit is better than fine gold; what I yield surpasses choice silver." (Prv. 8:19) "How much better to get wisdom than gold, to choose understanding rather than silver." (Prv. 16:16) "Of what use is money in the hand of a fool, since he has no desire to get wisdom?" (Prv. 17:16) "Gold there is, and rubies in abundance, but lips that speak knowledge are a rare jewel." (Prv. 20:15) "A faithful man will be richly blessed, but one eager to get rich will not go unpunished." (Prv. 28:20) "A greedy man stirs up dissension, but he who trusts in the LORD will prosper." (Prv. 28:24) "The poor man and the oppressor have this in common: the LORD gives sight to the eyes of both." (Prv. 29:13) This notion that wealth is not the end will be expanded upon in the discussion of idolatry in the next chapter. Suffice it to say here that love of God in order to gain prosperity is not love of God and is, therefore, sinful. Nevertheless, the point being made here is that God Himself defines prosperity as good and poverty as bad. Nowhere in Scripture is their even a hint that a vow of poverty leads to salvation.

A corollary of the foregoing caveat is the additional provision that only wealth obtained honestly is regarded as legitimate, an important distinction particularly made throughout Scripture. As Murphy notes in his commentary on Proverbs, "Wealth is normally preferable to poverty—put not any price.... Possessions, or the lack thereof, can be ambiguous; virtue is what counts."[140] Solomon eloquently makes this point. "Such is the end of all who go after ill-gotten gain; it takes away the lives of those who get it." (Prv. 1:19) "Dishonest money dwindles away, but he who gathers money little by little makes it grow." (Prv. 13:11) Of interest for our later discussion of pride, according to Murphy, "dishonest money" is literally "money from vanity."[141] "The house of the righteous contains great treasure, but the income of the wicked brings them trouble." (Prv. 15:6) "Better a little with the fear of the LORD than great wealth with turmoil." (Prv. 15:16) "Better a little with righteousness than much gain with injustice." (Prv. 16:8) "Honest scales and balances are from the LORD; all the weights in the bag are of his making." (Prv. 16:11) "Food gained by fraud tastes sweet to a man, but he ends up with a mouth full of gravel." (Prv. 20:17) "Better a poor man whose walk is blameless than a rich man whose ways are perverse." (Prv. 28:6) "… he who hates ill-gotten gain will enjoy a long life." (Prv. 28:16)

Even the prophets, who harshly condemned the idolatry of materialism and the sin of hedonism, nevertheless implied a favorable posture toward prosperity and wealth—as long as it was achieved righteously. "In that day I will restore David's fallen tent…. the reaper will be overtaken by the plowman and the planter by the one treading grapes. New wine will drip from the mountains and flow from all the hills…. They will plant vineyards and drink their wine; they will make gardens and eat their fruit." (Am. 9:11-14) "If you are willing and obedient, you will eat the best from the land." (Is. 1:19) "Yet her [Tyre's] profit and earnings will be set apart for the LORD;… Her profits will go to those who live before the LORD, for abundant food and fine clothes." (Is. 23:18) " the LORD Almighty will prepare a feast of rich food for all peoples, a banquet of aged wine—the best of meats and the finest of wines." (Is. 25:6) "He who walks righteously… His bread will be supplied, and water will not fail him." (Is. 33:15,16) "I will build you with stones of turquoise, your foundations with sapphires. I will make your battlements of rubies, your gates of sparkling jewels, and all your walls of precious stones…. In righteousness you will be established." (Is. 54:11-14) "Arise and shine, for your light has come, and the glory of the LORD rises upon you…. The wealth on the seas will be brought to you, to you the riches of the nations will come…. Instead of bronze I will bring you gold, and silver in place of iron…." (Is. 60:1,5,17) "…you will drink deeply and delight in her overflowing abundance." (Is. 66:11) "I will extend peace to her like a river, and the wealth of nations like a flooding stream;…" (Is. 66:12) Fascinatingly, when Isaiah talks about Israel's ultimate salvation, he describes it in economic terms, "Never again will I give your grain as food for your enemies, and never again will foreigners drink the new wine for which you have toiled; but those who harvest it will eat it and praise the LORD, and those who gather the grapes will drink it in the courts of my sanctuary." (Is. 62:8,9) "Behold, I will create new heavens and a new earth.... my chosen ones will long enjoy the works of their hands." (Is. 65:1,22) Owensby notes, "a life of plenty was the goal of creation and the outcome of faith."[142]

Later God, through Jeremiah, not only suggests the goodness of prosperity, but also asserts the validity of the trickle-down theory, a well-accepted concept in economics which nevertheless catches the ire of some contemporary social activists. Jeremiah writes in a letter to the Jews in exile in Babylon, "the LORD Almighty, the God of Israel, says...., seek the peace and prosperity of the city to which I have carried you into exile. Pray to the LORD for it, because if it prospers, you too will prosper." (Jer. 29:4,7) Jeremiah's other comments reflecting the legitimacy of prosperity include: "I brought you into a fertile land to eat its fruit and rich produce," (Jer. 2:5) "How gladly would I treat you like sons and give you a desirable land," (Jer. 3:19) "The shepherds are senseless and do not inquire of the LORD; so they do not prosper...." (Jer. 10:21) "Then I will fulfill the oath I swore to your forefathers, to give them a land flowing with milk and honey...." (Jer. 11:5) "...they will rejoice in the bounty of the LORD—the grain, the new wine and the oil,.... and my people will be filled with my bounty." (Jer.; 31:12,14) "...so I will give them all the prosperity I have promised them." (Jer. 32:42) "...they will be in awe and will tremble at the abundant prosperity and peace I provide for it." (Jer. 33:9) Again in Jeremiah we find the condemnation of riches gained by unjust means (Jer. 17:11), suggesting by inference that riches gained by just means are acceptable in God's eyes.

The same theme of the legitimacy of worldly possessions, wealth, money and financial transactions is continued by Ezekiel, "On that day I swore to them that I would bring them out of Egypt into a land I had searched out for them, a land flowing with milk and honey." (Ez. 20:6) "I will bless them..., I will send down showers in season;... The trees of the field will yield their fruit and the ground will yield its crops; the people will be secure in their land..... I will provide for them a land renowned for its crops, and they will no longer be victims of famine…. Then they will know that I, the LORD their God, am with them….” (Ez. 34:26-30) “I… will make you prosper more than before. Then you will know that I am the LORD…. I will call for the grain and make it plentiful…. I will increase the fruit of the trees and crops of the field. (Ez. 36:11,29,30,

A fascinating occurrence of treating material elegance positively is in one of Daniel’s visions, chapters 10-12, wherein a messenger from God (some scholars believe it was an appearance of Christ)— a spiritual being—is described in terms of material lavishness as a sign of royal authority. It is noteworthy that God’s word could just as easily have appeared in the prophets’ visions in plain, modest attire if God had intended that poverty be regarded as some virtue. Clearly God did not regard poverty as virtuous. This theme continues with the postexilic prophets. “… at that time I will bring you home…. When I restore your fortunes…” (Zep. 3:20) “My towns will again overflow with prosperity.” (Zec. 1:17) “How attractive and beautiful they will be! Grain will make the young men thrive, and the new wine the young women.” (Zec. 9:17) As LaSor observes, “Zechariah is filled with glorious promises for Jerusalem: the return of God’s presence, the renewal of the covenant, and economic prosperity.”[143]

To conclude the position of the Old Testament on wealth, certainly wealth is not in any way regarded as an end. Worship of God is to come first, and God is to be worshipped for God’s sake. The message of the Old Testament is that, if we let God run our lives, God will provide whatever is necessary. A second message, however, is that God did not regard wealth as bad; in fact, quite to the contrary, God explicitly declares prosperity—in the broad sense—as good and therefore as legitimate. While much of the foregoing material drawn from the Old Testament refers to the leader of the clan or the king, every family had its own land that it worked in order to lead a good life.

New Testament

One of the contrasting characteristics of the Old Testament and New Testament is their respective treatment of prosperity and wealth. While a promise of the Old Testament is prosperity, health and the good things of this world, the promise of the New Testament—the promise of the Cross—is the good things of the eternal world, the kingdom of God.

However, neither Jesus nor the Evangelists were suggesting that material possessions were irrelevant to life. In our earlier discussion of God as the source of material possessions and wealth, it was observed that in the Lord's Prayer, "Give us today our daily bread." (Mt. 6:11), Jesus acknowledges that in order to sustain life we have material needs.

Very early in the Gospels in the discussion of Jesus facing the first temptation of Satan suggesting that he turn stone into bread, Jesus responds by quoting the Old Testament (Dt. 8:3), "It is written, 'Man shall not live by bread alone." (Mt. 4:4 and Lk 4:4) Note that he did not say that man shall not live by bread. He said that man shall not live by bread *alone*. That is, bread is fine, but there is more to one's life than just bread. (Let us not lose sight, however, of the lesson being conveyed as Jesus refuses to turn from God to satisfy his needs, but rather reaffirms his obedience to and exclusive trust in God.)

Scripture well recognizes that living and functioning within the world requires worldly goods and, presumably, the financial wherewithal to acquire worldly goods. "Jesus traveled about ..., proclaiming the good news of the kingdom of God. The Twelve were with him, and also some women.... These women were helping to support them out of their own means." (Lk. 8:1-3) As church leaders and missionaries for the past two thousand years have known, doing God's work in the world requires worldly resources and doing more of God's work requires more worldly resources.

In the Marriage at Cana in the Gospel of John (Jn. 2:1-11), the very first miracle performed by Jesus as related by John is positioned in this Gospel just three days after Jesus' baptism and conveys three very important aspects of Jesus' attitude toward the worldly dimension. First, Jesus honored a social obligation (he had been invited to the wedding) and took time to enjoy himself. Second, Jesus' miracle dealt with turning a necessity (water) into a luxury (wine) or at least a utility (water) into an object of enjoyment (wine). Third, Jesus' wine was of very good quality. While this story has been the subject of numerous, wide-ranging interpretations, it seems reasonable that perhaps Jesus was using a relatively pedestrian miracle in this story to convey the message that God takes care of our *every* need. Further, perhaps he was showing that serving God need not be something that is unpleasant and dull and feared, but something filled with excitement and enjoyment which should be embraced.

John Alexander notes, "At the very least, Jesus was not an ascetic. His objection to material possessions was not based on a belief in the inferiority of the material world. He was always attending feasts and diners..... Certainly he enjoyed food and drink..... he doesn't try to stop the feasts—he doesn't tell people they should be too poor to have feasts. In Luke 14:12-14 Jesus tells one of his hosts to invite poor people to his feasts, which introduces a drastic note typical of Jesus' extreme teaching, but this suggestion still presumes keeping possessions."[144] Nash points out "Jesus did not teach that being rich means necessarily being evil. Jesus did not see anything sinful in the ownership of houses, clothes, and other economic goods. He had wealthy friends and followers (Lk. 14:1); he stayed in the homes of wealthy people; he ate at their tables (Lk. 11:37)"[145] "Yet," Alexander adds, "without doubt Jesus considered wealth dangerous."[146] We will address this concern in the next chapter, "Attitudes Toward material Possessions and Wealth."

Additionally, in the same way that Jesus preached that faith in God would lead to curing illness, restoring broken bones and eyesight and hearing, and to harmonious interpersonal relations—the full array of human needs—Jesus taught that such faith provided for our material needs as well: food, clothing, shelter, etc. "...he said to Simon,. 'Put out into the deep and let down your nets for a catch.' And Simon answered, 'Master, we toiled all night and took nothing! But at your word I will let down the nets.' And...they enclosed a great shoal of fish...and filled both the boats so that they began to sink." (Lk. 5:4-7) In the feeding of the five thousand and the four thousand (Mt. 14:15; Mt. 15:32; Mk. 6:35; Mk. 8:1; Lk. 9:12; Jn. 6:5.) Jesus turns to God. "Then enough bread and fish were distributed of such great abundance that everyone had eaten all that they wanted." In the Gospel of Luke Jesus "spoke to them of the kingdom of God." This emphasizes the function of this miracle as a demonstration of what it is like in the kingdom of God: infinite resources to address our needs. Jesus recognized that humanity is of the world and that worldly needs exist. Nevertheless it is clear that after this meal Jesus taught the people about a better "meal:" himself, who, as the "bread of life," would provide true nourishment.

The legitimacy of worldly goods, money and commerce seem to be reflected in some of the parables of Jesus. In The Prodigal Son, which conveys the lesson of God's constant, patient, welcoming love to all of His children, the father nevertheless expresses his joy by directing, "Bring quickly the best robe and put it on him; and put a ring on his hand, and shoes on his feet; and bring the fatted calf and....let us eat and make merry;" (Lk. 15:21) While nevertheless devoted to different messages, in The Parable of the Talents and the Parable of the Nobleman's Ten Servants, Jesus seems to condone the role of bankers in paying interest on deposits, and, therefore, I presume because it generates the income from which to pay interest on deposits, the role of lending money and receiving interest. "Then you ought to have invested my money with bankers, and... I should have received... interest." (Mt. 25:27; Lk. 19:23). Similarly, Jesus' saying "do not refuse him who would borrow from you." (Mt. 5:42) suggests that Jesus condoned lending. Elsewhere in his teachings Jesus seems to regard lending/borrowing as an accepted normal activity (Lk. 6:34, 7:41). (It should be noted that Scripture is somewhat confusing as to whether or not charging interest, particularly to fellow Israelites, is condoned. I will return to this later.)

In The Parable of the Unjust Steward (Lk. 16:1-9) Jesus is advocating to his disciples the shrewd—wise—use of worldly resources in order to overcome the countervailing shrewdness of many humans and/or in order to deal effectively within the worldly realm so as to bring the message of the kingdom of God. Later, when commissioning his twelve disciples Jesus states explicitly, "I am sending you out like sheep among wolves. Therefore be as shrewd as snakes and as innocent as doves." (Mt. 10:16) According to J. Dwight Pentecost, Professor of Bible Exposition at Dallas Theological Seminary, "He pointed out that the people of this world were often more shrewd in using their material possessions and their position than those who belong to God. Christ said worldly wealth should be used shrewdly with a view to the future, not used selfishly with a view only to the present."[147] Shephard agrees, "Jesus ...shows how to use money in such a way, for helping others and promoting the ends of the Kingdom that....they might find a welcome in heaven on the part of many who had been benefited....One cannot buy his way into heaven with money but by the right use of it for service of God on earth he may lay up treasure in heaven."[148]

However, are worldly things intrinsically sinful and therefore *not* of any concern to Jesus? In Jesus' rebuke of Peter, he says, "Get behind me, Satan! ...For you are not on the side of God, but of men." (Mt. 16:23; Mk. 8:33) Jesus seems to be equating "of men" with Satan. This message continues, "And if any man would come after me, let him deny himself...For whoever would save his life will lose it; and whoever loses his life for my sake will save it." (Mt.16:24; Mk. 8:34; Lk. 9:23; Jn. 12:25) Is Jesus implying that worldly achievement and heavenly achievement are mutually exclusive? I think not. Jesus seems to be suggesting two things. First, the key element is the mindset of humanity; i.e. humans' *attitude* toward wealth should be such that wealth is neither an impediment nor a distraction nor a displacement to seeking the kingdom of God. Second, while wealth and worldly possessions are all right, there is considerably more than that to one's life. "For what does it profit a man if he gains the whole world and forfeits his life?" (Mt. 16:26; Mk. 8:36; Lk. 9:25) Biblical scholar J. Ramsey Michaels concludes that in these passages Jesus is instructing his disciples to "give up the vested interest he or she has in the world and follow Jesus in the way of servanthood."[149] To the rest of us—nondisciples, but followers—perhaps it is a call to give up the pre-occupation with worldly matters, the single-minded, top priority placed on worldly objectives, and place one's top priority on Jesus Christ.

Finally, when looking at ways in which the legitimacy of wealth and material possessions seem to be acknowledged in the Gospels, it is notable to observe at almost the very end of the story, following the crucifixion, that it was a rich man, Joseph from Arimathea, who took down Jesus' body, wrapped it in a linen shroud and placed it in a tomb. The passage notes that this rich man was "good and righteous...and looking for the kingdom of God." (Mt. 27:57; Mk. 15:42; Lk. 23:50; Jn. 19:38)

It is important to emphasize that, although wealth and material possessions are legitimate, they are not the end. A major message of Jesus Christ was that earthly treasure was subordinate to heavenly treasure. Further, Jesus spent a considerable amount of his ministry warning the rich of the dangers of wealth; e.g., "But woe to you who are rich," (Lk.6:24), also the Parable of the Rich Fool, etc. We will return to this matter later in the discussion of idolatry in the next chapter on "Attitudes Toward Material Possessions and Wealth." In fact, humanity's greatest gift—salvation—has no price tag, having been given freely by God.

The book of Acts continues the messages found in the Gospels regarding material possessions and wealth, particularly providing insights regarding the source, the legitimacy, and the role of material possessions and wealth as well as the importance of one's attitude toward wealth. However, Paul seems to take a slightly different tact regarding wealth than Jesus. Jesus' message seemed to emphasize the folly of relying on materiality for one's wellbeing, reflecting the economic reality in Palestine that the masses were poor with little opportunity of gaining wealth. Jesus directed the disciples to renounce their material possessions as a demonstration of their exclusive reliance on God. On the other hand, Paul, who functioned in the Greco-Roman cities where wealth was more common, seems to view wealth as (1) a mechanism for spreading the gospel in the world and (2) something to be shared with the poor. "When money is being used to further the preaching of the gospel or to express the unity of all Christians in the gospel, Paul does not hesitate to ask for money.[150] Paul, nevertheless reaffirms the dangers of wealth and the fact that worldly wealth has nothing to do with eventual heavenly wealth.

Before proceeding further in the New Testament, it should be noted that both of the books of Luke and Acts, which are believed to have been written by Luke, are dedicated to Theophilus who, it is hypothesized, was Luke's patron, a wealthy man who supported Luke and who underwrote the publishing of the books of Luke and Acts. In so doing, Theophilus and his wealth contributed directly to the spread of God's word. Additionally, "... Stephanus (1 Cor. 16:15) was by inference wealthy enough to act as patron to the Pauline mission. The families of Aristobulus and Narcissus (Rom. 16:10-11) both had imperial connections."[151] Paul, himself, is believed to have been from a prominent well-to-do family in Tarsus.

As Paul carried the message of the Gospels on his three missionary journeys, all believers, including those who dealt in commercial trade, were regarded as children of God and were candidates for salvation. "One of those listening was a woman named Lydia, a dealer in purple cloth…who was a worshiper of God. The Lord opened her heart to respond to Paul's message." (Acts 16:14) "So he reasoned in the synagogue…, as well as in the marketplace…." (Acts 17:17)

Paul's attitude toward wealth is revealed in the instructions he gave to Timothy and Titus. "Now the overseer [church leader] must be above reproach,…, temperate, self-controlled, respectable, …., not a lover of money." (1 Tm. 3:3) Note that Paul did not say "not a *possessor* of money." Paul goes on to say "Deacons, likewise, are to be men worthy of respect, sincere, not indulging in much wine, and not pursuing dishonest gain." (1 Tm. 3:8) "…an overseer…must be blameless—not overbearing, not quick-tempered, not given to drunkenness, not violent, not pursuing dishonest gain." (Ti. 1:7) Actually, these passages have to do with leadership—deacons and elders—of the church, causing some commentators to suggest that "dishonest gain" refers to that from church service such as false teaching, rather than referring to commercial, business transactions. Note that in both cases Paul did not say "not pursuing gain." Presumably, then, pursuit of honest gain is acceptable. This would tend to support the legitimacy of the capitalist / Adam Smith model which provides for an acceptable level of profit as a return to the provider of capital or entrepreneurial effort, in the same way that the other factors of production, labor and land, receive their return: wages and rent.

Even in the context of his deep spirituality, Paul was very much a person of the world, dealing with worldly issues. Edwards notes in his commentary on Romans that Paul's statement, "For if the Gentiles have shared in the Jews' spiritual blessings, they owe it to the Jews to share with them their material blessings," reflects (among other things to be mentioned later) the notion that, "The church consists of both the spiritual and the material, and both are in equal measure a ministry."[152] Further, when teaching theology, Paul often made use of worldly analogies. For example, when discussing the promise of the eschatological reward, "The hardworking farmer should be the first to receive a share of the crop." (2 Tm. 2:6)

Griffiths summarizes, "The basic necessities for living are not provided like manna; the land has to be cultivated, the sea has to be harvested, minerals have to be extracted, the city has to be supplied with services. God created us with the capacity and the desire to do all these things. Life itself, therefore, demands that we use what God has given us to provide the necessities."[153] This leads us to the next section on work. First, however, Griffiths continues, "But God intended far more than that. We were not created to live our lives in hunger or on the breadline, in a state of poverty using only the barest minimum. God intended us to enjoy his world. The land which he promised Israel was to be flowing with milk and honey. No Christian should feel a sense of guilt from living in a decent house, driving a solid car, wearing a proper suit of clothes or eating a good meal. If we take seriously the fact that this world is God's world, then the business of creating wealth has a Christian foundation."[154]

Work

Related closely to the legitimacy of worldly possessions and wealth is the activity of work. The legitimacy of work is declared at the very outset of Scripture. "By the seventh day God had finished the work he had been doing; so on the seventh day he rested from all his work." (Gn. 2:2) Earlier God asserted that humans are made in God's image and likeness; therefore, humans are "wired" for work.

Work can be defined as the application of human capital to physical capital. It is the employment of human intelligence, skill, and ingenuity in concert with land, animals, natural resources, and manmade tools and equipment. This is a definition that applies throughout human history, including today. Human capital has always been the most important component of the factors of production, and increasingly human intelligence is replacing human strength in importance. As mentioned earlier, in today's economic environment capitalism unleashes the power of human capital.

The activity of work continues following the creation story. "The LORD God took the man and put him in the Garden of Eden to work it and take care of it...." (Gn. 2:15) Murray notes, "The significant feature for our present interest is that, notwithstanding the curse, there is still to be the fruit of labour; Adam would still eat bread. Labour and its appropriate reward are not abrogated.... When we arrive at the period of the three patriarchs, Abraham, Isaac, and Jacob, we read of the riches of Abraham, the toil of Jacob in Padanaram, and the wealth of Esau. The Scripture casts no reflection upon the riches accumulated in these instances. Wealth as the fruit of toil, or as an inheritance from the toil of others, carries no dishonour.... It is this background that places in proper perspective more than one of the precepts of the decalogue. If we think, for example, of the fourth commandment, it should not be forgotten that it is the commandment of labour as well as of rest. 'Six days shalt thou labour, and do all thy work.' If we will, we may call this an incidental feature of the commandment. But it is an integral part of it. The day of rest has no meaning except as rest from labour. It is rest in relationship to labour; and only as the day of rest upon the completion of six days of labour can the weekly Sabbath be understood."[155]

Work and wages paid for work appear throughout the Old and New Testaments as legitimate and expected activities of humanity. "Tell me what your wages should be." (Gn. 29:15) "Name your wages, and I will pay them." (Gn. 30:27) Clearly, in Genesis we see the concept of God's blessings and justice integrated with the notion of economic well-being and fairness. Jacob to Rachel regarding unfair treatment by Laban, "...I've worked for your father with all of my strength, yet your father has cheated me by changing my wages ten times. However, God has not allowed him to harm me." (Gn. 31:6,7) The concept of wages is further legitimized in the book of Numbers, "...it is your wages for your work at the Tent of Meeting." (Nm. 18:31) "My men will work with yours, and I will pay you for your men whatever wages you set." (1 Kgs. 5:6) "...when Solomon saw how well the young man did his work, he put him in charge of the whole labor force of the house of Joseph." (1 Kgs. 11:28)

King Solomon declared work as appropriate and honorable. Diligence is a common theme in Proverbs. "Go to the ant, you sluggard; consider its ways and be wise! It has no commander, no overseer or ruler, yet it stores its provisions in summer and gathers its food at harvest. How long will you lie there, you sluggard? When will you get up from your sleep? A little sleep, a little slumber,... and poverty will come on you like a bandit and scarcity like an armed man." (Prv. 6:6-11; 24:33,34; 30:25) "Lazy hands make a man poor, but diligent hands bring wealth. He who gathers crops in summer is a wise son, but he who sleeps during harvest is a disgraceful son." (Prv. 10:4,5) "He who works his land will have abundant food," (Prv. 12:11; 28:19) "The sluggard craves and gets nothing, but the desires of the diligent are fully satisfied." (Prv. 13:4) "All hard works brings a profit, but mere talk leads only to poverty." (Prv. 14:23) "One who is slack in his work is brother to one who destroys." (Prv. 18:9) "Laziness brings on deep sleep, and the shiftless man goes hungry." (Prv. 19:15) "A sluggard does not plow in season; so at harvest time he looks but finds nothing…. Do not love sleep or you will grow poor; stay awake and you will have food to spare." (Prv. 20:4,13) "The sluggard's craving will be the death of him, because his hands refuse to work." (Prv. 21:25) "Do you see a man skilled in his work? He will serve before kings;" (Prv. 22:29) "The sluggard buries his hand in the dish; he is too lazy to bring it back to this mouth." (Prv. 26:15) "He who tends a fig tree will eat its fruit, and he who looks after his master will be honored." (Prv. 27:18) Solomon even has something to say regarding priorities. "Finish your outdoor work and get your fields ready; after that, build your house." (Prv. 24:27) Obviously Solomon's foregoing comments reflect his attitude regarding the results of work—wealth—as favorable and the result of not working—poverty—as unfavorable.

King Lemuel similarly regarded work favorably, "A wife of noble character…. She… works with eager hands…. She gets up while it is still dark; she provides food for her family…. She sets about her work vigorously;… She sees that her trading is profitable, and her lamp does not go out at night." (Prv. 31:10-18)

Work is affirmed again in Ecclesiastes, "That everyone may eat and drink, and find satisfaction in all his toil—this is the gift of God." (Eccl. 3:14); "…, to accept his lot and be happy in his work—this is a gift of God." (Eccl. 5:19); and "Whatever your hand finds to do, do it with all your might,…" (Eccl. 9:10) The point being made in Ecclesiastes is that, although this material, temporal world in which humanity lives may be meaningless relative to the spiritual, eternal kingdom of God, nevertheless, all that we do here, including work, is to be to the glory of God.

The prophets also reflected the legitimacy of work. "…my chosen ones will long enjoy the works of their hands. They will not toil in vain…; for they will be a people blessed by the LORD." (Is. 65:22,23) "Woe to him who builds his palace by unrighteousness,… making his countrymen work for nothing, not paying them for their labor." (Jer. 22:13) "Be strong, all you people of the land,' declares the LORD, 'and work." (Hg. 2:4)

In Biblical times work also had a very important religious function. Because rabbi's had a trade, they were self-supporting which enabled them to provide education for free. This served three very important purposes. First, it enabled a broader group of students. Second, it enabled rabbi's to remain intellectually independent, speaking the truth as they saw it. Thirdly, it prevented them from having to burden others.

For most of his life—to support himself while studying and preparing for his ministry—Jesus worked as a carpenter. In teaching that humans were made in the image of God, Jesus must have included in that image God as a worker and who, after working, then rested.

Paul supported himself through working as a tentmaker. "...we worked night and day in order not to be a burden to anyone while we preached the gospel of God to you." (1 Thes. 2:9) To Paul proper love does not place a burden on others.[156] Paul was supporting himself not just to avoid burdening the Thessalonians, but also to achieve some other important objectives. First, it enabled him to evidence God's grace through presenting the Gospel as God's free gift to the people. Paul felt called by God to the ministry, and accepting pay for such activity would have been disobedient to the purity of God's calling. Second, Paul's working to earn his own money served to prevent tainting or diluting his message by precluding any suspicion that money might be his real motivation as it was with many of the philosophers and teachers who traveled and spoke for pay.[157] Third, Paul's financial independence enabled him to avoid any kind of patron/client relationship with the people and thereby avoid any chance that he might become beholden to them and lose his independence of thought.[158] "...work with your hands,...so that...you will not be dependent on anybody." (1 Thes 4:11,12) Paul continues with this message in other letters; see particularly Chapter Nine of 1 Corinthians. Clearly, then, Paul's worldly/material wherewithal contributed to the success of his spiritual mission.

The combination of lay employment and religious preaching was a consistent behavior pattern of Paul throughout his missions, reflecting his background as a Pharisee as well as reflecting his pursuit of the above objectives. The Biblical scholar R. J. Hock "has shown that, far from being peripheral to Paul's life, tentmaking was central to it.... 'His trade occupied much of this time.... His life was very much that of the workship...of being bent over a workbench...."[159]

Additionally, Paul clearly regarded work as a virtue per se and was particularly harsh on idlers. "...respect those who work hard....warn those who are idle,..." (1 Thes 5:12-14) "...keep away from every brother who is idle....We were not idle when we were with you, nor did we eat anyone's food without paying for it. On the contrary, we worked night and day, laboring and toiling so that we would not be a burden to any of you. We did this,...in order to make ourselves a model for you to follow. For even when we were with you, we gave you this rule: 'if a man will not work, he shall not eat'....We hear that some among you are idle....Such people we command and urge in the Lord Jesus Christ to settle down and earn the bread they eat....If anyone does not obey our instruction in this letter, ...Do not associate with him, in order that he may be ashamed." (2 Thes. 3:6-14) While in this passage he was specifically addressing idleness resulting from eschatological preoccupation; i.e., why work when the end is imminent, Paul nevertheless viewed work as a manifestation of a responsible life and necessary to functioning within a material world. Further, Paul observed that idleness on the part of some Thessalonians was leading them to sin. Hence, another reason for worldly productive activity: to reduce the tendency toward sinful behavior. Recall the adage, "idle hands are the devil's playground." In his commentary on both of these passages Williams notes, "The implication in the letters is that these disruptive persons were perfectly capable of supporting themselves instead by meddling in other persons' affairs, compounding the problems they were creating. An implication of the rule laid down...is that the ability to earn one's living is an important factor in human well-being.... Free-loaders had no place in Paul's concept of Christian community, which called for shared work in a context of personal responsibility.... There was no question, however, that those who could not work, whether through lack of opportunity or because of age or infirmity, should look to the church for their support."[160]

Finally, while directing his comments to slaves, Paul's message applies also to all workers, "Whatever you do, work at it with all you heart, as working for the Lord, not for men." (Col. 3:23) Paul's attitude toward the appropriateness of work is further reflected in his letter to the Ephesians, "He who has been stealing must steal no longer, but must work, doing something useful with his own hands,..." (Eph. 4:28) Note this passage ends with "that he may have something to share with those in need." The purpose of work is to gain something with which to express love through generosity. We will come back to this in Chapter VII, "Role of Material Possessions and Wealth."

While nevertheless discussing discipleship and church leadership respectively, both Jesus and Paul seem to acknowledge the appropriateness of paying wages for work. "for the worker deserves his wages." (Lk. 10:7); "The worker deserves his wages." (1 Tm. 5:18) While admonishing certain wealthy, James nevertheless confirms the legitimacy of working for wages. "The wages you failed to pay the workmen." (Jas. 5:4) Paul carries this notion of wages further in his letter to the Corinthians noting that workers in the church deserve their just wages. "If we have sown spiritual seed among you, is it too much if we reap a material harvest from you? If others have this right of support from you, shouldn't we have it all the more?... Don't you know that those who work in the temple get their food from the temple, and those who serve at the altar share in what is offered on the altar? In the same way, the Lord has commanded that those who preach the gospel should receive their living from the gospel." (1 Cor. 9:11-14)

All of the foregoing notwithstanding, Paul's comments regarding work cannot be interpreted as the advocation or even condoning of some sort of ethic of materiality, consumerism, or physical comforts. To Paul work clearly had a higher end: principally to (1) further the mission and (2) share with the poor. Additionally, Paul cherished the financial independence—and therefore independence of thought and action—which working enabled.

Related to the subject of work is the matter of the way in which workers are organized. In Scripture we find an appreciation of the benefits of the division of labor. Early organizational structures reflected an understanding of the efficient allocation of all productive resources, including workers.

The concepts of division of labor and organization structure appear earlier in Scripture in the Old Testament. An example is the workers required to build the temple in Jerusalem. "You have many workmen: stonecutters, masons and carpenters, as well as men skilled in every kind of work in gold and silver, bronze and iron— craftsmen beyond number." (1 Chr. 22:15,16) A related example is all of the various duties performed in the temple in Jerusalem:

supervisors, officials, judges, public administrators, priests, prophets, assistants for sacrifices, assistants for purification ceremonies, bakers, caretakers, bookkeepers, safekeepers, musicians, gatekeepers, scribes, treasurer, etc. (See 1 Kings 4:1-19 and 1 Chronicles 23-26) Also, "Solomon had seventy thousand carriers and eighty thousand stonecutters in the hills, as well as thirty-three hundred foremen who supervised the project and directed the workmen." (1 Kgs. 5:15,16) Later, when King Joash repaired the temple, "they gave the money to the men appointed to supervise the work on the temple. With it they paid those who worked on the temple of the LORD—carpenters and builders, the masons and stonecutters." (2 Kgs. 12:11,12) Later, King Josiah repaired the temple, utilizing privately donated money and division of labor, "...get ready the money that has been brought into the temple of the LORD, which the doorkeepers have collected from the people. Have them entrust it to the men appointed to supervise the work on the temple. And have these men pay the workers who repair the temple of the LORD—the carpenters, the builders and the masons." (2 Kgs. 22:4-6)

Perhaps the best example of superb organization skills is Nehemiah who rebuilt the wall of Jerusalem in just fifty-two days. Leaving a responsible position in the government of Persian King Artaxerxes, Nehemiah returned to Jerusalem where he organized people into groups which he assigned to rebuild specific sections of the wall. He oversaw the logistics of this immense project and at the same time provided for the defense against severe opposition, utilizing careful planning, teamwork, problem-solving and motivation. (See especially Neh. 4:16-22 and Neh. 5:16-18)

In the New Testament we observe that, as the early missionary work grew in numbers, administrative tasks seem to become more complicated and certain imperfections emerged. "In those days when the number of disciples was increasing, the Grecian Jews among them complained against the Hebraic Jews because their widows were being overlooked in the daily distribution of food." (Acts 6:1). In response, and in order to pursue efficiently and effectively their missionary objective, the apostles made a certain division of labor and organized themselves somewhat. "So the Twelve gathered all the disciples together and said, 'It would not be right for us to neglect the ministry of the word of God in order to wait on tables. Brothers, choose seven men from among you.... We will turn this responsibility over to them and will give our attention to prayer and ministry of the word." (Acts 6:2-4) Stephen and Philip were two of the seven leaders chosen to handle the distribution of food and other administrative and logistical tasks associated with the growth and expansion of the early church.

The implication of the foregoing is quite clear: those seven disciples involved in the distribution of food were as critical to the success of the mission as those actually doing the preaching. The former permitted the latter to devote themselves exclusively, therefore presumably more effectively, to preaching. Indeed, today are not those who create the financial and other resources used in religious work as important to the work as those who directly perform the work? David thought so. Regarding disposition of the spoils after defeating the Amalekites, he declares "The share of the man who stayed with the supplies is to be the same as that of him who went down to the battle. All will share alike.' David made this a statute and ordinance for Israel from that day to this." (1 Sm. 30:24,25)

The disciples employed an extremely important concept in microeconomics—the division of labor—in order to achieve an extremely important end of microeconomics: the efficient allocation of productive resources. As Adam Smith observes, "The greatest improvement in the productive powers of labour,…seem to have been the effects of the division of labour."[161] The early disciples readily saw the advantages of becoming more efficient through specialization by dividing duties. Paul, in his letter to the Romans also reflects on the division of labor and specialization. "Just as each of us has one body with many members, and these members do not all have the same function, so in Christ we who are many from one body, and each member belongs to all the others. We have different gifts, according to the grace given us." (Rom. 12:4-6) According to Paul each of the parts in making up the whole belong to each other—so similar to Adam Smith's division of labor, specialization! This in turn contributed to the early missionaries maximizing their "bottom line:" the number of persons to whom the Good News was delivered. (Notice the suggestion by Paul that our individual attributes are gifts resulting from God's grace. This has huge implications which are discussed in the following section, "Calling.")

This notion of specialization is reflected also in Paul's letter to the Corinthians, "The body is a unit, though it is made up of many parts; and though all its parts are many, they form one body.... But in fact God has arranged the parts of the body, every one of them, just as he wanted them to be. If they were all one part, where would the body be?.... Now you are the body of Christ, and each one of you is a part of it." (1 Cor. 12:12-27) Paul was imploring the Corinthians not to let their differences divide them, but to be a positive element in their working for Christ. As noted by Marion Soards, professor of New Testament at Louisville Presbyterian Theological Seminary, "Paul's theme becomes 'diversity in unity, and unity over diversity.'.... According to Paul, in Christ unity dominates diversity and makes diversity genuinely meaningful and constructive.... Not only has God enriched the unified body by granting distinctive gifts to the diverse parts of the body, but also God created the unified body per se.... God arranged the members of the body with all their diversity so that there was mutual dependence."[162] The same principle applies in the commercial world. Interestingly, Brown explicitly places this decision regarding organizational structure in the context of theology, "...the Holy Spirit given by the risen Christ guides the church in a way that allows basic structural development to be seen as embodying Jesus Christ's will for his church."[163]

In concluding our discussion of work, let me note that, while recognizing that God is the Source of all, "work" is the process of humans implementing the creation mandate, converting the resources which God has provided us into a physical form for the benefit of all of God's children while also providing an opportunity for self-expression on the part of the worker. One is reminded of the familiar joke: a prosperous farmer was proudly showing a visitor his flourishing farm. Finally the visitor commented, "what gorgeous abundant fruit and grain crops; you certainly have been blessed by God," to which the farmer replied, "yeah, well you should have seen this place when God had it all by Himself!" Work is the process through which we humans give manifestation to God as the Source. Indeed, wealth is the result of the co-creation process of humans with God.

Finally, The Oxford Declaration defines work as "all those activities done, not for their own sake, but to satisfy human needs. Work belongs to the very purpose for which God originally made human beings.... Because work is central to the Creators' intention for humanity, work has intrinsic value.... At the same time, we have to guard against over-valuation of work. The essence of human beings consists in that they are made in the image of God. Their ultimate, but not exclusive, source of meaning and identity does not lie in work, but in becoming children of God by one Spirit through faith in Jesus Christ.... God calls all Christians to employ through work the various gifts that God has given them.... The deepest meaning of human work is that the almighty God established human work as a means to accomplish God's work in the world."[164]

Of course, work has another theological end: to glorify God through full expression of our talents and skills which God has given us. This leads us to the next section, "calling," which is a broader concept than "work" and is therefore discussed separately here to emphasize this distinction.

Calling

While the term "calling" in Scripture refers to God's calling people to salvation and is used synonymously with "election," I agree with the assertion by Dr. William Klein, Professor of New Testament at the Denver Seminary, that action is implied in calling, "The apparently definitive divine acts of 'calling' and 'election' necessitate human actions if they are to be confirmed or made sure. Peter abhors the emptiness of a mere profession that produces no fruit in a believer's life. Not that one's acts earn salvation, but the confirmation of calling and election exists in a life of faithfulness."[165]

This notion of action is what bridges the Scriptural usage of the term "calling" and my use of the term "calling" here within the secular, more common usage, as defined by Webster, as, "one's work or profession." In this regard God has a purpose for each of His creations. "I make known the end from the beginning, from ancient times, what is still to come. I say: My purpose will stand, and I will do all that I please." (Is. 46:10) That God fills us "with skill, ability and knowledge in all kinds of crafts.... to make everything I have commanded" (Ex. 31:1-11, 35:31-35) and to otherwise achieve God's purposes is affirmed by God to Moses when preparing for construction of the tabernacle. And elsewhere in the Old

Testament, "May the favor of the Lord our God rest upon us; establish the work of our hands for us—yes, establish the work of our hands." (Ps. 90:17)

Jesus Christ was with purpose. "From the east I summon a bird of prey; from a far-off land, a man to fulfill my purpose.... what I have planned, that will I do." (Is. 46:11) Each of us, as God's creations, has a purpose. As God said to Jeremiah, I believe God says to each of us, "Before I formed you in the womb I knew you, before you were born I set you apart;..." (Jer. 1:5) I think that one of the most beautiful passages in the Bible regarding God's shaping each one of us into a purposeful creation is Isaiah's utterance, "Yet, O LORD, you are our Father. We are the clay, you are the potter; we are all the work of your hand." (Is. 64:8)

Jesus Christ could not have been more clear on this subject of calling: God has endowed each of us with certain talents, and one's purpose in life is to utilize these God-given talents with which one has been endowed to their maximum potential toward fulfillment of God's purpose and to the glory of God. At the present time in the history of the world we are in the in-between times: between the first and second comings of Christ. Jesus presents two very clear parables describing what we servants are to do in the absence of the Master, prior to his returning. In the Parable of the Talents (Mt. 25:14-30) and the Parable of the Nobleman's Ten Servants (Lk. 19:11-27) we are told four very important things. First, each of us has been given gifts, talents, attributes, resources, abilities. Second, each of us is to use these—put these to work—to the benefit of the Master. Third, furthermore, we are not simply to use the resources, but are to use them in a manner in which they will multiply, expand, grow. Fourth, each of us who uses our resources fruitfully will be rewarded with more resources and more opportunities for growth.

The role of one's physical, intellectual and spiritual resources is to achieve one's potential in such a manner that the glory of God is served. These parables can be further interpreted to include the understanding that our individual assets are not really ours; we are simply caretakers, not owners. They have been entrusted to us by our Master. When we ignore or squander that with which we have been entrusted, we are guilty of sin. "The message ...is one of...dedicated and fruitful response by the Christian to God's gift in and through Jesus."[166] (Interestingly, Brown suggests that Luke interprets a narrower application of this parable, "to challenge the disciples to make profitable use of all that Jesus has revealed to them."[167] Of further interest, Moxnes explains that one talent was sixty minas, and one mina was one hundred denari; therefore, five talents equaled 30,000 denarii,[168] one of which was equal to a days' wages for a laborer. Hence, the parable used a considerable amount of money, reflecting an infinitely wealthy Master.)

Many interpretations have been made of the Parable of the Talents. One interpretation emphasizes the relationship between the Master and the servants, noting that the Master holds much confidence and trust in the servants. Two of the servants understood that the Master had entrusted them with His money and they went out to do His work with His money, while the third servant hid the money, disappeared and was not engaged in the world. The Master expressed joy with the first two servants for their engagement in pursuing His purpose and further giving them the talent which He had given the third servant who had not been engaged in the world. Upon relating this interpretation, Sewall poses the question, "Do you view the Master with joy and gratitude and therefore are you engaged in the world for good, doing what He wants you to do? Do you invest your portion of the Master's love by expressing love in the world, or do you hide it?" [169]

Jesus Christ vigorously pursued the agenda he had been given by God, and each of us is to pursue the agenda given each of us by God, as Paul continuously reminds us. In his letter to the Romans he notes, "Therefore, I urge you, brothers, in view of God's mercy, to offer your bodies as living sacrifices, holy and pleasing to God— this is your spiritual act of worship. Do not conform any longer to the pattern of this world, but be transformed by the renewing of your mind…. Just as each of us has one body with many members, and these members do not all have the same function, so in Christ…. We have different gifts,…" (Rom. 12:1-6) The use of the term "gifts" suggests that there is a giver to whom we therefore owe gratitude. This suggests that the purpose of life is to live out our life in a manner that exhibits our gratitude to God for the gift of life and the gift of our individual attributes; i.e., in service to His glory.

In one of his letters to the Corinthians Paul points out that each of us has a unique calling, we each have a role; "each one should retain the place in life that the Lord assigned to him and to which

God has called him....each man, as responsible to God, should remain in the situation God called him to." (1 Cor. 7:17,24). Soards notes in his commentary on 1 Corinthians that "Paul maintains that God saves the believers regardless of their worldly social status; remaining in the social state in which one was called demonstrates that what humans do does not effect salvation; worldly social change is not equivalent to salvation."[170] In discussing the members' relationship to their church, and "the unifying purpose of the manifest diversity of the Spirit in the life of the church being the well-being of all those in the church,"[171] Paul states, "There are different kinds of gifts, but the same Spirit. There are different kinds of service, but the same Lord. There are different kinds of working, but the same God works all of them in all men. Now to each one the manifestation of the Spirit is given for the common good." (1 Cor. 12:4-7) To an economist, this passage leaps off the page, for it is remarkably similar to a passage in Adam Smith's *Wealth of Nations,* "...led by an invisible hand to promote .... [the interest] of the society...."[172] Indeed, *capitalism is an economic system so structured that the pursuit of one's personal calling accrues to the common good.*

Finally from Paul, "I urge you to live a life worthy of the calling you have received." (Eph. 4:1) Patzia elaborates, "In Ephesians, the Gentiles have been told that God has...appointed them to praise God's glory, called them to wonderful hope, and incorporated them into the body of Christ for a life of good works. Now they are admonished to demonstrate their calling...by living a worthy ethical life. They are part of God's grand design for the world, which includes the uniting of all things in heaven and on earth."[173] Is not each one of us a part of "God's Grand Design"?

But we should ever keep in mind that, because we are creations of God and therefore God has given us our individual characteristics, we are not free to use them in ways contrary to God's ways. We have a responsibility to the Giver in how we use our gifts. As Peter reminded his fellow Jewish Christians, "Each one should use whatever gift he has received to serve others, faithfully administering God's grace in its various forms." (1 Pt. 4:10) Rev. Dale Turner, retired Senior Pastor of University Congregational Church and widely regarded as the dean of Seattle clergy, states it beautifully, "What we are born with is God's gift to us. What we do with it is our gift to God."[174]

But we are not alone in pursuing our worldly calling. God is with us. "….for it is God who works in you to will and to act according to his good purpose." (Phil. 2:13) Theologian F. F. Bruce explains, "This is part of Paul's teaching about the Holy Spirit,…. The Spirit does what the law could not: the law could tell people what to do without supplying the power, or even the will, to do it; the Spirit supplies both,…imparting to believers the desire and the power to do the will of God,… and they do his will 'from the heart.'"[175]

On the subject of one's calling, I commend to you a marvelous spirit-filled book by Os Guinness, Senior Fellow at the Trinity Forum, *The Call*, and I share with you the following excerpts. "Answering the call of our Creator is 'the ultimate why' for living, the highest source of purpose in human existence…. What do I mean by 'calling'? For the moment let me say that *calling is the truth that God calls us to himself so decisively that everything we are, everything we do, and everything we have is invested with a special devotion and dynamism lived out as a response to his summons…*"[176] Guinness distinguishes between primary and secondary calling, noting, "*Our primary calling as followers of Christ is by him, to him, and for him…. Our secondary calling, considering who God is as sovereign, is that everyone, everywhere, and in everything should think, speak, live, and act entirely for him.* We can therefore properly say as a matter of secondary calling that we are called to homemaking or to the practice of law or to art history. But these … are 'callings' rather than the 'calling.' They are our personal answer to God's address, our response to God's summons. Secondary callings matter, but only because the primary calling matters most…. *God normally calls us along the line of our giftedness, but the purpose of giftedness is stewardship and service, not selfishness*…. Gifts are never really ours or for ourselves…. John Cotton [seventeenth century New England minister] expands… 'we live by faith in our vocations, in that faith, in serving God, serve men, and in serving men, serve God.'…. But we are not responsible to our calling. We are responsible to God, and our calling is where we exercise that responsibility….. We do what we do in life because we are called to it rather than because we get paid for it."[177] The conclusion, then, I believe, is that the key element is not *what* one does, but *why* one does what one does. It is appropriate that we return here to Paul's admonition, "Whatever you do, work at it with all you heart, as working for the Lord, not for men." (Col. 3:23)

Finally, in response to certain feelings of guilt weighing on one when one doesn't give up all of one's possessions and head off to some third-world country to dig irrigation ditches and share the Gospel, the point is that we are to identify our calling and pursue it with vigor and love and to the glory of God. In that way one will have the greatest impact on one's fellow humans. Thomas strongly addresses this common source of guilt with the assertion, "if men or women ignore their responsibilities in life with the excuse that they want to live 'spiritually' they are mocking God, not serving him."[178] Guinness relates a personal story, "In my early days of following Jesus, I was nearly swayed by others to head toward spheres of work they believed were worthier for everyone and right for me. If I was truly dedicated, they said, I should train to be a minister or a missionary…. Coming to understand calling liberated me from their well-meaning but false teaching and set my feet on the path that has been God's way for me."[179] Guinness also tells the story of the two Dutch priests who in the sixteenth century upon reading Martin Luther's *The Babylonian Captivity of the Church*, "locked the door of their church… as a statement that followers of Christ were to live their whole lives for God. The bricklayer with the trowel, the farmer behind the plow, the artist before the easel, the cook beside the oven, the magistrate presiding at the bench, the parent at the crib—each one was to live out his or her calling…. Locked out of the church… as a demonstration of the lordship of Christ over every inch and second of life."[180] Finally, as quoted by Guinness, Luther notes, "The works of monks and priests, however holy and arduous they be, do not differ one whit in the sight of God from the works of the rustic laborer in the field or the woman going about her household tasks, but that all works are measured in faith alone…." and Bishop Thomas Bacon reminds us, "Our Savior Christ was a carpenter. His apostles were fishermen. St. Paul was a tent-maker."[181]

The key point is that each one of us take our theology to our workplace and to our interaction with family and friends. Heed the words of Barry Rowan, former high-tech CFO, "We don't derive meaning from our work. We bring meaning to our work. We find our work meaningful when it becomes an opportunity for the expression of who we are. We are our talents and our passions but our ultimate identity is found in Christ. Therefore, we bring greatest meaning to our work when it becomes an expression of Christ in us."[182]

The key is that we identify our calling through listening to God. Let us be like the author of Psalm 119, "I run in the path of your commands, for you have set my heart free." (Ps. 119:32)

And when we listen to God and then respond to His call, we will live in the glory of a purposeful life. As Guinness notes, "... calling provides the story line for our lives and thus a sense of continuity and coherence in the midst of a fragmented and confusing modern world.... In any and all situations,... God's call to us is the unchanging and ultimate whence, what, why and whither of our lives. Calling is a 'yes' to God that carries a 'no' to the chaos of modern demands."[183] Finally, Guinness instructs that calling involves the totality of our lives, not just our vocations or professions, "We may retire from our jobs but never from our calling. We may at times be unemployed, but no one ever becomes uncalled."[184] Lee Hardy, professor of philosophy at Calvin College, agrees, "I have a calling as a father, a son, a citizen, a parishioner, and a teacher. My job is just one of my callings, one facet of my call from God.... Rather, my job is one of the ways in which I respond to my calling to love my neighbor."[185]

Our "calling" is one of the connecting links between our divine nature and the material world in which we live and function. Guinness points out, "The grace that constitutes the cross also constitutes calling. Seen one way, calling initiates in our lives what the cross completes. Seen another, what the cross concludes beyond question as its final verdict, calling declares as its opening statement."[186] Holland states its this way, "We are living in the tension between the Cross (which redeemed us for what we were) and the eschaton (what we are to become)."[187]

An integral part of serving others is determining our own earthly purpose, our own God-given potential, and actualizing on that potential. Fulfilling one's calling within God's scheme is one form of expressing our love to our fellow humans. Therefore, is it not sinful to fail to identify or to ignore one's God-given talents and thereby inadequately fulfill one's potential?

Money

Before leaving this discussion of the legitimacy of material possessions and wealth, some important distinctions should be made regarding money. Since the beginning of civilization money has had four functions:

- As a common denominator of value. All goods and services are stated in money terms and therefore their relative exchange value can be immediately known.

- As a medium of exchange. Commercial transactions are facilitated when the obvious inconvenience of barter can be avoided through exchanging money for goods and services.

- As a medium of philanthropy. Conveying wealth from one party to another is facilitated as in the same way as a medium of exchange.

- As a store of value. Money can be readily saved over time and utilized when needed.

The mercantilists exaggerated the importance of money as an end in itself. Rather, as particularly Adam Smith, Alfred Marshall and John Stuart Mill eloquently observed in their writings, money is merely an intermediary, a common unit of value into which one good or service can be converted from another.

Money is neutral—neither good nor bad. Money is simply a mechanism that can be used for both righteous and evil ends. Money first appears in Scripture as a medium of exchange when Abraham purchases land from Ephron, "Abraham...weighed out for him....: four hundred shekels of silver,..." (Gn. 23:16)

Money, because it is a common medium of exchange between parties, reflects the values of the parties. Because humans are sinful and engage in sinful practices and transactions, money has become tainted with the general sinfulness of humanity. Indeed, all materiality, not just money, is human-related and therefore could be asserted to be sinful. Two important points are made in this regard

in the case of the righteous prophet Elisha refusing a gift from
Naaman. First, Elisha points out that God's favor cannot be
purchased. "As surely as the LORD lives, whom I serve, I will not
accept a thing." (2 Kgs. 5:16) Second, both money and clothing are
involved in a sinful, greedy, fraudulent transaction as Gehazi,
Elisha's servant, chases after Naaman to extract "a talent of silver
and two sets of cloth." (2 Kgs. 5:20-27) Money is no more sinful
than clothing. Gehazi, not money, was sinful.

Even God, through humans, deals with money. One of the first
accounts in Scripture, "I am the LORD. To redeem the 273 firstborn
Israelites who exceed the number of the Levites, collect five shekels
for each one, ... Give the money for the redemption of the additional Israelites to Aaron and his sons." (Nm. 3:45-48) Under King
Joash, "a proclamation was then issued in Judah and Jerusalem that
they should bring to the LORD the tax that Moses…had required….
and all the people brought their contributions…. They did this regularly and collected a great amount of money…. They hired masons
and carpenters to restore the LORD's temple, and also worked in iron
and bronze to repair the temple." (2 Chr. 24:9-12; also similar in 2
Chr. 34:11)

Similarly, when Zerubbabel leads a group from exile back to
Jerusalem to build the temple, "Cyrus, king of Persia, says:…
'provide him with silver and gold, with goods and livestock, and
with freewill offerings for the temple of God'…. King Cyrus
brought out the articles belonging to the temple of the LORD, 5,400
articles of gold and silver…." (Ezr. 1:4,7,11) "… freewill offerings….they gave to the treasury for this work 61,000 drachmas of
gold, 5,000 minas of silver…" (Ezr. 2:68,69) "Then they gave
money to the masons and carpenters…" (Ezr. 3:7) "The costs are to
be paid by the royal treasury…. The expenses of these men are to
be fully paid out of the royal treasury, from the revenues of Trans-
Euphrates." (Ezr. 6:4,8) Indeed, taxation of income from commerce
rebuilt the temple! Then when Ezra lead a second group out of
exile, "… you are to take with you the silver and gold that the king
and his advisers have freely given… together with all the silver and
gold you may obtain from the province of Babylon, as well as the
freewill offerings of the people…. With this money be sure to
buy…. anything else needed for the temple…. You may provide
from the royal treasury." (Ezr. 7:15-20) "I weighed out to them 650

talents of silver,...100 talents of gold, 20 bowls of gold valued at 1,000 carics, and two fine articles of polished bronze, as precious as gold.... weighed out the silver and gold" (Ezr. 8:26,27,33) Indeed, taxation of income from commerce financed operations of the temple! Then later, when Nehemiah returns to rebuild the walls, "the governor gave to the treasury 1,000 drachmas of gold,... Some of the heads of the families gave to the treasury for the work 20,000 drachmas of gold and 2,200 minas of silver. The total given by the rest of the people was 20,000 drachmas of gold, 2,000 minas of silver and 67 garments for priests." (Neh. 7:70-72) The foregoing is just a sampling of the text material related to money and goods in the books of Ezra and Nehemiah. The return of the exiles and the rebuilding of the temple and the walls in Jerusalem were largely financed by the treasury of the Persian royalty and freewill offerings. Although the term "freewill offering" is used, "expropriation" is probably a more accurate term, as it was the king who was "suggesting" an offering.

And finally in the book of Ezra we discover the first recorded tax exemption of a religious organization as the Persian King Artaxerxes decrees, "... you have no authority to impose taxes, tribute or duty on any of the priests, Levites, singers, gatekeepers, temple servants or other workers at this house of God." (Ezr. 7:24)

God, through Ezekiel, confirms the legitimacy of money by even specifying the relative value of denominations, "This is what the Sovereign LORD says:.... The shekel is to consist of twenty gerahs. Twenty shekels plus twenty-five shekels plus fifteen shekels equal one mina." (Ez. 45:9,12)

While money is mentioned infrequently in the Gospels, it is interesting to note that, when it is mentioned, it is often done so in a negative light; e.g., driving out the merchants and money-changers in the temple, do not lay up treasures on earth, you cannot serve God and mammon, woe to you who are rich, the Rich Fool, unrighteous mammon, theft (Judas), defrauding (Zacchaeus), etc. Further, Judas, the one who betrayed Jesus, was also the disciple who was in charge of the disciples' money. Nowhere, however, is the evil that money can do more dramatically displayed than in the following two cases:

(1) The first is Judas going to the chief priests and offering to betray Jesus to them in return for payment; "Judas went to the chief

priests in order to betray him to them…and they engaged to give him money. So he agreed." (Mt. 26:14; Mk. 14:10; Lk. 22:4)

(2) The second is the chief priests bribing the soldiers to tell everyone that the disciples stole Jesus' body away during the night while the soldiers were asleep; "they gave a sum of money to the soldiers and said, 'Tell people his disciples stole him away." (Mt. 28:12)

However, it should be re-emphasized that money is neutral. It is simply a mechanism for facilitating transactions of any type, good or evil. It is not the money that was sinful; it was Judas, the chief priests, and the soldiers. In the Parable of the Shrewd Manager, Jesus points out how worldly mechanisms such as money can be used in worldly ways—e.g., shrewdly—to achieve righteous ends. "I tell you, use worldly wealth to gain friends for yourselves, so that when it is gone, you will be welcomed into eternal dwellings." (Lk. 16:9) Recall also Boaz's clever purchase of Naomi's land.

Nevertheless, one gets the feeling when studying the Gospels that, to the extent that money is related to wordily transactions and therefore subject to association with the basic sinfulness of the world, the Evangelists essentially regarded it with disdain, as they regarded all worldly things. Indeed, the more money one has the more worldly enjoyments one can have. Further, the symbol of worldly pursuits is money; hence, its intrinsic danger—not intrinsic sinfulness, but intrinsic susceptibility to sinfulness. We will explore this further in the next chapter, "Attitudes Toward Material Possessions and Wealth."

Throughout Scripture we read acknowledgment of the realism that functioning within the world requires money. To the extent that the founders of the early church required food, clothing, transportation and other material and supplies, money was required to purchase these things. Paul mentions this on several occasions. For example, "Now about the collection for God's people:…each one of you should set aside a sum of money in keeping with his income, saving it up…send…to Jerusalem." (1 Cor. 16:1-3)

Finally, as appears in several different places in Scripture, God's admonishment not to charge the poor interest on loans implies that lending money and charging interest thereon under normal circumstance is appropriate. "If you lend money to one of my people among you who is needy,… charge him no interest." (Ex. 22:25) "If one of your countrymen becomes poor.... Do not take interest of any kind from him." (Lv. 35:35,6) "Do not charge your brother interest, whether on money or food or anything else that may earn interest. You may charge a foreigner interest...." (Dt. 23:19-20) "Do not take a pair of millstones....as security for a debt,..." (Dt. 24:6) "When you make a loan of any kind to your neighbor, do not go into his house to get...a pledge." (Dt. 24:10) "who lends his money without usury..." (Ps. 15:5) "The wicked borrow and do not repay," (Ps. 37:21) "I and my brothers and my men are also lending the people money and grain. But let the exacting of usury stop!" (Neh. 5:10) "He does not oppress anyone, but returns what he took in pledge for a loan.... He does not lend at usury or take excessive interest." (Ez. 18:7,8,17), suggesting that lending money and charging reasonable rates of interest is acceptable. "You take usury and excessive interest and make unjust gain from your neighbors by extortion. And you have forgotten me, declares the Sovereign LORD." (Ez. 22:12) There is considerable disagreement among interpreters of the foregoing passages, with some asserting that they declare the outright prohibition of charging any interest on any loan (claiming to be closer to the intent of the Hebrew term that is translated as "usury") and others suggesting that their principal message is to express kindness to and refraining from oppression of the poor. Biblical scholars and historians generally agree that interest rates at this time were around 20%—clearly excessive, by any millennium's standards! Most of the concern regarding interest rates related to overcharging the poor on personal loans used for subsistence. The validity of interest charged on loans for commercial purposes has been affirmed for centuries, recognizing that capital is a factor of production and, as such, is deserving of a return for its employment. As an example, while noting that the financial condition and interests of the borrower must be considered when setting the terms of a loan, "Calvin recognized the right to receive money for the use of one's money.... Calvin and others fixed the maximum amount of interest for the parishes of Geneva at 5 percent.... [Calvin's] world was that of urban commerce and he affirmed it. The exchange of money and goods was affirmed.... God had provided the institution [of money] for the good of humanity.... Money is a test for humanity, it tests one's humility and it is to be used charitably."[188]

There are a disturbing number of instances in which a portion of Jesus' parable material has been extracted and quoted from the Bible to make a point regarding specifics of the story which in fact were unintended by Jesus or in some cases are even opposite from the parable's conceptual point. This, I think, has led to some guilt on the part of contemporary business people. In the Parable of the Unforgiving Servant, (Mt. 18:23-35) Jesus was talking about forgiveness. In the parable the king (God) forgave the debt of one of his servants (humanity) who in turn refused to forgive the debt of one of his fellow servants (fellow human). Jesus was discussing forgiveness in general and the importance of maintaining a forgiving mind-set. It would be naïve to conclude that Jesus was either opposed to borrowing or opposed to repaying debts. Jesus undoubtedly knew that the normal conduct of commercial affairs involved the continual incurring and repayment of debt. Because repayment of debt was regarded as a serious matter, Jesus used it in his parable.

An implied legitimacy of borrowing and lending money is reflected in Paul's directive to the Romans "Let no debt remain outstanding,…" (Rom. 13:8) although the purpose of this phrase as used here was simply as a lead to Paul's point that the debt to love one another is never extinguished. Further implicitly suggesting a basic legitimacy of money is the frequent advice in Scripture to be prudent in commercial affairs and all business judgments. "He who puts up security for another will surely suffer, but whoever refuses to strike hands in pledge is safe." (Prv. 11:15) "A man lacking in judgment strikes hands in pledge and puts up security for his neighbor." (Prv. 17:18) "Take the garment of one who puts up security for a stranger;…" (Prv. 20:16) "… the borrower is servant to the lender." (Prv. 22:7) "Like an archer who wounds at random is he who hires a fool or any passer-by." (Prv. 26:10)

When discussing Paul's letters to Timothy and Titus regarding church organization and function, Brown observes, "Christian presbyters…were to give the whole community direction, e.g., by guiding policy decisions and supervising finances."[189] It is clearly recognized throughout the Bible that functioning in the world, spreading the news of the Gospels and practicing the doctrines of Christianity, took worldly goods and therefore financial wherewithal—money. Accordingly, the production of worldly goods and the generation of money is very much an exercise in accordance with God's plan.

A final observation regarding money: its theological dimension. Unlike Biblical times when money consisted primarily of precious metals, today money, consisting primarily of paper and electronic balances in bank accounts, possesses no intrinsic value. Money has value only to the extent that people using that money have faith and trust in its value. Remove the faith and the trust and money has no value.

Conclusion

The Bible begins with God defining prosperity as a blessing, and it ends with poverty declared as the opposite. "I know your afflictions and your poverty...." (Rev. 2:9) Robert Wall, professor of biblical studies at Seattle Pacific University, notes in his commentary on Revelation, "The Lord's opening declaration of his resurrection reassures a community that lives on the economic margins of the social order.... Thus, the promise of an economic reversal is more forcefully given. As a motif of apocalyptic literature, the promise of a reversal in socioeconomic fortunes is an element of God's coming triumph over the Evil One.... [L]iberation from poverty is their experience of God's shalom."[190] This is, however, also an affirmation of the transitory nature of one's worldly condition. Nevertheless, while throughout Scripture worldly poverty is often referred to in juxtaposition to heavenly riches, it nevertheless must be acknowledged that poverty was regarded by God and by Jesus as an unfavorable condition. Does it not follow, then, that *un*poverty, prosperity, is deemed as favorable—assuming, of course, righteously gained prosperity?

Ronald Sider, professor of theology and culture at Eastern Baptist Theological Seminary, answers affirmatively, suggesting that in the Bible poverty "is a 'curse'.... Prosperity and wealth, on the other hand, are good and desirable."[191] This favor of prosperity is found equally in both the Old Testament and the New Testament. The poor are continuously mentioned as worthy of assistance; the prosperous are continuously implored to assist the poor. Of all God's creations, God expresses greatest concern for (1) the poor and (2) the sick or disabled. "..., there should be no poor among you..., do not be hardhearted or tightfisted toward your poor brother....be open handed toward your brother and toward the poor and needy in your land." (Dt. 15:4-11)

Similarly in the New Testament, Jesus expressed extraordinary concern for the sick or disabled and the poor. Jesus devoted an inordinate amount of his time on earth convincing the prosperous to assist the poor. When discussing the New Testament treatment of poverty it should be kept in mind that the economy of the world at the time of Jesus was essentially agrarian with some mineral extraction and fishing. Land ownership was key to wealth creation, accumulation and holding. Moxnes observes further, "This was also the way power worked. Power meant control of land and of agricultural production."[192] In such an economy, wherein there essentially was an absence of a meaningful middle class, there was a great economic disparity. There were a few rich landowners while the bulk of the populace were poor peasants, effectively indentured servants. Accordingly, Israel at the time of Jesus resembled a third-world country today, accompanied by oppression of the poor, rather than a contemporary capitalistic industrialized country with a broad middle class. In that context Jesus, recognizing that essentially the poor had no way out of their plight, carried to the poor the message that one can still lead a blessed life in poverty and that, when one became part of the kingdom of God, regardless of one's worldly material wellbeing or status, one would be truly blessed.

While prosperity may be regarded as more favorable than poverty and while God directly declares prosperity as good, it is not suggested that prosperity is the end. Prosperity is not the end. God is the end. Humans wrestle with this. The story of the Bible is in fact a story which humanity is still living out. We are in the in-between times, the "already" of Jesus's resurrection and the "not yet" of his second coming. We are still living out the story of sin and redemption, moving toward the restoration of the original relationship between God and humanity. Accordingly, Scripture is a manual dealing with humans functioning within the physical world. Scripture shows how the material and spiritual are related. However, while God explicitly links "blessings" and "prosperity," somewhere along the line this relationship became perverted by humans. The cause and effect order became reversed. "Prosperity" became the end, the idol, and was used to display one's alleged "Godliness." It is this perversion against which Jesus lashed out as he harshly rebuked those who "taught that material possessions were a sure sign of God's favor,"[193] that "wealth was the evidence of divine approval."[194]

It is this same perversion which characterizes so much of hedonistic contemporary humankind with its materialistic idols. Finally, it is this perversion which the "Have Nots" of today's world continually demonstrate through their envy and covetousness of the "Haves." The discussion of the idolatry of material possessions and wealth is discussed further in the next chapter, "Attitudes Toward Material Possessions and Wealth." One cannot help but wonder if we have reverted all the way back to the story of the Old Testament which relates how recalcitrant God's people are despite God's reaching out to them.

In summary, while we have discussed the legitimacy of worldly goods, it does not follow that they are the end nor does it follow that pre-occupation with obtaining worldly goods is legitimate human effort. Further, while wealth and material possessions are clearly legitimate and the use thereof is clearly part of functioning within God's world, it does not follow that "more is better." To both Jesus and Paul material *sufficiency* was the criterion. Alexander reminds us, "Nowhere in Scripture is anyone ever told to get rich, either to help the poor or for any other reason.... So the New Testament never encourages us to get rich—even in order to use our money well.... Belief in the importance of money runs so deep in our culture that even the church accepts it.... Ironically, most Christian discussion on poverty... give a materialistic analysis: sharing money will solve the problem. But if we are to make any progress against the horrors of our world, we're going to have to give a deeper ethical and spiritual analysis than that."[195] Let us remember our earlier discussion: God is the source. God will provide. All that is required on humans' part is faith.

Nevertheless, Christianity is very much a religion of this world. According to Guthrie, "We have seen that the Spirit we meet in scripture is the Spirit of a this-worldly God who (1) created, blesses, protects and defends the physical life of all of God's creatures; (2) is at work to establish just social conditions....; (3) came to us in a flesh-and-blood human being...; (4) called together the Christian community... to be empowered to serve the world God loves;... the Holy Spirit of the God enables people not to escape *from* the world but to live *in* it.... Truly spiritual people, therefore, are not recognized by how suspicious they are of physical needs and pleasures but by how joyfully, thankfully, and responsibly they acknowledge them as good gifts of God.... They are recognized not just by how much they pray but by how much they pray for the world. They are recognized not just by how much they 'praise the Lord' for what 'the Lord has done for me' but by how sensitive their praise makes them to the needs and hurts of other people and the protection of the natural environment. They are recognized not just by how much they read the Bible, but by how their Bible reading influences their business practices, political commitments and social relationships.... True Christian spirituality cheerfully and confidently plunges into the life of this world, for there is where we meet the Spirit of God of the Bible who is at work not to save us from but in and for the sake of the world."[196] Recall our prior discussion: work is the process through which we humans give manifestation to God as the Source. Indeed, wealth is the result of the co-creation process of humans with God.

Murray concludes, "The New Testament does not cast any aspersion or suspicion upon riches as such any more than does the Old. It would be foolhardy to say that Scripture is against capitalism. It is true that the severest kind of condemnation rests upon ill-gotten gain."[197] Murray continues, "the abuse of riches and the abuses of the rich do not, however, make wealth evil.... When Paul, for example, enjoins that the rich should not be high-minded nor have their hope set on the uncertainty of riches, he does not insinuate to the least degree that it was evil to possess these riches."[198]

Griffiths summarizes, ""Within a Judeo-Christian framework the legitimacy attached to wealth creation follows directly from the creation mandate. While materialism, injustice and greed are in fundamental conflict with the teaching of Jesus, there is nothing in Christian theology which suggests that the creation of wealth is anything other than desirable. Wealth creation is not only necessary to sustain life but provides a unique opportunity for people to express their creativity in the service to others."[199]

Finally, Fr. Sirico ties together the concepts of materiality, private property, work and wealth. "I came to understand the indispensable principle of private property for constructing a society that would be inclusive.... [W]hat the Bible begins with is the fact that God is the author of both the heavens and the earth.... God calls man to work before sin makes its appearance on the human scene....When God decides to redeem the world, He does it not just by fiat or abstract word, but the concrete Word (Jn. 1:14) The Incarnation is God's reiteration of His intention to be in relation to the world."[200]

Chapter VI

Attitudes Toward
Material Possessions and Wealth

Through a review of Scripture we have learned that all matter is intrinsically good, created and declared so by God. Further, God, as the source of all material possessions and wealth, is their ultimate owner, and therefore we have a huge accountability for responsible stewardship. We have also learned that God views prosperity rightfully gained as favorable and poverty as unfavorable.

In this context what is the appropriate attitude that one should hold toward material possessions and wealth? The answer is found throughout Scripture: we should be filled with gratitude which is expressed through service to God. Peter's exhortation to the church elders could be applied to all of us, "not greedy for money, but eager to serve..." (1 Pt. 5:2) In the next chapter, "Role of Material Possessions and Wealth," we will observe that the ultimate role of material possessions and wealth is to serve God's glory.

However, there is a strong tendency for us sinful humans to develop attitudes toward material possessions and wealth that get in the way of our pursuing God's purposes by displacing God with materialism. These sinful attitudes are idolatry, distraction, pride, covetousness, envy and hypocrisy. Rather, the righteous attitudes to hold toward material possessions and wealth are humility and gratitude, accompanied by a dedication to serving God. Each of these attitudes is explored in this chapter.

Idolatry / Addiction / Distraction

According to the *Dictionary of the Later New Testament and Its Developments*, "Idolatry is the offering of sacrifice to some deity other than the Creator, usually with a view to gaining temporal benefits...; by extension, a person dominated by anything in the created realm might be guilty of idolatry."[201] There is immense danger that worldly political and economic systems detract from humans' relationship to God and that worldly possessions can become the subject of idolatry, displacing God.

An interesting observation is made by LaSor regarding the ironic relationship between the notion that God is the source of all material possessions and the emergence of a pervasive idolatry. "The more abundantly God blessed Israel, the more they chased after idols."[202] Today the same thing occurs, as to many people wealth is the subject of idolatry. Wheeler asserts, "Possessions and the love of them stand as a continual temptation to idolatry,...taking wealth itself as the primary object of love, trust and attachment."[203] As noted by Pentecost, "Jesus viewed the desire to accumulate wealth as a substitute for faith. If one has material means, that person may not see the need to trust God for needs."[204] John Schwarz, business-man turned theologian and head of the Tabgha Foundation in Minneapolis, in discussing the seven deadly sins enumerated by Pope Gregory in the late sixth century, notes that avarice and greed are "the manipulation of people and circumstance to acquire possessions and power, which become 'gods' in which we place our hope and trust."[205]

In the context of this particular treatise dealing with economics and theology, it is interesting to note that immediately after giving Moses the Ten Commandments, God emphasizes, by repeating and expanding upon, the sin of idolatry with the admonishment: "Do not make any gods to be alongside me; do not make for yourselves gods of silver or gods of gold." (Ex. 20:23)

While many of the following passages were limited to the subject of monotheism and the nature of God and while in the Old Testament "idolatry" has to do with setting up other gods as a subject of faith and worship, certainly in a derivative sense this term "idolatry" can be applied to other subjects of faith and worship which replace God. God has been clear to humanity that God is to be the sole object of our worship. The Old Testament story includes the lesson of the consequences of turning from or even compromising one's faith in God.

> "Do not make idols....I am the LORD your God." (Lv. 26:1)

> "...do not prostitute yourselves by going after the lusts of your own hearts and eyes. Then you will remember....I am the LORD your God." (Nm. 15:39-41)

> "...do not become corrupt and make for yourselves an idol,....the LORD is God; besides him there is no other." (Dt. 4:16,35)

"I am the LORD your God, ...You shall have no other gods before me." (Dt. 5:6,7) But it goes beyond mere recognition. There is an action imperative. "Love the LORD your God with all your heart and with all your soul and with all your strength." (Dt. 6:4) It goes beyond mere love. We are to love with all of our heart, soul and strength. It is quite clear. God is to come first; and we are to devote our full heart, soul and strength to demonstrating our love. Wright emphasizes the force of this passage my noting further translations of the Hebrew words for "heart," "soul" and "strength" as "mind," "whole inner self," and "substance, possessions" respectively.[206] Further, "If you ever forget the LORD your God and follow other gods and worship and bow down to them, I testify against you today that you will surely be destroyed." (Dt. 8:19)
    "... commit yourselves to the LORD and serve him only,..." (1 Sm. 7:3) "... serve the LORD with all your heart. Do not turn away after useless idols. They can do you no good." (1 Sm. 12:20,21) "How great you are, O Sovereign LORD! There is no one like you, and there is no God but you,..." (2 Sm. 7:22) "You have made for yourself other gods,...; you have provoked me to anger...." (1 Kgs. 14:9) The folly of worshipping or relying upon anything other than God is no more dramatically illustrated than by Elijah's challenging his God to Baal of the 450 pagan prophets in 1 Kings 18:16-46.

"Answer me, O LORD, answer me, so these people will know that you, O LORD, are God,....' Then the fire of the LORD fell...." (1 Kgs. 18:37,38) Lest one fall into the sin of idolatry, keep in mind the ultimate disposition of the evil Jezebel who possessed immense wealth and mightily wielded power as Ahab's wife. "But when they went to bury her, they found nothing except her skull, her feet and her hands. They went back and told Jehu, who said, 'This is the word of the LORD that he spoke through his servant Elijah:... On the plot of ground at Jezreel dogs will devour Jezebel's flesh. Jezebel's body will be like refuse on the ground..., so that no one will be able to say, 'This is Jezebel." (2 Kgs. 9:35-37) "They worshiped idols, though the LORD said, 'You shall not do this.'.... So the people of Israel were taken from their homeland into exile in Assyria,..." (2 Kgs. 17:12) "Josiah got rid of ..., the idols and all the other detestable things seen in Judah and Jerusalem" (2 Kgs. 23:24) "They abandoned the temple of the LORD..., and worshiped...idols. Because of their guilt, God's anger came upon Judah...." (2 Chr. 24:18) "You praised the gods of silver and gold, of bronze, iron, wood and stone.... But you did not honor the God..." (Dn. 5:23)

> "If I have put my trust in gold or said to pure gold, 'You are my security,' if I have rejoiced over my great wealth,... then these also would be sins..." (Jb. 31:24-28)

"How long, O men, will you turn my glory into shame? How long will you love delusions and seek false gods? (Ps. 4:2) "In his arrogance the wicked man...boasts of the craving of his heart; he blesses the greedy and reviles the LORD." (Ps. 10:2) "The sorrows of those will increase who run after other gods." (Ps. 16:4) "He... who does not lift up his soul to an idol.... will receive blessing from the LORD." (Ps. 24:4,5) "I hate those who cling to worthless idols: I trust the LORD." (Ps. 31:6) "Blessed is the man who makes the LORD his trust, who does not.... turn aside to false gods." (Ps. 40:4) "...though your riches increase, do not set your heart on them." (Ps. 62:10) "But they soon forgot what he had done.... they gave in to their craving.... worshiped an idol.... exchanged their Glory...forgot the God who saved them... yoked themselves to the Baal of Peor... worship their idols,...sacrificed to the idols of Canaan,... Save us, O LORD our God,…Praise the LORD." (Ps. 106:13,14, 19-21,28,38,47,48) "The idols of the nations are silver and gold, made by the hands of men. They have mouths, but cannot speak, eyes, but they cannot see; they have ears, but cannot hear,…" (Ps. 135:15-17)

King David sums up the point being made, "You are my Lord; apart from you I have no good thing." (Ps. 16:2) and "O LORD, by your hand save me from…. men of this world whose reward is in this life." (Ps. 17:14) Indeed, wealth is transitory and powerless.

Solomon warns of the evil of materialism, hedonism and idolatry, noting wealth is not the end. God is the end. "A greedy man brings trouble to his family," (Prv. 15:27) "He who loves pleasure will become poor; whoever loves wine and oil will never be rich." (Prv. 21:17) "A good name is more desirable than great riches; to be esteemed is better than silver and gold." (Prv. 22:1) "Do not wear yourself out to get rich; have the wisdom to show restraint. Cast but a glance at riches, and they are gone," (Prv. 23:4,5) "Do not join those who drink too much wine or gorge themselves on meat, for drunkards and gluttons become poor, and drowsiness clothes them in rags." (Prv. 23:20,21)

In Ecclesiastes we are warned, "Whoever loves money never has money enough; whoever loves wealth is never satisfied with his income…. I have seen a grievous evil under the sun: wealth hoarded to the harm of its owner." (Eccl. 5:10,13) "All man's efforts are for his mouth, yet his appetite is never satisfied." (Eccl. 6:7) Finally, the derision, "…but money is the answer for everything." (Eccl. 10:19)

A dominant message of the prophets was the denunciation of idolatry which they saw as a manifestation of turning from God. Hosea, referring to the Northern Kingdom of Israel which had prospered under Jeroboam II but decayed spiritually, "she decked herself with rings and jewelry, and went after her lovers, but me she forgot." (Hos. 2:13) "Israel has forgotten his Maker and built palaces." (Hos. 8:14) "For you have been unfaithful to your God; you love the wages of a prostitute…. they consecrated themselves to the shameful idol and became as vile as the thing they loved." (Hos. 9:1,10) Finally, Hosea calls Israel to repent, "We will never again say 'Our gods' to what our own hands have made,…" (Hos. 14:3) Jonah, in his prayer inside the fish, finally realizing his dependence on God, notes the cost of idolatry, "Those who cling to worthless idols forfeit the grace that could be theirs." (Jon. 2:8)

The prophet Isaiah was quite forthright in his condemnation of idolatry in a way that readily applies today. "Their land is full of silver and gold; there is no end to their chariots. Their land is full of idols; they bow down to the work of their hands, to what their fingers have made. So man will be brought low and mankind humbled—do not forgive them.... Hide in the ground from dread of the LORD and the splendor of his majesty." (Is. 2:7-10) Isaiah condemns materialism and hedonism in general, "Woe to those who.... have harps and lyres at their banquets, tambourines and flutes and wine, but they have no regard for the deeds of the LORD,... Therefore my people will go into exile for lack of under-standing." (Is. 5:11-13) "But see, there is joy and revelry, ... eating of meat and drinking of wine! 'Let us eat and drink,' you say, 'for tomorrow we die!' The LORD Almighty has revealed this in my hearing: 'Till your dying day this sin will not be atoned for,' says the Lord, the LORD Almighty." (Is. 22:13,14) "I am the LORD;... I will not give my glory to another or my praise to idols.... But those who trust in idols, who say to images, 'You are our gods,' will be turned back in utter shame." (Is. 42:8,17) "Is there any God beside me? No, there is no other Rock; I know not one.' All who make idols are nothing, and the things they treasure are worthless." (Is. 44:8,9) "All the makers of idols will be put to shame and disgraced; they will go off into disgrace together.... Ignorant are those who carry about idols of wood, who pray to gods that cannot save." (Is. 45:16,20) "Some pour out gold from their bags and weigh out silver on the scales; they hire a goldsmith to make it into a god, and they bow down and worship it....Though one cries out to it; it does not answer;... I am God, and there is no other; I am God, and there is none like me." (Is. 46:6-9)

Isaiah also notes the addiction characteristic of idolatry, "They are dogs with mighty appetites; they never have enough....; they all turn to their own way, each seeks his own gain. 'Come,' each one cries, 'let me get wine! Let us drink our fill of beer! And tomorrow will be like today, or even far better." (Is. 56:11) The entire chapter fifty-seven of Isaiah is particularly vitriolic in its condemnation of idolatry, "But come here you sons of a sorceress, you offspring of adulterers and prostitutes!... Are you not a brood of rebels,... You burn with lust among the oaks....Whom have you so dreaded and feared that you have been false to me,.... When you cry out for help, let your collection of idols save you! The wind will carry all of them off, a mere breath will blow them away." (Is. 57:3-5, 11,13) "Surely the arm of the LORD is not too short to save, nor his ear too dull to hear, But your iniquities have separated you from your God…. Like the blind we grope along the wall, feeling our way like men without eyes." (Is. 59:1,2,10) "I will destroy your carved images…. You will no longer bow down to the work of your hands." (Mi. 5:13)

Jeremiah was equally forthright in condemning idolatry and calling to faithfulness in God as the ultimate Reality. "I will pronounce my judgments on my people because of their wickedness in forsaking me,….in worshiping what their hands have made." (Jer. 1:16) "They say to the wood, 'You are my father,' and to stone, 'You gave me birth.' They have turned their backs to me and not their faces;…. Where then are the gods you made for yourselves? Let them come and save you when you when you are in trouble!" (Jer. 2:27,28) "Your children have forsaken me and sworn by gods that are not gods. I supplied all their needs, yet they committed adultery…. They are well-fed, lusty stallions, each neighing for another man's wife. Should I not punish them for this?" (Jer. 5:7-9) "They are all senseless and foolish; they are taught by worthless wooden idols…. What the craftsman and goldsmith have made is then dressed in blue and purple—all made by skilled workers. But the LORD is the true God; he is the living God, the eternal King." (Jer. 10:8-10) "….every goldsmith is shamed by his idols. His images are a fraud;…" (Jer. 51:17)

Similarly, God through Ezekiel condemns "all your detestable idols." (Ez. 5:9) "…how I have been grieved by their adulterous hearts, which have turned away from me, and by their eyes, which have lusted after their idols…. They will know that I am the LORD when their people lie slain among their idols…." (Ez. 6:9,13) That God, and only God, is LORD was a dominant message of Ezekiel. "Their silver and gold will not be able to save them in the day of the LORD's wrath. They will not satisfy their hunger or fill their stomachs with it, for it has made them stumble into sin." (Ez. 7:19) "This is what the Sovereign LORD says: Repent! Turn from your idols and renounce all your detestable practices!" (Ez. 14:6) "But you trusted in your beauty…. You took some of your garments to make gaudy high places,…. You also took the fine jewelry I gave you,… and you made for yourself male idols…. Also the food I provided for you—

the fine flour, olive oil and honey I gave you to eat—you offered as
fragrant incense before them." (Ez. 16:15-19) Ezekiel continues on
throughout Chapter 16 with a vicious condemnation of idolatry and
likening the people to prostitutes. "Because you poured out your
wealth and exposed your nakedness in your promiscuity...." (Ez.
16:36) "their hearts were devoted to their idols." (Ez. 20:16) "You
will... bear the consequences of your sins of idolatry. Then you will
know that I am the Sovereign LORD." (Ez. 23:49)

All of the prophets challenged idolatry, forcing our introspection
regarding the following questions: who created me, in what do I
ultimately trust, to what do I look for security and happiness, who is
in charge of my future, and where do I look for ultimate truth?
Although the prophets condemn us for turning away from God,
they also offer hope that God, by God's grace-filled love, will
welcome us back under God's care. In the familiar passage,
Jeremiah foretells the ultimate solution of the New Covenant
wherein God, through Jesus Christ, "will put my laws in their
minds and write it on their hearts. I will be their God and they will
be my people." (Jer. 31:33) To what extent today have we turned
away from the New Covenant?

Early in the New Testament Jesus declares, "Away from me,
Satan! For it is written: 'Worship the Lord your God, and serve him
only." (Mt. 4:10) The supremacy of God is also reaffirmed by Jesus
in his response to the Pharisees and Herodians attempting to trick
him, "Give to Caesar what is Caesar's and to God what is God's."
(Mt. 22:21), noting that, while we have a responsibility to government, we have an overriding responsibility to God. Later, Jesus
goes further, suggesting worshipping idols can become an addiction, "...everyone who commits sin is a slave to sin." (Jn. 8:32-4)

Nowhere is the displacement by wealth from pursuing God more
poignantly related in the Bible than in the story of the rich young
man. "Good Teacher what must I do to inherit eternal life?'... 'You
know the commandments; all these I have observed; what do I still
lack?' 'Sell all that you have, and give it to the poor...and come
follow me.' At that saying his countenance fell and he went away
sorrowful; for he had great possessions." (Mt. 19:16; Mk. 10:17; Lk.
18:18) Wheeler notes that "Jesus' rigor in this case was the result of
something he perceived about the state of this particular rich man's
soul. Not only was he rich, ...but he loved and trusted" God and

otherwise kept the commandments so that the surrender of his property was the ultimate, remaining required task.[207] Of course, by the nature of his reaction the man knows that he is addicted to his material possessions. This story teaches several points: worldly possessions are not the basis of security or identity, they are less important than God, they have no relationship to gaining eternal life, and they can get in one's way by becoming a source of pride and a feeling of self-sufficiency. The message is that God is first—before all else. Further, the good deeds and keeping the commandments which the young man had done were insufficient; rather, he needed to start all over—as symbolized by selling all of his possessions—and humbly submit himself to God. Danker, in his commentary on Luke's version of this story, stresses that a major point is that action considerably more revolutionary than merely keeping the commandments is required. "Moses is not renounced, but more creative possibilities of moral existence are available to the one who is liberated from dependence on the code.... The future called for erasure of all pride in past achievement [in obeying the code]."[208]

Another important element of this story, as suggested by Wheeler and other commentators, is that Jesus perceived this particular man to be far enough advanced in his spiritual commitment that Jesus went one step further and suggested that the man in fact become a disciple. "The central concern of Mark's Gospel is not wealth but discipleship, and the punchline of the foregoing story is not 'whatever you have sell it' but rather 'come follow me.' It is important....to note the disvalue of wealth. For Mark,...Wealth has no importance at all except as a stumbling block."[209] L. W. Hurtado, professor of New Testament Language and Literature at the University of Edinburgh, agrees, "His possessions are a snare and hindrance,... precisely because they distract him from answering Jesus' invitation to follow him.... The issue is Jesus, the one who assures participation in the kingdom of God, and the point is that following him and joining his mission are to be put ahead of all other interests."[210] Of final note, the message of this story is not that poverty is the door to the kingdom of God. Mounce comments, "The requirement to divest oneself of all possessions is not a universal requirement for entrance into heaven. It was, for this specific person, a test of his willingness to place God's priorities first in his own life. The monastic requirement of poverty grew out of a misunderstanding of this verse."[211] Hurtado notes, "The man is called, however, not to poverty for its own sake, but to discipleship.... This is no mere advocacy of a social program involving redistribution of wealth or romantic praising of the idea of poverty."[212]

Our attitude toward wealth and material possessions is addressed clearly and effectively in *The Sermon on the Mount.* "Do not lay up for yourselves treasures on earth, where moth and rust consume and where thieves break in and steal, but lay up for yourselves treasures in heaven,...For where your treasure is, there will your heart be also." (Mt. 6.19; also a version in Lk. 12:33-34) "Lay up" is a key verb. Jesus seems to be talking against accumulating wealth and possessions as ends in themselves and just owning rather than utilizing them. He also is warning against a predisposition toward accumulating worldly goods rather than placing as first priority the accumulation of spiritual understanding and favor with God. If we are pre-occupied with worldly goods, our hearts will be there as well and it will follow that attention to God eventually will slip away altogether. Further, in the Parable of the Rich Fool, Jesus relates the futility and invalidity of collecting and storing worldly goods because they have no relevance to the kingdom of God; rather one must accumulate riches toward God: generosity, service, righteousness, etc. "The land of a rich man brought forth plentifully... I will store all my grain and goods. And I will say to my soul, Soul, you have ample goods laid up...But God said to him, 'Fool! This night your soul is required of you; and the things you have prepared, whose will they be?' So is he who lays up treasure for himself, and is not rich toward God." (Lk. 12:16-21) Danker elaborates, "At the top of the list of tyrannical forces is the despotic power of things..... The rich fool was not stupid because he took thought for the future, but because he planned on a future without God in it and thought that he was in charge of that future."[213]

Jesus becomes even more forceful in his distinguishing between worldly goods and heavenly goods. "No one can serve two masters; for either he will hate the one and love the other, or he will be devoted to the one and despise the other. You cannot serve God and mammon." (Mt. 6:24, Lk. 16:13) Here Jesus is saying that we have to go farther than implied in the preceding paragraph. We must make God our single, exclusive priority and then simply rest with the faith that all else will flow satisfactorily from our reliance on God. Of course Jesus and his disciples were the ultimate example of this. "…and he called the twelve together and he sent them out to preach of the kingdom of God and to heal. And he said to them, 'Take nothing for your journey,…nor money….'" (Mt. 10:5-10; Mk. 6:8-9; Lk. 9.1-3)

At this point an important distinction should be inserted in the discussion. The foregoing passage from the Gospel of Luke is from a discourse of Jesus to his disciples which ends with "Sell your possessions, and give alms; provide yourselves with…a treasure in the heavens that does not fail, where no thief approaches and no moth destroys. For where your treasure is, there will your heart be also." (Lk. 12:33-34) This is stronger than the account from the Gospel of Matthew above. But it should be noted that Jesus was speaking to his disciples, not to the public in general, and therefore it seems that the analysis by Schweizer is valid: "The disciples in the narrower sense are called to an exemplary radical renunciation, not as an act of human supererogation but as a way of showing a heart devoted totally to the One who is their Redeemer….That is where their hearts must beat so that God may once again become a truly present reality. Therefore, Luke sets the disciples before the community as a model…."[214]

Finally, when studying Jesus' treatment of wealth, it is important to note that the structure of society at the time of Jesus was highly bifurcated, consisting of one small group of an elite, privileged aristocracy comprised of wealthy landowners and political leaders and another immense group of peasants and minor tradespeople. Wealth went hand-in-hand with political and social oppression. There was no broad middle class characteristic of today's developed economies. In addition to the validity of the substance of Jesus' message, it is logical that Jesus' harshness regarding the wealthy was partially his reaction to the harsh arrogance of the wealthy group.

Turning to the book of Acts, we see that wealth can possess a seductive power that leads one to displace God by substituting material wellbeing. In Ephesus riots broke out in response to Paul's message being perceived as a threat to the demand for silver shrines of the Ephesian goddess Artemis. "A silversmith named Demetrius, who…brought in no little business for the craftsmen…called them together,…and said: 'Men, you know we receive a good income from this business. And you see and hear how this fellow Paul has convinced and led astray large numbers of people here in Ephesus....There is danger...that our trade will lose its good name." (Acts 19:24-7) Danker explains, "This combination of political-economic power with religious sanction is well-nigh irresistible, for there exists endemic opposition to change."[215]

The seduction of materialism and wealth can carry further into the notion that anything, even spiritual powers, can be purchased for a price. "When Simon saw that the Spirit was given at the laying on of the apostles' hands, he offered them money and said, 'Give me also this ability....' Peter answered, 'May your money perish with you, because you thought you could buy the gift of God with money!....you heart is not right before God." (Acts 8:20-2) This false notion that all it takes is money fails to recognize the limited nature of all materiality, the subordination of created matter to the Creator.

The limited role of wealth and material possessions is reaffirmed throughout Scripture and certainly in the book of Acts. When the crippled beggar outside the temple "saw Peter and John about to enter, he asked them for money. Peter looked straight at him, as did John....Then Peter said, 'Silver or gold I do not have, but what I have I give you. In the name of Jesus Christ of Nazareth, walk.'.....He jumped to his feet and began to walk." (Acts 3:1-8) Charette observes, "Power has nothing to do with wealth or position. Power comes from one's relationship with Jesus Christ.... Further, in fact, wealth tends to get in the way and weaken the church to the extent that the church can tend to become dependent upon and therefore pre-occupied with money."[216]

The apostle Paul admonishes us for the sinful human tendency to displace God by material possessions. "They exchanged the truth of God for a lie, and worshiped and served created things rather than the Creator...." (Rom. 1:25) "Those who live according to the sinful nature have their minds set on what that nature desires; but those who live in accordance with the Spirit have their minds set on what the Spirit desires." (Rom. 8:5) Hawthorne explains, "Paul links idolatry in all of its forms,...with...'works of the flesh' against which Christians must...continually flee."[217]

Paul in his letters to the Corinthians addresses the struggle of the Christians in Corinth in dealing with the full array of corporeal temptations surrounding them. While acknowledging the legitimacy of worldly goods, Paul, nevertheless makes the important distinction that worldly goods are only transitory—never to be idolized or worshipped. "If any man builds on this foundation using gold, silver, costly stones, wood, hay or straw, his work will be shown for what it is, because the Day will bring it to light. It will be revealed with fire, and the fire will test the quality of each man's work." (1Cor. 3:12) Reflecting his focus on the eschaton, Paul states, "…those who use the things of the world, as if not engrossed in them. For this world in its present form is passing away." (1 Cor. 7:31) Paul also notes, "We know that an idol is nothing at all in the world and that… there is but one God, the Father, from whom all things came and for whom we live; and there is but one Lord, Jesus Christ, through whom all things came and through whom we live." (1 Cor. 8:4,6) "Therefore, my dear friends, flee from idolatry." (1 Cor. 10:14) Paul further asserts, "Don't you know that you yourselves are God's temple and that God's Spirit lives in you?" (1 Cor. 3:16) "God…will not let you be tempted beyond what you can bear. But when you are tempted, he will also provide a way out so that you can stand up under it." (1 Cor. 10:13) God is faithful to us; all we need do in all of our worldly concerns is faithfully accept God's grace.

But a corollary to the foregoing is not to rid oneself of material possessions. It is to rid oneself of the idolatry of material possessions. It is a matter of priorities, of values. As Paul further reflects, "I have learned the secret of being content in any and every situation, whether well fed or hungry, whether living in plenty or in want…." (Phil. 4:12) Bruce observes, "Paul had a long experience of having less than sufficient at some times and more than sufficient at other times: it made little difference to him."[218] Paul also warns against making wealth and material possessions the end. "…many live as enemies of the cross of Christ. Their destiny is destruction, their god is their stomach,….Their mind is on earthly things." (Phil. 3:19) "No…greedy person—such a man is an idolater—has any inheritance in the kingdom of Christ and of God." (Eph. 5:5) "Set your minds on things above, not on earthly things….Put to death, therefore, whatever belongs to your earthly nature: sexual immorality, impurity, lust, evil desires and greed, which is idolatry." (Col. 3:2-5) Patzia notes, "Greed is idolatry because it leads one to focus attention and affection on things other than God."[219]

Paul warns in a letter to Timothy, "But if we have food and cloth-

ing, we will be content with that. People who want to get rich fall
into temptation and a trap and into many foolish and harmful
desires that plunge men into ruin and destruction. For the love of
money is a root of all kinds of evil. Some people, eager for money,
have wandered from the faith and pierced themselves with many
griefs." (1 Tm. 6:8-10) Note, it is the *love* of and *eagerness* for
money rather than the mere possession of money that is the problem. They can distract us from the pursuit of the end for which God
created us and to which God called us: faithful service.

This theme throughout the Gospels, Acts and letters of Paul
appears also in the other New Testament writings: "Keep your lives
free from the love of money....here we do not have an enduring city,
but we are looking for the city that is to come." (Heb. 13:5) "Now
listen, you who say, 'today or tomorrow we will go to this or that
city,... carry on business and make money.' Why, you do not even
know what will happen tomorrow. What is your life? You are in a
mist that appears for a little while and then vanishes. Instead, you
ought to say, 'If it is the Lord's will, we will live and do this or that.'
As it is, you boast and brag. All such boasting is evil." (Jas. 4:13-16)
"Do not love the world or anything in the world. If anyone loves the
world, the love of the Father is not in him. For everything in the
world—the cravings of sinful man, the lust of his eyes and boasting
of what he has and does—comes not from the Father...." (1 Jn.
2:15,16) "Dear children, keep yourselves from idols." (1 Jn. 5:21)
"Woe to them! They have.... Rushed for profit into Balaam's error."
(Jude 11) According to theologian Thomas E. Johnson, in the two
passages above from 1 John we are "warned to avoid an approach to
life wherein the thought, decisions,... [and] activities of everyday
life are dominated by the cravings of one's own 'flesh' and to refrain
from letting anything take the place that is rightly due God."[220]

And this theme of the transitory nature of earthly riches and God
as the sole definition of richness continues to the end of Scripture.
"I know your afflictions and your poverty—yet you are rich!" (Rev.
2:9) "To him who overcomes, I will give some of the hidden [spiri-
tual] manna." (Rev. 2:17) "Never again will they hunger; never
again will they thirst." (Rev. 7:16) Heavenly goods are eternal and
infinite; worldly goods are limited to worldly purposes and are transitory. They are immaterial to salvation and have no relationship to
one's heavenly standing. Wall notes, "For John, then, manna is yet

another symbol of eschatological fulfillment, when God's people receive the promised blessings of salvation."[221]

Even if among some people wealth does not reach the extreme of idolatry, it can certainly be a distraction, and Scripture warns against this. "...when you eat and are satisfied, be careful that you do not forget the LORD." (Dt. 6:11,12) As Wright notes regarding the foregoing passage, "God's desire for the people of God was (and still ultimately remains) a full life, enjoying the gifts of creation. But equally there is no illusion regarding the likely behavior of the people; in the enjoyment of the gift they might forget the giver.... Fullness can lead to forgetfulness,..."[222] Even the Spirit-filled David and wise Solomon, as well as other mortals, did so with dire consequences.

The prophet Zephaniah takes to task the business community who are so pre-occupied with business matters that they are indifferent toward God. "Wail, you who live in the market district; all your merchants will be wiped out, all who trade with silver will be ruined. At that time I will search Jerusalem with lamps and punish those who are complacent, who are like wine left in its dregs, who think, 'The LORD will do nothing, either good or bad." (Zep. 1:11,12) Similarly, Malachi states, "You have said, 'It is futile to serve God.... But now we call the arrogant blessed'.....Sure the day is coming;... All the arrogant.... will be stubble." (Mal. 3:14; 4:1)

King Solomon, also warns against distraction and complacency. "they will eat the fruit of their ways and be filled with the fruit of their schemes. For the waywardness of the simple will kill them, and the complacency of the fools will destroy them; but whoever listens to me will live in safety...." (Prv. 1:31-33)

Jesus warns that the pursuit of wealth can be a distraction from the pursuit of the kingdom of God. In Jesus' interpretation of the Parable of the Sower, the seed that "was sown among thorns,...are those who hear the word, but the cares of the world, and the delight in riches, and the desire for other things enter and choke the word, and it proves unfruitful." (Mt. 13:22; Mk. 4:19; Lk. 8:14) Mounce provides this instructive interpretation, "To be caught up in the worries of everyday living and to fall prey to the seductive appeal of financial well-being is to guarantee a spiritual crop failure."[223] This notion is addressed also in the Parable of the Great Supper: "The kingdom of heaven can be compared to a king who gave a marriage feast...and those who were invited....would not come....and made light of it and went off, one to his farm, another to his business...." (Mt. 22:2; Lk. 14:15-24) Wheeler observes, "In the gospels the concern for material wealth repeatedly thwarts the response to Jesus' teaching."[224]

Paul discovered the reaction of people whose livelihood was threatened by Paul's message and actions. One story involves Paul commanding the spirit within a fortune-telling slave girl who "earned a great deal of money for her owners..., 'In the name of Jesus Christ I command you to come out of her!' At that moment the spirit left her. When the owners of the slave girl realized that their hope of making money was gone, they seized Paul and Silas and dragged them into the marketplace to face the authorities." (Acts 16:16-19)

Humans tend to become so self-conscious that they lose God-consciousness. We tend to lose sight of Paul's reminder, "Now we know that if the earthly tent we live in is destroyed, we have a building from God, an eternal house in heaven, not built by human hands.... We live by faith not by sight." (2Cor.5:1,7) Often today a successful person is totally occupied with his/her worldly pursuits and simply does not take the time for many other things, including family as well as spiritual study and contemplation. Additionally, it follows that dealing all day with material goods, performing "objective" analyses and the like can cause the business or professional person to place a high value on being a pragmatist. The notion of faith can be anathema to conventional business decision-making. The greatest need among successful business people, as well as all humans, is to learn the ability to turn from their head to their heart.

It has been asserted that the very success of capitalism has exacerbated this pre-occupation with worldly goods. Indeed, daily we in economically developed countries lavish ourselves on a cornucopia of material goods, leading to what Guinness calls an insatiability.[225] The ease with which we pick the goods from the banquet table called capitalism has led to an obsession. We can hardly wait until tomorrow's banquet to gaze at what abundance has been set before us. And our banquet hosts keep enticing us to "take more, take more." As producers court consumers through advertising, hundreds of millions of dollars are devoted to inducing consumption—not only consumption of a particular product but consumption in general. Every device imaginable is used to lure the consuming maiden into the den of the lustful producer. Sider reports the tragedy that "We in the United States spend more on advertising than on all our public institutions of higher education…. The ever more affluent standard of living is the god of twentieth-century North America, and the adman is its prophet…. Perhaps the most demonic part of advertising is that it attempts to persuade us that material possessions will bring joy and fulfillment."[226]

From one's first waking moment in the day until finally falling asleep at night, one is bombarded with an unceasing, clanging barrage of urgings to consume this or that worldly good. Such activity has generated bizarre outcomes. Producers desire to get their messages to as many consumers as efficiently as possible, which has led to an explosion of usage of an incredibly effective device for accomplishing this: television advertising. The average American adult views 21,000 television commercials per year.[227] As huge numbers of consumers view certain professional sports, for example, the marginal utility of a message on a sports program is commensurately great. As the viewership reaches tens of millions of consumers, the marginal utility of advertising to producers reaches astronomical levels. Accordingly, it makes economic sense for the provider of the athletic event being shown on television to pay higher amounts of money to those athletes who generate the higher viewership (read: all-stars, champions, etc.). Hence, the similarly astronomical salaries paid to certain professional athletes. When one adds in product endorsements by athletes, the sums soar to beyond astronomical! It is testimony to the materialism of modern day capitalism that the dominant edifice in most major American cities is the professional sports stadium or arena. This is a particularly fascinating phenomenon when juxtaposed against the major edifice of most medieval European cities: the cathedral.

Of course, even a more prevalent luring of viewers to television than sports is, as everyone knows, that other worldly pre-occupation: sex. The awesome power of television is an extremely important subject in itself and has been the topic of many writings, but I mention it here only in the context of its role as an inducer of consumption. However, lest we use advertising as a convenient scapegoat, I suggest that advertising appeals to the instincts *already existing within* humans. These instincts were not placed within humanity by the system. As any college student who has taken Civilization 101 knows, lustful orgies were widely practiced long before capitalism or any other modern economic system came on the scene.

Nevertheless, it is the very success of capitalism—material abundance—that gives rise to its greatest point of criticism: materialism. George Gilder, one of capitalism's great champions, nevertheless observes, "Yet capitalism for all its productivity and creativity, has foundered in its own materialist superstitions and failed to produce or create a compelling argument for its own essential morality."[228] It is an indisputable empirical fact that the dominant characteristic of a successful, vibrant capitalistic economy is a pervasive culture of consumerism.

But do we blame capitalism or do we say such materialism is intrinsic to any economic system? Indeed, that is what economics deals with: the production and consumption of worldly goods. As suggested earlier, perhaps capitalism has been more successful than other economic systems in *all* economic respects, providing worldly goods to individuals included, and therefore it would follow that it has been accompanied by a commensurately great interest in worldly goods on the part of the populace. Many social scientists and theologians throughout the world agree. A common observation of the United States was reflected in Czech President Vaclav Havel's comments to the United States Congress, "…economic advances….have gradually altered humanity's very value system. We now worship a new deity: the ideal of perpetual growth of production and consumption… materialism,…. consumerism,…a selfish cult of material success, the absence of faith in a higher order."[229]

John Paul, II warns, "A given culture reveals its overall understanding of life through the choices it makes in production and consumption. It is here that the *phenomenon of consumerism* arises. In singling out new needs and new means to meet them, one must be guided by a comprehensive picture of man which respects all the dimensions of his being and which subordinates his material and instinctive dimensions to his interior and spiritual ones….. Of itself, an economic system does not possess criteria for correctly distinguishing new and higher forms of satisfying human needs from artificial new needs which hinder the formation of a mature personality. *Thus a great deal of educational and cultural work* is needed.... It is not wrong to want to live better; what is wrong is a style of life which is presumed to be better when it is directed toward 'having' rather than 'being,' and which wants to have more, not in order to be more but in order to spend life in enjoyment as an end in itself. It is therefore necessary to create life-styles in which the quest for truth, beauty, goodness and communion with others for the sake of common growth are the factors which determine consumer choices, savings and investments.... [T]he decision to invest, that is, to offer people an opportunity to make good use of their own labour, is also determined by an attitude of human sympathy and trust in Providence, which reveal the human quality of the person making such decisions."[230]

But Havel and John Paul II and others who bemoan the prevalence of consumerism are not entirely correct. The capitalistic system is inappropriately blamed as the villain of materialism. As stated earlier, consumerism—hedonism—has *always* existed. The Bible is replete with stories of lavish banquets and parties. Earlier in this chapter I have quoted numerous Scriptural passages with admonitions to abandon worldly delights. History books are filled with accounts of the opulent, indulgent, sensual lifestyles of the wealthy down through the ages, and such lavishness is depicted by the masters in every art museum in the world. What is different·today is that, thanks to capitalism, wealth is considerably more diffused, and a broad middle class can now also afford the decadence that previously was the exclusive ritual of the tiny, elite class of the particular society. "Consumerism" is only a term for "widespread hedonism." Hedonism has always been a pronounced characteristic of humanity. Don't blame advertising. Don't blame capitalism for corrupting humans; humanity has always been corrupted. Capitalism has just financed its wider display. Since the beginning of human life, we "peasants" would have indulged if we could have afforded to. (It must also be acknowledged that also today there is much greater interest among the masses in leading a meaningful life than at any previous time in history. While in Biblical times those peasants weren't living it up at wild parties, neither were they reading books on the meaning of life nor retiring at mid-life and devoting themselves to volunteer work.)

This is perhaps the greatest irony of capitalism. It is damned by its own success. Everyone agrees that the objective of any economic system, as distinguished from political, social, educational or religious system, is the maximization of material welfare, wealth. That is what economics is about; it is not about other, perhaps even more important, dimensions of human life. Capitalism, relative to other economic systems, has been so overwhelmingly successful in the widespread achievement of its objective, in fact over-shooting the mark to such an extent, that it has elicited severe criticism of an alleged corollary adverse affect on other dimensions of human life. Such criticism is, however, often lacking in genuiness, reflecting an equally grievous covetousness and envy on the part of the critic. Granted, those living in capitalistic countries are subjected to a barrage of annoyingly offensive advertisements. But advertising did not inject us humans with our hedonism. Humanity's hedonism has existed since the fall. Capitalism has simply enabled the masses to afford to satisfy their hedonistic desires, a luxury heretofore enjoyed only by a tiny elite.

If it could be asserted that capitalism is somehow to blame for the pervasive materialism today, it could also be asserted that Christianity is similarly to blame. Indeed, a dominant characteristic of the church today is its becoming, as Kristol suggests, "incorporated into our worldly efforts to 'better our condition,' and... redefin[ing] its task either as social reform or as providing us with a 'healthy and happy life-style.'"[231] If any sector of our society is at fault for the present manifest hedonism, it is less the business sector which, as noted earlier, is neutral, providing people with as many Bibles as "Playboys," and more the church whose role is to bring people to God. Capitalism simply says, "we'll produce the goods and services; what people do with them is up to them." It is the church that says, "we'll help them determine what to do with them." The present hedonism of our society reflects less a failing of the business sector and more a failing of the church. However, as suggested previously, I believe that neither the business firm nor the church is to blame for materialism which is an intrinsic human characteristic.

The immense cost of pre-occupation with consumption cannot be understated. Perhaps the most dramatic cost has been the neglect of children stemming from the perceived "need" for both spouses to work to generate sufficient household income to purchase all of the things they desire. Anyone who accepts the typical human trait of rationalizing this situation by saying "yes, but I spend more *quality* time with my child" just hasn't been home when their child bursts through the door with a joyful exclamation of pride over some accomplishment or, more critically, slumps through the door in need of an understanding hug because of some slight at school. A common characteristic of children, ignored by the "quality" (rather than quantity) of time adherents, is the need for spontaneous expression and sharing. Children do not respond effectively to appointments.

Finally, to those with inadequate faith in God there is another threat of capitalism that is somewhat related to the pre-occupation with the worldly, material realm. It is the psychological threat of anxiety and insecurity. An outcome of the incredible success of capitalism has been a mind-bogglingly rapid pace of creativity and innovation, springing to life new jobs, accompanied by an equally severe jettisoning of old jobs. There were two dominant economic themes in the 1990's: (1) ballooning of new jobs, particularly "high tech," and (2) "downsizing" by older American business firms. This lack of employment stability, while the source of excitement and stimulation and growth for some, has been the source of anxiety, even debilitating depression, for others. However, I purposely do not give this threat the dignity of its own major heading because I would then be contributing to the very invalid notion that I criticized above: placing inordinate importance on the material realm. To secure Christians with strong faith in God and the knowledge that true security comes only from the kingdom of God within oneself, rather than from some external worldly source, this is not a threat at all, but simply a bi-product of an extremely exciting outcome of economic success.

In concluding this discussion of idolatry, Os Guinness, Senior Fellow at Trinity Forum, sums up idolatry as follows. "God alone needs nothing outside himself, because he himself is the highest and the only lasting good. So all objects we desire short of God are as finite and incomplete as we ourselves are and, therefore, disappointing if we make them the objects of ultimate desire."[232] Turner states it this way, "Those who give centrality to the acquisition of more and more of life's goods, to the neglect of human values, miss life's deepest joys and choicest riches."[233] The major point is, while acknowledge the legitimacy of worldly possessions, it should be clearly understood that they are not the end. Pursuit of worldly power, success and wealth is not any part of the game of life. There is one and only one objective: justification through faithful acceptance of God's grace as demonstrated by our love of others. Nevertheless, in this discussion of capitalism and Christianity it must again be explicitly and forcefully affirmed that hedonism is not the result of or fault of the system. Hedonism is not a characteristic of the system. Hedonism is a human characteristic. As I will discuss later, capitalism is as efficient and effective in its production of Bibles as it is in its production of bourbon. The fact that one particular type of economic system excels on all fronts, including aiding the life of hedonists, is basis for celebration rather than condemnation. The fact that hedonism as well as the spread of the Gospel both benefit from capitalism's success does not in and of itself serve as a basis for criticism. Further, idolatry is a sin not confined to capitalists. Socialists have their idol: the state. This becomes apparent when, as identified earlier when discussing the prophets' admonitions regarding idolatry, the key questions regarding the matter of idolatry are: in what do I ultimately trust, to what do I look for security and happiness, who is in charge of my future, and where do I look for ultimate truth?

Pride

Let us now turn to another unfavorable attitude associated with material possessions and wealth. Ultimately the process of becoming wealthy can lead to arrogance and self-pride; i.e., "look what I have accomplished on my own." This feeling of self-reliance tends to be accompanied by a shunning of any notion of using any kind of "crutch" such as religion. Wheeler asserts, "The trouble with wealth is that, as a putative source of security, it usurps God's role as source and measure and guarantor of life."[234] This notion applies to both individuals and nations. Ironically, to the extent that capitalism has been overwhelmingly successful in causing nations to become wealthy, an unintended consequence could be a conduciveness to the displacement of God by a national self-confidence.

To guard against this human tendency every Christian capitalist should have the following passage from Scripture memorized and say it out loud every day. It is Moses' admonishment to the

Israelites when they were camped on the east bank of the Jordan River and about to cross over into the Promised Land, a land "filled with milk and honey" where God promised that they would prosper.

> "You may say to yourself, 'My power and the strength of my hands have produced this wealth for me.' But remember the LORD your God, for it is he who gives you the ability to produce wealth,..." (Dt. 8:17,18)

The foregoing is the connecting link between capitalism and Christianity. It should be adopted as the Christian capitalists' creed as a constant reminder that everything that we have of economic value, including "my power and the strength of my hands" are gifts from God. Wright declares this truth as "the first principle of biblical economics."[235]

Mann expands, "Israel is warned against the presumption of self-sufficiency, as if the land and all its rich blessing were a result of human achievement alone. Affluence is not inherently evil, but it is inherently dangerous. The way to avoid an attitude in which materialism replaces allegiance to Yahweh is to remember the story of the wilderness journey, and especially the provision of manna."[236]

Further, let us not forget another comment by Moses to the Israelites immediately prior to crossing over into the Promised Land, "Remember how the LORD your God led you all the way in the desert these forty years, to humble you..., causing you to hunger and then feeding you with manna,...to teach you that man does not live on bread alone, but on every word that comes from the mouth of the LORD. Your clothes did not wear out and your feet did not swell during these forty years. " (Dt. 8:2,3) Moses was instructing the Israelites who had failed to give thanks for their blessings from God. This, of course, was the passage that Jesus quoted (Mt. 4:4) when being tempted by the devil, reflecting Jesus' understanding that a complete life does not come from material possessions.

The condemnation of pride occurs throughout Scripture. "Do not keep talking so proudly..., for the LORD is a God who knows, and by him deeds are weighed." (1 Sm. 2:3) "You save the humble, but your eyes are on the haughty to bring them low." (2 Sm. 22:26) Pride was the most common sin of the leaders of the Old Testament. Even the most devout followers of God had their moments of arrogant self-reliance and sinful distractions. 2 Samuel and 1 Chronicles present both David's devotion and transgressions. 1 Kings presents the same for Solomon. LaSor observes, "That the vast majority of Israel's kings failed to fulfill their ordained role... as preparation for the King of Kings... is testimony to kingship's intrinsic dangers."[237]

Additionally, a reading of 2 Chronicles and 2 Kings reveals the pattern over the period of Judah's sixteen kings and Israel's twelve kings: obedient worship is accompanied by prosperity which leads to pride and apostasy which leads to downfall. As just one example, Hezekiah's boastful display of wealth to the Babylonians led to Judah's demise. "Then Isaiah said to Hezekiah, 'Hear the word of the LORD: The time will surely come when everything in your palace,.... will be carried off to Babylon." (2 Kgs. 20:18)

This pattern of prosperity leading to pride followed by downfall was also common among the various empires which dominated the Jews, as successively the Assyrian, Babylonian, Medo-Persian, Greek and eventually Roman empires met their demise, as God continues with God's purpose. The book of Esther presents such a story, but perhaps two of the most dramatic examples are King Nebuchadnezzar and his son King Belshazzar described in chapters four and five of the book of Daniel. "those who walk in pride he is able to humble...." (Dn. 4:37) "when his heart became arrogant and hardened with pride, he was... stripped of his glory." (Dn. 5:20) Then later during the reign of Cyrus, king of Persia, Daniel says, "...the king of the South filled with pride..., will not remain triumphant.... After this, he will...stumble and fall.... The king will... exalt and magnify himself.... Yet he will come to his end." (Dn. 11:12,19,36,45) Anyone afflicted with pride and arrogance should read the entire book of Daniel. The juxtaposition of Daniel's faith (remember the Sunday School stories of Daniel in the lion's den and Shadrach, Meshach and Abednego in the fiery furnace?) against several kings' pride presents a powerful lesson.

In the Psalms we find several exhortations against pride. "In his pride the wicked does not seek him; in all his thoughts there is no room for God. His ways are always prosperous; he is haughty and your laws are far from him;... He says to himself, 'Nothing will shake me; I'll always be happy, and never have trouble." (Ps. 10:4-6) "whoever has haughty eyes and a proud heart, him will I not endure…" (Ps. 101:5) "…do not grant the wicked their desires, O LORD; do not let their plans succeed, or they will become proud." (Ps. 140:8)

Perhaps Psalm 49 most eloquently repudiates the flawed notion of pride, and I refer you to Appendix D, "The Capitalist's Psalm," but highlight here the following verses:

Psalm 49

5,6   "Why should I fear… those who trust in their wealth and boast of their great riches?….

12   But man, despite his riches, does not endure; he is like the beasts that perish.

13,14   This is the fate of those who trust in themselves,… Like sheep they are destined for the grave,….

16,17   Do not be overawed when a man grows rich,… for he will take nothing with him when he dies,…

20   A man who has riches without understanding is like the beasts that perish."

Another particularly strong condemnation by King David of self-pride is found in Psalm 52, verses 5-7, and perhaps the harshest denunciation of self-pride of the wealthy is expressed in the entirety of Psalm 73. "Those who are far from you will perish." (Ps. 73:27)

King Solomon adds to the chorus condemning pride. "He mocks proud mockers but gives grace to the humble." (Prv. 3:34) "Does not wisdom call out?… I hate pride and arrogance," (Prv. 8:1,13) "When pride comes in, then comes disgrace, but with humility comes wisdom." (Prv. 11:2) "Whoever trusts in riches will fall, but the righteous will thrive like a green leaf." (Prv. 11:28) "The LORD tears down the proud man's house…." (Prv. 15:25) "The LORD detests all the proud of heart. Be sure of this: They will not go unpunished." (Prv. 16:5) "Pride goes before destruction, a haughty spirit before a fall." (Prv. 16:18) "The wealth of the rich is their fortified city; they imagine it an unscalable wall. Before his downfall a man's heart is proud, but humility comes before honor." (Prv. 18:11,12) "Haughty eyes and a proud heart, the lamp of the wicked, are sin!" (Prv. 21:4) (The Masoretic Text is stronger, using the word "tillage" rather than "lamp," suggesting, according to Murphy, that pride is the preparation for or undertaking of sin.)[238] "The proud and arrogant man—'Mocker' is his name; he behaves with over-weening pride." (Prv. 21:24) "Humility and the fear of the LORD bring wealth and honor and life." (Prv. 22:4) "A rich man may be wise in his own eyes, but a poor man who has discernment sees through him." (Prv. 28:11) "A man's pride brings him low." (Prv. 29:23) Finally, Agur makes explicit the dynamics of what is involved with pride: "give me neither poverty nor riches, but give me only my daily bread. Otherwise, I may have too much and disown you and say, "Who is the LORD? (Prv. 30:8,9)

> And we are reminded in Ecclesiastes, "Wisdom is as shel-ter as money is a shelter, but... wisdom preserves the life of it possessor." (Eccl. 7:12)

The evil of pride was a common exhortation among the prophets as they declared that God is in charge. A prayerful study of Scrip-ture reveals a major message of the prophets as: because God is in charge, reliance on anything other than God (e.g., one's wealth) is both folly and sinful, and similarly worldly challenges are not to be feared. Eventually justice and righteousness will prevail for the faithful. God's free gift of grace to us which is revealed in the New Testament is foretold by Isaiah, "Though grace is shown to the wicked, they do not learn righteousness,... they go on doing evil and regard not the majesty of the LORD. O LORD, your hand is lifted high, but they do not see it." (Is. 26:10,11) Of course the first step in turning toward God is turning from self.

The prophets define pride and arrogance as symptomatic of the same affliction: turning to self-reliance and from God. "Woe to you who are complacent... who feel secure.... I abhor the pride of Jacob and detest his fortresses; I will deliver up the city and every-thing in it." (Am. 6:1,8) "Israel's arrogance testifies against him, but despite all this he does not return to the LORD his God..." (Hos. 7:10) "When I fed them, they were satisfied; when they were satis-fied, they became proud; then they forgot me" (Hos. 13:6) "Ephraim (Israel) boasts, 'I am very rich; I have become wealthy. With all my wealth they will not find in me any iniquity or sin." (Hos. 12:8) This statement also reflects the Old Testament's notion that wealth reflected God's favor. The prophets attempted to correct this misunderstanding, and the New Testament further sets us straight on this misconception.

Obadiah, the shortest book in the Old Testament and which some say is a micro-statement of the message of the Old Testament, probably presents the pride—self reliance—downfall scenario more succinctly than any other prophet. Addressing the Edomites, "The pride of your heart has deceived you, you who live in the clefts of the rocks and make your home on the heights, you who say to yourself, 'Who can bring me down to the ground?' Though you soar like the eagle and make your nest among the stars, from there I will bring you down." (Ob. 3,4)

Isaiah, in a message to Hezekiah, "This is the word that the LORD has spoken against him [king of Assyria]:... Against whom have you raised your voice and lifted your eyes in pride?....'Have you not heard? Long ago I ordained it....." (2 Kgs. 19:20-34) And Isaiah's message to all of Judah, "The eyes of the arrogant man will be humbled and the pride of men brought low; the LORD alone will be exalted in that day." (Is. 2:11) All of chapter two of the book of Isaiah drives home the point that everything is subordinate to God and, therefore, there is no place for prideful self-reliance. Isaiah continues, "Woe to those who are wise in their own eyes and clever in their own sight." (Is. 5:21) "I will punish the king of Assyria for the willful pride of his heart and the haughty look in his eyes. For he says: 'By my strength of my hand I have done this, and by my wisdom , because I have understanding." (Is. 10:12,13) "I will put an end to the arrogance of the haughty and will humble the pride of the ruthless." (Is. 13:11) "You said in your heart, 'I will ascend to heaven; I will raise my throne above the stars of God;...." But you are brought down to the grave, to the depths of the pit." (Is. 14:13,15) "In that day men will look to their Maker.... They will not look to the altars, the work of their hands," (Is. 17:7,8)

Perhaps one of Isaiah's most pointed condemnations of pride related to economic achievement is in his prophecy about Tyre: "Wail O ships of Tarshish! For Tyre is destroyed.... Be silent, you people of the island and you merchants of Sidon whom the seafarers have enriched. On the great waters came the grain of the Shihor; the harvest of the Nile was the revenue of Tyre, and she became the marketplace of the nations.... Who planned this against Tyre, the bestower of crowns, whose merchants are princes, whose traders are renowned in the earth? The LORD Almighty planned it, to bring low the pride of all glory and to humble all who are renowned on the earth." (Is.23:1-3,8,9) Similarly, "Woe to those who go down to Egypt for help, who rely on horses, who trust in the multitude of their chariots and in the great strength of their horsemen, but do not…. Seek help from the LORD…. But the Egyptians are men and not God." (Is. 31:1,3) In Isaiah's foretelling the fall of Babylon, "Now then, listen, you wanton creature, lounging in your security and saying to yourself, 'I am, and there is none besides me.'…. Disaster will come upon you, and you will not know how to conjure it away. A calamity will fall upon you that you cannot ward off with a ransom;" (Is. 47:8,11) Zephaniah agrees, "Neither their silver nor their gold will be able to save them on the day of the LORD's wrath." (Zep. 1:18) "I will remove from this city those who rejoice in their pride. Never again will you be haughty on my holy hill." (Zep. 3:11) Therefore, "Seek the LORD,…. seek humility." (Zep. 2:3)

This theme continues with Jeremiah as God's agent, "My people have committed two sins: They have forsaken me, the spring of living water, and have dug their own cisterns, broken cisterns that cannot hold water." (Jer. 2:13) "Let not the …rich man boast of his riches, but let him who boasts about this: that I am the LORD,…" (Jer. 9:23,24) "They do not say to themselves, 'Let us fear the LORD our God who gives us autumn and spring rains in season, who assures us of the regular weeks of harvest.'…. They have become rich and powerful and have grown fat and sleek…. Should I punish them for this?" (Jer. 5:24,28,29) "Hear and pay attention, for the LORD has spoken. Give glory to the LORD your God…." (Jer. 13:15,16) "Cursed is the one who trusts in man, who depends on flesh for his strength and whose heart turns away from the LORD." (Jer. 17:5) "Does it make you a king to have more and more cedar?…I warned you when you felt secure, but you said, 'I will not listen!'" (Jer. 22:15,21) "Since you trust in your deeds and riches, you too will be taken captive,… We have heard of Moab's pride— her overweening pride and conceit, her pride and arrogance and the haughtiness of her heart. I know her insolence but it is futile." (Jer. 48:7,29) "The arrogant one will stumble and fall…." (Jer. 50:32)

Ezekiel also uses Tyre as an example of the truth that economic wealth alone does not bring real security. "You say, O Tyre, 'I am perfect in beauty.' Your domain was on the high seas; your builders brought your beauty to perfection….. But the east wind will break you to pieces... Your wealth, merchandise and wares, your mariners,... and everyone else on board will sink into the heart of the sea on the day of your shipwreck.... Your wares and all your company have gone down with you.... You have come to a horrible end and will be no more." (Ez. 27) To the king of Tyre Ezekiel says, "In the pride of your heart you say, 'I am a god;... But you are a man and not a god,...By your wisdom and understanding you have gained wealth for yourself and amassed gold and silver in your treasuries. By your skill in trading you have increased your wealth and because of your wealth your heart has grown proud.....You will be but a man, not a god, in the hands of those who slay you.... Your heart became proud on account of your beauty, and you corrupted your wisdom because of your splendor. So I threw you to the earth.... You have come to a horrible end and will be no more." (Ez. 28:2-19) Chapters 27 and 28 of Ezekiel, conveying the sobering experience of Tyre, should be required reading for all wealthy business people. (In fact, also Chapters 29-32 which convey the sobering experiences of Egypt and Assyria should be added to the list of required reading. In fact, the entire Old Testament, which conveys the sobering—and inspiringly hopeful—experience of the Jews of prosperity leading to pride followed by downfall should be required reading. In fact the New Testament, which presents the Redeemer who delivers our salvation and teaches us what we are to do about it, should be required reading. Hence, the Bible—a required read!!)

God and only God is God, and God is sovereign—as the Israelites, the Assyrians, the Babylonians, the Egyptians, the Medo-Persians, the Greeks, the Romans all learned. What are we in the process of learning today? Were the Nazi fascists a demonstration of turning from God to prideful self-reliance? Were the Soviet communists a demonstration of this? Will the United States be a demonstration of this? The dominant message of the Old Testament is clear: humans progress, not through reliance on self, but through reliance on God—reliance characterized by unequivocal faith and obedience. "Not by might nor by power, but by my Spirit." (Zec. 4:6) The message also is that God is in charge and uses our weaknesses to accomplish His ends. It is when, in a state of weakness, we rely on God that God delivers good to us. God utilized the weakness of Abraham, Isaac, Jacob, Joseph, Moses, Gideon, Samuel, David and others to demonstrate that God is in charge.

This was also a constant theme of the prophets.

As suggested in the foregoing discussion, a key to whether or not a wealthy person enters the kingdom of God is the person's *attitude* toward wealth as demonstrated by his/her actions or inaction. Humans seem particularly vulnerable to arrogance and self pride, and Jesus warns against this. "For everyone who exalts himself will be humbled, and he who humbles himself will be exalted." (Mt. 23:12; Lk.14:11) "Blessed are the meek, for they will inherit the earth." (Mt. 5:5) Further regarding humility, lack of pretense, and total dependency on the Father, "unless you turn and become like children, you will never enter the kingdom of heaven." (Mt. 18:3) and "whoever does not receive the kingdom of God like a child shall not enter it." (Mk. 10:15; Lk 18:15) Pentecost explains, "A child cannot depend on himself but must depend on his father. He does not exalt his own thinking above that of his father."[239]

Jesus devotes much of his ministry to combating the attitude of pride, none more dramatically than with the Beatitudes in *The Sermon on the Mount* and the "woes" in *The Sermon on the Plain* e.g., (Lk. 6:24) "But woe to you that are rich, for you have received your consolation"—your apparent worldly consolation of satisfied ego. Jesus' "target is the superfluity that has no need of anyone or anything, not even God."[240] But egoism is not limited to capitalists. Televangelists and even the local minister on whom so many in his congregation depend for psychological support must ask the question, why am I doing what I'm doing?

Paul also carries the message of admonishment of pride. "Therefore, as it is written: 'let him who boasts boast in the Lord.'" (1 Cor. 1:31) "Command those who are rich in this present world not to be arrogant nor to put their hope in wealth, which is so uncertain, but to put their hope in God, who richly provides us with everything for our enjoyment." (1 Tm. 6:17) Murray points out that Paul is suggesting that "We are, therefore, to put our hope in him who is the bountiful giver, not in the riches themselves—they are uncertain because they are at the disposal of God's sovereignty, and in the exercise of the sovereignty by which he dispensed them he can also take them away."[241] Gordon D. Fee, professor of New Testament at Regent College, focusing on the latter part of the foregoing passage, suggests that "Paul is no ascetic. That the wealthy should not place confidence in their wealth does not carry with it an attitude of total rejection…. Enjoyment, however, does not mean self-indulgent living. The reason everything may be enjoyed lies in the recognition that everything, including one's wealth, is a *gift*, the expressing of God's gracious generosity."[242]

To assist one in combating pride it is helpful to keep in mind the transitory nature of all matter, including wealth. Possession of wealth has nothing whatsoever to do with one's value or position in the kingdom of God. When it comes to salvation, our worldly possessions are irrelevant. James severely admonishes the wealthy. "The brother in humble circumstances ought not take pride in his high position. But the one who is rich should take pride in his low position, because he will pass away like a wild flower." (Jas. 1:9,10) "Humble yourselves before the Lord, and he will lift you up." (Jas. 4:10) "Now listen, you rich people, weep and wail because of the misery that is coming upon you. Your wealth has rotted, and moths have eaten your clothes. Your gold and silver are corroded. Their corrosion will testify against you and eat your flesh like fire….You have lived on earth in luxury and self-indulgence. Your have fattened yourselves in the day of slaughter." (Jas. 5:1-5) David observes, "what they [the rich] are at present proud about is indeed their humiliation…. [T]he very object of their joy, the evidence of their disobedience, will humiliate them…. James sees as tragic figures well-dressed men and women pondering investments over excellent meals; they act as if they were winners but in reality have lost the only game that matters."[243] Martin notes, "Rich merchants and landowners are condemned both because of their arrogant attitude that forgets God and because of their exploitation of the poor in general and their poor workers."[244]

Similarly, Peter admonishes, "All of you, clothe yourselves in humility toward one another, because, 'God opposes the proud but gives grace to the humble.' Humble yourselves, therefore, under God's almighty hand, that he may lift you up in due time." (1 Pt. 5:5,6) Finally, we should heed Christ's rebuke, through John, to the wealthy church at Laodicea, a community widely known for its great wealth, "So, because you are luke-warm—neither hot nor cold—I am about to spit you out of my mouth. You say, 'I am rich; I have acquired wealth and do not need a thing.' But you do not realize that you are wretched, pitiful, poor, blind and naked. I counsel you to buy from me gold refined in the fire [spiritual treasure], so you can become rich; and white clothes [righteousness] to wear so you can cover your shameful nakedness;...." (Rev. 3:16-18) Wall notes, "They are spiritually impoverished.... These symbolize repentance and also divine gifts that provide the repentant one with the spiritual goods necessary to turn around and follow Christ."[245]

Applying the foregoing discussion to contemporary society, a common thread among worldly successful people seems to be pride. "I have accomplished this" (not necessarily boastful, but certainly with self-pride), accompanied by the implicit and many times subconscious, " so who needs God?" The lesson of Scripture is to go beyond material wealth and submit to God. Although there is nothing wrong with wealth per se, nevertheless God-reliance should not be replaced by self-reliance. The severe impediment that wealth poses to the worship of God is the reason that Jesus asserted, "it is easier for a camel to go through the eye of a needle than for a rich man to enter the kingdom of God." (Mt. 19:24; Mk. 10:25; Lk. 18:25) This has become one of the most misinterpreted passages of Scripture. In the same way that, when Jesus rebuked the Pharisees and Sadducees for their hypocrisy, he was not rebuking religion, when Jesus rebuked the wealthy for their idolatry and pride, he was not rebuking wealth. He was referring to the notion that the distractions of pursuing wealth, the false self-reliance that the accomplishment of accumulating wealth can create, the arrogance that can accompany being wealthy and the indifference to others that pursuit of wealth can cause—all of these things—tend to draw one away from God. Each Gospel records that Jesus prefaced his comment above with: "It is *hard* [but not impossible] for those who have riches / a rich man to enter the kingdom of God / heaven." (Mt 19:23; Mk 10:23; Lk 18:24) (italics mine) This assertion of Jesus is understandable. It is hard because it is hard for a rich man to stay focused on God. As Mounce states in his commentary on Matthew, "What Jesus is saying is that the lure of possessions is so strong that a rich person is unable with his or her own strength to break its grip."[246]

Today a strong tendency for wealth-induced pride to displace God suggests that a great outreach need of the church is toward the affluent. The wealthy must be brought to understand Jesus' warning, "When a strong man, fully armed, guards his own house, his possessions are safe. But when someone stronger attacks and overpowers him, he takes away the armor in which the man trusted and divides up the spoils." (Lk. 11:21,22) The lesson: lasting security comes only from reliance on the most powerful: God.

Ethicist David Gill notes, "It is often difficult for the materially rich to experience profoundly the provision of the God who owns everything. It is sometimes difficult for the smile of God to light up the face of beautiful people. It is often difficult for the brilliant and educationally rich to be filled with the wisdom and discernment of the mind of Christ. It is difficult for those glorying in their own prosperity and accomplishment to exult in the glory and provision of God. If we are full of pride and our own spirit, there is no room for God's Spirit."[247]

Indeed, this sinfulness of pride and self reliance is not limited to successful capitalists. In answer to the question, would another economic system be more conducive to Christianity? I think not. Economic systems, such as socialism, which replace the free market with government decision-making tend to be accompanied by pre-occupation with political power and status as also reflected in material possessions. (Ah, those dachas and limousines of the Communist officials!) Political power and might, rather than wealth, become the cause of self-reliance displacing God-reliance. Further, in such politically-dominated systems, there emerges a strong tendency for centralization which tends to lead to domination and subordination of the individual, God's creation. In capitalism, on the other hand, power is diffused and thereby reduced.

Pride can be imperceptible. Sometimes pride—lack of humility—can be extremely subtle, existing within even the most devout believer. The story of Job is one of the most illuminating in the Bible regarding the relationship between humans and God; however, interpretation of the Book of Job is one of the most difficult in Scripture. Professor Pamela Scalise asserts, "No attempt to state succinctly the meaning or message of the book of Job is adequate."[248] Biblical scholars have puzzled over the lesson of Job. Nevertheless, I think that Job provides us with some insights regarding the critical importance of humility as well as the true nature of our relationship with God.

Job, a devout and righteous wealthy man, is subjected to intense suffering, losing his family and all of his possessions and inflicted with excruciating physical pain. Three friends, wanting to help, try to convince him that this suffering must be the result of sin, and therefore all Job need do is repent. Two problems exist, however: this approach introduces the possibility of the wrong motivation and, further, Job claims that he is innocent of sin (such a claim itself a prideful attitude), and therefore, to his credit, will not fabricate a phony repentance. A fourth participant, Elihu, points out that Job's demand for justice is a presumptuous expectation placed on God and therefore a form of arrogance. Finally, God responds noting particularly his omnipotence, omniscience and sovereignty as Creator of all—and therefore beyond Job's or anyone's ability to comprehend. God ends the discourse with "Nothing on earth is his equal—a creature without fear. He looks down on all that are haughty: he is king over all that are proud." (Jb. 41:33,4) Finally, Job falls in humble awe of God, understanding that submission to God is the first step toward wisdom. "I know that you can do all things; no plan of yours can be thwarted....Surely I spoke of things I did not understand, things too wonderful for me to know." (Jb. 42:2,3) The lesson: the ultimate is to know God rather than the "reasons." Later, in the New Testament Jesus, in denying Satan's temptation, declares, "Do not put the Lord your God to the test." (Mt. 4:7)

Then at the end of the book of Job one of the most fascinating, perplexing acts of God related in Scripture occurs. To demonstrate God's sovereignty and grace, God restores Job's possessions, family and prosperity "even beyond their initial state. This restoration preserves God's integrity: Job has passed the test. It disproves the friends' contention: Job's deprivation was not due to his sin. The restoration shows that poverty is not necessarily a more righteous state than prosperity. It shouts its word of grace...."[249] The lesson: all that we are and will become is due to God's grace—a grace that is beyond our ability to understand. Accordingly, there is no room for pride.

Indeed the story of Job reveals the inadequacy of the doctrine of retribution, and any capitalist who is operating on the basis of this doctrine is misdirected. The notion that God rewards goodness and punishes sinfulness is not an adequate basis for behavior and often leads to hypocrisy which is discussed later. We do not bargain with God. The issue, its seems to me, is submission—an all consuming fear of God—characterized by total, complete, unequivocal acceptance of, trust in and loyalty to God. This in turn is reflected in true, complete humility accompanied by our accepting certain things that occur to us that are beyond our momentary ability to understand. How many times after a painful experience has one looked back and in retrospect understood it as an opportunity for personal growth? Now, through God, we can declare victory over doubt, knowing that ultimately "… in all things God works for the good of those who love him,…" (Rom. 8:28) This passage is not simply a superficial affirmation that everything is going to work out all right. Rather, as explained by Edwards, "It means that for those who love God no evil may befall them which God cannot use for their own growth and his glory."[250] The prophet Jeremiah expresses this wisdom, "The LORD is good to those whose hope is in him, to the one who seeks him; it is good to wait quietly for the salvation of the LORD." (Lam. 3:25,26)

This notion exists throughout the New Testament, as observed by Gary Thomas, "Surely there has never been a more unequal relationship than the one Christ calls us to when He says, 'Come, follow me.' Our occasional lack of wonder at the absolute inequality of the relationship is evidence enough that we do not fully comprehend the greatness of the God who speaks and the humility of we who listen."[251] Thomas continues, "The twin pillars of a truly Christian spirituality are realizing our own lowliness and God's greatness…. These twin pillars can be combined into one word: *humility*…. There is no truly Christian spirituality without humility."[252] Thomas notes some huge benefits to humility, none the least of which is its liberating character. "Humility is at root a celebration of our freedom in Christ; we are freed from having to make a certain impression or create a false front…. Humility…is the dissolution of all pretense."[253]

Thomas concludes "Without a direct experience of God, humility is impossible because our frame of reference is distorted…. It's easy for a man or woman to be proud…. until they catch a glimpse of God's holiness…. If I want to be humble, I must remain lost in the Great Light. This true self-knowledge is found only in relation to God."[254] Therefore, the meaningful societal benefit from humility, "Spiritual maturity means we hold ourselves to a high standard while being gracious toward others."[255]

Guthrie issues similar instruction, "To say that we are God's creatures is to emphasize our total dependence on God…. But the God upon whom we are dependent is a God who is *for* us,…"[256]

Admitting such dependence is the first step toward complete reliance on the One who can conquer all other challenges to us, leading then to complete confidence and security. This totally giving himself over to Jesus Christ is what Paul meant when he said, "For when I am weak, then I am strong." (2 Cor. 12:10) "Paul in Acts has an unshakable confidence in God's providential care."[257] And of course the ultimate demonstration of strength through weakness: the Crucifixion.

In closing this section on pride, I must relate a story of Dr. Randy Rowland, Presbyterian minister in Seattle whose office is separated by a window from his wife's adjoining office in which she has a large poster strategically placed in eyesight of Randy's office. The poster reads in huge letters:

> Two fundamental truths in the Universe:
> I. There is a God.
> II. It's not you.

When we recognize that humans' ultimate salvation flows from God's grace which is given freely, any prideful boasting on human's part is a logical inconsistency and must, therefore be replaced by praise of God's goodness.

Schwarz notes that, of the "seven deadly sins…, pride is the first sin because it is the 'root' or core sin,… it is going our own way and doing our own thing,"[258] ignoring, in fact, superceding God. The second sin is envy, to which we now turn our attention. (The other five are anger, sloth, avarice, gluttony, and lust.)[259] Guinness concludes regarding pride, "Our human desire can go wrong in two ways: when we stop desiring anything outside ourselves and fall for the pathetic illusion that we are sufficient in ourselves, or when we desire such things as fame, riches, beauty, wisdom, and human love that are as finite as we are and thus unworthy of our absolute devotion."[260]

Covetousness / Envy

We have just observed the tendency for wealth to lead to the sin of pride. Similarly, there is a tendency for lack of wealth to lead to the sin of covetousness and envy. Both reflect a displacement of

God by materialism. Wright notes, "Thus the commandments come full circle. To break the tenth is to break the first. For covetousness means setting our hearts and affections on things that then take the place of God."[261] Both envy and pride are equally sinful attitudes toward material possessions and wealth.

God is quite clear: "You shall not covet your neighbor's wife. You shall not set your desire on your neighbor's house or land, his manservant or maidservant, his ox or donkey, or anything that belongs to your neighbor." (Dt. 5:21)

"Resentment kills a fool, and envy slays the simple." (Jb. 5:2)

"And I saw that all labor and all achievement spring from man's envy of his neighbor." (Eccl. 4:4) "Better what the eye sees than the roving of the appetite. This too is meaningless, a chasing after the wind." (Eccl. 6:9)

Jesus admonished us to avoid the sin of envy. "Take heed, and beware of all covetousness;" (Lk. 12:13)

Elsewhere in the New Testament we are warned, "But if you harbor bitter envy and selfish ambition in your hearts,....Such 'wisdom' does not come down from heaven but is earthly, unspiritual, of the devil. For where you have envy and selfish ambition, there you find disorder and every evil practice." (Jas. 3:14-16) James continues, "You kill and covet,...you quarrel and fight. You do not have, because you do not ask God. When you ask, you do not receive, because you ask with wrong motives,... Anyone who chooses to be friend of the world becomes an enemy of God....Wash your hands you sinners." (Jas. 4:1-8) James was addressing how "jealousy and rivalry were destroying the cohesiveness of the Christian community.... These evil impulses [lead] a person in their grip to resort to slander and verbal abuse of those who do have [what the person desires].[262]

Within any given society, envy and anger over what one doesn't have is simply another form of idolatry and lack of worshipping the one true God. "The rabble with them began to crave other food, and again the Israelites started wailing and said, 'If only we had meat to eat! We remember the fish we ate in Egypt at no cost—also the

cucumbers, melons, leeks, onions and garlic...." (Nm. 11:4-6) Such
an attitude on the part of the Israelites focusing on what God had
not done for them blinded them from seeing that God had set them
free from slavery and was giving them their own new land. Such
complaining and lack of faith added another forty years to their
wandering in the desert. In the specific passage cited above God
provided the people with quail which, upon eating, caused the
Israelites to be struck by a severe plague. Another Scripture story of
covetousness, envy and blind ambition is that of Korah, the Levite
whom God swallowed up.

Novak observes, "St. Augustine offers different wisdom in his
commentary on Psalm 72, v. 34: 'It is not a matter of income but of
desires.... Look at the rich man standing beside you: perhaps he has
a lot or money on him, but no avarice in him; while you, who have
no money, have a lot of avarice."[263] Thomas Aquinas defines envy
as "sorrow for another's good. The object of a man's sorrow is his
own evil"[264] and therefore is a sin. One of the fascinating things
about attitudes toward wealth and worldly possessions is that
wealth and worldly possessions often are more important to people
who don't have them than to people who do. A great myth in our
society is that upper income people are somehow, every minute of
every day from the moment of sunrise to the last moment of sunset,
totally consumed with a lustful lunging after possessions, the sole
purpose of which is to accumulate and display to others. As a
generalization of U.S. society, nothing could be farther from the
truth. If this myth were true, then what, for example, explains the
multitude of hours devoted by upper income people to a mind-
boggling array of volunteer activities as well as contribution of their
incomes to multitudes of charities? Indeed, the hackneyed image of
businesspeople as greedy, avaricious animals lusting after wealth is
empirically erroneous. Professors Thomas J. Stanley and William
D. Danko (formerly and currently, respectively, on the faculty of the
State University of New York at Albany), in their best-selling book,
The Millionaire Next Door, which presents the findings of their
massive research of millionaires, quote W.W. Allen, representative
of the millionaires whom they studied, "Money should never
change one's values.... Making money is only a report card. It's a
way to tell how you're doing" (in terms of economic contribution.)[265] Charles Lindblom, Sterling Professor emeritus of

economics and political science at Yale University, notes, "survey research seems to indicate that for most people in market societies, aspirations for a challenging job, friendships and the pleasures of children and family rank higher than do aspirations for more money or more market products."[266]

Most of the wealthy simply consume because they have the wherewithal—without any great lustful passion or unbalanced pre-occupation with the act of or result from consuming. One of the reasons that there tends to exist a common perception of successful business people as avaricious is that most of the sociological and economic research and writing on income and wealth in the United States has been performed by academicians and journalists who are not members of this group and therefore have no direct understanding of the wealthy, and, worse, tend to possess an envy and covetousness of the wealthy which clearly and unmistakably shines through in their utterances. Veblen was one of the first, "The motive that lies at the root of ownership is emulation;... The possession of wealth confers honor; it is an invidious distinction."[267] Such utterances, forms of which appear daily in the news media, help to promulgate envy, causing the nonwealthy to be more consumed with consumerism than the wealthy.

Chilton makes an important distinction, "Envy is the greatest disease of our age. It is often confused with jealousy and covetousness, which have to do with wanting the possessions...of others.... Envy is the feeling that someone else's having something is to blame for the fact that you do not have it."[268] Accordingly, envy reflects a zero-sum mentality which is in accord with neither capitalism nor Christianity. Chilton continues, "Envy destroys the man who commits it. He does not work for the future and the glory of God. He cannot fulfill the purpose for which he was created."[269]

A currently popular manifestation of covetousness is the "issue" of income disparity. However nowhere in Scripture is advanced the notion that there is some sort of virtue per se in the equality of incomes. 2 Cor. 8:13 is lifted and misused by some to advocate income equality, but that is not what is being addressed in this passage. As James Scott, professor of biblical studies at Trinity Western University, notes, "[F]rom Paul's perspective, Jerusalem, which has suffered impoverishment at the hands of the nations (Isa. 42:22; 55:1), requires the promised influx of tribute from the nations in order to complete the restoration of Israel (cf. Isa. 45:22; 53:12; 60:3-16; 61:6-7; 66:12). Only then will there be what Paul here calls equality, that is, between Israel and the nations. Just as Israel shares in the wealth of the nations, so also the nations share in the restoration of Israel. (cf. Isa. 2:2-5; 11:10; 25:6-10)."[270] Elsewhere in Scripture, it is acknowledged that some sort of notion of parity is reflected in God's providing land to each Israelite family and instituting the Year of Jubilee, a mechanism for those families who fell on hard times and lost their land to get it back. Beyond that, however, throughout Scripture just the opposite of income equality is implied: to be blessed by God included receiving economic prosperity. Assuming it was attained virtuously and not the subject of idolatry, wealth was viewed favorably; poverty was viewed unfavorably. Throughout the Bible people's incomes and levels of wealth differ. Hay expands, "Our biblical principles... do not speak of equality as an ideal. Instead, they affirm a man's right to a minimum basic standard of life, those basic needs to be met primarily through useful work, and place an obligation on the rich to help the poor who are unable to provide for themselves."[271]

Indeed, today income disparity is accompanied by three substantial advantages. First, income disparity reflects the efficient allocation of resources—by which we all benefit—from the market system functioning effectively. As consumers exercise their free wills, those resources which are in great demand receive relatively high incomes, and those in low demand receive relatively low incomes. The higher incomes of the highly demanded resources induce more to be supplied, satisfying consumer demand. The individual consumer is king, as his/her purchase preferences are signaled in the market place. Through this mechanism, resources are allocated to their most valuable use, and all of society wins. As was suggested earlier when discussing the market system, this is not just some theoretical meandering. Those societies relying on this system in fact experience the most efficient allocation and highest productivity of their productive resources resulting in abundant benefits to *everyone* in the society.

Second, income disparity is a common characteristic of societies lifting members out of poverty. As Gilder observes, "To lift the incomes of the poor, it will be necessary to increase the rates of investment, which in turn will tend to enlarge the wealth,..., of the rich." Again, these are not just theoretical meanderings. The current technological surge has created the multitude of thirty-something millionaires who in turn attend more movies and eat out more often, creating job opportunities for ticket-takers, ushers, waiters, janitors, dishwashers—the whole gamut of entry level positions giving the poor the opportunity to climb out of poverty. Today in the United States with so many benefiting from high paying jobs with lucrative stock options of the New Economy there has been an outpouring of newspaper articles on the growing income "gap." That statistic is completely irrelevant. The relevant statistic is how real incomes of people are changing over time. Would you rather be in the bottom fifth of a society in which the incomes of the top fifth rose 3% and the bottom fifth rose 6%? over the past decade or in a society in which the incomes of the top fifth rose 20% and the bottom fifth rose 10%? The answer is clear.

Third, income disparity results in huge public expenditures for the general benefit of all of us. Those people of relatively high economic value and therefore receiving high income do two important things for the rest of us: (1) donate a portion of those incomes to charities and a whole array of institutions from which we all benefit and (2) pay progressively higher taxes on those incomes, financing a plethora of government services and facilities enjoyed by all of us. Those persons of little economic value or not in the economic stream receive contributions from and public goods via taxes on those persons of high economic value. Further, as observed by Novak, "Often the wealthy invest grandly.... public monuments and centers of research, churches and universities. Where there are few or no wealthy, many amenities disappear from the social landscape, life becomes grayer, and the verve of the whole society declines"[272] To give a specific example. I live on Mercer Island in the middle of Lake Washington between Seattle and Bellevue, Washington. In this area, as a result of the recent soaring wealth particularly of the high-tech group, waterfront property has been bid up to inordinately high prices. Paul Allen, for awhile the second wealthiest man in the world, bought several waterfront lots and built a lovely estate. As a result of the influx of wealth to our island, the income disparity has become greater. But it doesn't take too much insight to see how the rest of us have benefited from increased parks, recreational programs, new fire engines, etc. which have flowed from the higher taxes and from the better equipment and expanded programs at the Boys and Girls Club, more computers from contributions to the schools, and even $6 million of improvements to our Presbyterian Church! Similarly, my friends in Medina, Washington, where Bill and Melinda Gates built their new home, raising the wealth disparity of that small community, are praising the over $1 million in property taxes which the Gates pay annually to support local services of all types.

The nonsensical nature of the concept of income equality is dramatized by a fascinating observation by *Forbes* publisher Rich Karlgaard, "I know how we *could* have solved the problem of inequality in America. Maybe Steve Jobs shouldn't have popularized the personal computer. If only Jeff Bezos had stayed in his hedge fund job instead of starting Amazon. Too bad Michael Dell didn't obey his parents and become a doctor. Wouldn't it be great if Tad Waitt had taken up cattle ranching instead of starting Gateway? And who can deny that David Filo and Jerry Yang [Yahoo founders] would have done more for society if they had finished their Ph.D. dissertations!"[273]

The foregoing discussion of income disparity applies solely to internal comparisons within democratic countries with developed economies, the dominant characteristic of which is a broad middle class. Indeed, within many underdeveloped, undemocratic countries and between such countries and developed countries income disparities can be great, with those at the bottom of the scale not receiving even the essentials for sustaining life, often with a tiny elite at the top oppressing a massive group in poverty. Such disparities—horrible by any criteria—have given rise to important global economic issues which I discuss later in Chapter XI. Such disparities also underscore the importance of generosity which I discuss in the next chapter, "Role of Material Possessions and Wealth." Concern for the poor is unequivocally a religious issue—well enunciated as such by Luther, Calvin, Knox and other leaders of the Reformation.

Finally it should be noted that the sins of covetousness and envy are promoted by the distributionist ethic which Schall observes in his critique of liberation theology and Bauer even notes in his critique of the encyclicals of Paul VI.[274] In concluding this brief discussion of covetousness and envy, let us heed the words of Guinness, "... envy by its very nature is comparative.... If someone else's success... is due to that person's calling, then finally my grudge is not simply against the other person but against God....We are called individually, accountable to God alone, to please him alone, and eventually to be approved by him alone. If ever we are tempted to look around, compare notes, and use the progress of others to judge the success of our own calling, we will hear what Peter heard: 'What is that to you? Follow me!'"[275] Schweizer, in his exegesis of Lk. 12:13 notes, "Luke takes it as a warning against covetousness, which does not quite fit either the question or the narrative that follows. But the real point is the general statement about human life: possessions are not its source of strength, and abundance does not lend it meaning."[276] Prideful wealthy fail to see this; covetous nonwealthy fail to see this.

Hypocrisy

Lastly, an attitude which is found to be despicable in Scripture is hypocrisy. The decrying of hypocrisy is a common biblical theme. "Does the LORD delight in burnt offerings as much as in obeying the voice of the LORD?" (1 Sm. 15:22) "Humans look at the outward appearance, but the LORD looks at the heart." (1 Sm. 16:7) "Sacrifice and offering you did not desire,... burnt offerings and sin offerings you did not require..... I desire to do your will, O my God; your law is within my heart." (Ps. 40:6-8) "All a man's ways seem innocent to him, but motives are weighed by the LORD." (Prv. 16:2) "To do what is right and just is more acceptable to the LORD than sacrifice." (Prv. 21:3) "He who conceals his sins does not prosper," (Prv. 28:13)

Hypocrisy was a common subject of the exhortations of the prophets. "Stop bringing meaningless offerings! Your incense is detestable to me.... Stop doing wrong, learn to do right!" (Is. 1:13,16,17) "You cannot fast as you do today and expect your voice to be heard on high." (Is.58.4) "Her leaders judge for a bribe, her priests teach for a price, and her prophets tell fortunes for money. Yet they lean upon the LORD and say, 'Is not the LORD among us? No disaster will come upon us.' Therefore, because of you Zion will be plowed like a field, Jerusalem will become a heap of rubble" (Mi. 3:11,12) "Her prophets are arrogant;.... Her priests profane the sanctuary." (Zep. 3:4) "From the least to the greatest, all are greedy for gain; prophets and priests alike, all practice deceit." (Jer. 6:13

and 8:10) "Will you.... follow other gods..., and then come and stand before me in this house, which bears my Name, and say, 'We are safe'—safe to do all these detestable things? Has this house, which bears my Name, become a den of robbers to you? But I have been watching! declares the LORD." (Jer. 7:9-11) "You live in the midst of deception; in their deceit they refuse to acknowledge me." (Jer. 9:6)

Ezekiel takes to task the people as well as the rulers and religious leaders of Israel while in exile, "With their mouths they express devotion, but their hearts are greedy.... they hear your words but do not put them into practice." (Ez. 33:31,32) "Woe to the shepherds of Israel who only take care of themselves!... You eat the curds, clothe yourselves with the wool and slaughter the choice animals, but you do not take care of the flock." (Ez. 34:2) "It is you, O priests, who show contempt for my name.... You have not set you heart to honor me..... you have turned from the way and by your teaching have caused many to stumble." (Mal. 1:6; 2:1,8)

Hypocrites were a major target of Jesus who taught that only those with pure motives would enter the kingdom of God. Jesus abhorred hypocrisy and rebuked it in many ways, including one of his characteristic hyperbole's, "You hypocrite, first take the plank out of your own eye, and then you will see clearly to remove the speck from your brother's eye." (Mt. 7:5; Lk. 6:42) "Not everyone who says to me, 'Lord, Lord,' will enter the kingdom of heaven, but only he who does the will of my Father." (Mt. 7:21) "You brood of vipers, how can you who are evil say anything good?" (Mt. 12:34) "You hypocrites! Isaiah was right when he prophesied about you: 'These people honor me with their lips, but their hearts are far from me." (Mt. 15:7,8; Mk.7:6) Mounce reminds and warns, "Out of our own mouths will come the words that condemn or acquit us...."[277] And then of particular relevance to this and all treatises on economic systems, "When man-made rules are taught as the laws of God, all worship become useless."[278]

Jesus focused particularly on the piosity and hypocritical outward display of righteousness by many of the religious leaders, giving long discourses on this, one of the most harsh of which is presented in chapter 23 of the book of Matthew, which commences, "The teachers of the law and the Pharisees sit in Moses' seat. So you must obey them.... But do not do what they do, for they do not practice what they preach." (Mt. 23:2,3) The *Sermon on the Mount* is filled with such rebukes. "For I tell you, unless your righteousness exceeds that of the scribes and Pharisees and Sadducees, you will never enter the kingdom of heaven." (Mt. 5:20) With some Jews at the time of Jesus wealth was accumulated as a device to show to others that one was favored by God. "The Pharisees... therefore sought material possessions to prove that they were accepted and approved by God."[279] Jesus continuously and forcefully rebuked and castigated the Pharisees (e.g., "woe to you Pharisees!" Mt. 23:23; Lk 11:42..."beware of the leaven of the Pharisees, which is hypocrisy." Mt. 16:6, Mk. 8:15; Lk. 12:1) (The Pharisees and Sadducees, who had it wrong, should have done a better job of studying Job. In life, as LaSor notes, "Since the righteous may suffer and the wicked prosper, it is dangerous to brand a sufferer as guilty of secret sin or to praise the prosperous as righteous. [God's] design of the universe is far too complex to yield to this simple principle."[280]) One of the very few places in the Bible where Jesus is depicted as angry to the point of appearing to lose his temper is in the passage on the cleansing of the Temple. Jesus seemed to be irate primarily with the hypocrisy of commercial activity dominating a place of worship and also with the merchants extorting their customers through selling sacrificial animals at inflated prices and exchanging currency at overstated rates. Jesus quotes Jeremiah, "... you have made it a den of robbers," (Mt. 21:13; Mk. 11:17; Lk. 19:46).

Condemnation of hypocrisy was also a component of the theology of the Evangelists. For example, Matthew and Mark observe and comment on the unconventionality of John the Baptist's clothing; "Now John wore a garment of camel's hair and a leather girdle around his waist;..." (Mt 3:4; Mk 1:6) John was certainly different from the Pharisees who dressed in a more opulent fashion in order to impress their followers with their "favor with God." John the Baptist made this physical demonstration of his separation from hypocrisy and a statement that his sole interest was with the praise of God.

Let us now apply the foregoing review of Scripture to an examination of contemporary society. In this context the sins of covetousness and hypocrisy are closely aligned. Today many of the high profile social, political, and economic "causes" are nothing more than an attempt by the "have nots" to dignify their covetousness by cloaking their envy in respectability and / or rationalize or avoid responsibility for their station in life by a common technique, use of a villainous scapegoat. Novak expands, "Of course envy never travels under its own name; it is the one vice that never calls itself what it is; it prefers prettier names, good names to which it has no right: 'justice,' 'fairness,' and the like.... Left-wing politicians feed on envy,..."[281]

The hypocritical rationalizations by those who view themselves as "have nots" are common: "well, money can't buy happiness;" "money can't buy health;" and of course the misinterpretation of the familiar passage, "it is easier for a camel to go through the eye of a needle than for a rich man to enter the kingdom of God." (Mt. 19:24; Mk. 10:25; Lk. 18:25) As discussed earlier, Jesus did not in any way mean that the mere possession of wealth was negative. That misinterpretation has been used hypocritically by "have nots" to curb their envy or salve their lack of worldly accomplishment.

James addresses a particular kind of hypocrisy on the part of the clergy. "Suppose a man comes into your meeting wearing a gold ring and fine clothes, and a poor man in shabby clothes also comes in. If you show special attention to the man wearing fine clothes and say, 'Here's a good seat for you,' but say to the poor man, 'You stand there' or 'Sit on the floor by my feet,' have you not discriminated among yourselves and become judges with evil thoughts? Listen, my dear brothers; has not God chosen those who are poor in the eyes of the world to be rich in faith and to inherit the kingdom he promised those who love him?" (Jas. 2:2-5) In this example James is admonishing the clergy who might hypocritically be favoring the rich in church.

Interestingly, however, today's clergy seem not only to have responded to James criticism, but to have swung over to the opposite extreme, giving rise to another form of hypocrisy which tends to be practiced predominantly by the clergy. In fact the clergy have put many business people in a sort of catch-22; that is, damned if they do and damned if they don't. To step back a moment, everyone understands that, ultimately, reducing poverty, by definition, requires increasing its opposite: wealth. Providing jobs for the poor or donating goods to the poor requires first the creation of the wealth—capacity—that brings forth the jobs and the goods. I am amazed at how many present-day clergy dive into this subject of wealth in its middle: the distribution stage, without any concern for its initial stage: generation. In fact, to the extent that the clergy voice opinions about the generation stage it is usually with some sort of disdain and condemnation of the "materialism" of capitalists. However, on the other hand, the clergy turn around and lead the charge, the battle cry of which is, "I don't understand what you've done, I don't even like what you've done, but now that you've done it, give some of the fruits to me and others."

Our tendency toward hypocrisy has given rise to many myths in our society. One of the most tragic myths is that somehow the plight of the poor is caused by the wealthy. As a trained economist, I find this nonsensical notion baffling and tragic—tragic, not only because it is precisely contrary to reality but because it can result in counterproductive public policy. Henry Ford became wealthy when he figured out how to build a car that the masses could buy. Michael Jordan became wealthy by providing entertainment to the masses. Sam Walton became wealthy by providing the highest value to the great mass of consumers. Bill Gates became the wealthiest man in the world by revolutionizing the life of the masses. It was not by accident that the initial slogan for the Macintosh computer was "Power to the People." Stanford economist Nathan Rosenberg and legal scholar L. E. Birdzell, Jr. observe, "the West's system of economic growth offered its largest financial rewards to innovators who improved the life-style not of the wealthy few, but of the less-wealthy many."[282] Business firms maximize profits by lowering prices, not by raising them. The erroneous notion that wealth causes poverty reflects a misunderstanding of how wealth is created. Wealth flows from economic contribution, and economic contribution creates job opportunities for all. The poor have a vested interest in the number of wealthy growing because of the three ways in which the poor benefit as mentioned before: jobs created by successful businesses, social programs funded by philanthropy of the wealthy, and government programs funded by taxes on the wealthy. As mentioned earlier, even Jeremiah understood the validity of the trickle-down theory. Similarly, the wealthy have a vested interest in the rise in incomes of the poor because the size and vibrancy of markets determines the potential up-side for business firms. In capitalism, with its orientation toward wealth creation, everyone benefits by everyone else being better off. This is why capitalism is referred to as a positive sum game.

As the late Senator Paul Tsongas declared in criticizing his fellow Democrats at their 1992 convention, "You cannot redistribute wealth you have never created. You can't be pro-jobs and anti-business at the same time. You cannot love employment and hate employers."[283] Perhaps the epitome of this hypocritical syndrome was the "class warfare" strategy of the Gore 2000 presidential campaign. Herein is where those politicians who are furthering their own career through promulgation of the "psychology of victimization" reveal their true motivation: it is not to raise the condition of the poor, but to further their own ambition. This hypocritical notion stems from a more basic cause, envy and covetousness. (The term "psychology of victimization" is from Thomas Sowell, an African-American scholar at the Hoover Institution of Stanford University who makes the observation that a scapegoat-generating paranoia on the part of many African-Americans has largely resulted from the Black leadership's promulgation of the tragic "psychology of victimization." His thesis is that not until Blacks shed themselves of this debilitating mindset will they have any hope of climbing out of the dark hole into which certain politicians and others who prey on the Blacks' feeling of inadequacy, keep shoving them. One of the reasons that other minority groups in our society have tended to climb out of their dark holes of discrimination and join the economic mainstream is that they, ironically, did not have an articulate, vocal, organized leadership that kept shoving them back down into that hole.) Herbert Schlossberg, senior research scholar at The Fieldstead Institute, while discussing global poverty, observes, "One of the most galling attributes of many who appear to bask in the glow of their own compassion is their damnable patronizing of poor people..., and...ersatz compassion that often not only dehumanizes them but uses them to advance extraneous and usually damaging ideological purposes...."[284]

As stated earlier, despite its many flaws and imperfections, capitalism at least has the virtue of intellectual honesty: the score of the game is measured as profit. Throughout my life I have tended to run across more hypocrites *outside* of the business community—the pastor silently seeking the power and fame of a larger church, the college professor silently seeking the status of the department chairmanship or college presidency, the politician running on a platform of do-goodism, expropriating my property to give to others in order to further his/her own political career, and—the worst of all—the political or religious leader who promulgates the "psychology of victimization" in order to further his/her own fame and power. As Guthrie observes, "Every sin that can be found outside the church can also be found in it.... Inside as well as outside the church there is prejudice and intolerance; personal immorality;... cut-throat competition; misrepresentation or misuse of the truth for personal or collective gain;... nationalistic arrogance,..."[285] When it comes to criticizing business per se, let you who "is without sin,... be the first to throw the stone...." (Jn. 8:7)

In addition to the pretense of virtue which I have just discussed, there is another type of hypocrisy which is even more pervasive and less obvious. It relates to the notion of, "You bet, I'll shed my worldly possessions and follow Jesus.... Heck, I have no worldly possession to shed, so what do I have to lose?" It's easy to say "I surrender all" when one has nothing to surrender. In one respect attracting destitute people to hear the Scriptures at the inner-city's gospel mission is considerably easier than attracting someone to church from an affluent neighborhood. Some of the formers' attitude could be, "heck, what do I have to lose—listen to a talk, get a hot meat, not bad." To what extent were some who needed healing who came to Jesus or were brought to Jesus by others in the state of mind of "We've tried everything else; maybe this itinerant preacher can do the trick?" Indeed, hypocrisy is not limited to the wealthy and the pious.

Jesus observed and reacted to the foregoing kind of hypocrisy. It is related in one of the most powerful passages of the Bible, Jesus' discourse, *The Bread of Life*, as recorded by John. In the synagogue at Capernaum he said to the people "...you seek me, not because you saw signs, but because you ate your fill of the loaves. Do not labor for the food which perishes, but for the food which endures to eternal life..." to which the people responded, "What must we do, to be doing the works of God? Jesus answered them, 'this is the work of God, that you believe in him whom he has sent....the bread of God is that which comes down from heaven, and gives life to the world....I am the bread of life; he who comes to me shall not hunger, and he who believes in me shall never thirst...." (Jn. 6:26-59) It is instructive to draw from Michaels' commentary, "The crowd had begun following him because of the miracles he had done…pursuing him as one who can satisfy their physical hunger…. They think they have found him, but they have not. They have been fed, yet they have not begun to receive what Jesus has to give… What they do not yet realize is that food is a metaphor….'I am the bread of life.' (vs. 35)"[286]

In the same way that the poor, lacking sustenance items, can be inclined to the foregoing type of hypocrisy, they also tend to be more susceptible to selling-out and therefore are particularly vulnerable to the hypocrisy of power-motivated public officials. Nebuchadnezzar utilized this dependency of the poor in his captivation policies. Unlike the Assyrians who moved out captives from their homelands which were resettled with "loyalists," the Babylonians moved out the wealthy and skilled, leaving only the poor who were then elevated to positions of responsibility, winning the grateful loyalty of the poor. "He carried into exile all of Jerusalem: all the officers and fighting men, and all the craftsmen and artisans—a total of ten thousand. Only the poorest people of the land were left…. He also took to Babylon the king's… officials and the leading men of the land." (2 Kgs. 24:14,15) "Nebuchadnezzar king of Babylon appointed Gedaliah… to be over the people he had left behind in Judah…. Gedaliah took an oath to reassure them…. 'serve the king of Babylon, and it will go well with you." (2 Kgs. 25:22,24) "Nebuzaradan left behind the rest of the poorest people of the land." (Jer. 52:16) Such preying on the vulnerabilities of the "have nots" continues today by many hypocritical politicians and other power-seekers.

Perhaps the clearest example of hypocrisy involving economics is the leftist college professor. Years ago while on the economics faculty of a small liberal arts college, I learned through my students of a colleague over in the Philosophy Department devoting considerable time in his class lectures to ravings against the "avarice and greed of the businessman." At the same time, this college professor assigned as a requirement for this particular class a textbook written by him which, in today's dollars, cost the students $69! This professor, like many others, was taking advantage of his monopolistic power to conspire with the publishing company to extract monopolistic profits out of his unfortunate students. When I asked him if he was donating the extraordinarily high portion of his royalty to the poor, he scoffed at me with an abruptness that made Ebinezeer Scrooge seem warm. No, capitalism is not sinful. Wealth is not sinful. Humans are sinful.

One of the reasons that hypocrisy is so rampant throughout the academic community is their strong identification with the "have nots" accompanied by an envy and covetousness which overwhelms the clarity of their thinking and writing resulting in their spewing a copious amount of intellectual dishonesty. In performing the research for this book I read volumes of works on contemporary social and economic issues such as poverty, the environment, international trade, labor relations, etc. Much of what I waded through were irrational diatribes characterized by faulty, incomplete research wrapped in pseudo-intellectual jargon (a common one is heavy, redundant use of Latin phrases). Additionally, so much of what comprises the conceptual foundation of their arguments has long ago been *empirically* debunked, the two most prominent cases being Malthus and Marx. (An economics professor assigning the writings of either Malthus or Marx in a college class in order to present "all sides" is like a physical science professor for the same reasons assigning a treatise asserting that the world is flat.) Kristol expands, "The simple truth is that the professional classes... are engaged in a class struggle with the business community for status and power. Inevitably, this class struggle is conducted under the banner of 'equality'.... Professors are genuinely indignant at the expense accounts which business executives have and which they do not.... So this, it appears to me, is what the controversy 'about equality' is really about. We have an intelligentsia which so despises the ethos of bourgeois society,... that it is inclined to find even collective suicide preferable to the status quo. (How else can one explain the evident attractiveness which totalitarian regimes possess....?) We have a 'New Class' of self-designated 'intellectuals' who share much of this basic attitude—but who, rather than committing suicide, pursue power in the name of equality."[287]

Hypocrisy has become so pervasive in our society that we have even dignified it by conferring a name upon it: political correctness. Every once in awhile someone comes along and dramatically opens our eyes to see that the emperor has no clothes. An example which was sweeping the airways and the Internet awhile ago was the story attributed to Rev. Joe Wright, pastor of the Central Christian Church in Kansas City who reportedly opened the new session of the Kansas Senate with the following prayer:

"Heavenly Father, we come before you today to ask Your forgiveness and to seek Your direction and guidance. We know Your Word says, 'Woe to those who call evil good' but that is exactly what we have done.

We have lost our spiritual equilibrium and reversed our values. We confess that we have ridiculed the absolute truth of Your Word and called it Pluralism;

we have worshipped other gods and called it multiculturalism;

we have endorsed perversion and called it alternative lifestyle;

we have exploited the poor and called it the lottery;

we have rewarded laziness and called it welfare;

we have killed our unborn and called it choice;

we have shot abortionists and called it justifiable;

we have neglected to discipline our children and called it building self-esteem;

we have abused power and called it politics;

we have coveted our neighbor's possessions and called it ambition;

we have polluted the air with profanity and pornography and called it freedom of expression;

we have ridiculed the time-honored values of our forefathers and called it enlightenment.

Search us, oh God, and know our hearts today; cleanse us from every sin and set us free. Guide and bless these men and women who have been sent to direct us to the center of Your will...."

No, wealth is not sinful. The market system is not sinful. Humans are sinful: idolatrous, prideful, covetous and hypocritical.

Summary of Sinful Attitudes Associated with Wealth and Material Possessions

We have discussed four sinful attitudes toward material possessions and wealth: idolatry, pride, covetousness/envy and hypocrisy. In each case attention toward personal wealth and material well-being has separated one from God. This is one of the dominant themes of the Old Testament, as the Israelites repeatedly alternate between obedience to and abandonment of God. This human tendency continues today.

While Scripture clearly acknowledges that poverty is unfavorable and that prosperity is favorable, often referring to the former as an affliction and the latter as a blessing, nevertheless, there are three immense dangers associated with wealth. The first is that prosperity and the accompanying intoxicating hedonism become the subject of idolatry, become one's primary objective. (Recall the bumper sticker, "He who dies with the most toys wins.") The second is that in the process of pursuing prosperity, one devotes one's entire attention to it, subordinating or abandoning all other interests and concerns, especially becoming distracted from one's relationship with God and one's fellow humans. Third, after achieving prosperity, there is the danger that one feels self-sufficient—"I did it on my own; who needs anything else?"—and a closely aligned attitude that all security is provided by one's prosperity. Wealth, luxuries, and ease can make mortals feel prideful: confident, satisfied and complacent, with no need for or interest in God. The first danger is wealth as a displacement, the second is wealth as a distraction, the third is wealth as an impediment.

Additionally, however, in the same way that the wealthy are particularly susceptible to certain types of sins, there are equally grievous sins that tend to be prevalent among the non-wealthy: covetousness and hypocrisy. These two sins converge in what has become the politically correct cloak of "economic rights." The assertion of such rights is an affront to Scripture. What Scripture focuses on is not "rights" but responsibilities. The poor do not have a divine right to be unpoor; the wealthy have a divine *responsibility* to be lovingly generous to the poor. The relatively recent emergence of the political issue of "economic justice" is not much more than an effort to put a cloak of respectability around the sins of envy and covetousness. Rather, in the context of Scripture the term "economic justice" does not refer to the rights of the poor; it refers to the unequivocal immeasurable responsibility of the wealthy. Finally, the poor tend to be particularly vulnerable to the hypocrisy of power seekers claiming to be motivated solely by the desire to do good when instead furthering their own ambition.

The common thread among all four sins of idolatry, pride, covetousness and hypocrisy is a displacement of God by materialism. This materialism pervades all economic systems. As discussed earlier, materialism is common to humans, and capitalism best accommodates it to the common good. Further, it should be noted that certain evils attributed to capitalism by some social scientists—conspicuous consumption, for example—flourished long before capitalism ever existed or the economic complexities to which capitalism applies ever existed. The decadent lives of the ancient empires testify to this. Hedonism is an intrinsic sin of humankind, independent of the economic structure of a particular society. Soviet communist leaders lived lavishly relative to their "comrades." Indeed, throughout the Bible are accounts of lavish feasts and partying—all occurring in the absence of any stimulation from a massive advertising industry. In the first century Paul warns regarding the impending eschaton, "But mark this: There will be terrible times in the last days. People will be lovers of themselves, lovers of money, boastful, proud, abusive, disobedient to their parents, ungrateful, unholy, without love, unforgiving, slanderous, without self-control, brutal, not lover of the good, treacherous, rash, conceited, lovers of pleasure rather than lovers of God...." (2 Tm. 3:1-5) As Gaylen Byker, president of Calvin College, observes, "Consumerism... has always been a major problem—just read the Old Testament of Jesus' parables. Having things define who one is and what is important in one's life has always been a problem."[288] I would go further and suggest that the current prevalence of hedonism throughout the world is not related to any particular economic system but rather receives its impetus from a dominant intellectual philosophy of secular humanism.

Therefore, we must conclude that the response to one who claims that capitalism is an economics system based on greed, socialism is an economic system based on envy and covetousness. Both deal with materiality. Both rich and poor are torn by the inner conflict of pursuing God or mammon. Sider notes, "When we focus on ourselves, we forget not only God but also the people he created. In our self-absorption, we are fooled by the pleasure of possessing."[289] Addressing this existence of dual, conflicting forces within humans, James admonishes all to "Come near to God and he will come near to you. Wash your hands, you sinners and purify your hearts, you double-minded." (Jas. 4:8)

At this point it should be emphatically asserted that neither capitalism nor the discipline of economics is any more susceptible to these dangers than any other human system, including religion and the church. The following table outlines various human systems and institutions and the idols associated therewith.

The Dangers of Worldly Systems and Institutions

Sector	Idol
Government	Position, Power
Business	Wealth, Fame
Politics	Position, Power, Fame
Church	Fame, Ingratiation
Entertainment	Wealth, Fame
Military	Rank, Power
Professional Athletics	Wealth, Fame
Education	Rank, Ingratiation, Fame
Arts	Fame, Wealth
News Media	Fame, Power, Wealth

Performance in all of these fields is driven by ego. All human activity is self-centered—even the apparent generous act which is done more for the self-centeredness of wanting to feel righteous for having done it—save that activity performed by the saints solely for the glory of God. As discussed previously, the genius of capitalism is that it admits this flaw of humanity and provides corresponding structural elements in order to serve the common good. Within socialism and within many totalitarian states, the first two fields above—government and business—are intertwined which explains why socialist governments and dictatorships tend to be corrupt. Further, as will be expanded upon later, under capitalism the power of the business sector is at least diffused and subjected to the discipline of the marketplace and the constraints imposed by government.

Whereas the Bible is virtually silent on worldly social, economic and political systems, except for the simple directive to endure and passively exhibit loyalty to the particular government leader, in

Revelation we find clear warning that these worldly systems can contribute to humans putting worldly matters—especially power, fame and wealth—before God. "And I saw a beast coming out of the sea....The dragon gave the beast his power and his throne and great authority....The whole world...followed the beast. Men worshipped the dragon because he had given authority to the beast,....All inhabitants of the earth will worship the beast—all whose names have not been written in the book of life belonging to the Lamb.... This calls for patient endurance and faithfulness on the part of the saints.....Then I saw another beast, coming out of the earth..... He exercised all authority....he deceived the inhabitants of the earth.....He also forced everyone, small and great, rich and poor, free and slave, to receive a mark on his right hand or on his forehead, so that no one could buy or sell unless he had the mark." (Rev. 13:1-17) "... 'If anyone worships the beast and his image and receives the mark on the forehead or on the hand, he, too, will drink of the wine of God's fury.... He will be tormented....for ever and ever....'" (Rev. 14:9-11) But still, nevertheless, God simply directs, "This calls for patient endurance on the part of the saints who obey God's commandments and remain faithful to Jesus." (Rev. 14:12)

There is a clear warning in Revelation that involvement with worldly systems detracts from our relationship with God. Pastor Jack Hayford, of "The Church on the Way," Van Nuys, California, and one of the national leaders of the impressive growth of the Pentecostal movement, agrees with this notion, stating "the church is called to a spiritual mission, not a political mission."[290] He also notes, by the way—relevant to the table on the previous page—that "there is nothing headier than political power. It is considerably more intoxicating than wealth.....The whole world's systems operate within a desire to control."[291] Wall goes further, "The beast's sociopolitical program, which pervades every political regime in any age, is inherently satanic and ultimately ends in chaos and death."[292]

The dramatic warning of the dangers of worldly systems such as governments and economies continues in Revelation, "Come, I will show you the punishment of the great prostitute who sits on many waters. With her the kings of the earth committed adultery and the inhabitants of the earth were intoxicated with the wine of her adulteries." (Rev. 17:1,2) "Fallen! Fallen is Babylon the Great!... The kings of the earth have committed adultery with her, and the merchants of the earth grew rich from her excessive luxuries... Therefore in one day her plagues will overtake her: death, mourning and famine. She will be consumed by fire,... The merchants of the earth will weep and mourn over her because no one buys their cargoes any more—cargoes of gold, silver, precious stones and pearls; fine linen, purple, silk and scarlet cloth; every sort of citron wood, and articles of every kind made of ivory, costly wood, bronze, iron and marble; cargoes of cinnamon and spice, of incense, myrrh and frankincense, of wind and olive oil, of fine flour and wheat; cattle and sheep; horses and carriages; and bodies and souls of men. They will say, 'the fruit you longed for is gone from you. All your riches and splendor have vanished, never to be recovered.' The merchants who sold these things and gained in their wealth from her will stand far off, terrified at her torment. They will weep and mourn and cry out: '...In one hour such great wealth has been brought to ruin!' Every sea captain,...will....cry out: '...Oh great city, where all who had ships on the sea became rich through her wealth! In one hour she has been brought to ruin!'.... 'No workman of any trade will be found in you again.... Your merchants were the world's great men.'.... 'Hallelujah! Salvation and glory and power belong to our God,.... He has condemned the great prostitute who corrupted the earth by her adulteries." (Rev. 18:2-24) And finally, "Behold, I am coming soon,...and I will give to everyone according to what he has done....Blessed are those who wash their robes, that they may have the right to the tree of life and may go through the gates into the city. Outside are the dogs,... the idolaters...." (Rev. 22:12-15)

Wall interprets, "secular power, conceived of in political terms, is self-corrupting because it forms a functional atheism that denies the sovereign rule of God.... [M]iddle-class materialism corrupts and enslaves human beings from inside out.... The apparent invincibility of secular power and human ingenuity, whether Tyrean, Roman, or North American, poses a threat to the believer. The compromise of faith is often viewed as expedient, gives the very real evidence of secular power which surrounds the church.... The optimism of nationalism (kings), of middle class affluence (merchants), and of secular humanism (mariners) wherever it exists, is exposed as lies and fictions."[293] In this passage in the Book of Revelation two things are being condemned by the apostle John: (1) the humanism of the world's political systems with a deification of human power manifest in lust for power and fame and (2) the materialism of the world's economic systems with a deification of wealth manifest in self-indulgence. The point being made in the book of Revelation is that all of these worldly things are transitory. Only through God will we experience the eternal.

It should be acknowledged that, whenever citing passages from the book of Revelation, extraordinary care should be taken in the interpretation process. Revelation, with its abundant use of symbolism, can easily be misinterpreted. As Brown points out, "Part of the misuse of Revelation is based on the misunderstanding that the message is primarily addressed to Christians of our time.... Rather the meaning of the symbolism must be judged from the viewpoint of the 1st Century addressees—a meaning that needs adaptation if we are to see the book as significant for the present era....Three sorts of problems confront the seven churches: false teaching (Ephesus, Pergamum, Thyatira); persecution (Smyrna, Philadelphia); and complacency (Sardis, Laodicea).... The struggle against complacency may be much more applicable to modern Christianity.... The false teaching is very conditioned by the 1st Century in one way..., and yet the underlying issue of Christians conforming in an unprincipled way to the surrounding society remains a very current problem."[294]

Indeed, Revelation does suggest the current human dilemma: the more effectively humans control and operate their economic and political systems and mechanisms, the more humans become seduced by and controlled by those systems. In Revelation, according to Martin. "John sought to overcome the tension between reality and faith....its ultimate motive is to reveal the fulfillment of God's purpose for his creation in a redeemed humanity in fellowship with himself."[295]

In closing this discussion of the sins associated with material possessions and wealth, let us listen to Jesus' admonition, "Watch out! Be on our guard against all kinds of greed: a man's life does not consist in the abundance of his possessions." (Lk 12:15) which reflects the Old Testament prayer, "Turn my heart toward your statutes and not toward selfish gain. Turn my eyes away from worthless things; preserve my life according to your word.... The law from your mouth is more precious to me than thousands of pieces of silver and gold....How sweet are your words to my taste, sweeter than honey to my mouth!... Because I love your commands more than gold..." (Ps. 119:36,37,72,103,127)

These sinful postures toward possessions lead us now to turn to a discussion of what ought to be humans' attitudes toward material possessions and wealth: humble gratitude for receiving them and dedication to their use toward God's purpose. As a transition, I offer the following summary by theologian Craig L. Blomberg: "Material possessions are a good gift from God.... Material possessions are simultaneously one of the primary means of turning hearts away from God.... A necessary sign of life in the process of being redeemed is that of transformation in the area of stewardship.... There are certain extremes of wealth and poverty which are in and of themselves intolerable.... Above all, the Bible's teaching about material possessions in inextricably intertwined with more 'spiritual' matters."[296]

Gratitude / Dedication

Having discussed four sinful attitudes toward material possessions and wealth, let us now turn our attention to the righteous attitude toward material possessions and wealth: gratitude.

All aspects of one's life is a repayment for the gift of life itself. Holland points out that "everything we do in living out our relationship with God is as an expression of gratitude for the grace given us by God."[297] Guinness reminds us that "calling is a reminder for followers of Christ that nothing in life should be taken for granted; everything in life must be received with gratitude."[298]

The importance of gratitude flows from the notion that we have received a free gift from God—our salvation flows from God's grace. This should place one in a constant state of gratitude and humility. Gratitude, as most concepts in Scripture, implies action. Gratitude unexpressed is nonexistent. Guinness notes, "The link between calling and gratitude, choseness and wonder touches our lives practically in two main places. First, it reminds us that with so much grace given to us, we should be givers of grace to others.... Second, the link between calling and grace reminds us that gratitude must be our first and constant response to God... Dvorak began writing his new music with words, 'with God' and ended 'God be thanked.'... Bach wrote in the margins of his music 'SDG'

(Soli Deo Glorie) and "Glory to the Lamb."[299]

Gratitude for our material gifts from God and dedication to using those material gifts in accordance with God's purposes is expressed continuously throughout Scripture. "When you have eaten and are satisfied, praise the LORD your God for the good land he has given you." (Dt. 8:10) "Be sure to fear the LORD and serve him faithfully with all your heart; consider what great things he has done for you." (1 Sm. 12:24) Solomon, reflecting his great wisdom, sums up beautifully the notions that God is the source, and we are to remain humble and express our gratitude for God's gifts by dedicating ourselves to fulfilling God's purpose: "Now, O LORD my God, you have made your servant king.... But I am only a little child and do not know how to carry out my duties.... So give your servant a discerning heart to govern your people and to distinguish between right and wrong.... The Lord was pleased that Solomon had asked for this, so God said to him,.... I will do what you have asked.... Moreover, I will give you what you have not asked for—both riches and honor...." (1 Kgs. 7-13) The message here is that, when we genuinely dedicate ourselves to God, we are provided with what we need to carry out God's purpose. The dedication must come first. This is reaffirmed in Solomon's prayer of dedication of the temple which he built in Jerusalem, "But your hearts must be fully committed to the LORD our God,..." (1 Kgs. 8:61) (The entire prayer, which expresses Solomon's wise and spirit-filled insights regarding the nature of God, the nature of humanity and the relationship between the two, is found in 1 Kings 8:22-61.)

An attitude toward material possessions and wealth held by Jesus, the disciples and many followers since has been gratitude and dedication: gratitude to God for providing for our needs and dedication to utilizing material possessions and wealth to fulfilling God's purpose for me. This notion of gratitude and dedication brings us full circle back to the concept of stewardship. We evidence our gratitude for God's gifts by dedicating ourselves to acting responsibly toward them.

Underlying these attitudes of gratitude and dedication is the view that material possessions and wealth are not the end. One understands that material possessions and wealth are simply a means to our glorifying God. When viewed this way, God understands profit maximization. Profits are simply the fuel for the engine from which flows an abundance of goods and services which can be used for improving the well-being of humanity. It is profits that (1) induce the miraculous efficiency with which God's resources are used, (2) through reinvestment build an immense level of wealth to support *all* of God's children, and (3) provide the capacity to support humans' overwhelming generosity as capitalistic nations of the world transport in cargo aircraft their life-saving and poverty-alleviating goods and services in immediate response to any disaster or other need that befalls God's children anywhere on the globe.

Oh, the splendor of the market system and profits! We are grateful for the incredibly efficient allocation of God's resources that flows therefrom. We dedicate ourselves to utilizing this miraculous productivity to the glory of God.

In this context Novak asserts, "Under God, a wealthy nation faces an especially harsh judgment, but that judgment will not be aimed so much at the existence of wealth as at the character of the uses made of it. On Judgment Day, the rich may find it especially hard to get through the eye of the needle, but this will not be because they had money but because their use of it will be subjected to an accounting on different ledgers from those scrutinized by the Internal Revenue Service. The rich have reason to tremble. If their wealth has been productive for others, though, the world has reason to be merciful to them even if God's standards are higher."[300] Guinness expresses this notion as follows, "calling means that, for the follower of Christ, there is a decisive, immediate, and moment-by-moment authority above money and the market. The choice between Masters has been made. There is one God, there is no God but God,...."[301]

An important point to be made in the context of dedication is that *faith* is not a passive concept; it implies action. God does not intend for us simply to sit passively and wait for God's will to be done to us. No, God expects us to act toward fulfilling God's purpose. Indeed, works are the outward manifestation of one's faith. Scripture is filled with such examples; virtually every book of the Bible—common to and throughout both the Old and New Testaments—relates stories of faithfilled people acting out their faith. One of the most intriguing stories utilizing ingenuity and cunning combined with the courage to take a risk—all based on faith—is that of Esther who saved the Jews from destruction while under

Persian rule. A similar story of ingenuous faithful action was Nehemiah's stealthily surveying the damage to the walls of Jerusalem and quietly devising a plan for their reconstruction so as not to alert his opponents. "I set out during the night with a few men. I had not told anyone what my God had put in my heart to do.... By night I went out examining the walls....The officials did not know where I had gone or what I was doing...." (Neh. 2:11-16)

Holland notes the relationship between gratitude and dedication, "When one expresses gratitude for God's willingness to draw near to a sinner like me, gratitude becomes life-changing."[302] This leads us to one of the most beautiful statements of dedication in Scripture, Isaiah's commission as a prophet, "Then I heard the voice of the Lord saying, 'Whom shall I send? And who will go for us?' And I said, 'Here I am. Send me!" (Is. 6:8) So elegant in its simplicity; so inspirational in its sincerity. Is this not what one should say every day upon rising?

Gratitude and dedication as the appropriate attitudes toward material possessions and wealth lead us now to examining the role of material possessions and wealth.

Chapter VII

Role of Material Possessions and Wealth

W hen we acknowledge that God is the source of material possessions and wealth, it becomes obvious that the use to which material possessions and wealth are put must be in accordance with God's purpose. What God's purpose is has been the subject of substantial interpretation and misinterpretation over the centuries. To bring some clarity to God's intent it is important that we first examine the legal framework which Scripture has established.

God's Laws

At the beginning of Scripture God explicitly, clearly and forcefully sets down various laws related to material goods and human relationships. The entire Pentateuch relates many of God's specific laws by which people are to live which reflect the covenant relationship between the Israelites and God. "If you obey me full, and keep my covenant, then out of all nations you will be my treasured possession." (Ex. 19:5) The major presentation of the laws are the Ten Commandments (Ex. 20:3-17; Dt. 5:6-21), the Book of The Covenant (Ex. 20:22-23:33), and the Holiness Code (Lv. 17-26) See Appendix E wherein I have related some of these laws to

213

contemporary business considerations. Suffice it to say at this point that these laws reflected some economic institutions and practices at that time, including private property, commercial transactions, opportunity cost, bankruptcy, tithing, and the economic role of humans, animals and land. These economic institutions and practices obviously were deemed acceptable to God because it was God who decreed the laws relating to their preservation and adherence. "Then the LORD said to Moses,....'These are the laws to set before them." (Ex. 20:22; 21:1)

The laws reflected somewhat the norms and mores of the day and may or may not have literal applicability today. A clear example of literal inapplicability today are most of those laws related to women and slaves. The Rev. Dr. John Goldingay, former Principal of St. John's College in Nottingham, suggests that God's laws could be viewed as "...a gracious gift to Israel. It was not a collection of limitations imposed by God, but a body of loving guidance to lead God's people in the best way.... the outworking of grace.... See obeying God's laws as the grateful and appropriate response that God's people give to what God has done for them.... Loyalty to the Lord is of fundamental significance."[303] It remains so.

As a careful study of Exodus, Leviticus, Numbers, Deuteronomy, and the entire Bible clearly reveals, the specifics of laws were dynamic, ever-changing to reflect changing conditions to which the laws must be applied. Further reflecting the evolutionary nature of laws, it is interesting to note that after the Pentateuch "the various kings and judges in making legal rulings do not site laws in the Pentateuch."[304] Joshua, Judges, Samuel and Kings focus only on Pentateuchical rules regarding worship and religious practices. Nevertheless, even certain religious laws were broken in order to comply with higher laws or principles. When Ahimelech the priest gave David consecrated bread to feed his men, it was to pursue God's end for David. Therefore, today the enactment, interpretation and application of laws is, appropriately, a dynamic exercise. Accordingly, it is exceedingly dangerous, in fact often simply incorrect, to justify one's position on a contemporary matter by quoting Scriptural law. Indeed, as asserted by Turner, "God's revelation didn't stop with the publication of the Bible." Guthrie agrees, "The God we come to know in the history of Israel and Jesus Christ speaks and acts—above all in and through the church....God is a living God,... who goes with the people of God in every time and place, promising to reveal to them what they need to know, say , and do in their particular situation, So God's self-revelation does continue."[305]

Most Biblical interpreters feel that God's laws were intended to serve the following purposes:[306]

- establish and maintain an awareness of the accessibility of God's presence,
- counteract certain attitude problems reflected in disrespect and sinful behavior,
- make the philosophical point that acts have consequences,
- establish the expectation that certain values and virtues such as compassion and truthfulness are to be upheld, i.e., underlie ethics,
- set a standard of behavior toward which people are to strive,
- establish a means of maintaining justice through accepted ways of resolving conflicts and thereby facilitate the Israelites functioning as a group, and
- distinguish and separate the Israelites from other nations, thereby contributing to their cohesiveness and spiritual development.

C. J. H. Wright expands, "The law was designed to mold and shape Israel in certain clearly defined directions within their own historico-cultural context. That overall shape...becomes the model or paradigm intended to have a relevance and application beyond the geographical, historical and cultural borders of Israel itself.... The point is that this paradigmatic nature of Israel is not just a hermeneutical tool devised by us retrospectively, but theologically speaking, was part of God's design in creating and shaping Israel as he did in the first place."[307]

Applied to material possessions and wealth, the general directive of the laws was to use these things moderately and with justice. The emphasis was on providing for the necessities of life and for sharing. "When you reap the harvest of your land, do not reap to the very edges of your field or gather the gleanings of your harvest. Do not go over your vineyard a second time or pick up the grapes that have fallen. Leave them for the poor and the alien." (Lv. 19:9-10; 23:22) At least two of God's laws reflect the notion of some sort of economic justice. As discussed earlier, God provided equally to every Israelite family its own land with which to generate a decent living. If, for whatever reason, the family lost ownership of its land, after fifty years, ownership would revert back to the original owner. (Year of Jubilee, Lv. 25:8-54) Additionally, every seven years debts were to be forgiven. (Dt. 15:1-11) Wright notes an interesting distinction, "Even cancellation... in the seventh year, therefore, would not have meant a forfeiture of the *total* debt, but a writing off of whatever remained unpaid by then."[308] Regardless, the purpose of these laws was to restore one's ability to be a productive, digni- fied member of society. Applying this biblical concept to today, there is Scriptural foundation for providing the poor with those things which enable them to be productive, dignified members of society: an adequate level of sustenance, education and health care, and to provide to those, who, because of disabilities or otherwise, cannot become productive, with the necessities of life. Sider suggests the foregoing as a definition of "economic justice" and further warns that, "if an individual chooses not to act responsibly, then only sustenance be provided. Otherwise such gifts become an unloving act by contributing to the person persisting in being less than what God wants her/him to be."[309] Sider further notes that "while the right of a family to have the means to earn a living takes precedence over the right of ownership, failure to act responsibly has consequences, e.g., loss of land for up to 49 years."[310] Further. it is in this context of scriptural passages implying some sort of "economic justice" that Sider asserts, "There is an implication here that private property is so good that God wants everybody to have some!"[311]

The over-riding purpose of God's laws was to assure people that (1) God is present and must be worshipped above all else and (2) God is in charge with final authority. "I will walk among you and be your God, and you will be my people....If after all this you will not listen to me, I will punish you..." (Lv. 26:12,18) The same is true today. Our sinful behavior has dire consequences. The laws were to convey the general notion that, according to LaSor, "Faithful worship supports holy living, and a moral life finds fulfillment in worship....It is not a surprise, then, that the great commandment to love a neighbor as oneself comes here. Behavior governed by love is at the heart of holy living."[312]

Mann, when discussing the laws of Moses in Deuteronomy, observes that "If ever human beings are properly to attempt to be 'like God' (Gn. 3:11) it is in this imitation of divine redemption. 'Justice, and only justice, you shall follow, that you may live and inherit the land which Yahweh your God give you' (Dt. 16:20 RSV). In the chapter preceding the corpus of laws, we have seen that the inheritance of the land is conditional on a number of basic attitudes, all of which are part of a proper righteousness: trust, loyalty, gratitude, humility."[313] "Israel is the community of the redeemed, but only if also a redemptive community."[314] That applies to humanity today. We must accept our relationship with God and then act in accordance with it. The classical scholar and ethicist Darrel Amundsen notes, "By the grace of God one is declared righteous when one is not yet righteous. Out of gratitude we seek to keep God's laws which are guides for behavior."[315]

The purpose of God's laws was to serve as a guideline, reflecting a set of general principles, for people as to how to live a life toward holiness and to identify certain types of sin applicable at the time the laws were written so that the fear of God will be with us to keep us from sinning. Viewing the Ten Commandments in this respect, Commandments 1—4 can be summarized as the Great Commandment, "Love God," and Commandments 6-10 can be summarized as the Second Commandment, "Love Others." LaSor notes, "the Ten Commandments were never intended to institute a system of legal observances by which one could earn God's acceptance. Rather, they are the stipulations of a covenant relationship anchored in grace....Redemption already has been accomplished."[316] Of course the entire Reformation turns on this notion as Martin Luther asserts that faith, not works, is the avenue to salvation. Our great leader John Calvin suggests that contemporary use of the Ten Commandments is facilitated by thinking of them in terms of their opposite; that is, "Do not steal" becomes "Share;" "Do not kill" becomes "Live to contribute to the life of others."[317]

Jesus devoted a considerable amount of his ministry to distinguishing between compliance with the law and expression of the heart, asserting clearly and forcefully that the latter is what mattered.

Jesus' opponents made heavy use of technicalities of the law in endeavoring to trap him, but he always effectively rebuts them. "I tell you that one greater than the temple is here..... Therefore it is lawful to do good on the Sabbath. (Mt. 1-14; see also Lk. 13:10-17; Lk. 14:1-6 and Jn. 5:1-18) "My Father is always at his work to this very day, and I, too, am working." (Jn. 5:17)

Of course, this is revealed earlier in God's new covenant prophesied through Jeremiah, "I will put my law in their minds and write it on their hearts." (Jer. 31:33) Goldingay explains, "...the New Testament offers an entirely different attitude to law.... Attachment to the law can become legalism. People can think that obeying the law earns them God's favor.... Keeping God's Commandments is not a way of earning a relationship with God. The relationship is given, and obedience is a response. Christians are in at least as great a danger of trying to live by legalism."[318] Bruce asserts, "The age of law, in fact, was a temporary dispensation: the law served to bring home to men their inability to fulfill the will of God and left them no option but to embrace the way of release proclaimed in the gospel."[319]

This was a notion expressed often by Paul. For example, "... but Israel, who pursued a law of righteousness, has not attained it. Why not? Because they pursued it not by faith but as if it were by works. They stumbled over the 'stumbling stone." (Rom. 9:31,32) Rather, Paul asserts, "So the law was put in charge to lead us to Christ that we might be justified by faith. Now that faith has come, we are no longer under the supervision of the law." (Gal. 3:24,5) Paul sums up his instructions regarding the law in his letter to the Romans, "Therefore love is the fulfillment of the law." (Rom. 13:10) and in his letter to the Galatians, "The entire law is summed up in a single command, 'Love your neighbor as yourself" (Gal. 5:14) as a demonstration of one's faith.

Tithing

Some of God's decrees which have been subject to misunderstanding are those related to tithing. More important than the specific portion of one's possessions that must given, is the general notion that the first use of our material possessions is as an expression of our love of God. That is, first things first. In order to recognize and express gratitude to God as the source of all material possessions and wealth, the first role is to tithe. This practice is affirmed at the very outset of Scripture.

"Then Melchizedek, king of Salem brought out bread and wine. He was priest of God Most High, and he blessed Abram saying,
'Blessed be Abram by God Most High,
   Creator of heaven and earth.
And blessed be God Most High
   Who delivered your enemies into your hand.
Then Abram gave him a tenth of everything." (Gn. 14:18-20)

Later, when Jacob makes his vow to God, he ends it with "and of all that you give me I will give you a tenth." (Gn. 28:20-22)

"I give to the Levites all the tithes in Israel as their inheritance..... When you receive from the Israelites the tithe I give you as your inheritance, you must present a tenth of that tithe as the LORD's offering." (Nm. 18:21,26)

After defeating the Midianites, the Israelites were instructed by God through Moses, "Divide the spoils,... set apart as tribute for the LORD one out of every five hundred,..." (Nm. 31:27,28)

"A tithe of everything from the land,...belongs to the LORD;..." (Lv. 27:30)

"...bring your tithes...to the LORD your God..." (Dt. 12:6,11)

"Be sure to set aside a tenth of all that your fields produce each year." (Dt. 14:22)

"They brought a great amount, a tithe of everything." (2 Chr. 31:5)

"We assume the responsibility for carrying out the commands to give a third of a shekel each year for the service of the house of our God:... We also assume responsibility for bringing to the house of the LORD each year the firstfruits of our crops and of every fruit tree." (Neh. 10:32,35)

"All Judah brought the tithes of grain, new wine and oil into the storerooms." (Neh. 13:12)

"This is the special gift you are to offer: a sixth of an ephah from each homer of wheat and a sixth of an ephah from each homer of barley. The prescribed portion of oil,.... Also one sheep is to be taken from every flock.... These will be used for the grain offerings, burnt offerings and fellowship offerings..." (Ez. 45:13-15)

"Bring the whole tithe into the storehouse..." (Mal. 3:10))

"....Abraham gave him a tenth of everything.....collect a tenth from the people..." (Heb. 7:2-10)

Of course, the bringing of offerings to the Lord throughout Scripture is another indication of God's recognition of the legitimacy of material possessions and wealth. But the major point being made is that, more important than the amount, is the order of the gift. That is, the first disposition of any of our material possessions and wealth is as a gift back to God to express our gratitude for God's gifts to us and our love of God.

Beyond reflecting our acknowledgment that God is the source of all of our supply, tithing is also a clear demonstration of one's faith that God will continue to supply all of one's needs. The specific percentage is not the important element. The important element is regular and sacrificial giving. Tithing is an important aspect of "The Circular Flow of Prosperity," which I discuss later in this chapter.

Old Testament: Wealth to the Glory of God.

In addition to the on-going tithing of income, the periodic support of major funding requirements is also an activity described in Scripture which further reflects God's acknowledgment of the legitimacy of material goods and wealth.

In the latter part of Exodus (Ex. 25-31; 35-40) we see that all of the silver and gold obtained from the Egyptians was used to construct a tabernacle with an ark with rings and poles and cheribums, table with rings and poles, altar with horns all overlaid with bronze, ornate lampstand and lamps, linen and yarn curtains with gold clasps and embroidery, goat hair curtains with bronze clasps, tent frames with silver bases, crossbars overlaid with gold, entrance posts overlaid with gold and with cast bronze bases, pitchers, bowls, dishes, utensils, grating and metalwork for the fireplace, and a courtyard with fine linen embroidered curtains and posts with bronze bases and silver hooks, bronze wash basins as well as elaborate priestly garments, a robe, ephod, tunic, turban, sash, gold bells and breastpiece with precious stones and engravings—all to the glory of God. These items consumed huge amounts of fine materials: gold, silver, bronze, fine linen, yarn, goat hair, ram skins, dyed hides of sea cows, acacia wood, precious stones and gems, clear pressed olive oil for light and spices for anointing oil and incense. Additionally, design and fabrication of all of this required highly skilled craftsmen.

Consecration of the priests was done with perfect bulls and rams as well as bread and cakes made from fine wheat flour with oil. Also, anointing oil and baskets were used. The altar was consecrated by daily offering two yearling lambs. Finally, recognizing that all people belonged to Him, God commanded that "each one must pay the Lord a ransom for his life..." and, interestingly, the rich and the poor were both to give the same amount: a half shekel (Ex. 30:12), reflecting God valuing all His children equally.

All of the foregoing was done for the glory of God at God's command, utilizing material goods. This was an immense task, utilizing huge amounts of material and a wide variety of manual skills (woodworking, stoneworking, metalworking, silver and gold design and fabrication, inlaying precious stones, etc.) "All who are skilled among you are to come and make everything the Lord has commanded:..." (Ex. 35:10) Note the implicit acknowledgment that people differed in their type and level of skill. Additionally, all were invited to participate financially. "From what you have take an offering for the Lord. Everyone who is willing is to bring to the Lord....and everyone who was willing and whose heart moved him came and brought an offering to the Lord...." (Ex. 35:5,21) Accordingly, there was a very real connection between the material world and the spiritual world—the former used to the glory of the latter.

Clearly, money provides the capacity to pursue God's ends. One of the purposes to which it was put was financing the Israelites trip from Egypt to the Promised Land. Moses, when quoting God's instructions regarding their travel through Seir, "You are to pay them in silver for the food you eat and the water you drink." (Dt. 2:6)

Later in the Old Testament we again see material goods lavishly devoted to the glory of God in the building and the rebuilding of the temple in Jerusalem. "He provided a large amount of iron..., and more bronze than could be weighed.... More cedar logs than could be counted,...a hundred thousand talents of gold, a million talents of silver, quantities of bronze and iron too great to be weighed, and wood and stone" (1 Chr. 22:3-14) "Then David gave his son Solomon the plans for the portico of the temple, its buildings, its storerooms, its upper parts, its inner rooms and the place of atonement...., for the treasuries of the temple of God and for the treasuries for the dedicated things...., as well as for all the articles to be used in its service...gold articles...silver articles...gold lampstands...silver lampstand...gold for each table for consecrated bread;...silver tables;...pure gold for the forks,...gold dish...silver dish...gold for the altar.... chariot, that is, the cherubim of gold that spread their wings and shelter the ark of the covenant of the LORD.... Every willing man skilled in any craft will help you in all the work." (1 Chr. 28:11-21) (See also 1 Kings 5:5—6:37 and 7:13—51 for a complete description of the lavish materials and workmanship that went into the temple.)

Building the temple was funded largely by wealth confiscated by the king. Perhaps the ultimate example of giving of one's wealth to the glory of God is King David. "With all my resources I have provided for the temple...gold..., silver..., bronze..., iron..., wood..., onyx..., turquoise..., stones..., marble—all of these in large quantities...." (1 Chr. 29:2) The temple was also partially privately funded from personal contributions from individuals. "Then the leaders of families, the officers of the tribes of Israel, the commanders of thousands and commanders of hundreds, and the officials in charge of the king's work gave willingly. They gave...five thousand talents and ten thousand darics of gold, ten thousand talents of silver, eighteen thousand talents of bronze and a hundred thousand talents of iron. Any who had precious stones gave them....freely and wholeheartedly to the LORD." (1 Chr. 29:6-9)

Then, when Solomon builds the temple he uses many skilled craftspeople, tens of thousands of workers and common laborers and several thousand foremen, reflecting the requirement for management and some sort of organizational structure. The temple was large. "The foundation… was sixty cubits long and twenty cubits wide…" (2 Chr. 3:3) An abundance of resplendent material was used. "…overlaid the inside with pure gold…pine…covered…with fine gold and decorated it with…palm tree and chain designs… precious stones…overlaid the ceiling beams, doorframes, walls and doors of the temple with gold…. gold nails…. wingspan of the cherubim was twenty cubits….curtain of blue, purple and crimson yarn and fine linen….pillars….thirty-five cubits long….bronze altar….ten gold lampstands….hundred gold sprinkling bowls…. overlaid the doors with bronze….four hundred pomegranates for the two sets of network….pots, shovels, forks and related articles…of polished bronze….gold floral work….pure gold wick trimmers, sprinkling bowls,…gold doors of the temple." (2 Chr. 3,4) One must read chapters three and four of 2 Chronicles to understand fully the immensity and grandeur of the temple. Abundant material goods and personal wealth were used in its construction and furnishing. LaSor notes the critical role played by wealth in this and in preparing Solomon personally for this role. "Solomon, aware of his wide and weighty responsibilities,… took full advantage of his international contacts, wealth, and respite from war to dedicate himself to literary pursuits…. The most lasting and influential legacy of Solomon's era was the temple at Jerusalem. Only during this period did Israel have the combination of wealth, centralized government and relief from enemy attack necessary to complete a project of this scale."[320]

Clearly a message of the Old Testament is a confirmation of the legitimacy of material goods and wealth through God's expectation of their use for the glory of God and God's creations. One's contribution to the capital campaign of one's church or to mission construction projects abroad or to producing and distributing Bibles and other Christian literature or to myriad other examples are all demonstrations that God uses material goods and wealth toward His ends. It is interesting to observe that Joash led one of the first church capital campaigns: "Joash said to the priests, 'Collect all the money that is brought as sacred offerings to the temple of the LORD—the money collected in the census, the money received from personal vows and the money brought voluntarily to the temple. Let every priest receive the money from one of the treasurers, and let it be used to repair whatever damage is found in the temple." (2 Kgs. 12:4,5)

What was demonstrated millennia ago continues to apply today: that many things used in the worship of God; e.g., church structures, furniture and fixtures, heat and light, clergy salaries, etc., require financial capacity. Is not wealth, therefore, a part of God's plan? Of course it is. The $6 million recently used to remodel and expand the church which I attend on Mercer Island came from private accumulations, most *directly* from the flourishing high-tech industry in the Seattle area.

I do not want to imply that in the Old Testament wealth was used only for righteous purposes. As noted earlier in the discussion of the market system, wealth is neither intrinsically good nor bad. Accordingly, there are a multitude of occurrences in the Bible wherein sinful humanity put wealth to sinful purposes. In fact all of the Jewish kings used a portion of their wealth for sinful purposes. Further, money was commonly used for extortion and bribery, particularly between nations. As we noted earlier, money is neutral; humans are sinful.

New Testament: Wealth for the Spread of the Gospel

As wealth played a key role at the outset of the Old Testament, it similarly played a key role at the outset of the New Testament. It is hypothesized by some that the gifts of the Magi provided the financing for the escape by Mary, Joseph and Jesus into Egypt, saving Jesus from being killed under Herod's program.

Throughout his ministry Jesus implores us to use our possessions and wealth for one general purpose: to glorify God. Jesus tell us to abandon the false notion that one's security comes from one's wealth, to leave all of our possessions and "follow me."

The book of Acts clearly exhibits the major, direct role played by material possessions and wealth in the spread of Christianity. Four major elements are described below.

First, Paul was from a family of means in Tarsus. It is generally believed that Paul was able to request a hearing before Caesar because he was a Roman citizen, suggesting a certain level of wealth. Hawthorne notes, "But much more important than the family's possession of Tarsian citizenship was its acquisition of Roman citizenship—an honor rarely granted to provincials....: his father or grandfather must have been so honored for conspicuous services rendered to a military proconsul."[321]

Second, Paul was a manufacturer, a relatively affluent producer of tents and other items of cloth and leather. This production of tents and the revenue produced therefrom helped to finance his three missionary journeys. "After this, Paul went to Corinth.... Claudius had ordered all the Jews to leave Rome. Paul went to see them [Aquila and Priscilla], and because he was a tentmaker as they were, he stayed and worked with them." (Acts 18:1-3) Further, "the reference to tentmaker at the beginning of Paul's stay at Corinth reminds us of the indication in his letters that he normally supported himself and did not ask his hearers for personal financial help."[322] This emphasized the sincerity and genuiness of Paul's message, separating him from the charlatans who spoke and taught for money, often, therefore, telling the audiences what they wanted to hear. Paul's position of independence and therefore, presumably genuineness, is further highlighted in Acts in his farewell speech to the Ephesian elders, "...I declare to you today that I am innocent of the blood of all men. For I have not hesitated to proclaim to you the whole will of God....I have not coveted anyone's silver or gold or clothing. You yourselves know that these hands of mine have supplied my own needs and the needs of my companions." (Acts 20:25-34) Additionally in several of his letters, Paul points out that being financially independent enabled him to preach the gospel unencumbered and free from any taint of being compromised by being beholden to any financial sponsor. "Am I not free...Don't we have the right to food and drink?...Though I am free and belong to no man, I make myself a slave to everyone, to win as many as possible." (1 Cor. 9:1-19) Paul is saying, I, being my own financially independent self, have told it the way it is. Today, financial independence can play this same role.

Third, most of the early church meetings were held in private homes large enough to accommodate a group of Christians in the particular community. This suggests that the meetings were held in the home of relatively wealthy people who had generated the financial capacity to own a large home. Hawthorne explains, "Affluent believers in various cities, including a number of women, became hosts to Paul, and some opened their homes for the services of a local congregation."[323] "Households were not the private residences of today but were most likely large houses which provided shops at the front and living accommodations at the rear. There would also have been room for workshops and living quarters for dependents and visitors. Such an arrangement would have ideally suited Paul's purposes by both enabling him to finance his mission through his work as a tentmaker and by providing him with a ready-made platform from which preaching and teaching could be conducted daily among the many who would have been around the workshop."[324] From the very beginning of the church, Christianity and economics intertwined! Apparently Paul approached the affluent by design. "Owning a fine house and property was one of the leading indicators of wealth.... Thus the conversion of a household...was a strategic means of establishing the new cult in unfamiliar surroundings, and the household remained the soundest basis for the meeting of Christians.... This explains the prominence Paul accords to various heads of households, ...who served as patrons of the fellowships meeting in their houses."[325] For example, "There was an estate nearby that belonged to Publius,... He welcomed us to his home... They honored us in many ways and when we were ready to sail, they furnished us with supplies we needed." (Acts 28:7-10)

Fourth, Acts provides many examples of lay persons who use their wealth and material possessions to contribute directly and indirectly to spreading The Word. Paul was joined by others who combined lay employment and religious preaching, two of the most noteworthy being Priscilla and Aquila, owners of a tentmaking business who met Paul in Corinth, accompanied him to Ephesus and eventually formed one of the "house churches" in Rome. Similarly, Lydia, the wealthy businesswoman dealing in purple cloth, a luxury, "may have been a contributor, [and] no doubt her home became the first 'church' in Philippi."[326] Also, Phoebe, a businesswomen, was a benefactor to the church. Finally, it is hypothesized that some of Paul's letters were delivered by business travelers.

Additionally, earlier in Acts Cornelius, the Roman centurion, "....gave generously to those in need....gifts to the poor.... had called together his relatives and close friends....Peter said, 'They have received the Holy Spirit'....he ordered that they be baptized in the name of Jesus Christ. Then they asked Peter to stay with them for a few days." (Acts 10:1-48) Another example, because Dorcas who made robes and clothing was always doing good and helping the poor in her community, her revival by Peter "became known all over Joppa, and many people believed in the Lord." (Acts 9:42). Interestingly, this passage in Scripture continues, "Peter stayed in Joppa for some time with a tanner named Simon." (Acts 9:43) Presumably this was possible because Simon, as a result of his tanning business, possessed a sufficient house and furnishings and food which he was able to make available for missionary work in this way. Additionally, Barnabas, a landowner, "sold a field he owned and brought the money and put it at the apostles' feet." (Acts 4:36-7). Finally, "all the believers...shared everything they had....There were no needy persons among them. For from time to time those who owned lands or houses sold them, brought the money from the sales and put it at the apostles' feet, and it was distributed to anyone as he had need." (Acts 4:32-5)

One thing that comes through loud and clear in Acts is that functioning within the world—for example, performing missionary work for the church such as that by the apostles—requires worldly goods: food, clothing, shelter, transportation, etc. Presumably, the more worldly possessions made available to the missionary cause, the greater the effort to spread Christianity. Ergo, the greater material wealth available, the greater the spread of Christianity.

When considering missions, a very important distinction should be made. Those who contribute their wealth and material possessions to the work of the Lord are playing a role in taking the message to the world that is just as important as those doing the actual direct missionary work. "Dear friend, you are faithful in what you are doing for the brothers....You will do well to send them on their way in a manner worthy of God....We ought therefore to show hospitality to such men so that we may work together for the truth." (3 Jn. 5-8) Johnson notes, "Not every Christian has the gifts or opportunity to be...a missionary, but nearly everyone can, like Gaius, be a 'fellow worker in the truth' (RSV) by supporting those who go forth to bring the gospel to others."[327] Providing food, shelter, clothing, transportation, and contributing to all of the other logistical elements of spreading the Gospel is critically important and just as much a part of "God's work" as performing the direct ministry or going on the mission. Indeed, it is no wonder that the major support for worldwide mission work comes from the capitalistic nations.

Their societies possess the wealth available for these purposes. Interestingly, capitalistic societies also possess the character values most in concert with those of Christianity as I will discuss later in the chapter, "Conduciveness of Capitalism to Christianity."

Finally, one of the most poignant passages in Acts describing the role of wealth in the growth of the early church was the voluntary sharing of possessions by the infant church in Antioch which sent goods to the poorer believers in Judea in response to the prophet Agabus predicting "a severe famine would spread over the entire Roman world....The disciples, each according to his ability, decided to provide help for the brothers living in Judea. This they did, sending their gift to the elders by Barnabas and Saul." (Acts 11:27-30). This had important symbolism beyond an act of love. Antioch, where the followers of Jesus were first called Christians, at this time was the third largest city of the Roman empire, including a relatively large number of Gentile Christians, and this act of sharing enabled them to "display *koinonia*,"[328] (fellowship/ community) with the Hebrew Christians in Judea, an important occurrence in the early development of the church.

This brings us to the subject of generosity.

Generosity: Wealth for the Expression of Love

As suggested earlier in this book, the *possession* of wealth is neither intrinsically good nor bad per se. What matters is what one does with one's wealth. This includes, among other things, the nature and degree of one's generosity. As we observed earlier, humans have responsibility for stewardship of all of God's creations. This includes each other!

"Carry each other's burdens, and in this way you fulfill the law of Christ." (Gal. 6:2) This passage is particularly important for two reasons beyond simply the implication to be generous. First, it declares something that often gets lost in the notion of giving: generosity is a two-way street, a mutual act—"carry *each other's* burdens." The receivers of generosity, if they are to "fulfill the law of Christ," have a responsibility to be generous in return and/or to others. Such generosity can be expressed in many, many ways beyond simply financial. So often among contemporary recipients of philanthropy this gets lost. The second reason that the passage is so significant is the implication that generosity and mutual support is an ongoing, never-ending responsibility and therefore there is a strong implication that it is the responsibility of the Christian to continuously go through life with an attitude of generosity. An attitude of generosity is a manifestation of obeying the commandment "love one another." Furthermore such an attitude reflects an understanding of the theological interpretation of financial blessings received from God. Such blessings are first to give the recipients the opportunity / responsibility to share and, then, secondarily, as something from which to receive benefit themselves.

The other conceptual notion underlying generosity is the fact that all of our possessions are results of God's gifts to us. Even if they appear to be the result of one's hard work, talent, intelligence, perseverance, etc., from where did those gifts of character come? God, of course. It follows, therefore, that, if all that one has reflects God's generosity, then it is incumbent upon one in turn to express similar generosity to God's other children, one's brothers and sisters.

The concept of generosity is reaffirmed throughout Scripture, and no more pleasing than in the book of Psalms, "...the righteous give generously;" (Ps. 37:21) "Good will come to him who is generous.... He has scattered abroad his gifts to the poor," (Ps. 112:5,9)

Generosity was also addressed by the wise Solomon. "Do not withhold good from those who deserve it, when it is in your power to act." (Prv. 3:27) "He who despises his neighbor sins, but blessed is he who is kind to the needy..... Whoever is kind to the needy honors God." (Prv. 14:21,31) "He who mocks the poor shows contempt for their Maker;" (Prv. 17:5) "He who is kind to the poor lends to the LORD." (Prv. 19:17) "If a man shuts his ears to the cry of the poor, he too will cry out and not be answered." (Prv. 21:13) "A generous man will himself be blessed, for he shares his food with the poor." (Prv. 22:9) "The righteous care about justice for the poor," (Prv. 29:7) And King Lemuel says, "A wife of noble character.... She opens her arms to the poor and extends her hands to the needy." (Prv. 31:20) Note that, reflected in most of the foregoing passages, demonstrating love of the poor is equivalent to expressing love of God. This notion is enunciated throughout Scripture and is of critical importance to all of us.

The prophets also preached generosity. "Is it not to share your food with the hungry and to provide the poor wanderer with shelter—when you see the naked, to clothe him,... then your righteousness will go before you, and the glory of the LORD will be your rear guard....if you spend yourselves in behalf of the hungry and satisfy the needs of the oppressed, then your light will rise in the darkness, and your night will become like the noonday." (Is. 58:7-10) Ezekiel expressed it in the negative, "The people of the land.... Oppress the poor and needy and mistreat the alien, denying them justice.....So I will pour out my wrath on them..., declares the Sovereign LORD." (Ez. 22:29,31)

That worldly goods are to be given generously and particularly directed toward God is reflected in the New Testament first in the Gospel of Matthew (Mt. 2:1-12), when the wise men, believed to be astrologers, who "...have come to worship him...who has been born king of the Jews...fell down and worshipped him. Then, opening their treasures, they offered him gifts, gold and frankincense and myrrh." Prior to the birth of Jesus John the Baptist preached "The man with two tunics should share with him who has none, and the one who has food should do the same." (Lk. 3:11)

Generosity, of course, is a manifestation of the second great commandment, "You shall love your neighbor as yourself." (Mt. 22:39; Mk. 12:31; Lk. 10:27) Therefore, the true measure of one's relationship with God, is not whether or not one possesses wealth or how much wealth, but it is what one does with one's wealth with no expectation of return. This is because our love of God, as explicitly directed by Jesus Christ, is expressed by our demonstrated love of our fellow humans, particularly the destitute. "Lord, when did we see thee hungry and feed thee, or thirsty and give thee drink...see thee a stranger and welcome thee or naked and clothe thee? ....as you did it to one of the least of these my brethren, you did it to me....and the righteous will go into eternal life." (Mt. 25:37)

In *The Sermon on the Mount* and *The Sermon on the Plain* we are told to "give to everyone who begs from you." (Mt. 5:42; Lk. 6:30) In John's relating the feeding of the five thousand, the introduction of the young boy apparently willing to give his five loaves and two fish further dramatizes the importance of generosity and further demonstrates that, if we provide whatever we have in faith and trust, God will augment it to satisfy our need. (See later discussion, "Circular Flow of Prosperity.") Our generosity should be simply one aspect of an outpouring of love to all in many different ways, the general message of these two sermons of Jesus.

In the book of Luke one of the major messages is that the extent to which a person has internalized Godliness and grace is revealed by the extent of the person's generosity. Jesus states, "When you give a feast, invite the poor, the maimed, the lame, the blind, and you will be blessed because they cannot repay you. You will be repaid at the resurrection of the just." (Lk. 14:12-13) Joel Green, associate professor of New Testament at Graduate Theological Union, Berkeley, California, points out that "Luke borrows from widespread conventions for sharing among friends in the community, [and] presents the question of possessions as less a question about wealth and more an issue of treating others as members of one's own extended family.... Closely related is the counsel of Luke that followers of Jesus adopt the perspective of those in need."[329]

Moxnes notes, "People with resources are urged (by Jesus) to be generous without limits....and without expectation of return. This redistribution to the needy is the practical implementation of the divine reversal. This emphasis upon the nonexpectance of a return is balanced, however, by a promise of return and generous reward from God."[330] In this way, God is establishing himself as the only patron, with both wealthy and poor ultimately receiving their possessions from Him. We acknowledged this in the earlier chapter, "The Source of Material Possessions and Wealth."

Recognizing that God is the source of all wealth, material possessions are to be shared. "All the believers were together and had everything in common. Selling their possessions and goods, they gave to anyone as he had need."(Acts 2:44-5) "No one claimed that any of his possessions was his own, but they shared everything they had..... There was no needy persons among them. For from time to time those who owned lands or houses sold them, brought the money from the sales and...it was distributed to anyone as he had need." (Acts 4:32-5) While most theologians interpret these texts as reflecting an overwhelming overriding voluntary mutual love and concern among the first believers, interestingly, these passages have been subject to misinterpretation by some as advocating communism. However, there are three arguments that such an interpretation is unsound.

First, to draw the conclusion that such passages are advocating a form of government for a particular society is too far of a stretch.

Indeed, these passages refer to a group of private individuals in Jerusalem who had a common bond, belief in Jesus Christ, who were voluntarily joining together and pooling their resources to facilitate pursuit of their common interest. This is done in capitalistic societies all of the time. A multitude of voluntary groups of people with a common interest exist throughout the United States and in other capitalistic countries. Indeed, the legal form of corporation represents a pooling of resources by a group of people, shareholders, to pursue a common objective. Williams expands in his commentary, "From Luke's expression, however, it is clear that the believer still 'owned' his belongings until such time as he saw fit to dispose of them, that is, they were not practicing a thoroughgoing communalism but were simply a caring community responding to the needs of others as they arose. The response was purely a voluntary one."[331] To assert that *any* passage in the Bible which refers to communal sharing implies advocation of a communistic form of government is an affront to Scripture. The message of the Bible is *love*, intrinsically a voluntary act.

Second, empirically it is interesting to note that those communal believers in Jerusalem who abandoned their sources of livelihood and sold all of their possessions eventually had to be "bailed out" and supported by other Christians elsewhere who had kept their sources of income. The apostle Paul (who interestingly maintained his private business) had to devote an inordinate amount of his time collecting money from the various churches to send to the group in Jerusalem who had fallen into a state of poverty—not too unlike Americans sending food to the communal experiment of North Korea today. Williams notes, "It may be…true that…their willingness to sell their belongings…contributed to their later state of acute need."[332]

Third, Calvin comments, "For neither doth Luke in this place prescribe a law to all men which they must of necessity follow, while that he reckoneth up what they did in whom a certain singular efficacy and power of the Holy Spirit of God did show itself; neither doth he speak generally of all men, that it can be gathered that they were not counted Christians which did not sell all that they had."[333] Stotts explains, "Calvin… concludes that Luke was not proposing a law for all to follow when he refers to all things being held in common. Luke was showing that those in need must always be cared for and that those who had much were given the heart to share what they had. Calvin in dealing with Acts 2 and 4 retains the voluntary character of sharing in the church and the assumption of private ownership of goods."[334]

Returning to another example of sharing, "...Ananias, together with his wife Sapphira, also sold a piece of property. With his wife's full knowledge he kept back part of the money for himself, but brought the rest and put it at the apostles' feet. Then Peter said, 'Ananias, how is it that...you have lied to the Holy Spirit, and have kept for yourself some of the money you received for the land?...You have not lied to men but to God.' When Ananias heard this, he fell down and died.....later his wife came in....Peter asked her.... 'how could you agree to test the Spirit of the Lord?'...she fell down at his feet and died." (Acts 5:1-10) The lesson of Ananias and Sapphira is that lying is a sin. It was not expected or necessary that all of one's property be shared. However, they implied that they had given all, and such deceit was sinful. Nowhere is there in Scripture the command to share all that we have. There is the command to love one another, which implies sharing at least to serve the needs of others.

In his farewell speech to the Ephesian elders Paul summarizes the end of all wealth accumulation: "In everything I did, I showed you that by this kind of hard work we must help the weak, remembering the words the Lord Jesus himself said: 'it is more blessed to give than to receive." (Acts 20:35) As Paul relates in his letter to the Galatians regarding his initially becoming a missionary, "James, Peter and John, those reputed to be pillars, gave me and Barnabas the right hand of fellowship when they recognized the grace given to me. They agreed that we should go to the Gentiles, and they to the Jews. All they asked was that we should continue to remember the poor, the very thing I was eager to do." (Gal. 2:9,10) Another example is Paul's advice to the Romans to "Share with God's people who are in need." (Rom. 12:13) and to the Ephesians, "He who has been stealing must steal no longer, but must work, doing something useful with his own hands, that he may have something to share with those in need." (Eph. 4:28) Greaves observes, "Care for the poor has ample biblical sanction, and has consequently been advocated by men of all types of the history of Christianity."[335] Patzia notes, "The ultimate goal for work is to have something to give away."[336] As I stated earlier, concern for the poor is clearly a religious issue, reflecting humans' relationship with each other as being reflective of our relationship with God.

Paul, who devoted considerable effort and time on his travels to collecting money for the poor believers in Jerusalem, in his letter to the Corinthians noted, "But just as you excel in everything—in faith, in speech, in knowledge, in complete earnestness and in your love for us—see that you also excel in this grace of giving....For you know the grace of our Lord Jesus Christ, that though he was rich, yet for your sakes he became poor, so that you through his poverty might become rich..... For if the willingness is there, the gift is acceptable according to what one has, not according to what he does not have." (2 Cor. 8:7-12) Paul introduces the very important concepts of grace and sacrifice to which we will return in the next chapter.

Paul continues in his letter to the Corinthians expanding his concept of generosity, "Our desire is not that others might be relieved while you are hard pressed, but that there might be equality. At the present time your plenty will supply what they need, so that in turn their plenty will supply what you need. Then there will be equality, as it is written, 'He who gathered much did not have too much, and he who gathered little did not have too little." (2 Cor. 8:13-15) Here, Paul was suggesting the magnitude of generosity that seemed appropriate as well as introducing the concept of reciprocity. He was not introducing, as some contemporary social theorists have misapplied, a theory of "economic justice" involving the concept of coerced income redistribution. As Scott explains "what Paul here calls 'equality,' [refers to the notion that] as Israel shares in the wealth of nations, so also the nations share in the restoration of Israel."[337]

Paul understood that sharing the wealth not only provides the practical benefit of helping the poor, put it also provides a very important psychological benefit of drawing the receiver and giver closer together as mutual children of God. Paul viewed financial sharing as a device not only to reflect unity but to generate unity. When he implored the Galatians, Corinthians and others to "set aside a sum of money..., saving it up...send...to Jerusalem." (1 Cor. 16:1-3), he knew that this would draw the Gentile churches closer psychologically to the Jewish believers and vice versa. "For if the Gentiles have shared in the Jews' spiritual blessings, they owe it to the Jews to share with them their material blessings."

(Rom. 15:27) This drawing giver and receiver closer together continues to be an important relationship today. God's family works most effectively when all of its members work together cooperatively.

Paul frequently makes the point that intrinsic to the notion of generosity is that generosity be from the heart, genuine. "Love must be sincere." (Rom. 12:9) Paul conveys the Christian notion that love, generosity, kindness and other righteous acts cannot be legislated or brought about by edict. These are acts of the soul, not statutory regulations. Therefore, implicit in Christianity is individual freedom—to choose faith or not, to choose salvation or not, to choose to believe in Jesus Christ or not, to choose to love God or not, to choose to accept God's grace or not. "Therefore no one will be declared righteous in his sight by observing the law;..." (Rom. 3:20)

Paul explicitly points out that the establishment of laws and adherence thereto is insufficient for salvation. "Since they did not know the righteousness that comes from God and sought to establish their own, they did not submit to God's righteousness. Christ is the end of the law so that there may be righteousness for everyone who believes." (Rom. 10:3) "...know that man is not justified by observing the law, but by faith in Jesus Christ." (Gal. 2:16) "Clearly no one is justified before God by the law, because, 'the righteous will live by faith." (Gal 3:11) Throughout this letter Paul focuses on the distinction that good works cannot "buy" salvation; rather, good works are what naturally flow forth from one who has achieved salvation through faith.

While recognizing that we cannot "buy" our salvation through insincere good deeds, nevertheless, "What good is it...if a man claims to have faith but has not deeds?...Suppose a brother or sister is without clothes and daily food. If one of you says to him, 'Go I wish you well; keep warm and well fed,' but does nothing about his physical needs, what good is it?... faith by itself, if it is not accompanied by action, is dead." (Jas. 2:14-17) The foregoing passage has been used, along with others, to fabricate the so-called Paul/James, faith/works debate. I concur with those who see no conflict. James was not advocating legalism, and Paul agreed that faith was an active term and argued against only those "works" related to legalistic and ritualistic compliance with the law. Both Paul and James viewed faith as a relational trust in Christ, with Paul noting that

"The only thing that counts is faith *expressing* itself through love."
(Gal. 5:6) (italics mine) Jervis suggests, according to Paul, "faith
comes to expression by means of love.... Paul states that faith is not
an abstract but a way of life that is made effective, visibly and daily,
through love."[338] Further, Paul affirms in his letter to the
Ephesians, "For we are God's workmanship, created in Christ Jesus
to do good works,..." (Eph. 2:10) (italics mine)

Generosity flows from the very essence of our being. Justification comes from righteousness; righteousness comes from faith and
is manifest in love; and an expression of love is generosity. Hence,
generosity is a manifestation of our purpose as children of God.
"Command those who are rich....to do good, to be rich in good
deeds, and to be generous and willing to share. In this way they will
lay up treasure for themselves as a firm foundation for the coming
age, so that they may take hold of the life that is truly life." (1 Tm.
6:17-19) In his commentary Fee notes, "True 'riches' is found in
the giving , not in the having.... For the rich to give riches away is
not to suffer loss but rather to lay up treasure for themselves of a
different kind."[339]

Lack of generosity as manifest by indifference and lack of care
and concern towards one's fellowman will result in not entering
heaven, as dramatically related in The Parable of the Rich Man and
Lazarus. (Lk. 16:19) According to Pentecost, "since the man did
not use his wealth on earth to help the needy, there could be no
blessing for him upon his death."[340] Schweizer expands: "Neither
is the rich man a villain, but his innocence does not excuse
him...."[341] The rich man was guilty, not of a sinful act of commission, but of the equally sinful act of omission. His preoccupation
with his prosperity resulted in his neglecting the needs of Lazarus.
(This parable has been misinterpreted by some to suggest that
Lazarus was received by God simply because he was poor, but such
a conclusion, according to Griffiths, "would be in violation of
everything which Jesus ever taught about sin, repentance, new birth,
redemption and entry into his Kingdom."[342])

Calvin, while preaching on the Ten Commandments also affirms
that righteousness requires more than the avoidance of evil; it is
pro-active notion. "For God... did not create us simply to abstain
from evil.... Rather it is crucial for men to give and apply themselves to accomplishing good. Therefore let us understand that

when our Lord wills for the life of our fellowmen to be precious and dear in our sight,…. When we do not help them in their need and do not attempt to engage ourselves in their behalf when they need our help, we are guilty before God."[343]

Finally, regarding generosity in the New Testament, John admonishes, "We should love one another….If anyone has material possessions and sees his brother in need but has not pity on him, how can the love of God be in him?….love one another…God is love. Whoever lives in love lives in God , and God in him." (1 Jn. 3:11,17; 4:7,16) And in Hebrews we read "And do not forget to do good and to share with others,…." (Heb. 13:16) "May the God of peace…equip you with everything good for doing his will…" (Heb. 13:20,21)

Alexander summarizes, "The New Testament proposes sharing as a way of life….. The New Testament doesn't offer programs to be copied, but it does offer a mindset to work toward: we are to be totally economically available to others in the Christians community; we are to accept unlimited economic liability for them."[344]

The Circular Flow of Prosperity

There is a considerably broader perspective in which generosity can be viewed. If one views God as the provider of the great material abundance that flows throughout humankind, then one's giving is just part of the flowing prosperity, and, indeed, *not* to give would impede or even halt the flow. This has both practical and moral dimensions.

This concept is enunciated in both the Old Testament and the New Testament. As the wise, insightful Solomon expresses this relationship, "Honor the LORD with your wealth, with the firstfruits of all your crops; then your barns will be filled to overflowing, and your vats will brim over with new wine." (Prv. 3:9,10) "One man gives freely, yet gains even more; another withholds unduly, but comes to poverty. A generous man will prosper; he who refreshes others will himself be refreshed. People curse the man who hoards grain, but blessing crowns him who is willing to sell. (Prv. 11:24,5,6) "Do not eat the food of a stingy man,… for he is the kind of man who is always thinking about the cost…. his heart is not with you." (Prv. 23:6,7) And from the prophet Malachi, "Return to me, and I will return to you." (Mal. 3:7)

In the Old Testament we find an eloquent illustration of the concept of the circular flow of prosperity. The prophet Haggai, reacting to a fifteen year standstill of work on rebuilding the temple in Jerusalem while people devoted all of their efforts to their own homes and other personal interests, says, "Now this is what the LORD Almighty says:.... 'Is it a time for you yourselves to be living in your paneled houses, while this house remains a ruin?.... Give careful thought to your ways. You have planted much, but have harvested little. You eat, but never have enough. You drink, but never have your fill. You put on clothes, but are not warm. You earn wages, only to put them in a purse with holes in it..... You expected much, but see, it turned out to be little. What you brought home, I blew away. Why?' declares the LORD Almighty. 'Because of my house, which remains a ruin, while each of you is busy with his own house. Therefore, because of you the heavens have withheld their dew and the earth its crops. I called for a drought on the fields and the mountains, on the grain, the new wine, the oil and whatever the ground produces, on men and cattle, and on the labor of your hands." (Hg. 1:2-11)

In this respect, then, let us keep in mind the conclusion of LaSor, "Just as it was important for Zerubbabel to build Yahweh's temple, we need to build structures today through which God can work. They may be actual buildings, such as churches and hospitals or societal structures, such as missionary organizations and humanitarian agencies."[345]

The Circular Flow of Prosperity is also enunciated in Malachi wherein God is upset because the people have not been tithing. "Bring the whole tithe into the storehouse, that there may be food in my house. Test me in this,' says the LORD Almighty, 'and see if I will not throw open the floodgates of heaven and pour out so much blessing that you will not have room enough for it." (Mal. 3:10)

In the New Testament the circular flow has a broader meaning, including the notion of enlightened response to Jesus' teachings and demonstrations regarding the kingdom of God. "...give and it will be given to you; good measure, pressed down, shaken together, running over will be put into your lap. For the measure you give will be the measure you get back." (Lk. 6:38) The Gospel of Mark goes even further, "...the measure you give will be the measure you get, and still more will be given you. For to him who has will more be given;..." (Mk. 4:24-5) Of course Jesus' message has to do with the circular flow of spiritual understanding and eventual salvation. As Hurtado explains, "The sayings...have to do with recognizing and receiving the kingdom of God.... A positive response to the present manifestation of the kingdom in Jesus will entitle one to still more light and the blessings of the future salvation, whereas those who show no readiness to perceive God at work in Jesus now will suffer rejection at the judgment to come."[346] Additionally, however, material goods were involved in the circular flow, "Freely you have received, freely give." (Mt. 10:8) as Jesus instructs his disciples upon sending them out to proclaim Jesus Christ's message. As Mounce notes, "There is no need to take along money or extra provisions, because a worker should receive those things from the people served."[347]

And in the Parable of the Talents (Mt. 25:14-30) and the Parable of the Nobleman's Ten Servants (Lk. 19:11-27) Jesus goes even further, suggesting that it is a sin to break the circular flow. After noting that some servants had used their talents fruitfully and others had not, the master directs, "Take the talent from him and give it to the one who has the ten talents. For everyone who has will be given more, and he will have in abundance. Whoever does not have, even what he has will be taken from him. And throw that worthless servant outside..." (Mt. 25:28-30) "Take his mina away from him and give it to the one who has ten minas.... I tell you that to everyone who has, more will be given, but as for the one who has nothing, even what he has will be taken away." (Lk. 19:24-26) Mounce notes in his commentary on Matthew, "In context it means that faithfulness is rewarded by expanded opportunities, whereas the lack of fidelity leads to impoverishment. The law of spiritual atrophy is that when gifts are not exercised they are withdrawn.... The warning is appropriate for Christians who rest upon their religious profession without any apparent desire to live out its implications."[348]

Perhaps the clearest statement of the Circular Flow of Prosperity is in Paul's Letter to the Corinthians regarding their providing financial support to the church in Jerusalem:

> "Whoever sows sparingly will also reap sparingly, and whoever sows generously will also reap generously. Each

man should give what he has decided in his heart to give, not reluctantly or under compulsion, for God loves a cheerful giver. And God is able to make all grace abound to you, so that in all things at all times, having all that you need, you will abound in every good work....Now he who supplies seed to the sower and bread for food will also supply and increase your store of seed and will enlarge the harvest of your righteousness. You will be made rich in every way so that you can be generous on every occasion, and through us your generosity will result in thanksgiving to God.

"This service that you perform is not only supplying the needs of God's people but is also overflowing in many expressions of thanks to God. Because of the service by which you have proved yourselves, men will praise God...., and for your generosity in sharing with them and with everyone else. And in their prayer for you their hearts will go out to you because of the surpassing grace God has give you. Thanks be to God for his indescribable gift!" (2 Cor. 9:6-15)

Hawthorne notes, "The most theologically interesting part of Paul's fund-raising appeal is found in the extended sowing / reaping metaphor of 2 Corinthians 9:6-15.....Sowing was seen as a sign of trust in God, who could alone guarantee the harvest. In this context, any gift given to God was understood as a thank offering for blessing received.... A thankful giver gives cheerfully and abundantly, knowing that both seed and harvest come from God.... God provides everything, including the means to be generous. In fact, since liberal sowing results in liberal harvest, one can expect progressively larger harvests as one is provided with more seed to be sown. God will not only provide for the needs of the generous giver, but will multiply the giver's resources for even more generous giving. Generous giving glorifies God by providing for the needs of the saints, showing obedience to the gospel of Christ....Generous giving is an act of worship which gives thanks to God for his gifts. Since material and spiritual wealth are both gifts of divine generosity, one should share with others."[349] The key, however, is the sincerity of the giver. Giving is not to enrich the giver. Giving is to recognize God as the source and therefore share with our fellow humans. James reflects an understanding of the circular flow of prosperity in this admonition, "Your gold and silver are corroded. Their corrosion will testify against you and eat your flesh like fire. You have hoarded wealth...." (Jas. 5:3)

A clear, explicit message of Scripture is that our physical and spiritual lives are one in the same. Accordingly, the relationship between theology and economics is intertwined. When we regard material possessions as God's gifts, we more readily immerse ourselves in the Circular Flow of Prosperity, recognizing that by sharing, we are acknowledging and reaffirming the Source of our good. Furthermore, by contributing to the flow of prosperity we contribute to increasing its velocity and to an ever-widening circle. Christianity is a positive sum game. As we share the love of God, the goodness of God flows through us to others, multiplying as it goes through this process. Remember, capitalism also is a positive sum game—a win-win exercise. All enlightened capitalists readily understand this. Henry Ford understood it when he decided to pay wages sufficient for his workers to be able to afford the cars his company produced. General Grant understood it when, after the Civil War, he commanded that the defeated Southern troops be "sent home with a horse." He knew that the entire country would benefit by the economy of the defeated South reviving as quickly as possible. A contemporary manifestation of the "Circular Flow of Prosperity" is expressed by Rev. Robert Schuller, when describing building the Crystal Cathedral in Garden Grove, California, "gifts... were brought to us by God's friends whom He inspired to help build His dream..... All the money went to workers. They spent it on food, house payments, gifts to charities and children's college savings funds."[350]

If one ever wanted to relate Adam Smith to Jesus or relate Smith's *Inquiry into the Nature and Causes of the Wealth of Nations* to the Bible, the foregoing discussion of the Circular Flow of Prosperity accomplishes it. Capitalism is a mechanism—in fact the most effective mechanism yet devised—for converting God's resources to prosperity. Indeed, the whole theory of production and trade in a free, competitive economy is based on a continuous circular flow of giving and receiving—a continuous flow of goods and services and money between buyers, sellers, investors, entrepreneurs and consumers. To explain more specifically, in a free market the prevailing, equilibrium price of any product will be that price at which marginal revenue equals marginal cost. That is, in a free market the price at which a good or service is exchanged will be that price which reflects the value of the product to the buyer and which reflects the seller's production cost plus minimum profit. Value received by the buyer equals value given by the seller. This is true by definition. If the price were higher than the value to the buyer, the buyer would not buy the product, and, if the price were lower than its cost plus profit to the producer, then the producer would not supply the product. To repeat, then, in free market there is a continuous flow of equal value between buyers and sellers.

Further, as a producer becomes more efficient, more cost-effective, the price of the product will fall, more buyers will be satisfied and the producer will sell more, receiving greater income. Additionally, as a producer creates a product of higher quality at the same price, buyers will receive greater value and the producer will sell more products, receiving greater income. In these processes, workers are employed at increasing higher value jobs enabling higher wages. Everyone wins—just like it says in Scripture! Capitalism is a positive sum game.

This circular flow mindset is fascinating to observe in individuals. The Circular Flow of Prosperity is readily apparent all around us today. People who have a genuine openness to the circular flow of wealth see their own wealth increase; those who are miserly or fearful or focusing on preserving what they have or otherwise not totally open to the flow, constrain their level of wealth. Indeed, full participation in the flow of prosperity is glorious—it is the economic demonstration of the power of faith.

The concept of the "Circular Flow of Prosperity" is reflected in the familiar charge by John Wesley to "gain all you can [righteously], save [invest] all you can, give all you can."[351] Finally, Turner sums up the "Circular Flow of Prosperity" as follows: "God gave us two hands—one to receive with and one to give with; we are not made for hoarding, we are channels made for sharing." God, in return for His active, generous love of us, demands our actively generously loving others who in turn actively love others out of gratitude for the love which they receive and on and on and on, so the circle of love and prosperity continues.

Conclusion

Let us not get so enamored of the "Circular Flow of Prosperity" that we see virtue per se in an ever-accelerating flow and ever-expanding abundance. Nowhere in Scripture is there the suggestion that the purpose of worldly possessions and wealth is to satisfy the hedonism of humanity.

Worldly possessions and wealth have one and only one role: to glorify God through serving as instruments to express our love to our fellow children of God. In addition to generous philanthropy, examples of the results of capitalism include better medicines, improved education, fulfilling careers, income levels which permit free time to devote to pursuits other than subsistence, more comfortable and convenient travel, quicker and broader sources of information, refreshing recreation and entertainment, more cost-effective church facilities, and so on including the vast array of products produced by capitalistic systems at relatively high value and low cost and enjoyed broadly.

However, capitalism has stimulated the generation of wealth to such a degree that materialism and consumerism have been propelled to a level so high as to divert our attention from God's directives to use material goods moderately and with justice. "Woe to you who add house to house and join field to field till no space is left…." (Is. 5:8) "The women of Zion are haughty, walking along with outstretched necks, flirting with their eyes, tripping along with mincing steps, with ornaments jingling on their ankles. Therefore the Lord will bring sores on the head of the women of Zion." (Is. 3:16) "Woe to you who are complacent in Zion…. You lie on beds inlaid with ivory and lounge on your couches. You dine on choice lambs and fattened calves. You strum away on your harps…. You drink wine by the bowlful and use the fine lotions, but you do not grieve over the ruin of Joseph. Therefore you will be among the first to go into exile;" (Am. 6:1-7)

Clearly hedonism is not unique to capitalism, being inherent to humanity at all times and within all economic systems. As discussed in the previous chapter, "Attitudes Toward Material

Possession and Wealth," the danger of capitalism emerges from its success: that its abundant output distracts us from the sole role of wealth: to glorify God through love of all of God's creations. But, relative to generosity, capitalism also presents a major virtue to which we now turn our attention.

Chapter VIII

The Virtue of Capitalism

n the foregoing discussion of the role of material possessions and wealth we observed that the primary role of wealth was as a vehicle through which humans could pursue the Great Commandments: love God and love one another; namely, the expression of generosity.

There are two ways in which capitalism contributes to fulfilling this role: first, by permitting and emphasizing the voluntary expression of love, and, second, by embodying structural and attitudinal elements that are intrinsically generous.

Love: Voluntarism—the Great Deal Maker / Breaker

When discussing generosity in the previous chapter, we observed that a major message of Scripture is that God wants sincere hearts, not insincere heads. One of the differences in emphasis between the Old Testament and the New Testament is humanity's movement from legalism to love from the heart. "I will put my law in their minds and write it on their hearts." (Jer. 31:33) "I will put my laws in their hearts,...." (Heb. 10:16) Indeed, a common theme of Jesus regarding generosity was that tithing alone is not sufficient. "Woe to you Pharisees, because you give God a tenth of your mint, rue and all other kinds of garden herbs, but you neglect justice and the love of God." (Lk. 11:42)

Paul carries this notion further in pointing out that the establishment of laws and adherence thereto is insufficient for salvation. "Since they did not know the righteousness that comes from God and sought to establish their own, they did not submit to God's righteousness. Christ is the end of the law so that there may be righteousness for everyone who believes." (Rom. 10:3) Further, Paul asserted, "Love must be sincere." (Rom. 12:9)

The key element of the foregoing is that the act of sharing must be *genuine*. Therefore, voluntarism is regarded as the great deal maker / breaker of a society because the extent of one's voluntarism reflects the genuiness of one's love for one's fellow humans. Generosity, to be an expression of love, must be voluntary. Accordingly, therefore, some sort of political intrusion is not implied because, *coerced* sharing is not an act of love.

Presented quite clearly and profoundly throughout all of the Gospels is the notion of genuiness. It follows that all acts of love and generosity be voluntary. Nowhere in the message of Jesus is there even the hint of taxes and laws and other forms of coercion. Jesus' concern is with one's heart. Jesus never offers up any sort of social/economic/political agenda. If all were following him, pursing the kingdom of God as Jesus taught, such programs would be unnecessary, as their results would all be forthcoming voluntarily. Fr. Sirico expresses it this way, "it is dangerous to reduce our moral and civic obligations merely to paying taxes.... We need to work faithfully in our vocations and give charitably in our communities. Surely these obligations cannot be, nor should be, codified into tax law.... Each one of us has a responsibility to become intimately and personally involved in the human needs most immediate to us."[352] Nash observes, "One of the great ironies of Christian socialism is that its proponents in effect demand that the state get out its weapons and force people to fulfill the demands of Christian love."[353] Fr. James Schall, Jesuit priest on the political science faculty of Georgetown University, views this with concern, "The most important public issue today,... is that our religion and our ethics again start preaching and teaching about what we can do ourselves by the initiatives and graces that come to each of us. Otherwise, our passage from compassion to coercion will be steady and irreversible."[354]

Brown notes, "An important aspect described in Acts.... is voluntarily sharing goods among the members of the community."[355] While there was no higher priority of Paul than the collection of funds for the poor in Jerusalem, as noted by the *Dictionary of Paul and His Letters*, "It is hard to imagine any campaign more embracing of the northern Mediterranean and any project that occupied Paul's attention more than this collection for the saints,"[356] there was never any *requirement* for such giving. Financial support back to Jerusalem was given voluntarily by the churches founded by Paul who knew the critical importance of such generosity being an act of love.

Utilizing a worldly system to appease God reflects a misunderstanding of our relationship with God. We do not earn salvation through good deeds; rather our gratitude for the gift of salvation through God's grace and our complete faith in God leads us to a loving heart. "...let us draw near to God with a sincere heart in full assurance of faith..." (Heb. 10:22) As Bruce notes, "Paul taught that...Christian charity could not be a matter of external dictation; it must be exercised spontaneously and voluntarily."[357]

It is interesting to contrast the two tracks below.

"Sincere" order:

God ──▶ grace ──────▶ faith / love ──▶ trust, hope, ──▶ good deeds;
                                      obedience   prosperity

"Insincere" order:

Man ──▶ obey laws; ──▶ appearance of ──▶ "buy" God's ──▶ conspicuous
        good deeds   righteousness   favor, blessings   wealth

In summary, then, love and genuine generosity cannot be legislated, coerced. If one voluntarily gives to the poor, one is generously expressing love. Simply paying one's taxes, part of which support welfare programs for the poor, is not necessarily, although it may be, an act of generosity. To conform to the message of Scripture, generosity *must* be voluntary, *must* come from the heart. A loving heart is manifest in obedience to God and service to others, reflective of a genuine generosity. Generosity is an individual matter; a matter of each individual's heart.

Socialism, to the extent that it relies on legislated coercion to share, represents a sort of giving up on humanity. That is, socialism assumes that, because humanity is incapable of growing in righteousness, we have to formally organize ourselves in a way that statutorily requires benevolence. How contrary to the hope of Christianity! To think that legislated statutes have anything to do with true generosity is to misunderstand the matter. Therefore, by definition, socialism, by statutorily coerced preemption, is neither logically nor empirically congruous with Christianity.

A summary is provided by the late William E. Simon, former U.S. Treasury Secretary, "Gospel principles require us to give of ourselves, to be personally generous with our money and our time. Spending someone else's money through government programs is not the same thing as personal sacrifice. Sadly, all the government programs have to some extent crowded out individual initiative in helping the poor; many people figure they are already doing their fair share through the high taxes they pay.... For many decades now, politicians have spent taxpayer money as a way to ensure their own re-election."[358] (Recall our earlier discussion of hypocrisy.) Simon is not just hypothesizing. It is interesting to observe in the 1980's when President Reagan cut taxes, philanthropic contributions increased as a percent of income.[359]

Alexander concludes, "Promise. The message of the New Testament is not that we must sell our possessions and become servants. It's that we can. By God's grace we have that power. Jesus promised. We're *free to serve*."[360] (Italics mine.) Danker adds, "One cannot codify all the possibilities of neighborly behavior. Instead, one must think in terms of being a neighbor, even as God is the benefactor of humanity."[361] Heyne agrees, "the bishops' [*U.S. Bishops' Pastoral Letter on Catholic Social Teaching and the U.S. Economy*] concrete recommendations for government economic policy, far from being a concept of justice found in the New Testament, run *directly counter to it*.... What does the institution of government have to do with the radically new relationships that are to characterize the kingdom of God?.... Government is fundamentally a coercive institution. The New Testament provides no agenda for government"[362] Socialism—neighborly generosity by edict; love by law—is anathema to the Christian notion of liberation in order to express love. Socialism (of the law) and Christianity (of the heart) are logically inconsistent.

The Intrinsic Generosity of Capitalism

The economic equivalent of genuine giving is capitalism which embodies more individual freedom and is more voluntary and less statutorial than alternative economic systems.

Generosity is an area where the capitalist shines. Indeed, capitalists lead all humanity in assistance to the poor as will be discussed in a later chapter, "The Brilliant Outcomes of Capitalism." In fact, alleviating the plight of the poor might be defined as the "divine role of the capitalist."

This **Grand Contribution of the Capitalist** comes in three immense ways:

- First, the capitalist, as investor, owner and/or businesses manager, makes the capital available, primarily through reinvested profits, to finance new and expanded businesses which produce the products which, while satisfying consumer demand, create the jobs which certain of the poor can take with which to earn incomes and become unpoor. There are essentially two ways to help the poor: give them the material necessities they need or provide them the opportunity to obtain their own material necessities. The latter is often accompanied by the corollary, and probably more important, benefit of improved psychological well-being. (See Chapter X, "The Brilliant Outcomes of Capitalism.")

- Second, the capitalist, as the owner of property and generator of incomes, creates the wealth that can be taxed to support public programs to feed, house, transport and train the poor to enable them to become qualified for jobs which they can take with which to earn incomes and become unpoor.

- Third, the capitalist, as the possessor of wealth, makes voluntary contributions to a broad array of social services for the poor. An important point that is often ignored in these types of discussions is that, unless one possesses wealth and has the *capacity* to be generous, this matter of generosity is a less relevant question. The good Samaritan (Lk. 10:29-37) was able to be the good Samaritan because he was able to provide the wrappings for the wounds, the oil and wine and the cost of the inn. Indeed, he gave the innkeeper two denarii, equal to two days' wages of a laborer.[363] Joseph from Arimathea possessed the linen for a shroud for Jesus' body and had the "connections" and relationships that led to his receiving permission to take down Jesus' body. (Mt. 27:57; Mk. 15:42; Lk. 23:50: Jn. 19:38) Stated from another perspective, in order to redistribute wealth, we first have to have produced the wealth.

There is another way in which the structure of capitalism is intrinsically generous. As observed by Gilder, "Capitalism begins with giving. Not from greed, avarice, or even self-love can one expect the rewards of commerce, but from a spirit closely akin to altruism, a regard for the needs of others, a benevolent, outgoing, and courageous temper of mind.... Not taking and consuming, but giving, risking, and creating are the characteristic roles of the capitalist...."[364] Indeed, if one concentrates on the giving (on the customer), the receiving (income/profit) will take care of itself—almost a direct quote from Ray Kroc, founder of McDonald's, and straight out of the Nordstrom employee manual! This concept that sufficient profits will flow from focusing on the quality of goods or services and treating employees well is accepted by most enlightened capitalists. It is not an exaggeration to assert that every business person I know holds the attitude, "take care of the customers and employees and profits will take care of themselves."

Actually, capitalism as a system gives more than it receives. Virtually all buyers get more than they pay for. That's true. "Consumer Surplus" is the well-known economics term that describes this phenomenon. I'll explain.

Recall that the demand curve represents the various prices at which various amounts of a good or service will be demanded by consumers in any given society or market. Some consumers are willing to pay a relatively high price, and other consumers are willing to pay only a relatively low price, reflecting their individual preferences. As explained previously, the actual market price of the particular good or service is determined by the intersection of the supply and demand curves, price P in the graph below. This means that all of the consumers who were willing to pay a higher price than the market equilibrium price are paying less than the value which they are receiving. Stated another way, they are receiving greater value than they are paying for.

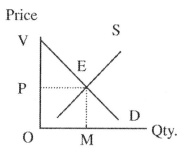

The total amount of money spent by the total market for the particular product is represented in the graph above by the area OPEM, while the aggregate value to consumers is represented by the larger area, OVEM. The excess area, PVE, is the amount by which the aggregate value exceeds the aggregate amount paid. This is referred to as "Consumer Surplus" and is an intrinsic outcome of the market system. Consumers, in the aggregate, receive more value than the amount which they pay—the generous outcome of capitalism's market system.

Capitalism is also intrinsically generous to workers. Assume the following supply and demand curve for a certain type of worker, say carpenters.

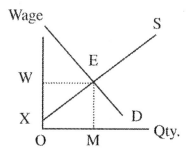

Although there are workers (OM) who would be willing to work for a lower wage than W, as represented by the supply curve of workers, they all get paid W, the market equilibrium price. The aggregate "opportunity cost" of all of the workers, that is, the total of each wage which each worker must receive in order to be induced to work as a carpenter is represented by the area OMEX. However, the total amount which all of the workers get paid is represented by the area OMEW. The "excess" going to the workers is represented by the area XEW. Workers in the aggregate receive more in wages than they would have been willing to work for.

Another way in which capitalism generates a generous surplus is through the borrowing and lending of money. Interest rates are nothing more than the price for the use of money and, as such, they are determined in the free market by the law of supply and demand. Presumably people act rationally and only borrow money when the return to them exceeds the cost of the money to them. This return can be in the form of a dollar amount such as a cash return when the money borrowed is placed into a particular investment. Or this return can be stated as a psychic return such as the utility one receives from using a car purchased with borrowed money. The amount by which the real or psychic return exceeds the interest rate paid on the loan is the "excess" or "generous" return to the borrower from the transaction. This excess return can be called a "gift" to the borrower.

A third demonstration of the intrinsic generosity of capitalism, why capitalism is a positive sum—win-win—game, is expressed by economist Peter Hill, "There can be no coerced institutional order that can be appropriately called a market... What we call a free market society is really just one based upon private property rights with certain individuals deciding to enter into voluntary exchanges. To the extent that each one decides that he or she would be better off engaging in a voluntary transaction with another individual or group of individuals, a market can be said to exist."[365] That is, one doesn't buy a ticket to a movie unless one feels that the movie is going to generate an amount of utility of a value that equals or exceeds the price of the ticket or unless the value of the utility from watching the movie equals or exceeds the value of the utility of doing something else during that same time and spending (or saving) the money elsewhere. *By definition*, we participants in the market win.

Finally, in commenting on the intrinsic generosity of the market to each of us, Turner observes, "We receive more in life that we are able to return to others. We live in houses we did not build. We sleep in beds we did not construct, in sheets and blankets we did not weave. We wear clothes we did not make. We eat food we did not grow. We read books and papers we did not write. We go to worship in buildings we did not erect."[366]

Philanthropy

Philanthropy is a way of life in most democratic capitalistic nations. Huge amounts of data have been gathered in the United States from which we can draw conclusions regarding the degree of philanthropic generosity in this particular country. Michael S. Hamilton, Assistant Professor of History at Seattle Pacific University observes, "Annual per-person disposable income in the U.S., adjusted for inflation, climbed from $8,281 to $14, 569 between 1945 and 1993.... The result was a flurry of nonprofit institution-building—religious and secular—that persuaded Americans to devote ever-larger portions of the national treasure to charitable activities. Between 1950 and 1990 the total number of nonprofit corporations increased eighty-fold, while the number of for-profit corporations increased but sevenfold. Since 1970, the amounts Americans have donated to nonprofits have outstripped the increases in Gross Domestic Product, personal income, and personal consumption expenditures."[367] The data for 1999 reflect this long term phenomenon: nearly $40 billion was donated to America's major charities, a 13% increase over the preceding year, which was more than triple the growth in the economy as measured by Gross Domestic Product of 4.2% and more than double the rise in total personal income of 5.4% and increase in corporate profits of 5.0%.[368]

One of the most fascinating characteristics of corporate philanthropy is its subordinating its own direct, short-run business interests to the general interest of society, clearly reflecting an attitude on the part of American business that a socially healthy society characterized by divergent views is good for the long run health of the economy. The multitude of "anti-business" causes funded by the Ford

Foundation, Kellogg Foundation, Carnegie Foundation, and many, many others are legendary. Indeed, Henry Ford II, upon resigning from the board of the Ford Foundation, "was moved to remind it that it was 'a creature of capitalism' and 'the system that made the foundation possible very probably is worth preserving.'"[369]

Some corporate generosity comes back to haunt some business firms. Perhaps the most dramatic example—emerging as a major issue in the 2000 Presidential campaign—is the case of U.S. pharmaceutical companies selling drugs in poorer countries at below full production costs. As observed by Lenzer and Kellner, "Price discrimination makes economic sense for a product that has a huge fixed cost (namely, the R&D that found it) and a small marginal cost (the cost of pillmaking). You charge full price to a base of prosperous customers large enough to cover the R&D…, then get whatever you can from poorer customers…. If AIDS-fighting proteases cost $14,000 a year in the U.S. but something close to manufacturing costs—$2,000 a year—in Africa, that could be seen as a humanitarian gesture. But at some point uninsured, unprosperous patients in the U.S. want to receive the humanitarian rate…. Here come price controls. There goes the R&D budget."[370]

The upsurge in philanthropy is no more dramatically demonstrated than by the new high-tech wealth. I happen to live in the midst of one of the country's high-tech centers, and I have talked with many of the new super-wealthy "techies." The most common answer to the question, "what are you going to do with all of this money?" is "Give it away." That is easy to understand; with this group money wasn't the driving force in the first place. It was the opportunity to create. *The Seattle Times* performed a study of this group, finding that "The new money is opening doors for the community. Hopelink, where the largest gifts were once $2,000 or $3,000, just received its third $1 million gift and successfully completed a $10 million capital campaign…. Julie Edsforth, 34, returned to her dream of being a social worker after nearly four years at Microsoft, leaving before she was fully vested with stock options. She co-founded… a nonprofit that helps empower girls in public schools."[371] The *Eastside Journal*, the newspaper serving the communities surrounding Microsoft's headquarters, found similar stories, "After working grueling days at Amazon.com,… Nicholas Lovejoy… and his wife, Barbara Gordon,…. 'were able to think of giving away money as a vocation,'.... After researching different causes, he and Gordon settled on environmentalism. They founded the Seattle-based Gordon-Lovejoy Foundation to make grants to projects that promote earth-friendly practices, such as the Organic Farming Research Foundation.... Julie Edsforth said she had always wanted to be a social worker. So, when she left Microsoft, she pursued a master's degree, then founded Powerful Voices, a program aimed at helping teenage girls build self-esteem."[372]

Time magazine also has studied this phenomenon of the new high-tech wealthy. "Lily Kanter, 35, is the sort of 'ordinary' multi-millionaire that Microsoft has churned out by the thousands.... as her stock doubled and redoubled. Yet she lives an ordinary life in most ways, ferrying her three dogs around in a seven-year-old Ford Explorer..... Kanter says she gets her real kicks these days mostly from the Sarosi-Kanter Charitable Foundation that she and her husband Marc started with $2 million..... 'I'm not just into writing checks... I want to see and feel the results.' Those results include Paulo Liwanag, 20, for whom Kanter's foundation paid $3,500 in tuition for a technology course.... It prepared him for a more promising career—and a $45,000 salary."[373]

It is interesting that the epitome of the new high tech wealth is also the epitome of the new philanthropy. Bill and Melinda Gates have clearly enunciated their intention to give away essentially all of their money. High on the priority for their $24 billion foundation, which gives away over $1 billion annually, have been minorities, libraries, education and health programs, particularly those oriented toward children and infectious diseases. The energy and creativity which Gates is pouring into philanthropy rivals that which he devoted to entrepreneurialism. According to *Time*, "There is a room in the Gates Foundation's new Seattle office complex that is command central for that [equipping libraries] initiative, where huge national maps are studded with pins showing which library districts have been wired—22,530 computers in 4,540 libraries in the U.S. and 4,024 computers in 1,435 libraries in Canada.... This is a war room of a battle Bill is winning. The wiring project will last until 2005, and is being expanded to libraries around the world.... The Gates Foundation has made finding a malaria vaccine a priority, along with eradicating scourges such as hookworm, hepatitis B, leishmaniasis (a parasitic disease transmitted by sand flies that affects 15 million people a year), HIV, guinea-worm disease, polio and tuberculosis. The foundation is spending nearly $400 million a year on its global-health initiative, mainly by developing new vaccines and cures and making existing cures more available to people who need them. Bill Gates scrutinizes each project and often asks very specific questions."[374]

All of the foregoing is in addition to the awesome humanitarian benefits flowing from the technological computer-oriented innovations from Gate's commercial enterprise: Microsoft.

Further, in addition to pursuing its commercial purpose, Microsoft is a leader in corporate social responsibility. As just one example of its social activities, in 1999 the company formed a national organization aimed at assisting the nation's 17 million disabled obtain jobs. Many of the kingpins of the New Economy are similarly engaged: Jim Barksdale, former Netscape CEO, giving $100 million to teach kids to read in his home state of Mississippi; Larry Ellison, founder of Oracle, providing $100 million to wire public schools for the Internet; Jim Clark, founder of Silicon Graphics, giving $150 million for biomedical research at Stanford University; Ted Turner, founder of CNN, providing $1.1 million to the United Nations; Pierre Omidyar, founder of eBay, eventually transferring 99% of his wealth to the Omidyar Foundation with the purpose of aiding programs which build a sense of community and helping nonprofits become self-sustaining[375] as well as hundreds of others giving an aggregate of billions of dollars to fund children's programs, environmental causes, medical research and delivery, cultural opportunities and myriad other humanitarian programs.

Interestingly, as a result of the overflowing prosperity in the United States today, so much money will be pouring into charities (an estimated $6-20 trillion over the next fifty years)[376] that a common subject among philanthropy professionals, both givers and receivers, is: can the charities handle all of that money in management and operations? This is what is giving rise to the new philanthropists taking an extraordinary interest in the management effectiveness of their recipient charities. As dramatic as the upsurge in the quantity of money devoted to charities is the quantity of time devoted to charities by the new wealthy providing all types of consulting. "They have a different way of seeing the world, with their charts, graphs and deadlines,' says Patti Skelton, executive director of Youth Eastside Services, which counsels kids and parents on issues such as better parenting and preventing teen violence. Two Microsoft retirees, Irene Pasternack and her husband, Edward Mills, volunteer at YES. Irene manages the volunteers, while Ed is wiring the building—and three like it—to a single network…. Venture capitalist John Doerr has spent 10% of his time on the New School Venture Fund, a $20 million organization that funds public school projects…."[377] Using their business training, the new wealthy are demanding measurable results and providing management advisory services, increasing considerably the efficiency and effectiveness with which the non-profit social service organizations deliver their services. Sometimes this is formalized. An effective example is Social Venture Partners founded in 1977 by Paul Brainerd, founder of Aldus Corp. SVP, which parcels out to charities the funds contributed by a group of donors, also provides advice and oversight to the nonprofits in much the same way that venture capital companies relate to their portfolio companies.

In short, as a result of the application of business techniques by these new young philanthropists—"social entrepreneurs"—society is not only getting more bucks, but more bang for the buck as nonprofits become better managed organizations. This contribution of time and attention has as great a dollar value as the monetary contribution and also is as beneficial, if not more so, to society.

There are millions of examples of ways in which economic growth and technological advance are flowing directly to social ends. In 1977 "Jay Backstrand left a high-paying job as marketing manager at Sun Microsystems to create VolunteerMatch.org…. [which] connects nonprofits with potential volunteers. Visitors interested in helping a child learn how to read or in working at a homeless shelter can quickly find their choice of opportunities at VolunteerMatch.org. So far, the site has matched 150,000 people with volunteer opportunities across the country. It has signed up 8,400 nonprofit organizations….:[378] The numerous African American "Gates scholars" around the country and multitude of others receiving the benefits of massive contributions and tax dollars flowing from the New Economy into education suggests that the "Digital Gap" is a misnomer. Digital profits flowing through taxes and contributions are financing impressive improvement in technological understanding and competency throughout the world. Yes, at differing rates among different societies, but almost all improving to some degree or another.

My own bank was privileged to play a role in this in-kind philanthropy by providing banking services and training to The Compass Center in Seattle, a transition program for the homeless which provides beds, meals, clothing, laundry facilities, a hygiene center, counseling and referral services, mail, and now an array of banking services (accounts, safekeeping, smart cards, and electronic deposit of social security and other federal payments). Our bank's director of administration as well as several people on his staff devoted considerable hours to this project. Ironically, much of this time was spent trying to get some of what we wanted to do for the homeless approved by the federal banking regulators. Several other business firms joined us. Easy Systems provided the teller software at no charge. Diebold donated an automatic cash dispensing machine. Loomis Wells Fargo provides cash deliveries in their armored cars at no charge. Even the American Institute of Banking is providing their course on Principles of Banking to five of the volunteer staff of the center. This project is just one tiny example of the millions of such types of corporate activity occurring in every corner of the country. It has neither been measured nor estimated, but I imagine it is safe to conjecture that the dollar value of corporate in-kind contributions as well as the work time of employees contributed to philanthropy far exceeds the billions of dollars of annual cash contributions.

Lest the foregoing examples create the incorrect impression that this burgeoning philanthropy is primarily a U.S. phenomenon, the following are noted: Dietmar Hopp, (SAP, Germany) $3.2 billion to support technical education, Li Ka-shing (Cheung Kong, Hong Kong) $19.3 million to aid disabled persons, Barry Sherman (Apotex, Canada) $17.2 million to fund health care and children's causes, Kumar Mangalam Birla (Aditya Birla Group, India) $11.2 million to support schools and hospitals, Dhirubai Ambani (Reliance, India) $10 million for drinking water in draught-prone areas, etc., etc., etc.[379] Until it was surpassed by the Gates Foundation, the UK's Wellcome Trust was the world's largest private foundation and today has assets of $20 billion. The Cairpolo Foundation, Milan, Italy, with $10 billion in assets, is one of the world's largest. Perhaps the most dramatic recent example of global philanthropy facilitated by the new high technology economy is, on September 11, the day of the terrorists attacks in New York and Washington D.C., Amazon.com converted a part of its home page to a donation box for the Red Cross. Within fifteen minutes contributions totaling $12,000 had been received; within a day contributions exceeded $1.5 million, and within two weeks 174,000 people from over 130 countries had donated nearly $7 million.

These examples are just a minuscule portion of the cornucopia of philanthropic offerings by private business firms and individuals. The outpouring of money *and personal time* devoted to helping others is probably one of the most noteworthy characteristics of the capitalistic countries of the world. Reflective of the enormous magnitude of this current phenomenon is *Forbes,* "the capitalist tool," now regularly devoting an article to philanthropy by corporations and business people. As suggested earlier, an important aspect of philanthropy that tends to get ignored in the statistics is the amount of people's time that is contributed to worthy causes, none the least of which is aiding the poor. At one time or another Boeing, Seattle's largest employer, has donated a "loaned executive" to virtually every major civic organization in this area, and I have no doubt that every major U.S. corporation has done likewise in the communities in which they are located. Adding both time and dollars, we can conclude that a common characteristic of most capitalistic nations is an overwhelming generosity on the part of the rich to the poor. Every time I see that "donations full" sign at the local Salvation Army and the Family Services Thrift Shop or observe on a fall day the throngs flowing into any college football stadium carrying their canned food donations or hearing about another record-breaking year of fund raising by the local YMCA, I see in my mind that sentence in Ron Sider's book about rich Christians, "The resources of the entire community of obedient disciples would be available to anyone in need."[380] While falling far, far short of the extent of generosity implied by the message of Jesus, the wealthy individuals in capitalistic nations are behaving in a generous manner that at least must be described as commendable.

There is no group on the face of the earth, including all of the government and church workers combined, that does as much for the world's sick, poor and downtrodden as the capitalists. As one looks around the board tables of the various philanthropic organizations in any community, it is readily observed that most of the people there are associated with business and professional firms. Stated another way, no group has benefited more from the recent burgeoning global economic growth over the past decade than the world's sick, poor and downtrodden. Nevertheless, it is recognized that enormous tasks still need to be accomplished. In terms of helping the world's sick, poor and downtrodden, the surface has barely been scratched. However, that reality should not obscure the fact that, to the extent that the global hunger and health condition has improved at all—albeit with considerable distance yet to go, it is economic prosperity that has enabled that improvement.

Special Case: Giving to One's Church

There is no lack of opportunities to contribute one's funds, and certainly active church members tend to give generously also to many worthwhile secular organizations involved in education, the arts, and human services. However, we should consider our gifts to our churches in an entirely different way than we do our gifts to, say, our alma mater, the food bank or the YMCA. It seems to me that there are at least three reasons to be extraordinarily generous in giving to one's church.

First, the church has fewer categories of sources to draw upon. Secular civic organizations receive donations not only from individuals, but also from corporations, foundations and government. Additionally, most churches have a much smaller constituency than most civic organizations. Therefore, because any church has fewer resources to call upon, it is critical that each of us members dig deep into our pockets and step forward generously.

Second, and more important, the church is related to the very source of all of the financial wherewithal that each of us has in the first place: God. Therefore, in the case of church donations, we are not giving *to*...., we are giving *back*. In this way we are explicitly recognizing the divine source of all of our good, we are demonstrating our faith in God as the source of all of our funds in the first place and that God will continue to replenish, indeed, multiply, our supply. Recall, "Everything comes from you, and we have given you only what comes from your hand." (1 Chr. 29:14) We are living within God's principles of prosperity by participating in an uninterrupted flow. And by so doing we put ourselves in a frame of mind to continue to receive His growing abundance. Recall the earlier discussion of the "Circular Flow of Prosperity."

Third, suggested by Bud Paxon, co-founder of Home Shopping Network and founder of the PAX TV Network, "God created all commerce on earth for two reasons. One is to feed and clothe His people, and the other is to fund The Great Commission."[381]

An important element of philanthropy, of course, is that genuineness and sacrifice are more important than amount. When the newborn Jesus was presented at the Temple, Mary and Joseph offered a sacrifice of "a pair of turtledoves or two young pigeons." Such a modest sacrifice, rather than a lamb, was offered by the poor. We are brought to understand that what matters to God is the sincerity and genuiness of the person making the sacrifice. The value of the sacrifice relative to the person's wealth is considerably more important than the value of the sacrifice relative to that of the sacrifices of others. "...this poor widow has put in more than all those who are contributing to the treasury. For they all contributed out of their abundance; but she out of her poverty has put in everything she had." (Mk. 12:44; Lk. 21:4) In contemporary society perhaps some wealthy people and the charities to which they give lose sight of this. Certainly, in many, many (perhaps, most) instances, a charitable donation of high market value tends to be given greater acknowledgment than the donation of low market value, regardless of the relationship of the value of the donation to the level of wealth of the donor. Hurtado reminds us, "The virtue of the widow's gift lies in her giving all she had, illustrating... the wholesale commitment for which Jesus called. Her action exemplifies...complete devotion...[and] commitment to God. The elevation of this simple woman to such an exemplary place captures the essence of Jesus' words that in God's judgment 'many who are...last [will be] first."[382]

Before leaving this discussion of philanthropy, it is of particular interest in this discussion of capitalism and Christianity to note that the great bulk of charitable contributions go to religious organizations. The $190 billion contributed in 1999 was distributed as follows:[383]

Religion	43%	Arts, Culture	6%
Education	14	Environment	3
Health	9	International	
Human Services	9	Affairs	1
		Other	15

Finally, lest the foregoing discussion create the impression that philanthropy is largely a recent phenomenon, let us repeat that an abundant generosity has been part of the fabric of America since its founding, an engrained characteristic of our culture. According to *Forbes*, in 1913 banking heiress Eleanor Widener gave $2 million to Harvard where today the Widener Library houses 3.5 million volumes, one of the most important academic collections in the world; in the 1930's Sears chairman Julius Rosenwald started a school for African-Americans; in the 1950's oil billionaire J. Paul Getty bequeathed $700 million to a charitable trust which today is now worth $5.6 billion (thanks to the profitable growth of the companies represented by the stock in which the trust invested); reclusive Howard Hughes founded the Hughes Medical Institute in the 1940's to fund genetics, cell biology, immunology and neuro-science researches at academic labs; in the early 1900's A. N. Pritzker, founder of Hyatt Hotels, donated millions of dollars to Michael Reese Hospital in Chicago which had treated him in 1881 when a young Russian immigrant.[384] Emory University's Candler School of Theology reflects the generosity and values of Asa G. Candler, the founder of Coca-Cola, and Moody Bible Institute similarly benefited from the spiritual commitment of Henry P. Crowell of Quaker Oats. Indeed, virtually every major seminary in the United States has received a substantial portion of its funding from wealth generated through capitalism. Today corporate and personal generosity flourishes as an expected part of our culture. Economist Paul McCracken observes, "Most corporations today have a contri-butions budget, and corporate funds are flowing to ... eleemosynary activities. Corporate managers are expected to give time and energy to civic projects."[385]

Included for completeness sake in this discussion is the argument by some that philanthropy is not in any way an appropriate activity by business firms for two reasons. First, it is argued that humanity benefits most by the corporation devoting all of its time and attention and financial resources to doing solely what it was created to do: produce and distribute goods and services as efficiently as possible in order to minimize cost and at a quality that maximizes value. Milton Friedman and John Hood have made convincing arguments that aggregate social welfare is maximized when firms act solely to maximize profits. Their argument is eloquently clear and simple: a nation's social welfare is a function of a nation's wealth, and a nation's wealth is maximized by business firms acting in a way to maximize profits. In this way tax payments to government are maximized and wages and dividends to employees and owners are maximized in turn maximizing individual philanthropy. This argument makes a great deal of sense. The second reason for business firms refraining from making philanthropic contributions holds that, rather than make the philanthropic allocation decision corporately, the firm should instead increase the wages to employees and dividends to the owners who then can make the philanthropic allocation decision individually. While I do not subscribe to this notion, instead feeling that a legitimate activity of a business firm is expressing the collective love of its employees and owners, nevertheless it is worthy of serious consideration.

An Important Consideration: Self Interest

There are those who assert that, rather than love and generosity, the key mind-set of capitalistic societies is self-interest as reflected in the profit motive. But there are two very important distinctions to keep in mind in this regard.

First, self-interest, as distinguished from selfishness, is acknowledged as an acceptable human trait in the Bible. In the Old Testament God declares so through Moses, "love your neighbor as yourself." (Lv. 19:18), and in the New Testament Jesus instructs, "Love your neighbor as yourself." (Mt. 22:39) While clearly this passage is not advocating selfish self-love, there seems to be general agreement among theologians that a reasonable level of personal concern is natural and legitimate. Regardless of the economic system or even if one's vocation is other than business, humans' motivation to achieve stems to a large degree from self-interest—to be a high ranking government official, an accomplished violinist, an effective pastor—even if the self-interest is solely complete self-actualization or achievement of potential. Even, indeed, is the desire to be the most selfless human God ever created an expression of self-interest? Is it not "self" who has that desire?

Second, to the same extent and in the same way as capitalism, Christianity embodies self-interest. While Jesus exhorted us to love one another simply because we all are creations of God, he nevertheless on occasion positions God as the Great Patron, the Great Benefactor. "But love your enemies, do good to them,…. Then your *reward* will be great, and you will be sons of the Most High." (Lk. 6:35) (italics mine) Green notes, "Jesus observes people can guarantee God's future, eternal hospitality by assisting the poor in the present (Lk. 16:9)"[386] Paul and every single preacher since have sought to bring people to Jesus Christ by appealing to people's self-interest in receiving God's gift of salvation. The apostle Paul utilizes an amazing array of metaphors to capture our attention and receive his message, even equating achieving salvation to winning a gold medal at the Olympic Games! "Do you not know that in a race all the runners run, but only one gets the *prize*? Run in such a way as to get the *prize*. Everyone who competes in the games goes into strict training. They do it to get a crown that will not last; but we do it to get a crown that will last forever. Therefore, I do not run like a man running aimlessly; I do not fight like a man beating the air. No, I beat my body and make it my slave so that after I have preached to others, I myself will not be disqualified for the *prize*." (1 Cor. 9:24-27) Even when appearing to abandon all worldly concerns, it is for the purpose of self-interest: "…*that I may gain* Christ….I want to know Christ…., becoming like him in his death, and so, somehow, *to attain* to the resurrection from the dead." (Phil. 3:7-11) "Everyone who calls upon the Lord will be saved." (Rom. 10:13) "So do not throw away your confidence; it will be *richly rewarded*. You need to persevere so that when you have done the will of God, you *will receive* what he has promised. (Heb. 10:35,36) "do good,…and…be generous and willing to share. In this way they will *lay up treasure for themselves* as a firm foundation for the coming age, so that they may *take hold* of the life that is truly life." (1 Tm. 6:18-19) (all italics mine) These are just five passages of many of such appeals found throughout the New Testament. Paul, ever the salesman, repeated his consistent message: faithfully accept God's grace *so that* you *gain* salvation. From Genesis through Revelation God endeavors to motivate particular attitudes and behavior on the part of humans by holding out the reward of receiving God's blessings. The *Dictionary of Paul and His Letters* observes, "Rewards as Paul views them therefore play a most important role in encouraging Christ's followers to be faithful and diligent in the ministries to which each is called. Far from being questionable in any way, they are a most gracious provision by God to motivate his children to run the race successfully, and so to enjoy both in this life and in that to come the blessing of salvation."[387] And from the *Dictionary of the Later New Testament and Its Developments*, "This same understanding of rewards is carried on in the remainder of the New Testament.... Like the teaching of Jesus and Paul, here the prospect of rewards is used to motivate the readers to turn from sinful ways and to live holy lives."[388] There may be reasons for the Christian to object to capitalism but mere self-interest is not one of them.

The notion of self-interest is expanded further upon by Griffiths who notes, "it is easy to misunderstand the expression of self-interest.... Self-interest is a characteristic of the highest as well as the lowest kind of human behaviour. A person may act in a self-interested way for a host of reasons, such as the carrying out of responsibilities on behalf of family, friends, colleagues, community or Church. Indeed, as Christians we can go further and argue that self-interest as a characteristic of human behaviour cannot be divorced from that self-respect of which our Lord spoke when he instructed us to love our neighbours as ourselves.... [I]f we take the Bible seriously when it says that God loves each one of us, then we should be able to love ourselves.... Not only that, but in the ministry of our Lord the call to repent, to believe, to follow, to forgive is an appeal to a legitimate human self-interest. It is not selfishness."[389]

Finally, Griffiths observes, "It is frequently thought that because business depends on the pursuit of profit, this reduces those in business to the level of economic man,... In business, behaviour is selfish and aggressive while in the home or in the community people are caring and considerate, concerned with the good of others rather than their own narrow self-interest. Such a Jekyll-and-Hyde existence is impossible to justify either logically or empirically. There is no doubt that certain individuals in business are selfish, aggressive and brutish, but it requires more than guilt by association with money to show that this is an inevitable outcome. Similar individuals exist in all walks of life. In principle, there is no reason whatsoever why people should behave in a dualistic manner. For the person who decides to live by certain moral principles, there need be no difference between behaviour in a market and in a non-market situation. An executive in a business corporation can if he so wishes be just as concerned for his staff as a school teacher might be for pupils, an officer for soldiers, a community worker of the elderly or a vicar for parishioners…. Selfishness, aggression and rivalry may be just as common in schools, local authorities and even families as in business…. Moral and immoral behavior occurs in all human institutions. What determines the morality of behaviour is not the institutions in which decisions are made but the individuals who are making the decisions."[390] And is it not the role of the church to bring individuals to righteous behavior?

Finally, often accompanying the criticism of self-interest within capitalism is the criticism of competitiveness within capitalism. Competitiveness has nothing to do with the system. Competitiveness has to do with two things: the nature of humanity and the scarcity of resources. As noted by Nash, "Competition exists whenever the scarcity of something people prize or value results in more people wanting it than can have it."[391] Students compete for grades, workers compete for promotions, performers compete for accolades, churches compete for members, government officials compete for power. The beauty of the market system is its providing a rational, voluntary, peaceful method for resolving competitive situations, as buyers and sellers daily freely exchange. Furthermore, in order to prevail against competitors a business firm is required to provide the cooperative, creative, responsive service to others, which I will address in Chapter XII.

Conclusion

It is in Romans that we find the statement of *The Great Privilege and Great Responsibility of Christianity:* "Through him and for his name's sake, we received grace and apostleship to call people…to the obedience that comes from faith." (Rom. 1:5) Christians are privileged in that God has forgiven our sins and we have been given the gift of righteousness through faith. Christians are responsible to maintain an unwavering belief in Jesus Christ, to accept him as Lord and Savior and in our daily lives witness to God's Good News through loving our fellow humans. Stated another way, the privilege of Christianity is the gift of freedom from the power of sin and from the domination of the law. The responsibility of Christians is to serve God by serving God's creations. Loving generosity is a divine imperative.

It follows, then, that the ultimate role of material possessions is their being used toward this end. "In a large house there are articles not only of gold and silver, but also of wood and clay; some are for noble purposes and some for ignoble. If a man cleanses himself from the latter, he will be an instrument for noble purposes, made holy, useful to the Master and prepared to do any good work." (2 Tm. 2:20-21) This notion will be expanded upon later in Chapter XIII, "Implications for Capitalists." It is not the possession of wealth that is relevant. It is what one does with wealth that is relevant, and more particularly, one's ability to distinguish between worldly riches and heavenly riches, that is relevant. Further, "so whether you eat or drink or whatever you do, do it all for the glory of God." (1 Cor. 10:33)

Practicing a high level of generosity flows from four considerations.

> First is the belief that we all are creations of God and therefore are brothers and sisters and therefore love each other and therefore share a responsibility for each other. "... so in Christ we who are many form one body, and each member belongs to all the others." (Rom. 12:5)

> Second is the notion that every good thing comes from God and, therefore to the extent that I give something I possess to God via giving to the less advantaged ("...whatever you did for one of the least, you did for me." Mt. 25:40), I am not giving something of mine *to;* rather, I am giving something of God's *back.*

> Third is the concept that, because every good thing comes from God, to the extent that I possess some of it, I am

simply in the flow of prosperity from God. In turn, I have the responsibility not to block the flow, but rather to serve as a conduit through which the flow continues and, interestingly, grows.

Fourth, the act of generosity implies the material capacity to be generous.

In this regard the type of economic system becomes relevant to the extent that it is conducive to (1) generating the wealth with which to be generous and (2) embodying a practice of free choice in order to permit voluntary, genuine generosity to occur and therefore be reflective of love. A lesson of Paul in Romans is the message that by trusting in the Holy Spirit, life can be a process of *growth* in our relationship with Jesus Christ. One way we participate in this growth is through freely, voluntarily serving God by serving all mankind. Capitalism, with its emphasis on creation and freely serving the marketplace, is an economic system that is compatible with this notion.

Novak sums up this notion in an interesting way, "If such a society were to be formally committed in its central institutions to a Christian vision of justice and love, it might still retain some elements of democracy and some elements of markets and incentives. For there is an inner consonance between the acts of faith and conscience common to Judaism and Christianity and the rights protected by democracy."[392] Finally, an empirical observation by Novak, "Under democratic capitalism in Great Britain, the United States and elsewhere, the history of community service, universal education, social work, philanthropy, and concern for the needy.... rivals in quantity, quality, organization, and dedication any other era of church history."[393]

As discussed above, one of the roles of material possessions is to serve God by loving one's neighbor through sharing one's money and possessions. If we are to give to the poor and to the church and to other ends that further the pursuit of the kingdom of God, then it is implied that we have the material wherewithal to do that. What is needed is an attitudinal mindset, rather than the pursuit of some over-riding socio-economic structure. Indeed, we have seen the economic degeneration and suffering in those societies whose primary emphasis is on distribution rather than production. Further, Fuller and Rice note, contrary to the utterances of utopians, "Christians can never 'build the kingdom of God' on earth—such language is completely foreign to the New Testament....you can *receive* the kingdom of God, *enter* it, *seek* it. But you can never *build* it....Rather, it is the Christian task, by obeying the commandment of love, to shape society....(without) taking this world too seriously."[394]

Finally, a critical point. The true test of the genuineness of one's generosity, the clear indicator of the sincerity of one's heart, the manifest reflection of the fullness of one's love is the degree of *sacrifice* involved. As Scott notes in his commentary on 2 Corinthians 8:1-15, "Paul...wants them to respond...voluntarily and from the heart. Only in this way would their gift be an expression of grace..... The Corinthians are to abound in the grace of self-sacrificial giving to the Jerusalem saints, because Christ gave himself.... [W]hat counts is not the kind of offering but the heart of the offerer. Giving sacrificially of one's substance,...makes the offering acceptable to God."[395]

Chapter IX

The Conduciveness of Capitalism to Christianity

===================

Before proceeding, it must again be acknowledged that the primary message of Christianity has to do with the attitudes and behavior of individuals. As I have asserted earlier, Jesus was not advocating any particular social, political or economic system. Nowhere in Scripture is there a discussion of economic theory or of economic systems. Rather, Jesus' message, love God and love each other, transcended such a mundane topic. Furthermore, ultimate achievement of Jesus' message will bring about the right social, political and economic order as a matter of course.

Accordingly, the title of this chapter is not intended to be presumptuous. History has shown that in order to flourish Christianity does not need the conduciveness of capitalism nor of any human system. Commencing with a small band of eleven, God has shepherded his flock through horrible persecutions and vicious oppression until today the followers of Jesus Christ extend to all the corners of the earth. God has been in charge in fostering Jesus Christ's church from the beginning when God freed Peter from Herod's prison where he was "sleeping between two soldiers, bound with two chains, and sentries stood guard at the entrance,..." (Acts 12:6) to modern times, as an example, from Mark Noll, professor of Christian thought and professor of history at Wheaton

271

College, "… the story of Christian survival… will show how the number of Christians in China grew from less than one million Protestants and three million Catholics in 1949, when the Western missionaries were expelled and Mao unleashed his campaign against the churches, to the tens of millions that exist today…."[396] God is in charge. God works in ways that are incomprehensible to us humans. Perhaps one of the greatest examples is the transformation of Saul. "On that day a great persecution broke out against the church at Jerusalem, and all except the apostles were scattered throughout Judea and Samaria. Godly men buried Stephen…. But Saul began to destroy the church." (Acts 8:2,3) But then, "Those who had been scattered preached the word wherever they went." (Acts 8:4) And eventually, "Placing his [Ananias'] hands on Saul, he said,… 'Jesus, who appeared to you on the road as you were coming here has sent me so that you may see again and be filled with the Holy Spirit'…. Saul spent several days with the disciples in Damascus. At once he began to preach in the synagogues that Jesus is the Son of God." (Acts 9:17-20)

No, Christianity does not need the conduciveness of capitalism. Noll further notes, "The church survives by the mercy of God, not because of the wisdom, purity or consistent faithfulness of Christians."[397] Moxnes explains further, "Since the flow of resources was structured according to the *power* in a society, Luke saw them as ultimately subject to the power of God, the creator and keeper of life."[398] God has been in charge, is in charge and will be in charge.

The foregoing notwithstanding, because humankind is now in the in-between times, the "already" of God's incarnation on earth as Jesus and the "not yet" of Parousia, the second coming, and humankind has not yet accomplished Jesus' charge and remains sinful, this book will proceed with its discussion of the connection between religion and economics. More specifically, we will examine the ways in which capitalism is conducive to the practice of Christianity.

Capitalism wins on two fronts. It wins on the theoretical and conceptual front, being in accord with the true nature of humankind and with the relationship between God and humans, as shown in the previous discussion. The following discussion will show that capitalism also wins on the empirical front, how it has affected the actual behavior and condition of humanity. To summarize the conclusion first, let me present the observation of the finance minister of Sweden in the 1980's as quoted by Stanford Professor Seymour Martin Lipset, "The market economy's facility for change and development and therefore economic growth has done more to eliminate poverty and the exploitation of the working class than any political intervention in the market's system of distribution."[399] Why is this the case? It is because of capitalism's empirical performance being in accord with Christianity.

Hope and Optimism

The message of hope and optimism is found throughout Scripture. "For I know the plans I have for you,' declares the LORD, 'plans to prosper you and not to harm you, plans to give you hope and a future." (Jer. 29:11) Former pastor and World Bank economist David Beckman observes, "The modern sense of progress is... rooted in the biblical experience. Ancient Israel, unlike the rest of the ancient world, believed that history was going somewhere new and better.... Their Lord was always on the move—freeing them from slavery, taking them to a new land,... and promising a new creation, finally even taking on human flesh. He would never allow his people to become too settled."[400] Wright expands, "Yet the Old Testament is actually full of boundaries that God's people were challenged to cross,... Abraham leaving Ur for the land of promise; Jacob...to Egypt; the exodus generation crossing the Sea of Reeds from slavery to freedom; the Deuteronomic generation, about to cross the Jordan into the land; the generation that went to Babylon; and the generation that faced the challenge of returning.... In each case, the primary challenge was faith and loyalty in the midst of change."[401]

Commencing with the resurrection, Christianity has been a religion of hope—"the Gospels," "the Good News." Christianity, with its emphasis on the eschatological question, points us toward the future. "... he who stands firm to the end will be saved." (Mt. 24:13) "Then the end will come, when he hands over the kingdom to God the Father...." (1 Cor. 15:24) "Therefore, since we have been justified through faith, we have peace with God through our Lord Jesus Christ, through whom we have gained access by faith into this grace in which we now stand. And we rejoice in the hope of the glory of God." (Rom. 5:2) Even in the face of adversity, there is reason for hope. "...we also rejoice in our sufferings, because we know that suffering produces perseverance; perseverance, character; and character, hope. And hope does not disappoint us, because God has poured out his love into our hearts by the Holy Spirit,..." (Rom. 5:3-5) Edwards in his commentary on Romans notes, "Hope, which both begins (v.2) and ends (vv. 4-5) the sequence, means to live by the promises of God. The stimulus to this chain reaction is *faith*."[402]

Milnes asserts, "As the creation of the Holy Spirit, the church looks constantly towards the future. The Spirit is the life of the new era of the fulfilled kingdom of God, and hence the foretaste of the coming glory."[403] "Hope, the assured and joyful anticipation of the future triumph of God's purposes and the glorious coming of our Lord Jesus, is a shining mark of the religion of the New Testament."[404] Guthrie notes, "Between the times' (between Easter and the end), the deadly battle between God and the powers of darkness still goes on, but the victory of Christ that has been won is the guarantee of the final victory that is surely on the way."[405] Bruce agrees, "The crucial event of all time is the sacrifice of Calvary; that was the decisive victory which has ensured the final triumph of God's cause and God's people over the forces opposed to them."[406]

Perhaps the clearest statement of hope and optimism is found in the discussion of faith in the book of Hebrews. "Now faith is being sure of what we hope for and certain of what we do not see." (Heb. 11:1) Christians understand that connecting with God through prayer, combined with complete faith and the righteous thoughts and behavior which complete faith leads to, combined with gratitude for God's grace, is leading to eternal life in the Kingdom of God. As Goldingay observes, throughout the Bible "... the stories challenge readers to be faithful to God and their faith, to trust that God is the Lord of the secrets of world history, and to expect to find that even in an alien environment, they may be able not only to survive, but to triumph."[407]

Faith is not a static concept implying sit and wait. Rather, faith is a dynamic concept; it is an active response to God, demonstrating expectation of God's blessings. "But my righteous one will *live* by faith." (Heb. 10:38) (italics mine) As noted by Donald A. Hagner, professor of new Testament at Fuller Theological Seminary, "It is the expression of faith rather than the conviction of faith that is the author's point in this chapter. The obedient response of faith substantiates what is promised.... The author's argument is that faith results in conduct that points unmistakably to the reality of what is not yet seen.... Faith that is authentic recognizes the reality of the unseen and allows itself to be governed by that reality."[408] And in 1 Peter we are told, "...he has given us a new birth into a *living* hope..." (1 Pt. 1:3) (italics mine)

Capitalism is the economics of hope. While Christian hope is spiritual hope, nonetheless, the contemporary economics equivalent is capitalistic entrepreneurialism wherein one ventures forth taking risks and expending effort, persevering in *expectation* of a return. Capitalism, with its emphasis on investment with an expectation of return, points us toward the future. Creativity—expressing our God-given talents through our calling—combined with sound analysis and planning accompanied by enlightened, righteous behavior, leads to satisfactory outcomes for all parties involved. Satisfactory earthly returns reflecting the value of economic contribution accrue to all participants. Further, as discussed earlier, the circular flow of prosperity, with ever-expanding circles of wealth, reflects a positive sum game. Everyone wins; some more than others; but everyone— even one outside of the game—wins.

Both systems, religious (Christianity) and economic (capitalism), are oriented toward the future with hope and positive expectation. The present is devoted to connecting with God in order to receive insights regarding one's purpose, to express gratitude for God's grace, to unleash one's creative abilities, and, in community with others, to express love toward one's fellow human beings.

In Chapter III, "The Genius of Capitalism: Accommodating Both Characteristics of Humanity," I presented a table displaying the attributes of socialism and of capitalism. Going back and reviewing that table clearly reveals capitalism as a dynamic system of positive expectation, oriented toward others. Fascinatingly, the very first step that any and every capitalistic entrepreneur must take is *identifying others' needs*. If your teen-age child said to you "this summer I want to go into business for myself," and asks, "what do you suggest I do?" your first response would be, "identify what people need that you have the ability to provide."

Capitalism, and particularly the misunderstood and therefore maligned supply-side economics, is built on a psychology of saving and self-discipline with an eye toward the future reflected in capital accumulation, investment and creative innovation—in short, on economic and social progress. And it is capitalism's empirically demonstrated and clearly evident record of progress that sustains continued hope—not just materialistic progress and hope, but progress and hope for many other dimensions of humanity: improved health care, more vibrant cultural experiences, job opportunities for the poor, unleashed outlets for expressing one's creativity, expanded and quickened communication, better education materials and facilities, expanded and more suitable religious facilities, even extra largess to transport in huge quantities to the poor around the globe. If the definition of hope is optimism toward the future, than capitalism is the economics of hope.

The foregoing is amply demonstrated throughout the world. In 1962 and 1963 economists Rose and Nobel laureate Milton Friedman traveled to twenty-one countries, reporting in *Harpers*, "Whenever we found any large element of individual freedom, some beauty in the ordinary life of the ordinary man, some measure of real progress in the material comforts at his disposal, and a live hope of further progress in the future—there we also found that the private market was the main device being used to organize economic activity."[409]

Of course the present day epitome of capitalistic optimism are the new high-tech entrepreneurs and operatives. The distinguished scholar Dinesh D'Souza has dubbed them, "The Party of Yeah." These enthusiastic optimists, according to D'Souza "assert that in previous eras the priest, the intellectual, and the bureaucrat have all tried to lead society, and all have failed miserably. They were unable to solve the problem of scarcity. So all they did was redistribute resources or try to reconcile people to living in degradation."[410] Capitalism, and the entrepreneurial fervor it unleashes, while not "solving" the problem of scarcity, has overcome the problem of scarcity by its abundant wealth creation.

Gilder summarizes, "Capitalism... [is based] on optimism and faith.... Capitalist production entails trust—in one's neighbors, in one's society, and in the compensatory logic of the cosmos. Search and you shall find; give and you will be given unto;.... In a socialist economy,... rationality rules, and it rules out the awesome uncertainties and commensurate acts of faith that are indispensable to an expanding and innovative system. Under capitalism, the ventures of reason are launched into a world ruled by morality and Providence. [Products] will succeed only to the extent that they.... spring from an understanding of the needs of others. They depend on faith in an essentially fair and responsive humanity. In such a world... one can take initiatives amid radical perils and uncertainties. When faith dies, so does enterprise.... The man who seeks assurance and certainty lives in the past,... and his policies, ... are necessarily reactionary. The man who shapes the future must live ever in doubt and thus thrive on faith."[411] Therefore, to the extent that they both have as their primary focus the future and as their primary mind-set, hope and optimism, capitalism and Christianity are compatible.

However, lest I be misinterpreted, an important distinction should be made. When relating the "hope and optimism" of capitalism to the "hope and optimism" of Christianity the only similarity I am talking about is a mind-set. I do not in any way want to imply that the characteristics of capitalism are making the world a more God-like world. Christian hope and optimism do not refer only, nor even primarily, to the worldly condition, as I will return to at the end of this book. As Guthrie notes, "The justice, freedom, and peace of the kingdom of God will not come *within* history as the result of human efforts; it will come at the *end* of history as the result of what only God can and will do."[412] Further, as Gasque points out, "While the kingdom of God remains the eschatological hope, between now and then we live in the realism of sin. Therefore the concept of present utopianism is invalid. The implications are that all human structures and systems must take man's fallenness into consideration."[413] Accordingly, therefore, Christian hope and entrepreneurial hope are two different things, but, nevertheless, they both embody a consistent, faith-based optimism.

Societal Values and Norms

Capitalism, in order to work, requires the same societal values and norms as those embraced by Christianity; namely, liberty, trust, genuineness, egalitarianism, integrity, and justice. Further, capitalism, to remain viable, requires a democratic political system, a respected legal system, and a moral ethical system, the very characteristics of a society conducive to the church flourishing.

This point cannot be made strongly enough and often gets ignored. When the history books on the 21st Century are written, the great dramatic lesson of the conversion by the Soviet Union from communism to "capitalism" is its demonstration that the critical requirement—the necessary precedent condition—to capitalism functioning is the existence of (1) political stability and (2) the unequivocal commitment of the populace to a high moral order. When graft and corruption, common to many government-dominated societies, are pervasive, chaos and collapse ensue as we have observed first hand today in Russia at the end of the 21st Century. When the government dominated economy of Russia converted to a market economy, the top Communist officials took with them their former values and practices, resulting in a graft-ridden economy dominated by an elite group of corrupt oligarchs and their sordid organizations. Certainly, this is a major lesson of the Old Testament as the Israelites experienced a long series of unrighteous rulers and unrighteous societies.

It is exciting to observe that the spread of capitalism, particularly in the form of microenterprise, is contributing to the promulgation of societal values that are in concert with the values of Christianity. Listen to a report by K. W. Taylor, chairman of the Oxford Conference committee that directed a study of nongovernmental organizations and entrepreneurialship, "In our training seminars as well as personal consultancy…, we emphasize the value of doing the right thing in all areas of the business: to offer the best services to the customer, to deal with competition healthily and to pay taxes whenever due. In short, we promote the practices of the right business ethics in a climate where dishonesty, corruption and expediency are the rule."[414]

Indeed, it is the similarities of the cultural values which cause capitalism and Christianity to be so compatible. Had Russia been a Christian state committed to trust and justice with the attendant institutions such as the rule of law, perhaps the conversion to a market economy would have been easier. Hay observes, "A market economy can only operate successfully if there is acceptance of standards of honesty, truth, trust…."[415] Fr. Sirico agrees, "To function effectively, markets require a certain moral context and perspective on the part of entrepreneurs who participate in market activities. What business could long exist without a reputation for honesty, quality workmanship, civility, and courtesy? For if a firm establishes a reputation for abusing its customers, people will cease to do their business there; in a market system based upon the principle of voluntary exchange, consumers have the freedom to refuse to do business with such firms.... In a free-market system, people succeed not by oppressing their neighbors but by serving them."[416]

Other phony, pseudo-capitalistic nations have been exposed by the recent economic collapses in Southeast Asia. "Crony capitalism," wherein business firms appear to be but in fact are not subject to the disciplines of a free market but are propped up by political favoritism or family connections, eventually implodes. This deception of pseudo-capitalism can be dangerous to those doing business with such firms and must be guarded against. Pseudo-capitalism has failed in certain countries, not because of an intrinsic deficiency of capitalism, but because of the absence of the necessary cultural, political and social framework. Accordingly, eventual recovery and sustainability of many of the Southeast Asia economies is more of a cultural than an economic challenge.

It must be acknowledged that even in enlightened capitalistic economies such as the United States and Western Europe there are many rogue players. As a result, such economies are not laissez faire, but are regulated in order to make certain anti-social behavior illegal. Hay notes, "Examples are the regulation of securities and insurance markets to prevent fraud, the development of consumer protection legislation, and the increased sophistication of competition authorities in regulation behaviour in markets where the participants no longer have any agreed basis for what is 'fair' competition."[417] Regulating capitalism is also intended to prevent monopolies, predatory pricing, tied products, raping resources, etc.

One final introductory comment before discussing society values. Conspicuous in the following discussion to some will be the absence of the value of "security" which seems to be the primary goal of many social welfare economists. It is unfortunate that so many embrace the goal of "security" because in a world of sinful humans security is an illusive goal. To a child of God there is only one kind of security worth contemplating: that which comes from within—that total and complete security which comes from total and complete faith in and reliance upon God. Material "security" lacks sufficient dignity and even practical reality to be considered here.

Liberty

Flowing from the nature of humans as creations of God is the notion of the intrinsic virtue of individual liberty. As Britain's Lord Acton observed in "The History of Freedom in Christianity" written in 1877, the origin of liberty can be traced to the ancient Hebrew doctrine of a higher law that applies to everyone, including rulers. Further, Acton asserts, "Liberty is not a means to a higher political end. It is itself the highest political end.... Liberty alone demands for its realisation the limitation of the public authority.... Power tends to corrupt and absolute power corrupts absolutely."[418] However, individual liberty does not imply some sort of "go it alone" social system. Equally intrinsic as liberty to our nature as children of God is the state of all being brothers and sisters and therefore in the same family and therefore with mutual responsibility for each other's wellbeing. Christianity is a religion of community.

Therefore, we are talking about a particular type of liberty. An inspiring Biblical discourse on spiritual liberty is found in the entire first half (chapters 1-8) of Paul's letter to the Romans. "... through Christ Jesus the law of the Spirit of life set me free from the law of sin and death." (Rom. 8:2) Similarly, Paul's letter to the Galatians, which has been called the "Magna Charta of Christian liberty," asserts, "It is for freedom that Christ has set us free." (Gal. 5:1) However, a critically important qualification must be made. Paul is referring to a completely different type of freedom: spiritual freedom. As noted by Edwards, "The cross of Christ has once and for all broken the claim and power of evil over the lives of believers..... [but] Christians may still live with the effects of sin, but they do not live under its *authority*.... Christians are alerted to the ways of sin and are no longer ignorant and unresisting accomplices to its work."[419]

Further, freedom and liberty are not license. The ultimate liberator is Jesus Christ in that He liberates us from the bondage of sin by granting us, not the freedom to do what we want, but the liberty to choose what we ought. God even permits us to choose sin—so great is His commitment to our dignity that He will never force our free will. Accordingly, perhaps the second part of that verse in Galatians is more important: "Stand firm, then, and do not let yourselves be burdened again by a yoke of slavery." (Gal. 5:1) To a broad extent we humans in capitalistic societies have willingly put on the yoke of consumerism, as I discussed in the chapter, "Attitudes Toward Material Possessions and Wealth."

Believers in Jesus Christ immediately surrender to a new type of bondage as they become willing slaves of their Lord Jesus Christ. Accordingly, while one becomes liberated, one becomes liberated to pursue a life of righteousness. "You have been set free from sin and have become slaves to righteousness." (Rom. 6:18) As creations of God, we are meant to be free to express our love of God and love of one another. Indeed, such freedom is accompanied by huge responsibilities. As Lacordaire, 19th Century priest at the Cathedral of Notre Dame, asserts, "Therefore the Gospel, which is the very naturalization of charity, was not a declaration of the rights of man, but a declaration of his duties."[420]

Capitalism, which is based on individual choice and private property functioning within a free market system, both requires and is protective of a political system embodying individual liberty. Many classic tomes have been written on this subject including the works of Say, Bastiat, Hayek, von Mises, Acton and more recently the works of Kristol, Friedman and Novak. It therefore would be redundant and of considerably inferior quality for me to expand further on this subject in this space. I simply will summarize by a statement of Novak, "... modern democracy and modern capitalism proceed from identical historical impulses. These impulses had moral form before institutions were invented to realize them; they aimed (1) to limit the power of the state, in defense against tyranny and stagnation; and (2) to liberate the energies of individuals and independently organized communities."[421] Novak asserts further, "Liberty is the reason God made the universe. He wanted one creature... to be able to *choose* to reciprocate his proffered friendship."[422]

A common thread among the writings of all of the great scholars and philosophers on liberty is that political freedom requires private property. Without private property the means and security for political dissent do not exist, and therefore there is no genuine political freedom. Nash states, "Private ownership of property is an important buffer against any exorbitant consolidation of power by government."[423] The economic system embodying private property is capitalism. Irving Kristol observes, "to collectivize economic life you have to coerce all sorts of other institutions (e.g. the trade unions, the media, the educational system) and to limit individual freedom in all sorts of ways (e.g., freedom to travel, freedom to 'drop out' from the world of work, freedom to choose the kind of education one prefers) if a 'planned society' is to function efficiently."[424]

Indeed, liberty is important not only as an end in itself, recognizing humans as creations of God, but it also performs the very utilitarian function of unleashing the creative and innovative skills and proclivities of humans which in turn advances all of humankind. Heyne notes, "Reasonably secure property rights and their important corollary, freedom to exchange those rights, are necessary conditions for the evolution of a successful commercial society in which people cooperate effectively in creating and using resources to serve one another's wants, so economic growth occurs. In the absence of these conditions, poverty is assured,...."[425]

Schall makes the empirical observation, "[W]hen the state owns the property, schools, bureaucracies, farms, and industry, not to mention the newspapers and TV, not only is their little prosperity, there is even less personal freedom and dignity.... When individuals are free to pursue their own goals within a truly limited, responsible state, there will be real development and liberty."[426] Sider notes, "Biblical principles point in the direction of decentralized private ownership that allows families to control their economic destinies. As stewards of...economic resources that belong ultimately to God, they have the responsibility and privilege of earning their own way and sharing generously with others. This kind of decentralized economic system empowers all people to be coworkers with God. It also protects everyone against centralized economic power that might threaten freedom and promote totalitarianism."[427]

Finally, the perspective from John Paul II, "The modern *business economy* has positive aspects. Its basis is human freedom.... Economic activity is indeed but one sector in a great variety of human activities, and like every other sector, it includes the right to freedom, as well as the duty of making responsible use of freedom."[428] Beckman warns, "Much of the freedom of the West is wasted. Too many people trudge ahead in a bland, consumerist conformity, taking whatever jobs pay best.... Most people, also

Christians, will probably continue to conform more closely to the affluent life-styles we have come to consider normal.... But,... time and energy we are not spending in unsatisfying ways can be freed for other purposes, if we are at all open to God."[429]

Irving Kristol provides us with a bridge between the previous discussion of liberty with the following examination of egalitarianism, "It is the diffusion of wealth and power and status in a market economy that creates the 'social space' within which civil and political liberty can flower or at least be preserved to some degree."[430] Nash expands, "Economic freedom is a necessary condition for personal and political liberty.... Economic freedom aids the existence and development of political liberty by helping to check the concentration of too much power in the hands of too few people. As long as a large percentage of the people in a society exercise ownership control, power within that society will be more widely diffused.... When the master becomes the state, obedience becomes a prerequisite to employment and to life itself."[431]

Egalitarianism

When it came to bringing people to the kingdom of God, Jesus was all-inclusive. As Green observes, "The message of Jesus is that..... anyone may freely receive the grace of God. Anyone may join the community of Jesus' followers. All are welcome.... We have observed the degree to which this community [of disciples] cannot have closely prescribed boundaries. Jesus himself disallows any such concerns by his willingness to open the doors of discipleship to anyone,...."[432] Similarly, capitalism is all-inclusive; anyone who desires to can participate, even the neighborhood children selling lemonade.

Free markets are neutral. All that counts to the consumer is the quality and price of goods and services. In the system there are no other considerations. In the complex capitalistic system with its multitude of players involved in all of the steps of production, extraction, transportation, fabrication, assembly, distribution, etc. normally a consumer neither knows nor cares about the nationality, race, color, religion, national origin, sex, sexual preference or any other characteristic of the people involved in the long, complex chain of producing and distributing products. All that matters is the value—the price and quality—of the particular product.

Further, capitalism detaches a connection between wealth and social status and power. In Jesus' time the wealthy were the elite and vice versa. Today, that connection does not necessarily hold. The virtue of this situation is that this contributes to a general condition of egalitarianism in a society. Novak points out, "Yet it is in the interest of markets to include all. In a market system things move; wealth grows; opportunities open; breakthroughs are made; new groups rise to wealth. Practical intelligence assesses existing arrangements in order to invent others, to offer new services, to meet unmet needs, to discover better ways."[433]

Regarding upward mobility, Stanley and Danko note that "Eighty percent of America's millionaires are first-generation rich.... Wealth is more often the result of a lifestyle of hard work, perseverance, planning and, most of all, self-discipline.... We discovered seven common denominators among those who successfully build wealth. (1) They live well below their means. (2) They allocate their time, energy, and money efficiently,... (3) They believe that financial independence is more important than displaying high social status. (4) Their parents did not provide economic outpatient care. (5) Their adult children are economically self-sufficient. (6) They are proficient in targeting market opportunities. (7) They chose the right occupation."[434] Sounds like a group which Jesus might view with some degree of favor!

Nowhere is the upward mobility of capitalism more dramatically demonstrated than in the high tech centers of the United States. *The Seattle Times* performed considerable research on this matter, finding that "Many of today's suddenly rich... never aimed to become wealthy.... many, before they became rich in the high-tech boom, were secretaries, programmers, sales people. They are people like Tom Ikeda, 44, a Microsoft retiree who grew up in a working–class home.... Or former software designer Charles Gust, 35, whose inner-city Chicago family's annual vacation was one day at an amusement park. Cheryl Hafer, 45, remembers... her mother went to work nights as a printer, and Hafer, the eldest of four, cared for her siblings.... remembers her mother cried as she paid bills, and how embarrassed she was to shop at thrift stores. Later, Hafer lived in her car for most of a semester, unable to pay both rent and community-college tuition. She married, adopted a child... then, over the course of a few years, after her husband's computer-services company struck gold, 'we found ourselves with a great deal of money.'.... For Hafer part of the solution was to give away money and time.... Most of these newly wealthy live in homes that appear modest from the street and dress in Seattle mufti: jeans, natural fabrics and good-quality rain gear."[435]

An additional observation of Stanley and Danko addresses the point of why so many clergy and other nonwealthy may have such disdain or envy of the wealthy. Their research found that "Being frugal is the cornerstone of wealth-building. Yet far too often the big spenders are promoted and sensationalized by the popular press.... But the lavish lifestyle sells TV time and newspapers. All too often young people are indoctrinated with the belief that 'those who have money spend lavishly'.... Could you imagine the media hyping the frugal lifestyle of the typical American millionaire? What would the result be? Low TV ratings and lack of readership, because most people who build wealth in America are hard working, thrifty, and not at all glamorous.... [Further, their] traditional family values and ... lifestyle of hard work, discipline, sacrifice, thrift, and sound investment habits might threaten the audience."[436] Stanley and Danko provide many examples of spending patterns of millionaires that are contrary to popular belief. "Only 23.5 percent of millionaires have purchased a car in the last two years....."[437]

D'Souza makes similar observations. "They routinely dress down....; they love to be seen in torn jeans and baseball caps... Offer them a plate of fancy hors d'oeuvres, and they'll go for the cheese and crackers; give them a choice of beers, and they'll pick a Bud.... America's new rich are fanatically determined to appear middle class in public.... Pierre Omidyar drives the same Volkswagen Jetta he's owned for years. Jeff Bezos,... still commutes to work in a Volvo station wagon. Warren Buffett... inhabits the modest Omaha house that he bought several decades ago."[438] In fact, when we look at the changes in American society over the past century nowhere is there a more dramatic improvement evident in the human condition than the attitude of the wealthy toward their wealth and possessions today compared with that of the "robber barons" and corporate titans of yore with their household servants and named estates.

The findings of Stanley and Danko and observations of D'Souza coincide with the conclusions of George Gilder, "America's entrepreneurs... work fanatically hard. In proportion to their holdings or their output, and their contributions to the human race, they consume less than any other group of people in the history of the world.... [They] display discipline and self-control, hard work and austerity that excel that in any college of social work, Washington think tank, or congregation of bishops. They are a strange riffraff, to be sure, because they are chosen not according to blood, credentials, education, or services rendered to the establishment. They are chosen for performance alone, for service to the people as consumers.... America's entrepreneurs in no way resemble the plutocrats of socialist and feudal realms who get government to steal their winnings for them and then revel in their palaces with eunuchs and harems. The American rich, in general, cannot revel in their wealth because most of it is not liquid. It has been given to others in the form of investments. It is embodied in a vast web of enterprise that retains its worth only through constant work and sacrifice."[439] Nevertheless, there are many of the new wealthy who live quite comfortably. In fact large homes have become so common around the country that those suffering from covetousness refer to them as "McMansions," nevertheless testifying to these new homes' commonplace position in our egalitarian society. In most cases the owners of these commonplace mansions—the largest room of which is the family room—are out mowing their own lawn and coaching their kids' Little League games.

Gilder has collected interesting statistics that reflect how capitalism enables even politically and religiously persecuted groups to break out of their political and religious shackles. "The Japanese, for example, were interned in concentration camps during World War II, but thirty years later they had higher per capita earnings that any other ethnic group in America except the Jews. Three and one-half million Jewish immigrants arrived on our shores around the turn of the century with an average of nine dollars per person in their pockets,... Six decades later the mean family income of Jews was almost double the national average."[440]

Women have tended to fare better in business firms than in other types of human institutions. Women were officers of major corporations long before they were ordained clergy in most mainline denominations. Women were in responsible positions in business firms long before they were even allowed to enroll in some universities. Today there are more women bank presidents than women university presidents and there are more women business CEO's than government CEO's (governors, mayors, etc.) Yes, the "glass ceiling" is very real in the business world, but not any more so than in the church, the academy or government. To repeat a mantra of this book, capitalism is not sinful; humans are sinful.

Another way in which capitalism has fostered egalitarianism is through the corporation serving as a mechanism for spreading out business ownership. Novak points out, "... the ownership of publicly owned companies extends through more than half the American adult population. The largest holders of stocks and bonds are the pension plans of workers, in the public sector as well as the private sector. To cite just two examples, TIAA-CREF, the pension plan of educators, researchers, and university staffs, as of the end of 1995 owned over $69 billion in stocks and bonds, and the pension plan of the public employees of California owned over $50 billion.... Total stock owned directly by individuals at the end of 1995 was worth $3.6 trillion. Seventy percent of families owning such stock have annual incomes under $75,000."[441] The most common descriptive statement that can be made about a typical American household is that it is a business owner! We Americans probably have business ownership more in common than any other characteristic, certainly than religious orientation, education level or ethnicity.

When discussing egalitarianism, I am not suggesting economic equality. Nowhere in Scripture is the notion of income equality proposed nor even the values that would lead to adoption of such a notion. Further, as Novak observes, "No traditional society, no socialist society—indeed, no society in history—has ever produced strict equality among individuals or classes. Real differences in talent, aspiration, and application inexorably individuate humans. Given the diversity and liberty of human life, no fair and free system can possibly guarantee equal outcomes. A democratic system depends for its legitimacy, therefore, not upon equal results but upon a sense of equal opportunity. Such legitimacy flows from the belief of all individuals that they can better their condition. This belief can be realized only under the conditions of economic growth."[442] These comments by Novak notwithstanding, it can be asserted that to the extent that it is concerned solely with freely rewarding economic contribution, capitalism has resulted in (1) a virtual absence of class barriers as a result of fluid upward economic mobility and (2) the emergence of a broad middle class which I discuss later in Chapter X, "The Brilliant Outcomes of Capitalism." In this way, then, capitalism has fostered egalitarian conditions.

Another way in which capitalism fosters egalitarianism is through education. This is done in three ways, and, again, profits are the key. First, reinvested profits generate economic expansion creating job opportunities which in turn provide a return to one continuing one's education. Secondly, taxes on these profits generate the social capital with which to invest in educational facilities and to pay the salaries of educators. Third, private contributions to private colleges and universities have enabled these higher education institutions to make available the opportunity to attend them to every admitted applicant. Virtually every private college and university in the United States has a need-based financial aid program which provides a complete financial support package enabling every single person admitted, regardless of level of financial need, to attend. All over the United States the new super-rich are funding a wide variety of scholarship programs and other forms of financial support for minority primary and secondary students, some including the commitment to see kindergartners all the way through college if their academic performance warrants. No element contributes to equality in a society more than education. Of course, education has considerable value far beyond its utilitarian economic function in creating a more liberal, enlightened populace in general.

Another way in which the market system directly contributes to an egalitarian society is its reducing geographical disparities. As signaled by the price system through differing wage rates, businesses look more and more to lower income communities to locate facilities. Decades ago Citibank moved its credit card processing operations from New York to South Dakota. Particularly facilitated by high-tech communication devices, daily business firms are building facilities and hiring people in remote locations throughout the nation and the world. As previously low-wage areas receive investment by businesses accompanied by higher wage jobs, the global incomes and standards of living are becoming more similar. A note of caution: one must be very careful in utilizing short run data. It is recognized that in the robust, burgeoning economies of the developed countries of the world, personal income today is soaring to new heights, outstripping the pace of some undeveloped countries. While the relationships are not constant, without any doubt the soaring incomes of the developed countries are bringing along, albeit sometimes with a lag effect, the incomes of the underdeveloped countries.

Before concluding this discussion of egalitarianism, it must be observed that at least among socialist intellectuals there is a disdain of the free market wherein "consumer sovereignty" enables us commoners to choose things that are bad for us. Ah, the typical war-cry of the leftists: we masses should be protected from ourselves by the elitists in the upper echelons of the socialist bureaucracy. Perhaps capitalism's egalitarian nature is its most distinguishing characteristic. Novak observes, "Conventions of ridicule extend to polyester suits, McDonald's, American-made automobiles, televised football games, shopping malls, and other forms of what is called, with audible disdain, 'mass culture' and 'consumerism.' An underlying assumption seems to be that, if intellectuals were in command of markets and behaviors, people would soon purchase what is good for them and learn their place."[443] Kristol agrees, "The elitist attitude is basically suspicious of, and hostile to, the market precisely because the market is so vulgarly democratic.... A civilization shaped by market transactions is a civilization responsive to the common appetites, preferences, and aspirations of common people. The 'new class'... has little respect for such commonplace civilization"[444] Therefore, a word to the intellectual elites: when criticizing materialism and hedonism, one must be very careful not to commit an equally grievous sin—intellectual arrogance and suppression of liberty. Pomposity and oppressiveness were not high on Jesus' list of acceptable personality traits. (Interestingly, Kristol goes on to note that it is the very success of capitalism that has generated a level of affluence supporting its greatest critics, the 'new class' of intellectual elites.) At any rate, any system that removes the ultimate decision-making from the individual flies in the face of the reality that each and every one of us is a creation of God, and God, in His creation of humanity, did not impose any kind of hierarchy. Contrary to the implicit assumptions of most intellectual socialists, each of us—the fool who devotes every waking hour not at work to watching inane television and the loving Christian who devotes every waking hour not at work to volunteering for the church—is equal in God's eyes.

Indeed, capitalism with its opportunity for upward mobility and its focus on economic value, ignoring such extraneous considerations as race, creed, etc. has proven itself empirically to be the most egalitarian economic system yet devised. Its very basis is the respect of humans as creations of God. Increasingly, the individual is becoming empowered relative to the corporation. Heretofore, the employer seemed to hold most of the cards. Today, however, particularly related to the high-tech explosion, employees are more like independent contractors, selling their services to the highest bidder (monetary and nonmonetary) and remaining with an employer only as long as the employee's needs (financial and nonfinancial) are satisfied.

Finally, the business firm is probably the most multi-cultural, multi-racial, multi-ethnic, multi-educational, multi-social institution in our society—considerably more so than the university or the church. In the context of egalitarianism and diversity I am compelled to compare the bank for which I worked with my church. Obviously, at my church are only those people who are like me theologically. At my bank I worked closely with people of all faiths as well as agnostics and atheists. Until just a few years ago, the minorities represented among the bank's employees and customers exceeded that of my church's staff and congregation. My bank is more pro-active in soliciting minority customers than my church is in soliciting minority members. The staff time which my bank devotes to volunteering in the community probably exceeds that outreach work performed by my church. The point here is not to compare the righteousness of my bank to that of my church. *Indeed, it is acknowledged that, to the extent that my bank operates on tenets compatible with Christian tenets, it is my church and other churches that have lifted our consciousness to that point.*

As I have asserted previously, no institution in our society is subject to less understanding and therefore is more maligned than the business firm. As a further example, the reality at my bank is that anytime a loan application is submitted by a minority, it receives extraordinarily creative effort in endeavoring to accommodate the request, and, only after every conceivable way to make it work is explored, would the application be denied. However, thanks to the convenient scapegoat of the "psychology of victimization" promulgated particularly by the African-American leadership, the person denied the loan by my bank clearly attributes the denial, not to any deficiency in the loan proposal, but clearly to racial bias. What a tragedy. Not until we overcome this gigantic hurdle of mutual misunderstanding do we have any hope of getting to where God wants us to be in our interpersonal relationships.

Trust

I will address two types of trust. One is trust in God, or faith. The other is interpersonal trust, or honesty with others, their trust of you and your trust of them.

The theme throughout all of the stories of the Bible is that God is in charge. The message of both the Old and New Testaments is simply to trust, to have faith in God. Commencing with Abraham faithfully obeying God's command to venture forth, the story of the Israelites is one of recurrent exercise of faith and lack thereof.

Two of the most famous, frequently quoted passages in the Bible embody the notion of trust.

> "For God so loved the world that he gave his one and only Son, that whoever believes in him shall not perish but have eternal life." (Jn. 3:16)

> "I am the way and the truth and the life. No one comes to the Father except through me." (Jn. 14:6)

Our path to salvation commences with our faith in God evidenced by our trust in Jesus Christ. Note that trust is a dynamic concept; it implies behavior reflecting faith in the trusted object. The two statements above imply that we are to *do* and *act* in accordance with our trust in Jesus Christ.

As discussed previously, humility is the opposite of pride. And humility leads to faith and faith leads to trust and trust leads to risk-taking! One of the ironic conditions of humanity is that a humble attitude leads to bold actions. Winston Gooden, associate dean of the School of Psychology at Fuller Theological Seminary, concludes from his research that "faith and risk taking are also

closely related. Abraham, for instance, is the father of faith because
he believed God, took his family and possessions, and went toward
a place promised but not seen…. Risk taking involves making decisions in a climate of uncertainty, where information is incomplete
and potential for gain is balanced by a potential for loss or
harm"[445] This seminary professor could not have described more
accurately capitalism. Wooden continues, "Faith helps leaders
remain aware of their vulnerabilities without eroding their confidence, and it sustains them when they must pursue values and
visions that put them and their organizations at risk….When we
invest ourselves in work and construe work as vocation, we do so
with no firm or concrete evidence that our investment will yield the
hoped-for return…. Faith is about staking everything on a future we
can't determine or predict. Yet without this investment of ourselves,
life remains absurd. When we start a new business, enter a new
market, or develop a new product line, there is no firm assurance
that the business will do well, that the new product will be accepted,
or that we will make a return on our investment…. Success, meaning, and fulfillment, in business as in personal life, require the exercise of faith.[446] When a private timber company plants a Douglas
fir seedling on the western slope of the Cascade Mountains in
Oregon or Washington, the profit—if any—from harvesting that
tree will not occur until half a century later. What a statement of
faith! Indeed, trust is the first step to entrepreneurialism.

Gilder expands, "Religious faith takes many forms from church
attendance to prophetic visions. But they all entail a commitment to
ideas or concepts that are unprovable at the outset, that are empirically incalculable because they refer not to statistical probability
but to singular outcomes, whether personal salvation or the success
of a business innovation."[447]

To summarize,

God's → Gratitude, → Faith, → Confidence → Risk taking, → Return
Grace   Humility   Trust   Perseverance

Looking to the other type of trust, honesty, Solomon reminds us
that "The LORD abhors dishonest scales." (Prv. 11:1) "The LORD
detests lying lips, but he delights in men who are truthful." (Prv.
12:22) and "Differing weights and differing measures—the LORD

detests them both." (Prv. 20:10,23) Daily trillions of dollars of financial instruments are traded all over the globe verbally over the telephone or by fax or e-mail across national borders by people, most of whom have never seen each other and many of whom do not even know each other, of every conceivable religion, race, nationality, color, sex, sexual preference, etc. There are no written, signed contracts. It all depends upon trust. The first time that any participant fails to honor a verbal commitment, he/she will be excluded from the game.

Interestingly, nowhere is economic activity more closely tied to Godly virtues than with the virtue of trust. The effective functioning of the entire global financial and commercial system is dependent upon it. Without trust the global economy would grind to a halt. This is because business is voluntary and therefore success requires persuading, rather than coercing or oppressing, others, and persuasion requires trust. As expressed by David Gill, Professor of Applied Ethics of North Park University, "Without trust, we cannot do business. This is both intuitively and experientially clear,.... And, without integrity, individuals and companies will, over time, fail to persuade others to do business with them."[448]

In *The Sermon on the Mount* Jesus states that one's word ought to be enough, without requiring an oath or vow. "Do not swear at all, …Let what you say be simply 'yes' or 'no;' anything more than this comes from evil." (Mt. 5:34-36) Later, Jesus asserts that one cannot be just a tiny bit untrustworthy and that there is a relationship between earthly integrity and heavenly trust. "He who is dishonest in a very little is dishonest also in much. If then you have not been faithful in unrighteous mammon, who will entrust to you the true riches?" (Lk. 16:10-12)

Jesus understood the important role that trust and consistency play in commercial transactions, and that absent them, much of our economic activity would come to an end. Accordingly, when Jesus talks about forgiveness, including forgiving our debtors, he is not advocating abandoning the reciprocal honoring of commitments. What he is saying is that in the situation wherein someone has defaulted on an obligation to us and after we have legally and morally attempted to obtain payment but have been unable to do so, we must forgive the debtor as we forgive anyone who wrongs us in some fashion.

Judas, of course, is the personification of lack of trust. In the story of the woman with the ointment at the dinner with the Pharisees Judas asks "Why was this ointment not sold for three hundred denarii and given to the poor?' This he said, not that he cared for the poor, but because he was a thief and as he had the money box, he used to take what was put into it." (Jn. 12:5-6) Later, of course, Judas presents us with the ultimate example of absence of trust when he betrays Jesus—which he does for money, even a trifle amount. (Mt. 26:14; Mk. 14:10; Lk. 22: 4)

It is utterly fascinating to observe that the multitude of international business transactions that occur daily on the basis of trust between the parties are in many, many cases occurring between political enemies and even religious opponents, yet the profit motive causes them to be economic friends. And the key component of this economic friendship is trust.

Enlightened Leadership

It should be kept in mind that in this book I am discussing *contemporary* economics. Indeed, it is acknowledged that American business went through a stage of pretty unseemly behavior. Regretfully, many people today still view corporate leaders as akin to the "robber barons" of yore. Nothing could be further from the truth. Today's corporate executive is a professional manager, formally educated in such concepts as "participative management" and "social entrepreneurship" and possessing an enlightened regard for *all* of his/her stakeholders: employees, customers, suppliers and the community at large as well as shareholders. Most corporate leaders not only understand but are unequivocally committed to the concept that a socially healthy and vibrant community is conducive to maximizing profits over the long run.

Today's corporate leader understands clearly and is firmly committed to the notion that profits are maximized by (1) low worker turnover resulting from just wages, good working conditions, attractive benefits, and fair treatment, (2) productive workers resulting from support of educational institutions, additional job-related training, safe working conditions, advanced equipment, excellent community health care and recreational and cultural opportunities, (3) conserving and maximizing the growth of renewable resources, (4) minimizing the number of units of inputs required per unit of output, and (5) myriad other measures that also have a social benefit dimension to them. Additionally, they view workers not as simply costly input factors, but as human beings worthy of treatment as ends in themselves, giving rise to the company satisfying the human needs of actualization and fulfillment. (Which gives rise to another advantage of the capitalistic system: if a worker finds oneself in a situation not as that described above, one can quit and go work elsewhere, in such an environment!)

It should be observed that most leaders of publicly held corporations are not, in fact, profit maximizers. They are profit satisfiers. Further, notwithstanding the common, now trite, exhortation by journalists that investment advisors and stock analysts can't see past the end of the current quarter, most capitalists are profit satisfiers over the long run. That is, they know that over the long run the most positive effect on valuation of the company's stock is achieved by generating a pattern of sustained consistent growth in earnings. Hence, the huge investment in research and development and productivity-enhancing equipment as well as training which do not have pay-offs until much later. Any firm which greedily maximizes immediate profits fails to make the expenditures and investments necessary to sustain its future health and therefore eventually dies, destroyed by competitor firms or by itself. Sir John Templeton, one of the pioneers of mutual funds, observes, "In almost fifty years of studying over ten thousand corporations, I learned that the best long-term results flowed to those who focused on providing increasingly beneficial products and services.... One of the world's wealthiest men, Sam Walton, said that he always had been doing the best possible thing for humanity by finding ways to sell higher quality goods at lower prices. He felt that his career had been a ministry of helping people, especially the poor, through the efficiency of his operation."[449]

And the new high tech entrepreneurs are driven more by the desire to create than to generate profits. Many also are driven by a loftier human goal. According to D'Souza, "This promise, or what cybercowboy John Perry Barlow terms the Great Work, is a spectacular one: to eliminate scarcity, to feed and clothe and heal the world.... Dewang Mehta, a leading software entrepreneur in India, told me he believes that the computer industry will realize 'Gandhi's dream of wiping a tear from every Indian face."[450] They also have a more philosophical view of wealth and understanding of the role of wealth in a capitalistic society. D'Souza quotes Jay Walker's (founder of Priceline.com) prophetic response to an inquiry regarding what it was like to be worth several billion dollars, "Let me put it differently.... My paper wealth is based on a promise to my shareholders that over time I will deliver value corresponding with that wealth. If I don't deliver [economic value in the market place], that wealth will disappear as quickly as it came."[451]

Most proprietorships, the common form of small business organization, are profit-satisfiers. The business is used by the proprietor as a platform for civic involvement and a healthy family life while providing a satisfactory financial base. As Novak states, "The real interests of individuals, furthermore, are seldom merely self-regarding. To most persons, their families mean more than their own interests;.... Their communities are also important to them. In the human breast, commitments to benevolence, fellow-feeling, and sympathy are strong. Moreover, humans have the capacity to see themselves as others see them, and to hold themselves to standards which transcend their own selfish inclinations.... The 'self' in self-interest is complex, at once familial and communitarian as well as individual, other-regarding as well as self-regarding, cooperative as well as independent."[452] D'Souza adds, "The desire of people to support themselves and their families is not a wicked impulse, it is a decent impulse."[453]

As suggested above under the discussion of trust, enlightened leadership, characterized by confidence and a broad perspective of concern flows to a high degree from faith. To draw again from Professor Gooden, "Faith is a unique source of confidence for those who lead from within a spiritual framework..... Christian faith is a response of the total person—heart, mind, will, and body—to the initiative God has taken with respect to humanity,.... This response involves an intentional acceptance of who God is and what God intends for our lives. People of faith commit themselves to living a new life patterned after God's loving expectations, as found in scripture and church teachings and as mediated through the presence of the Holy Spirit."[454] Faith-based leadership, flowing from an understanding and appreciation of humans as created in the image of God, translates into a broader, genuine concern for the interests of all persons affected by the business leader: employees, customers, suppliers, owners, community, etc.

The enlightened leader understands that the purpose of life is to glorify God. This leader then adopts an ethical stance that is in accord with this understanding and that reflects one's relationship with God through Christ. "Since we live by the Spirit, let us keep in step with the Spirit. Let us not become conceited, provoking and envying each other." (Gal. 5:25,26) The enlightened leader agrees with Jervis' interpretation, "By means of the Spirit the Galatian believers are to enact the life they already have in the Spirit."[455]

In this discussion of enlightened leadership of business following the discussion of egalitarianism it is appropriate to focus on an important aspect of leadership: interpersonal relations. In the context that we all are creations of God, one of the baffling elements of the Bible to me is the apparent condoning of slavery, a practice viewed as abhorrent today, as well as condoning social class stratifications, a practice viewed as anathema today. While recognizing that slavery in the Roman Empire was considerably different than slavery in early America, the former including some highly educated slaves who handled important administrative matters, a wide range of social status, many legal rights, and relatively common emancipation, nevertheless, the notion of one human owning another is intolerable. I reconcile the early Christians' apparent tolerance of the horrible practice of slavery in two manners. First, the focus of Jesus, Paul and the other apostles was on our heavenly status to which our earthly status was subordinate and further, as Jervis suggests, believers "gained a new identity, one rooted in and defined by Christ. This identity transcended all typical social distinctions..."[456] Patzia agrees, "The creation of a new humanity...is one of the wonderful truths of the gospel.... At the foot of the cross the ground is level!.... [Worldly] distinctions no longer have any significance when it is realized that Christ is everything and that he dwells in all people."[457] Paul declares, "You are all sons of God through faith in Christ Jesus, ... There is neither Jew nor Greek, slave nor free, male nor female, for you are all one in Christ Jesus." (Gal. 3:26-28) "For we were all baptized by one Spirit into one body—whether Jews or Greeks, slave or free...." (1Cor. 12:13) "Here there is no Greek or Jew, circumcised or uncircumcised, barbarian, Scythian, slave or free, but Christ is all, and is in all" (Col. 3:11) Second, Jesus and his Christian followers were focused on the individual's relationship with God, rather than on social, political or economic relationships. They felt that if individuals achieved righteousness accompanied by unbounded faith and love, human relationships and interactions would take care of themselves. As Professor Blaine Charette notes, "The Christian life helps one transcend the particular social situation in which one found oneself. But, indeed, the logical conclusion of the Christ message is the abolition of abhorrent societal practices. For example, when the Roman Empire became more Christianized, slavery eventually went by the wayside."[458]

Another school of thought suggests that the primary reason for the apostles not advocating the abolishment of slavery was that it was so entrenched in the life of the Roman Empire that such "treasonous" acts would have brought the wrath of the rulers down upon the Christians, eradicating them. Such a view, however, flies in the face of the omnipotence of God and therefore any ability of anything to confound God's plan. Finally, a further school of thought contends that Jesus and Paul "had an apocalyptic approach in which the death and resurrection of Christ marked the changing of the times. Strong apocalypticism does not encourage long-range social planning. Structures in society that prevent the proclamation of the gospel must be neutralized. Yet precisely because Christ is coming back soon, other structures that do not represent gospel values can be allowed to stand provided that they can be bypassed to enable Christ to be preached......to overturn the massive Roman societal institution of slavery is not a feasible accomplishment in the very limited time before Christ comes."[459]

One of the most beautiful, loving books of the Bible is Paul's letter to Philemon, asking him to receive back Onesimus, his slave who had stolen from him and run away and whom Paul apparently had converted to Christianity. (As a measure of Paul's love of others it is interesting to note that he was asking for another's freedom while he himself was a prisoner.) "...I appeal to you on the basis of love....Perhaps the reason he was separated from you for a little while was that you might have him back for good—no longer as a slave, but better than a slave, as a dear brother. He is very dear to me but even dearer to you, both as a man and as a brother in the

Lord. So…, welcome him as you would welcome me." (Phlm. 9-17) In his commentary on this passage Patzia notes the truth that holds today, "Partnership in the Lord has broken down all barriers."[460]

While the directive of Scripture is a universal "love one another," there is very little in the Bible specifically about employer/employee relationships, except in the context of poor employees (primarily day laborers) and slave/master relationship. Such passages are helpful, however, in guiding one's attitude and behavior as an employer. "Do not take advantage of a hired man who is poor.... Pay him his wages each day before sunset,…"(Dt. 25:14,15) Wright comments, "The law is concerned that the *conditions* of work should be fair…and that the *payment* for work should be prompt.... Workers' rights are responsibilities before God. Unjust pay and conditions are not just social problems, they are sins against God."[461] There is a parallel situation in the New Testament. "The wages you failed to pay the workmen who mowed your fields are crying out against you. The cries of the harvesters have reached the ears of the Lord Almighty." (Jas. 5:4) New Testament scholar Peter Davids interprets, "The cries have not gone unheard.... All Jews knew…that God's ears were open to the poor, so James' statement implies a threat of judgement."[462] Also in the New Testament, Paul instructs, "Slaves, obey your earthly master with respect…, and with sincerity of heart…, doing the will of God from your heart.... *And master, treat your slave in the same way. Do not threaten them, since you know who is both their Master and yours is in heaven and there is no favoritism with him.*" (Eph. 6:9) *"Masters, provide your slaves with what is right and fair, because you know that you also have a Master in heaven."* (Col. 4:1) (italics mine) Underlying the eventual ridding humankind of the institution of slavery and standing over all employer/employee relationships is the basic notion that we all are creations of God and therefore are brothers and sisters intrinsically worthy of each other's respect, concern and love. Made explicit by Paul is that in all relationships, husband and wife, parent and child, slave and master, there is a third party involved: God to whom both of the other two are equally responsible. Therefore, in contemporary employee/employer relationships, as the subordinate must answer to the boss, the boss must answer to the Ultimate Boss over both.

Interestingly, John Murray, former Professor of Systematic Theology at Westminster Theological Seminary in Philadelphia, in *Principles of Conduct*, regarded as one of the contemporary masterpieces on ethics, continues with his interpretation of the passage cited in the previous paragraph, focusing on the words "right and fair" ("just and equal"), "Here the necessity of wages is implied, but the emphasis rests upon the obligation that wages be proportionate to the service rendered."[463]

The foregoing should not stand in the way of appropriate disciplining an employee for infraction of rules or terminating an employee for poor performance. In fact, in many cases the foregoing notion should *support* the termination. When one recognizes that people / employees are not "good" or "bad" per se and that job performance reflects the particular employee's skills, personality, disposition—the full array of personal characteristics—*related to the particular job*, terminating an employee for poor performance is in fact doing the employee a favor. It is forcing the employee to find a situation that is more suitable. In my three decades as an employer I cannot recall any incident in which I terminated an employee for poor performance that within a relatively short period of time the employee was not in a job that was more suitable for him/her.

Recognizing all humans as created in the image of God helps in not only employee / employer relations, but in all human relationships. Capitalism, the positive sum game emphasizing win-win solutions, is in accordance with this.

Many people who do not understand economics or business have a perverted concept of the practice of negotiation. Negotiating is not the process of one party attempting to beat the other party over the head, extracting a loss out of the other party. Negotiation is not oppression. Negotiation is the process of two parties mutually exploring different alternatives in an effort to identify a way in which their separate interests can come in concert. Only when each party reaches a point wherein his/her interest is met will a transaction occur. If a party's interest is *not* met in a business transaction, that party has simply made an irrational decision. In bona fide negotiations wherein the interests of both parties are met, both parties, by definition, win. This is not to say that they win equally. One might win more that the other, but, by definition, they both are better off, or one party has acted irrationally. For example, in a weak real estate market the tenant may end up paying a relatively low rental rate, but the landlord has at least rented the space; in a strong real estate market, the landlord may end up receiving a relatively high rental rate, but the tenant at least has the use of the space for his particular need. If the tenant is paying more for the space than his particular need can generate in benefit, then he has simply made an ignorant or irrational decision, which is not the "fault" or "blame" of the landlord.

Conclusion

Christianity does not "need" capitalism nor any other human system. The last two thousand years have clearly demonstrated that God's plan can overcome any obstacle. What I mean by the conduciveness of capitalism to Christianity is that for us humans it is nevertheless comforting to know that the values upon which the effective functioning of capitalism depends are precisely those values espoused by Christianity.

As Christianity is a religion of hope and optimism, capitalism is an economic system of hope and optimism. While liberty, egalitarianism and enlightened leadership, particularly in employer/employee relationships, flow from the view that *all* humans are creations of God, Christianity explains what it means to be a child of God. And, while a key tenet of Christianity is faith and a value embodied in Christianity is trust, key components of capitalism are faith, which leads to confidence which leads to innovation, and trust which permits transactions among participants. Capitalism, to succeed, requires tenets and values which are in accord with the tenets and values of Christianity.

Perhaps the most significant practice in those countries with constitutional separation of church and state such as the United States which would be precluded by the socialist model is bringing religious faith into the workplace. In the United States practicing religion outwardly in a government workplace is difficult—witness the recent brouhaha over U.S. Attorney General Ashcroft's prayer group. Guinness is concerned about what he sees as "an emerging separationism, the absolute separation of church and state so that religion is inviolably private and the public sector is inviolably secular, threatening the circular relationship of freedom requiring virtue, virtue requiring faith and faith requiring freedom."[464]

While discouraged or prohibited in government agencies, increasingly private business firms are explicitly bringing God into the company. Throughout the United States there is an accelerating trend of companies explicitly practicing their Christian faith within the company. Some examples include Herman Miller, Inc., Barnhart Crane & Rigging Co., Hobby Lobby Stores, Inc., CARDONE Industries, Amway Corp., TLC Beatrice International, Amick Farms, Grace Software Marketing Co., Chick-fil-A, and International Trade Group, LLC, and there are hundreds of thousands of others. Also, there is an increasing partnering by business firms with churches and other religious organizations. Bank of America's partnering program is headed up by a Senior Vice President for Faith-Based Initiatives.[465] This phenomenon of business firms integrating spirituality and work has become so great as to give rise to a magazine devoted to it. *The Life@Work Journal*, the spiritual / commercial entrepreneurial effort of Tom Addington, Stephen Graves, and Sean Womack, has as its mission: "to blend Biblical wisdom and business excellence...." Perhaps one of the reasons that these and other firms in the private sector outperform the typical government agency is their explicitly turning to God in their daily business affairs! At any rate, we have identified another area in which Christianity and socialism are incompatible. In a socialistic society there is only one producer, supplier and employer, the state, and that employer may or may not permit one to outwardly practice one's Christianity on the job. In a capitalistic society, if one's employer prohibits the practice of Christianity on the job, one has an array of alternative employers which do.

The trend of a growing spirituality in the workplace gives hope to the notion that capitalism will be able to avoid its greatest threat as perceived by Kristol, nihilism. "Only liberal capitalism doesn't see nihilism as an enemy, but rather as just another splendid business opportunity."[466] Fortunately, such tendencies, though quite pronounced as discussed previously, are also accompanied by other offsetting trends, perhaps the most pronounced of which is growing *practiced* spirituality among business leaders. The compatibility of virtue and freedom is being excellently catalogued and reported by Fr. Sirico and his Acton Institute.

Finally, capitalism is in accord with the creation mandate. As

Griffith explains, "When we put together the Christian views of the physical world and of work, they have major implications for economic life. Man has been created with an urge to control and harness the resources of nature in the interests of the common good, but he is subject to his accountability to God as trustee to preserve and care for it. This process is precisely what an economist would refer to as a responsible form of wealth creation. Anything which transforms the material world so that it can be of greater use to fellow human beings is an act of wealth creation.... A businessman concerned with construction, manufacturing, agriculture, extraction or services is involved therefore in the complex task of fulfilling the creation mandate.... At heart the process of wealth creation stems from a fundamental human drive, the result of man being made in the image of God."[467] As stated earlier, creation is a divine imperative.

Chapter X

Brilliant Outcomes of Capitalism in the Context of Christianity

$$\rule{4in}{0pt}$$

R elative to the particular interests of Christianity, capitalism is generating seven brilliant outcomes. Six are discussed in this chapter. The seventh is so monumental that it deserves a chapter of its own.

Before focusing on the seven outcomes related to Christianity, it should be noted that, in addition to achieving these outcomes, capitalism has overwhelmingly achieved its primary goal of economic growth. The material standard of living of the broad general populace of the capitalistic nations of the world far, far exceeds that of the noncapitalistic nations, and in some, such as the United States, the material well-being can only be described as luxurious. Further, the breakneck speed with which capitalism is creating new products and services boggles the mind. Many of today's "necessities" (e.g., e-mail) did not even exist just a few years ago. In fact, it is the impressive economic growth accomplishments of capitalism that is permitting many of its other corollary achievements discussed in this chapter.

First, capitalism has most readily empowered the poor.

As observed earlier in our discussion of the legitimacy of worldly possessions and wealth, Jesus was concerned predominantly with two groups: the sick or disabled and the poor. Throughout Scripture are laments regarding the poor and exhortations to demonstrate love of the poor. Empowering the poor—a dominant concern of many clergy—is most effectively achieved by enabling them to become unpoor. This is most readily achieved through the job opportunities, higher incomes, and expenditures on social goods such as job training and health care which result from and are financed by a vibrant economy stimulated by the incentives of private ownership under capitalism.

The most effective device to convert the poor from their status of poor to unpoor is the creation of job opportunities. Aided by the vibrant economic expansion and egalitarianism of capitalism, opportunities abound in capitalistic countries and new ideas keep popping up hourly. Latte stands have brought a whole new group of people into economic prosperity! In the United States in the 1990's new jobs were created at a rate of over 5,000 per day—365 days per year! These new jobs were created, not by some umbrella government program, but by hundreds of thousands of business firms making individual staffing decisions. Interestingly, over the past two decades 85% of the new jobs created have been done so, not by the large mega-corporations, but by firms employing less than 500 people. Nearly one-third of the new jobs are in firms with less than twenty employees.[468] Each year over the past decade 165,000 new businesses have started up.[469]

This job-creating economic expansion comes through reinvestment of profits. Economic expansion requires the accumulation of capital, and capital accumulates by a firm generating excess income over expenses. The definition of this excess is profit. The greater the profits, the greater the reinvestment; the greater the reinvestment, the greater number of job opportunities created; the greater the number of jobs, the lesser number of poor. This is not to imply by any means that perfection has been reached. During the past two decades the average rate of unemployment has been about 6%,[470] reflecting nearly 7 million people looking for jobs. Nevertheless much of this is "frictional" unemployment, people changing jobs and others requiring retraining, reflecting a dynamic, growing, changing economy. Accordingly, unemployment will never reach zero. Most economists define "full employment" as about 4.0%

unemployment. One of the vagaries of the market system, it must be acknowledged, is the existence of business cycles with an accompanying rise and fall in demand for workers. While counter-cyclical efforts will always be made by government and while it appears that the "information" explosion and business management advances such as "just in time" inventory control appear to be reducing both the magnitude and duration of economic fluctuations, business cycles never will be completely done away with, and therefore there will always be a need for generosity to the unemployed.

Returning to my general assertion that capitalism has empowered the poor, Gilder observes, "What system that continues to admit immigrants in huge numbers, what system that embraces some 210 million souls across a giant continent could ever have succeeded in raising its lowest ranks of earners above a line of poverty that exceeds the median family income of the Soviet Union by perhaps $1,000 per year?"[471] Michael Novak adds another perspective on poverty in the United States, "For virtually all Americans, coming to America has brought good fortune. Even for American blacks, who have suffered much injustice and faced unequalled obstacles, America has brought success that neither Africa nor any other place ever has. The combined income of America's 32 million blacks alone is larger that the GDP of all but ten nations of the world, and nearly as large as that of all of Africa's 800 million people combined."[472] Today the percentage of families living in poverty in the United States is about half of what it was forty years ago.[473] From a different perspective, D'Souza observes, "An [American] family that subsists at the poverty line, as defined by the U.S. government, has a standard of living that is higher than 80 percent of the world's population,"[474] virtually all of whom live in non-democratic, non-capitalistic countries.

Before proceeding any further, a very important characteristic of income statistics should be observed. *The Wall Street Journal* has noted the dynamic nature of wealth. "Over time most bottom quintilers *moved up*. The University of Michigan's Panel Survey on Income Dynamics tracked over 3,000 people from 1975 to 1991. After 17 years, only 5% of bottom dwellers were still on the bottom. That means 95% move up—over half made it to the middle-class quintiles and 29% were... in the top fifth. Moreover,

... .[the bottom quintile] in 1975 saw an average gain in real income of $25,322 by 1991 while [the top quintile] were only $3,975 richer.... Some [of the bottom quintile] were low-skill adults new to the work force and some were kids, either part timers... or first-time full-timers.... The U.S. Treasury, using entirely different data, tracked 14,351 households from 1979 to 1988. Over this nine-year period, the survey found that 86% of those in the lowest income bracket moved up..... The Michigan survey shows that almost 98% of the lowest quintile in 1975 had higher income over the following 17 years—two-thirds scoring a higher standard of living than the middle-fifth in 1975." The *Journal* concludes, "Problems of course remain. In particular, some schools don't provide the education necessary to fulfill opportunity. Financing cutting-edge health care without rationing has yet to be solved by any society.... The human condition, being what it is, will always produce stories that rend the heart. Yet we should not lose sight of what we have achieved. Each decade marks advancement in which most people live longer, in better health and with higher standards of living. This is a society that takes seriously its great and grand opportunity to make things better."[475]

Rising real incomes result largely from productivity increases which enable wages to rise to a greater degree than prices. This has been dramatically demonstrated in the United States throughout our history and recently in the 1990's when wage increases exceeded the average annual rate of inflation. From 1970 to 1998 in the United States business sector productivity measured as output per hour rose by 52%, enabling a five-fold increase in compensation per man hour in the business sector to translate into only a tripling of unit labor costs.[476] Impressive productivity achievements by American business firms has allowed them to raise worker compensation more than prices, causing a marked increase in the standard of living at all levels.

Looking at productivity another way, per capita real GDP (that is, Gross Domestic Product adjusted downward to remove the effect of price increases) has risen by over one-third over the past twenty years and has more than doubled over the past forty years.[477] That is, in the United States each man, woman and child receives more than twice the amount of physical goods and services as their grandparents did. This is largely due to extensive investment in productivity measures by American industry over this period of time. Today, annually over $200 billion is being spent on computers and communications hardware, in addition to the tens of billions spent on software and systems.

Education is another device for converting the poor from poor to unpoor. Perhaps nowhere is the superiority of private enterprise over public enterprise more dramatically demonstrated than in education. After business firms hire generally inadequately educated workers, they turn around and spend over $100 billion annually on training.

We have discussed capitalism helping the poor by generating job opportunities and providing education. But it is recognized that the market system rewards only economic contribution and therefore economic value. Clearly there are many, many people who due to bad luck, limited capabilities or by choice doing things with relatively little or no economic value have low incomes. For example, it is tragic that teachers and the clergy receive economic returns far below the value of their non-economic contributions. Nevertheless, capitalism and its attendant prosperity helps these people also. Prosperity helps the poor and others with low economic value or otherwise outside of the economic stream in three ways:

1. Generates job opportunities for them.
2. Increases the level of charitable contributions to them.
3. Increases tax revenue which supports programs for the poor and which transfer income and/or wealth to those making an important non-economic contribution.

In the decade of the 1980's and 1990's an unmatched prosperity in the United States was abundantly manifest in the three elements above. First, the creation of 1.8 million new jobs per year was mentioned earlier. Second, over the past twenty years individuals, households, business firms and private foundations have more than tripled the amount of funds they contribute to the full array of private philanthropies in the United States from $49 billion per year in 1980 to over $150 billion in 1999. Today in the United States approximately 45,000 private foundations distribute to the full array of charities and cultural, educational and civic organizations from a total private asset pool of nearly $400 billion. Interestingly, households with annual incomes under $100,000 voluntarily contribute 2.3% of their income to charity, while those with annual incomes over $100,000 contribute 3.4% of their income.[478] Third, over the past twenty years tax revenues to federal, state and local governments have more than tripled, slightly exceeding the tripling of Gross Domestic Product over the same period of time.[479] This enormous increase in tax revenue has financed a commensurately enormously generous and broad variety of transfer payments which have reallocated wealth from the prosperous to the poor and to others outside of the economic value arena. Indeed, not only have the rich not exploited the poor, but the second and third elements above are ways in which the rich have subsidized the poor. Which, I must say, is appropriate. Let us rid ourselves of the incorrect notion that somehow the rich have become so on the backs of the poor. Nothing could be farther from the truth; in fact, the rich have provided huge benefits for the poor.

Of even greater significance than the economic benefits stated above, are the abundant social benefits that flow from prosperity. Perhaps the most noteworthy corollary statistic to the record economic expansion in the United State in the 1990's was the plummeting of crime rates during the same period. The seven and a half year period of "1991 to the first half of 1999 witnessed the longest streak of declining crime reports since the FBI began collecting national crime data in 1930."[480] Further, as noted by Father Gorski, "in the broader church's social thinking,... employment is seen as a central issue in the economy because it is so important for human dignity."[481] A 1999 study of low-wage men in 322 metropolitan areas by Richard Freeman at Harvard University and William Rodgers III at the College of William and Mary indicates that "black men aged 16 to 24 with a high school education or less— many saddled with prison records—are working in greater numbers, earning bigger paychecks and committing fewer crimes than in the early 1990's.... The surge in legitimate employment has gone hand in hand with a drop in criminal activity... Indeed, crime has fallen rapidly in regions where joblessness has fallen most.... Brian Burnett, 19, is typical of many young blacks who have benefited from the extended period of low unemployment in fast-growing parts of the United States. He graduated from an inner city high school.... After working at a series of temporary jobs for about a year and completing a federally financed job readiness program, he landed a $7-an-hour, full-time position as a front-desk clerk at an Embassy Suites hotel. Now Burnett is planning to study hotel management part time with tuition help from his employer.... 'The market is more powerful than any government program,' Freeman said."[482]

It is clearly demonstrated that *there is no greater source of benefit to the poor and others outside the economic stream than economic prosperity.* As former President John F. Kennedy observed, "A rising tide lifts all ships." This notion was also supported by John Paul II's 1991 encyclical, *Centesimus Annus,* which notes that "the poor are empowered best through participation in a free economy."[483] Fr. Schall agrees, "In general, the best way business can help the poor is to provide for a growing, fair economy in which the vast majority of the population work for their own living. Without a growing, free economy, each person finds it difficult to take care of himself and his family."[484] Capitalism keeps ever-present the future hope and reality of upward movement by the poor and others with low economic value.

The foregoing perspective on raising the plight of the poor was understood clearly by Victor Hugo, humankind's greatest champion of the poor, and who put his money where his mouth is, reportedly donating about a third of his income to charity. Powell notes, "while *Les Miserables* exudes generous sympathy for the most wretched among us, Hugo stood apart from the socialist trend of his time. He seemed to be countering the Marxist dogma of class warfare when he wrote, 'There has been an attempt, an erroneous one, to make a special class of the bourgeoisie. The bourgeoisie is simply the contented portion of the people. The bourgeois is the man who has now time to sit down. A chair is not a caste.... Communism and agrarian law think they have solved the second problem [distribution of income]. They are mistaken. Their distribution kills production.... To kill wealth is not to distribute it.' He expressed confidence that private enterprise and peace would alleviate poverty: 'All progress is tending toward the solution. Some day we shall be astounded. The human race is rising, the lower strata will quite naturally come out from the zone of distress. The abolition of misery will be brought about by a simple elevation of level."[485] Hugo's predictions have been born out by the impressive gains of capitalistic nations and their generosity to the citizens of noncapitalistic nations.

In addition to the great income raiser, capitalism has been the great income leveler. This has been achieved through mind-boggling advances in productivity, stimulated by the profit motive, which in turn has generated commensurate rises in real wages which has fostered a broad middle class. It is this massive middle class that most distinguishes contemporary capitalism from other contemporary economic systems and other economic systems of the past. Throughout the period of history covered by Scripture there was virtually no middle class. All of a nation's wealth was in a few hands, distributed thereto by the ruler, and the great mass of the population was relatively poor. Now, as a result of the achievements of capitalism's technology, as D'Souza notes, "Wealth has exploded and spread beyond the confines of a narrow caste; suddenly, it has become accessible to a large segment of society. Mass affluence, once a philosopher's dream, is now a social reality. What could be more exhilarating than for people—and entire societies—to relish the victory over necessity!"[486]

In this context, then, let us listen to the words of Ronald H. Stone, Professor of Social Ethics at Pittsburgh Theological Seminary, "The goal [of Christianity as seen by Calvin and his followers] is a society of neither the poor nor the rich, but a working, contributing class with sufficiency for life at a modest level."[487] Democratic capitalism of the United States and Western Europe, the most distinguishing characteristic of which is an immense middle class, has come closer to achieving that goal than any other economic system yet devised by humans. Further, capitalism has enabled a continuous upward revision of "poor" and has so overshot the mark of "a modest level" for the broad middle class that a pervasive hedonism is its major point of criticism.

In this regard money has played a critical role. Money, as well as a medium of exchange, is a store of value. As Adam Smith observes, "By what a frugal man [or corporation] annually saves [retains earnings], he not only affords maintenance to an additional number of productive hands, for that or the ensuing year, but,...he establishes a perpetual fund for the maintenance of an equal number in all times to come."[488] At this point it can be observed that the business corporation, which has perpetual life, is the economic version of "eternal life."

The banking system has also played a role in "The Great Redistribution" in that banks are the intermediary through which excess capital is channeled from those who are holding it idle (savers) to those who can put it to productive use (borrowers). A loan will occur anytime the marginal utility of (return on) the capital borrowed exceeds the interest rate on the loan, transferring the capital to it highest and best use. Daily, banks participate in channeling funds from savers to users, paying savers interest and charging users a higher level of interest, taking the spread between the two as its compensation for performing this service. Interest rates—the price of "renting" otherwise idle money—are determined by the market forces of supply and demand in the identical way in which prices of all goods and services are set. Banks compete ferociously with each other, and the winners are the savers who get as high a rate of interest as the market conditions determine and the borrowers who pay as low a rate of interest as the market conditions determine, and, most importantly, all members of society benefit as one of the economy's key resources, money, is channeled via the market system to its most productive use. Mutual funds are another important financial intermediary transferring funds from savers to users, generating job opportunities.

Having earlier mentioned greater economic parity as an outcome of capitalism, let me assert that there is no intrinsic virtue to economic parity. Sider notes, "These is no explicit declaration of a system of economic justice in the Bible."[489] Dr. R. C. Sproul, founder and chairman of Ligonier Ministries, Orlando, Florida, points out, "God makes no provisions for the equal distribution of wealth in the Bible. He makes many provisions for people being treated justly according to the law and according to ethics.... [J]ustice is not the same thing as equality..... When the prophets are speaking of 'social justice' in the Old Testament, the principal people who are guilty of exploiting and oppressing the poor are those in offices of government."[490] Fuller and Rice observe, "Jesus has no social theory about the redistribution of wealth.... 'You have the poor among you always, and you can help them if you like.' (Mk. 14:7) Jesus simply came to confront men with the challenge of the kingdom of God. Rich men, poor men were confronted with that challenge.... there was no virtue in poverty as such, just as wealth in itself was not an unsupportable barrier..., since with God all thing were possible."[491] Wheeler agrees, "poverty...does not define discipleship,...the importance of possessions (or their lack) in these texts (Gospels) is entirely derivative and instrumental....all that matters is that one follows."[492] Preston Williams, Houghton Professor of Theology and Contemporary Change, Harvard Divinity School, notes, "Calvinism has no doctrine of abstract equality. It affirms instead an inequality of earthly vocations and an essential inequality of human life."[493] In Calvin's own words, "I acknowledge indeed that we are not bound to such an equality as would make it wrong for the rich to live more elegantly that the poor; but there must be such an equality that nobody starves and nobody hordes his abundance at another's expense."[494] Finally, Fr. Schall quotes his friend Eugene Poirier, a Canadian Jesuit economist, on this matter of justice, "It is extremely important to keep the problem of justice in the civil order, as distinguished from the religious order, clear to avoid the confusion too often created by modern day discussion of faith and justice, which fail to distinguish adequately between justice as the revealed holiness and sanctity of God and justice as a social virtue. The religious order, especially in divine revelation, is founded on an authority of service based on charity (love of God and neighbour) which knows no minimal standards, no sanctions, and no penalties, but only the mercy and compassion of one who gives his own life that others may live eternally."[495]

Despite the proclivity of the contemporary media and other social liberals toward covetousness, there is no per se virtue in wealth equality. In fact, in the earlier discussion of covetousness and envy in Chapter VI, I asserted that the opposite can be argued. Income disparity has significant social benefits to the extent that the society in general benefits from the philanthropy and tax payments of the higher income group. Further, as suggested in the earlier discussion of liberty in Chapter IX, it can be asserted that liberty and parity are logically and practically inconsistent. Equal rights implies unequal results. Equal results (outcomes) implies unequal rights. Reflecting this relationship, the United States Constitution and the accompanying Bill of Rights guarantee equal rights, not equal outcomes. Nevertheless, in an attempt to provide a cloak of respectability, envy and covetousness have been enshrouded by the contemporary politically correct phrase, "economic justice." Some contemporary social theologians have misapplied scriptural passages to economic systems, when, in fact the matter being addressed was generosity. As discussed earlier in the section on generosity, when Paul suggests to the Corinthians that they give money to the Jerusalem churches so that "there might be equality" (2 Cor. 8:13), he was referring to spiritual equality, their sharing in the ultimate salvation of all Israel. Further, Paul prefaced his discussion with "I am not commanding you, but I want to test the sincerity of your love." (2 Cor. 8:8) What some have attempted to pass as a biblical theory of economic justice is not that at all. Rather, it is a theory of theological genuiness. There is no concept of mandatory redistribution of wealth put forward by Paul whose major concern was the expression of love. In this regard perhaps John Stackhouse, professor of theology at Regent College, provides the most appropriate definition for "economic justice," one that is practical, workable and within the teachings of Jesus: "The operative word is 'enough.' The poor should have enough, and the rich should say 'enough.'"[496]

There are two considerable problems associated with a society pursuing income equality as an objective. First, is the practical, empirical one that, anywhere it has ever been done, the equal income is at a very low level. Sociologist Peter Berger declares, "Socialist equality is shared poverty by serfs, coupled with the monopolization of both privilege and power by a small (increasingly hereditary) aristocracy.... It seems to be the intrinsic genius of socialism to produce these facsimiles of feudalism."[497] In Cuba, for example, rather than the poor becoming unpoor, everyone—save a small political elite—becomes poor. Another example: "The poorest one fifth of the population in South Korea is wealthier than the richest one fifth in North Korea."[498] Would you rather live in less-equal Switzerland or more-equal China? Financial equality is a meaningless concept. Second, given the sinful nature of humanity, the programs and organizations required to implement such a policy require the elimination of liberty. Novak sums up as follows, "Yet if one keeps uppermost in mind the material needs of the poor, the hungry, and the oppressed,.... I have come to think that the dream of democratic socialism is inferior to the dream of democratic capitalism, and that the latter's superiority in actual practice is undeniable..... the record of existing socialism is plain,... Whatever the high intentions of its partisans, the structures they build by their actions promise to increase poverty and to legitimate tyranny."[499] Empirically, capitalist economies have made the greatest achievement in the reduction of poverty, the severest economic injustice of all.

Professor Murray lays to rest this subject of equality of outcome. "It is simply a fact that God has not ordained equality of distribution of gift or possession. And because this is so, it is impossible to put equality into effect. Some are more capable of increasing their possessions; they are more provident, diligent, industrious, progressive. Are we to suppose that the qualities which make for the development of natural resources are to be discouraged? Are we to engage in a leveling process that will secure uniformity and make all conform to a stereotyped average? How absurd would be the attempt, and how futile! Equality is not a fact of God's providence, and it is not a rule to be practiced in the order he has instituted; diversity is a fact to be recognized and the rule to be followed. Liberty itself must take account of inequality. Unequal distribution of wealth is indigenous to the order God has established and to the natures with which he has endowed us."[500]

Nevertheless, to return to the main point, one of the most distinguished characteristics of developed capitalistic countries has been the emergence of a broad middle class. This condition is dramatically opposite of that of the societies of Biblical times. For example, to borrow from LaSor's research, "This is the picture of society Amos painted so vividly. Two classes had developed: rich and poor (Am. 5:10,15; 6:4). The poor were oppressed (2:6; 5:11; 6:3-6) and even sold into slavery (2:6-8). The rich had summer and winter palaces crammed with ivory-inlaid art and furniture(3:15), great vineyards for choice wines, and precious oils for hygiene and perfume (5:11; 6:4-6). The women, fat as pampered 'cows of Bashan,' drove their husbands to injustice so they might live in luxury (4:1). Justice was a commodity to be purchased."[501] This bears no resemblance whatsoever to any democratic capitalistic society today, and therefore, these images should not be permitted to influence one's thinking about contemporary economic matters. However, viewed on a global scale, the battle against poverty still has a long, long way to go. The great bulk of the world's population are poor. Further, throughout Scripture there is a special concern for the poor; the poor are explicitly identified as needful of special attention. This was particularly noted in our discussion of Generosity, and we will return to this in the next chapter when discussing the global social and economic common denominator.

Before leaving this discussion of the poor, let us explicitly acknowledge a very important distinction, the common ignoring of which casts considerable confusion on the subject of poverty. The distinction is simply that, *by definition*, we will *never* eradicate poverty. This is because in our society "poverty" is a relative term. In wealthy, egalitarian, generous societies such as the western capitalistic nations there will always be concern for those on the bottom rungs. Further, the definition of "subsistence" and "necessities" has always been rising and can be expected to continue to rise. Each year the United States federal government re-establishes the official "poverty line" income of families of various sizes. Because this number is related to a particular minimum acceptable standard of living which itself is a dynamic, ever-changing level, then, the objective of ridding a society of poverty is a nonsequitur. Therefore, while it has been and always will be logically impossible to rid a society of poverty, the condition of poverty is continuously being improved over time. For example, today in the United States most poor people enjoy television information and entertainment. Each Christmas the employees of the bank of which I served as Managing Director gave gifts to poor families. First, we contacted the State of Washington Department of Health and Social Services or, in some years, a private social service agency and received the names of each of the members of two families deemed "poor." All of our bank employees became lovingly and enthusiastically involved in shopping for or making the gifts, wrapping them, and then delivering them. It is interesting to note that in all of the cases, upon delivering the gifts, we observed that all of the people had a television set and a telephone and most had a car. That is wonderful that they do. What percentage of people in the world have television sets, telephones and automobiles? Beckman comments, "I remember trying to explain to friends in Bangladesh—people for whom bicycles are luxuries—how it could be that some people in the United States who own cars consider themselves poor."[502] D'Souza presents some interesting statistics: "Today poor people in the United States spend less than half their income on basic necessities.... 50 percent of Americans defined by the government as 'poor' have air-conditioning, 60 percent have microwave ovens and VCR's, 70 percent have one or more cars, 72 percent have washing machines, 77 percent have telephones, 93 percent have at least one color television and 98 percent have a refrigerator."[503] Therefore, it is irrational to be on some sort of an overwhelming guilt trip over the mathematical truism that there will always be the bottom X%. Do not misunderstand what I am saying. Indeed, raising the standard of living of all humans remains a glorious opportunity and responsibility for us all. And, as displayed quite clearly in the foregoing discussion, has been a major accomplishment of capitalism.

Accordingly, the foregoing discussion notwithstanding, it must be emphasized that, because by definition we will never eradicate poverty, we will never rid ourselves of the need for generosity. Today a disturbing statistic continues: despite a decade of continuous economic prosperity and an uninterrupted vibrant expansion of the U.S. economy, there still remain over 30 million people (approximately 11% of the population) in poverty (annual income below $16,660 for a family of four).[504] After adjusting for the dynamic characteristic of young people and students just getting started in vocations and careers earning low wages and salaries, the number of actual poor in the United State is probably around 5%, or 15 million of God's creations—far too high by any standards. Such a situation is a national disgrace, and those committed to attacking this disgrace are to be commended. Nevertheless the most effective device for combating poverty remains a two-fold mechanism. First, incent the vibrant creation of wealth. Second, incent the broad distribution of wealth. Capitalism, with its dependence on healthy markets, does both.

Taking a global perspective on the subject of poverty, I agree with Beckman's observation as a World Bank economist that, "The extent of absolute poverty is intolerable," and, quoting Kurt Waldheim, former Secretary-General of the United Nations, "mass poverty is 'the single most devastating indictment of current world civilization."[505] It is fascinating to observe that, while the great majority of the world's population can be described as poor, those who have been raised up out of poverty have been done so in economies in which the following are the distinguishing characteristics: private property accompanied by individual incentives, productive resources allocated in a relatively free price system, and a democratic political system. Obviously Western Europe and the United States are the stellar examples, particularly juxtaposed against Eastern Europe and the former Soviet Union, perhaps the most resource-rich region of the world. It is dramatic to compare the economic achievements of South Korea to North Korea, Taiwan to Red China, Hong Kong and Singapore to Pakistan and Cambodia. Certainly differing natural resources do not explain the differences. They are explained entirely by differences in political and economic systems. The economic successes are characterized by accumulated profits reinvested in technological advancements which increased productivity—done within a stable political environment upholding the rule of law. Novak makes the empirical observation, "In the Third World,... the nations least touched by market economics are poorest,..."[506]

Rich Karlgaard, publisher of *Forbes*, points out another cause of poverty in many countries: the absence of private property. "Property laws unlock wealth.... Hernando de Soto, the South American economist [and author of] *The Mystery of Capital*,....thinks that the world's postcommunist poor—some 4 billion souls out of the world's 6 billion—own more assets than most economists ever stop to consider. The problem is title, not wealth. Lacking title to his land patch or milk cow, and bedeviled by local bureaucrats from getting it, the poor man remains a squatter. What wealth he owns may feed him but is otherwise 'dead.' He can't tap it as collateral to buy another cow or a two-stroke engine or a PalmPilot. He can't grow. His road out of poverty is blocked."[507]

One of the most baffling discoveries of my three-year research underlying this book is that many of those who profess a concern for global poverty are the very ones who decry the very mechanism that offers the greatest hope to the world's poor: capitalism. The typical book on the subject of world poverty starts out with a chapter denouncing the growing gap between the rich and the poor nations. Yes, the gap is growing. And the gap is growing largely because so many of the poor nations and those who profess a concern for the poor nations fail to get the message, fail to draw the logical conclusion from empirical evidence. The growing gap between the capitalistic nations and the noncapitalistic nations is testimony to a very clear, simple message: the success of capitalism in generating *and distributing* wealth. The logical reaction to the fact of a growing gap is an embracement, not a denunciation, of capitalism. As Sider notes, "Market economies have been far more successful than existing alternatives in creating wealth. Those who care about the poor should endorse market-oriented economics—rather than state-owned, centrally planned ones—as the best basic framework currently known for economic life."[508] Indeed, those who seek a solution to poverty in various places in the world would be well-advised to cease their pre-occupation with the question, "why are the poor nations poor?" (particularly when massive poverty has been the natural condition of humanity for all of the thousands of years of our existence, right up to just the past hundred years) and rather embrace the clear answer to "why are the rich nations rich?" The widespread distribution of affluence is a miraculous occurrence of just a flicker of time in the history of humanity and among just a small portion of humans alive today. One would think that anyone concerned with poverty would be fascinated by the unusual phenomenon of wealth and investigate it. The greatest victims of a lack of understanding and commitment to capitalism are the world's poor. They remain destined to continue the bleak existence of their ancestors of the prior tens of thousand of years.

The final testimony as to how far capitalistic countries have come in raising people out of poverty is in fact the indignation toward poverty that exists in capitalistic countries. Even throughout Scripture, while a major concern of God, Jesus and others is the plight of the poor, particularly how the poor are treated, nowhere in Scripture can be found surprise or indignation over the fact of poverty's existence nor can be found any sort of declaration that poverty ought to be eliminated. Throughout the history of the church, while all of the great historical religious leaders express loving concern for the poor, nowhere is there the declaration that poverty ought to be done away with. This did not reflect any value judgement; it simply reflected the overwhelming, dominant reality that—because of the pervasiveness of poverty; it being the natural condition of the masses—an objective of eliminating it would have been deemed such an impossibility that its mere suggestion was beyond realistic consideration. Perhaps the greatest testimony to the triumph of capitalism in reducing poverty is the outrage that is expressed in capitalistic societies that some people even continue in the state of

poverty. Not until the emergence of a broad affluent middle class—
a recent occurrence within human history—has humanity become
indignant over the mere fact of poverty.

Second, in a capitalistic society economic power is diffused.

Nash observes, "One of the more effective ways of mitigating the
effects of human sin in society is dispersing and decentralizing
power. The combination of a free market economy and limited
constitutional government is the most effective means yet devised
to impede the concentration of economic and political power.[509]

Unlike socialistic societies wherein a monolithic state is
producer and distributor, in capitalistic societies production and
distribution comes forth from hundreds of thousands of unrelated,
enterprises many of which have conflicting, countervailing interests. For example, anyone who thinks that the over 10,000 separate
banks in the United States have a singular position on most issues
just doesn't understand. There are big banks, little banks, urban
banks, rural banks, consumer banks, corporate banks, commercial
banks, mortgage banks, etc., etc., etc.

One of the great myths of modern America is that large corporations have almost omnipotent power. For some reason Americans
have arbitrarily conveyed an image of power to corporations far
beyond that which exists in reality. Despite hundreds of millions of
dollars spent on research, engineering, design, tooling, organizing
and promoting the Edsel, Ford Motor Company was brought to its
knees by the individual American consumer who rejected this product. Similarly, giant Xerox, which was poised for the introduction
of a personal computer which it had spent millions of dollars developing, was pre-empted by a nimble end-run by a small band of
entrepreneurs and venture capitalists. Recently Bethlehem Steel
and Polaroid, once innovative industrial leaders which became
giants of American capitalism, declared bankruptcy. There are tens
of thousand of other examples wherein the consumer is king.

Those alleging inordinate power held by American corporations
lose sight of the fact that, thanks to increasing economic globalization, these firms are also competing vigorously with foreign suppliers, automobiles being an excellent example. In fact, in this day of a
global economy, analyzing economic issues in the context of the

boundaries of any particular country—especially the United States—is invalid. Boeing competes vigorously against Airbus. And virtually every American supplier of any product faces not only domestic competitors but competitors from abroad as well. Further, any business firm is not only competing with other producers of the same product, but with all producers of all products. We sovereign consumers are not only deciding which car to buy, but whether or not to spend these funds on a car, a trip, a second home down payment, a remodel of the kitchen, or any number of alternatives. It is interesting to hear Beckman's personal testimony, "I went from seminary to graduate school in economics primarily because I was concerned about charges of U.S. imperialism. At that time my analysis of big corporations, for example, was primarily in terms of power.... But in studying economics I learned the subtler logic of trade, and came to appreciate that even big corporations have to earn their keep, also in developing countries, by providing goods and services their clients cannot get as cheaply elsewhere."[510]

When discussing capitalism's diffusion of economic power, it should nevertheless be acknowledged that even in most capitalistic economies the government plays a dominant role in the economy in two respects:

(1) as a regulator to inhibit anti-public behavior by business firms, and
(2) as a participant through monetary and fiscal policy to stimulate or dampen down the economy.

Implementing fiscal policy continues as a government function in the United States even though the prescriptions of John Maynard Keynes, who erroneously assumed a constant production function, have been debunked by such stalwarts as Milton Friedman, who showed that economic cycles were more tied to the money supply, and Margaret Thatcher, who as Prime Minister of Britain stimulated the economy in the early 1980's by instituting fiscal constraints and expansionary monetary policy. The role of government in the economy is a subject of continuing widespread debate and is outside the scope of this book. Certainly government regulation of private enterprise is highly appropriate in order to protect the interests of consumers by overseeing the safety of products, maintaining a competitive market and otherwise insuring that economic power is diffused.

Nevertheless, it should be noted that certain types of limitations on the free market work against power diffusion. Powell discusses the work by Nobel laureate George Stigler: "Until the early 1960's, almost everybody seemed to assume government regulations did what they were supposed to: protect consumers.... University of Chicago economist George J. Stigler realized that nobody had ever tried to measure the actual effects of laws and regulations. He began measuring, and he either couldn't find any effects of a regulation or the effects were the opposite of what was intended. Stigler went on to make a revolutionary case that government regulations were lobbied for by interest groups to restrict competition, raise prices, and in other ways gain a privileged position not available in an open market.... By the 1970's there was substantial consensus in the economics profession that many regulations were counterproductive, and the movement to deregulate the economy gained momentum."[511] The reason that this is so, as identified by von Mises, is that interference with the market system often can eliminate the critical role of prices in providing information to producers and consumers and thereby lead to an inefficient allocation of economic resources.

Suffice it to conclude with the observation that at least with capitalism the loci of economic power and of political power are separate, not one and the same as in socialism. Therefore, regardless of the size of the participants, at least under capitalism we benefit from the effects of countervailing powers as eloquently enunciated by J. K. Galbraith.[512] Even if the large U.S. corporations had the colossal power erroneously attributed to them by some people, that power would be offset by the power of labor unions, state governments, the federal government, consumer groups, trade associations, and, most noteworthy, foreign suppliers.

Finally, in this discussion of economic power, considering sinful humans we should heed Novak's assertion, "Lust for power is deeper, more pervasive, and more widespread than lust for wealth."[513] When the arena of political power and economic power are combined, all sorts of opportunities for foul play emerge. Within the government sector personal relationships and "loyalties" play an inordinately important role. In determining one's advancement economically, getting to know the right people becomes considerably more important than effectively serving consumers. Further, when one represents the sole supplier of a good or service, extortion and bribery become the accepted common practice. The dominant ethic of the entire country becomes, not serving the consumer, but advancing one's own political status through relationships or economic status through bribery. Again, these are not just theoretical musings on my part. Substantial empirical evidence exists to support the notion that bribery at *all* levels is the common practice in nondemocratic socialistic countries. Indeed, in the ethics classes of business schools in universities throughout the United States the most common case study of an ethical challenge to businesses is, how do we deal with the demand for a bribe by a government official abroad?

In socialistic countries it all comes down to one bureaucrat who is going to decide how many widgets are produced, by whom, where, and sold at what price. In capitalistic countries individual consumers bring about those decisions through daily "voting" their dollars, and the multitude of existing and potential producers respond accordingly. And as we observed previously when discussing the market system, the great irony is that under the disjointed, separate, uncoordinated, conflicting individual decisions of millions of consumers and hundreds of thousands of suppliers within capitalism, the outcome is elegantly efficient. So under a system of a multitude of producers and distributors two marvelous outcomes occur:

(1) consumers determine what is produced and at what price, and
(2) economic power is diffused among multitudes of participants.

When discussing diffusion of power, a final dimension of this issue must be mentioned. While most business firms, save Nordstrom and a few others, are hierarchical in the organizational structure, no corporations are as top-down oriented or autocratic in their behavior as the typical government agency. A good friend of mine who left a prominent corporate position to take a high-level post in the Reagan Administration commented to me once that "managing government workers is a piece of cake. You send out a directive, and they comply—do what they're told—no back-talk, better idea, different observation of the marketplace, or any of a number of inputs that I am used to getting from subordinates in the private sector." Power and the opportunity to effect decisions is as diffused within business firms as in any human organization and considerably more so than in government. Recall the earlier discussion of "Enlightened Leadership" in Chapter IX. Today, most effective business leaders manage by consensus.

Novak summarizes, "An economic system in which private corporations play a role, in turn, alters the political horizon. It lifts the poor, creates a broad middle class, and undermines aristocracies of birth. Sources of power are created independent of the power of the state."[514] Let us conclude this section with a statement in The Oxford Declaration: "economic power is diffused within market-oriented economies to a greater extent than in other systems."[515]

Third, capitalism has led to enlightened stewardship of God's resources.

As stated earlier, Malthus, who couldn't be bothered with trivia such as evidence, and his latter day disciples in the Club of Rome have been fully discredited by empirical data. The demand for the world's resources has not outrun supply. This has resulted from two elements: first, productivity advances; second, the price system.

In its vigorous pursuit of productivity, efficiency and maximum value, capitalism has contributed to the incredibly efficient utilization of the world's resources. In 1900 in the United States 841 million acres were in farmland. Today, there are 954 million acres in farmland, a 13% increase, while output has increased fourfold, feeding over triple the number of Americans—and a large portion of the world's population as well![516] Over just the past two decades U.S. farm productivity has increased by over 50%.[517] Griffiths notes, "The primary source of wealth creation in the Western world over the past one hundred years has been the increasing efficiency with which resources are used rather than the growth of the resources themselves."[518]

The price system assures that the lowest cost, most plentiful resources are used for any economic activity. As we observed in discussing the price system and the law of supply and demand, when the supply of a resource commences to become relatively scarce, its price rises, causing two things to occur. First, consumers will start to use substitutes. As the price of a redwood picnic table rises, an increasing number of people will be satisfied to use a less expensive fir or cedar or metal picnic table. Second, producers will start to use substitute inputs.

The other way in which capitalism contributes to enlightened stewardship of natural resources is the self-interest and long range perspective of capitalism which was discussed earlier. To the extent that the most common form of business organization is the corporation most of which exist in perpetuity, the mind-set of the business leader is one of perpetuity, eternity if you will. Clearly there are pressures for short-run performance, none the least of which come from the masses of workers who quarterly track the performance of their 401k investment plans. Other short-run thinking stems from the corporate officer who wants to achieve a stellar performance while the company or division or department is under his watch. Nevertheless, the perspective of most corporations as an entity is eternity—either as is or as merged into another entity. Most corporations plan and behave as if they are going to exist forever. (This is not to suggest that they will make it. One of the great benefits of the free market system is its "selecting out"—failing—those firms that do not effectively perform their role of efficiently satisfying consumer demand.)

Let me give an example of how this leads to responsible resource management. Because the decision horizon of the owners of the Weyerhaeuser Company is eternity, the company has a policy and practice of sustained yield forestry. In fact it was Weyerhaeuser, not a government agency, which seventy years ago came up with the idea and instituted the practice of sustained yield forestry. This refers to the notion that in any given year the volume of timber cut is limited to the volume of timber growth. This way the timber resource is never depleted. Further, because it is the objective of the owners to increase the earnings over time, the timber resource is managed so that the volume of timber growth exceeds the volume of timber cut. Currently Weyerhaeuser plants more than 100 million seedlings annually throughout the world.[519]

There is another major way in which capitalism contributes to responsible, efficient use of God's natural resources. Reflecting the objective of increasing earnings over time, Weyerhaeuser invests hundreds of millions of dollars in research, developing improved fertilizers, implementing advanced thinning practices and other silvaculture measures—all toward increasing the volume of wood grown per acre. This effectiveness is supported by empirical data. Today, globally the timber growth rate (volume per acre per year) on well-managed corporate timberland is ten-times as great as the growth rate of timber on natural timberland. In other words, by utilizing advanced forest management practices, one-tenth of the forests of the globe are required to supply the wood and paper products used by the world's population.[520] According to the U.S. Forest Service, annual timber growth in the United States exceeds harvest by 37 per cent and has exceeded harvest every year since 1952.[521] Interestingly, while as a youngster attending YMCA camp on the shores of pristine Spirit Lake at the base of then majestic Mt. St. Helens and hiking on trails throughout both U.S. Forest Service land and Weyerhaeuser land on the west slopes of the Cascade Mountains, we would observe that the elk and other wildlife were more abundant on Weyerhaeuser land where berries and other edibles benefited from the fertilizing and thinning practiced by Weyerhaeuser! (Two decades later I observed a somewhat similar phenomenon: the caribou on Alaska's North Slope attracted to the nourishing, abundant and easily accessed lush grasses planted in the open space along the route of the trans-Alaska oil pipeline. Certain elitist environmentalists may not, but those caribou say a prayer of thanks every night for that pipeline!)

Despite the passion that the president of the Sierra Club might have for protecting forests and fish, none is as passionate as the private owners of those resources. To repeat for emphasis, it was private timber companies, not the government, that developed the concept of sustained yield management to ensure adequate forest resources in perpetuity. Today there is less timberland in the United States than thirty years ago,[522] but the output of wood and paper products serves a population base 25% greater while also exporting considerable quantities.

This leads us to observe a huge problem of socialism: when everyone collectively owns everything, no-one owns anything. This in turn leads to inefficient use and waste of God's resources. There are a multitude of testimonies to this. Why, for example, was the output per acre from the former USSR communal farms so far below that of the small pieces of land carved out for the farmers' own output?

This impact of capitalism was discussed at length under "Stewardship" in Chapter IV, "Source of Material Possessions and Wealth." Let me at this point summarize by quoting Novak, "The combustion engine was invented under democratic capitalism barely a century ago. The first oil well was dug in Titusville, Pennsylvania in 1859, and the first oil well in the Middle East was dug only in 1909. If oil is today to be considered a 'resource,' one must recall how short a time ago the entire human race lay in ignorance of its potential. Most of the materials we today call resources were not known to be such before the invention of a democratic capitalist political economy; many were not known to be such even one hundred years ago. (Presumably, there are others which we do not yet appreciate.) Dumb material remains inert until its secrets are discovered and a technology for bending it to human purposes is invented."[523] The key is instituting a mechanism for stimulating such discovery and innovation. Let me remind the disciples of Dr. Malthus, the false teacher, "resource" is a dynamic economic notion, not a static, physical notion.

There is another, more indirect and subtle, but also more profound element of capitalism underlying responsible stewardship of God's resources which has only recently appeared: the creation of a level of wealth that finances such stewardship. As prelude to discussing this cause of capitalism being responsible for enlightened stewardship of God's resources, let me first give some background.

There is no question that the greatest blemish on the United States landscape occurred simultaneously with the rapid industrialization in the 19th and early 20th centuries. *But the cause of this was not the particular economic system.* Three observations lead to this conclusion.

First, when we finally were able to peer into the USSR following the drawing of the Iron Curtain at the end of the 20th Century, we discovered three astonishing conditions:

- widespread corruption,
- pervasive poverty and
- extensive environmental degradation.

The first, corruption, had occurred because the political and economic systems were combined, leading to political and economic rewards based on patronage. The second, poverty, existed because of severe inefficiencies resulting from inadequate or nonexistent incentives to create and innovate, particularly related to improving productivity and quality. The third, environmental degradation, occurred because of economic immaturity characterized by the country grasping for any kind of industrial growth, similar to the United States in the 19th and early 20th centuries. Interestingly, in 1988 the amount of sulfur emissions in East Germany was triple that of West Germany; that of Poland was nearly triple that of France;[524] and at the same time the volume of production output of France and West Germany exceeded by far that of Poland and East Germany. This tragic grasping for economic growth continues today. It is pathetic that in order to obtain an estimated $21 billion in foreign currency, Russia is advertising itself to become the world's garbage dump for radioactive nuclear waste.[525]

The second observation of inadequate environmental stewardship in a noncapitalistic economy are those underdeveloped third-world countries wherein rudimentary methods are being used to scratch and claw out an existence accompanied by raping soils of their ability to sustain either agriculture or forestry. In many of these countries the environment is being severely damaged by inadequate or nonexistent sanitation, the primitive use of wood fuel, the use of inefficient rudimentary methods of agricultural and the improper disposal of waste.

The third argument for the assertion that the capitalistic system is not the villain of environmental degradation emerges when we more closely examine the period of horrible environmental stewardship in the United States—the 19th and early 20th centuries. We discover that municipal governments were as bad as industrial business firms. These are the very governments that are closest—and presumably most responsive—to the wishes of the people. It was the cities and towns, as well as business firms, across America that were dumping raw sewage and other pollutants into lakes and rivers. Like certain low level animals, we humans on our own volition through our elected officials chose to wallow around in our own excrement. (An abhorrent example is my own community, as surrounding municipalities dumped their waste into Lake Washington.) It was not the economic system. It was our lacking a will which translated into our not allocating the resources to the purpose of preventing pollution.

The common thread through these three observations is the actual or perceived lack of financial resources to allocate to environmental protection. The major cause of deficient stewardship of God's resources has been people's perceptions that "we cannot afford to"—people placing a higher priority on other collective community objectives, jobs for example.

The emergence of the strong environmental movement in the late 20th Century was not because environmental degradation had finally reached an intolerable level—it had reached that point long before. It was because of the following three conditions:

(1) scientific advances and discoveries that raised our level of knowledge regarding environmental risks and costs, the effects of asbestos and lead, for example, and

(2) more importantly, the American economy having finally reached a level of wealth that was perceived as adequate to be able to "afford" spending money for this purpose, and

(3) most importantly, having essentially reached the top of the economic mountain; i.e., having achieved in an aggregate sense our economic goals, people now commenced to place a higher priority on non-economic goals—the arts commenced to thrive, parks and bike paths proliferated, and environmental restoration and protection programs have flourished.

Indeed, the very system—capitalism—that has been used as the scapegoat for pollution is in fact the very system that brought about the strong economic growth which has created a level of wealth that has finally convinced people to allocate the scientific and financial resources to improving and protecting the environment. Regretfully, many of the citizens of the economically backward or immature countries of the world have not yet made this commitment.

It is not capitalism that lies behind environmental degradation. It is poverty and inadequate financial resources which translate into a lack of will to pursue protection of the environment. Accordingly, to the extent that capitalism has been most effective in creating and increasing the level of wealth of countries, it is capitalism that has provided both the will and the financial resources necessary for appropriate stewardship of God's natural resources. This has been the most profound, albeit indirect and subtle, element of capitalism underlying responsible stewardship.

In fact in the United States huge amounts of financial resources are being devoted to environmental restoration and protection, giving rise to a whole new industry as entrepreneurs respond to this new opportunity. In the nearly two decades from 1980 to 1998 employment in the environmental industry nearly tripled from 452,000 to 1,348,000 and revenues more than tripled from $59 billion to $192 billion.[526] As a result, while the U. S. economy has been growing strongly over the past two decades, pollution has been declining. Another interesting observation, during the past decade of the high-tech boom in the Pacific Northwest, the number of private foundations oriented toward environmental issues has multiplied five-fold.

The Environmental Protection Agency, funded, of course, by taxes on individuals and corporations, has spent nearly $15 billion on hazardous waste clean-up since the establishment of the Super-fund program in 1980. The Superfund list has included 1,450 sites over the past twenty years, having completed cleanup of 229 of those sites and currently working on 759 of the sites. Although much has been made—appropriately—of the government's relatively recent role in environmental restoration and protection, interestingly, quietly fifty years ago Weyerhaeuser revolutionized pollution control by developing the vaporsphere to reduce odor emissions of its pulp mills and designed and installed wet air scrubbers for removal of particulates, including difficult sea salts. Further, Weyerhaeuser uses "virtually every portion of the logs [brought to] sawmills, reuses 98 percent of the chemicals required for making paper, and generates two-thirds of the energy needed for pulp and paper mills from the use of biomass fuels.... [and] obtains 40 percent of the wood fiber needed for paper products from recycled wastepaper. [527] Twenty-five years ago Weyerhaeuser entered the recycling business. Currently the company spends annually an estimated $80-100 million on environmental restoration and protection.[528] Weyerhaeuser is not an aberration; rather, just a normal public corporation operating like most large public corporations do. I have just included them here as an example of the way most major U.S. companies function.

Perhaps the most profound example of wealth-induced devotion of resources to stewardship of God's creations is the annual flow of hundreds of millions of dollars into the Nature Conservatory, The Trust for Public Lands, Loomis Forest Fund and other such private organizations, the primary purpose of which is to acquire land in order to maintain its natural state. It is well known that the genesis for Grand Teton National Park in Wyoming was John D. Rockefeller's Snake River Land Company. Further, today enlightened real estate development is embodying high density "urban pockets" between green belts rather than simply expanding urban sprawl. An example is Snoqualmie Ridge, a development east of Seattle done by an affiliate of Weyerhaeuser Company. 45% of the land is devoted to open space including timbered slopes, stream buffers, wetlands and their buffers, neighborhood 'pocket parks,' a community pea patch and a 222 acre golf course. Indeed, in a wealthy society, the demands of consumers even cause the profit motive to translate into environmentally friendly use of land. The story gets more interesting. The nearby town of Snoqualmie, Washington, a picturesque historic logging community, was discharging treated waste water into the Snoqualmie River. While the sewage had been treated up to the standards of several years ago, it was below current standards, and the U.S. Environmental Protection Agency faced two alternatives: either close down the town or look the other way. EPA had selected the latter. When Weyerhaeuser submitted its application for developing Snoqualmie Ridge, indicating its intent to utilize the latest state-of-the-art sewage treatment technology and also to use much of the treated waste water for watering the proposed golf course, government officials negotiated an agreement to include treatment of the existing sewage from the town of Snoqualmie in the new system of Snoqualmie Ridge. Accordingly, as a result of this real estate development project, the town of Snoqualmie is today no longer discharging below-standard waste into the Snoqualmie River. Here is a clear case of economic growth and the attendant real estate development directly *reducing* pollution! All of this is possible solely because the level of wealth of the Western Washington economy is such that wages and salaries are at a level that permits people buying homes in Snoqualmie Ridge at high enough prices that include the cost of cleaning up the prior sewage from the people who had been living in the nearby town of Snoqualmie.

The foregoing discussion of the positive environmental effect of wealth can be summarized as follows:

FIVE STAGES OF STEWARDSHIP RELATED TO ECONOMIC STAGES IN THE UNITED STATES

Stage One	Stage Two	Stage Three	Stage Four	Stage Five
Prior to 18th Century	18th Century	19th Century	Early and mid-20th Century	Late 20th Century
U.S. pre-colonization	Cottage industries, Agriculture	Agriculture, Early industrialization	Industrialization, Mass production	Services, High technology
Subsistence	Economic Infancy	Economic Adolescence	Economic Acceleration	Economic Adulthood
		Low Wealth	Moderate Wealth	High Wealth
Negligible Impact	Minor Impact	Clearing, Desecration	Pollution	Substantial investment in protection and restoration

Accordingly, it can be argued that, once a society commits itself to economic growth, getting to the high wealth level as quickly as possible is advantageous in that it enables the allocation of resources to protection of the environment. This is the point of "ecological breakthrough"—that point when a society's wealth reaches a level which enables the society to absorb the opportunity cost of environmental restoration and protection. It is estimated that today private business firms spend over $10 billion annually on environmental restoration and protection. Note, those expenditures essentially have no effect on productivity, therefore translate into higher prices for consumers and/or lower profits for shareholders. The foregoing is expressed by Peter Huber, senior fellow at the Manhattan Institute, "Green is what people become when they feel personally secure, when their own appetites have been satisfied.... It is the rich who can cherish the wilderness because they no longer have to choose between their own survival and nature's"[529]

In summary, then, capitalism induces responsible stewardship of Gods resources in six ways. First, the price system makes scarce resources more expensive, discouraging their use. Second, the profit motive places a high value on productivity, minimizing the quantity of inputs required for a quantity of output. Third, the decision horizon for most business firms is eternity inducing the practice of sustained yield management. Fourth, a relatively high level of wealth is attained giving the populace the will to commit resources to protecting the environment. Fifth, separating producers from regulators (business from government) enables the government to maintain pressure on the private sector to behave responsibly. Sixth, the population growth rate of affluent capitalistic countries is considerably lower than that of poorer countries, limiting the pressure of population on the environment. On the sixth factor, Sider notes, "Affluence and decline in population growth seem to go together.... Fortunately, empowering the poor is a quick way to reduce the population explosion."[530]

In conclusion, it should be noted that the matter of environmental stewardship probably is accompanied by more misinformation, myths and hypocrisy than any other issue in American economics and politics. As just one example, during the election campaigns of 2000, I, who have been on Alaska's North Slope and the Arctic National Wildlife Refuge dozens of times, was continuously aghast to hear some congressman from the eastern U.S., who for that matter may never have been west of the Mississippi River, refer to that Alaska frozen tundra as a pristine jewel and that "saving" it is worth incurring the enormous opportunity cost of higher energy prices and greater risk of energy supply. Another related example, it is an interesting fact that the seepage of hydrocarbons from the oil rigs in Cook Inlet, Alaska, actually contributes to the vitality of sea life in that body of water. But the "have nots" attacking the oil companies do not seem to want to let these facts get in their way. It is interesting to note that Britain and Norway, whose fishing industries are integral to their social and economic fabric, have not permitted such fanaticism to block sensible offshore oil drilling.

Volumes have been written on such unscientific and even nonsensical and hypocritical misapplication of environmental stewardship, and I refer you to them. For the record, let me state that I cherish my cabins on Dabob Bay, Washington and at Mt. Bachelor, Oregon and I possesses the typical Westerner's reverence for the majestic surroundings in which I am fortunate to live. Further, as a Christian, I view all of God's creations as reflecting His glory. Therefore, ignoring the pervasive diatribes of the ignorant, I thank God for capitalism's contribution to responsible environmental stewardship. Capitalism has provided both the incentives and the wealth to underwrite such enlightened stewardship. Reflecting their enlightened leadership, today the boards of directors of virtually every major transnational corporation have adopted official policies related to their stewardship of God's creations. Just a tiny sampling of Weyerhaeuser's approach is included in Appendix L.

Fourth, capitalism has fostered political stability.

Most of the social atrocities in the world that are so disturbing to the Christian mind can be attributed to severe political instabilities, particularly in underdeveloped nations. Capitalism has fostered political stability in several different ways.

First, intrinsic to capitalism is private property. As we observed earlier, private property, by protecting the rights of minorities and protecting the ability to dissent, undergirds democracy.

It is private property which protects one against political oppression, because when the state owns all property, dissent and the protection of minorities is impossible.

Second, the rule of law is a critical element to capitalism. While at the same time providing consistent and constant protection of the rights of participants in business transactions, it provides the same protection to all individuals. Further related, one of the advantages of separating the economic sector (producers and distributors) from the government is that it prevents a sort of muddling of interests wherein the government in general and individual bureaucrats and officials in particular face continuous conflicts of interests. Having two distinct sectors—the private sector which is focused on serving consumers and generating earnings for shareholders and a government sector which is focused on regulating and otherwise overseeing the private sector—is a model that ensures responsible behavior which benefits the populace in general. All of this occurring within the rule of law establishes a legal and political environment that tends to be accompanied by consistency, predictability and, thereby, stability.

Third, capitalism made possible the emergence of a massive, stable middle class. In addition to being brought about by the impressive productivity advancements discussed earlier, much of the credit for achieving a massive middle class in the United States goes to the labor unions. Unlike many of their foreign brethren who aimed toward overthrowing the very economic system, most American labor unions in the nineteenth and early twentieth centuries focused on wages, benefits, and working conditions. This enlightened focus on economic rather than political issues; that is, on obtaining their share of the pie rather than changing the pie or constraining the size of the pie, resulted in American workers participating in the benefits of growth of the United States economy. Conversely, a great disparity of wealth in a society characterized by a small wealthy elite and the remainder in poverty often gives rise to political instability accompanied by revolutions reflecting an attitude of "what do we have to lose?" Beckman agrees, "Capitalism in developing countries also leads to the formation of an independently minded middle-class, which is eventually likely to demand representative government and civil liberties."[531]

Fourth, the very existence of private property and economic security in turn gives rise to a general independence of thought pervasive in a capitalistic society. The apostle Paul articulated often to his followers that the genuiness of his message was demonstrated by his having relied on no one else for his worldly needs. "I have not hesitated to proclaim to you the whole will of God....I have not coveted anyone's silver or gold or clothing. You yourselves know that these hands of mine have supplied my own needs and the needs of my companions." (Acts 20:27,33,34) "... others have this right of support from you,... But we did not use this right... I am free and belong to no man,..." (1 Cor. 9:12-19) Financial independence assured Paul's theological independence. Genuine independence of thought accompanied by freedom of expression of course prevents the accumulation of pent-up political frustrations which eventually explode in upheaval.

This contribution of capitalism to political stability was observed by Adam Smith over two centuries ago, "...commerce and manufacturers gradually introduced order and good government, and with them, the liberty and security of individuals,...who had before lived [in the feudal system] almost in a continual state of war.... A revolution of the greatest importance to the public happiness was brought about. To gratify...was the sole motive of the great proprietors.... It is this that through the greater part of Europe commerce...instead of being the effect has been the cause and occasion of the improvement and cultivation of the country."[532]

As observed earlier, capitalism is oriented to the future. It is the future return from today's investments and it is the future value of today's wealth that investors are most concerned with. Accordingly, everyone within a capitalistic society has a vested interest in ensuring a stable, consistent and tranquil future.

Fifth, capitalism has set free and stimulated economic creativity.

Creation is an on-going activity of God. Humans' ability to create is God-originated; it is a reflection of our having been created in the image of God. Humans' creativity is a reflection of the Holy Spirit within. The form which any particular individual's creativity takes is a reflection of that person's God-given talents. The ultimate economic manifestation of the creation process is entrepreneurialism, the bringing into being of a new business enterprise offering a new or higher quality good or service. Capitalism, sets free this creativity.

Gilder expresses this concept in the following manner. "It is these capitalists, extending the division of labor by launching new goods and services, who expand the market,...extend the frontiers of human possibility. The greatest damage inflicted by state systems of redistribution is not the 'distortion of markets,' the 'misallocation of resources,' or the 'discoordination' of producers and consumers, but the deflation of capitalist energy, the repression of … ideas,…. Steeply 'progressive' tax rates not only destroy incentives; more important they destroy knowledge…."[533]

Nevertheless, in certain circles it is popular to bemoan the use of the term "progress" to describe the outcome of technological advance, noting the social costs such as crime, pollution, etc. which can accompany economic growth. However, we have observed how creation of jobs reduces crime and how, after achieving a certain threshold level of wealth, today general economic growth is *conducive* to improving the environment. We must keep in mind a point made at the beginning of this book that the market system and the profit motive are neutral. Their output is not progress per se. Whether or not their output can be dubbed progress depends upon the use to which we humans put that output.

It is acknowledged, and will be addressed as the final topic of this book, that economic creativity and the resultant technological advance and material gains, to the extent that they are only of this world, are meaningless—neither good nor bad per se—to God. As noted by Guinness, "Capitalism, for all its creativity and fruitfulness, falls short when challenged to answer the question 'Why?' By itself it is literally meaning-less, in that it is only a mechanism, not a source of meaning."[534] Further reflective of this position of the irrelevance of worldly systems, in Revelation we are not called upon to change the system, rather to abandon it and simply remain faithful and true. However, such a position conflicts with the common message throughout Scripture that God want us to be prosperous in a worldly sense in this life.

We are still talking about life in the world. And creativity expressed through technological advance has done much to serve God. Indeed, a technological invention—the Gutenberg printing press—is given credit as a major contributor to the explosion of Christianity during the Reformation. Today one can now download the Bible over the Internet—in whatever language one desires. Similarly, the millions of discoveries emanating from the research and development departments of capitalistic corporations have saved lives, improved health, advanced education, fought crime, even facilitated spiritual growth (by reducing the construction costs of churches, introducing sound systems benefiting the hearing impaired listening to sermons, enlarging the size of print and reducing the unit production costs of Bibles, etc.), and otherwise contributed to the progress of all aspects of humanity. Simply to list all of these creations flowing from private enterprise which improve human life would take volumes. Suffice it to conclude here that, clearly, technological advance is all part of God's plan, all part of Divine order.

Interestingly, Schumpeter, one of the great champions of capitalism, saw in its success the seeds of its undoing: as business firms grew in size, entrepreneurs would be replaced by managers. He failed to see that corporate size creates the ability to devote massive amounts of capital to research and development as well as investment in new ventures, maintaining the entrepreneurial role of the corporation. Schumpeter also failed to foresee the present New Economy revolution propelled by millions of small high-tech and low-tech entrepreneurs throughout the world. As observed earlier, virtually all of the jobs created since 1980 have come from small firms. Start-ups are growing at three times the pace of the national economy. No economist alive or dead ever foresaw that at the end of the twentieth century, with the U. S. economy having achieved massive size, not only would the continued upward propulsion not be primarily due to gigantic corporations, but that the average size of the business firm would be *declining!*

Entrepreneurialism—economic creativity—is thriving! While the Industrial Revolution was characterized by many drudgery jobs associated with mass production, the chief characteristic of the economy of the 20th and 21st centuries is creativity and fulfillment. The ethic of not only small high-tech firms, but most huge corporations as well, places a very high value on innovation and coming up with ways of doing one's job better—an expectation even among the "lowest" job holders of a firm. In today's fast-paced economy with change occurring at ever-accelerating speed, "routine" is not an acceptable term. Further, the meaningfulness of work is very much a major concern of the present enlightened business leadership. Employee benefits made portable have removed a major impediment to job transfer, and now multiple careers—related to fulfilling a broader spectrum of an individual's needs or actualizing a greater degree of one's potentialities—are becoming the norm. Much stimulation of individual creativity has resulted from the increasingly widespread use of stock options which puts workers and owners in the same mindset.

The critical elements that have unleashed and will continue to induce in the future this impressive vibrant, widespread creativity is the freedom of the marketplace and incentive of the profit motive. Novak summarizes, "The Creator locked great riches in nature, riches to be discovered gradually through human effort.... This potential was hidden for thousand of years until human discovery began to release portions of it for human benefit. Yet even today we have not yet begun to imagine all the possibilities of wealth in the world the Creator designed..... What the entire human race meant by energy until the discovery of the United States and the inventions promoted by its political economy were the natural forces of sun, wind, moving water, animals, and humans muscle.... The primary capital of any corporation is insight, invention, finding a better way."[535]

Sixth, capitalism has generated a high level of non-economic goods.

The relentless pursuit of efficiency among capitalists leads to the most efficient allocation of productive resources in turn minimizing the cost thereof. This applies not only to secular entities but to religious as well: the printing of Bibles, the construction and furnishing of churches, etc., in turn maximizing the number of souls reached.

Further, the high level of national wealth generated by capitalism in turn permits our turning attention from satisfaction of basic economic needs to satisfaction of important non-economic needs. Perhaps the most dramatic example is the environmental movement. As observed earlier, only after achieving a certain level of wealth did the people of the United States have the will to bear the opportunity costs of transferring productive resources from generating economic goods and services to generating and/or protecting assets associated with psychic income. Stated another way, only after a certain level of achievement of economic goals was attained, did Americans turn attention to greater achievement of our *non-*economic goals. This also was addressed in the earlier discussion of stewardship of God's resources.

Enough evidence exists to draw the conclusion that not only is capitalism responsible for impressive economic achievements, but also has been responsible for equally impressive non-economic achievements. Novak observes, "The chief funder of the many works of civil society, from hospitals and research institutes to museums, the opera, orchestras, and universities is the business corporation. The corporation today is even a major funder of public television"[536] which, I will add, presents many programs which run counter to the very interests of the corporations which fund them. Former Prime Minister Margaret Thatcher asks rhetorically, "How could we respond to the many calls for help, or invest for the future, or support the wonderful artists and craftsmen whose work also glorifies God, unless we had first worked hard and used our talents to create the necessary wealth?"[537] D'Souza reminds us that *all* of the income of philanthropies and of governments is the donated and taxed surpluses generated by capitalism. A major area of non-economic benefits from the capitalistic system is health care. Largely as the result of research and development by pharmaceutical and bio-tech companies as well as grants to universities and taxes to government from individuals and corporations, medical research in the capitalistic countries has dwarfed that of the non-capitalistic countries. The results have been impressive. Today in the United States a person lives nearly two-thirds longer than in 1900. (Life expectancy at birth was 47 years in 1900 and 77 years in 1997).[538]

There are myriad examples of social benefits from private enterprise in every community of America. I will relate one example which I experienced. In the 1960's Alaska was a rural, extractive economy with a paucity of public goods and services which is normally characteristic of such an economy. After risking hundreds of millions of dollars in exploration, several major oil companies discovered oil in the northernmost part of the state. In 1974, shortly after I arrived to serve as chief economist of the National Bank of Alaska, the state's largest bank, the oil companies commenced construction of a pipeline to transport the oil nearly 800 miles across the state to a terminal at the Port of Valdez for shipment to the "Lower 48." In 1977 pipeline construction was completed, and the shipment of oil commenced. While the large number of workers and families brought into Alaska for oil production placed commensurately heavy pressure on public goods and services— police, water, sewer, schools, etc., nevertheless, the public revenues generated by the royalties, taxes and fees associated with the oil production exceeded by far the additional requirement for public goods—huge excesses were available for a whole array of discretionary public goods—parks, bike paths, performing arts facilities, better health care, etc. Petroleum firms finance over 80% of the expenditures by the State of Alaska. Even more significantly, from the moment they arrived in Alaska, the oil companies and their employees *voluntarily* donated huge amounts of money and personal time for the arts, recreation, education, etc., enhancing the whole array of cultural opportunities in a previously culturally-deficient society. Relatively high skilled, highly paid and well-educated employees of these firms served as Sunday school teachers, volunteers in homeless shelters, classroom assistants in public schools, museum docents and on and on. Indeed, the social/public benefit from the petroleum industry may very well have exceeded its economic/private benefit!

Sowell presents another example. "The tragic earthquake that has killed more than 25,000 people in India was not as large as the 1989 earthquake in California that killed fewer than a hundred people. The difference is that Californians are affluent enough to build their homes, buildings, and other structures to earthquake-resistant standards, while the poverty-stricken people of India are not. Moreover, California has far more rescue equipment, more motor vehicles to rush people to hospitals, and far better medical facilities waiting in those hospitals. Wealth is one of the greatest savers of lives, whether in earthquakes or in a thousand other ways."[539] There are thousands upon thousands of other examples, empirically demonstrating the substantial social benefit of capitalism.

This discussion of non-economic goods generated from capitalism includes of course the general topic of philanthropy discussed earlier. To repeat for emphasis, in addition to the jobs Microsoft has created are the symphony halls, parks, bike paths, library facilities, YMCA programs, churches and myriad other social goods that have flowed from the corporate and personal wealth generated from that and other business enterprises. The notion of generously giving to support the betterment of one's fellow humans implies that one has the financial capacity to give. This explains why people in the United States and Western Europe are so overwhelmingly generous. It is not that Americans and Europeans are kinder, more compassionate people than others in the world. It is because their capitalistic economies have generated the high level of wealth which permits the commensurately high level of generosity. But the growth in giving has been more than commensurate as we observed in the previous discussion of philanthropy. Over the past several decades in the United States the growth in charitable contributions has surpassed the general growth of the economy and people's incomes and levels of wealth. The greatest manifestation of the economic boom of the 1990's was not a proliferation of Mercedes and BMW's or designer dresses, but rather the explosion of private charitable foundations. In fact, among the new high-tech millionaires the family foundation has become the new status symbol.

I find it amusingly ironic that the very nation that has been criticized for "the avarice and greed upon which its business system is based" is in fact the most generous nation on the face of the earth. According to a recent survey by the Johns Hopkins Comparative Nonprofit Sector Project, "13% of German respondents and 19% of French volunteered their time for civic activities in the previous year, in contrast to 49% of Americans.... And while 43% of French and 44% of Germans said they gave money to charity last year, 73% of Americans reported doing so. To be sure, many prosperous Europeans and Japanese pay far higher taxes than Americans, in part to finance social-welfare programs. Yet the private efforts of Americans make an impressive addition to what they do through government. Charitable gifts by Americans totaled $190 billion in 1999— equivalent to one-third of the domestic federal budget."[540]

Interestingly, that $190 billion given to charity equates to about 2% of national income—considerably below the biblical notion of tithing. Yet it can be asserted that the conceptual message of Scripture—the importance of establishing a pattern of regular giving—is an engrained cultural characteristic of the United States and most other capitalistic societies. Further, it can be argued that to some extent private contributions for welfare, education and other such purposes are below what they otherwise would be had government not injected itself into this arena. It is not too far a stretch of logic to suggest that some government welfare programs run counter to Christian values of love and charity to the extent that they permit members of a society to abrogate their personal responsibility by adopting the attitude of "the government takes care of that."

Related to the notion of capitalism's role in the pursuit of noneconomic ends is the increased discretionary time available to the individual as a result of rising real incomes discussed previously. It takes considerably less hours of work to earn enough to buy the necessities of life today than ten, fifty, a hundred years ago. In 1929 the average family spent 24% of its disposable income on food; in 1997 that portion of income required for food had declined to 11%.[541] According to a study by the Hudson Institute, over just the past two decades median household wealth, in constant dollars; i.e., real purchasing power, has increased by over one-third.[542] The average worker today enters the work force at a much higher age and works considerably fewer hours than previous generations as well as retiring earlier with a good twenty years of meaningful life left. Today in our economically developed society one has both the funds and the time available to read, walk in the park, go fishing, attend a concert, take courses in religion, etc. However, it is of major significance that this opportunity created by capitalism has been offset to a large degree by an overriding negative effect of capitalism: the stimulation of an inordinate pre-occupation with consumption that has placed men and women on a working tread-mill of which they feel unable to get off. This major danger of capitalism—the intensification of materialism and consumerism and thereby the increased secularization of society—was noted in our earlier discussion in Chapter VI, "Attitudes Toward Material Possessions and Wealth" and should not be understated. It is a meaningful deficiency common to most capitalistic societies. (But, again, capitalism did not cause hedonism—which has existed since the beginning of humankind;—capitalism has simply facilitated and broadened hedonism.)

Nevertheless, it cannot be denied that the miraculous increases in productivity have reduced the amount of time that one must devote to working to earn enough for subsistence. David Henderson, research fellow at Stanford University's Hoover Institution quotes from *In Praise of Commercial Culture*, the 1998 book by Tyler Cowen, an economist at George Mason University, "whereas in 1760, a common laborer had to work two whole days to earn enough money to buy a cheap book, today the cost of a paperback is slightly more that the hourly minimum wage. As wealth has increased relative to the cost of books, people have bought more books. In 1989, for example, the average American bought eight books, up from three in 1947. Presumably also because of increased wealth, in 1997, 35 percent of Americans visited an art museum, up from 22 percent in 1982."[543] Novak observes, "The productivity of the new economics has freed much human time for questions other than those of mere subsistence and survival. The workday has shrunk and 'weekends' have been invented. After work [and even increasingly on company-donated time], millions now take part in voluntary activities.... [R]oom has been created for the emergence of the private self."[544] Schall agrees, "Yet, a life devoted to work or craft or production and distribution would be a most constricting one if it prevented any higher sort of activity..., even though an economic purpose was a good purpose as such.... Leisure,...in its contemplative acts of knowing and loving the highest being,... concerns what human life is about in its highest forms."[545] D'Souza adds this perspective, "At a time when people in poor countries are desperately trying to better their condition, you cannot lecture them about the moral and social perils of affluence; they would surely think you were joking. It's not that they would disagree with you; they simply wouldn't know what you were talking about.... But now there are millions of people all over the world—most of them in the West, and the greatest proportion in America—for whom the struggle for existence has effectively ended.... They are able to ask, as only a handful of people in any given society have been able to in the past, What do I want to do with the rest of my life? What is my life for? As affluence spreads, I believe that tens and eventually hundreds of millions of people will be asking that question. That they can ask it is in and of itself a great moral achievement, because it opens up to innumerable ordinary people avenues of human fulfillment that were previously open only to aristocrats."[546]

In this regard, capitalism has been the object of invalid criticism. Certain critics make the observation that the proliferation of self-help books and books dealing with the meaning of life and other non-economic interests is testimony to the "emptiness" of the results of capitalism. That is not the case. Rather, we are seeing a triumphant result of capitalism. For thousands of years, lasting right up through the 1930's, the average person had little time for such pursuits, devoting virtually all of her / his time to earning a living. Not until the overwhelming prosperity of the latter half of the twentieth century and the accompanying ability to afford leisure time and more contemplative activity have the masses been able to afford the "luxury" of contemplating the meaning of life and giving oneself over to more meaningful activity—family activity and volunteering—that generates a spiritually full life. In the context of Jesus' assertion that 'Man shall not live by bread alone." (Mt. 4:4 and Lk 4:4), how wonderful it is to see the diminishment in the amount of time that man must devote to the "bread" side of man's life. The astronomical increase in productivity and the accompanying time for spiritual study, contemplation and prayer just might be capitalism's greatest contribution to humanity. Today more and more people are retiring in their 50's and devoting full time to serving others. This positive relationship between economic prosperity and increased time for spiritual thought and activity is why I am so optimistic about humanity's future.

No institution has benefited more from the achievements of capitalism than the Christian church. *Capitalism*, by generating a high level of wealth throughout the society, *contributes directly to religious worship, education and mission.* As noted earlier, many things used in the worship of God; e.g., churches, furniture and fixtures, heat and light, clergy salaries and benefits, etc., require financial capacity. Therefore, it can be argued that to the extent that capitalism is a proven mechanism for efficiently allocating the world's productive resources and stimulating economic growth, generating greater financial capacity, capitalism is a mechanism conducive to the construction and employment of items that aid in our worship of God. Schall observes, "The general prosperity of the American economy at every state,… allowed religion, if it chose, to build schools, churches, hospitals, clubs, and other institutions on the basis of free giving in a manner unique in the world."[547] Indeed, is not wealth part of God's plan? Let me add here a personal example. In 1998 the Presbyterian Church on Mercer Island, Washington, a small residential suburb of Seattle populated by about 26,000 people, raised $6 million during a capital campaign to enlarge and improve the existing church. I had the privilege of serving on one of the fund-raising committees and was able to view directly the statistics that reflected that one-half of those funds came from God directly through high-tech business firms. Had less than a dozen specific, particular high-tech firms not existed in the Seattle area, the Mercer Island Presbyterian Church would not be improving the choir rehearsal space, enhancing the adult education program, improving the facilities to attract the community's youth to the church, purchasing additional vehicles to bring to church senior citizens, and sending funds to missions in the inner city and abroad. Thank you, God, for creating high tech! I am not in any way suggesting that capitalists are more righteous. But what can be suggested is that perhaps, in the same way that God used Cyrus to free the Israelites and used many sinful humans to serve His ends, God is using the capitalists to build churches, feed the hungry and heal the sick. Is capitalism, with its amazing effectiveness, an instrument of God?

The seventh and ultimate brilliant outcome of capitalism in the context of Christianity will be world peace.

Capitalism, through raising the global social and economic common denominator and fostering an interdependence among the nations of the world, is creating a growing force for international political stability. I regard this as such an important contribution from the private enterprise system that I am discussing it in a separate chapter.

Chapter XI

The Ultimate Contribution of Capitalism to Humanity

D espite our sinfulness, God loves us and intends for all humanity to be blessed as revealed by His first covenant with
Abraham, "I will make you into a great nation and I will bless
you....and all people on earth will be blessed through you." (Gn.
12:2,3) Later God reaffirms this with Isaac, Abraham's son,
"...through your offspring all nations on earth will be blessed,..."
(Gn. 26:4) and then again with Jacob, Issac's son, "All peoples on
earth will be blessed through you and your offspring..." (Gn.
28:14; see also Gn. 48:3,4,15-22) Wright notes, "God's call of
Abraham was explicitly for the ultimate purpose of blessing the
nations. This fundamentally missionary intention of the election of
Israel echoes through the Old Testament at almost every level."[548]
As summarized by LaSor et al, "the salvation promised Abraham
will ultimately embrace all humankind."[549]

The prophets proclaimed the same message. God to Jonah with
the rhetorical question reflecting God's love and concern extending
throughout all the earth: "But Nineveh has more than a hundred and
twenty thousand people who cannot tell their right hand from their
left, and many cattle as well. Should I not be concerned about that
great city?' (Jon. 4:11) This is also a dominant theme of the prophet
Isaiah. "From the ends of the earth we hear singing: 'Glory to the

Righteous One." (Is. 24:16) "On this mountain the LORD Almighty will prepare a feast of rich food for all peoples,…" (Is. 25:6) "And the glory of the LORD will be revealed, and all mankind together will see it." (Is. 40:5) "Bring my sons from afar and my daughters from the ends of the earth—everyone who is called by my name, whom I created for my glory, whom I formed and made." (Is. 43:6,7) "…my house will be called a house of prayer for all nations." (Is. 56:7) "They will proclaim my glory among the nations." (Is. 66:19) Isaiah, in one of his foretelling of the Messiah and the Messiah's Great Commission, states, "I will also make you a light for the Gentiles, that you may bring my salvation to the ends of the earth." (Is. 49:6) Earlier Isaiah had declared, "For to us a child is born,…. And he will be called… Prince of Peace." (Is. 9:6)

One of the most interesting stories in the Bible reflecting God's universality is God anointing Cyrus, a gentile ruler who would allow the exiles to return and Jerusalem to be rebuilt. In Isaiah's relating this, he notes God's words, "I am the LORD, and there is no other; apart from me there is no God, I will strengthen you, though you have not acknowledged me, so that from the rising of the sun to the place of its setting men may know there is none besides me…. Turn to me and be saved, all you ends of the earth;" (Is. 45:5,6,22)

And even king Hezekiah acknowledged in a prayer, "…you alone are God over all the kingdoms of the earth. You have made heaven and earth." (Is. 37:16) Ezekiel, in referring to Israel's role in bringing the word of God to all people, "Then the nations will know that I am the LORD, declares the Sovereign LORD, when I show myself holy through you before their eyes." (Ez. 36:23) "I will show myself holy through them in the sight of many nations." (Ez. 39:27) Zechariah proclaims, "Many nations will be joined with the LORD in that day and will become my people…. Be still before the LORD, all mankind,…" (Zec 2:11,13) Finally, in prophesying the Messiah, "He will proclaim peace to the nations. His rule will extend from sea to sea and from the River to the ends of the earth." (Zec. 9:10)

The notion that all humans are included in the process of salvation is also proclaimed in the New Testament, "I bring you good news of great joy that will be for all the people." (Lk. 2:10) and is a major theme of Jesus, "I have other sheep that are not of this sheep pen. I must bring them also…., and there shall be one flock and one shepherd." (Jn. 10:16) "Go into all the world and preach the good news to all creation. Whoever believes and is baptized will be saved. (Mk. 16:15) "...go and make disciples of all nations,..." (Mt. 28:19) This is expressed again following the resurrection as Jesus appears before the apostles and directs them, "But you will receive power when the Holy Spirit comes on you; and you will be my witnesses in Jerusalem, and in all Judea and Samaria, and to the ends of the earth." (Acts 1:8)

Paul reaffirmed that there is one global community of humanity. "For this is what the Lord has commanded us: 'I have made you a light for the Gentiles, that you may bring salvation to the ends of the earth." (Acts 13:47) "From one man he made every nation of men, that they should inhabit the whole earth;..." (Acts. 17:26) "...the gospel...is the power of God for the salvation of everyone who believes:..." (Rom. 1:16) "You are all sons of God.... for you all are one in Christ Jesus. If you belong to Christ, then you are Abraham's seed, and heirs according to the promise." (Gal. 3:26-29) "There is one body and one Spirit....one Lord, one faith, one baptism; one God and Father of all, who is over all and through all and in all." (Eph. 4:4-6) "For by him all things were created: things in heaven and things on earth, visible and invisible,...and in him all things hold together." (Col. 1:16,17) Patzia notes, "The concepts express God's transcendence, his omnipresence, and his immanence."[550]

At the time that Paul and the other disciples embarked upon their grand mission, the Roman trade roads, shipping routes and communication systems protected by *Pax Romana* facilitated travel and communication by the disciples and thereby contributed hugely to the spread of Christianity. The book of Acts is filled with the travels of the disciples, switching from cargo ship to cargo ship sailing from port to port and traveling the roads among the various commercial centers, from the launching pad and home base of Antioch ["and they sent Barnabas to Antioch" (Acts 11:22)] to Paul's ultimate destination of Rome ["...we would sail for Italy..." (Acts 27:1)].

"Antioch of Syria, one of the principal cities of the roman Empire, was the focal point of Christianity as it spread beyond the border of Palestine to the Diaspora....A thriving, wealthy and cosmopolitan city where barriers of religion, race and nationality were easily crossed—and where toleration may have been a matter of civic pride—it was a perfect base of operations for the spread of Christianity."[551]

From Antioch the missionaries carried The Word well over 6,000 miles via the Roman trade roads and shipping routes primarily to existing population centers where many people could be addressed. Nine—one-third—of the twenty-seven books of the New Testament are given their names from letters to people in the communities in which Paul and the other apostles were founding churches:

- Rome, the political and commercial center of the Roman Empire.
- Corinth, a major trade center controlling the overland movement between Italy and Asia and traffic between the two ports of Lechaeum and Cenchreae to avoid sailing the treacherous waters around Peloponnesus. It was a pluralistic melting pot of cultures.[552]
- Ephesus, a major seaport on the western edge of Asia Minor, on the main route from Rome to the east. Regarded as the leading city of the richest region of the Roman Empire.[553]
- Philippi, a major commercial center on the *Via Egnatia*, an extension of the *Via Appia,* a trade route joining Rome with Asia Minor.
- Colosse, a textile center inland from Ephesus near Laodicea, a larger textile and banking center.
- Thessalonica, a major seaport and wealthy trade center on the *Via Egnatia* and capital of Macedonia.
- Galatia, a province in Asia Minor "crisscrossed by Roman roads which tied the cities and villages together in a remarkably efficient communications system."[554]

A common thread among these geographical places is that they played significant economic roles and were prosperous population centers, facilitating the spread of the church by enabling the disciples to come in contact efficiently with large communities of people. Further, the transportation and communication channels within and between these communities served to the advantage of the early church as well—just as such devices contribute to the spread of the gospel today. "...Paul's mission strategy involved selecting important cities of repute and strategic location as ideal centers from which the good news of the gospel might radiate out."[555] Ordinary merchants—business people—in their normal coming and going, traveling and buying and selling, heard and carried the Good News. Finally, conducting his missionary work in business centers enabled Paul to work at his trade of tentmaking which provided financial support for himself and his entourage.

Another interesting common characteristic of these cities was the presence of an ethic of toleration and pluralism, resulting largely from their economic and social upward mobility. These societies were relatively open to the emergence of new ideas—an ideal condition for the establishment of a new church. These very conditions are also those necessary for free trade.

Perhaps the most dramatic example of international trade's contribution to the early church is Paul's being saved from the wrath of the Jewish leaders by appealing to Caesar and thereby being sent to Rome, first by cargo ship north from Caesarea to various ports along the coast to Myra where he transferred to another cargo ship sailing west to Italy, ending up on Malta from which he eventually caught a northbound cargo ship to Italy.

It is interesting that God chose as "lead missionary" Paul, truly a citizen of the world. Paul was well traveled, spoke four languages (Aramaic, Hebrew, Greek and Latin), was a Roman citizen, heir of a Greek culture, possessed a Jewish heritage as a member of the tribe of Benjamin and was well educated under the great rabbi Gamaliel. Paul's ability to move freely between cultures contributed substantially to his effectiveness in establishing churches throughout the Roman empire. Undoubtedly, Paul viewed the world as one society under God.

Similarly, capitalism views the world as one global marketplace and invites all people to participate regardless of race, creed, nationality, color, sex, religion, etc. In the earlier discussion of the market system I noted that it is neutral, impersonal. It is open to all throughout the globe. This is in dramatic contrast to socialism wherein the economic system is tied to the government, and therefore national political divisions define the economic divisions.

Additionally, as we observed earlier, the charge of God through Scripture is clear and simple: love God and love each other—live in peace. This is to be done regardless of the human political, economic or social system. Nevertheless it can be shown that capitalism is bringing about two conditions compatible with humanity expressing love toward each other. The first is capitalism raising the global social and economic common denominator. The second is capitalism fostering an interdependence, mutual self-interest, among people around the globe.

These two conditions combine to create a force for international political stability manifest in world peace. Each is discussed in this chapter.

Global Social and Economic Common Denominator

The economic expression of humanity's global unity is international trade. It is very simple to see how the economic common denominator is raised. It reflects simply the law of supply and demand at work globally. When a relatively wealthy country imports goods from a relatively poor country, demand for workers in the poor country rises, in turn causing wage rates to rise. As the wages of these workers in export industries rise, these workers in turn demand additional goods and services of all types, creating an increase in demand for workers of all types, in turn causing their wages to rise over time. It is very clear and straightforward.

It is tragic that those who have short run selfish interests oppose free trade. Nowhere is humanity's unity and interdependence as well as the ever-growing circle of prosperity more clearly demonstrated than by the flow of goods, services, investments and money between countries. Today, *all* nations benefit from international trade—some more than others—but *all* nations are better off than if they did not trade. This flows from a very simple and well-known law of economics, the Law of Reciprocity, which states simply that "to sell abroad a nation must buy abroad." As George Gilder notes, "It was this belief that David Hume proclaimed in 1742, at the end of his essay, 'of the Jealousy of Trade:' 'I shall therefore venture to acknowledge, that, not only as a man, but as a British subject, I pray for the flourishing commerce of Germany, Spain, Italy, and even France itself. I am at least certain that all nations would flourish more [with] such enlarged and benevolent sympathies toward each other."[556]

To understand the foregoing assertion and get a quick lesson in international trade, work backwards. That is, imagine that "in order to protect jobs in our state" an ignorant and ill-advised program to raise trade barriers was adopted by each of the fifty states. What would happen to the standard of living in every single state? It is clear. The same is true among countries.

Law of Comparative Advantage

The benefits from trade result from the Law of Comparative Advantage which states that anytime countries have differing economic resources and therefore differing production advantages, each country benefits from each focusing on producing those things in which it has a comparative advantage and trading with the others. This concept is so clear and fundamental to anyone who has had a basic Principles of Economics course that it is exceedingly frustrating when free trade is opposed by those with a selfish, short run interest. Granted, for international trade to work, the rules of the game must be the same for all players. Therein lies the "rub" in many current trade relationships. Indeed, trade negotiations aimed toward "leveling the playing field" lead to further opening the international flow of prosperity and therefore the aggregate economic benefit.

The Law of Comparative Advantage and the benefits of international trade can be made clear by a simple example. Assume two countries, Country A and Country B, and each has the resources—natural, human, human-made—to produce corn flakes and/or plywood.

Domestic Production and Consumption Only

Country A's characteristics are such that, if it devoted all of its resources to producing corn flakes, it could produce ten units per year, or, if it devoted all of its resources to producing plywood, it could produce fifteen units per year, or it could produce some combination of both.

Country B's characteristics are such that, if it devoted all of its resources to producing corn flakes, it could produce five units per year, or, if it devoted all of its resources to producing plywood, it could produce fifteen units per year, or it could produce some combination of both.

Therefore, without trade, producing and consuming domestically only, each country's production and consumption alternatives are plotted on the graphs below.

Production Possibilities Curves

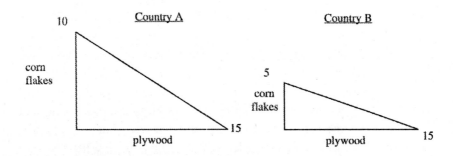

Note, Country A has an absolute advantage in producing corn flakes, and neither country has an absolute advantage in producing plywood, which they both can produce equally.

Benefits From Productivity Increases

Before proceeding further with the discussion of foreign trade, let us stop a moment and take a look at the advantages within each separate country of productivity increases. In each country, producers of corn flakes and plywood, in order to increase profits and dividends to their shareholders, will invest in myriad ways in which to increase productivity: fertilizers, pesticides, irrigation, timber thinning programs, education, more advanced equipment, etc. This enables the country to get more output from the same amount of input of natural and human resources devoted to producing goods, in turn, in economics jargon, shifting out the production possibilities curve.

Production Possibilities Curves

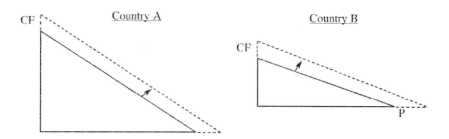

With productivity increases raising the output per unit of input of natural and human resources, exhibited by a shift out of the production possibilities curve, consumption opportunities increase, raising the standard of living in each country.

Before proceeding with the discussion of international trade, let us note the assumption, for example, that the preferences of consumers in each country are such that in Country A four units of corn flakes and nine units of plywood are produced and consumed and in Country B four units of corn flakes and four units of plywood are produced and consumed.

The production and consumption levels of each country are displayed in the graphs below.

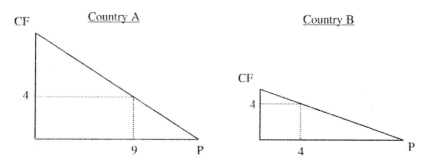

Benefits from Foreign Trade

Now let us switch from two separate economies, each operating exclusively domestically, to one global economy, with each country specializing in producing the product in which it has a comparative advantage, consuming part of its production, and exporting the other part of its production for imports of the other product which it then consumes. Country A has an absolute and comparative advantage in producing corn flakes; Country B has a comparative advantage in producing plywood. The graph below presents the outcome of this arrangement.

Country A produces only corn flakes, 10 units. Country B produces only plywood, 15 units,

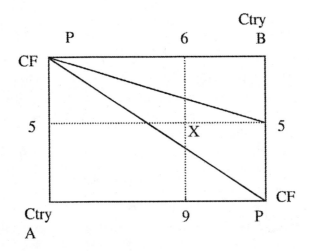

Country A consumes 5 units of corn flakes and exports 5 units to Country B. Country B consumes 6 units of plywood and exports 9 units to Country A. Each country consumes at a point, X, beyond its production possibilities curve—each country wins!

The foregoing outcome of international trade is summarized in the following table.

Without Trade

	Production		Consumption	
	Corn Flakes	Plywood	Corn Flakes	Plywood
Country A	4	9	4	9
Country B	4	4	4	4

With Trade

	Production		Consumption	
	Corn Flakes	Plywood	Corn Flakes	Plywood
Country A	10	0	5	9
Country B	0	15	5	6

The Conclusion

Even though Country B has no absolute advantage in either product and Country A has an absolute advantage producing corn flakes and is equally good at producing plywood, it still makes more sense to specialize and trade. *Both* countries are better off operating together as one global economy rather than separately as two domestic economies.

Further, as a greater amount of all goods and services is produced at relatively lower costs, the global demand for workers increases, causing wage rates to rise, in turn increasing the demand for goods and services of all types and therefore workers of all types. Everyone wins.

The Law of Comparative Advantage is as irrefutable as the Law of Supply and Demand and the law of gravity. The benefits of foreign trade are clear and indisputable. There may be rational reasons—political and otherwise—to constrain free trade, but such action will *always* be accompanied by a significant cost, the foregone benefits that otherwise would have occurred.

It should already be apparent from where opposition to free trade comes. Going back to our example prior to trade, when neither country was trading with the other, when they commence to have trade discussions, clearly the plywood workers in Country A and the corn flakes workers in Country B would be vehemently opposed to such discussions and would be loudly demonstrating out in front of the building where the discussions were taking place! While in terms of their own *short run* self-interest, they may be acting rationally, nevertheless, in their demonstrations and press releases they should in no way try to hoodwink the rest of us into thinking that they are only interested in the public good.

Rather, everyone—even they—would be better off if they were retrained to produce the other product. Their wages and their standard of living would rise. This is not to minimize the short run dislocations and social costs as corn farms and cereal plants in Country B are closed and loggers and plywood workers in Country A lose their jobs. The attendant increases in crime, the costs of unemployment benefits, the adverse effect on mental health, the retraining costs, and myriad other financial, psychological and social costs are significant. But this is not to deny the truth of the more than commensurate foregone benefit of international trade. In the longer run the people in both countries are worse off, facing a lower level of prosperity.

The example above is a very simple description of how, even though one country clearly has the absolute advantage, both countries benefit from trading with each other when the other country has a comparative advantage. Granted, what I have presented above is a simple conceptual framework of economic considerations only. Obviously, many valid political, social, cultural and other considerations exist when dealing with foreign trade. Nevertheless, the truth holds: anytime foreign trade is constrained, for whatever sound, valid reason, there is a significant economic cost.

Professor Heyne offers some illumination by example. "United States farmers can surely produce rice at a lower opportunity cost than Japanese farmers can do it. But the Japanese nonetheless choose to grow domestically most of the rice they consume rather than import it from the United States. There are some Japanese,... who insist that foreign rice just doesn't taste as good as Japanese rice, and that is why Japanese consumers prefer the domestic product. The flaw in this argument is that it doesn't explain why the Japanese government would restrict rice imports. If the Japanese people really didn't want to eat foreign-grown rice, the government would not have to keep it out; the market would do the job. Japanese farmers faced with this counterargument often respond that rice produced in Japan is a symbol of Japanese culture,... and therefore deserves a market protected from foreign competition. They may be right. How does one place a monetary value on national symbols? The undeniable fact is that Japanese consumers pay a great deal more than they would otherwise have to pay for the food they eat,... Similarly, American motorists pay more for the cars they drive when U.S. automobile manufacturers, labor unions and suppliers persuade the government to restrict the importation of Japanese automobiles. Some calculations have suggested that government restrictions on automobile imports protect the jobs of U.S. automobile workers at a total cost to automobile buyers of about $250,000 per job. That is a lot to pay to preserve just one job. It seems altogether likely that a payment of half that amount would be far more than enough to persuade each and every automobile worker who would lose his job to drop his objection to Japanese imports and look for a job elsewhere."[557]

To illustrate the absurdity of protectionism, in 1845 Bastiat wrote a satire in which candlemakers appealed to the French Chamber of Deputies for the passage of laws requiring the closing of all windows and other sources of outside light to protect them from the ruinous competition from a gigantic source of low cost light which was flooding the French domestic market: the sun.

The Law of Comparative Advantage is seen at work early in Scripture as Solomon buys timber products from Lebanon. "Send me also cedar, pine and algum logs from Lebanon, for I know that your men are skilled in cutting timber there. My men will work with yours to provide me with plenty of lumber [for the temple].... Now let my lord send his servant the wheat and barley and the olive oil and wine he promised, and we will cut all the logs from Lebanon that you need and will float them in rafts by sea down to Joppa. You can then take them up to Jerusalem." (2 Chr. 2:8-16) This account is also related in 1 Kings 5:1-12, explicitly acknowledging the concept of comparative advantage, "... we have no one so skilled in felling timber as the Sidonians." (1 Kgs. 5:6) and noting one of the first trade agreements, ",... and the two of them made a treaty." (1 Kgs. 5:12) LaSor observes, "Solomon's alliance with Hiram of Tyre was also profitable. The Phoenicians supplied.... many materials, especially Lebanese timber, for the temple and palaces. They built and manned his ships and provided a market for Israel's wheat and olive oil. This tie proved especially lucrative when Hiram extended to Solomon a substantial loan."[558] The transactions between Solomon and Hiram gave rise to foreign letters of credit, a common mechanism used today, with Solomon collateralizing the loan with twenty towns in Galilee (1 Kgs. 9:11). Hiram, through trade with Solomon, was repaid many times over. God uses the Law of Comparative Advantage to raise the economic common denominator of all humanity.

Sider summarizes the advantages of free trade. "Scores of careful studies show that greater concentration on goods for export almost always produces economic growth. International trade also tends to increase real wages in developing countries. Wages in export-oriented firms in developing countries are, of course, very low in comparison to wages in developed nations…. But those 'low wages' are usually substantially higher…than the average wages in the country. Thus,…two beneficial things can result: poor people receive higher wages and all of us pay lower prices for the products…. [T]hose who care about the poorest should accept markets as an important, useful tool for empowering the poor."[559]

Social common denominator

In addition to the economic common denominator, the social common denominator is also raised. Capitalism, characterized by power in the hands of consumers, is enlightening the treatment of God's children by each other. The abominable conditions and treatment faced by some workers particularly in many of the lesser developed countries is dramatically clear through both visible observation by the casual traveler and through well documented official studies and reports.

It must be recognized that exploitation of the poor in undeveloped countries has been at the hands of their own countrymen who employ them. Today, however, consumers in the developed capitalistic nations are expressing widespread indignation at the practice of major retailers buying from sweatshops or from oppressive plantation owners. Responding to their customers, retailers are in turn demanding of their foreign suppliers that they implement more enlightened employment practices. Starbucks, Nordstrom and hundreds of thousands of other business firms have already made a major contribution to humans abroad by providing them with a job, raising their economic well-being as noted above. Now it is going beyond that. Today, responding to demands by their customers as well as reflecting the Judeo-Christian values of their corporate leaders, Starbucks, Nordstrom and hundreds of thousands of other business firms are requiring their foreign suppliers to implement more enlightened employment practices related to working conditions, health care, vacations and many other elements effecting workers' quality of life as well as meeting additional social and environmental standards.

The market system is a marvelous communications vehicle—direct and quick. Rather than trying to use moral suasion to apply political pressure on governments to achieve certain social ends, the NGO's (nongovernmental organizations) are increasingly turning to applying economic pressure on private producers and sellers. An impressive example has been Global Witness obtaining De Beers' agreement to certify the specific geographical source of its diamonds, guaranteeing that they are not from areas where the proceeds are used to finance insurrections. Around the world thousands of these NGO's are championing the full array of social causes, including the environment, healthy working conditions, adequate medical care, product safety, etc., and the most effective mechanism for achieving their goals is economic pressure on the business firm.

Could it be that the business firm has become the most efficient and effective mechanism for transmitting God's enlightened employment practices? See the diagram on the following page.

METHODS FOR AFFECTING IMPROVEMENTS IN EMPLOYMENT PRACTICES

METHOD A:

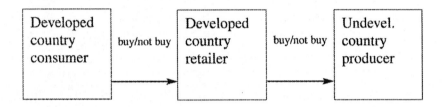

METHOD B:

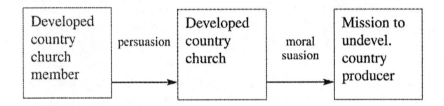

Clearly, Method A is the more effective.

Indeed, to the extent that working conditions in many underdeveloped countries have improved, much of the credit can go to American consumers through American capitalists demanding it from their foreign suppliers. God clearly understands the free enterprise system as evidenced by the use which God is making of it. Ask the foreign workers who work for producers who sell to Starbucks, Nordstrom and others. They feel God's work. Eventually God will get to the others. Recent market research studies are revealing that, everything else being equal, consumers feel a strong preference toward buying from sellers viewed as socially responsible.

Interestingly, the flow chart above can be applied not only to improved employment practices but to an array of social objectives, including improved environmental practices. As environmentally sensitive consumers bring pressure on business firms, threatening to withhold purchasing from firms which are not environmentally responsible, business firms respond by adopting environmentally responsible practices. As a result, globalization of trade is resulting in the convergence of good business practices with good environmental practices.

Debunking a Tragic Myth

A pervasive myth throughout the Western world, which has been promulgated by myriad organizations, universities, churches, journalists, the former Communist bloc, even the United Nations, is that somehow the "West" bears the responsibility for the economic backwardness of the Third World. This notion has been effectively debunked by many highly regarded economists. Lord Peter T. Bauer at the London School of Economics notes, "throughout the underdeveloped world, large agricultural, mineral, commercial, and industrial complexes have been built up through profits that have been reinvested locally....The poorest and most backward countries have until recently had no external economic contacts and often have never been Western colonies, so their backwardness cannot be explained by colonial domination or international social stratification. And industrial corporations are not notable for their presence in the least developed countries of the Third World (the so-called Fourth World), such as Afghanistan, Chad, Bhutan, Burundi, Nepal, and Sikkim."[560] William Scully agrees, "Actually, much of the developing world that has had contact with the West owes its economic development to such contact, which provided access to Western markets, Western enterprise, capital, and ideas. Today's poverty in [areas like Latin America] is much more the result of domestic mismanagement and unsound domestic policies than of Western interference and domination."[561]

And even theologians weigh in, with Nash declaring, "The West did not become rich at the expense of the poor... [Further, when] proper attention is given to the necessary role that the creation of wealth must play in relieving poverty, it is clear that capitalism offers the poor their only real hope of economic deliverance.... Nations that give greater place to market systems exhibit much greater rates of economic growth than those that have controlled economies.... [M]ost important causes of Third-World poverty are internal, not external; many of these internal reasons are noneconomic factors such as morals, attitudes, and motivation of the people along with relevant features of the culture [e.g., India]...conduct of nation's rulers with respect to providing political and economic stability. "[562] Schall agrees, "The best way to discover why Tanzania, for example, remains poor and depends on handouts is not to examine its soil or its rainfall, but to read the collected speeches of Mr. Julius Nyerere.... The fact is that many people are poor in highly endowed areas of the world, while others live in places seemingly abandoned by nature, yet are rich. What is the difference? In almost every case the difference has to do with how the individual, property, reward, work, and inventiveness are looked upon."[563] The lack of greater internal economic development strides made by the poorer countries also is explained somewhat by the "scapegoat factor." Local politicians further their own ambitions by serving as champion of the people against a common adversary: "The West."

Larry Diamond, fellow at Stanford's Hoover Institution, observes, "The indispensable key to development is good governance.... The real goal of political leaders is to extract wealth from their own society and distribute it to themselves and their cronies. No formal policy direction—and no amount of foreign aid—can turn the country around.... In such autocratic systems, from Cameroon to Cambodia, from Egypt to Uzbekistan, leaders stay in power by distributing corrupt largesse to their narrow circles of supporters, rather than by providing the schools, clinics, markets, courts, roads, and other public goods that could eventually make the whole society rich.... [T]hey also...violate human rights and the rule of law."[564]

In fact, one of the reasons that economic conditions of many undeveloped nations are so tragically deplorable is because, where the profit motive is absent, there has been so much waste and so many failures. The economic aid programs of the governments and nongovernment organizations, including the churches, have been characterized by mismanagement, waste and siphoning to corrupt local officials. Listen to Robert L. Strauss, "I took a position with a... firm in Washington D.C. that promoted appropriate technology... in developing countries. I spent two fascinating years at this company but never quite knew whether to be amused, appalled or ashamed by the waste I witnessed and occasionally abetted.... The long string of short-term [foreign economic development] assignments I've taken has given me plenty of opportunity to wonder if anyone really has an answer for poverty and whether good intentions alone justify the billions that are squandered. Some developing countries have prospered largely on their own, while others remain chronically malnourished after 50 years on the teat of development....Back in Manila,.... it became apparent that my boss, who had a significant say in how $3 million was spent each year, didn't understand the basics of finance—like the difference between debt and equity. When I returned to Washington, I discovered that most of the firm's staff didn't either. I was learning that good intentions and a precocious understanding of multiculturalism were enough to land people in high positions. Hard skills—the ability to actually do or produce something—counted for much less. On my next assignment, I was sent to assess a small-scale cement plant in Northern India. I spent two weeks calculating capacities and cash flow and watching in awe as Indian laborers loaded cement into porous jute bags—the public health equivalent of smoking cigarettes laced with asbestos and arsenic. My report to the home office was blunt: the plant could never be commercially viable, even though it was selling cement at three times the world price thanks to India's protectionist policies. Nevertheless, we continued to fund it. The plant managers, I later learned, were old pals of our executive director.... At a brick works we supported in Botswana... I had been struck by the manager's apparent incompetence.... The numbers in his financial reports didn't add up—literally. Two plus two summed to five, for example. [Checking invoices,] invoice number 1234 indicated that the United Nations Development Program had recently paid for a tractor-trailer [which had previously been paid for].... With the German [supervisor] and local manager in tow, I went to Barclay's Bank and seized the project's funds. I cabled the news back to Washington, where I expected to be greeted with a hero's welcome, if not a ticker-tape parade. What I got was nearly fired. My bosses furiously and profanely wondered aloud how I imagined I had the authority to seize a project's assets. Did I have any idea how bad it would make them look at the U.S. Agency for International Development (our chief backer) to 'deobligate' the funding?.... It's disheartening to realize that few in the international development business ever question the system itself.

Sure, every now and then a book comes out that decries the emperor's state of undress. UNICEF or some other program may be doing enough good to compensate for the harm and waste that occur elsewhere. My dressing-down finally came in an unlikely corner of the world, [the small island of] Tonga, a Polynesian kingdom with 110,000 subjects. There I paid a call on the secretary for labor, commerce, industries and tourism. Before I could finish telling him why I was there, the secretary began screaming, 'Another consultant! What do all you people do? USAID, UN, EEC, World Bank. Come here. Expect soft drinks. Ask me questions. Act important. When are you going to *do* something?"[565]

Oh, for the effective discipline which the profit motive brings! The late William E. Simon, former U.S. Treasury Secretary, agreed. "Foreign aid is rarely effective in promoting development; indeed, the evidence is the fact that aid filtered through corrupt governments with no commitment to economic freedom makes matters worse. We know that the development success stories—Taiwan, South Korea, Hong Kong, Singapore—have happened because these countries have been integrated into the Western economic system and have welcomed foreign investment. We know that private enterprise is the only way to create lasting development;...."[566] Hay agrees, "[T]hose countries which have favoured market capitalist systems have apparently experienced faster growth than those that have not. The difference is particularly dramatic in developing economies, where market-oriented economies such as South Korea, Singapore and Kenya in the 1970's outperformed countries such as Liberia, Sri Lanka and India, where planned development was more significant."[567]

Bauer, having performed considerable research on the subject of Third World poverty, is armed to refute some of the trite, unsubstantiated accusations commonly made. "...a student group at Cambridge published a pamphlet on the Third World, asserting, "We took the rubber from Malaya, the tea from India, raw materials from all over the world and gave almost nothing in return.' This is as nearly opposite of the truth as one can find as the British took the rubber *to* Malaya and the tea *to* India. There were no rubber trees in Malaya or anywhere in Asia until ...the British took the first rubber seed there out of the Amazon jungle. From these sprang the huge rubber industry—now very largely Asian-owned. Tea plants were brought to India by the British from China."[568] Bauer continues in his lengthy article, disproving, one-by-one, many false yet commonplace accusations, concluding, "...the most prosperous areas in the Third World are those with the most commercial contacts with the West.... Commercial contacts...generally established by the West have eliminated the worst diseases, reduced and eliminated famine, extended life expectancy, and improved living standards."[569]

Bauer observes that much of the contemporary diatribe revolves around the false notion of "exploitation," that the rich have become rich by "exploiting" the poor. Bauer notes, "Whatever one thinks of colonialism, it cannot be held responsible for Third World poverty. Some of the most backward countries never were colonies: Afghanistan, Tibet, Nepal, and Liberia, for instance. Ethiopia,...an even more telling example,...was an Italian colony for only six years in its long history....Nor is the prosperity of the West the result of colonialism. The richest and most advanced countries, Switzerland and the Scandinavian countries, for example, never had colonies.... [Finally,] the European countries were already far ahead of the others when they established colonies.... [P]rivate investment....[has] expanded opportunities and raised incomes and government revenues in the Third World."[570]

Finally, let us pursue this argument from another perspective. Let us suppose that international trade were taken away. Let us suppose, for example, that Starbucks—purveyor of an expensive, luxury item—closed down, ceased doing business. What happens to the market demand for coffee beans? What happens to the price of coffee beans? What happens to employment on the plantations? What happens to the standard of living of the plantation workers? In response to certain naïve social theorists who incorrectly assert that the poor are poor because the rich are rich or that the hungry are not fed because the satiated have exploited them, Fr. Schall asserts, "Ironically, the best way to starve the poor would be for the rich of the world to stop eating, to stop being rich."[571] Bauer expands further on this notion, asserting that even if it were true that the Third World faces unfavorable terms of trade, "which it does not, this would *not* mean that external trade is damaging to the Third World, but only that it is not quite as beneficial as it would be under more favorable terms of trade."[572]

In fact, as Bauer concludes, "external commercial relations... benefit people by opening up markets for exports, by providing a large and diverse source of imports, and by acting as channels for the flow of human and financial resources and for new ideas, methods, and crops. Because of the vast expansion of world trade...and the development of technology in the West, the material advantages from external contacts are now greater than ever before."[573]

Further to this argument, Novak explains the appeal by President Robert Mugabe for United States' aid to Zimbabwe, "President Mugabe invites transnational corporations for several reasons. Through their efforts, Zimbabwe stands to gain: (1) industrial plants that otherwise would not be there; (2) the products those plants produce (which otherwise would have to be imported); (3) the salaries paid to employees; (4) related investments in infrastructure (roads, electricity, sewage); (5) the teaching of skills to the work force; (6) an industrial tax base for the locale; and (7) the amenities foreign corporations usually import with them (clinics, schools, services).[574] Novak further observes, "Yet any foreign investment in Zimbabwe necessarily: (a) is largely immovable insofar as it goes into buildings, infrastructure, and salaries; and (b) owes its origins to profits earned somewhere else. Today's investments in place P are yesterday's profits in place Q."[575]

Finally, when discussing raising the social and economic common denominator, philanthropy must be included. We observed earlier how growth in wealth translated into environmental restoration and protection as well as a more than commensurate growth in philanthropy. This wealth-permitted generosity is an international phenomenon through both private organizations and government programs. In 1999 and 2000 Royal Dutch / Shell spent over $100 million on hospitals, roads and schools in Nigeria (where it produces oil, having invested over $14 billion in facilities and created 3,700 jobs for Nigerians) as well as hiring a local Nigerian to work in community development.[576] This is just one of millions of such activity by private firms all over the world. Unocal is building schools and medical clinics in Burma, Nike is working with World Vision to provide education and vocational training for their 70,000 workers, mostly women,[577] and similar activity is occurring in every free place in the world. In addition to direct aid in the form of money and goods, it is interesting to note that in October, 2000

Congress approved a foreign aid package—funded by taxes on corporations and individuals—that included cancellation of $435 million of debt owed by 30 countries and permission to the International Monetary Fund to release $800 million of gold reserves to pay off debt. The Old Testament principles embodied in the Year of Jubilee have even found their way into the halls of Congress!

A case study: General Electric

Reginald H. Jones, former Chief Executive Officer of General Electric, reports:

"We have found over many years that the key to business success in any country is to consult with the people who are there.... Find out what they are trying to do—discover their priorities, their plans for the nation, their most urgent needs, their rules for participation in the local economy. Then figure out the best way to make your capabilities and products and services fit those needs and regulations....

"Characteristically, the first contact is made through a local agent helping us to develop some export business. General Electric's main exports are products that help a country build up its economic infrastructure.... We provide equipment for electric power systems, transportation systems, communication systems, and health-care systems. Our first sales to a developing country are usually high-technology equipment and construction services that help that nation lay its economic foundations.

"After we have developed such an export relationship with a country, the need arises for people and facilities to service our equipment. So we establish an international network of service and repair facilities, which also involves training foreign nationals in the maintenance of such equipment—an early form of technology transfer. The pressures then build up for us to establish manufacturing facilities in the country. Many countries establish "local content" laws, requiring that at least part of a product they are going to import, such as locomotives, be assembled in local factories. These factories in turn become the basis of their own export industries. We cannot establish such production facilities in all countries, of course, but where there is enough political stability to assure that the investment has a good chance of surviving and prospering, we set up the facility—often in a joint venture with local partners, since that is what most countries want....

"Some of our oldest and most productive connections are in Latin America. Our Brazilian affiliate, General Electric do Brazil, with major manufacturing facilities in Campinas, Rio de Janeiro, and Sao Paulo, has been an important supplier of heavy apparatus to the country's infrastructure. Large industrial motors, controls, switchgear, generators, and complete industrial drive systems are supplied to the nation's utility system and its basic industries. We produce a range of consumer goods for the growing Brazilian market.... Brazil is anxious to build up its own export industries, so we recently signed an agreement with the government to expand several of our operations there...which will provide about $700 million in export business for Brazil....

"Another country important to General Electric...is our neighbor to the south, Mexico. GE's operations have been a part of Mexico since 1896. Today GE-Mexico is the country's leading electrical manufacturer, producing lamps, consumer appliances, electrical and electronic industrial components, and electrical power line equipment. This is a strongly Mexican operation. With more than five thousand employees, less than half of one percent are Americans. This is characteristic of U.S. multinational corporations,... We move as fast as we can toward putting the business in the hands of foreign nationals, which means bringing people to the United States for training and also conducting training courses in foreign countries.

"Smaller affiliates are located in Venezuela, Argentina, Uruguay, Chile, and Colombia, and where we do not have manufacturing operations of our own, we license technology to local manufacturers for products ranging from television receivers...to distribution transformers...and washing machines. We are highly flexible in our business arrangements, depending on local circumstances and desires. We are not so flexible, however, that we lose sight of our own standards and principles. In some Latin American countries, for example, the institutions of graft and kickbacks are so deeply ingrained that it is impossible to do business in accordance with our own policies and principles of attracting business on the merits of our products and prices. This is especially true in construction work, for example. So we have simply closed down our construction businesses in some locations and decided to forgo the business. There are plenty of other opportunities....

"As an illustration of the role that a transnational company can play in a very poor country, consider GE's experience in helping to bring electricity to rural villages in the Dominican Republic. In the little Dominican town of Lagunia de Nisibon in the early 1970s, farmers dried their rice crops by setting them out in the sun, and workers produced concrete blocks with a primitive manual press. Electricity had still not reached this town, which was typical of 160 such unelectrified rural villages in the country. In 1971, the Dominican government embarked on an ambitious rural electrification plan. On the basis of previous experience with General Electric in electrification work, the Dominican government gave us a contract to expand their steam power generation facilities, and our Italian construction company, Sade/Sadelmi, was hired to do the arduous work of stringing miles of lines from the power plant through swamps and timberland and across mountains to some of the villages involved....

"Electrification has wrought dramatic changes in the village of Lagunia de Nisibon. An electric concrete-block maker now churns out building blocks for homes. Electric grain-dryers prepare rice for storage in the town's food co-op. GE mercury lamps light the main street. Young workers attend evening classes at the electrically lit one-room school. Television brings news of the outside world, and refrigerators keep food and antibiotics from spoiling....

"GE has provided much of the economic infrastructure to African nations such as Nigeria, Ghana, and Egypt. In Asia we have been involved with the successes of Singapore, South Korea, and Taiwan. But the real message from these three Asian countries is that nations that make themselves attractive to industry and that encourage their own entrepreneurs can, with the help of transnational suppliers, turn economic miracles. Tom Snedeker, manager of our Korea Liaison Office, says, "Current headlines don't tell the real story here. Much more important over the long run is the rise of Korea...to one of the world's fastest-growing economies, with a solid GNP of $25 billion in 1977, and with a *steadily growing middle class....* [italics mine]

"This is an all too brief picture of how one company, General

Electric, has been able to participate significantly in the development of nations on all continents. Our strategy is basically to learn what nations need and want, what *their* plans and priorities are, what rules and regulations they have for participating in their local economy, and then be flexible enough and creative enough to match our business strategies to their perceived needs and desires. This is a far cry from the imperial multinational corporations of popular fiction and Marxist caricature. And I hope it demonstrates that large business firms can and do operate in such a way as to help the people of the world achieve their legitimate aspirations for a better life.

"When we first put in a plant to make household wiring devices at Juana Diaz, we put in a paved parking lot. I remember noticing just five or six cars in the lot…. On my next trip to Juana Diaz I was amazed to see the lot full and employees' cars parked all over the place. We enlarged the parking lot, and I think that example demonstrates that we are not underpaying or exploiting our employees. Another example in Puerto Rico [is a case where GE was asked to take over a failing plant.] It was something of a mess by our standards, so we installed new lighting, air-conditioning, and better equipment and gave the place a fresh coat of paint—dark green up to waist height, and a lovely soft green from there to the ceiling. A couple of months after the plant opening,…the women [employees] went to San Juan and bought some cloth and made skirts to match the dark green and blouses to match the soft green. The attitude of those employees speaks volumes. It gives me a lift to see those women wearing their handmade uniforms, clearly so proud of themselves and their bright and cool workplace.

"Leafing through a recent publication produced under a grant from the Episcopal Church Publishing House and advocating class war and a rejection of capitalism, I noticed a headline that said, 'To most people, the world of work is a place of crucifixion.' I wondered what the author would think if he could see that plant in Puerto Rico and sense the pride, the sociability, the feeling of status and personal fulfillment that work has brought to those women. For most people, work is not a crucifixion; it is a salvation.….

"About four years ago, [1976] George Gallup reported on the largest opinion survey ever conducted, a worldwide project covering nearly seventy nations on six continents. Fundamental questions were asked about attitudes and expectations in life, and the most important finding was the huge discrepancy, in terms of human happiness, between the technologically developed and the underdeveloped nations. Says Mr. Gallup, 'On the average, people in the richest countries—those who live in North America, Australia, and Western Europe—report themselves as being far happier, find their lives more interesting, worry less, and would like few, if any, changes in their own existences. They are also more content with their family life, their countries, their communities, their education, and with themselves. By stark contrast, only 28 percent of the Latin Americans, 8 percent of the Africans, and a mere 6 percent of the Indians surveyed consider themselves fully satisfied with their lives.' Do these unhappy people reject industrial society? On the contrary, they want it desperately. As Gallup says,... 'The inhabitants of the Third World want more industry in their countries by ratios exceeding 20 to 1.' The only question is how to get it, and that is largely a political and social question....."[578]

"As I said to our managers at the first management conference after I had become chairman of General Electric, in January, 1973, we are stewards for some of the most valuable resources of the nations, or of the world. General Electric is a unique configuration of assets, one of the most productive enterprises on the globe. Those assets are truly significant to the progress of humankind, and must not be squandered, mismanaged, or directed toward socially destructive ends. So we recognize our public franchise, and how easily it could be lost."[579]

The fascinating aspect of the foregoing example is that it is not unusual. It is the norm. It is reflective of how virtually every major U. S. and European multinational corporation actually functions. It mirrors my own personal experience at Weyerhaeuser. It mirrors my own personal internal observation of ARCO and Exxon. It mirrors my observation of friends and acquaintances in the business world. Oh, certainly, there are scoundrels in business—just as there are in government, educational institutions and the church. But the general reality is that corporations and people who work for corporations have a broad and deep social commitment.

Another observation on this matter comes from Professor Gary Quinlivan, Saint Vincent College, "[F]rom 1980 to 1998, world child labor rates (the percentage of children working between the ages of ten and fourteen) tumbled from 20 to 13 percent.... Interestingly, regions lacking multinational corporations had the worst child labor rates and the smallest reductions.... This reduction in rates was attributable to increased family income, which permitted families to.... provide their children with more educational opportunities.... The United Nations' *World Investment Report 1999* notes several studies that confirm foreign affiliates have higher environmental standards than their domestic counterparts." Professor Quinlivan goes on to report some other statistics shedding light on the nature of the global economy. For example, contrary to popular image that a few mammoth corporations hold a static stranglehold on the global economy, comparing the top 100 largest public companies in 1990 with the list just nine years later, "remarkably, there were sixty-six new members in the 1999 list.... According to the conventional wisdom, an increase in monopoly power should also lead to fewer and larger multinational corporations, but, as reported by the United Nations, the number of multinational corporations tripled from 1988 to 1997."[580]

Clearly, increased foreign trade has opened our eyes to the great economic disparities between the developed countries and the underdeveloped countries of the world. We should not let the gruesome sights in some of these countries blind us to the reality that, slowly, gradually, in myriad separate individual transactions by private firms, international trade is serving as the great economic and social leveler. Recognizing the benefits of economic growth, Beckman observes, "A generation ago perhaps a third of all adults in developing countries could read; now about half can read. The proportion of children in primary school has risen almost everywhere, and the proportion in secondary school has doubled. In the past two or three decades the developing countries have registered increases in life expectancy that took the developed countries a century to achieve. Infant mortality is down, and several killer diseases are under control."[581] D'Souza notes, "life expectancy in the Third World today has more than doubled to nearly seventy years. That's six years behind the United States, but still, who can deny that the doubling of the life span is not only an immense achievement but also an egalitarian achievement? Technological capitalism deserves the main credit for this achievement, because it has produced advances in medicine and food production, as well as countless other amenities, making them available to ordinary citizens."[582]

Finally, when focusing on this issue of the global social and economic common denominator, perhaps the most common vision that enters one's mind is the pervasive hunger around the world. The foregoing discussion notwithstanding, a shameful, tragic reality remains: the world "is divided into the one-third of its people who are affluent and the two-thirds who are poor. Of the affluent, a small percentage are super-rich; of the poor a large number are miserably impoverished.... The average diet [of these two thirds] is insufficient. According to the Food and Agriculture Organization and the World Bank, almost... one-tenth of all people regularly consume less than the 'minimum critical diet' without which it is impossible to maintain body weight and stay healthy.... It is estimated... that every year 40 million people die from hunger and hunger-related diseases. Nearly half of them are children."[583] These statistics are particularly meaningful in this discussion of capitalism, because the solution to the world's hunger problem, identified by Irving Kristol,[584] is so simple, direct and more than adequate. If agricultural productivity of the vast arable lands of Russia, China and India were equal to that of the United States, Canada, Taiwan and other capitalistic societies and if the generosity of those countries matched that of the affluent capitalistic nations, world hunger would not exist. Yet, the collectivization of such land omitted the incentives that would generate such productivity and the wealth that would induce such generosity. Nobel laureate Theodore Schultz agrees, "For lack of incentives the unrealized economic potential of agriculture in many low-income countries is large."[585] So does "Norman Macrae [who] in *The Economist*...held that we could easily produce a glut on the international food market so great it would dwarf all other issues. The Ganges Valley in India, the Yangtze in China, the Mississippi Valley in the Midwest, and even the smaller San Joaquin Valley in California can by themselves come fairly close to supplying the world's basic food needs.... What causes insufficient food production are fundamentally the theories, values, and ideologies that interfere with or fail to foster those means of achieving the planet's capacity in this area."[586] Yet, never have I seen any clergy, who profess an appropriately extraordinary concern for the world's hungry, demonstrating in front of the Washington D.C. embassies of Russia, China and India for more enlightened agricultural polices that would permit productivity incentives! (It should be noted that over the past twenty years agricultural reforms in China have led to a soaring increase in output, leading China to becoming a net exporter of grain.)

In concluding this discussion of the global economic and social common denominator, it must be explicitly acknowledged that the "gap" between the "wealthy" nations and the "poor" nations is likely to widen for as far as one can imagine. This is because a major cultural characteristic firmly engrained in capitalistic societies is innovation. The competitive market system places a pronounced value on commercial creativity and innovation. It is a simple empirical observation that in most capitalistic societies scientific research, discovery and application is growing exponentially, resulting in dramatic increases in per capita income and wealth. Absent the commitment to innovation and the other previously discussed cultural characteristics required for capitalism to flourish, the "poor" nations are simply not going to catch up. But viewing the relationship as some sort of race which one "wins" and another "loses" is nonsensical. The only thing that matters is not how one country is doing relatively to another, but how a country is doing relative to its past and to its potential. Accordingly, the preoccupation of many with the "gap" should be abandoned as an invalid perspective accompanied by the potential negative result of covetousness and envy leading to counter-productive policies and programs. The differing rates of growth notwithstanding, most countries *which so choose* are advancing economically and the global median level is rising. Also, to the extent that some countries are lagging severely and other countries are leading dramatically, the capitalistic leaders, reflecting their Spirit-filled generosity, are aiding the laggers by gifts.

Global Interdependence

> "They will beat their swords into plowshares and their spears into pruning hooks. Nation will not take up sword against nation, nor will they train for war anymore" (Is. 2:4)

Can you today in your most bizarre thought-process or most

wild, outlandish thinking even imagine the Japanese bombing Peal Harbor? Of course not. Even raising the question seems nonsensical for one simple, clear reason: they would be declaring war on their best customer. The well-being of the typical Japanese family is directly related to the well being of the United States and vice versa. And everyone knows that.

The key to achieving and maintaining world peace is interdependence; that is, a condition wherein it is in each of our own self-interest to further the well-being of the other.

To the extent that it is individual, private capitalistic firms which are bringing about this interdependence, the ultimate contribution of capitalism to humankind will be the achievement of a secure, sustained world peace. Indeed, it is the multinational business corporation, serving as a vehicle to channel funds and goods and employment across borders and thereby contributing to this interdependence, which is emerging as the creator and guarantor of world peace. Not only is the multinational corporation not the Satanic, evil, oppressive institution portrayed by certain journalists, but it indeed has established itself as the vehicle through which all God's children have mutual interests. (Again, we must acknowledge that the corporation as a concept is a neutral mechanism. It can be used for international arms sales and sex trade as well as international sales of Bibles and medicines.)

Certainly governments, emphasizing geographical borders and separation, cannot claim this contribution. Indeed, a primary raison d'etre of government has been to organize around our differences and protect us from those different from us. Therefore, by definition socialism, wherein the government is the sole economic agent, accentuates our separateness and shields us from interaction and interdependence with others across the border. While governments formalize our separateness, business firms formalize our connectedness. The intrinsic nature of a government is to, for a variety of reasons, separate us from others. The business firm reconnects us by crossing over the boundary and actively, on a day-to-day basis connecting individuals, person-to-person.

Even the organized church or organized religion cannot claim this achievement of creating mutual dependence as the business firm can. Denominations and churches, too, are organized around our differences. Regretfully, and ironically to some observers, religion has been one of the most divisive forces throughout the history of the world. Like governments, religious denominations are based upon, and therefore intrinsically emphasize, our differences. I acknowledge that, yes, it is my church that raises my consciousness to embrace the message of Jesus Christ which gives rise to my love of my fellow humans and therefore my feeling of and acting upon my responsibility for my fellow humans. Nevertheless, this Sunday, after I hear, appropriately, a plea to contribute to our church's missions abroad, my wife and I will stop at Starbucks for our latte, directly contributing to providing a coffee plantation worker a job, bringing pressure on his or her employer to provide enlightened working conditions and compensation, not to mention leaving off a book in the collection barrel which Starbucks, through CARE, will distribute abroad to help increase literacy. Without the profits, Starbucks would not be able to contribute to such extent in improving the wellbeing of humankind. There are multitudes of other examples.

The institution bringing about world peace by encouraging cooperation and communication and instilling mutual dependence is a small quiet player. It is the business firm quietly, individually, without any fanfare, going around creating the links between suppliers and demanders, that is giving rise to global interdependence. Every issue of every business magazine and newspaper is filled with articles related to international investment. While writing this book I received my *Forbes* in the mail, and on the cover noticed, "The World's Best-Run Bank." It was an article by Richard Morais about London's Hong Kong & Shanghai Bank Corp. In his article Mr. Morais states, "It's 3 p.m. Vans from HSBC's London branches and wholesale clients swarm into the backroom service center in South London, where 300 employees annually process 475 million checks. A change of address from a British customer is fed into an industrial scanner. A picture of the handwritten change of address is routed to a central queuing system. Operator RCX066 is free, looks at the change of address up on the screen and seconds later has made the simple change to the woman's London account. The operator sits in China.... HSBC is aggressively taking advantage of the worldwide drop in telecommunications charges and advances in technology to industrialize the back room on a global scale."[587] Then, let's follow that operator in China who recently was hired for this job. She moves into a nicer apartment, listens to relaxing music, performs well on her job and gets promoted to supervisor, sends her daughter to college, maybe even takes a vacation to London and takes in an Andrew Lloyd Weber production and on and on and on the wonderful story goes.

Myriad examples exist. Fareed Zakaria, managing editor of Foreign Affairs and fellow at the Hoover Institution at Stanford University, notes, "Thousands of goods, services, and even ideas are manufactured globally, creating complex interconnections between states. A book, for example, can be written in New York, copyedited in India, typeset in the Caribbean, printed in Singapore, and then shipped worldwide. The Internet has made global manufacturing, distribution, and communication simple and cheap."[588]

Further, as Novak observes, "Transnationals have a real interest in the self-protection afforded by stimulating local ownership. They have urgent capital needs elsewhere…., Galbraith makes the classic case for free international trade. In a free world economy, technology is spread more rapidly; the international division of labor follows more realistic and intelligent lines; productivity increases; prices fall (as efficiencies earned in one place displace older inefficiencies); and a greater aggregate of employment around the world is achieved."[589]

One of the most baffling phenomena of capitalism to those who do not understand economics is how a system based on the separate, uncoordinated decisions of thousands of small individual players can lead to such an elegantly efficient and orderly outcome. One thing a New York officer worker has never lain awake worrying about is whether or not he/she will have a pencil to use tomorrow, but, indeed there is no one anywhere in the world responsible for seeing that he/she does. Indeed, capitalism has demonstrated that "microism," individual free producers, works and works far superior to "macroism," central, aggregate planning. Nowhere is this being more clearly demonstrated than in the international arena. The myriad individual private producers and consumers around the globe with their mutual dependence are achieving what no treaty or political agreement or church program or non-profit social service agency is able to achieve—relationship stability. Further, to the extent that churches and social service agencies are effective in generating international harmony, it is through small, individual units—church-to-church, family-to-family, local organization-to-local organization that this is most effectively being done. In fact, some have asserted that the individual local church is the religious embodiment of the economics concept of free enterprise!

Another form in which microism is being effective is in the microlending programs proliferating around the globe. In such programs local small business people or potential business people are granted very small loans to embark upon small enterprises. For example, a woman may borrow $50 with which to buy a used sewing machine for making an item to sell to locals. Typically she is a member of a support group that provides advice and encouragement to each other, and not until the first borrower in the group demonstrates consistent repayment performance on the loan is a loan made to the next borrower, and so on. Commencing with Dr. Muhammad Yunus' Grameen Bank in Bangladesh, these microlending programs have proliferated throughout the world because, by pursing economic development through tiny bite-sizes they are proving effective. They are upstaging the unwieldy grandiose economic development schemes, many of which find funds siphoned off through corruption. Instead, viable entrepreneurs are sprouting up all over the globe. By the early 1990's two billion dollars of such loans had been made—with a repayment rate of over 90%.[590] According to Joe Remenyi, professor of economics at Deakin University, Australia, "The seeds of a successful credit-based income generation program are identified as putting people first; working *with* the poor instead of *for* the poor; the combined discipline of market forces; individual self-interest, and peer group acclaim, support, and discipline; and rejection of modernization as the primary goal of development.... Social welfare and well-intentioned charities do not alleviate poverty on a sustained basis because they do nothing to augment the productivity of the poor. Credit-based income generation projects that are successful... generate jobs because the increase in productivity and improved demand for the output of microenterprises make it profitable for employers to take on additional labor.... The financial results [of a sampling] for the typical loan can be summarized as follows: the permanent income of borrowers increased by not less than 25 percent, jobs were created at ... one-tenth the typical cost of job creation programs in Third World economies,... default rates were minimal, and estimated social rates of return were typically much greater than those calculated for investments in the modern sector.... Poverty alleviation policies must tap the vitality and potential of the private enterprise driven economic goals of the thousands on thousands of small businesses that employ and service the consumption needs of the poor."[591] Capitalistic microism is working!

In this discussion of global economic interdependence, I am not asserting that all is "sweetness and light." Indeed, quite to the contrary; economic cycles have not been done away with, and at any give time one country might benefit from trade to a greater or lesser degree than another country. Considerable problems continue in the arena of international relationships, giving rise to voluminous writings and recommendations by economists, political scientists, sociologists, theologians and others outlining their respective versions of what Beckman refers to as the "New International Economic Order." It is fascinating to observe that most problems defined as international are really domestic. It is not the "fault" of the United States that Brazilian teen-agers are embracing the decadence of our MTV. Further, most impediments to social and economic advance in various developing countries reflect primarily corruption and oppression by their own leaders.

Summary

All of the problems and shortcomings notwithstanding, we should remain steadfastly mindful of the truth of the Law of Comparative Advantage that countries are better off if they focus on producing those items in which they have a comparative advantage and trade with each other. While one of the two countries may win more than the other country, both countries still win in the sense of being ahead of where each otherwise would have been without trade. Just because one country is behind the other country, it should not let envy blind itself to its improved condition.

To summarize this *ultimate* contribution of capitalism, as people become increasingly inter-dependent upon one another and have a stake in each other's wellbeing, we become more loving toward each other. Peace, prosperity and loving treatment—globally— three of God's objectives for humanity are unfolding, albeit excruciatingly gradually, unevenly and interruptedly. But to the extent that God's objectives of peace, prosperity and loving treatment are emerging at all, the chief mechanism for bringing this about is the business firm. Today the most powerful force leading to world peace is not the church, nor government nor political agreements, but the corporation, providing global interdependence of people through international trade and ownership. Granted, this is not out of altruism. I am not suggesting an extraordinary righteousness on the part of the business firm. It is in the business firm's self interest to perform this role. As explained in the earlier chapter, "The Genius of Capitalism," Adam Smith's Invisible Hand operates not just within a particular political boundary, but globally, and all of the attendant economic and social benefits discussed in that earlier chapter accrue to all peoples participating in the capitalistic economic activity.

This concept was graphically presented in a recent magazine advertisement by Interland, an enlightened firm providing a full array of consulting services to organizations using the Internet. This simple yet dramatic advertisement effectively conveys the whole point regarding the new state of the world:

> **WWI**
>
> **WWII**
>
> **WWW.**

God's primary mechanism for pursuing God's objective of global peace, prosperity and loving treatment is the business firm: it crosses government boundaries and it is blind to race, creed, color, sex, religion, nationality and all other differences as it serves as the conduit for directly connecting God's children to one another. The *Dictionary of Paul and His Letters* makes the strong assertion, "In a very real sense the *Pax Romana* could be seen as a divine preparation for the evangelistic activity of the church."[592] Could it be that a similar assertion—Divine expression—could be made regarding today's global expansion of individual business firms and all of the attendant communication channels and inter-dependence?

While the prophets were describing the eschaton, "the last days," it is with some degree of intrigue that we listen to Micah and Isaiah while observing the current apparent progress of international relations, a key element of which are free trade agreements and disarmament treaties.

> They will beat their swords into plowshares
>> and their spears into pruning hooks.
> Nation will not take up sword against nation,
>> nor will they train for war anymore.
> Every man will sit under his own vine
>> and under his own fig tree,
> and no one will make them afraid,
>> for the LORD Almighty has spoken.
> All the nations may walk
>> in the name of their gods;
> we will walk in the name of the LORD
>> our God for ever and ever.
>
> (Mi. 4:3-5)

> They will beat their swords into plowshares
>> and their spears into pruning hooks.
> Nation will not take up sword against nation,
>> nor will they train for war anymore.
> Come, O house of Jacob,
>> let us walk in the light of the LORD.
>
> (Is. 2:4,5)

Chapter XII

Conclusion

═══════════════════════════════════

In the context of viewing all of humanity as created in the image of God, perhaps the most distinguishing characteristic of capitalism is its egalitarianism. Kristol summarizes: "What did capitalism promise? First of all, it promised continued improvement in the material conditions of all its citizens, a promise without precedent in human history. Second, it promised an equally unprecedented measure of individual freedom for all of these same citizens. And lastly, it held out the promise that, amidst this prosperity and liberty, the individual could satisfy his instinct for self-perfection—for leading a virtuous life that satisfied the demands of his spirit (or as one used to say, his soul)—and that the free exercise of such individual virtue would aggregate into a just society."[593] Henry Hazlitt observes, "Capitalism has enormously raised the level of the masses. It has wiped out whole areas of poverty. It has greatly reduced infant mortality, and made it possible to cure disease and prolong life. It has reduced human suffering. Because of capitalism, millions live today who would otherwise have not even been born. If these facts have no ethical relevance, then it is impossible to say in what ethical relevance consists."[594]

What a wonderful environment conducive to Christianity flourishing!

The key element that causes capitalism, among economic systems, to be most in accord with Christianity is private ownership which permits *voluntary* acts. The existence of private property sets up the precedent condition to the expression of love. To give to others requires that I first possess. Further, not only does capitalism with its voluntarism *permit* genuine exercise of certain Christian virtues, generosity for example, but the very nature of capitalism *requires* the genuine expression of certain Christian virtues, stewardship and trust for example.

Summarizing the seven brilliant outcomes of capitalism, a thorough analysis leads to the clear, unassailable conclusion that today democratic capitalism has made immense achievements in the following:

- Empowering the poor.
- Diffusing economic power.
- Enlightening stewardship of God's resources.
- Fostering political stability.
- Stimulating economic creativity.
- Generating a high level of non-economic—social—goods.
- Creating the conditions conducive to sustainable world peace.

We also observe that the six chief attributes of capitalism are the following:

- Hope and optimism
- Liberty
- Trust
- Egalitarianism
- Voluntarism (outward demonstration of love)
- Enlightened leadership

Note that the seven outcomes of capitalism listed above are the direct opposite of those conditions against which the prophets, Jesus Christ and the disciples vehemently cried out and that the six attributes listed above are key elements embodied in Christianity. Could it be that capitalism, with its emphasis on (1) genuine generosity reflecting love from each individual's *heart* rather than orientation toward coercive redistribution by compliance with the *law*, combined with (2) corralling us sinners through the discipline, "Invisible Hand," of the market system, is God's ingenuous creation? Rick Baugh, a successful participant in Seattle's high-tech community, expressed it this way: business—which unleashes the creativity of God's children and constrains the self-interest of sinners—is "God's delivery system."

That is not such an outlandish notion when we acknowledge that, when the seven outcomes are combined with the six attributes, we see that the chief behavior component is *cooperation*. The capitalistic society is comprised of a multitude of business firms voluntarily brought into existence and comprised of virtually every culture, race, language, religion, sex, education level, societal position, and nationality of humankind. In order to function and achieve its purpose each of these millions of entities within the capitalistic society must *cooperate*—even business competitors which must cooperatively abide by the rules of the game. Contrary to the naïve, superficial beliefs of some, capitalism involves a greater degree of cooperation than of competition. While competition in the marketplace is a component of capitalism, the chief characteristic of capitalism is cooperation.

To illustrate:

To the extent that each capitalistic entity involves intra-entity cooperation by the members comprising the entity and inter-entity cooperation by the various entities comprising a larger unit, for example, a market, such entities are said to comprise a *community*. Novak observes, "Consider the institutions of capitalism: the corporation, the labor union, banking, the stock exchange. Each of these is communal.... Each depends upon bonds of trust which go beyond coercive force. Ironically, a society supposedly based upon competitive individualism and possessiveness seems to favor in its citizens forms of generosity, trust, extroversion, outgoingness, and reliance upon the good faith of others.... Liberty, basic trust, and communal purpose underlie the theory of the corporation."[595] Novak expands on this notion of community, "To be sure, the *forms* of each of these communities—families, neighborhoods, local agencies, interest groups, voluntary associations, churches, unions, corporations, guilds, societies, schools—are transformed under democratic capitalism into modalities unfamiliar in previous history. Less and less are they rooted in kith and kin, blood and status, propinquity and immobility. They have become more voluntary, fluid, mobile."[596]

Hardy puts it this way, "Again, God, could have created the world differently. He could have made us self-sufficient. But God chose to connect us to each other in a circle of need and care, to make us a society of inter-dependent persons who serve each other and are served by each other. Each connection in the social bond is made where human need and human ability meet.... We are born naked, and there are those involved in the design, manufacture, and distribution of clothing; we are born hungry, and there are those involved in the production, distribution, and preparation of food. Soon we grow and come to find our own place in this system of mutual service."[597] D'Souza agrees, "capitalism channels greed in such a way that it is placed at the service of the want of others. Destructive forms of greed, in which we seek to seize and appropriate other people's possessions, are outlawed in a capitalist society. We can acquire what others possess only by convincing them to give it to us, and the best way to do this is to give them something in exchange. The point isn't just that capitalism makes society better off; it is that capitalism makes us better people by limiting the scope of our vices."[598]

Bernard Murchland, professor of philosophy at Ohio Wesleyan

University, enunciates this point from a different perspective, "I have often argued with socialist friends that the corporation might be considered one of the principal forms of community in our time because it allows very different kinds of people to work in harmony for common goals, to form friendships, make choices, and deploy their talents; it generates an esprit de corps and common loyalties and it distributes power—in brief, it affords the opportunity to practice a significant range of democratic virtues."[599] It is interesting to note that the words *company* and *companionship* have the same root.

Griffiths expresses the embodiment of community within capitalism as follows: "The act of employment is not just a legal transaction...; it becomes a personal relationship between two human beings and the work situation becomes a network of such relationships. The act of selling is not just finding a point on a demand curve, but a transaction between two people with a God-given sense of absolute standards. The 'market' is not just some construct... but a series of individual exchanges between people in which mutual trust is extended and accepted."[600]

John Paul II concurs, "Many goods cannot be adequately produced through the work of an isolated individual; they require the cooperation of many people in working towards a common goal.... It is his disciplined work in close collaboration with others that makes possible the creation of ever more extensive *working communities* which can be relied upon to transform man's natural and human environments. Important virtues are involved in this process, such as diligence, industriousness, prudence in undertaking reasonable risks, reliability and fidelity in interpersonal relationships...."[601]

Finally, The Oxford Declaration weighs in, "Christians should encourage governments everywhere to foster vigorous voluntary associations." What better example than the business firm—embodying a community of God's children voluntarily joining together to cooperatively provide a good or service to God's other children.

The Christian doctrine of the church reflects the notion that our practice of Christianity, our demonstration of Jesus's teachings, is to be done in community with others. This relates to our very nature. To be born in the image and likeness of God means to be in relationship with each other. This community is referred to as the "church." The *Westminster Dictionary of Theological Terms* defines "church" as "The community of those who profess faith in Jesus

Christ."[602] The *Dictionary of Paul and His Letters* notes further, "Integral to Paul's teaching about the people of God is his use of the important word *ekklesia,* a term meaning "congregation," "church," "gathering" or "assembly." Burton states the role of the church as fourfold: "worship (*latreia*), fellowship (*koinonia*), ministry (*diakonia*) and mission/witness (*martyria*)."[603] Interestingly, each of these general roles has its counterpart in economics.

Fellowship: the business firm is a subset of society, a form of voluntary community. Further, it can be a manifestation of the ideals promulgated by the church. But in order to be genuine this act of community must be voluntary. It must reflect a relationship between our heart and God that leads to our desire to relate to other humans. It cannot be a coercive act. If it is, God sees the falsity within our hearts. Hence, the free market—the economics manifestation of free will—facilitates this act of genuine community.

Ministry, from the Greek *diakonia* and Latin *ministerium* meaning "service." Capitalism, humans voluntarily serving one another through the production and distribution of goods and services and free exchange in the marketplace, is a mechanism for carrying out ministry in the physical world, if such service is "to God in Jesus Christ rendered by the church and by individuals through the power of the Holy Spirit."[604] Entrepreneurialism, the act of forming a business firm, is nothing more than a form of creative service.

Mission/witness, from the Greek word *martyria,* refers to our bearing witness to Jesus through every aspect of how we live, including at work.

Finally, capitalism has expanded the boundaries of humanity's communities to include the globe. While governments are organized with walls, corporations have leaped over, crawled underneath and opened gates, broadening communication and cooperation to include the entire globe (even penetrating the tightest barricade, North Korea for example). Another way in which the expansion of communities has flowed from capitalism is the plethora of brand new global communities emerging on the Internet. Now small groups of people all over the world who share an interest in the most esoteric subject are chatting about it all day long every day if they so desire.

So we can describe capitalism in terms of its behavior requirements: *cooperation,* and in terms of its organizational characteristics: voluntary *communities*. Have we not, then, come full circle back to the universality of God; i.e., all humans are creations of God, and therefore giving rise, as brothers and sisters, to our two great commandments: love God and love one another? Calvin, according to Andre Bieler, seems to agree with this theological dimension of economics, "God has created man' Calvin says, 'so that man may be a creature of fellowship'.... Companionship is completed in work and in the interplay of economic exchanges. Human fellowship is realized in relationships which flow from the division of labor wherein each person has been called by God to a particular and partial work which complements the work of others. The mutual exchange of goods and services is the concrete sign of the profound solidarity which unites humanity."[605]

Lest I appear naïve, I want to acknowledge that considerable cooperation within the community of the business firm, as well as within the church, schools and other human institutions, is nothing more than superficial friendliness practiced in order to further individual ambition rather than a reflection of deep, spirit-filled interpersonal love. Nevertheless, superficial or not, at least the business firm, the primary institution of capitalism, requires the same values—cooperation and harmonious interpersonal relations—to succeed as the values espoused by Christianity.

Finally, capitalism is communitarian in another sense. As I pointed out earlier in this book, in capitalism, a positive sum game, everyone benefits by everyone else being better off. As a business, one of the ways I can sell more widgets is to have more people out there capable of buying them. Accordingly, I as a business person have a direct vested interest in everyone else being better off. Humans' mutual interest in each other's well-being is reflected in Guthrie's assertion regarding Christian doctrine, "The Christian answer is, 'I believe in the God who is the Creator, Preserver, Ruler, and Renewer of heaven and earth.' To believe in *this* God is to give ourselves with confidence and hope to the struggle for the improvement of human life in *this world*. We can do it and we must do it, because the struggle against poverty, ignorance, disease, injustice, war, and oppression is not our fight alone. It is the fight of a loving and powerful God who not only saves us at the end of time but invites and commands us to participate in God's creating and recreating work here and now, in 'secular' history, for the good of all people everywhere."[606] If one agrees with Guthrie, and presumably most Christians do, then the notion that capitalism is an economic system created by God is a very real possibility—particularly when one considers the outcomes outlined at the outset of this chapter. As an added test, let's apply capitalism to the challenges enumerated by Guthrie in the passage just quoted:

Poverty: Capitalism more than any other economic system has raised people's standard of living throughout the world and has been particularly distinguished by the emergence of broad middle classes.

Ignorance: The creation of wealth to support education and the training of workers in capitalistic nations dwarfs that of non-capitalistic nations.

Disease: The development of pharmaceuticals and the creation of wealth and contribution of funds to support scientific and medical research of the capitalistic nations dwarfs that of non-capitalistic nations.

Injustice: Pluralism, economic parity, and a broad middle class, which tend to thwart injustice, exist to a much greater degree in capitalistic nations than in non-capitalistic nations. Further, the creation of wealth to support public defenders and accessible judiciaries in capitalistic nations exceeds that of non-capitalistic nations.

War: As discussed at length in the previous chapter, establishing the incentive for peace is where capitalism, through individual business firms, towers in its contribution to humanity.

Oppression: Capitalism, which tends to be accompanied by democracy and conducive to societal values of pluralism and egalitarianism tends to be found

in countries where oppression is absent or relatively low.

Applying strictly the reasoning and the examples of challenges
enumerated by Guthrie, one has to accept the possibility that capitalism just might be a demonstration of Guthrie's assertion that
God's creation is on-going in today's secular world. Certainly the
foregoing achievements and other social benefits funded by capitalistic wealth are what led T. J. Rodgers, Chief Executive of Cypress
Semiconductors to assert, "my own view is that money is the root of
all good."[607] D'Souza agrees, "the movement from poverty to
affluence represents a kind of moral progress. It is a beneficial thing
for individuals and societies because it expands the opportunity to
act virtuously and help others."[608] Fr. Schall states it this way, "The
fact is that a healthy materialism is part of what the Incarnation
taught us."[609]

To Guthrie's implications of the positive relationship between
capitalism and Christianity we add Gilder's conclusions regarding
same. [The entrepreneurial initiative] "will most essentially express
an impulse of faith, a belief in the future, and a sensitivity to the
needs of others.... God is the foundation of all living knowledge;
and the human mind, to the extent it can know anything beyond its
own meager reach, partakes of the mind of God.... To overcome
[economic challenges] it is necessary to have faith, to recover the
belief in chance and providence, in the ingenuity of free and God-
fearing men. This belief will allow us to see the best way of helping
the poor, the way to understand the truths of equality before God
that can only come from freedom and diversity on earth. It will lead
us to abandon, above all, the idea that the human race can become
self-sufficient, can separate itself from chance and fortune in a
hubristic siege of rational resource management, income distribution, and futuristic planning. Our greatest and only resource is the
miracle of human creativity in a relation of openness to the
divine."[610]

Even if a valid conceptual argument could be made for socialism—and many intellectuals have tried—the unassailable empirical
fact is that socialist countries come in a distant second place to
capitalistic countries in terms of all dimensions of humankind:
economic, social, psychological, spiritual, etc. As Kristol observes,

"All that the various 'socialist' regimes have to show for the sacrifices they have demanded of their citizens is tyranny and scarcity, or bureaucracy and bankruptcy.... They do not promote superior economic growth or a greater degree of individual freedom, though they can make us all share more equally in the diminution of both.... Surely freedom and affluence are preferable, whatever the problems generated by this freedom and this affluence." Novak agrees, "When the state owns the means of production, not much improvement in the human condition appears to become visible. Workers seem no happier, wages are not higher, and neither sullenness nor alcoholism nor 'alienation' seems to be diminished."[611] He continues, "Social democratic societies are not notably happy or contented societies.... In an obverse paradox, while extolling the language of community and social sharing, social democracy necessarily excites envy,... and it inevitably divides citizens into factions that make on the state unceasing claims of favor, entitlement, and privilege. Each faction jealously and militantly claims its own 'just' stake."[612]

The foregoing discussion ought to resolve the capitalism / socialism debate. But let's finally lay it to rest by an empirical observation by Michael Boskin, the distinguished economist at Stanford University, "On the relative merits of capitalism and socialism, we hear today calls from economies in transition to return to central planning. History has already performed that experiment. Compare the former East and West Germany. Both were shattered by World War II. Both had similar problems and opportunities. One was dosed with communism—the heavy hand of state planning, controls and government intervention, regulation and state ownership of virtually everything. The other was dosed with capitalism. The West grew into an economic superpower... while the East stagnated. When the two Germanys were reunited, the standard of living in the West was five times that in the East, which had a spoiled environment, a decrepit capital stock, and a demoralized labor force.... That is about as close as we get to a natural experiment in economics. And the answer is unambiguous."[613]

Another comparison is Poland before and after communism. Upon visiting the village of Niepolomice in 1999, Lori Montgomery, reporter for Knight Ridder Newspapers, reports "When communism fell in 1989, this village... had no running water, four bankrupt state businesses and 700 telephones for 17,000 people. Today [a mere ten years later], nearly every home has not only a phone and indoor plumbing, but also a computer. There are 35 major employers, including 10 foreign companies.... But the village is most proud of its modern high school, with its computer lab and annual trips abroad."[614]

Looking at another less dramatic example. France, hobbled by a monstrous public sector, "according to the London Business School, has a business startup rate of 1.8 per 100 people, compared with 8.5 for the U.S. and 4.4 for Germany."[615] While privatization is gathering momentum with stellar results of increased efficiency and creativity (e.g. Renault), France, dominated by reactionary, distribution-oriented labor unions, lags behind its neighbor, Germany, in both economic and social advance. A decade ago Sweden finally understood. After the Conservatives were elected in 1991 and instituted market-oriented liberalizing policies, implemented considerable privatization, cut the national debt, slashed tax rates and otherwise incented the private sector, Sweden finally experienced meaningful entrepreneurial effort and accelerating economic growth. On the other side of the globe, in China, the communist regime is evidencing an understanding of the benefits of capitalism. It is estimated that somewhere between one and six million private business firms exist in China, producing nearly two-thirds of that country's gross domestic product.[616]

It is a statement, not of theory or conjecture, but of empirical fact that, as practiced by humankind today, communism enslaves, socialism debilitates and democratic capitalism liberates. The final nail was put in the coffin of the socialism/capitalism debate in 1991 by none other than one of the world's leading socialists, historian and philosopher Robert Heilbroner of the New School of Social Research in New York, "Less than seventy-five years after it officially began, the contest between capitalism and socialism is over: capitalism has won."[617] In this context, Schall notes, "What is disturbing is...how little the actual experience of socialist systems, particularly their failures, seems to affect socialist theory."[618]

To the person who asserts that there are still huge economic deficiencies remaining in capitalistic societies, perhaps the two most noteworthy being environmental degradation and the many people still in poverty, I respond with the observation that the very fact that there is widespread outrage over the mere existence of poverty and environmental damage is testimony to the triumphs of capitalism. The pervasive indignation regarding these two conditions did not emerge until an unprecedented magnitude and breadth of wealth was achieved by capitalistic societies. The emergence of poverty and the environment as major political issues in the United States did not occur until the general populace perceived that a level of wealth finally had been attained such that solving these problems has finally become a practical possibility. Not throughout human history has this occurred until today—thanks to the level and breadth of wealth generated by capitalism. Despite Scripture's preoccupation—appropriate in my view—with the state of the poor and the importance of loving and showing justice and generosity to the poor, nowhere in Scripture is there any advocation of eliminating the state of poverty. The reason is simple: the means were not available. The recent popular issues of "economic justice" accompanied by certain groups claiming "economic rights" as goals perceived as attainable is an outcome of the great achievement of democratic capitalism. Can one imagine, for example, the pervasiveness of such issues in the context of feudalism?

To summarize, throughout the world the individual business firm—directly in its own operations and indirectly through its philanthropy—is privately (far beyond what it pays in taxes) doing more to raise humanity out of poverty, heal the sick, feed the hungry, educate the ignorant and bring peaceful inter-dependence among all of God's creations than any other human institution. This is not in any way to suggest that much has been accomplished. Humanity has a far, far way to go in eradicating poverty, sickness, hunger, illiteracy, war and all of the other maladies facing humanity. The point is not to beat the chest of capitalism regarding its accomplishments. The point is simply that capitalism and the business firm have done more in this regard than any other economic system or human institution. Further, it is the very material achievements of capitalism that give rise to heightened attention to satisfying those needs not yet satisfied. Rosenberg and Birdzell observe, "it is only as a result of the material success of the Western [capitalistic] world that the pronounced shift in values... such as social justice, equality and a concern for the environment...occurred."[619] As observed earlier, perhaps the most distinguishing characteristic of both the new corporate executive and the new wealthy entrepreneurs is their commitment of their firms' and their personal resources and time to the pursuit of social causes. At no time in human history has the active concern for our fellow humans been manifest by the bulk of the members of a society to the extent as it is today in capitalistic societies. As equally impressive as the material prosperity achievements of capitalistic societies are their advances in stewardship and their demonstration of generosity.

Gilder expresses this notion as follows: "Most of all, the entrepreneurs learn the deepest truths of giving and sacrifice, the miraculous powers of commitment and faith. They give themselves, their time, their wealth, their sleep; they give it year after year, reinvesting every profit, mortgaging every property. They leverage their lives to their private belief in a redemptive idea. And their long outpouring of belief and faith and funds and sacrifices, seemingly wasted and lost in the maws and middens of the world economy, somehow mysteriously coheres and collects.... It is an irrational process, but it is the classic experience of the entrepreneur, the endlessly recurrent miracle of capitalism, by which orphans and outcasts vastly and repeatedly excel the works and wealth of emperors, the reach and rule of armies, the dreams of kings, the calculus of expertise, the visions of state. 'Do unto others as you would have them do unto you' and 'Give and you will be given unto' are the central rules of the life of enterprise (you cannot give what you do not own) and personal freedom (a planned economy cannot allow the surprising gifts of entrepreneurs). But it is a life that most deeply springs from religious faith and culture.... The act of committing your work and wealth, over a period of years, to bring into the world a new good that the world may well reject—the act of putting your own fate into the hands of unknown others, freely deciding your future in a market of free choice—these are the essential acts of a religious person...., the entrepreneur finds a higher source of hope than reason, a deeper well of faith than science, a farther reach of charity than welfare. His success is the triumph of the spirit of enterprise—a thrust beyond the powers and principalities of the established world to the transcendent sources of creation and truth."[620] In another book, Gilder summarizes the foregoing as the "Law of Reciprocity, that one must supply in order to demand, save in order to invest, consider others in order to serve oneself"[621] and notes that such relationships are crucial to all life in society. To paraphrase: within capitalism (1) in order to receive one must first give which in turn requires (2) initiating action based on faith.

Gilder continues, "the moral core of capitalism is the essential altruism of enterprise.... The circle of giving (the profits of the economy) will grow as long as the gifts [products] are consistently valued more by the receiver than by the givers. In deciding what new goods to assemble or create, the givers [producers] must there-fore be willing to focus on the needs of others.... Profit is a measure of the extent to which an investment reflects an accurate under-standing of the needs of others.... The altruism of the capitalist goes further. Not only must the entrepreneur comprehend the wants of others; he must also collaborate with others in his business. And most of all, he must wish that others succeed. The businessman must be full of optimism and hope for his potential customers. He must want them to prosper. Above all he must want the poor to prosper, if only because the poor always compose the world's largest untapped market.... The spirit of enterprise is generous and optimistic about human nature. 'Give and you will be given unto' is its fundamental theme. Altruism—an orientation toward the needs of others—is its moral and commercial compass.... If they [capital-ists] hoard their wealth, the system tends to fail. It succeeds by inducing the capitalist continually to give his wealth back to the system in the form of new...investments. The belief that good fortune of others is also finally one's own does not come easily or invariably to the human mind. It is, however, the golden rule of economics, a key to peace and prosperity.... It is the absolutely crucial Christian source of wealth creation."[622]

D'Souza, who immigrated to the United States from India, makes this observation regarding the historical development of America, "It has delivered... unprecedented material prosperity within a framework of exhilarating freedom.... America is now the model for the world...based on the simple fact that its formula has been tried and has proven successful... Moreover,... America's... principles of commerce and technology... have produced not just material but moral progress: the abolition of slavery, the elevation of countless people from poverty to comfort, the relief of suffering produced by disease, humanitarian campaigns against torture and famine all over the world, and a widely shared conception of human rights, human freedom and human dignity."[623] The overwhelmingly abundant outcome—financial and nonfinancial—of capitalism just might give rise to capitalism being defined as the economic manifestation of that large enough lever with which Archimedes said he could move the world.

Finally, contrary to popular belief, the distinguishing characteristic of capitalism is not consumption; it is saving. As mentioned previously, all of the benefits of capitalism—job creation, productivity increases, improved products, economic growth—and all of the attendant social benefits which have been discussed depend upon the reinvestment of retained earnings. That is, capitalism, which focuses on the future, foregoes present consumption in favor of savings—retained earnings, in accounting vernacular—which are reinvested in the business. As Griffiths notes, "Historically it has been the accumulation of increasing amounts of capital, embodying as they did new technology, which raised dramatically the productivity of labour. The source of this increase in capital is saving; that is, it is income which is currently received but not consumed…. It is only when an individual or a society make a conscious decision to forgo consumption that it is possible to accumulate capital…. If the wages, tax payments and dividends of a corporation are less than its total revenue then it is enabled to increase its investment…. It is important to notice that saving always involves thinking beyond the present. Alfred Marshall, the distinguished Cambridge economist of the turn of the century, expressed it by saying that saving was associated with 'man's prospectiveness; that is, his faculty of realising the future.' But less consumption always involves some element of sacrifice, self-denial or abstinence."[624] Indeed, the reality of capitalism—in direct contrast to the image with which it has been tarnished—is its embodying a mindset of deferred consumption; i.e., savings.

Both the conceptual and empirical evidence is clear. The tenets of capitalism are in accord with the tenets of Christianity, and capitalism has functioned in concert with the objectives of Christianity. It just might be that, at least for this period in human history, capitalism is God's delivery system. Let me quickly point out that by using the term, "God's delivery system," that I am *not* suggesting that the system is "Godly." I am suggesting the following. We know that God uses all sorts of worldly, unrighteous mechanisms to achieve His ends. He even used Satan and Satan's temptations to demonstrate the divine nature of Jesus. As mentioned earlier, he used Cyrus, the pagan Persian leader. Therefore, could it be that God is using capitalism—a human system—to generate medicines for the sick, food for the hungry, reclamation and protection of God's natural resources, the leisure for all to devote time to spiritual pursuits, and even a conduit for world peace?

Before closing, an important modifier must be noted. As observed in my earlier discussion of societal values and norms, it is clear that in order to function effectively capitalism requires cultural norms and political and social systems embodying trust, liberty, democracy, private property, and egalitarianism. Those societies in which these characteristics are absent are not suitable for capitalism. "Michael Novak [in his] review of Peter Berger's... *The Capitalist Revolution: Fifty Propositions About Prosperity, Equality, and Liberty*,...says we have to consider that there cannot be private property without respect for law, markets without respect for contracts, enterprise without confidence in creative practical intellect, or investments without willingness to defer reward."[625] Nash agrees, "There are several necessary conditions without which a market could not exist,... They include an enforced right to own and to exchange property, an enforcement of contracts, and laws forbidding the use of force, fraud, and theft. Government has several important roles to play. It must set up a stable system of rules within which exchanges can take place."[626] Accordingly, my praise of capitalism notwithstanding, I do not want to imply an adherence to the naïve notion that capitalism is the preferred or even appropriate economic system for all societies at all times. Scholossberg reports, "the endemic corruption of most poor countries can entangle the most dedicated and energetic entrepreneur in a morass of restrictions and the financial drain of bribery, thus sapping the enterprise."[627] Michael Novak attributes much of the economic backwardness of Latin America to "refusing to recognize the moral validity of [capitalism's] requisite habits and institutions of invention: forethought, saving, investing, punctuality, workmanship and the like."[628] Indeed, much harm has been done by endeavoring to introduce a capitalistic system into a society lacking the requisite cultural norms and characteristics. Further, the pace of the conversion of a society to capitalism may be significant. The gradualism of China toward privatization may in the long run be more successful to the eventual emergence of a capitalist society than the abrupt upheaval of some of the former Soviet Union countries. No, I am only asserting that in societies in which the tenets of Christianity are present democratic capitalism is the preferred political / economic system.

Interestingly, however, Beckman makes the following empirical observation, "economic development... does tend toward satisfaction, health, beauty, truth, justice and increased power for good or ill—cogent arguments in favor of change for people from almost any culture or religious background."[629] Hernando de Soto, director of Peru's Institute for Liberty and Democracy, goes even further "Capitalism stands alone as the only feasible way to rationally organize a modern economy. At this moment in history, no responsible nation has a choice."[630] de Soto goes on to insist that the precedent condition to capitalism functioning in any society is the granting of legal title of ownership of the possessions of the masses of people in poor countries. Private property supported by appropriate law and documentation is the key to liberating the world's poor. To return to my point, any given country must first be willing to adopt and implement such law and documentation.

All of the foregoing discussion notwithstanding, the developed capitalistic societies of the world as a result of their overwhelming economic success are at a fork in the road. One fork leads to heightened materialism, consumerism, hedonism and therefore drifting away from God. The other fork leads to heightened cultural interests, contemplation, meaning and spirituality, drawing nearer to a relationship with God. Which fork we take is not a function of the system but depends solely on we humans who live in the capitalistic society. This leads us to the next chapter, "Implications."

Chapter XIII

Implications

===

A s suggested at the end of the previous chapter, what we humans do with the enormous success of capitalism is up to us. In this chapter I want to suggest some considerations for two groups: capitalists and clergy.

Implications for Capitalists

When we understand that God is the beginning and the end, that humans have only two things to do: love God and love each other, what are the implications for those who function in the business world?

First, rejoice at your vocation as a capitalist! Look upon your vocation as exactly what it is: within your calling from God. Recognizing the immense good for humankind that flows from capitalism and that the work of Christianity requires the whole array of worldly goods and services, be the best practitioner you can. Compete vigorously by innovating continually, improving the quality of your products and driving down their prices through improved efficiency. Be grateful for your calling as a capitalist that has led you to the privilege of participating in a system that generates immense economic and noneconomic benefits to humankind throughout the globe. You and your fellow capitalists, as God's agents, have done more to eradicate disease, reduce the numbers of the poor, improve communication, lighten the burden of work, disseminate information, broaden exposure to the arts, even contribute to world peace than any other group of humankind. The practice of Christianity takes food, clothing, shelter, transportation, communication—the whole array of worldly goods and services. And the more effectively and efficiently these can be produced and distributed, the more effectively and efficiently Christianity functions. Be the best capitalist you can! But be so solely in the context of your Christianity. It has been helpful to me to dwell on the words of William Covey, the English evangelist and missionary, which, when in the course of performing some of the research for this book, I would see on the wall of the Seattle Pacific University library: "Expect great things from God; attempt great things for God." Remember that the term "calling" is not limited to one's occupation but refers to one's total relationship with God and with God's creations. Remain mindful of Byker's words, "When you see your life as a calling, you understand that you do everything before the face of God."[631]

Second, adhering to the message that exists throughout Scripture, commencing with Abraham and ending in Revelation, faithfully seek and obey divine guidance in all that you do. Recall the admonition of James, "Now listen, you who say, 'today or tomorrow we will go to this or that city,... carry on business and make money.' Why, you do not even know what will happen tomorrow.... Instead, you ought to say, 'If it is the Lord's will, we will live and do this or that." (Jas. 4:13-15) Davids explains, "This advice is to plan with God. Each plan is evaluated by his standards and goals; each plan is laid before God in prayer with adequate time spent in *listening* for God's ideas."[632] Because God alone controls what we can or cannot, such plans made in accord with God are secure plans. Go back and read all of the book of Romans to receive Paul's exhortations not to let sin have dominion over oneself, never wavering from the understanding that "....God works for the good of those who love him...." (Rom. 8:28)

Third, always view private ownership in its theological context. Although private property is a human institution for efficiently and fairly allocating resources, recognize that God, the creator of everything, is the owner of everything. All of our material possessions are simply on loan from God; we are trustees on behalf of God.

Heed Guthrie's admonition, "Any neglect, abuse or destruction of any part of God's creation,... is not just an offense against our natural environment and a threat to the future of humankind; it is an offense against the Creator of heaven and earth."[633] The freedom embodied in the market system of capitalism is accompanied by commensurate responsibilities to voluntarily follow God's way. Further, keep continuously in mind the dialectic nature of material goods as described by Gilbert Meilaender, Professor of Christian Ethics at Valparaiso University, "So possessions are to be received with thanksgiving and enjoyed as gifts.... [But] renunciation becomes necessary as a continual reminder that the good gifts of God, good as they are, are still not where our heart's longing can finally find its rest. So both poles of this dialectic—enjoyment and renunciation—are necessary. One enjoys these good thing because God gave them, and they point us toward him. One renounces them because, finally, they are not the Giver, the One in whom our hearts are to rest."[634] Give your "net worth" a whole new definition, reflecting your whole self and reflecting our understanding that the sole purpose of all creation is to glorify God. Therefore the value of all assets are in their role as serving God's purpose, and we also possess the huge liability—debt of gratitude—to God for having been granted His grace.

Fourth, view capitalism as simply a mechanism—and the most effective mechanism yet devised—to achieve high efficiency and optimum allocation of resources, contributing to the common good, the general well-being of humanity. View yourself and your vocation as tools in this marvelous mechanism. View return on investment not as the end, but as simply a measure of how well you are performing your role as a capitalist and as an analytical tool when choosing among alternative investments. Adhere to the Christian doctrine that God's people are "chosen... to be God's *servants*, chosen not to receive and enjoy for themselves all the benefits of God's saving grace others do not have but to be instruments of God's grace so that others may receive and enjoy these benefits also."[635] Accordingly, follow Paul's admonition to the Philippians, "Do nothing out of selfish ambition or vain conceit, but in humility....look not only to your own interests, but also the interests of others." (Phil. 2:3,4) Keep in mind that capitalism is just one of the sub-games in the larger tournament of life. While profit is both the nourishment of the players and the "score" of the game of capitalism, the overall objective of the tournament of life is the glory of God as reflected in the good of mankind. Adopt a spiritual definition of "riches," according to Paul's usage throughout his letters. One example: "And my God will meet all your needs according to his glorious riches in Christ Jesus." (Phil. 4:19) Consider adopting a mission statement similar to that of AES, a global energy company producing and distributing electricity to millions of customers throughout the world, earning profits of over $300 million on revenues of over $3 billion: "The mission of the company is to give glory to God by stewarding the resources of the world."[636] In this regard keep in mind the words of John Paul II, "...the free market is the most efficient instrument for utilizing resources and effectively responding to needs. But this is true only for those needs which are 'solvent,' insofar as they are endowed with purchasing power, and for those resources which are 'marketable'..... But there are many human needs which find no place in the market."[637] Being an advocate of the free market does not mean supporting some sort of economic anarchy. As Christians we recognize that it is adherence to God's commandments which frees us from the bondage of the various human conventions that enslave us. Indeed, our continuing to function in a sustained free market depends upon our unwavering commitment to our Christian ideals.

Fifth, remain vigilant to the natural tendency of sinful humans to allow wealth to become a distraction, impediment or displacement from putting God first. That is, do not idolize material goods or comforts. "You shall have no other Gods before me." (Ex. 20:3; Dt. 5:7). Endeavor to follow Jesus Christ's admonishment to be in the world but not of the world, and remember Paul's reminding us that the very God who said, "I will live with them and walk among them" also said, "Therefore come out from them and be separate." (2 Cor. 6:17) Both Jesus and Paul were instructing us not to permit our values to be determined by worldly influences. In addition to being an affront to God, idolatry has the practical negative effect of shifting faith from God to the idolized object, shifting reliance on God to reliance on worldly devices, removing from one the protective shield of God. "To believe that God is the Creator and Ruler of 'all things visible' means we do not have to surrender... to any [worldly] things...."[638] That is, abandon the tyranny of false idols, of viewing money as the source of one's security which in turn leads to a life of anxiety and fear. Reaffirm, as observed in our earlier discussion of the *Circular Flow of Prosperity*, that God's world is one of a circular flow, just as the seasons of the year. Prosperity does not come from hoarding and thereby stopping the flow but by dynamic participation in the flow.

Particularly to leaders of major corporations I exhort you to abandon the inordinately high compensation levels which—you know—far exceed what is necessary to motivate and appropriately reward performance. A justifiable criticism of major corporate boards of directors is that they function somewhat like "old boys clubs" wherein A serves on B's board and compensation committee and B serves on C's board and compensation committee and C serves on A's board and compensation committee each ratcheting up the other's rewards to absurd and obscene levels. This, more than any other phenomenon, has given rise to the widespread animosity of "big business" and must compel a self-analysis of the ethics of compensation.

While resisting hedonism and rejecting materialistic decadence, do not over-react in the opposite direction. Nowhere does Scripture assert that poverty per se is good. In fact Scripture asserts just the opposite, prosperity is good. What is bad is the love of maximizing prosperity. Keep the mindset that earthly status is irrelevant to—neither in concert with nor opposite from—status in heaven. A major message preached by Jesus, and particularly emphasized in the theology of Luke, is that, contrary to the message of the Pharisees, God is the God of all humankind. This concept arises early in Luke in the *Magnificat* (Lk. 1:46-55), "...the mighty he has toppled...and exalted those of low degree...filled the hungry...and rich sent away empty..." Indeed, God's son is brought into the world through a poor person: "the low estate of His handmaiden." God is the great leveler; in His eyes all humans are equal. The point here is not a condemnation of the rich; rather, the structure of this poem is being used to make the point that worldly status has nothing to do with one's relationship with God. This was declared centuries earlier by Solomon, "Rich and poor have this in common: the LORD is the Maker of them all." (Prv. 22:2) The apostle Paul expressed it this way: "I know what it is to be in need, and I know what it is to have plenty. I have learned the secret of being content in any and every situation..... I can do everything through him who gives me strength." (Phil. 4: 12,13) To summarize this point, as you earn money and gain wealth, be mindful of the kind of person you are becoming and maintain a steadfast dependence on God. Daily ask yourself, do I own my possessions or do they own me?

Sixth, in your role as employer and co-worker continue to view all of God's creatures as that, creations of God, and therefore worthy of one's love and stewardship. The "end" is each individual created in the image of God. People always come before products and profits. Paul exhorts us to look at people in a new way. "Therefore, if anyone is in Christ, he is a new creation; the old has gone, the new has come! All this is from God, who reconciled us to himself through Christ and gave us the ministry of reconciliation:...." (2 Cor. 5:17,18) Remember also in all of our human relationships that "There is no such thing as reconciliation with God without reconciliation with our fellow human beings."[639] Therefore, functioning as a Christian in the business world requires going beyond simply enlightened self-interest and embodying genuine love of our fellow humans. Each of our employees and co-workers—indeed every human—should be viewed as a redeemed person in Jesus Christ and a deserving recipient of one's love; "Not just love as a sentimental feeling, but the kind of no-strings-attached, no-one-excluded, no-cost-too-great love of God in Jesus Christ."[640] Carefully re-read Paul's explanation of love in 1 Corinthians 13. 2000 years later Professor Morrie Schwartz reminded us through his former student Mitch Albom, "We must love one another or we die."[641] There is no challenge that cannot be overcome by love. In our family—particularly when it comes to interpersonal relations among the array of personalities of the extended family—we have a saying, "Love conquers all." But love does not mean some sort of namby-pamby acquiescence. Jesus Christ was the opposite of a door mat, vigorously pursuing his agenda. Tough love—as every effective parent knows—is a valid concept. The hardest business challenge I ever faced was successfully met by approaching it in a very tough, loving manner.

Seventh, as Jesus directed, while being driven toward achievement *in* this world, be not *of* this world. In the context of the breath-taking speed and exponential rate of change in the world, remain steadfast to your Christian principles. Insure that you house is built on a solid rock foundation of eternal, unchanging principles. Maintain an unequivocal faith in God through good times and bad as demonstrated by Job. Maintain the Christian doctrine that "the Spirit does not always save us *from* our weakness but helps '*in* our weakness' to give us the comfort, help, courage, and strength to endure and entrust our lives to God."[642] In the face of new challenges and opportunities springing up daily—a scientific breakthrough, a new competitor, a cross-country move to a new job, the venture capitalist cutting off the funds, losing a job, forgetting about a child's piano recital, best friends moving away—remember Ecclesiastes 1:9, "there is nothing new under the sun," and rely exclusively on the eternal truths from your one Source of guidance.

Eighth, maintain an appreciation for the benefits to *all* members of our society from the economic structure of capitalism and, therefore, refrain from advocating laws and taking other actions that would diminish the effectiveness and therefore the immense social benefits flowing from this system. Continue to appreciate that intrinsic to the notion of genuiness is the concept of voluntarism. Do not mistake coerced social welfarism for the political equivalent of Christian love. Continue to view life as a positive sum game rather than a zero sum game because God's supply is unlimited. That is, keep focused on production rather than on distribution because a fascinating outcome of such a perspective is that in societies dominated by such an attitude there tends to be (1) a more even distribution of wealth and (2) a higher average level of wealth. Nevertheless, in your vigorous pursuit of output maintain an understanding of and sensitivity toward opportunity costs, especially the social costs of private actions. Private development often is accompanied by significant environmental costs, and these should be factored in when making investment decisions. Opportunity cost is one of the most often-ignored concept of economics, yet more than any other concept, it prevents making ineffective decisions or taking courses of action with negative unintended consequences. But also communicate to the public in general the economic opportunity costs associated with pursuing social objectives. As the Friends of the Earth, Wilderness Society, Sierra Club and Environmental Defense Fund held up construction of the trans-Alaska oil pipeline in the early 1970's, the severe energy crisis was further exacerbated, with the bill picked up by the American public.

Ninth, practice genuine generosity, viewing all of your possessions as loans from God, viewing money simply as a conduit or
mechanism for exchange, and sharing your wealth so as not to
impede the universal circular flow of prosperity. Include in your
generous gifts your time and your professional or management
expertise to contribute to the effective functioning of your church
and other organizations which serve God's children. Keep in mind
Milne's teaching, "Creation asserts our utter dependence upon God.
All that we are and have is from him; our every breath is quite literally a gift. Our proper response is therefore true humility before
him, both explicitly in our acts of worship and implicitly in the
whole spirit of our living.[643] Go back and read 3 John and commit
yourself to an emulation of Gaius, John's friend of means who
extended his hospitality and help with food and shelter to the traveling evangelists and teachers. Acknowledge that you who help by
contributing money to missionary work are just as important to
spreading the Gospel as those who are actually out in the field
preaching and teaching. They could not do it without your vital
support. But do not lose sight of Gasque's words, "the Old Testament provides certain models. It is not sufficient to be honest and
fair and just and not take advantage of people but to do concrete
things that really help...."[644] Such pro-action is reaffirmed in the
New Testament. Never forget the story of Lazarus, recognizing that
your possessions are to be used by you to help those less fortunate.
As Calvin notes, "Having mentioned love [Paul] now refers to
Christ as the perfect and unique pattern of it.... By Christ's example
we are incited to beneficence so that we should not spare ourselves
when our brethren require our help."[645]

Tenth, maintain the humility that results from the continuous
acknowledgment that God is the source of all of one's good. Reject
the false prideful notion of "look what I have accomplished." Maintain a decentered perspective. Daily through prayer acknowledge
that you are nothing more that an instrument of God. God, not we,
is the source of all of our good. "I am the LORD your God, who
teaches you what is best for you, who directs you in the way you
should go."(Is. 48:17) Never lose sight of the notion that humility is
"the anchor of our calling and vocation."[646] Thomas explains that
humility, to the extent that it "moves us to depend on God" rather
than ourselves causes us to become more courageous, more confi-

dent, noting "Sometimes pride and the fear of embarrassment can hold us back."[647] Isaiah made this same point, "Who are you that you fear mortal men,…that you forget the LORD your Maker…. For I am the LORD your God, … I have put my words in your mouth and covered you with the shadow of my hand…." (Is. 51:12,15,16) As God said to Moses, "I will be with you." (Ex. 3:12) and said to Jeremiah "I am with you and will rescue you." (Jer. 1:8), he says to all of his creations, including each of us. (Note that God says "rescue" you, not prevent anything from happening from which you need to be rescued—an important distinction.) Jesus stated it another way, "Peace I leave with you; my peace I give you. I do not give to you as the world gives. Do not let your hearts be troubled and do not be afraid." (Jn. 14:27) Gill notes, "To be meek means to be able to live…relying on God's power and control…. 'Submission' is an important aspect of… humble servanthood."[648] The foregoing can be summed up in a saying that has been in my family for years, "Let go and let God." For assertive, "can-do," take charge business people this is easier said than done. Perhaps the following analogy from biblical scholar Norman Hillyer will be helpful. "A drowning man must submit to the one who comes to his aid. If he struggles in his own strength to try to save himself—in effect in the pride of self-sufficiency—he is likely to defeat the best efforts of his would-be rescuer, who in the end may even have to disable him before getting him to safety."[649]

Eleventh, do not compartmentalize your life, separating your Christian self from your vocational self. View your business or professional organization as the work of the church, which it is. The business firm is an environment conducive to sharing in the practice and study of spirituality. Remember, the entire Protestant Reformation was based on the notion that all believers, every Christian, is a priest, a minister. We all, in everything we do, are to take the church's message to the world and this is most effectively done through demonstrating the message of the Gospels in all that we do. As Erasmus of Rotterdam directs us, "Make Christ the only goal of your life. Dedicate to Him all your enthusiasm, all your effort, your leisure as well as your business."[650] Specifically related to business, Professor R. Paul Stevens of Regent College suggests, "see the marketplace as a 'mission' field—one of the many arenas where people of faith may share their good news and bring the presence of

God, with or without words. As Fancis of Assisi put it, 'preach the gospel constantly and, if necessary, use words.'... [I]t is important to ask whether the marketplace itself is not only a 'field' for mission, but *is* mission itself—or at least could be. If mission is joining God in his caring, sustaining and transforming activity in the world,... business then could be a part, though not all, of God's mission."[651] As Fr. Sirico suggests rhetorically, "If Jesus is Emmanuel, God with us, then must He not be God with us on the floor of the New York Stock Exchange? Must He not be God with us in our boardrooms? Must He not be God with us in front of the computer terminal? In all of the ingenuity that goes into forming business plans and balancing budgets and establishing bottom lines and being responsible and taking risks in enterprise, must Jesus not be present with us there?"[652]

Recognizing that you are more than a capitalist, that you are a complete human, follow Jesus Christ's directive in the Sermon on the Mount, and in all that you do, in business and otherwise, "let your light shine before men, that they may see your good deeds and praise your Father in heaven." (Mt. 5:16) Remember that we each have a role in carrying out the Great Commission, "All authority in heaven and on earth has been give to me. Therefore, go and make disciples of all nations, baptizing them in the name of the Father and of the Son and of the Holy Spirit, and teaching them to obey everything I have commanded you. And surely I am with you always, to the very end of the age." (Mt. 28:18-20) And the resurrected Christ directs, "But you will receive power when the Holy Spirit comes on you; and you will be my witnesses... to the ends of the earth." (Acts 1:8) In the Old Testament Isaiah proclaims, "How beautiful on the mountains are the feet of those who bring good news, who proclaim peace, who bring good tidings, who proclaim salvation, who say to Zion 'Your God reigns!" (Is. 52:7)

That is, we are to go out into the world and dwell among others in the Spirit of Christ. "Then they asked him, 'What must we do to do the works God requires?' Jesus answered, "The work of God is this: to believe in the one he has sent." (Jn. 6:28,29) Wall notes in his commentary on Revelation "The result was to make Christ Lord only over one's personal and interior life, while tolerating the social evils that shaped one's public conduct.... This kind of religious schizophrenia is outlawed by the one who is Lord over both the private and public dimensions of human existence."[653] Randy Rowland reminds us, "The imperative of the Gospel is to be a person who belongs to Jesus Christ twenty-four hours per day 365 days per year.... Unleash your spirituality at work."[654] Living all of life in the face of God leads us away from pride and toward humility and away from greed and idolatry and toward gratitude. Living a life based on faith and rooted in prayer maintains a connectedness with God's power. God's gifts to each of us are "enablements out of our uniqueness in order to allow us to represent the Living Christ to the world."[655] It is the responsibility of each of us to identify the characteristics of one's uniqueness. Often this is reflected in that activity about which one can become passionate because, "we best reflect the image of God when we are authentic."[656]

Twelfth, move forward confidently in God pursuing your calling. Realizing that we will experience our moments of trial, temporary setbacks, growth opportunities—or whatever you want to call them—but continued reliance on God will ensure our spiritual growth. "See I have refined you, though not as silver; I have tested you in the furnace of affliction. For my own sake, for my own sake, I do this. How can I let myself be defamed?" (Is. 48:10) From the wise Solomon, "My son, do not despise the LORD's discipline and do not resent his rebuke; because the LORD disciplines those he loves, as a father the son he delights in." (Prv. 3:11,12) And from the book of Job, "Blessed is the man whom God corrects; so do not despise the discipline of the Almighty." (Jb. 5:17) Webster reminds us, "discipline: training that develops self-control, efficiency, etc.; strict control to enforce obedience; orderly conduct."[657] And the perspective from the New Testament, Hebrews teaches, "the Lord disciplines those he loves." (Heb. 12:5) Paul reminds us, "Therefore, since we have been justified through faith, we have peace with God throughout our Lord Jesus Christ, through whom we have gained access by faith into this grace in which we now stand. And we rejoice in the hope of the glory of God. Not only so, but we also rejoice in our sufferings, because we know that suffering produces perseverance; perseverance, character; and character, hope.... we also rejoice in God throughout our Lord Jesus Christ, through whom we have now received reconciliation." (Rom. 5:1-11)

Note that this section on the implications for capitalists is intentionally brief, serving essentially to summarize the prior material.

Suffice it to say at this point that the essence of Christian ethics is to listen for and follow the will of God, "Not my will but thine be done." Jesus Christ is the ultimate example of placing God's will first. Hence, the wide-spread use by teenagers of bracelets and other apparel articles with the initials, "W.W.J.D."—"What would Jesus do?" Should this not be the credo of every human being and human organization, including the business firm?

An immense volume of writings exist on the subject of business ethics, enlightened management, and value-based leadership. Some of the more helpful works which I commend to you are listed below.

Banks, Robert and Powell, K.S., ed. *Faith in Leadership.* Jossey-Bass Publishers, 2000.

Beckett, John D. *Loving Monday.* Inter-Varsity Press, 1998.

Briner, Robert and Pritchard, Ray. *The Leadership Lessons of Jesus.* Broadman & Holman, 1997.

Coffee, Rob and Jones, Gareth. *The Character of a Corporation.* Harper Business, 1998.

Covey, Stephen. *Principle-Centered Leadership.* Fireside, 1992.

DePree, Max. *Leadership is an Art.* Dell, 1990.

Drucker, Peter. *The Effective Executive.* Harper Business, 1993.

Drucker, Peter. *Innovation and Entrepreneurship.* Harper Business, 1993.

Drucker, Peter. *Management: Tasks, Responsibilities, Practices.* Harper Business, 1993.

Greenleaf, Robert. *Servant Leadership.* Paulist Press, 1983.

Hood, John. *The Heroic Enterprise: Business and the Common Good.* The Free Press, 1996.

Jones, Laurie Beth. *Jesus CEO.* Hyperion, 1995.

Maxwell, John. *The 21 Irrefutable Laws of Leadership.* Thomas Nelson, 1998.

Niebuhr, H. Richard. *Christ and Culture.* Harper Collins, 1986.

Novak, Michael. *Business as a Calling: Work and the Examined Life.* Free Press, 1996.

Pascarella, Perry. *Christ Centered Leadership.* Prima, 2000.

Sanders, J. Oswald. *Spiritual Leadership.* Moody Press, 1994.

Sherman, Douglas and Hendricks, William. *Your Work Matters to God.* Navpress, 1987.

Zigarelli, Michael A. *Management by Proverbs*. Moody Press, 1999.

If you can read only one, I would read *Business as a Calling* by Michael Novak. In addition to being a faith-filled brilliant scholar, Novak is an accomplished writer. His works read quite well. You will note that Novak's *The Spirit of Democratic Capitalism* is in the bibliography of this book. This marvelous insightful work which I first read two decades ago was the initial stimulation to my delving into the subject of this book. In addition to these books, I commend to you subscribing to *The Life@Work Journal* (P.O. Box 469048, Escondido, CA 92046) which "serves as a resource for facilitating the integration of spiritual life and work" (quoting from its mission statement published in each edition). Finally, two books of a slightly different nature from those listed above, but which I found both inspiring and practical and which also played an important role in initiating my researching and writing this book, are *Halftime* and *Second Half* by Bob Buford. They are Spirit-filled works essential for anyone with an itch toward vocation repotting. (The term "repotting" comes from Ernest Arbuckle, Dean of the Stanford Business School when I was a student there, who in his graduation address suggested strongly that "every ten years or so one ought to repot.")

While the foregoing books are substantive works worthy of thoughtful reading, there is one source on management and leadership which towers above them all: the Bible. Jesus Christ, our leader, invites others to leadership positions and to become "fishers of men." (Mt. 4:19) Throughout Scripture are accounts of outstanding leaders/managers and examples of horrible leaders/managers. An example of positive leadership which I find particularly noteworthy is Nehemiah, the quintessential general contractor of the Bible who extremely effectively oversaw the rebuilding of Jerusalem's walls. For further inspiration, particularly in the context of the loneliness of leadership under adverse conditions, go back and read the book of Nehemiah. Nehemiah, using superb leadership and organization skills, rebuilt the wall of Jerusalem in just fifty-two days. "...the people worked with all their heart.... So the wall was completed in fifty-two days." (Neh. 4:6; 6:15) An example of poor leadership skills is Rehoboam whose failure to practice participative management gave rise to the division of Israel, a critical event in its history. "When all Israel saw that the king refused to listen to them, they answered the king: 'What share do we have in David.... So Israel has been in rebellion against the house of David to this day." (1 Kgs. 12:16,19) But there are numerous other examples—good and bad. Indeed, the Bible is the finest "How to..." manual ever written, and any business practitioner should obtain a deep understanding of its lessons and messages.

It is important to observe that the first step taken by all of the effective leaders in the Bible in any task was to pray. It is important for all capitalists before making any decision to reconnect through prayer with our Divine Guidance. The first step in all leadership activity is to pray. This is one of the greatest lessons of Scripture wherein we find numerous examples throughout the Bible. Jesus often went away to a place of solitude to pray. (Mk. 1:35, 6:46, 14:35; Lk. 3:21, 5:16, 6:12, 9:18,28, 11:1, 22:32,41) Hurtado notes, Mark's account shows the source of Jesus' power... and also provides in Jesus' behavior an example for his readers in Jesus' earnest and dedicated pursuit of God in prayer."[658] Connecting with God through prayer is an affirmation that our foundation is God, our foundation is not our job, our career, our family or even our church. Our foundation is God which we reaffirm and demonstrate through prayer. Faithful prayer is done with an *expectation* of its fulfillment because, basing all of one's decisions on faithful prayer means prayer involving *listening* to God's guidance. And guidance from God, our loving parent, is always fulfilled.

Jesus "told his disciples... that they should always pray and not give up." (Lk. 18:1) Mounce instructs, "Prayer requires stamina and persistence."[659] Don Jennings, our minister when my family lived in Alaska, used to say that we should stay "prayed-up," not just turning to prayer as the last resort. Accordingly, a continuous element of exercising leadership is prayer.

Remaining in a receptive prayerful mode is a continuous affirmation of, to use Bonhofer's words, our willingness to be the creature of the Creator. When we go it alone, presuming, for example, that within one is the moral grounding and authority to decide what is right and wrong, we breach the bonds of creaturehood. In your business change the definition of ASAP to "Always Say A Prayer." We say grace before meals; why not before a board meeting? We give an invocation before our church meetings; why not before our employee meetings? (Non-believers can simply remain silent.)

Recognizing that the first step to all thought and action is prayer, I offer to my fellow capitalists a suggested prayer.

CAPITALIST'S PRAYER

Lord, I give thanks for the privilege of participating in an activity that benefits all humanity. Recognizing that you are the source and owner of everything, I acknowledge that I am simply a steward of what is yours.

I commit myself to behavior reflective of your moral and ethical standards demonstrated on earth by Jesus Christ and of your directive simply to love my fellow humans, each of whom is your creation.

In all my dealing in the material realm let me remain ever focused on you. As the apostle Paul taught me, you are my creator in whom I live, move and have my being. In all that I do I listen for your guidance.

In concluding this discussion of the implications for capitalists, let us follow Sider's suggestion to emulate Jesus' "carefree life" which he defines as an abandonment of society's materialism, focusing on Jesus' directive to "not worry about your life, what you will eat, drink or wear... but seek first His [God's] kingdom, and these things will be provided." (Mt. 6:25-33; Lk. 12:22-31) and "delight in the splendor of the material world but not forget that things cannot ultimately satisfy,...enjoy the good earth and celebrate its abundance without neglecting sacrificial sharing with the needy,...distinguish between necessities and luxuries,...enjoy possessions while recognizing their seductive danger,... When forced to choose between Jesus and possessions,... gladly forsake the ring for the Beloved."[660]

As a capitalist and in all of one's calling, Thomas reminds us, "This relationship [inequality between humans and God] calls us to the chief goal of humankind, 'to glorify God and enjoy Him forever."[661] "True fulfillment comes in receiving God's love, and then responding to that love by loving others. This is the essence of Christian spirituality."[662] And nowhere is there greater opportunity to practice this than in the business world with its multiplicity of human relationships.

Griffiths summarizes, "First, the major purpose of life is to serve and worship our Creator and Redeemer;... Second, the service of God demands that we be involved in the service of man;... Third, we are trustees for everything which God has given us; and he has given us everything;... Fourth, we have been created to live in a series of communities: school, workplace, church, parish; and we have a responsibility within these communities to serve and care. Fifth, we are to strive for justice in the small and the large.... The business corporation is a community. It requires leadership, and at present it is desperately in need of a renewed vision of what is possible in business life in terms of ideals of service, stewardship, community and justice under God."[663]

The implication, then, for capitalists, follow God's words through Micah:

> He has showed you, O man, what is good.
>   And what does the LORD require of you?
> To act justly and to love mercy
>   and to walk humbly with your God."
> (Mi. 6:8)

Implications for the Clergy

Note that this section is very brief. This is because, not being one among them, I am not so presumptuous as to suggest what the clergy ought do or not do. Nevertheless, two very obvious suggestions emerge from the foregoing discussion. I have summarized these below.

First, learn economics.

Before uttering another word on poverty, income distribution or any other economics issue, commit yourself to understanding economics. Economics issues are matters on which all citizens have strong opinions, but about which most citizens understand little.

(Perhaps the former flows from the latter—nothing like a good dose of ignorance to lead to a firm opinion!) The clergy are not alone in their ignorance of economics, as Kristol observes, "It is indeed amazing that, in a society in which business plays so crucial a role, so many people come to understand so little about it—and, at the same time, to know so much about it which isn't so."[664] Theologian Nash cautions, "when good intentions are not wedded to sound theory, especially sound *economic* theory, good intentions can often result in actions that produce consequences directly opposite to those we planned. There is growing evidence that this is precisely what has happened in the case of the social policies to help the poor adopted in the United States since 1965." Nash continues, "American writer Dinesh D'Souza decided to interview a number of the bishops associated with the *U.S. Bishops' Pastoral Letter on Catholic Social Teaching and the U.S. Economy* in order to assess the extent of their economic knowledge…. He discovered that the typical Catholic bishop whose authority is being used to support debatable economic policies knows less about economics than a college freshman in the third week of a basic economics course…. It turns out, D'Souza discovered, that the bishops themselves have no idea what they're talking about…. It is both foolish and ultimately harmful to attempt to use economics without understanding it. We cannot do a very good job of improving the economic order if we do not know how it works."[665]

In my search for the reasons why so many of the clergy seem to hold wealth in disdain, I have discovered a very logical, valid and understandable explanation: most clergy's first exposure to the subject of wealth is not as economics students where they see wealth as the earned logical, justified result of economic contribution, but as biblical students where they see wealth as the result of plunder following military conquests or the outcome of political oppression or obtained through extortion. Most of the military engagements related in the Bible were for the purpose of gaining an economic advantage. "…because Tyre has said of Jerusalem, 'Aha! The gate to the nations is broken, and its doors have swung open to me; now that she lies in ruins I will prosper,'…" (Ez. 26:1) "I have sinned against the LORD, the God of Israel….. When I saw in the plunder a beautiful robe from Babylonia, two hundred shekels of silver and a wedge of gold weighing fifty shekels, I coveted them and took them." (Jos. 7:20,21) "…each man threw a ring from his plunder onto it. The weight of the gold rings… came to seventeen hundred shekels,…" (Jgs. 8:25,6) "Why did you pounce on the plunder and do evil in the eyes of the LORD?" (1 Sm. 15:19) "… and there they were, scattered over the countryside, eating, drinking and reveling because of the great amount of plunder they had taken from the land of the Philistines and from Judah." (1 Sm. 30:16) "So the Moabites became subject to David and brought tribute…., and the Arameans became subject to him and brought tribute….. David took the gold shields that belonged to the officers of Hadadezer and brought them to Jerusalem…. King David took a great quantity of bronze." (2 Sm. 8:2,6-8) "These countries brought tribute and were Solomon's subjects all his life." (1 Kgs. 4:21) "Jehoiakim paid Pharaoh Neco the silver and gold he demanded. In order to do so, he taxed the land and exacted the silver and gold from the people of the land….." (2 Kgs. 23:35) "… and they found among them a great amount of equipment and clothing and also articles of value—more than they could take away. There was so much plunder… " (2 Chr. 20:25) "the plunder from the poor is in your houses. What do you mean by crushing my people and grinding the faces of the poor?" (Is. 3:14,15) "Your wealth and your treasures I will give as plunder, without charge, because of all your sins…" (Jer. 15:13) "They will plunder your wealth…" (Ez. 26:12) "He will distribute plunder, loot and wealth among his followers." (Dn. 11:24) "Plunder the silver! Plunder the gold!" (Na. 2:9)

Habakkuk delivers a diatribe regarding pride, plunder and wealth which is presented below. Habakkuk lived in Judah during the reign of Jehoiakim and prophesized during the period of approximately 612 B.C. (fall of Nineveh, capital of Assyria) and 588 B.C. (Babylonian invasion of Judah), with the Babylonians having replaced the Assyrians as the dominant world power.

God, through Habakkuk, tells the people of Jerusalem:

> "I am raising up the Babylonians,
>   that ruthless and impetuous
> people, who sweep across the
>   whole earth to seize dwelling
> places not their own.
>
> …..

                          guilty men, whose own
                          strength is their god.

Habakkuk observes: The wicked foe pulls all of them
                          up with hooks, he catches
                          them in his net,

                          .....

                          Therefore he sacrifices to his net
                          and burns incense to his drag-
                          net,
                          for by this net he lives in luxury
                          and enjoys the choicest food.

God answers: See, he is puffed up;

                          .....

                          Woe to him who piles up stolen
                          goods
                          and make himself wealthy by
                          extortion!"

                          Selected from Hb. 1 and 2

Of course the New Testament records events that take place within the Roman Empire, the wealth of which was derived by military conquests followed by oppression. Cicero writes, "...we Romans are loathed abroad because of the damage our generals and officials have done... There is now a shortage of prosperous cities for us to declare war on so that we can loot them afterwards."[666] The books of the New Testament are replete with admonitions of the wealthy. "Now listen, you rich people, weep and wail because of the misery that is coming upon you. Your wealth has rotted, and moths have eaten your clothes. Your gold and silver are corroded. Their corrosion will testify against you and eat your flesh like fire....You have lived on earth in luxury and self-indulgence. You have fattened yourselves in the day of slaughter." (Jas. 5:1-5)

Then to drive home the point in the closing book of the Bible, "You say, 'I am rich; I have acquired wealth and do not need a thing.' But you do not realize that you are wretched, pitiful, poor, blind and naked. I counsel you to buy from me gold refined in the fire, so you can become rich; and white clothes to wear so you can cover your shameful nakedness..." (Rev. 3:17)

And further,

"Fallen! Fallen is Babylon the Great!
.....
For all the nations have drunk
    the maddening wine of her adulteries.
The kings of the earth committed adultery with her,
    and the merchants of the earth grew rich from her
    excessive luxuries."

(Rev. 18:2,3)

Oh, such a picture presented to first-year seminarians! Conquest, plunder, wealth, materialism, hedonism, idolatry, pride, rejection of God—no wonder so many clergy have a disdain for wealth! Also contributing to seminarians' distaste for wealth, conspicuous throughout Scripture is the courts favoring the rich, denying justice to the poor. The courts were one of the dominant centers of corruption, and the victims commonly were the poor. Further, most of the trade centers in biblical times—Tyre, Nineveh, Corinth, Capernaum and others—were also the centers of immorality. Perhaps the final blow to capitalism among seminarians is from the writings of the Greeks and Romans who, while holding in high esteem aristocratic landowners, princely courtiers, military officers and government officials, regarded with contempt the lowly merchant. (See especially Cicero's *De officiis*.)

It is regretful that the introduction to the subject of wealth by most Biblical students is to view wealth as the result of military conquest or political oppression. Given its predatory connection, it is no wonder that wealth has a negative connotation among Biblical students. At the time of history covered by Scripture affluence was not distributed to a broad middle class characteristic of capitalistic countries today, but was possessed by a tiny group of elite. A negative perception of affluence, while perhaps valid in ancient biblical days, has no validity in today's egalitarian democratic capitalistic developed nations. While Scripture often refers to the wealthy as "wicked oppressors" and to the poor as "pious sufferers," such generalizations are not applicable to twenty-first century capitalistic societies. Beckman notes, "the moral character of wealth has changed since Bible times. In ancient Israel, a simple agricultural society, the only means to accumulate wealth was military aggression: booty and tribute. Modern technology, however, produces riches which do not depend on rapacity."[667] Today in democratic capitalistic countries most wealth is the logical, valid return from economic contribution. (It is acknowledged that extortion and bribery remain a common form of wealth accumulation in some government-dominated economies today.) Regretfully, the Biblical introduction to economics has created some fallacious notions regarding the realities of contemporary economic relationships and laws. If the clergy are going to make public pronouncements regarding economic matters—and in my opinion they should—then it is critically important that they understand contemporary economics.

As Father Sadowsky notes, "There is the economic way of enrichment and there is the political way of enrichment.... The economic means of enrichment... comes about as a result of voluntary exchange; it is entered into because both parties expect to benefit by it. This, in other words, is trade. The political means of enrichment consists basically of gaining wealth by exploitation. That is, one becomes rich not by exchanging what one has for what somebody else has, but simply by taking from somebody what he has produced. This enrichment is parasitical of the peaceful production of others.... I think this is relevant to what we read about riches in the Bible,.... Almost all the riches of that day,... were suspect—in almost every case they were gained as the result of extraction or exploitation. In other words, one could almost assume that a rich person was either the extractor of goods from somebody else, or at least the possessor of goods that had been previously taken from others. The idea that 'property is theft' thus applied, all too often, in the time of the Bible. But to apply this idea to a society in which individuals become rich as a result of economic means of enrichment is perhaps anachronistic."[668] To understand how wealth is created and distributed today is not to understand military operations or the psychology of rulers, but to understand how economies function. This, of course, requires an understanding of economic laws and principles.

Capitalism should be celebrated as a system which has been introduced wherein people prosper by serving others rather than by killing or oppressing them. Profit-seeking capitalists have a vested interest in a broadly prosperous market of consumers, as Henry Ford was one of the first and Bill Gates one of the most recent to demonstrate. Sam Walton and every successful business executive in the world understands this. D'Souza observes, "the typical business or professional practice that is successful is one that supplies the everyday needs of ordinary people.... [I]f there is a single trait that most distinguishes entrepreneurs from others, it is this: they have an uncanny ability to anticipate and supply what large numbers of people want."[669] Capitalism, with its focus on satisfying the needs of consumers is the economic manifestation of the Christian charge to serve others. Gilder expands, "Zero-sum assumptions have led inevitably to conflict. If wealth cannot expand, the nation must. Countries must choose between famine and decline, or aggression and war. It was only capitalism that overcame this immoral predicament. As Walter Lipton put it, capitalism 'for the first time in human history,' gave men 'a way of producing wealth in which the good fortune of others multiplied their own.' At long last 'the golden rule was economically sound.... Until the division of labor had begun to make men dependent on the free collaboration of other men, the worldly policy was to be predatory... [But now] the ancient schism between self interest and disinterestedness, was potentially closed."[670] I imagine that most clergy would be surprised to learn that corporate profits are maximized by getting prices as low as possible, not as high as possible.

D'Souza notes, "America [the cradle of capitalism] was nothing less than a new experiment in what it means to be human."[671] D'Souza continues, restating the genius of capitalism. "Historically, selfishness and greed have been in the same abundant supply that they are now. But they had a different outlet: conquest... seized possessions, concubine, slave.... What capitalism does is to channel [greed and selfishness] in such a way that their destructive power is minimized and they actually work to promote the common good.... Indeed, the actual workings of capitalism do more than steer greed into a socially beneficial outlet;.... Capitalism encourages empathy, consideration, and fair dealing with others. The reason is that, to be successful, a businessman must anticipate the wants and needs of his customers, and if he wants his business to prosper he has to keep treating the customer relationship as special.... The moral judgement for capitalism is that it makes us better people because it puts our imagination and our efforts at the behest of others. Success is defined as the ability to serve the needs and desires of others."[672]

In his book *Wealth and Poverty*, Gilder describes the foregoing aspect of capitalism as "the golden rule of economics," namely, "the good fortune of others is also finally one's own."[673] Sam Walton couldn't have said it any better, nor could have John Nordstrom. It was this relationship that led my friend to describe capitalistic business firms as "God's delivery system." I think that is an apt description, and it would behoove the clergy to gain an understanding of how this economic system works before forming opinions or making suggestions related to economic matters. I commend to the clergy two helpful books: *The Economic Way of Thinking* by the late Paul Heyne, an ordained Lutheran clergyman and a professor of economics, and *The Spirit of Democratic Capitalism* by Michael Novak, theologian, historian, social critic and winner of the 1994 Templeton Prize for Progress in Religion. A clear understanding of both of these works would contribute greatly to the economic enlightenment on the part of any reader. It is noteworthy that Novak, has concluded "Ignorance of economics has probably caused,... more harm to more people in more places than any other ignorance.... a huge systematic task awaits the theologians of the coming generation, as they apply sustained theological reflection to economic realities. They need clear and critical concepts about such realities as scarcity, work, money, capital accumulation, production, distribution, inequality, technology, division of labor and the like.... To think theologically about economics is, first of all, to learn some economics."[674]

Interestingly, the answer to poverty does not lie in studying the poor, but in studying the wealthy. As I suggested earlier in this book, in the context of the thousands of years of humans occupying the globe the normal state of the masses being wretched poverty, more interesting than the question of "why are there so many poor today?" is the question "why are so many today not poor?" How, after thousands of years, did in just the past hundred years or so a few particular societies of the world develop the distinguishing characteristic of a broad affluent egalitarian middle class? The proper way to phrase the question regarding contemporary poverty in the world is not why are the poor poor, but rather why are the wealthy wealthy. Only when the matter is analyzed from that perspective will the answers emerge as to conquering world poverty. Understanding economics is the first step in arriving at the insights required for eliminating global poverty.

As a result of an inadequate understanding of economics, one of the tragedies of contemporary Christianity is its having laid a guilt trip on multitudes of people working for profit-making organizations. Too many business people feel estranged from Christian churches today because too many Christian clergy have sent out a message of scorn. During all of the years that I was in business, I noted that I was surrounded by colleagues who possessed and acted consistent with qualities advocated in Scripture: loving, generous, compassionate, honest, helpful, and truthful. They also behaved consistent with the commandment to love. Most served as Sunday-school teachers, church elders, little league coaches, United Way fundraisers—indeed, in a whole array of religious and charitable activities.

The assertion that possession and/or pursuit of wealth is sinful is a myth. Indeed the whole broader question of the relationship between economic systems and religious systems; more specifically, between capitalism and Christianity, has been subjected to unfortunate misunderstandings. It is regretful that, if not explicitly, certainly inadvertently, in so many ways the clergy have contributed to the promulgation of these misunderstandings.

It is ignorance of economics that causes some clergy to commit an error common to most anti-business activists: *The Fallacy of Starting in the Middle.* That is, they focus on the *distribution* of income and wealth without first understanding the economic concepts and laws related to the *generation* of income and wealth in the first place. Many clergy and other social activists jump right in waving their arms and issuing proclamations regarding distribution without the slightest understanding of the first step, generation. Apparently, they just sort of assume that the goods to be redistributed just happen into existence without any thought as to why and how goods come into being and without any thought about what stimulates more output from a given amount of inputs and without any thought to many other crucial economic questions regarding economic output. If there is a genuine concern for the poor on the part of those who profess such concern, the first step is to learn about the creation of wealth, the production of food, clothing and building materials. The Catholic Bishops reflected an understanding of the primary role of wealth creation when, while asserting "a strong presumption against inequality of income and wealth as long as there are poor, hungry and homeless people in our midst," also noting, "This presumption can be overridden... if unequal distribution stimulates productivity in a way that truly benefits the poor."[675] That is, contrary to the long-ago debunked zero-sum view of the socialists that the rich became so at the expense of the poor, the positive-sum reality of capitalism is that the rich become rich by the creation of new, previously non-existent wealth from which both the poor and the rich then benefit.

This *Fallacy of Starting in the Middle* takes many forms, the common characteristic of which is a blatant inconsistency on the part of those inflicted with this malady, making them often look silly. An example is the WTO demonstrators driving, rather than walking, up I-90 from Eugene, Oregon to Seattle, Washington, stopping to get gas for the trip to take them to demonstrate against the oil companies, without any thought as to how that gasoline got into the pump and why that gasoline station was so conveniently located. Indeed, the innovations and efficiencies of capitalism have even contributed to the effectiveness of those fighting capitalism! Recall, one of the great attributes of the market system is its neutrality. Everyone can participate in its benefits—even those fighting it.

Another "Fallacy" characteristic of many anti-business activists which an understanding of economics will help one avoid is the *Fallacy of Even Number Demonstrations*. When my daughter arrived home for Christmas from her first term at college she enthusiastically told us about her joining in a demonstration on campus advocating protecting more open space and greenbelts in the area where her school was located. We congratulated her on putting her knowledge to work and expressing her ideals, particularly related to stewardship of God's creations. Then, she said, the next day she participated in a demonstration opposing the high cost of housing. While admiring her activism, we nevertheless responded that now, attending *both* demonstrations, she was looking irrational. The major cause of rising housing cost in the area of her college has been soaring land prices. As an economist, I explained to her the concept of opportunity cost, that nothing is free, and that a cost associated with keeping land out of the hands of real estate developers was higher cost housing. Accordingly, she could have rationally attended one or the other of the two demonstrations, but not both. To this she responded, "I know. That night, thinking about what I had done, I looked silly to myself. I also had learned in my freshman economics class that prices are determined by both supply and demand, so to correct the situation, I organized for the next day a demonstration to hold down the demand side, opposing economic growth which attracted population and the demand for housing. I responded, "Great. You no longer look silly." I decided to wait four years and discuss with her that, when she joins the demonstration decrying the lack of job opportunities for graduating seniors, in the context of her earlier decrying economic growth, she might look silly. Accordingly, if you're going to demonstrate, do it for an odd, not an even, number of issues! Understanding economics will help you.

Viewing another example of how economic ignorance makes one look silly, in an otherwise commendable treatise theologian John Alexander states the following: "Or consider black beans in Brazil. There farmers used to grow black beans that poor people ate. However, farmers have learned that they can earn more by growing soybeans for American cows. So naturally Brazilian farmers grow soybeans, our cows eat the soybeans, and Brazilian kids eat air. Those Brazilian farmers probably aren't malicious; they are just making a sound business decision prompted by a vicious system."[676] How preposterous. Presumably the Brazilian farmers are switching from growing and selling black beans to soybeans because the latter bring more money. What does Alexander think that the farmers are going to do with that money? Burn it or bury it? No, they are going to hire workers whom they can afford to pay a higher wage and they and their workers are going to spend that money locally for all kinds of goods and services, generating additional jobs and incomes. (Had Alexander taken Econ. 101, he would have learned about the multiplier effect.) Now, instead of subsisting on a monotonous diet of black beans, some of those previously poor people can occasionally have one of those great Brazilian steaks. Further, as the new soybean farmers earn more, they are going to pay higher taxes supporting an array of social services and they are also going to increase their charitable contributions, helping the poor and supporting the local church capital campaign for an expanded all-purpose room for children's' programs. My scenario is not just some theoretical meandering on my part, but is being repeatedly demonstrated daily all over the globe. But Alexander would prefer that they and future generations remain eking out a mere existence on black beans. The system which Alexander describes as "vicious" is in fact *glorious*! It provides for the Brazilian poor the way out of a life of poverty. Alexander's goofy conclusion severely undermines his credibility, revealing either faulty analysis or over-riding bias or both. When Alexander and others learn economics, they will understand that not only is international trade not the problem, but is in fact the solution to world poverty.

Alexander continues in his next paragraph with a similar example of the importance of economic understanding: "A more complex case is the present urban housing crisis. Many middle-class people have decided that urban living has advantages over suburban living. They are moving back to the city, and naturally prices are skyrocketing. Naturally poor people can't even afford to live in the slum anymore."[677] This is exactly what is currently happening in my community, Seattle, Washington. In fact *The Seattle Times* did a feature article *celebrating* how the rising housing prices in Seattle's urban areas has been the major factor enabling many minorities previously living in the central core area now to be able to sell their homes and afford to move out to the suburbs if that is their desire. Finally, after years of being trapped in an urban ghetto, the owners of those "slum" houses are obtaining prices for them which liberates these owners, enabling them, if that is their desire, to move to brand new houses in the suburbs with generally better schools, greater diversity, less crime and superior public goods and services of all types. Further, for those homeowners choosing not to sell and to remain in the previously "slum" area, they see homes around them being refurbished, yards being spruced-up, greater diversity, less crime, greater community pride. Oh, the glories of the free market system!

This is not to imply that all is sweetness and light for the Brazilian poor and the U.S. urban blacks. Many problems persist and new problems arise. Some of Brazil's poor may have to move to a new job, being disrupted from family perhaps causing certain social problems; the urban blacks now see their property taxes rise. The point, which Alexander missed entirely because of his faulty economic analysis, is that there are both costs and benefits involved, and what is relevant is the *net* effect.

As an economist, I find it curious that not more of the clergy with their concern for the sick have asked the question why the United States leads in the development of pharmaceuticals; or for the poor, why is the percentage of the population in poverty in Venezuela with huge resources so much higher than in Belgium with considerably fewer resources; or for the hungry, why were Moscow's grocery shelves empty while unharvested food rotted in the fields; or for the environment, what caused the decimation of soils in Africa and vibrancy of soils in Canada; or for building churches, what is the difference between and the role played by each average cost, marginal cost, sunk cost, variable cost, social/spillover cost, opportunity cost, transaction cost, and fixed cost and how is my church construction project affected by elasticity of supply and externalities? I've spent a lifetime pestering clergy with multitudes of questions regarding theology. Never has one ever asked me a question regarding economics—yet they certainly have well-expressed opinions on wealth, poverty, products, wages, natural resources, etc.

Returning to comments by Reginald Jones, former Chairman of General Electric, "The other day I saw a new report out of Indianapolis, dated April 17, 1980. The Methodist Church was holding its General Conference, and Bishop Dale White was fit to make the following statement to a press conference. 'All of us, really are hostages, those in the developed countries as well as those in developing nations. Hostages to a vast political economics system of cruelty structures which are pre-ordaining that the rich get richer and the poor get poorer.... These systems are so pervasive, so corrupting of the good intentions of decent people, so powerful, so destructive of human well being, so intractable and self-defensive, that perhaps the word which Khomeini uses for them, the word "satanic," is the only word which is aptly descriptive.' Statements like that—and we hear them oh-so-frequently from the church hierarchy, echoing the 'liberation theology'—leave me stunned.... I am puzzled as to where or how one starts to reason with a prejudice of such profound character. What does one say to people who ask, 'Can a person be a Christian and still work for a corporation?'

"If I may witness from my own experience of forty-one years working in a large corporation, the General Electric Company, I must confess that we are imperfect human beings operating in an imperfect environment, and we have made mistakes and committed sins along the way; but I will not accept that our work has been the work of Satan. We have been inventing and manufacturing useful products, good ones, with an excellent reputation for quality, that help to make life more enjoyable and more productive for people everywhere. We are providing jobs that most employees deem satisfying and fulfilling, jobs that grant a good measure of economic security to about 400,00 families—300,000 here in the United States and 100,00 in other countries. We have also been bearing our share of civic duties in many communities where we have operations, not only through the taxes we pay and the charitable contributions we make, but more importantly, through the offering of our time and talents."[678]

As stated previously, my experience at Weyerhaeuser, where I worked alongside hospice volunteers, Sunday School teachers, Little League coaches, church fundraising drive volunteers, etc, and my observation of major U.S. corporations mirrors that of General Electric. Further, as I look around the table at the board meetings of various local philanthropies, I observe that most there are associated with business and professional firms. So the obvious implication for clergy: learn economics. And also learn and understand the "corporate mind," the thought process of people associated with business firms. I am always bemused by the knee-jerk reaction of people outside the business community to a major recall of a defective product or a major environmental catastrophe. The fact is that, regardless of how irate—appropriately—we all were with Exxon for the Valdez oil spill or with Ford and Firestone for the tire recall, we were not as livid as the shareholders of those companies who, in addition to being upset along with us with the problem, also were upset with having to bear the cost of remediation and bearing the burden of lower earnings on their stock prices and therefore their wealth. The public at large received a single-whammy: the particular adverse event. The shareholders received a double whammy: the particular adverse event (Exxon shareholders enjoy seeing pristine Prince William Sound and Ford shareholders who own Explorers prefer them to be safe) and the cost of rectifying it. While we sinful, fallible humans will always make mistakes, fortunately, owners of corporations have a direct vested interest in seeing that mistakes are minimized. Profits and social welfare are in concert, not in conflict as many of those ignorant of economics and the "corporate mind" suppose.

The critical importance of understanding economics to the achievement of the human goals advocated by most clergy is under-scored by Rosenberg and Birdzell. "The Western achievement has surely opened up new possibilities of advancing many other values, among them those embraced within the connotations of social justice, environmentalism, and equality. But anyone who seeks to advance them needs to understand the sources of Western achieve-ment in order to avoid cutting off at the source the opportunities future generations may have to develop a society which can afford higher aspirations."[679] To underscore its importance, with which I wholeheartedly agree, Rosenberg and Birdzell end their important work by repeating the foregoing observation and warning. "Western advance in material welfare has raised social and political aspira-tions and made it easier to think of ways to create a society better in ways other than being richer. There is a danger that in thus trying to better our own society, we may pursue policies that will reduce the capacity of future generations to achieve still higher standards of material well-being, within a social and political framework more humane and compassionate than our own. To understand the sources of past growth is, we hope, in some measure to lessen the risk that we may unintentionally curtail the economic opportunities of future generations by our actions."[680]

Finally, it is interesting to note that when Christian clergy commence reading books on economics, they are going to be surprised to discover that the great champions of socialism are the secular welfare economists to whom acquisitiveness is the principle activity of humanity. In fact, "welfare" is defined exclusively in material terms. To the social welfare economist the more material goods and services one is able to acquire, the greater "welfare" one has. Production, creativity, faith, and other theological concepts do not enter into the socialist, secular welfare model.

However, all of the foregoing notwithstanding, *it is clearly recognized that a role of the church will always be to help the poor regardless of the "how" or "why" of their poverty.* In this regard the demands on the church are considerable. Also, *it will always be the role of the church to bring the wealthy to a compassion for the poor and to serve as a conduit through which the wealthy can be generous to the poor.*

It will always be a role of the church to bring all people, including the wealthy, to God. In fairness to the subject, in addition to its predatory dimension portrayed in the Bible, there is a second reason that wealth is held in such disdain by the clergy: its idolatry dimension. As Hay observes, "In that condemnation of the prosperous commercial city of Tyre in Ezekiel 28 and Isaiah 23… there is a strong association drawn between commerce and idolatry. The link perhaps lies in the greed for material things that biblical writers associate with trade and commerce. In the absence of God, man makes his idols from those things which give him security and power."[681] This, then, brings us to the second implication for the clergy.

Second, intensify your missionary work among the affluent.

By Jesus' own reckoning, the toughest challenge concerning salvation are the wealthy because of their strong tendency toward arrogance, pride and self-reliance. This is the reason that Jesus asserted, "it is easier for a camel to go through the eye of a needle than for a rich man to enter the kingdom of God." (Mt. 19:24; Mk. 10:25; Lk. 18:25) Beckman notes, "All the New Testament writers agree,… that it is exceptionally difficult for any rich person to be saved."[682] Yet, today they are the very group given the least attention by the clergy!

Scripture describes a time in the history of the world when there was no middle class, and the lower class—poor—tended to exist at and for the pleasure of the upper class—wealthy. Further, at this time in Israel the clergy, focused on its own material well-being, tended to placate the wealthy, leaving the poor to fend for themselves. In this context Jesus devoted an immense amount of time to addressing the plight of the poor. However, this should not cause us to forget that, as Rowland reminds us, "God loves both the 'up and outers' and the 'down and outers."[683]

Therefore, I make this second suggestion to the clergy: extend as much love and active compassion to the "up and outers" as you do to the "down and outers." Recognize that materialism is just as much an affliction in our hedonistic society as poverty and that self-pride is just as ruinous as low self-esteem. Look upon the affluent with as much understanding love as you do upon the poor. Devote as much time to curing spiritual poverty as you do to curing material poverty. Indeed, many of the poor know that they should place reliance on Something Greater; many of the affluent do not know they should place reliance on Something Greater. Dr. Ward Gasque, biblical scholar and expert on Saint Paul, when lecturing on the book of Acts and commenting on the hypothesis that Paul first conveyed the Gospel in his home town of Tarsus, noted the importance of witnessing to one's own existing relationships. In reflecting on the contemporary need to save souls within our own neighborhoods, he states "It takes more than an ocean to make a missionary."[684]

Therefore, do not avoid one of the greatest challenges facing you: converting the prideful who feel that they do not need God. Recall a major message of the Old Testament as we follow the Israelites through their progression of recurrent blessing and punishment: the point of greatest vulnerability in people's reliance on God is when everything is going well in our lives—health, wealth, friends, professional achievement, happy family, etc. This is the critical point when we are most vulnerable to drifting away from God, susceptible to thinking that we do not need God, that self-reliance is all that is needed. In the context of the story of the Bible it should not be surprising that the group in our society in greatest need of being brought back into an understanding of their relationship with God is the wealthy, the professionally successful, the happy, those who "have everything." Yet this is the very group that tends to be taken for granted. Mission and outreach efforts by churches should be reinvigorated toward taking the Gospel to the wealthy.

Step up to your role to save humanity. We have observed the abundant material benefits of capitalism—far in excess of those generated by any other type of economic system. The challenge now is to ensure that the functioning and the material output of capitalism are in line with God's purpose for humanity. Accordingly, step up to your role to bring capitalists to Jesus Christ. You, and only you, are the Great Connectors—God's chosen servants to connect private effectiveness to public goodness. Bauer notes, "It is paradoxical that the clergy are preoccupied with material conditions and progress [of the poor] at a time when the failure of material prosperity to advance and secure happiness, satisfaction and tranquillity is everywhere evident."[685] The greatest challenge facing humanity today is insuring that our daily activity reflects the divine imperatives. The clergy's primary God-given role, it seems to me, is to bring capitalists—and everyone—to (1) an understanding of what their divine imperative is and (2) a commitment to think and behave accordingly. When this is accomplished, many of humanity's other concerns; e.g., the poverty, health, and meaning of humanity, will be solved.

Combine your understanding of economics with your ministering to the wealthy to reinvigorate a major transformation of the relationship between Christianity and capitalism, between the clergy and the business community. To draw again from Gilder, "If the church is truly concerned with the material problem of world hunger and poverty, it should temper its own efforts at distributing food and instead promote the moral and spiritual conditions of capitalist farming.... Capitalism is suffering from the increasing betrayal of its moral, spiritual and religious foundation by churches... who believe that the paramount natural laws of giving and faith are irrelevant to the great dramas of human creativity and production, science and art. The problem is a crisis of religion. Too many clerics have renounced the claims of spirit in favor of inept ventures of materialism and social politics, thus depriving capitalism of its indispensable moral rules and roots and spreading famine and poverty in the name of social justice."[686] Fr. Schall agrees and expands, "What we ought to be doing is not sending our easily manipulated nuns, college students, and seminarians to slums and barrios to have them routinely return reciting canned ideology in the name of faith without a clue about the difference. Rather, we should send them, if we think religion really is about nothing else, to places where men, indeed, are rapidly learning to produce, to Hong Kong or Tokyo, rather than to Lima or Dar-es-Salaam.... Until we study why men came to be productive in the first place, until we stop preaching doctrines that prevent any real progress from even beginning, the message of religion in the modern world will be seen by the real poor as twofold in its betrayal of them: (1) the God of their ultimate destiny will have been taken away from them by making faith into politics, and (2) meanwhile they will find themselves locked up in non-productive systems which merely "redistribute" static economic goods and then proclaim there is no "distortion." Such a religion is, indeed, the opiate of the people. They do not deserve it."[687]

Recall my earlier observation that capitalism is neutral, producing both Bibles and liquor, family theme parks and brothels. Capitalism, like any economic system, is concerned with material production. That is its role. What capitalism produces and how the income generated thereby is used is up to humans. This is the role of the church. As I stated earlier, capitalism should not be blamed for doing its job well. The present hedonism of our society reflects less a failing of the business sector and more a failing of the church. The primary role of the church is to bring all God's children—including the affluent—to the enduring, spiritual values of God. If, as D'Souza asserts, today the new leaders of society are business people and scientists, replacing royalty, military leaders, political elites, intellectuals and religious leaders at various times in past ages, it becomes critically important that this new leadership be imbued with an understanding of Christian doctrine and committed to following Jesus Christ.

The clergy and capitalists have a great deal in common. In addition to all of the commonalties noted heretofore, perhaps the major one is that the social / political condition precedent to capitalism flourishing is the same as that precedent to religious practice flourishing: liberty. Remember the coerced sharing of socialism precludes the loving giving of democratic capitalism. Accordingly, celebrate the virtues of capitalism and imbue capitalists with your message of service to all of God's creations. Together you and the capitalists will be responsible for the emergence of a new economic order with a broadened expression of love and a firmer reliance on faith in God.

The wealthy are "ripe" for your message. An immensely important consequence of the impressive achievement of capitalism as a generator of wealth and leisure is that today more and more people, particularly the wealthy, are turning to the satisfaction of a need that only you can satisfy: meaning and significance. As Novak suggests in his expressing optimism regarding a resurgence of religion in capitalistic nations, in the past the suffering of the poor brought them to God; today the emptiness of the wealthy is bringing them to God. As more and more people conquer the mountain of financial wealth, as they stand on the top of that peak unfulfilled and incomplete, you are the one to whom they look for the answers they seek. One cannot discover that wealth is not the answer until one is wealthy. The spiritual emptiness of affluence is not experienced until one is first affluent.

Indeed, many observers view capitalistic civilization as hurling itself toward meaningless consumption and materialistic idolatry. (I asserted earlier that, if this is the case, it is not the system's fault.) Others, and I am among them, see capitalism as being the great liberator of civilization from preoccupation with earning a living to possessing the financial wherewithal, the time availability, and the intellectual and spiritual curiosity to come to grips with the essential questions of being a human. The great triumph of capitalism is that for the first time in human history, members of a broad middle class—not just a tiny aristocratic elite—have the opportunity to escape from the shackles of mere existence and, if they so choose, deal with the matter of their spirituality. You, the clergy, must step forward to your responsibility and divine appointment as mentor. Capitalism has provided you with a huge "market." No longer are there hordes of poor sulking to your door for the answers to their misery. Today the massive affluent middle class are coming to your door for the answer to the meaning of their wealth. Be there for them as they come to you in droves. No; pro-actively go out and seek them, as many are still afflicted with their debilitating arrogance and pride.

In conclusion, with (1) a renewed understanding of economics and therefore an enthusiastic appreciation for the extensive benefits flowing from capitalism and (2) a renewed commitment to ministering to the affluent and therefore evidencing an appreciation for the business community's role in society, you will then be positioned to make your meaningful contribution to the well-being of *all* humans: imbuing capitalists, through their renewed understanding of the Gospel and renewed commitment to its principles, with a love of humankind that they will daily demonstrate through all of their human interactions.

However, the question must be posed: has your church's role as a place of worship and learning Christian doctrine become diluted by social activism? Have you become so focused on those lacking materiality that you have become less concerned about those suffering from spiritual poverty? Explicitly deal with the question: is the role of my church (1) to save souls by leading people to God or (2) social service or (3) some combination of the two, and what is the relationship between the two? Wall warns, "The most subtle secularism is the one promoted by those charged with the spiritual care of a congregation of believers, when the proclamation of the Christian gospel takes its primary cues from the surrounding social order rather than from 'the world of God and the testimony of Jesus Christ."[688] To repeat the warning of Bruce from his commentary on John, "When the Christian message is so thoroughly accommodated to the prevalent climate of opinion that it becomes one more expression of that climate of opinion, it is no longer the Christian message. The Christian message must address itself in judgment and mercy to the prevalent climate of opinion, and can do so only when it is distinct from it. If it fails to do so, it has succumbed to that godless worldliness against which John warns his readers."[689] If the church adequately performs its primary role of bringing the world to a prayerful commitment to God, imbuing humanity with the values and priorities in the message of Jesus Christ, will not solutions to the world's economic, political and social challenges flow?

Clergy and business people, embrace each other! The former, focused on using wealth, and the latter, focused on creating and distributing wealth, have much good to do together. You have much in common. All of the advantages of the separation of church and state have their corollary advantages in the separation of producer and state. All of the disadvantages of one state religion have their corollary disadvantages of one state producer. The two groups in the global society that are focused on the needs of others are the clergy and the capitalist. Remember, the genius of capitalism is its dealing with the reality of humanity's dual nature: created in the image of God, yet sinful. If you want to elevate capitalism, elevate humanity. While the capitalist has done more than even you to feed the poor and heal the sick, you come first, it is you and only you that raises the spiritual consciousness of the capitalist.

Finally, be a positive force in the accelerating trend to take mission into the marketplace. Equip business leaders with an understanding of God's word and fill them with the Spirit and the commitment to take their love of God with them into the workplace. Affirm your congregation's serving God in the secular world.

Affirm their ministry in their vocations, charging them every Sunday to "take the Gospel to work tomorrow." If business people are going to follow God's Great Commission and take God's Great Commandment into the marketplace, you are going to have to fulfill your responsibility to minister to business people. Recommit yourself to saving the souls of the affluent.

Chapter XIV

Reflections

Jesus Christ presented no social/economic/political agenda; he advocated no particular social/economic/political structure or system. Gasque notes "Jesus' whole life was a parable teaching the real definition of riches, the limited subsistence role of material possessions, the virtue of humility, faith in the one God and love."[690] His only two agenda items, "love God" and "love one another" implied that all of the necessary behavior will be voluntary. Pursuit of the kingdom of God is intrinsically a voluntary act.

If the role of human life is to accept God's grace through faith and if faith-filled acceptance is manifest in becoming progressively more righteous, then the key element is a free heart as well as the freedom within human systems (political, social, economic and moral) to move toward a faith-filled life. Capitalism, which is accompanied by individual freedom and therefore voluntary—from the heart—action, is such an economic environment. Socialism, which is accompanied by coercion via statutory requirements to share, is not such an environment. Contrary to the unsound assertion of Tillich, socialism and Christianity are logically and structurally inconsistent. Coerced love is an oxymoron. Socialism *forecloses* the opportunity to practice Christianity! Recall Paul's admonition, "Since they did not know the righteousness that comes from God and sought to establish their own, they did not submit to God's righteousness. Christ is the end of the law so that there may be righteousness for everyone who believes." (Rom. 10:3)

Michael Novak observes further: "Of all the systems of political economy which have shaped our history, none has so revolutionized ordinary expectations of human life—lengthened the life span, made elimination of poverty and famine thinkable, enlarged the range of human choice—as democratic capitalism"[691] Christians should celebrate the genius of capitalism which accommodates the dual nature of humankind by serving as an outlet for humans' expressions as children of God while at the same time corralling, by the Invisible Hand of the free market, the sinfulness of humans to serve the general good. In the context of studying the historical development of economies over the ages, James Q. Wilson, emeritus professor of management at UCLA, concludes, "Capitalism... substituted the struggle for money for the struggle for power.... It permitted ambition—a natural human instinct—to be fulfilled in the attainment of commercial wealth rather than through conquest and brutality."[692]

Further, capitalism should be celebrated by Christians for providing a marvelous laboratory for practicing our Christian principles: the business firm. Through work to satisfy the needs of others we *serve*. Through cooperative interaction with others we *trust*. Through innovation we *create*. Through reinvesting profits we exercise *faith and hope*. Through enlightened management we *love*. Through private ownership and voluntarily sharing our possessions and funds with others we also *love*. Through both long range planning and efficient production we are responsible *stewards*. Through free enterprise we exercise self-discipline, responding to Jesus' call to *pursue righteousness*. Through creating jobs we *help the poor and reduce other social ills*. Through expanding markets and sources, creating international interdependence, we contribute to world *peace*. Through gratitude for our economic rewards we pay tribute to their *source, God*. Through our efficient production and distribution of religious goods and our contribution of our earnings to mission, we contribute to the *spread of God's word*. Finally, the business firm is private, *protecting our ability to practice our spirituality*, unlike a government agency where the practice of spirituality is unlawful or controlled by the state.

But it is solely for these practical reasons that Christians should celebrate capitalism. It is not in any way to be inferred that Scripture advocates capitalism. I agree with Johnson's assertion, "There is no Christian economic structure to be found in the Bible, any more than there is a Christian political or educational system. The Bible does not tell us how to organize our lives together, and still less which things we should call private and which public. Nor does it propose a clear program of social change."[693] The Bible's sole message is to love each other for the glory of God. The best human system for fulfilling this charge just possibly might be private enterprise limited by democratic government and operating on the basis of Biblical principles.

Interestingly, there is no evidence of opposition to wealth per se in Scripture. Indeed, wealth has certain characteristics that are in concert with spiritual objectives, enabling love-filled generosity, for example. The danger associated with wealth is the subtle seduction of material possessions that can rob us of our commitment to spirituality. Wheeler summarizes, "while material wealth may no longer be attributed to the virtues of the rich or as a sign of God's approval (as under ancient Israel), neither is it attributed to the devil. There is in the New Testament no pure asceticism that deprecates material reality as intrinsically evil, and no talk of a mystical ascent to God by means of a withdrawal from bodily reality. The dangers of distraction and entanglement, of misplaced trust and loyalty that is inherent in ownership are all brought forward, but there is no repudiation of material goods as such….The necessity and goodness of wealth as a resource for meeting of human needs are affirmed;"[694]

Wealth, commerce, trade, economic activity are neither good nor bad per se. Economics is neutral—as demonstrated in Scripture. In the same way that Jonah used trading vessels bound from Joppa to Tarshish to flee from God's assignment to preach in Nineveh, Paul used the trading vessels in the Mediterranean to spread the gospel. The neutrality of capitalism has been eloquently affirmed by Griffith (*The Creation of Wealth*), Weber (*The Protestant Ethic and The Spirit of Capitalism*) and others. As I identified before, one of the most noteworthy achievements of capitalism is its achieving a level of economic productivity that makes it no longer necessary for humans to devote literally every waking hour to producing enough to sustain life. Rather, today abundant time is available for other pursuits. Whether humans devote that time and their wealth to hedonistic pursuits or to spiritual pursuits is up to humans. As

Schall notes, "In themselves neither wealth nor poverty could automatically guarantee virtue or ensure vice. Wealth could be used nobly; poverty could foster bitterness and hatred.... Wealth makes good things possible. It also makes more substantial vices possible."[695] It is interesting to observe in an historical sense, however, that despite the miraculous achievements of capitalism in terms of wealth and leisure, humanity seems neither more nor less virtuous today than in Biblical times nor at any other time in human history. *The notion that capitalism, as a system is neutral, and therefore its behavior and outcomes depend upon the values of the participants, emphasizes the role of the clergy to bring the participants within capitalism to an understanding of and commitment to the teachings of Jesus Christ*, as I suggested in the previous chapter and repeat here for emphasis.

Indeed, contrary to the misunderstandings of many, affluence is not the problem. Humanity's sinful nature is the problem. Affluence, which provides the wherewithal for attacking social problems and lifts humanity to a higher plane than mere subsistence, is the solution. Affluence, rather than being feared should be celebrated and used to God's ends.

In their rebuking of the wealthy, both Jesus and the Evangelists seemed to be opposed not to wealth per se. Rather, they seemed to be conveying the following two messages:

(1) Earthly status has nothing to do with receiving God's love. Earthly wealth is irrelevant in terms of entering the kingdom of God; "for a man's life does not consist in the abundance of his possessions." (Lk. 12:15)

(2) We should put our top priority on God as manifest in *total devotion* to Him and *complete reliance* upon Him, and therefore praise of Him. "You shall love the Lord your God with all your heart, and with all your soul, and with all your mind, and with all your strength." (Mt. 22:37; Mk. 12:30; Lk. 10:26) All material needs will follow.

These two notions reflect a very important distinction embodied in the message of Jesus Christ, "Whoever finds his life will lose it, and whoever loses his life for my sake will find it." (Mt. 10:39, Lk. 9:24, Jn. 12:25)

On the other hand, Scripture has very much to do with the physical world. The connecting link between the two is stated by Jesus to his disciples, "do not worry about your life, what you will eat or drink…or wear…. Seek first his [heavenly Father's] kingdom, and these things will be provided to you as well." (Mt. 6:25-33; Lk. 12:22-31)

The Holy Bible is a manual for mortal human beings living in the world. In the Old Testament as God creates all materiality, six times God declares it good. Then, when the creation story is complete, "God saw all that he had made, and it was very good." (Gn. 1:30) However, the creation story is not complete. Creation is an ongoing activity of God. Humans' ability to create is God-originated; it is a reflection of our having been created in the image of God. Humans' creativity is a reflection of the Holy Spirit within. Our ability to create is not only a gift; it is a responsibility. It is the responsibility of each of us to use our God-given talents to create. Creation is a way in which we can pay tribute to our God—whether that creation be poetry, art, scientific theories, medicines, classroom methodologies, structure designs, manufacturing processes, product innovation—whatever. Indeed, the capitalist who participates in the efficient utilization of God's resources is an important participant in the creation process.

Business people and professionals engaged in economic activity are to bring to that activity, just like all people are to bring to all aspects of their lives, the entire lessons of the Bible. Indeed, one does not get meaning *from* one's occupation; one brings meaning *to* one's occupation. Capitalism is a vehicle through which we can practice our Christian principles. Private property allows one to express sacrificial love; communal property does not. Business and professional leaders, just like all leaders of all types, are to "Let your light shine before men, that they may see your good works and give glory to your Father who is in heaven." (Mt. 5:16). As an aid in this regard I have found it useful to reaffirm certain confessional statements of my particular denomination, the Presbyterian Church (U.S.A.):

"The Protestant watchwords—grace alone, faith alone, Scripture alone—embody principles of understanding which continue to guide and motivate the people of God in the life of faith....

Related to this central affirmation of God's sovereignty are other great themes of the Reformed tradition:

(1) The election of the people of God for service as well as for salvation.
(2) Covenant life [gathered in community]....
(3) A faithful stewardship that shuns ostentation and seeks proper use of the gifts of God.
(4) The recognition of the human tendency to idolatry and tyranny, which call the people of God to work for the transformation of society by seeking justice and living in obedience to the Word of God."[696]

Throughout Scripture there is the expectation by God regarding prosperity that we will (1) tithe in recognition of the true Source of our good and (2) lovingly share with the nonprosperous. The second great commandment, "Love your neighbor as yourself." (Dt. 6:5 and Mt.22:39) was commanded by God, reaffirmed by Jesus and reaffirmed again by Paul, "...if I have faith that can move mountains, but have not love, I am nothing. If I give all I possess to the poor and surrender my body to the flames, but have not love, I gain nothing....And now these three remain: faith, hope and love. But the greatest of these is love." (1 Cor. 13:1-13)

Love—to love our fellow humans—employees, employers, customers, suppliers, owners, shareholders, even competitors as we appreciate their role in motivating us to do our best.

Faith—faith undergirds hope. Hope sustains optimism. Optimism unleashes one's creativity which in turn frees us for accomplishing God's purpose for each of us.

The particular type of economic system is relevant only to the extent that one or another type of human system may be more or less in concert with the nature of humanity and more or less conducive to individual humans pursuing the kingdom of God. Furthermore, it must be acknowledged that the creation story, the Incarnation and the entire message of Scripture teach us that God is very much of the material world, and God uses humans and human systems and institutions for God's purposes and ends. Jean Cardinal Villot notes, "The Gospel, without identifying terrestrial progress with the increase of the Kingdom of Christ, shows the bonds between the two."[697] Schall continues, "there exist layers of human purpose and good which are not exhausted by economic efficiency.... On the other hand,... the light of the higher ends or goals enables those who think about economics and deal with its realities to be better...."[698] Capitalism has been analyzed in this book solely in this perspective.

Throughout the Gospels Jesus drives home the point over and over again: neither keeping the commandments nor reliance on material goods nor a false self-assurance provided by worldly accomplishments can lead one to eternal life. "Sell all that you have and distribute to the poor, and you will have treasure in heaven; and come, follow me." (Mt. 19:16; Mk. 10:17; Lk. 18:18) While Jesus was not advocating selling all of one's worldly goods, nevertheless he was dramatically making the revolutionary point that salvation ultimately depends upon total and exclusive love of God as reflected in complete faith in God and only God—"follow me." Alexander points out that, while in his extreme admonitions to sell all our possessions, Jesus' was not actually advocating such drastic action, "he was trying to *do* something to us. His teaching was meant to alter our perception of reality. He wanted us to have a change of heart, a reversal of values.... Jesus and the rest of the New Testament are trying to get through our heads the irrelevance and unimportance of wealth."[699]

The general admonishment being made is "...keep oneself from being polluted by the world." (Jas. 1:27) True religion requires a changed life. Heed Peter's words, "Praise be to the God and Father of our Lord Jesus Christ! In his great mercy he has given us new birth and a living hope through the resurrection of Jesus Christ from the dead, and into an inheritance that can never perish, spoil or fade—kept in heaven for you, who through faith are shielded by God's power until the coming of the salvation..." (1 Pt. 1:3-5) And heed John's words, "The world and its desires pass away, but the man who does the will of God lives forever." (1 Jn. 2:17)

Finally, let us turn our attention to the most important and closing point to be made in this book. Having spent three years praying, researching, and writing on this subject of the relationship between Christianity and capitalism, I come to the conclusion that its relevancy is limited—limited to the less important, subsidiary aspect of our lives.

To repeat what I stated earlier when making a distinction about the nature of hope and optimism, in my praise of capitalism I do not in any way want to imply that the characteristics of capitalism are making the world a more God-like world. Christian hope and optimism do not refer to the worldly condition. As Guthrie notes, "The justice, freedom, and peace of the kingdom of God will not come *within* history as the result of human efforts; it will come at the *end* of history as the result of what only God can and will do. For Christians that means the end of all idealistic or utopian confidence in any political or social ideology."[700] And I add economic ideology. Wall states it even more strongly, "Human efforts to build a great world or a lasting peace will only self-destruct..... Indeed, the myths of national security and economic contentment are from the false gods which cast the magic spell not only on John's Roman world but on every other society of human history."[701]

Therefore, the particular type of economic system has limited relevancy in relationship to any notion of its effect on salvation. Fr. Sirico explains, "In a grand, eschatological sense, the freedom for which the heart of man most deeply longs is freedom from the bondage of sin and death. Political, economic and personal freedom are critical, but the fundamental freedom is salvation."[702] Schall concurs, "for the Christian mind these political, economic and social issues are subordinate to the central importance of the salvation of each individual person in whatever society he might live."[703] Achtemeier expresses it as follows, "There is no good outside of God, no virtue, no ideology, no civil, political or religious [nor, I add, economic] scheme that can qualify unless it accords with God's desire for human life.... God has created human life on this earth, and as its creator, God alone can say what and how it should be lived."[704]

From the Old Testament:

As one would expect, the wise Solomon puts it directly and

succinctly: "Wealth is worthless in the day of wrath, but righteousness delivers from death." (Prv. 11:4) In other words, according to
Murphy's commentary, "you can't take it with you."[705]

The awesome contributions of the books of Job and Ecclesiastes,
which should be read in their entirety, is that this matter of our relationship with God surpasses our understanding and our ability to
understand.

> "Where then does wisdom come from?
>   Where does understanding dwell?
> It is hidden from the eyes of every living thing,...
>
> God understands the way to it
>   And he alone knows where it dwells,..."
> (Jb. 28:20,21,23)

Therefore, Job discovers, the purpose is not to know, but to know
God.

> "I know that you can do all things; no plan of yours can
> be thwarted....
>   Surely I spoke of things I did not understand, things
> too wonderful for me to know." (Jb. 42:2,3)

And with this acknowledgment by Job, God then bestows his
grace on Job.

This same message of the transcendent and incomprehensible
nature of God is found in the book of Ecclesiastes,

> "Meaningless! Meaningless!'
>   says the Teacher.
> 'Utterly meaningless!
>   Everything is meaningless." (Eccl. 1:2)

Most other versions of the Bible, translate the word "meaningless" as "vanities"—"vanities, vanities....everything is vanities."
This highlights the interpretation offered by LaSor and other scholars that "At stake was the difference between God and humankind.... and the limits that divine sovereignty has placed on human

understanding.... Failure to reckon with that gulf has caused humankind to overvalue it accomplishments in wisdom, pleasure, prestige, wealth and justice."[706]

Ecclesiastes continues,

> "I denied myself nothing my eyes desire;
>   I refused my heart no pleasure.
> My heart took delight in all my work,
>   and this was the reward for all my labor.
> Yet when I surveyed all that my hands had done
>   and what I had toiled to achieve,
> everything was meaningless, a chasing after the wind:
>   nothing was gained under the sun." (Eccl. 2:10,11)

> "There was no end to his toil,
>   yet his eyes were not content with his wealth.
> 'For whom am I toiling,' he asked,
>   'and why am I depriving myself of enjoyment?'
> This too is meaningless...." (Eccl. 4:8)

> "As a man comes, so he departs,
>   and what does he gain,
>   since he toils for the wind?" (Eccl. 5:16)

"Consider what God has done:

> Who can straighten
>   What he has made crooked?
> When times are good, be happy;
>   but when times are bad, consider:
> God has made the one
>   as well as the other.
> Therefore, a man cannot discover
> Anything about his future." (Eccl. 7:13,14)

"... then I saw all that God has done. Despite all his efforts to search it out, man cannot discover its meaning." (Eccl. 8:17)

"…here is the conclusion of the matter:
Fear God and keep his commandments.
    for this is the whole duty of man." (Eccl. 12:13)

Accordingly, while we are on earth striving to be the best capitalists and Christians that we can, we realize that such pursuits are not the end; they are temporal. God, the eternal, is the end. So all that we do, we do faithfully to the glory of God toward the end of knowing God, but not of understanding God.

As with Job, God does not leave us groping in confusion and despair, but grants us God's grace, "There is a time for everything, and a season for every activity under heaven:…. He has made everything beautiful in its time…. I know that there is nothing better for men than to be happy and do good while they live. That everyone may eat and drink, and find satisfaction in all his toil— this is the gift of God." (Eccl. 3:1,11-13) Elizabeth Huwiler, Associate Professor of Old Testament and Hebrew at The Lutheran Theological Seminary in Philadelphia, explains in her commentary on Ecclesiastes, "There is a possibility of joy, but it exists only within the context of human limitations and the ultimate limitation, death…. [A]ll life is *hebel* [meaningless], and yet joy is both possible and good."[707] Further, we live with an underlying joy knowing that God is in charge, and God is with purpose.

But the major point, of which we should never lose sight, is: "The fear of the LORD is the beginning of knowledge." (Prv. 1:7) "For the LORD gives wisdom, and from his mouth comes knowledge and understanding." (Prv. 2:6)

All of this is succinctly and beautifully stated by Isaiah:

Come, all you who are thirsty,
    come to the waters;
and you who have no money,
    come, buy and eat!
Come, buy wine and milk
    without money and without cost.
Why spend money on what is not bread,
    and your labor on what does not satisfy?
Listen, listen to me, and eat what is good,
    and your soul will delight in the richest of fare.

> Give ear and come to me;
> hear me, that your soul may live. (Is. 55:1-3)

<u>From the New Testament:</u>

As we Christians have learned, the Old Testament sets up the context for the New Testament, and Ecclesiastes, with its contrasting the human with the divine, plays a key role in this. As LaSor observes, in Ecclesiastes the "insistence on the inscrutability of God's ways underscores the magnificent breakthrough in divine and human communication which the Incarnation effected."[708] The divine and the human are very much connected, commencing with one of the most beautiful passages in Scripture when the angel Gabriel tells Mary, "for nothing is impossible with God," and Mary responds, "I am the Lord's servant,... May it be to me as you have said." (Lk. 1:37,38) Indeed, Jesus of Nazareth provides us with hope. "With man this is impossible, but with God all things are possible." (Mt. 19:26) "If you hold to my teaching,.... Then you will know the truth, and the truth will set you free." (Jn. 8:31,32)

Relating this more specifically to the subject of economics, in the Gospel of John the resurrected Jesus says to the disciples, "Cast the net on the right side,...so they cast it, and now they were not able to haul it in, for the quantity of fish." (Jn. 21:6) The miracles demonstrated what it is like in the kingdom of God: infinite resources to address our needs. Indeed, in the kingdom of God economics which deals with resource allocation, production, income distribution and the like is irrelevant. Furthermore in the kingdom of God "rich" and "gain" take on a completely different meaning than the definition found in economics textbooks. "For you know the grace of our Lord Jesus Christ, that though he was rich, yet for your sakes he became poor, so that you through his poverty might become rich." (2 Cor. 8:9) "For to me, to live is Christ and to die is gain." (Phil. 1:21)

Bruce, in his commentary on the *Sermon on the Mount,* notes, "Worldly wealth, which passes away, is not the chief end of man; God's kingdom and righteousness must be sought above all else, and other interests will then take their appropriate place."[709] Griffiths eloquently addresses this distinction and summarizes the essence of the point to which my study has brought me on this matter of the relationship between economics and religion. "There is within the life and teaching of Jesus a basic unity which is centered around what is called the kingdom of God.... Despite the poverty around him and the oppression and injustice of the colonial situation in which in found himself, he rejected a secular interpretation of salvation. When tempted, he refused to turn stones into bread. In a similar vein he refused to establish a government which would throw off the shackles of Roman domination. His primary task was to establish a kingdom but it was a kingdom whose dimensions were spiritual and not secular. Whenever and wherever anyone accepted the authority of God over their life, there and then the Kingdom of God was extended. The Kingdom meant the reign of God over the lives of individuals. As a result it was impossible for mortals to build this Kingdom. It was established by God; and its extension depended on the Holy Spirit. The essence of the Kingdom was that it viewed man's fundamental problem as spiritual and not political; it was established in response to the deepest and most intractable of human problems, namely man's independence of God. Jesus was no legislator or political activist by today's standards,... Even if Jesus had been handed political power...., it would have been an irrelevance to his basic purpose. It would have been then, and remains to this day, impossible to legislate the things about which he talked and preached, simply because the ethic of his Kingdom was love and the source of its power is supernatural."[710]

Edwards expresses this same thought as follows, "good citizenship is neither the sum of nor a substitute for true Christianity. Beneath civic duties and good causes,... lies the essential and indispensable characteristic of Christian faith, love for others."[711] As Danker notes in his commentary on Luke, "The Christian proclamation is a call to recognize that all systems of the world are now under the mastery of Jesus Christ and that within those systems the prior authority of Jesus Christ is to be recognized."[712]

Perhaps the most inspiring demonstration of giving oneself over to Jesus Christ is the apostle Paul. "But whatever was to my profit I now consider loss for the sake of Christ. What is more, I consider everything a loss compared to the surpassing greatness of knowing Christ Jesus my Lord, for whose sake I have lost all things. I consider them rubbish, that I may gain Christ and be found in him, ...—the righteousness that comes from God and is by faith." (Phil. 3:7-9) F. F. Bruce instructs, "Christ alone must be the object of

Paul's confidence, and...all these former objects of confidence have lost the value they once had.... When he entered the service of Christ on the Damascus road, that meant the renunciation of all that he had chiefly prized up to that moment.... 'Knowing Christ Jesus my Lord' is personal knowledge; it includes the experience of being loved by him and loving him in return...a knowledge so transcendent in value that it compensates for the loss of everything else.... To explore the fullness of this relationship was...Paul's inexhaustible joy.... Paul [had] received through faith in the Son of God the new durable foundation of righteousness freely bestowed by God's grace."[713]

As Paul notes to the Corinthians, "... as it is written: 'No eye has seen no ear has heard, no mind has conceived what God has prepared for those who love him." (1 Cor. 2:9); then, "....the wisdom of this world is foolishness in God's sight" (1 Cor. 3:19); and Paul observing about himself, "... poor, yet making many rich; having nothing, and yet possessing everything." (2 Cor. 6:10) And, as Paul further instructed the Colossians, "... set your hearts on things above... Set you minds on things above, not earthly things... Put to death, therefore, whatever belongs to your earthly nature:..." (Col. 3:1-5)

Let us listen to the apostle Paul's beautiful declaration of the transcendence of Truth and Reality:

> Oh, the depth of the riches of the wisdom and knowledge
> of God!
>   How unsearchable his judgment,
>   and his paths beyond tracing out!
> Who has known the mind of the Lord?
>   Or who has been his counselor?
> Who has ever given to God,
>   that God should repay him?
> For from him and through him and to him are all things.
>   To him be the glory forever! Amen. (Rom. 11:33-36)

Griffiths offers a beautiful reconciliation of the material and the spiritual, "the world which God created is a spiritual world as well as a material world. God is a spirit, and being created in his image we are possessed of spirit as well. Being made, therefore, from the dust of the earth but endowed with spirit, we are to pursue our lives in a material world, yet in the context of a spiritual order.... The injunction to seek first the Kingdom of God and his righteousness... is not the same as saying that the life of the spirit is superior to the life of the material world or that the life of the spirit is good while the concerns of the material world are bad. It is rather to expose priorities. The call to seek first the Kingdom of God is not a call to the life of the monastery or to a narrow-minded form of personal piety which rejects the material world. We are to seek God and live by the laws of his Kingdom within the material world which he himself has created and of which we are part. The challenge for the Christian then is not to reject the material world and the creation of wealth in favour of some higher spiritual priority but to serve others through the process of wealth creation in the perspective of serving God."[714]

The proper perspective to maintain, then, on the subject of Christianity and economics is, as suggested by Nash, "Christians who want to help the poor need capitalism. Rational economic activity is quite simply impossible apart from a market system. But, and let all friends of a market system pay heed, capitalism needs Christianity."[715] The question is, will our wealth dominant us or will we dominate our wealth? Will we own our possessions or will our possessions own us? The answer to questions posed by capitalism—like all of the essential questions of humans—lies with Christianity. But the answers will be different from what we expect. The revered British theologian John Stott reminds us, "God's word is designed to make us Christians, not scientists, and to lead us to eternal life through faith in Jesus Christ. It was not God's intention to reveal in Scripture what human beings could discover by their own investigations and experiments."[716]

Which brings us full circle. Certainly, God does not need capitalism nor any other economic system. God is in charge. Humankind has been given a free will, but God has a purpose. And ultimately God is in charge. But God works in mysterious ways: Abraham offering up his son, Isaac; Joseph in prison, then becoming Minister of Economic Development; Cyrus defeating Nebac, then letting the exiles return to rebuild the Temple; Jesus displaying kingship through his limpness on the cross; all of the martyrs..... Further, some great ironies have appeared. Christianity flourished under

Nero's vicious persecution as Christians passionately pursued the Good News, then languished after being adopted by Constantine and Christians became complacent.

As Job displayed and as enunciated in the book of Ecclesiastes and as stated by Paul, it is not for us to understand. Suffice it to say that Christianity does not *need* any human system or institution, neither capitalism nor socialism nor any other economic system. The Incarnation, God coming to be with humankind, demonstrated that humanity is an integral part of God's purpose. As our Lord Jesus Christ reminds us, "The kingdom of God does not come with your careful observation, nor will people say, 'Here it is,' or 'There it is,' because the kingdom of God is within you." (Lk. 17:20,21) In just the same way that God has used human institutions since God created us, could it be that today God is using capitalism and, its chief institution, the business firm, for God's ends?

Therefore, my fellow Christian capitalists—business people and professionals—as I salute you, I regard you the same way that Paul regarded the believers in Thessalonica (italics and bold mine): "We always thank God for all of you, mentioning you in our prayers. We continually remember before our God and Father your *work* produced by **faith**, your *labor* prompted by **love**, and your *endurance* inspired by **hope** in our Lord Jesus Christ." (1 Thes. 1:2,3) Such is the Christian basis of capitalism.

Notes

[1] Edwards, James R. *New International Biblical Commentary: Romans.* Peabody (Massachusetts: Hendrickson Publishers, Inc., 1992), pp. 291,2.

[2] McKim, Donald K. *Westminster Dictionary of Theological Terms* (Louisville: Westminster John Knox Press, 1996), p. 164.

[3] Pelikan, Jaroslav. *The Illustrated Jesus Through the Centuries* (New Haven: Yale University Press, 1997), p. 178.

[4] Griffiths, Brian. *The Creation of Wealth* (Donners Grove, Illinois: Inter-Varsity Press, 1984), pp. 45,6.

[5] Jervis, L. Ann, *New International Biblical Commentary: Galatians* (Peabody, Massachusetts: Hendrickson Publishers, Inc., 1999), p. 23.

[6] Gasque, W. Ward. *New Testament 101, Koinos Program* (Seattle: Pacific Association for Theological Studies, Fall, 1999), lecture notes.

[7] Danker, Frederick W. *Luke; Proclamation Commentaries,* Second Edition, ed. Krodel, Gerhard. (Philadelphia: Fortress Press, 1987), pp. 120,1.

[8] Nash, Ronald H. *Poverty and Wealth: The Christian Debate Over Capitalism* (Westchester, Illinois: Crossway Books, 1986), pp. 61,2.

[9] Bruce, F.F. *The Message of the New Testament* (Grand Rapids: William B. Eerdmans Publishing Company, 1972), p. 98.

[10] Schlossberg, H., Vinay, S. and Sider, R. ed. *Christianity and Economics in the Post-Cold War Era: The Oxford Declaration and Beyond* (Grand Rapids, Michigan: William B. Eerdmans Publishing Company, 1994), p. 9.

[11] Nash, p. 59.

[12] Ibid., p. 110.

[13] Ibid., pp. 169,70.

[14] Gibbon, Edward, quoted in Pelikan, p. 199.

[15] Novak, Michael. *The Spirit of Democratic Capitalism* (New York: Simon and Schuster, 1982), p. 56.

[16] Zakaria, Fareed. "The American Age," *Hoover Digest: Research and Opinion on Public Policy* (Stanford: Hoover Press, Summer, 2000), p. 129.

[17] McKim, p. 29.

[18] Holland, Jeffrey, lecture, Mercer Island Presbyterian Church, April 1, 2001.

[19] Bruce, p. 24.

[20] Stotts, Jack L. "By What Authority…?" in *Reformed Faith and Economics* ed. Stivers, Robert L. (Lanham, Maryland: University Press of America, 1989), pp. 9-10.

[21] LaSor, W.S., Hubbard, D.A., and Bush, F. W. *Old Testament Survey: The Message, Form and Background of the Old Testament*, 2d ed. (Grand Rapids, Michigan: William B. Eerdmans Publishing Co., 1996), p. 587.

[22] Hawthorne, Hawthorne, G.F. and Martin, R.P. ed. *Dictionary of Paul and His Letters*. (Downers Grove, Illinois: InterVarsity Press, 1993), p. 396.

[23] Ibid., p. 396.

[24] Milne, Bruce. *Know the Truth, Rev. Ed.* (Downers Grove, Illinois: InterVarsity Press, 1998), p. 64.

[25] Guthrie, Shirley C. *Christian Doctrine* (Louisville, Kentucky: Westminster/John Knox Press, 1994), p. 31.

[26] *The Scots Confession: 1560*. Ed. Henderson, G. D., trans. Bulloch, J. (Edinburgh: The Saint Andrew Press, 1960) quoted in *Book of Confessions: The Constitution of the Presbyterian Church (U.S.A.) Part I* (New York: The Office of the General Assembly, Presbyterian Church (U.S.A.), 1983), 3.01.

[27] LaSor, p. 23.

[28] Mann, Thomas W. *The Book of the Torah* (Atlanta: John Knox Press, 1988) p. 14.

[29] Guthrie, p. 146.

[30] Murphy, R. E. and Huwiler E. *New International Biblical Commentary: Proverbs, Ecclesiastes, Song of Songs* (Peabody, Massachusetts: Hendrickson Publishers, Inc., 1999), p. 24.

[31] Williams, David J. *New International Biblical Commentary: Acts* (Peabody, Massachusetts: Hendrickson Publishers, Inc., 1990), p. 305.

[32] Burton, Bryan. *Christian Theology 101, Koinos Program* (Seattle: Pacific Association for Theological Studies, Winter, 2000) lecture outline.

[33] Milne, p. 108.

[34] Guthrie, p. 151.

[35] Patzia, Arthur G. *New International Biblical Commentary: Ephesians, Colossians, Philemon* (Peabody, Massachusetts: Hendrickson Publishers, Inc., 1990), p 31.

[36] Pelikan, pp. 66,7.

[37] Scalise, Pamela, Ph.D.. *PENTATEUCH. Course OT501* (Seattle: Fuller Theological Seminary, Fall, 1999), lecture notes.

[38] LaSor, p. 23.

[39] Rowland, Randy, D.Min. *Christian Ministry 101, Koinos Program* (Seattle: Pacific Association for Theological Studies, Spring 2000), lecture outline.

[40] Scalise, lecture notes.

[41] Milne, p. 114.

[42] Ibid., pp. 14,15.

[43] Ibid., p. 16.

[44] Gasque, Laurel, *Christianity and the Arts 101, Koinos Program* (Seattle: Pacific Association for Theological Studies, Winter, 2000), lecture notes.

[45] Amundsen, Darrel W. *Christian Ethics 101, Koinos Program* (Seattle: Pacific Association for Theological Studies, Spring 2000), lecture notes.

[46] Gronbacher, Gregory M.A. *Economic Personalism: A New Paradigm for a Humane Economy* (Grand Rapids: Acton Institute, 1998), p. 8.

[47] Burton, lecture outline.

[48] Mann, p. 568.

[49] Guthrie, p. 216.

[50] Edwards, pp. 91,102.

[51] Scalise, lecture notes.

[52] Amundsen, lecture notes.

[53] Powell, Jim, *The Triumph of Liberty* (New York: The Free Press, 2000), p. 257.

[54] Schlossberg, Vinay and Sider, p. 14.

[55] Mounce, Robert H. *New International Biblical Commentary: Matthew* (Peabody, Massachusetts: Hendrickson Publishers, Inc., 1991), p. 235.

[56] Gilder, George. *Recapturing the Spirit of Enterprise* (San Francisco: ICS Press, 1992), p. 13.

[57] Sirico, Robert A. *Acton Notes.* (Grand Rapids: Acton Institute, February, 1999), p. 1.

[58] Waterman, A. M. C. "Mind Your Own Business: Unintended Consequences in the Body of Christ," *Faith and Economics* (Wenham, Massachusetts: Association of Christian Economists, Spring, 2000), p. 4.

[59] Burton, p. 8.

[60] Smith, Adam, *An Inquiry into the Nature and Causes of the Wealth of*

Nations (New York: Random House, Inc., 1937), p. 422.

[61] Novak, *The Spirit of Democratic Capitalism,* p. 79.

[62] Nash, p. 73.

[63] Novak, *The Spirit of Democratic Capitalism,* p. 209.

[64] Powell, p. 247.

[65] Ibid., p. 252.

[66] Cassidy, John. "The Hayek Century," *Hoover Digest: Research and Opinion on Public Policy* (Stanford: Hoover Press, Summer, 2000), p. 192.

[67] U.S. Census Bureau, *Statistical Abstract of the United States: 1999* (119th edition) (Washington D.C., 1999), p. 464.

[68] Ibid., p. 571.

[69] Romer, Paul M. "It's All in Your Head," *Hoover Digest* (Stanford, CA: Hoover Press, 1999), p. 14.

[70] Heyne, Paul. *The Economic Way of Thinking, Ninth Edition* (Upper Saddle River, N.J.: Prentice Hall, 2000), p. 264.

[71] "The Good Company," *WRF Comment* (Mississauga, ON, Canada: Work Research Foundation, Winter, 2000), p. 1.

[72] Novak, *The Spirit of Democratic Capitalism,* pp. 174,5.

[73] John Paul II.. *Centesimus Annus,* Encyclical Letter. (Rome: May 1, 1991), p. 68.

[74] Powell, p. 358.

[75] Novak, *The Spirit of Democratic Capitalism,* p. 114.

[76] Heyne, *The Economic Way of Thinking, Ninth Edition,* p. 81.

[77] Cassidy, pp. 196,7

[78] Keynes, John Maynard. *The General Theory of Employment, Interest and Money* (London: Macmillan, 1936), p. 374.

[79] Charette, B. B. *NEW TESTAMENT 1.,* Course NS500 (Seattle: Fuller Theological Seminary, Fall, 1999), lecture notes.

[80] Hay, Donald A. *Economics Today: A Christian critique* (Grand Rapids: William B. Eerdmans Publishing Company, 1989), p. 175.

[81] Novak, *The Spirit of Democratic Capitalism,* p. 95.

[82] Novak, p. 330 quoting Reinhold Niebuhr, "Biblical Faith and Socialism: A critical Appraisal," in *Religion and Culture: Essays in Honor of Paul Tillich,* ed., Walter Leibrecht (New York: Harper and Bros., 1959), p. 51.

[83] Gilder, *Wealth and Poverty,* (San Francisco: ICS Press, 1993), p. 29.

[84] Heyne, Paul. *The Catholic Bishops and the Pursuit of Justice.* (Washington D.C.: Cato Institute), pp. 6-16.

[85] Nash, p. 53.

[86] Von Mises, Ludwig. *Socialism* (New Haven: Yale University Press, 1951) paraphrased in Nash, Ronald H. *Poverty and Wealth: The Christian*

Debate Over Capitalism (Westchester, Illinois: Crossway Books, 1986), pp. 82,6.

87 Gibson, William E. "An Order in Crisis, and the Declaration of New Things," in *Reformed Faith and Economics* ed. Stivers, Robert L. (Lanham, Maryland: University Press of America, 1989), p. 149.

88 Mann, p. 121.

89 LaSor, p. 288.

90 Edwards, pp. 98,9.

91 Ibid., p. 30.

92 Thomas, Gary L., *Seeking the Face of God* (Eugene, Oregon: Harvest House Publishers, 1944), pp. 79-81.

93 West, John G., Jr. *Public Life in the Shadowlands* (Grand Rapids: Acton Institute, 1998), p. 8.

94 Ibid., p. 9.

95 Lovejoy, Arthur O. *Reflections on Human Nature* (Baltimore: Johns Hopkins University Press, 1961) p. 42, quoted by Murchland, Bernard, "The Socialist Critique of the Corporation," *The Corporation: A Inquiry,* ed. Novak, Michael and Cooper, John W., (Washington D.C.: American Enterprise Institute for Public Policy Research, 1981), p 162.

96 Moltmann, Jurgen, *The Trinity and the Kingdom: The Doctrine of God* (Minneapolis: Fortress Press, 1993), pp. 198,9.

97 Smith, p. 442.

98 Sewall, Dale. Sermon preached at Mercer Island Presbyterian Church, March 18, 2001.

99 Mann, p. 107.

100 LaSor, p. 176.

101 Mounce, p. 66.

102 Ibid., p. 155.

103 Wheeler, S.E. *Wealth as Peril and Obligations* (Grand Rapids: William. B. Eerdmans Publishing Company, 1995), p. 65.

104 Ibid., p. 64.

105 Bonhoeffer, D. *The Cost of Discipleship* (Simon & Schuster, 1959), p. 156, quoted in Fuller, R.H. and Rice, B.K. *Christianity and the Affluent Society* (Grand Rapids: William B. Eerdmans Publishing Co., 1967), p. 31.

106 Wheeler, p. 70.

107 Ibid., pp. 68-71.

108 Ibid., p. 71.

109 Davids, Peter H. *New International Biblical Commentary: James* (Peabody, Massachusetts: Hendrickson Publishers, Inc., 1989), p. 52.

110 Mann, p. 48.

111 LaSor, p. 90.

112 Lindsel, Harold. *Free Enterprise: A Judeo-Christian Defense*

(Wheaton, Illinois: Tyndale House Publishers, Inc., 1982), pp. 56,7.

[113] LaSor, p. 273.

[114] Achtemeier, Elizabeth. *New International Biblical Commentary: Minor Prophets I* (Peabody, Massachusetts: Hendrickson Publishers, Inc., 1996), pp. 308,9.

[115] Nash, pp. 163,4.

[116] Heyne, *The Economic Way of Thinking, Ninth Edition,* p. 390.

[117] Aquinas, Thomas. *Summa Theologica, Vol. II* (New York: Benziger Brothers, Inc., 1947), p. 66.

[118] Conquest, Robert. "The Spector Haunting Russia," *Hoover Digest: Research and Opinion on Public Policy* (Stanford: Hoover Press, Spring, 2000), p. 119.

[119] Morse, Jennifer Roback. "Who Puts the Self in Self-Interest?" *Religion & Liberty* (Grand Rapids: Acton Institute, November and December, 1998), p.6.

[120] Owensby, Walter L. *Economics for Prophets* (Grand Rapids: William B. Eerdmans Publishing Co., 1988), p. 40.

[121] Gasque, W. Ward. "Religion, Egalitarianism and Economic Justice," *Theology, Third World Development and Economic Justice,* ed. Walter Block and Donald Shaw (Vancouver, B.C: The Fraser Institute, 1985), p. 3.

[122] Nash, p. 166.

[123] Mounce, p. 101.

[124] Shepherd, J.W. *The Christ of the Gospels* (Grand Rapids: William B. Eerdmans Publishing Co., 1946), p. 384.

[125] Amundsen, lecture notes.

[126] Lewis, C.S. *The Abolition of Man.* (London: Macmillan, 1953).

[127] Interfaith Council for Environmental Stewardship, *The Cornwall Declaration on Environmental Stewardship* (Grand Rapids: Acton Institute, February 1, 2000).

[128] Gibson, p. 155.

[129] Schlossberg, Vinay and Sider, p. 14.

[130] Sowell, Thomas. *Barbarians Inside the Gates* (Stanford, California: Hoover Institution Press, 1999), p. 49.

[131] Heyne, *The Economic Way of Thinking*, Ninth Edition, p. 49.

[132] Heyne, Paul. "Controlling Stories: On the Mutual Influence of Religious Narratives and Economic Explanations" (paper presented at a session of the Southern Economic Association conference on "The Influence of Religion on Economics and Vice Versa," November, 18, 1990), p. 7.

[133] Nash, p. 164.

[134] LaSor, p. 47.

[135] Mann, pp. 30 and 43.

[136] Ibid., p. 68.

[137] Ibid., p. 77.

[138] Murphy and Huwiler, p. 106.

[139] LaSor, p. 463.

[140] Murphy and Huwiler, pp. 76, 138.

[141] Ibid., p. 65.

[142] Owensby, Walter L. *Economics for Prophets* (Grand Rapids: William B. Eerdmans Publishing Co., 1988), p. 167.

[143] LaSor, p. 407.

[144] Alexander, John F. *Your Money or Your Life: A New Look at Jesus' View of Wealth and Power* (San Francisco: Harper & Row, Publishers, 1986), pp. 52, 67.

[145] Nash, p. 163.

[146] Alexander, p. 53.

[147] Pentecost, J.D. *The Words and Works of Jesus Christ; A Study of the Life of Christ* (Grand Rapids: Zondervan Publishing House, 1981), p. 339.

[148] Shepherd, p. 425.

[149] Michaels, J. Ramsey. *New International Biblical Commentary: John.* Peabody (Massachusetts: Hendrickson Publishers, Inc., 1989), p. 225.

[150] Hawthorne, p. 299.

[151] Ibid., p. 889.

[152] Edwards, p. 349.

[153] Griffiths, p. 61.

[154] Ibid., p. 61.

[155] Murray, pp. 82,3.

[156] Charette, lecture notes.

[157] Brown, pp. 926,7.

[158] Charette, lecture notes.

[159] Hock, R. F. "Paul's Tentmaking and the Problem of His Social Class," *JBL* 97 (1978) pp. 555-64, quoted in Hawthorne, G.F. and Martin, R.P. ed. *Dictionary of Paul and His Letters* (Downers Grove, Illinois: InterVarsity Press, 1993), p. 926.

[160] Williams, David J. *New International Biblical Commentary: 1 and 2 Thessalonians* (Peabody, Massachusetts: Hendrickson Publishers, Inc., 1992), pp. 77,78,146.

[161] Smith, p. 3.

[162] Soards, Marion L. *New International Biblical Commentary:1 Corinthians* (Peabody, Massachusetts: Hendrickson Publishers, Inc., 1999), pp. 263,5.

[163] Brown, R.E. *An Introduction to the New Testament* (New York: Doubleday, 1997), p. 295.

164 Schlossberg, Vinay and Sider, pp. 16,17.
165 Martin, R.P. and Davids, P.H. ed. *Dictionary of the Later New Testament & Its Developments* (Downers Grove, Illinois: InterVarsity Press, 1997), p. 319.
166 Brown, p. 199.
167 Ibid., pp. 252-3.
168 Moxnes, Halvor. *The Economy of the Kingdom* (Philadelphia: Fortress Press, 1988), p. 67.
169 Sewall, October 15, 2000.
170 Soards, p. 153.
171 Ibid., p. 257.
172 Smith, p. 422.
173 Patzia, p. 229.
174 Turner, Dale E. *Different Seasons* (Homewood, Illinois: High Tide Press, Inc., 1997), p. 106.
175 Bruce, F. F. *New International Biblical Commentary: Philippians* (Peabody, Massachusetts: Hendrickson Publishers, Inc., 1983), p. 82.
176 Guinness, Os. *The Call* (Nashville: Word Publishing, 1998), p. 4.
177 Ibid., pp. 31,46,47,74,93,141.
178 Thomas, p. 211.
179 Guinness, p. 5.
180 Ibid., p. 163.
181 Ibid., pp. 34,5.
182 Rowan, Barry. *A Search for Meaning in Work* (Seattle: Barry Rowan, 1996), p. 15.
183 Guinness, pp. 179,80.
184 Ibid., p. 244.
185 Hardy, Lee. "My Job Is Not My Calling," *WRF Comment* (Mississauga, Ontario, Canada: Work Research Foundation, Summer, 2000), p.7.
186 Guinness, p. 209.
187 Holland, February 18, 2001.
188 Stone, Ronald H. "The Reformed Ethics of John Calvin" in *Reformed Faith and Economics* ed. Stivers, Robert L. (Lanham, Maryland: University Press of America, 1989), pp. 40,2.
189 Brown, p. 645.
190 Wall, Robert W. *New International Biblical Commentary: Revelation* (Peabody, Massachusetts: Hendrickson Publishers, Inc., 1991), pp. 73,4.
191 Sider, Ronald J. *Rich Christians in an Age of Hunger* (Dallas: Word Publishing, 1997), p. 101.
192 Moxnes, p. 28.
193 Pentecost, p. 338.
194 Ibid., p. 314.

[195] Alexander, pp. 78-80.

[196] Guthrie, p. 300.

[197] Murray, p. 89.

[198] Ibid., p. 91.

[199] Griffiths, p. 116.

[200] Sirico, Robert. "Capitalism and Morality," *Is Capitalism Morally Bankrupt?* lecture series. Sparks, John A. ed. (Grove City, Pennsylvania: Grove City College, June, 2000), pp. 5,6.

[201] Martin, p. 528.

[202] LaSor, p. 267.

[203] Wheeler, p. 129

[204] Pentecost, p. 185.

[205] Schwarz, John E. *Word Alive! An Introduction to the Christian Faith* (Minneapolis: Tabgha Foundation, 1993), p. 251.

[206] Wright, Christopher. *New International Biblical Commentary: Deuteronomy* (Peabody, Massachusetts: Hendrickson Publishers, Inc., 1996), p. 99.

[207] Wheeler, p. 46.

[208] Danker, p. 118.

[209] Wheeler, p. 51.

[210] Hurtado, Larry W. *New International Biblical Commentary: Mark* (Peabody, Massachusetts: Hendrickson Publishers, Inc., 1989), p. 165.

[211] Mounce, p. 184.

[212] Hurtado, p. 165.

[213] Danker, pp. 112,3.

[214] Schweizer, Eduard. *The Good News According to Luke*, trans. Green, D. E. (Atlanta: John Knox Press, 1984), p. 210.

[215] Danker, p. 113.

[216] Charette, lecture notes.

[217] Hawthorne, p. 426.

[218] Bruce, *New International Biblical Commentary: Philippians,* p. 150.

[219] Patzia, p. 73.

[220] Johnson, Thomas F. *New International Biblical Commentary: 1, 2, and 3 John* (Peabody, Massachusetts: Hendrickson Publishers, Inc., 1993), pp. 53,141.

[221] Wall, p. 77.

[222] Wright, C., p. 101.

[223] Mounce, p. 129.

[224] Wheeler, p. 129.

[225] Guinness, Os. "Rediscovering 'Calling' Will Revitalize Church and Society," *Religion & Liberty* (Grand Rapids: Acton Institute, 1998), p. 4.

[226] Sider, *Rich Christians in an Age of Hunger*, pp. 21,2.

[227] Sider, Ronald J. "Concrete Strategies for Implementing the Biblical Vision of Economic Justice." (paper presented at the *Christian in the Marketplace* annual conference, Regent College, Vancouver, Canada, February 10, 2001.), conference notes.

[228] Gilder, George. "The Soul of Silicon," *Forbes ASAP* (New York: Forbes, Inc., June 1, 1998), p. 114.

[229] Havel, Vaclav quoted in Ericson, E.E., Jr. "Living Responsibly: Vaclav Havel's View," *WRF Comment* (Ontario, Canada: Work Research Foundation, Winter, 1999), p. 7.

[230] John Paul, II, pp. 71-3.

[231] Kristol, Irving. *Two Cheers for Capitalism* (New York: Basic Books, Inc., Publishers, 1978), p. 251.

[232] Guinness, Os. *The Call* (Nashville: Word Publishing, 1998), p. 13.

[233] Turner, p. 137.

[234] Wheeler, p. 71.

[235] Wright, C., p. 128.

[236] Mann, p. 151.

[237] LaSor, p. 173.

[238] Murphy and Huwiler, p. 104.

[239] Pentecost, p. 267.

[240] Schweizer, p.122.

[241] Murray, p. 91.

[242] Fee, Gordon D. *New International Biblical Commentary: 1 and 2 Timothy, Titus* (Peabody, Massachusetts: Hendrickson Publishers, Inc., 1988), p. 157.

[243] Davids, pp. 33,116.

[244] Martin, p. 879

[245] Wall, pp. 86,7.

[246] Mounce, p. 184.

[247] Gill, David W. *Becoming Good* (Downers Grove, Illinois: InterVarsity Press, 2000), p. 129.

[248] Scalise, P. OT 504, Writings.

[249] LaSor, p. 483.

[250] Edwards, p. 218.

[251] Thomas, p. 11.

[252] Ibid., pp. 122,4.

[253] Ibid., p. 130.

[254] Ibid., pp. 132,3.

[255] Ibid., p. 137.

[256] Guthrie, p. 200.

[257] Martin, p. 886.

[258] Schwarz, p. 250.

[259] Ibid. p. 251.

[260] Guinness, p. 13.

[261] Wright, C., p. 86.

[262] Davids, pp. 90-9.

[263] Novak, *The Spirit of Democratic Capitalism*, p. 258.

[264] Aquinas, p. 567.

[265] Stanley, T. J. and Danko, W. D., *The Millionaire Next Door* (New York: Simon & Schuster, Inc., 1996), p. 110.

[266] Lindblom, Charles E. *The Market System: What It Is, How It Works, and What To Make of It* (New Haven: Yale University Press, 2001), p. 163.

[267] Veblen, Thorstein. *The Theory of the Leisure Class* (London: Macmillan, 1899), p. 219.

[268] Chilton, David. *Productive Christians in an Age of Guilt Manipulators*. (Tyler, Texas: Institute for Christian Economics, 1985), p. 139.

[269] Ibid., p. 148.

[270] Scott, James M. *New International Biblical Commentary: 2 Corinthians* (Peabody, Massachusetts: Hendrickson Publishers, Inc., 1998), pp. 180,1.

[271] Hay, p. 215.

[272] Novak, *The Spirit of Democratic Capitalism*, p. 213.

[273] Karlgaard, Rich. "Wealth Gap Follies," *Forbes*, October 11, 1999, p. 45, quoted in D'Souza, *The Virtue of Prosperity*, p. 70.

[274] Schall, James V. *Religion, Wealth and Poverty* (Vancouver, Canada: The Fraser Institute, 1990), p. 114.

[275] Guinness, pp. 132,3.

[276] Schweizer, Eduard, p. 207.

[277] Mounce, p. 120.

[278] Ibid., p. 149.

[279] Pentecost, p. 338.

[280] LaSor, p. 495.

[281] Novak, Michael. *The Fire of Invention: Civil Society and the Future of the Corporation* (Lanham, Md.: Rowman & Littlefield Publishers, Inc., 1997), pp. 111,3.

[282] Rosenberg, Nathan and Birdzell, L. E., Jr. *How the West Grew Rich* (New York: Basic Books, Inc., 1986), p. 27.

[283] Tsongas, Paul quoted in Zelnick, Bob. "Why the New Populism Won't Go Away," *Hoover Digest: Research and Opinion on Public Policy* (Stanford: Hoover Press, Winter, 2001) p. 44.

[284] Schlossberg, Herbert. "Destroying Poverty without Destroying Poor People," in Schlossberg, H., Vinay, S. and Sider, R. ed. *Christianity and Economics in the Post-Cold War Era: The Oxford Declaration and*

Beyond. (Grand Rapids, Michigan: William B. Eerdmans Publishing Company, 1994), p. 118.

[285] Guthrie, p. 356.

[286] Michaels, pp. 109-10.

[287] Kristol, pp. 177,83.

[288] Byker, Gaylen. "Free Market Requires Legal, Moral, and Religious Foundations," *Religion & Liberty* (Grand Rapids: Acton Institute, November and December, 1998), p. 5.

[289] Sider, *Rich Christians in an Age of Hunger*, p. 95.

[290] Hayford, Jack, *Studies In The Book Of Revelation* (Van Nuys California: Soundword Tape Ministry, 1991), sound cassettes CO438-447.

[291] Ibid.

[292] Wall, p. 169.

[293] Ibid. p. 183.

[294] Brown, p. 782.

[295] Martin, pp. 1035,6.

[296] Blomberg, Craig L. *Neither Poverty Nor Riches: A Biblical Theology of Material Possessions* (Grand Rapids: William B. Eerdmans Publishing Co., 1999), pp. 243-6.

[297] Holland, February 18, 2001.

[298] Guinness, p. 206.

[299] Ibid., pp. 209-10.

[300] Novak, *The Spirit of Democratic Capitalism,* p. 349.

[301] Guinness, p. 141.

[302] Holland, March 25, 2001.

[303] Goldingay, John *How to Read the Bible* (London: Triangle, 1997), pp. 38,9,43.

[304] Scalise, lecture notes.

[305] Guthrie, pp. 63,4.

[306] Scalise, lecture notes.

[307] Wright, C. J. H. "The Ethical Authority of the Old Testament," *TynBull*, pp. 227, quoted in Wright, C., p. 13.

[308] Wright, C., p. 188.

[309] Sider, Ronald J. "Is There a Biblical Definition of Economic Justice?" (paper presented at the *Christian in the Marketplace* annual conference, Regent College, Vancouver, Canada, February 10, 2001.), conference notes.

[310] Ibid.

[311] Sider, *Rich Christians in an Age of Hunger*, p. 77.

[312] LaSor, pp. 89,90.

[313] Mann, p. 154.

[314] Ibid., p. 156.

[315] Amundsen, course notes.
[316] LaSor, p. 75.
[317] Charette, lecture notes.
[318] Goldingay, p. 78.
[319] Bruce, p. 29.
[320] LaSor, p. 194.
[321] Hawthorne, p. 683.
[322] Fuller and Rice, p. 312.
[323] Hawthorne, p. 23.
[324] Ibid. p. 884.
[325] Martin, p. 503.
[326] Williams, D., pp. 282,3.
[327] Johnson, T., p. 174.
[328] Brown, p. 302.
[329] Green, Joel B. *The Theology of the Gospel of Luke* (Cambridge, England: Cambridge University Press, 1995), p. 149.
[330] Moxnes, pp. 155-6.
[331] Williams, D., p. 92.
[332] Ibid., p. 92.
[333] Calvin, John. *Commentary Upon the Acts of the Apostles* (Grand Rapids: Eerdmans, 1948), p. 130 quoted in Stivers, p. 10.
[334] Stotts, p. 10.
[335] Greaves, Richard L. *Theology and Revolution in the Scottish Reformation: Studies in the Thought of John Knox* (Grand Rapids: Christian University Press, 1980), p. 185.
[336] Patzia, p. 254.
[337] Scott, pp. 180,1.
[338] Jervis, p. 132.
[339] Fee, p. 158.
[340] Pentecost, p. 341.
[341] Schweizer, p. 262.
[342] Griffiths, p. 47.
[343] Farley, Benjamin W., trans. and ed., *John Calvin's Sermons on the Ten Commandments* (Grand Rapids: Baker Book House, 1980) pp. 162-3 quoted in Little, David. "Economic Justice and the Grounds for a Theory of Progressive Taxation in Calvin's Thought," in Stivers, p. 74.
[344] Alexander, p. 77.
[345] LaSor, p. 413.
[346] Hurtado, p. 76.
[347] Mounce, p. 92.
[348] Ibid., p. 235.
[349] Hawthorne, p. 298.

[350] Schuller, Robert H. *Prayer: My Soul's Adventure With God* (Nashville: Thomas Nelson, Inc., 1995), p. 76.

[351] Wesley, John. "The Use of Money" (read by Reed, Ronald at the *Christian in the Marketplace* annual conference, Regent College, Vancouver, Canada, February 10, 2001.), conference notes.

[352] Sirico, Robert A. *Acton Notes* (Grand Rapids: Acton Institute, April, 1997), p. 1.

[353] Nash, p. 64.

[354] Schall, p. 46.

[355] Brown, p. 287.

[356] Hawthorne, p. 144.

[357] Bruce, *The Message of the New Testament,* p. 33.

[358] Simon, William E. "Talents and Stewardship," *Religion & Liberty.* (Grand Rapids: Action Institute, 2000), p. 3.

[359] D'Souza, Dinesh. *The Virtue of Prosperity* (New York: The Free Press, 2000), p. 159.

[360] Alexander, p. 219.

[361] Danker, p. 118.

[362] Heyne, Paul. *The Catholic Bishops and the Pursuit of Justice*, p. 21.

[363] Moxnes, p. 66.

[364] Gilder, *Wealth and Poverty*, p. 21.

[365] Hill, Peter J. "Private Rights and Public Attitudes: A Christian Defense of Capitalism," unpublished, Department of Economics, Montana State University, p. 6, quoted in Nash, Ronald H. *Poverty and Wealth: The Christian Debate Over Capitalism* (Westchester, Illinois: Crossway Books, 1986), p. 54.

[366] Turner, Dale. "Jesus a great giver, and receiver, also," *The Seattle Times* (Seattle: The Seattle Times Publishing Company, March 7, 1998), p. B12.

[367] Hamilton, Michael S., "We're in the Money!" *Christianity Today*, June 12, 2000, p. 41 .

[368] U.S. Census Bureau, *The White House Economics Statistics Briefing Room*, Internet, Washington D.C., 2000.

[369] Kristol, p. 141.

[370] Lenzner, Robert and Kellner, Tomas. "Corporate Saboteurs," *Forbes* (New York: Forbes, Inc, November 27, 2000) p. 161.

[371] Ostrom, Carol M. "Sudden wealth, hard questions" *The Seattle Times* (Seattle: The Seattle Times Publishing Company, November 5, 2000), p. A12.

[372] Gillis, Cydney, "High-tech millionaires discuss ways they cope with newfound wealth," *Eastside Journal* (Bellevue: Horvitz Newspapers, September 23, 2000), p. D2.

[373] Greenfeld, K. T. "A New Way of Giving," *Time* (New York: Time, Inc., July 24, 2000), p. 53.

[374] Ibid., pp. 52,3.

[375] Ibid., p. 50.

[376] Hardy, Quentin. "The Radical Philanthropist," *Forbes*. (New York: Forbes, Inc., May 1, 2000), p. 117.

[377] Ibid., pp. 119,121.

[378] Baum, Geoff. "Different.com," *Forbes ASAP* (New York: Forbes, Inc, May 29, 2000), p. 220.

[379] "Sharing the Wealth," *Forbes* (New York: Forbes, Inc., July 3, 2000), p. 254.

[380] Sider, *Rich Christians in an Age of Hunger,* p. 79.

[381] Paxon, Bud, quoted in Caldwell, Stephen. "Funding the Great Commission," *The Life@Work Journal.* (Fayetteville, Arkansas: The Life@Work Company, March/April, 1999), p. 53.

[382] Hurtado, pp. 206,7.

[383] Giving USA 2000 / AAFRC Trust for Philanthropy.

[384] Hardy, p. 121.

[385] McCracken, Paul W. "The Corporation and the Liberal Order," *The Corporation: A Theological Inquiry* ed. Novak, Michael and Cooper, John W. (Washington, D.C: American Enterprise Institute, 1981), p. 40.

[386] Green, p. 116.

[387] Hawthorne, p. 820.

[388] Martin, p. 1038.

[389] Griffiths, pp. 68,9.

[390] Ibid., p. 67.

[391] Nash, p. 73.

[392] Novak, *The Spirit of Democratic Capitalism,* p. 67.

[393] Ibid., p. 261.

[394] Fuller and Rice, p. 36.

[395] Scott, pp. 178-80.

[396] Noll, Mark A. *Turning Points: Decisive Moments in the History of Christianity* (Grand Rapids: Baker Book House Company, 1997), p. 313.

[397] Ibid., p. 314.

[398] Moxnes, p. 97.

[399] Lipset, Seymour Martin. "Still the Exceptional Nation?" *Hoover Digest: Research and Opinion on Public Policy* (Stanford: Hoover Press, Spring, 2000), p. 157.

[400] Beckman, David M. *Where Faith and Economics Meet* (Minneapolis: Augsburg Publishing House, 1981), p. 42.

[401] Wright, C., p. 9.

[402] Edwards, p. 137.

[403] Milnes, p. 305.

[404] Ibid., p. 238.

[405] Guthrie, p. 284.

[406] Bruce, *The Message of the New Testament,* p. 84.

[407] Goldingay, p. 56.

[408] Hagner, Hagner, Donald A. *New International Biblical Commentary: Hebrews* (Peabody, Massachusetts: Hendrickson Publishers, Inc., 1990), p. 180.

[409] Powell, p. 383.

[410] D'Souza, *The Virtue of Prosperity*, p. 37.

[411] Gilder, Wealth and Poverty, pp. 37,8.

[412] Guthrie, p. 375.

[413] Gasque, W. Ward, *Christianity Monday Through Friday* (Mercer Island, Washington: Mercer Island Presbyterian Church lecture series, January, 1999), lecture notes.

[414] Taylor, K. W. "The Role of Evangelism, Christian Values, and Christian Community," quoted in Schlossberg, Herbert. "Destroying Poverty without Destroying Poor People," in Schlossberg, H., Vinay, S. and Sider, R. ed. *Christianity and Economics in the Post-Cold War Era: The Oxford Declaration and Beyond.* (Grand Rapids, Michigan: William B. Eerdmans Publishing Company, 1994), p. 117.

[415] Hay, p. 158.

[416] Sirico, Robert A. *Toward a Free and Virtuous Society.* (Grand Rapids: Acton Institute, 1997) pp. 6,7.

[417] Hay, p. 158.

[418] Powell, pp. 345-9.

[419] Edwards, p. 200.

[420] Lacordaire, Henri Dominique. *God: Conference Delivered at Notre Dame in Paris* (New York: Scribner, 1870)

[421] Novak, *The Spirit of Democratic Capitalism,* p. 14.

[422] Novak, Michael. "In God We Trust," *Hoover Digest: Research and Opinion on Public Policy* (Stanford: Hoover Press, Spring, 2000), p. 162.

[423] Nash, p. 68.

[424] Kristol, p. 14.

[425] Heyne, *The Economic Way of Thinking, Ninth Edition,* pp. 390,1.

[426] Schall, p. 69.

[427] Sider, *Rich Christians in an Age of Hunger*, p. 94.

[428] John Paul II, p. 63.

[429] Beckman, pp. 77,8.

[430] Kristol, p. xi.

[431] Nash, p. 78.

[432] Green, pp. 82,117.

[433] Novak, *The Spirit of Democratic Capitalism,* p. 106.

[434] Stanley, pp. 2-4.

[435] Ostrom, Carol M. "Sudden wealth, hard questions" *The Seattle Times,* (Seattle: The Seattle Times Publishing Company, November 5, 2000), p. A11.

[436] Stanley, pp. 29, 30.

[437] Ibid., p. 112.

[438] D'Souza, *The Virtue of Prosperity,* p. 54.

[439] Gilder, *Recapturing the Spirit of Enterprise,* pp. 5,6.

[440] Gilder, *Wealth and Poverty,* p. 11.

[441] Novak, *The Fire of Invention: Civil Society and the Future of the Corporation,* pp. 40,1.

[442] Novak, *The Spirit of Democratic Capitalism,* p. 15.

[443] Ibid., p. 111.

[444] Kristol, p. 29.

[445] Gooden, Winston, E. "Confidence Under Pressure," *Faith in Leadership* (Banks, Robert and Powell, Kimberly S., ed.) (San Francisco: Jossey-Bass Publishers, 2000), p. 44.

[446] Ibid., pp. 46-51.

[447] Gilder, George, "The Faith of a Futurist," *The Wall Street Journal.* (New York: Dow Jones Publishing Company, January 1,2000), p. R28.

[448] Gill, David W. "No Integrity, No Trust; No Trust, No Business," *Ethix* (Bellevue, Washington: Institute for Business, Technology & Ethics, October, 2000), p. 3.

[449] Templeton, Sir John M. interviewed in "Ministries of Service in the Marketplace," *Religion & Liberty* (Grand Rapids: Acton Institute, November and December, 2000), pp. 1,2.

[450] D'Souza, *The Virtue of Prosperity,* p. 38.

[451] Ibid., p. 55.

[452] Novak, *The Spirit of Democratic Capitalism,* p. 93.

[453] D'Souza, *The Virtue of Prosperity,* p. 239.

[454] Gooden, pp. 50,1.

[455] Jervis, p. 150.

[456] Ibid., p. 107.

[457] Patzia, p. 77.

[458] Charette, lecture notes.

[459] Brown, p. 506.

[460] Patzia, p. 114.

[461] Wright, C., p. 259.

[462] Davids, p. 116.

[463] Murray, John. *Principles of Conduct: Aspects of Biblical Ethics.* (Grand Rapids: William B. Eerdmans Publishing Co., 1957), p. 92.

464 Guinness, Os. Lecture, Seattle, Washington: Discovery Institute, February 26, 2001.
465 Crosby, Cindy. "Engaging the Community," *The Life@Work Journal*. (Fayetteville, Arkansas: The Life@Work Company, January/February, 2000), p. 11.
466 Kristol, pp. 66,9.
467 Griffiths, p. 53.
468 U.S. Census Bureau, *Statistical Abstract of the United States: 1999* (119th edition) (Washington D.C., 1999), p. 555
469 Ibid., p. 560.
470 Ibid., p. 411.
471 Gilder, *Wealth and Poverty*, p. 12.
472 Novak, *The Fire of Invention: Civil Society and the Future of the Corporation*, p. 14.
473 Heyne, *The Economic Way of Thinking, Ninth Edition*, p. 302.
474 D'Souza, *The Virtue of Prosperity*, p. 230.
475 "Movin' On Up," *The Wall Street Journal* (New York: Dow Jones and Company, August 17, 2000), p. A22.
476 Ibid., p. 695.
477 Ibid., p. 464.
478 U.S. Census Bureau, *Statistical Abstract of the United States: 1999* (119th edition) (Washington D.C., 1999), pp. 644,6,7.
479 Ibid., pp. 324, 349 and 459.
480 "Murder rate, serious crime plunge in U.S." *The Seattle Times* (Seattle: The Seattle Times Publishing Company, November 22, 1999), p. A1.
481 Gorski, Fr. Isidore, "Ethical Reflections on the Economic Crisis," *Theology, Third World Development and Economic Justice,* ed. Walter Block and Donald Shaw (Vancouver, B.C: The Fraser Institute, 1985), p. 80.
482 Nasar, Sylvia and Mitchell, Kirsten B. "Rising tide lifts young black men from joblessness," *The Seattle Times* (Seattle: The Seattle Times Publishing Company, May 23, 1999), p. A14.
483 Simon, p. 2.
484 Schall, p. 44.
485 Powell, p. 306.
486 D'Souza, *The Virtue of Prosperity*, p. 229.
487 Stone, p. 39.
488 Smith, p. 322.
489 Sider, "Is There a Biblical Definition of Economic Justice?" conference notes.
490 Sproul, "The Law and the 'Profits," *Is Capitalism Morally Bankrupt?* lecture series. Sparks, John A. ed. (Grove City, Pennsylvania: Grove City

College, June, 2000), p. 14.

[491] Fuller, R.H. and Rice, B.K., *Christianity and the Affluent Society* (Grand Rapids: William B. Eerdmans Publishing Co., 1967), p. 33.

[492] Wheeler, p. 129.

[493] Williams, Preston N. "Calvinism, Racism, and Economic Institutions," in Stivers, p. 50.

[494] Calvin, John. *Second Epistle of Paul the Apostle to the Corinthians* (Grand Rapids: Eerdmans Pub. Co., 1964) quoted in Little, David. "Economic Justice and the Grounds for a Theory of Progressive Taxation in Calvin's Thought," in Stivers, p. 66.

[495] Schall, p. 66.

[496] Stackhouse, John. "Money and the Church." (paper presented at the *Christian in the Marketplace* annual conference, Regent College, Vancouver, Canada, February 10, 2001.), conference notes.

[497] Berger, Peter. "Underdevelopment Revisited," *Commentary* (July 1984), pp. 41,3 quoted in Nash, Ronald H. *Poverty and Wealth: The Christian Debate Over Capitalism* (Westchester, Illinois: Crossway Books, 1986), p. 87.

[498] Templeton, Sir John quoted in Hall, Elizabeth. "Competition Seen As Spur to Expansion of Prosperity, Ethics, and Knowledge," *Progress in Theology* (Radnor, Pennsylvania: John Templeton Foundation, August, 2000), p. 1.

[499] Novak, *The Spirit of Democratic Capitalism*, pp. 26,7.

[500] Murray, p. 92.

[501] LaSor, p. 245.

[502] Beckman, p. 17.

[503] D'Souza, *The Virtue of Prosperity*, p. 75.

[504] U.S. Census Bureau, *Statistical Abstract of the United States: 1999* (119th edition) (Washington D.C., 1999), p. 485.

[505] Beckman, p. 82.

[506] Novak, *The Spirit of Democratic Capitalism*, p. 109.

[507] Karlgaard, Rich, "Room at the Bottom," *Forbes* (New York: Forbes, Inc, December 11, 2000), p. 55.

[508] Sider, p. 232.

[509] Nash, p. 68.

[510] Beckman, p. 72.

[511] Powell, p. 370.

[512] Galbraith, John Kenneth, *American Capitalism: The Concept of Countervailing Power.*

[513] Novak, *The Spirit of Democratic Capitalism*, p. 33.

[514] Novak, Michael. "A Theology of the Corporation," *The Corporation: A Theological Inquiry*, ed. Novak, Michael and Cooper, John W. (Washington D.C.: American Enterprise Institute for Public Policy Research,

1981), p. 220.
[515] Schlossberg, Vinay and Sider, p. 27.
[516] U.S. Census Bureau, *Statistical Abstract of the United States: 1999* (119th edition) (Washington D.C., 1999), p. 886.
[517] Ibid., p. 684.
[518] Griffiths, p. 23.
[519] *1999 Annual Environment, Health and Safety Report*, Weyerhaeuser Company (Federal Way, Washington, 2000), p.3.
[520] Phillips, Cassie "Identifying Problems and Challenges Associated with Private Forest Lands," *Washington Private Forest Forum* (Federal Way, Washington: Weyerhaeuser Company, March 29, 2000), p. 2.
[521] Kwong, Jo. "Suburban Sprawl and Human Ecology," *Religion & Liberty* (Grand Rapids: Acton Institute, March and April, 1999), p. 9.
[522] U.S. Census Bureau, *Statistical Abstract of the United States: 1999* (119th edition) (Washington D.C., 1999), p. 678.
[523] Novak, *The Spirit of Democratic Capitalism,* p. 301.
[524] Sider, *Rich Christians in an Age of Hunger*, p. 251.
[525] Glasser, Susan B. "Cash-poor Russia lobbies for nuclear waste," *The Seattle Times,* (Seattle: Seattle Times Publishing Company, March 18, 2001), p. A18.
[526] Census Bureau, *Statistical Abstract of the United States: 1999* (119th edition) (Washington D.C., 1999), p. 251.
[527] *1999 Annual Environment, Health and Safety Report*, Weyerhaeuser Company (Federal Way, Washington, 2000), p. 20.
[528] *1999 Annual Report*, Weyerhaeuser Company (Federal Way, Washington, 2000), pp. 40,46.
[529] Huber, Peter W. "No, the Sky Is *Not* Falling," *Hoover Digest: Research and Opinion on Public Policy* (Stanford: Hoover Press, Winter, 2001), pp. 91,2.
[530] Sider, *Rich Christians in an Age of Hunger*, p. 16.
[531] Beckman, p. 73.
[532] Smith, pp. 385, 91.
[533] Gilder, *Wealth and Poverty*, p. 34.
[534] Guinness, p. 4.
[535] Novak, "A Theology of the Corporation," p. 208.
[536] Novak, *The Fire of Invention: Civil Society and the Future of the Corporation*, p. 40.
[537] Thatcher, Margaret. "Speech to the General Assembly of the Church of Scotland," 1988 quoted in Schall, p. 175.
[538] U.S. Census Bureau, *Statistical Abstract of the United States: 1999* (119th edition) (Washington D.C., 1999), p. 874.
[539] Sowell, p. 56.

[540] Greenfeld, p. 49.

[541] U.S. Census Bureau, *Statistical Abstract of the United States: 1999* (119th edition) (Washington D.C., 1999), p. 876.

[542] D'Souza, Dinesh. "The Virtue of Prosperity," *Hoover Digest: Research and Opinion on Public Policy* (Stanford: Hoover Press, Winter, 2001), p. 114.

[543] Henderson, David R. "Capitalist Culture," *Hoover Digest: Research and Opinion on Public Policy* (Stanford: Hoover Press, Fall, 1999), p. 17.

[544] Novak, "A Theology of the Corporation," p. 220.

[545] Schall, p. 118.

[546] D'Souza, *The Virtue of Prosperity,* pp. 232,242.

[547] Scholl, p. 140.

[548] Wright, C., p. 11.

[549] LaSor, p. 47.

[550] Patzia, p. 234.

[551] Hawthorne, p. 23.

[552] Ibid., p. 173.

[553] Ibid., p. 249.

[554] Ibid., p. 326.

[555] Ibid., p. 708.

[556] Gilder, George. *Wealth and Poverty,* p. 9.

[557] Heyne, p. 140.

[558] LaSor, p. 383.

[559] Sider, *Rich Christians in an Age of Hunger,* pp. 140,1.

[560] Bauer, P.T., "Western Guilt and Third World Poverty," *The Corporation: A Theological Inquiry,* ed. Novak, Michael and Cooper, John W. (Washington D.C.: American Enterprise Institute for Public Policy Research, 1981), p. 105.

[561] Scully, William L. "The Brandt Commission: Deluding the Third Word," *The Heritage Foundation Backgrounder,* No. 182, April 30, 1982, p. 16 quoted in Nash, Ronald H. *Poverty and Wealth: The Christian Debate Over Capitalism* (Westchester, Illinois: Crossway Books, 1986), p. 109.

[562] Nash, pp. 109,98.

[563] Schall, pp. 15,68.

[564] Diamond, Larry. "Debt for Democracy," *Hoover Digest: Research and Opinion on Public Policy* (Stanford: Hoover Press, Winter, 2001), p. 128.

[565] Strauss, Robert L. "My Road To Nowhere," *Stanford* (Stanford, California: Stanford University Alumni Association, May/June, 2000), pp. 76-79.

[566] Simon, p. 2.

567 Hay, p. 157.

568 Bauer, p. 106.

569 Ibid., p. 111.

570 Ibid., pp. 113,4.

571 Schall, p. 16.

572 Bauer, p. 114.

573 Ibid., p. 117.

574 Novak, *The Spirit of Democratic Capitalism,* p. 227.

575 Ibid., p. 228.

576 Lenzner and Kellner, p. 166.

577 Erisman, Albert E. "20/20 Vision in a Myopic World," *Ethix*, interview of Richard E. Stearns. (Bellevue, Washington: Institute for Business, Technology & Ethics, August, 2000), pp. 7,8.

578 Jones, Reginald H. "The Transnational Enterprise and World Economic Development," *The Corporation: A Theological Inquiry,* ed. Novak, Michael and Cooper, John W. (Washington D.C.: American Enterprise Institute for Public Policy Research, 1981), pp. 132-8.

579 Ibid., pp. 131-8.

580 Quinlivan, Gary M. "Multinational Corporations: Myths and Facts," *Religion & Liberty* (Grand Rapids: Acton Institute, November and December, 2000), pp. 8-10.

581 Beckman, p. 19.

582 D'Souza, *The Virtue of Prosperity,* p. 104.

583 Gibson, pp. 150,1.

584 Kristol, pp. 40-3.

585 Schultz, Theodore. "The Economics of Being Poor," *Journal of Political Economy*, #4 (1980), p.645, quoted in Schall, James V. *Religion, Wealth and Poverty* (Vancouver, Canada: The Fraser Institute, 1990), p. 11.

586 Schall, p. 51.

587 Morais, Richard D., "Bullterrier Banking," *Forbes* (New York: Forbes, Inc, July 24, 2000), p. 68.

588 Zakaria, p. 126.

589 Novak, p. 233, also referencing John Kenneth Galbraith, "the Defense of the Multinational Company," Harvard Business Review, 56 (March-April 1978), pp. 83-93.

590 Remenyi, Joe. *Where Credit is Due* (London: Intermediate Technology, 1991) quoted in Remenyi, Joe and Taylor, Bill. "Credit-Based Income Generation for the Poor," in Schlossberg, H., Vinay, S. and Sider, R. ed. *Christianity and Economics in the Post-Cold War Era: The Oxford Declaration and Beyond.* (Grand Rapids, Michigan: William B. Eerdmans Publishing Company, 1994), p. 48.

591 Remenyi, Joe and Taylor, Bill. "Credit-Based Income Generation for the Poor," in Schlossberg, H., Vinay, S. and Sider, R. ed. *Christianity and Economics in the Post-Cold War Era: The Oxford Declaration and Beyond.* (Grand Rapids, Michigan: William B. Eerdmans Publishing Company, 1994), pp. 51-4.
592 Hawthorne, p. 945.
593 Kristol, p. 257.
594 Hazlitt, Henry. *The Foundations of Morality* (New York: Von Nostrand, 1964), p. 325 quoted in Nash, Ronald H. *Poverty and Wealth: The Christian Debate Over Capitalism* (Westchester, Illinois: Crossway Books, 1986), p. 76.
595 Novak, *The Spirit of Democratic Capitalism*, p. 226.
596 Ibid., p. 339.
597 Hardy, p. 4.
598 D'Souza, *The Virtue of Prosperity*, p. 126.
599 Murchland, Bernard, "The Socialist Critique of the Corporation," *The Corporation: A Theological Inquiry*, ed. Novak, Michael and Cooper, John W. (Washington D.C.: American Enterprise Institute for Public Policy Research, 1981), pp. 65,6.
600 Griffiths, p. 54.
601 John Paul II, pp. 62,3.
602 McKim, p. 49.
603 Burton, lecture outline.
604 McKim, p. 174.
605 Bieler, Andre. *Social Humanism of Calvin* (Richmond, Virginia: John Knox Press, 1964) quoted in Little, David. "Economic Justice and the Grounds for a Theory of Progressive Taxation in Calvin's Thought," in Stivers, p. 63.
606 Guthrie, p. 161.
607 Rodgers, T. J. quoted in D'Souza, Dinesh. "The Virtue of Prosperity," *Hoover Digest: Research and Opinion on Public Policy* (Stanford: Hoover Press, Winter, 2001), p. 116.
608 D'Souza, *The Virtue of Prosperity*, p. 131.
609 Schall, p. 63.
610 Gilder, *Wealth and Poverty*, pp. 280-2.
611 Novak, *The Spirit of Democratic Capitalism*, p. 151.
612 Novak, *The Fire of Invention: Civil Society and the Future of the Corporation*, p. 45.
613 Boskin, Michael J. "Capitalism and Its Discontents," *Hoover Digest: Research and Opinion on Public Policy* (Stanford: Hoover Press, Fall, 1999), p. 24.
614 Montgomery, Lori. "After Communism's Fall," *The Seattle Times*

(Seattle: Seattle Times Publishing Company, November 8, 1999), p. A3.

615 Murphy, Cait, "The Next Revolution," *Fortune* (New York: Time, Inc., June 12, 2000), p. 96.

616 Doebele, Justin. "Chinese Capitalism Gets a Face," *Forbes*. (New York: Forbes, Inc., November 29, 1999), p. 175.

617 Heilbroner, Robert. "Was the Right Right All Along?" *Harper's*, January, 1991, p. 18 quoted in Novak, Michael, *The Fire of Invention: Civil Society and the Future of the Corporation*. (Lanham, Maryland: Rowman & Littlefield Publishers, Inc., 1997), p. 23.

618 Schall, p. 143.

619 Rosenberg and Birdzell, p. 303.

620 Gilder, *Recapturing the Spirit of Enterprise*, pp. 308,9.

621 Gilder, *Wealth and Poverty*, p. 30.

622 Gilder, "The Soul of Silicon," pp. 114-124.

623 D'Souza, *The Virtue of Prosperity*, pp. 186,7.

624 Griffiths, p. 20.

625 Schlossberg, Herbert. "Destroying Poverty without Destroying Poor People," in Schlossberg, H., Vinay, S. and Sider, R. ed. *Christianity and Economics in the Post-Cold War Era: The Oxford Declaration and Beyond*. (Grand Rapids, Michigan: William B. Eerdmans Publishing Company, 1994), p. 116.

626 Nash, p. 53.

627 Ibid., p. 121.

628 Novak, Michael. *Freedom with Justice* (San Francisco: Harper and Row, 1984), p. 192 quoted in Nash, Ronald H. *Poverty and Wealth: The Christian Debate Over Capitalism* (Westchester, Illinois: Crossway Books, 1986), p. 108.

629 Beckman, p. 105.

630 de Soto, Hernando. *The Mystery of Capital: Why Capitalism Triumphs in the West and Fail Everywhere Else* (New York: Basic Books, 2000), p. 1.

631 Byker, p. 1.

632 Davids, p. 113.

633 Guthrie, p. 149.

634 Meilaender, Gilbert C. "To Be Drawn Out of Ourselves Toward God," *Religion and Liberty* (Grand Rapids: Acton Institute, January and February, 2001), p. 2.

635 Guthrie, pp. 139,40.

636 Berman, Phyllis. "Throwing away the book," *Forbes* (New York: Forbes, Inc., November, 2, 1998), p. 177.

637 John Paul, II, pp. 66,7.

638 Guthrie, p. 162.

[639] Ibid., p. 267.

[640] Ibid., p. 303.

[641] Albom, Mitch.. *Tuesdays With Morrie: An Old Man, a Young Man and Life's Greatest Lesson.* (New York: Doubleday, 1997).

[642] Guthrie., p. 302.

[643] Milne, p. 154.

[644] Gasque, W. Ward "Religion, Egalitarianism and Economic Justice," p. 3.

[645] Calvin, John. *Second Epistle of Paul the Apostle to the Corinthians* (Grand Rapids: Eerdmans Pub. Co., 1964) quoted in Little, David. "Economic Justice and the Grounds for a Theory of Progressive Taxation in Calvin's Thought," in Stivers, p. 68.

[646] Thomas, p. 140.

[647] Ibid., p. 142.

[648] Gill, pp. 139,42.

[649] Hillyer, Norman. *New International Biblical Commentary: 1 and 2 Peter, Jude* (Peabody, Massachusetts: Hendrickson Publishers, Inc., 1992), p. 145.

[650] Erasmus, *Enchiridion*, 1503, quoted in Pelikan, p. 166.

[651] Stevens, R. Paul. "Mission field or Mission?" *Vocati* (Vancouver, Canada: Regent College Foundation, December, 2000), p. 1.

[652] Sirico, "Capitalism and Morality," p. 9.

[653] Wall, p. 86.

[654] Rowland, Randy, *Christian Ministry 101, Koinos Program,* Seattle: Pacific Association for Theological Studies, Spring 2000, lecture notes.

[655] Ibid.

[656] Ibid.

[657] *Webster's New World Dictionary* (New York: Simon and Schuster, Inc.) 1900.

[658] Hurtado, p. 29.

[659] Mounce, p. 65.

[660] Sider, pp. 104,7.

[661] Thomas, p. 11.

[662] Ibid., p.18.

[663] Griffiths, p. 122.

[664] Kristol, p. 26.

[665] Nash, pp. 9,10,198.

[666] Powell, p. 3.

[667] Beckman, p. 71.

[668] Sadowsky, Fr. James, "Religion, Egalitarianism and Economic Justice," *Theology, Third World Development and Economic Justice,* ed. Walter Block and Donald Shaw (Vancouver, B.C: The Fraser Institute,

1985), pp. 9,10.

[669] D'Souza, *The Virtue of Prosperity,* pp. 89, 95.

[670] Gilder, George. "Zero-Sum Folly, From Kyoto to Kosovo," *The Wall Street Journal* (New York: Dow Jones Publishing Company, May 6, 1999).

[671] D'Souza, *The Virtue of Prosperity,* p. 181.

[672] Ibid., p. 240.

[673] Gilder, *Wealth and Poverty,* p. 9.

[674] Novak, *The Spirit of Democratic Capitalism,* pp. 57,239,241.

[675] U.S. Catholic Conference, "First Draft of the U.S. Bishops' Pastoral Letter on Catholic Social Teaching and the U.S. Economy," *Origins,* National Catholic Documentary Service, 15 November 1984, Vol. 14, no. 22/23, pp. 52ff, quoted in Stivers, p. 101.

[676] Alexander, p. 102.

[677] Ibid., p. 102.

[678] Jones, pp. 129-30.

[679] Rosenberg and Birdzell, p. 304.

[680] Ibid., p. 334.

[681] Hay, p. 24.

[682] Beckman, p. 49.

[683] Rowland, lecture notes.

[684] Gasque, W. lecture notes.

[685] Bauer, P.T. *Reality and Rhetoric: Studies in the Economics of Development* (Cambridge: Harvard University Press, 1984), p. 89 quoted in Schall, p. 128.

[686] Gilder, "The Soul of Silicon," p. 124.

[687] Schall, pp. 23,4.

[688] Wall, p. 173.

[689] Bruce, *The Message of the New Testament,* p. 98.

[690] Gasque, lecture notes.

[691] Novak, *The Spirit of Democratic Capitalism,* p. 13.

[692] Wilson, James Q. "Capitalism Cuts Crime," *The Wall Street Journal* (New York: Dow Jones Publishing Company, August 17, 2000), p. A17.

[693] Johnson, Luke T. *Sharing Possessions* (Philadelphia: Fortress Press, 1981), p. 115 quoted in Stivers, p. 7.

[694] Wheeler, p. 134.

[695] Schall, pp. 120,1.

[696] *Book of Order: The Constitution of the Presbyterian Church (U.S.A.) Part II* (Louisville, Kentucky: The Office of the General Assembly, Presbyterian Church (U.S.A.), 1998), G-2.0400—G-2.0500.

[697] Jean Cardinal Villot, "The Christian Practice of Economics," 1978, quoted in Schall, p. 129.

[698] Schall, p. 129.

[699] Alexander, p. 71.

[700] Guthrie, p. 375.

[701] Wall, pp. 217-19.

[702] Sirico, Robert A. *Acton Notes* (Grand Rapids: Acton Institute, December, 2000), p. 1.

[703] Schall, p. 112.

[704] Achtemeier, p. 352.

[705] Murphy and Huwiler, p. 54.

[706] LaSor, pp. 500,1.

[707] Murphy and Huwiler, pp. 159,165.

[708] LaSor, p. 509.

[709] Bruce, *The Message of the New Testament,* p. 67.

[710] Griffiths, pp. 44,5.

[711] Edwards, p. 311.

[712] Danker, p. 117.

[713] Bruce, *New International Biblical Commentary: Philippians,* pp. 112-5.

[714] Griffiths, pp. 61,2.

[715] Nash, p. 199.

[716] Stott, John R. W., *Christian Basics,* quoted in "Reflections: On the occasion of John R.W. Stott's 80th birthday," *Christianity Today,* April 2, 2001, p. 64.

Appendices

Appendix A

"THE ECONOMIST'S PSALM" — PSALM 104

1   Praise the LORD, O my soul.

O LORD my God, you are very great:
    you are clothed with splendor and majesty.
2   He wraps himself in light as with a garment;
    he stretches out the heavens like a tent
3   and lays the beams of his upper chambers on their
    waters.
    He makes the clouds his chariot
    and rides on the wings of the wind.
4   He makes winds his messengers,
    flames of fire his servants.

5   He set the earth on its foundations;
    it can never be moved.
6   You covered it with the deep as with a garment;
    the waters stood above the mountains.
7   But at your rebuke the waters fled,
    at the sound of your thunder they took to flight;
8   they flowed over the mountains,
    they went down into the valleys,
    to the place you assigned for them.
9   You set a boundary they cannot cross;
    never again will they cover the earth.

10 He makes springs pour water into the ravines;
    it flows between the mountains.
11 They give water to all the beasts of the field;
    the wild donkeys quench their thirst.
12 The birds of the air nest by the waters;
    they sing among the branches.

13 He waters the mountains from his upper chambers;
    the earth is satisfied by the fruit of his work.
14 He makes grass grow for the cattle,
    and plants for man to cultivate –
    bringing forth food from the earth:
15 wine that gladdens the heart of man,
    oil to make his face shine,
    and bread that sustains his heart.
16 The trees of the LORD are well watered,
    the cedars of Lebanon that he planted.
17 There the birds make their nests;
    the stork has its home in the pine trees.
18 The high mountains belong to the wild goats;
    the crags are a refuge for the coneys.
19 The moon marks off the seasons,
    and the sun knows when to go down.
20 You bring darkness, it becomes night,
    and all the beasts of the forest prowl.
21 The lions roar for their prey
    and seek their food from God.
22 The sun rises, and they steal away;
    they return and lie down in their dens.
23 Then man goes out to his work,
    to his labor until evening.

24 How many are your works, O LORD!
    In wisdom you made them all;
    the earth is full of your creatures.
25 There is the sea, vast and spacious,
    teeming with creatures beyond number —
    living things both large and small.
26 There the ships go to and for,
    and the leviathan, which you formed to frolic there.

27 These all look to you
    to give them their food at the proper time.
28 When you give it to them
    they gather it up;
    when you open your hand,

they are satisfied with good things.
29 When you hide your face,
        they are terrified;
        when you take away their breath,
        they die and return to the dust.
30 When you send your Spirit,
        they are created,
        and you renew the face of the earth.

31 May the glory of the LORD endure forever;
        may the LORD rejoice in his works —
32 he who looks at the earth, and it trembles,
        who touches the mountains, and they smoke.

33 I will sing to the LORD all my life;
        I will sing praise to my God as long as I live.
34 May my meditation be pleasing to him,
        as I rejoice in the LORD.
35 But may sinners vanish from the earth
        and the wicked be no more.

Praise the LORD, O My Soul.
Praise the LORD.

Appendix B

HOUSING COSTS AND THE LAW OF SUPPLY AND DEMAND

"Affordable Housing" is a current major public issue in almost every community across America. This is because in those few communities not experiencing rapid growth income levels is a concern. In those many communities experiencing strong growth shrinking land supply (the major component of the cost of a residence) and soaring demand are exacerbated by relatively inelastic supply and demand curves. The result has been skyrocketing prices for homes.

Because the quantity of land is somewhat fixed, regardless of its price, the supply curve for land is described as relatively inelastic. That is, for any given change in price, the quantity supplied does not change much. A relatively elastic supply curve is one that for any given change in price, the quantity supplied changes greatly. These supply curves are indicated below.

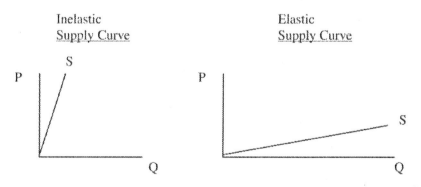

Housing is a necessity, that is, regardless of price, everyone has to live somewhere. Furthermore, everyone needs only one house. Accordingly, the demand curve for residential land, similar to the supply curve, is relatively inelastic. That is, because the quantity of residential land demanded is somewhat fixed, regardless of its price, the demand curve for land is described as relatively inelastic. For any given change in price, the quantity demanded does not change much. To make the point further by contrast, the demand curve for products which are not necessities, tickets to athletic events, for example, is relatively elastic. That is, for any given change in price, the quantity demanded changes greatly. These demand curves are indicated below.

Inelastic
Demand Curve

Elastic
Demand Curve

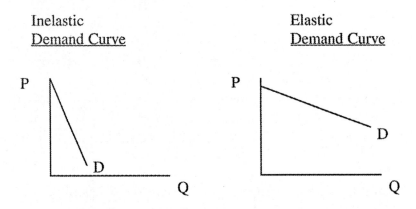

The dramatic effect of a city or county constraining the supply of land available for residential development accompanied by strong population growth and rising wealth levels experienced in most of the centers of high technology in the United States today is readily observed in the chart on the following page.

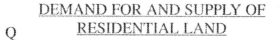

DEMAND FOR AND SUPPLY OF
RESIDENTIAL LAND

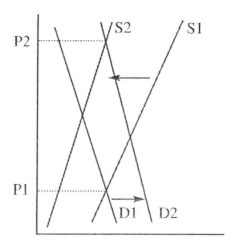

To may of us preserving greenery and the benefits of economic prosperity are both wonderful things, but they do have a dramatic cost, as the price of residential land soars from P1 to P2, commensurately pushing up the cost of housing.

These graphs explain why in Seattle, Washington during the twenty years from 1980 to 2000 when general consumer prices rose 42% the average price of a home more than tripled.

Lest an incomplete conclusion be drawn that such increases in the price of homes has a universally adverse result, let me note, for completeness in this discussion, that the soaring housing prices in Seattle's urban areas has been the major factor enabling many minorities living in the central core to now be able to sell their homes and afford to move out to the suburbs if that is their desire. Additionally, over the past ten years the rise in incomes in the greater Seattle area have exceeded the rise in annual housing costs, making home buying in this area more affordable to more people than ten years ago. Switching from time comparisons to geographic comparisons, while housing prices in Seattle exceed the national average and many other metropolitan areas, incomes also exceed by a more than commensurate amount. Accordingly, the dramatic headlines bemoaning Seattle's high housing costs deliver a false message.

Appendix C

MINIMUM WAGE LAWS AND THE LAW OF SUPPLY AND DEMAND

Another example of how public policy, regardless of how well-intended, cannot overcome the law of supply and demand is the effect of minimum wage laws. Such legislation occurs when politicians feel the prevailing wage of certain unskilled or entry level workers is simply "too low."

Assume the following demand and supply for such workers and their natural market wage is "W," indicated on the left-hand graph below. Congress or the legislature passes a law that says the minimum wage is now decreed to be "M," indicated in the right-hand graph below. Those employers not able to employ workers at the higher rate with not do so, and total employment will be at the lower level, Q2. The workers represented by Q1—Q2 will be out of work.

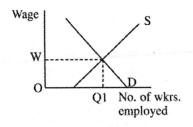 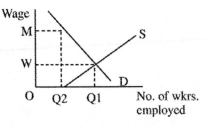

Again, this is not simply some theoretical construct. This is exactly what occurs in the real world as confirmed by many empirical studies. The opportunity cost of some workers (OQ2) earning higher wages is the unemployment of other workers (Q2Q1). That might be exactly in accord with what any given society might want to do, but too often those promulgating the minimum wage laws are masquerading as the champion of the lower rung workers. What about the lowest rung workers that they have put out of work? And, of course, regretfully, often the lower rung workers are those just entering the work force, the less experienced, less skilled, and some are minorities. Opportunities for on the job training diminish. Further, there are also considerable additional social costs: unemployment benefit payments to the unemployed workers and the costs associated with increased crime, drug abuse and other social problems associated with unemployment.

I am not arguing against minimum wage laws. I am arguing against the intellectual dishonesty of the "spin" given them by those wanting to appear as the champion of the downtrodden, but preying on the ignorant. The people who bear the burden of the minimum wage laws are the most marginal workers, those ending up unemployed.

Appendix D

"THE CAPITALIST'S PSALM" — PSALM 49

1 Hear this, all you peoples;
    listen, all who live in this world,
2 both low and high,
    rich and poor alike;
3 My mouth will speak words of wisdom;
    the utterance from my heart will give
    understanding.
4 I will turn my ear to a proverb;
    with the harp I will expound my riddle:

5 Why should I fear when evil days come,
    when wicked deceivers surround me —
6 those who trust in their wealth
    and boast of their great riches?
7 No man can redeem the life of another
    or give to God a ransom for him —
8 the ransom for a life is costly
    no payment is ever enough —
9 that he should live on forever
    and not see decay.

10 For all can see that wise men die;
    the foolish and the senseless alike perish
    and leave their wealth to others.
11 Their tombs will remain their houses forever,
    their dwellings for endless generations,
    though they had named lands after themselves.

12 But man, despite his riches, does not endure;
    he is like the beasts that perish.
13 This is the fate of those who trust in themselves,

and of their followers, who approve their sayings.
14 Like sheep they are destined for the grave,
     and death will feed on them.
   The upright will rule over them in the morning;
     their forms will decay in the grave,
     far from their princely mansions.
15 But God will redeem my life from the grave;
     he will surely take me to himself.

16 Do not be overawed when a man grows rich,
     when the splendor of his house increases;
17 for he will take nothing with him when he dies,
     his splendor will not descend with him.
18 Though while he lived he counted himself blessed —
     and men praise you when you prosper —
19 he will join the generation of his fathers,
     who will never see the light of life.

20 A man who has riches without understanding
     is like the beasts that perish.

Appendix E

THE LAWS AND THEIR RELATIONSHIP TO ECONOMICS

Economics Application:

THE TEN COMMANDMENTS (Ex. 20:3-17; Dt. 5:6-21)

"You shall have no other gods before me."	Not wealth nor power nor prestige.
"You shall not make for yourself an idol."	Not materialism nor position.
"You shall not misuse the name of the LORD you God."	Oaths need not be necessary.
"Remember the Sabbath day by keeping it holy."	No paid work on Sabbath; devote to God.
"Honor your father and your mother."	All relationships; e.g., employer/employee.
"You shall not murder."	Do not kill the spirit of any human.
"You shall not commit adultery."	Infidelity / disloyalty / betrayal.
"You shall not steal."	Dishonesty / mistrust / fraud.
"You shall not give false testimony."	Deception / misleading / double dealing.
"You shall not covet."	Greed; "have not's" vs. "have's"

SELECTED LAWS FROM THE "BOOK OF THE COVENANT"
(Ex. 20:23-23:33)

"If you buy a Hebrew servant, he is to serve you for six years. But in the seventh year, he shall go free,"

Similar concept to bankruptcy laws, giving one a clean, fresh start.

"If men quarrel…., must pay the injured man for loss of his time."

Notion of "opportunity cost."

"If ox or donkey falls into…a pit, …must pay."

Animals have economic role, value.

"If a man steals ox or sheep, must pay back…"

Animals have economic role, value.

"If a man's livestock graze in another man's field, he must make restitution from own field or vineyard."

Private property; land has economic role, therefore value.

"If silver or goods …are stolen, …pay back double."

Economic value.

"Illegal possession of animals, clothing or other,…pay back double."

Economic value.

"If you lend money to one… *who is needy*, …charge him no interest." (my italics)

Generosity should dominate; Charging interest to non-needy is acceptable.

"Do not hold back offerings from granaries or vats."

Tithing; generosity.

"Do not spread false reports."

Commercial relations require honesty/trust.

"Do not deny justice to your people."

Poverty regarded as poor unfavorable.

SELECTED LAWS FROM THE HOLINESS CODE (Lv. 17-26)

"Do not turn to idols…"

Not materialism nor position.

"Do not steal…, lie. Do not deceive one another."

Dishonesty, mistrust.

"Do not defraud your neighbor."

Fraud.

"Do not hold back the wages of a hired man overnight."

Forthright treatment of employees.

"Do not show partiality to the poor or favoritism to the great."

The market is neutral; offer the same to all.

"Do not seek revenge or bear a grudge."

No place for vengeance in business dealings.

"Do not use dishonest standards when measuring."

Fraud.

"The seventh day is a Sabbath of rest. Do no work."

No commercial transactions or activity.

"In this Year of Jubilee everyone is to return to his own property."

Similar concept to bankruptcy laws, giving one a clean, fresh start.

"If one of your countrymen becomes poor,…help him."

Generosity; poverty regarded as unfavorable.

SELECTED LAWS OF MOSES JUST PRIOR TO ENTERING THE PROMISED LAND (Dt. 5—25)

The Ten Commandments (see p. 498)

"Love the LORD you God with all your heart and with all your soul and with all your strength."

Tokenism is insufficient; substantial resources are to be devoted to generosity.

"Do not follow their gods, the gods of the peoples around you."

Not materialism nor position.

"Do what is right and good."

Beyond refraining from not doing wrong and bad; pro-actively pursue goodness.

"At the end of every seven years, ...cancel debts."	Similar concept to bankruptcy laws, giving one a clean, fresh start.
"...in the seventh year let a fellow Hebrew servant go free..."	Similar concept to bankruptcy laws, giving one a clean, fresh start.
"Do not charge your brother interest,...You may charge a foreigner interest,..."	Implies lending is acceptable and concept of interest is valid.
"Do not take a pair of millstones... as security."	Implies lending and collateral acceptable.
"Do not take advantage of a hired man is poor..." pay him his wages each day before sunset."	Forthright treatment of employees.
"When men have a dispute... take it to court."	Quick resolution; third party opinions.
"You must have accurate and honest weights and measures..."	Fraud is unacceptable.

Appendix F

WEALTH, PROPERTY AND COMMERCIAL TRANSACTIONS IN PROVERBS

Wealth is not the end. God is the end.

"Blessed is the man who finds wisdom, the man who gains understanding, for she is more profitable than silver and yields better returns than gold. She is more precious than rubies;" (Prv. 3:13-15)

"My fruit is better than fine gold; what I yield surpasses choice silver." (Prv. 8:19)

"Wealth is worthless in the day of wrath, but righteousness delivers from death." (Prv. 11:4)

"Whoever trusts in riches will fall, but the righteous will thrive like a green leaf." (Prv. 11:28)

"A greedy man brings trouble to his family," (Prv. 15:27)

"How much better to get wisdom than gold, to choose understanding rather than silver." (Prv. 16:16) "Of what use is money in the hand of a fool, since he has no desire to get wisdom?" (Prv. 17:16)

"Gold there is, and rubies in abundance, but lips that speak knowledge are a rare jewel." (Prv. 20:15)

"He who loves pleasure will become poor; whoever loves wine and oil will never be rich." (Prv. 21:17) "A good name is more desirable than... riches; to be esteemed is better than silver and gold." (Prv. 22:1)

"Do not wear yourself out to get rich;.... Cast but a glance at riches, and they are gone," (Prv. 23:4,5) "Do not join those who drink too much wine or gorge themselves on meat, for drunkards and gluttons become poor, and drowsiness clothes them in rags." (Prv. 23:20,21)

"Better a poor man whose walk is blameless than a rich man whose ways are perverse." (Prv. 28:6)

"A faithful man will be richly blessed, but one eager to get rich will not go unpunished." (Prv. 28:20)

"A greedy man stirs up dissension, but he who trusts in the LORD will prosper." (Prv. 28:24)

"The poor man and the oppressor have this in common: the LORD gives sight to the eyes of both." (Prv. 29:13)

God is the ultimate creator of all property, worldly possession, wealth, humanity.

"By wisdom the LORD laid the earth's foundations, by understanding he set the heavens in place: by his knowledge the deeps were divided, and the clouds let drop the dew." (Prv. 3:19)

"The LORD brought me forth as the first of his works, before his deeds of old; I was appointed from eternity, from the beginning, before the world began...., I was given birth, before he made the earth..... I was there when he set the heavens in place, when he marked out the horizon...., when he established the clouds above.... when he gave the sea its boundary...., and when he marked out the foundations of the earth.... I was filled with delight...., rejoicing in his whole world." (Prv. 8:22-31)

Because God is the creator of all, good stewardship is humans' responsibility.

"The lazy man does not roast his game, but the diligent man prizes his possessions." (Prv. 12:27)

"In the house of the wise are stores of choice food and oil, but a foolish man devours all he has." (Prv. 21:20)

"If you find honey, eat just enough –" (Prv. 25:16)

"Be sure you know the condition of your flocks, give careful attention to your herds; for riches do not endure forever, and a crown is not secure for all generations." (Prv. 27:23,24)

One should be prudent in commercial affairs and all business judgments.

"He who puts up security for another will surely suffer, but whoever refuses to strike hands in pledge is safe." (Prv. 11:15)

"A man lacking in judgment strikes hands in pledge and puts up security for his neighbor." (Prv. 17:18)

"Take the garment of one who puts up security for a stranger;..." (Prv. 20:16)

"... the borrower is servant to the lender." (Prv. 22:7)

"Like an archer who wounds at random is he who hires a fool or any passer-by." (Prv. 26:10)

<u>Material possessions and wealth are regarded as legitimate in Scripture.</u>

"keep my commandments..., for they will prolong your life and bring you prosperity." (Prv. 3:2)

"pay attention to my wisdom,... lest strangers feast on your wealth and your toil enrich another man's house. (Prv. 5:1,10)

"With me are riches and honor, enduring wealth and prosperity." (Prv. 8:17,18)

"The blessing of the LORD bring wealth, (Prv. 10:22)

"The wealth of the wise is their crown," (Prv. 14:24)

"he who cherishes understanding prospers." (Prv. 19:8)

"He who pursues righteousness and love finds life, prosperity and honor." (Prv. 21:21)

"The plans of the diligent lead to profit as surely as haste leads to poverty." (Prv. 21:5)

"A wife of a noble character.... She considers a field and buys it; out of her earnings she plants a vineyard...She sees that her trading is profitable .... She makes linen garments and sells them, and supplies merchants with sashes." (Prv. 31:10,16,18,24)

<u>Only wealth obtained honestly is regarded as legitimate.</u>

"Such is the end of all who go after ill-gotten gain; it takes away the lives of those who get it." (Prv. 1:19)

"Ill-gotten treasures are of no value, but righteousness delivers from death." (Prv. 10:2)

"The LORD detests lying lips, but he delights in men who are truthful." (Prv. 12:22)

"Dishonest money dwindles away, but he who gathers money little by little makes it grow." (Prv. 13:11) "The house of the righteous contains great treasure, but the income of the wicked brings them trouble." (Prv. 15:6)

"Better a little with the fear of the LORD than great wealth with turmoil." (Prv. 15:16)

"All a man's ways seem innocent to him, but motives are weighed by the LORD." (Prv. 16:2)

"Better a little with righteousness than much gain with injustice." (Prv. 16:8)

"Honest scales and balances are from the LORD; the weights in the bag are of his making." (Prv. 16:11)

"Better a poor man whose walk is blameless than a fool whose lips are perverse." (Prv. 19:1)

"Differing weights and differing measures—the LORD detests them both." (Prv. 20:10)

"Food gained by fraud tastes sweet to a man, but he ends up with a mouth full of gravel." (Prv. 20:17)

"The LORD detests differing weights, and dishonest scales do not please him." (Prv. 20:23)

"He who conceals his sins does not prosper," (Prv. 28:13)

"... he who hates ill-gotten gain will enjoy a long life." (Prv. 28:16)

<u>Because the result of work is regarded favorably, work is regarded as appropriate and honorable.</u>

"Go to the ant, you sluggard; consider its ways and be wise! It has no commander, no overseer or ruler, yet it stores its provisions in summer and gathers its food at harvest. How long will you lie there, you sluggard? When will you get up from your sleep? A little sleep, a little slumber,... and poverty will come on you like a bandit and scarcity like an armed man." (Prv. 6:6-11; 24:33,34; 30:25)

"Lazy hands make a man poor, but diligent hands bring wealth." (Prv. 10:4)

"He who gathers crops in summer is a wise son, but he who sleeps during harvest is a disgraceful son." (Prv. 10:5)

"He who works his land will have abundant food," (Prv. 12:11; 28:19)

"The sluggard craves and gets nothing, but the desires of the diligent are full satisfied." (Prv. 13:4)

"All hard works brings a profit, but mere talk leads only to poverty." (Prv. 14:23)

"One who is slack in his work is brother to one who destroys." (Prv. 18:9)

"Laziness brings on deep sleep, and shiftless man goes hungry." (Prv. 19:15)

"A sluggard does not plow in season; so at harvest time he looks but finds nothing.... Do not love sleep or you will grow poor; stay awake and you will have food to spare." (Prv. 20:4,13)

"The sluggard's craving will be the death of him, because his hands refuse to work." (Prv. 21:25)

"Do you see a man skilled in his work? He will serve before kings;" (Prv. 22:29)

"The sluggard buries his hand in the dish; he is too lazy to ring it back to this mouth." (Prv. 26:15

"He who tends a fig tree will eat its fruit; he who looks after his master will be honored." (Prv. 27:18)

"Finish your outdoor work and get your fields ready; after that, build your house. (Prv. 24:27)

"A wife of noble character.... She... works with eager hands.... She gets up while it is still dark; she provides food for her family.... She sets about her work vigorously;...and her lamp does not go out at night." (Prv. 31:10-18)

<u>While wealth is legitimate, it can be accompanied by sinful complacency, self-pride and arrogance.</u>

"they will eat the fruit of their ways and be filled with the fruit of their schemes. For the waywardness of the simple will kill them, and the complacency of the fools will destroy them; but whoever listens to me will live in safety...." (Prv. 1:31-33)

"Does not wisdom call out?.... I hate pride and arrogance," (Prv. 8:1,13)

"When pride comes in, then comes disgrace, but with humility comes wisdom." (Prv. 11:2)

"A man's riches may ransom his life," (Prv. 13:8)

"The LORD tears down the rich man's house...." (Prv. 15:25)

"The LORD detests all the proud of heat. Be sure of this: They will not go unpunished." (Prv. 16:5)

"Pride goes before destruction, a haughty spirit before a fall." (Prv. 16:18)

"The wealth of the rich is their fortified city; they imagine it an unscalable wall. Before his downfall a man's heart is proud, but humility comes before honor." (Prv. 18:11,12)

"Haughty eyes and a proud heart, the lamp of the wicked, are sin!" (Prv. 21:4)

"The proud and arrogant man—"Mocker" is his name; he behaves with overweening pride." (Prv. 21:24)

"Humility and the fear of the LORD bring wealth and honor and life." (Prv. 22:4)

"A rich man may be wise in his own eyes, but a poor man who has discernment sees through him." (Prv. 28:11)

"A man's pride brings him low." (Prv. 29:23)

"give me neither poverty nor riches, but give me only my daily bread. Otherwise, I may have too much and disown you and say, "Who is the LORD? (Prv. 30:8,9)

A major role of material possessions and wealth is generously supporting the less fortunate.

"Do not withhold good from those who deserve it, when it is in your power to act." (Prv. 3:27)

"blessed is he who is kind to the needy..... Whoever is kind to the needy honors God." (Prv. 14:21,31)

"He who mocks the poor shows contempt for their Maker;" (Prv. 17:5)

"A gift opens the way for a giver and ushers him into the presence of the great." (Prv. 18:16)

"He who is kind to the poor lends to the LORD." (Prv. 19:17)

"If a man shuts his ears to the cry of the poor, he too will cry out and not be answered." (Prv. 21:13)

"A generous man will himself be blessed, for he shares his food with the poor." (Prv. 22:9)

"The righteous care about justice for the poor," (Prv. 29:7)

"A wife of noble character.... She opens her arms to the poor and extends her hands to the needy." (Prv. 31:20)

A broader perspective in which generosity can be viewed: the Circular Flow of Prosperity.

"Honor the LORD with your wealth, with the firstfruits of all your crops; then your barns will be filled to overflowing, and your vats will brim over with new wine." (Prv. 3:9,10)

"One man gives freely, yet gains even more; another withholds unduly, but comes to poverty."(Prv 11:24)

"A generous man will prosper; he who refreshes others will himself be refreshed." (Prv. 11:25)

"People curse the man who hoards grain, but blessing crowns him who is willing to sell. (Prv. 11:26)

"Do not eat the food of a stingy man,... for he is the kind of man who is always thinking about the cost.... his heart is not with you." (Prv. 23:6,7)

The profit motive plays a key role in stimulating the generation of wealth.

"The laborer's appetite works for him; his hunger drives him on." (Prv. 16:26)

Appendix G

WEALTH, PROPERTY AND COMMERCIAL TRANSACTIONS IN THE GOSPELS

	Location			
	Matt.	Mark	Luke	John
"In the beginning…all things… made through him"				1.1
Magnificat, "…and the rich he has sent empty away…"			1:53	
Magi, "…gifts, gold and frankincense and myrrh"	2:11			
"and to offer a sacrifice…turtledoves and pigeons"			2:24	
"John wore a garment of camel's hair and a leather girdle…."	3:4	1:6		
Jesus, "Man shall not live by bread alone."	4:4		4:4	
Marriage at Cana, "the water now become…good wine…."				2:1
Gallilean base established in Capernaum, merchant center	4:13	1:21	4:31	2:12
"Jesus, 'The Spirit of the Lord is upon me, because he has anointed me to preach good news to the poor…captives…blind…oppressed."			4:18	
"to Simon, '…let down your nets for a catch.'…filled both the boats so that they began to sink."			5:4	
From *The Sermon on the Mount* and *The Sermon on the Plain:* Beatitudes	5:3		6:20	

	Matt.	Mark	Luke	John
"Do not swear at all, …Let what you say be simply 'yes' or 'no;'	5:34			
"if one sues you and takes your coat, let him have your cloak as well"	5:40			
"your alms my be in secret"	6:1			
"Do not lay up for yourselves treasures on earth,…where your treasure is there will your heart be also"	6:19			
"You cannot serve God and mammon."	6:24		16:13	
"do not be anxious about what you eat…drink….wear….But seek first his kingdom… and these things shall be yours."	6:25		12:22	
"Ask, and it will be given you; seek, and you will find; knock, and it will be opened to you."	7:7		11:9	16:24
			15:7	
"But woe to you who that are rich, for you shall hunger"			6:24	
Jesus to the disciples, "Freely you have received, freely give."	10:8			
Jesus to the disciples, "Take nothing for your journey…nor money…"	10:9	3:8	6:3	
Parable of the Sower, "worldly cares and the delight in riches choke the word,"	13:22	4:19	8:14	
Jesus in feeding the 5,000, "and all ate and were satisfied."	14:20	6:42	9:17	6:12
Jesus in feeding the 4,000, "and all ate and were satisfied;"	15:37	8:8		
"not to give offense to them (tax collectors) go to the sea and cast a hook and take the first fish…, and when you open its mouth…. find a shekel."	17:24			

	Matt.	Mark	Luke	John
"Take heed, and beware of all covetousness; for a man's life does not consist in the abundance of his possessions."			12:15	
Parable of the Rich Fool, "Fool!...So is he who lays up treasures for Himself, and is not rich toward God."			12:20	
"Sell your possessions, give alms; where your treasure is, there will be your heart..."				12:33
Parable of the Prodigal Son: "Bring the best robe...a ring...shoes... the fatted calf"			15:11	
Parable of the Unjust Steward: "sons of this world are more shrewd... mammon..."			16:1	
"If you have not been faithful in the unrighteous mammon, who will entrust you..."			16:10	
"Pharisees, who loved money,...'what is exalted among men is detestable in God's sight."			16:14	
Parable of the Rich Man and Lazarus: error of omission; inattention			16:19	
Zacchaeus, "half of my goods I give to the poor; and if I have defrauded anything, I restore it four-fold."			19:1	
To the rich young man, "Sell all that you have, give it to the poor, follow me."	19:16	10:17	18:18	
"it is easier for a camel to go through the eye of a needle than for a rich man to enter the kingdom of God."	19:23	10:23	18:24	
Parable of the Nobleman's Ten Servants: "... money on deposit... collected interest"			19:23	

	Matt.	Mark	Luke	John
Cleansing the Temple, "you shall not make my Father's house a house of trade"	21:12	11:15	19:45	2:14
Parable of the Talents: "entrusted to them his property…gave them… money….banks…interest."	25:27			
Parable of Wicked Husbandmen: "planted vineyard…build tower… let it out."	21:33	12:1	20:9	
"Render to Caesar the things that are Caesar's and to God things that are God's"	22:21	12:17	20:25	
"poor widow put in more than all who are contributing to the treasury. For they contributed out of abundance; but she out of poverty put in everything she had."		12:44	21:4	
"to betray him to them…and they engaged to give him money. So he agreed."	26:14	14:10	22:4	
"Judas…pieces of silver… priests…blood money…bought… Field of Blood"	27:3			
"And cast lots to divide his garments."	27:36	15:24	23:43	19:24
"took the body down and wrapped it in a linen shroud"	27:59	15:46	23:53	19:40
"they gave a sum of money to the soldiers and said, 'Tell people his disciples stole him away."	28:12			

Appendix H

DISTINCTION BETWEEN MATERIAL AND SPIRITUAL IN THE GOSPELS

Related to this discussion of wealth and possessions is the notion that Jesus often points out the distinction between that which is material and that which is spiritual, further teaching that only the spiritual is of God and therefore is everlasting.

The following are some selected passages in the Gospels wherein this distinction is made.

	Location			
Description	Matt.	Mark	Luke	John
Jesus tells Nicodemus, "...unless one is born of water and the Spirit, he cannot enter the kingdom of God. That which is born of the flesh is flesh and that which is born of the Spirit is spirit."				3:6
Further in Jesus' discussion with Nicodemus, "For God so loved the world that he gave his only Son, that whoever believes in him should... have eternal life. For God sent his Son into the world...that the world might be saved through him."				3:16
John saying to his disciples at Aenon, "He who comes from above is above all: he who is of the earth belongs to the earth."				3:31

	Matt.	Mark	Luke	John
Jesus to the Samaritan woman at the well: "Everyone who drinks of this water will thirst again, but whoever drinks of the water that I shall give Him will never thirst:…"				4:13
The disciples to Jesus at the Samaritan's well, "Rabbi, eat." Jesus responds, "I have food to eat of which you do not know."				4:41
The Lord's Prayer: "Thy will be done on earth as it is in heaven."	6:10			
The Sermon on the Mount:				
"Do not lay up treasures on earth, but lay up treasures in heaven."	6:19			
"You cannot serve God and mammon."	6:24			
"But seek first his kingdom… and all these things shall be yours."	6:33			
J. to disciples "do not fear those who kill the body but cannot kill the soul;"	10:28		12:4	
"taking the five loaves and two fish he looked up to heaven, and blessed….and gave them to the crowds, and all ate and were satisfied."	14:19	6:41	9:16	6:11
"Do not labor for the food which perishes, but for the food which endures to eternal life…the bread of God is that which comes down from heaven, and gives life to the world….I am the bread of life; he who comes to me shall not hunger and believes in me shall never thirst…."				6:26

	Matt.	Mark	Luke	John
"Every plant which my heavenly Father has not planted will be rooted up."	15:13			
"It is the spirit that gives life, the flesh is of no avail;"				6:63
"Get behind me, Satan! …For you are not on the side of God, but of men."	16:23	8:33		
"if any man would come after me, let him deny himself….For whoever would save his life will lose it; and whoever loses his life for my sake will save it."	16:24	8:34	9:23	12:25
"For what will it profit a man, if he gains the whole world and forfeits his life?"	16:26	8:36	9:25	
"From whom do kings of the earth take toll or tribute? From their sons or others?…..From others,…Then the sons are free."	17:25			
"Sell your possessions; provide yourselves with…a treasure in the heavens."			12:33	
"the sons of this world are more shrewd in dealing….than the sons of light"			16:1	
"If you have not been faithful in the unrighteous mammon, who will entrust to you true riches?"			16:10	
To the Pharisees: "you are those who justify yourselves before men, but what is exalted among men is an abomination in the sight of God."			16:14	
Jesus in the Temple: "if any one thirst, let him come to me and drink. He who believes in me 'out of this heart shall flow rivers of living water."				7:14

	Matt.	Mark	Luke	John
"I am the light of the world; he who follows me will not walk in darkness, but will have the light of life."				8:1
"If any one keeps my word, he will never see death."				8:52
"I am the resurrection and the life; he who believes in me, though he die, yet shall he live,…"				11:25
"Render to Caesar the things that are Caesar's…to God the things that are God's"	22:21	12:17	20:25	
"inherit the kingdom prepared for you from the foundation of the world"	25:34			
"and he who hates his life in this world will keep it for eternal life."			12:25	
"when Jesus knew that his hour had come to depart out of this world to the Father,"				13:1
The Last Supper	26:26	14:22	22:15	
Promise of Paraclete, Peace, Love, World's Hatred, Intercessory Prayer				14:17
"My kingship is not of this world"			18:36	
"Father, into thy hands I commit my spirit!"			23:46	
"he has risen"	28:7	16:6	24:5	
"I am ascending to my Father and your Father, to my God and your God"				20:17
"for a spirit does not have flesh and bones"			24:39	
"Receive the Holy Spirit"				20:22
"the Lord Jesus…was taken up to heaven,"		16:19		
"All authority in heaven and on earth has been give to me"	28:18			

	Matt.	Mark	Luke	John
"in the name of the Father and of the Son and of the Holy Spirit"	28:19			
"was carried up into heaven"			24:51	
"you may have life in his name"				20:31
"until I come"				21:23

Appendix I

ECONOMIC CONCEPTS AND WORLDLY POSSESSIONS MENTIONED IN ACTS

"All the believers were together and had everything in common. Selling their possessions and goods, they gave to anyone as he had need." (Ac 2:44-5)

"There was no needy persons among them (the apostles) for from time to time those who owned lands or houses sold them, brought the money from the sales and put it at the apostles' feet, and it was distributed to anyone as he had need." (Ac 4:34-5)

"...Ananias, together with his wife Sapphira, also sold a piece of property. With his wife's full knowledge he kept back part of the money for himself, but brought the rest and put it at the apostles' feet. Then Peter said, 'Ananias, how is it that...you have like to the Holy Spirit, and have kept for yourself some of the money you received for the land?...You have not lied to men but to God.' When Ananias hear this, he fell down and died.....later his wife came in....Peter asked her....'How could you agree to test the Spirit of the Lord?'...she fell down at his feet and died." (Ac 5:1-10)

Manufacturing:"After this, Paul went to Corinth....Claudius had ordered all the Jews to leave Rome. Paul went to see them, and because he was a tentmaker as they were, he stayed and worked with them." (Ac 18:1-3)

Distribution and organizational structure: "So the Twelve gathered all the disciples together and said, 'It would not be right for us to neglect the ministry of the word of God in order to wait on tables. Brothers, choose seven men from among you.... We will turn this responsibility over to them and will give our attention to prayer and ministry of the word." (Ac 6:2-4)

"When Simon saw that the Spirit was given at the laying on of the apostles' hands, he offered them money and said, 'Give me also this ability....' Peter answered, 'May your money perish with you, because you thought you could buy the gift of God with money!....you heart is not right before God." (Ac 8:20-2)

Several passages mentioning travel on trade roads or on cargo ships by disciples provide evidence that international trade facilitated the rapid spread of Christianity, from the launching pad and home base of Antioch ["and they sent Barnabas to Antioch" (Ac 11:22)] to Paul's ultimate destination of Rome ["...we would sail for Italy..." (Ac 27:1)] and many ports and trade centers between.

The message which the missionaries were preaching included, "We are bringing you the good news, telling you to turn to the living God, who...provides you with plenty of food and fills your hearts with joy." (Ac 14:15,16)

"One of those listening was a woman named Lydia, a dealer in purple cloth...who was a worshiper of God. The Lord opened her heart to respond to Paul's message." (Ac 16:14)

"So he reasoned in the synagogue..., as well as in the marketplace...." (Ac 17:17)

"A silversmith named Demetrius, who...brought in no little business for the craftsmen...called them together,...and said: 'Men, you know we receive a good income from this business. And you see and hear how this fellow Paul has convinced and led astray large numbers of people here in Ephesus....There is danger...that our trade will lose its good name." (Ac 19:24-7)

Paul, in his farewell to the Ephesian elders, "I have not coveted anyone's silver or gold or clothing.....these hands of mine have supplied my own needs and the needs of my companions....by this kind of hard work we must help the weak,..." (Ac 20:33-5)

Appendix J

WEALTH AND WORLDLY POSSESSIONS IN THE PAULINE LETTERS

"They exchanged the truth of God for a lie, and worshiped and served created things rather than the creator." (Rom. 1:25)

"Share with God's people who are in need." (Rom. 12:13)

"Let no debt remain outstanding,..." (Rom. 13:8)

"For if the Gentiles have share in the Jews' spiritual blessings, they owe it to the Jews to share with them their material blessings." (Rom. 15:27)

"...God is able to make all grace abound to you, so that in all things at all times, having all that you need, you will abound in every good work....Now he who supplies seed to the sower and bread for food will also supply and increase your store of seed and will enlarge the harvest of hour righteousness. You will be made rich in every way so that you can be generous on every occasion,...Thanks be to God for his indescribable gift." (2 Cor. 9:8,10,15)

"Do not be anxious about anything, but in everything, by prayer and petition, with thanksgiving, present your requests to God...." (Phil. 4:6-9)

"And my God will meet all your needs according to his glorious riches in Christ Jesus." (Phil. 4:19)

"All they asked was that we should continue to remember the poor,..." (Gal. 2:10)

"Carry each other's burdens,....for each should carry his own load." (Gal 6:2,5)

"...we worked night and day in order not to be a burden to anyone while we preached..." (1 Thes 2:9)

"...work with your hands,...so that...you will not be dependent on anybody." (1 Thes 4:11,12)

"...respect those who work hard....warn those who are idle,..." (1 Thes 5:12-14)

"...keep away from every brother who is idle....If anyone does not obey our instruction in this letter, ...Do not associate with him, in order that he may feel ashamed." (2 Thes. 3:6-14)

"The earth is the Lord's, and everything in it." (1 Cor. 10:26)

"Now about the collection for God's people:...each one of you should set aside a sum of money in keeping with his income, saving it up...send...to Jerusalem." (1 Cor. 16:1-3)

"I think it is necessary to send back to you Epaphroditus...., whom you sent to take care of my needs." (Phil. 2:25)

"...not one church shared with me, except you only;...you sent me aid again and again when I was in need.... I am amply supplied, now that I have received from Epaphroditus the gifts you sent." (Phil. 4:15-18)

"Now the overseer must be above reproach,..., temperate, self-controlled,...., not a lover of money." (1 Tm. 3:3)

"Deacons, likewise, are to be men worthy of respect, sincere, not indulging in much wine, and not pursuing dishonest gain." (1 Tm. 3:8)

"The worker deserves his wages." (1 Tm. 5:18)

"The hardworking farmer should be the first to receive a share of the crop.....In a large house there are articles not only of gold and sliver, but also of wood and clay; some are for noble purposes and some for ignoble." (2 Tm. 2:6, 20)

"...an overseer...must be blameless—not overbearing,... not pursuing dishonest gain." (Ti. 1:7)

"Those who live according to the sinful nature have their minds set on what that nature desires; but those who live in accordance with the Spirit have their minds set on what the Spirit desires." (Rom. 8:5)

"...we also rejoice in our sufferings, because we know that suffering produces perseverance; perseverance, character; and character, hope. And hope does not disappoint us, because God has poured out his love into our hearts by the Holy Spirit,..." (Rom. 5:3-5)

"No... greedy person—such a man is an idolater—has any inheritance in the kingdom of Christ and of God." (Eph. 5:5)

"If any man builds on this foundation using gold, silver, costly stones, wood, hay or straw, his work will be shown for what it is, because the Day will bring it to light. It will be revealed with fire, and the fire will test the quality of each man's work....the wisdom of this world is foolishness in God's sight." (1Cor. 3:12,19)

"Already you have all you want! Already you have become rich!" (1 Cor. 4:8)

"...those who use the things of the world, as if not engrossed in them. For this world in its present form is passing away." (1 Cor. 7:31)

"We know that an idol is nothing at all in the world and that... there is but one God, the Father, from who all things came and for who we live; and there is but one Lord, Jesus Christ, through whom all things came and through whom we live." (1 Cor. 8:4,6)

"Therefore, my dear friends, flee from idolatry." (1 Cor. 10:14)

"But whatever was to my profit I now consider loss for the sake of Christ. What is more, I consider everything a loss compared to the surpassing greatness of knowing Christ Jesus my Lord, for whose sake I have lost all things. I consider them rubbish, that I may gain Christ and be found in him, ….—the righteousness that comes from God and is by faith." (Phil. 3:7-9)

"I have learned the secret of being content in any and every situation, whether well fed or hungry, whether living in plenty or in want…." (Phil. 4:12)

"…many live as enemies of the cross of Christ. Their destiny is destruction, their god is their stomach,….Their mind is on earthly things." (Phil. 3:19)

"Set your minds on things above, not on earthly things….Put to death, therefore, whatever belong to your earthly nature: sexual immorality, impurity, lust, evil desires and greed, which is idolatry." (Col. 3:2-5)

"Command those who are rich in this present world not to be arrogant nor to put their hope in wealth, which is so uncertain, but to put their hope in God, who richly provides us with everything for our enjoyment." (1 Tm. 6:17)

"But if we have food and clothing, we will be content with that. People who want to get rich fall into temptation and a trap and into many foolish and harmful desires that plunge men into ruin and destruction. For the love of money is a root of all kinds of evil. Some people, eager for money, have wandered from the faith and pierced themselves with many griefs." (1 Tm. 8-10)

"each one should retain the place in life that the Lord assigned to him and to which God has called him….each man, as responsible to God, should remain in the situation God called him to." (1 Cor. 7:17,24)

"There are different kinds of gifts, but the same Spirit. There are different kinds of service, but the same Lord. There are different kinds of working, but the same God works all of them in all men." (1 Cor. 12:4-7)

"set aside a sum of money…, saving it up…send…to Jerusalem." (1 Cor. 16:1-3

"Am I not free…Don't we have the right to food and drink?…Though I am free and belong to not man, I make myself a slave to everyone, to win as many as possible." (1 Cor. 9:1-19)

"I have kept myself from being a burden to you in any way,…" (2 Cor. 11:9)

"so whether you eat or drink or whatever you do, do it all for the glory of God." (1 Cor. 10:33)

"In a large house there are article not only of gold and silver, but also of wood and clay; some are for noble purposes and some for ignoble. If a man cleanses himself from the latter, he will be an instrument for noble purposes, made holy, useful to the Master and prepared to do any good work." (2 Tm. 2:20-21)

"But just as you excel in everything—in faith, in speech, in knowledge, in complete earnestness and in your love for us—see that you also excel in this grace of giving….For you know the grace of our Lord Jesus Christ, that though he was rich, yet for your sakes he became poor, so that you through his poverty might become rich….. For if the willingness is their, the gift is acceptable according to what one has, not according to what he does not have." (2 Cor. 8:7-12)

"Whoever sows sparingly will also reap sparingly, and whoever sows generously will also reap generously. ….God loves a cheerful giver….Now he who supplies seed to the sower… will also supply and increase your store of seed and will enlarge the harvest of your righteousness. You will be made rich in every way so that you can be generous on every occasion, …. Thanks be to God for his indescribable gift!" (2 Cor. 9:6-15)

"...men of corrupt mind, who have been robbed of the truth and who think that godliness is a means to financial gain." (1 Tm. 6:5)

"women to dress modestly, ...not with braided hair or gold or pearls or expensive clothes,..." (1 Tm. 2:9)

"Do nothing out of selfish ambition or vain conceit, but in humility....look not only to your own interests, but also the interests of others." (Phil. 2:3,4)

"Command those who are rich....to do good , to be rich in good deeds, and to be generous and willing to share. In this way they will lay up treasure for themselves as a firm foundation for the coming age, so that they may take hold of the life that is truly life." (1 Tm. 6:17-19)

Appendix K

ECONOMIC SYSTEMS, WEALTH AND PROPERTY IN REVELATION

"A quart of wheat for a day's wages, and three quarts of barley for a day's sages, and do not damage the oil and the wine!" (Rev. 6:6) Represents opulence, luxurious oil and wine existing simultaneously with famine conditions.

"Then the kings of the earth,...the rich,...hid in caves and among the rocks of the mountains....For the great day of their wrath has come , and who can stand?" (Rev. 6:15-17)

"The rest of mankind that were not killed by these plagues still did no repent of the work of their hands; they did not stop worshiping demons, and idols of gold, silver, bronze, stone and wood—idols that cannot see or hear or walk." (Rev. 9:20)

"You are worthy, our Lord and God, to receive glory and honor and power, for you created all things, and by your will they were created and have their being." (Rev. 4:11)

".... 'Fear God and give him glory,....Worship him who made the heavens, the earth, the sea and the springs of water." (Rev. 14:7)

"I know your afflictions and your poverty—yet you are rich!" (Rev. 2:9

"To he who overcomes, I will give some of the hidden [spiritual] manna." (Rev. 2:17)

"Never again will they hunger; never again will they thirst." (Rev. 7:16)

"You say 'I am rich; I have acquired wealth and do not need a thing.' But you do not realize that your are wretched, pitiful, poor, blind and naked. I counsel you to buy from me gold refined in the fire [spiritual treasure], so you can become rich; and white clothes [righteousness] to wear." (Rev. 3:16-18)

"And I saw a beast coming out of the sea....The dragon gave the beast his power and his throne and great authority....The whole world...followed the beast. Men worshipped the dragon because he had given authority to the beast,....All inhabitants of the earth will worship the beast—all whose names have not been written in the book of life belonging to the Lamb.... This calls for patient endurance and faithfulness on the part of the saints.....Then I saw another beast, coming out of the earth..... He exercised all authority....he deceived the inhabitants of the earth.....He also forced everyone, small and great, rich and poor, free and slave, to receive a mark on his right hand or on his forehead, so that no one could by or sell unless he had the mark." (Rev. 13:1-17)

"... 'If anyone worships the beast and his image and receives the mark on the forehead or on the hand, he, too, will drink of the wine of God's fury.... He will be tormented....for ever and ever...." (Rev. 14:9-11

"This calls for patient endurance on the part of the saints who obey God's commandments and remain faithful to Jesus." (Rev. 14:12)

"Come, I will show you the punishment of the great prostitute who sits on many waters. With her the kings of the earth committed adultery and the inhabitants of the earth were intoxicated with the wine of her adulteries." (Rev. 17:1,2)

"Fallen! Fallen is Babylon the Great!... The kings of the earth have committed adultery with her, and the merchants of the earth grew rich from her excessive luxuries...Therefore in one day her plagues will overtake her: death, mourning and famine. She will be consumed by fire,... The merchants of the earth will weep and mourn over here because no one buys their cargoes any more—

cargoes of gold, silver, precious stones and pearls; fine linen, purple, silk and scarlet cloth; every sort of citron wood, and articles of every kind made of ivory, costly wood, bronze, iron and marble; cargoes of cinnamon and spice, of incense, myrrh and frankincense, of wind and olive oil, of fine flour and wheat; cattle and sheep; horses and carriages; and bodies and souls of men. They will say, 'the fruit you longed for is gone from you. All your riches and splendor have vanished, never to be recovered.' The merchants who sold these things and gained in their wealth from her will stand far of, terrified at her torment. They will weep and mourn and cry out: '...In one hour such great wealth has been brought to ruin!' Every sea captain,...will ...cry out: '...Oh great city, where all who had ships on the sea became rich through her wealth! In one hour she has been brought to ruin!'... 'No workman of any trade will be found in you again.... Your merchants were the world's great men.'... 'Hallelujah! Salvation and glory and power belong to our God, ...He has condemned the great prostitute who corrupted the earth by her adulteries." (Rev. 18:2-24)

"Behold, I am coming soon,...and I will give to everyone according to what he has done....Blessed are those who wash their robes, that they may have the right to the tree of life and my go through the gates into the city. Outside are the dogs,... the idolaters...." (Rev. 22:12-15)

Appendix L

EXAMPLE OF CORPORATE STEWARDSHIP OF GOD'S CREATIONS

Reflecting their enlightened leadership, today the boards of directors of virtually every major multinational corporation have adopted official policies related to their stewardship of God's creations.

As just one of hundreds of thousands of examples, Weyerhaeuser Company has large staffs and voluminous policies and procedure manuals and spends hundreds of millions of dollars for the sole purpose of protecting and improving all of God's creations: air, water, people, fish, wildlife, plantlife, minerals, even the aesthetics of God's landscape and seascape, addressing specific matters such as timber growing and harvesting practices, environmental management, recycling, threatened and endangered species, toxic release, watersheds, risk management, safety, etc.

The following, readily lifted from Weyerhaeuser's website, is just a tiny sampling of Weyerhaeuser's approach to stewardship.

Environmental Management Systems & Forestry/ Forest Products Certification

Weyerhaeuser's EMS Commitment

Since 1997, Weyerhaeuser has been committed to developing an Environmental Management System (EMS). An EMS is a systematic approach to implementing the company's environmental core policy to manage and continually improve its environmental impacts. It includes a set of reliable processes and procedures and combines policy, planning, education, performance standards, accountabilities, improvement plans and auditing into one system of reliable, documented processes.

This approach is improving efficiency and environmental performance, reducing costs, reducing risk, engaging our people and creating a competitive advantage. It also supports the company's Citizenship value of holding ourselves to the highest standards of ethical conduct and environmental responsibility.

Trend Toward Certification

Over the past few years, however, certification of forestry and forest products has become an important issue for the forest products industry. Customers—primarily at the wholesale level, but also some retail customers—are beginning to seek independent verification that the products they buy are produced in an environmentally responsible way.

Certification uses an outside party to audit a company's compliance with certain standards. Forest certification offers assurances that forests are managed in ways that:

- Maintain forest productivity and biodiversity.
- Protect soil and water
- Offer aesthetic, recreational, cultural and wildlife benefits as well as economic benefits.

Some certification standards require environmental practices, such as prompt reforestation of logged areas. Others focus more on the management practices, such as employee training and management accountability, needed to carry out a set of standards.

Weyerhaeuser's ISO 14001 Commitment

During 1999, Weyerhaeuser's senior management team conducted a thorough review of several certification systems and determined that the ISO 14001 international standard is best suited to the company's large-scale forestry and manufacturing operations in the United States, Canada and the Southern Hemisphere. They have committed that by the year 2005, all Weyerhaeuser units (manufacturing and timberlands) will have an EMS capable of being certified to the ISO 14001 standard. Decisions regarding independent certification of specific business units will be determined by each business based on customer or other stakeholder requirements. This commitment includes:

- Timberlands units in Canada will be third party certified to the ISO 14001 standard by 2002 and to the Canadian Standards Association (CSA) Sustainable Forest Management (SFM) standards by 2003.
- Financial responsibility
- U.S. timberlands units will incorporate the American Forest & Paper Association_s (AF&PA) Sustainable Forestry InitiativeSM (SFI) standard into their environmental management systems.
- U.S. manufacturing units will establish raw material supplier specifications based on the AF&PA SFISM standard, and Canadian manufacturing units will establish supplier specifications based on provincial and Weyerhaeuser requirements.
- Because of the unique conditions in coastal British Columbia, Weyerhaeuser's B.C. Coastal Group is working with other companies and stakeholders to develop a Forest Stewardship Council (FSC) regional standard for that province.

We expect this commitment to help ensure that reliable processes are in place to improve our performance, meet regulatory and other stakeholder requirements, and to protect our preferred-supplier position with key customers.

Current Status

Several Weyerhaeuser operating units have already received independent certification to the ISO 14001 EMS standard. These include: Weyerhaeuser New Zealand timberlands operations - 193,000 acres (78,000 hectares), June 1996; Interior B.C. timberlands - 3.09 million acres (1.2 million hectares), March 1999; North Island Woodlands, Coastal B.C. operations - 567,000 acres (230,000 hectares), ISO 14001 and CSA, March 1999; Grande Prairie/Grande Cache Alberta forestlands - 3.2 million acres (1.3 million hectares), May 2000; Chemainus sawmill on Vancouver Island was the company's first manufacturing facility to achieve ISO 14001 registration in August 2000.

Several approaches to certification
A variety of environmental certification systems are in use around the world.

Sustainable Forestry Initiative^{SM} (SFI)
The AF&PA Sustainable Forestry Initiative^{SM} standard is the forest industry standard for sustainable forestry practices on private land in the United States. It includes auditing, environmental performance evaluation, labeling and life cycle analysis.

Forest Stewardship Council (FSC)
The Forest Stewardship Council is an independent, nonprofit organization. It promotes a set of sustainable forestry principles, accredits organizations that certify the quality of forest management according to localized FSC standards, and promotes the use of certified forest products through use of the FSC label.

ISO 14001 Environmental Management System Standard
This standard, developed under the auspices of the International Organization for Standardization, focuses on the management processes and practices needed to meet SFISM, FSC or other environmental requirements. It includes auditing, environmental performance evaluation, labeling and life cycle analysis.

The Canadian Standards Association (CSA)
The Canadian Standards Association, the national standards body of Canada, has developed the national Sustainable Forest Management System Standard. Modeled after ISO 14001, it uses an environmental-management-system framework, internationally recognized criteria and indicators of sustainable forest management and includes a local public consultation process to set performance standards for a defined forest area.

Salmon

Overview
Salmon are an integral part of the Pacific Northwest's economy, culture and heritage. Native salmon populations have been declining throughout much of Oregon and Washington. Dams, fishing,

hatcheries and habitat loss or damage have all contributed to the problem. Weyerhaeuser is committed to maintaining and enhancing fish habitat across its private, commercial forestland in the Northwest.

The following information highlights what Weyerhaeuser is doing to help conserve this important natural resource.

Industry efforts

In Oregon, Weyerhaeuser is working with the Oregon Forest Industries Council to implement the forest industry's commitments made in the state coho/steelhead salmon plan. Weyerhaeuser is also working with the Oregon Board of Forestry and Governor to identify any improvements in the Oregon forest practices rules which are reasonably needed to support state salmon recovery efforts.

In Washington, the company is committed to helping develop effective statewide recovery plans for salmon. Weyerhaeuser supports the Forests & Fish agreement endorsed by federal and state fisheries and environmental agencies, a number of treaty tribes, county government and private forest landowners. This innovative collaborative plan will improve salmon habitat and water quality on private forestlands.

Watershed analysis

Weyerhaeuser manages its forests for the sustainable production of wood and other forest products. The company's foresters and scientists are developing new ways to accomplish this goal while better protecting water quality and fish habitat. One such success is watershed analysis.

A watershed is the land surrounding and draining into a river or stream. Watershed analysis recognizes that every watershed has a unique set of characteristics, including soils, topography, geology, stream network, fish populations and land use history. It uses scientific processes to evaluate the watershed's characteristics and determine how to reduce the cumulative effects of harvesting, road construction and other forest practices on fish habitat and water quality. The process involves:

1. Assessment-collecting data and describing the watershed's conditions and sensitivities.

2. Prescriptions-developing specific harvest methods and management plans with the participation of foresters, engineers, harvest managers, scientists and outside groups.
3. Implementation-putting plans in place on a schedule.
4. Monitoring-testing the plans' effectiveness.

Watershed analysis is a regulatory process in Washington. Weyerhaeuser piloted the state's first full-scale analysis in 1993 in the Tolt River watershed. The company has voluntarily extended this process to its Oregon forests as well. Weyerhaeuser has completed over watershed analyses in Oregon and Washington, covering more than 731,000 acres of its private forestland.

Improved practices

As a result of these scientific assessments, Weyerhaeuser has begun modifying on-the-ground practices to better protect water quality and fish habitat, including:

1. Road maintenance and repair. Improperly built or poorly maintained roads can produce sedimentation and landslides, so Weyerhaeuser is repairing and maintaining its forest roads to new, higher standards. In some cases, it is also closing or reseeding old, unused roads.
2. Streamside buffers. When harvesting, Weyerhaeuser leaves buffers of various widths to protect stream banks, furnish shade, and contribute trees that fall into streams and provide fish habitat.
3. Culvert repair and replacement. Weyerhaeuser is inventorying, repairing and replacing troublesome culverts that block upstream passage to fish. This reopens upper reaches of streams for year-round and seasonal fish use.
4. In-stream enhancements. Where indicated by fish biologists, Weyerhaeuser is placing boulders or logs into streams to create pools and provide cover for fish.

Scientific research

Weyerhaeuser's scientists and biologists are involved in a number of private and cooperative research projects to determine how private forestlands can contribute to salmon recovery:

1. Salmon carcass distribution. A former Weyerhaeuser biologist discovered the importance of spawned-out salmon carcasses as a source of nutrients and organic matter for animals and plants living in or near streams. In cooperation with the Washington Department of Fish and Wildlife, Weyerhaeuser added salmon carcasses to Washington streams to study the relationship between carcass availability and the density, growth rate and condition of fish populations in the stream. Based on research findings, conservation groups are placing carcasses of spawned-out hatchery fish in streams to restore naturally occurring nutrient levels and improve survival of juvenile salmon.

2. Effects of structural enhancements on fish populations. Working with other landowners and government agencies, Weyerhaeuser is studying the relationship between fish populations and in-stream structures. The study identifies what type of structures (e.g., boulders, logs) work best in aiding fish populations and where they should be located.

3. Fish inventory. Weyerhaeuser is gathering data on the types, distribution and abundance of fish species on its Washington and Oregon forestlands. This information will aid in development of forest management plans and correct errors in state agencies' stream classification systems.

Cooperative partnerships

Weyerhaeuser partners with numerous governmental, environmental, tribal, community, academic and landowner groups to develop far-reaching solutions to declining salmon populations, including:

- Bring Back the Natives
- King County
- Long Live the Kings
- National Marine Fisheries Service
- McKenzie Watershed Council
- Northwest Indian Fisheries Commission
- Oregon Dept. of Environmental Quality
- Oregon Dept. of Fish & Wildlife
- Oregon Dept. of Forestry
- Pacific Rivers Council
- Quinalt Tribe
- Seattle Water Dept.
- Showalter Bay Tribe
- Tulalip Tribes
- U.S. Bureau of Land Management
- U.S. Forest Service
- U.S. Fish & Wildlife Service
- University of Washington
- Washington Dept. of Ecology
- Washington Dept. of Fish & Wildlife
- Washington Dept. of Natural Resources
- Washington Environmental Council
- Washington Sea Grant
- Washington State Governor's Salmon Policy Office
- Washington Trout
- Willapa Alliance

AF&PA Sustainable Forestry Initiative™

Overview

The Sustainable Forestry Initiative™ (SFI) is a comprehensive program of forestry and conservation practices designed to ensure that future generations of Americans will have the same abundant forests that we enjoy today. The SFI was developed nationally through the American Forest and Paper Association (AF&PA), whose members—including Weyerhaeuser—produce 90 percent of the paper and 60 percent of the lumber produced in America today. Compliance with the SFI guidelines is mandatory for AF&PA

companies to retain AF&PA membership.

Weyerhaeuser's position

Weyerhaeuser fully supports the SFI and is applying its principles to all its private forestlands in the United States. The company views SFI as a natural extension of its long-standing commitment to sustainable forestry.

Weyerhaeuser practices meet the objectives of the SFI, and through the company's forestry resource strategies provide more specific goals and measurements for each of the company's operating regions.

Weyerhaeuser expects its contractors to meet SFI principles and objectives and encourages landowners supplying it wood to do the same.

SFI principles

Private forest landowners have an important stewardship responsibility and commitment to society. In keeping with this responsibility, AF&PA members support the following principles:

1. **Sustainable forestry** — To practice sustainable forestry to meet the needs of the present without compromising the ability of future generations to meet their own needs by practicing a land stewardship ethic which integrates the managing, growing, nurturing, harvesting and reforesting of trees for useful products with the conservation of soil, air and water quality, wildlife and fish habitat, and aesthetics.

2. **Responsible practices** — To use in its own forests, and promote among other forest landowners, sustainable forestry practices that are economically and environmentally responsible.

3. **Forest health & productivity** — To protect forests from wildfire, pests, diseases and other damaging agents in order to maintain and improve long-term forest health and productivity.

4. **Protecting special sites** — To manage its forests and lands of special significance (e.g., biologically, geologically or historically significant) in a manner that takes into account their unique qualities.

5. **Continuous improvement** — To continuously improve the practice of forest management and also to monitor, measure and report the performance of our members in achieving our commitment to sustainable forestry.

SFI guidelines
The following guidelines are intended to provide measures for evaluating AF&PA members' compliance with the SFI Principles:

1. Broaden the practice of sustainable forestry by employing an array of scientifically, environmentally and economically sound practices in the growth, harvest and use of forests.
2. Promptly reforest harvested areas to ensure long-term forest productivity and conservation of forest resources.
3. Protect the water quality in streams, lakes and other water bodies by establishing riparian protection measures based on soil type, terrain, vegetation, and other applicable factors, and by using EPA-approved Best Management Practices in all forest management operations.
4. Enhance the quality of wildlife habitat by developing and implementing measures that promote habitat diversity and the conservation of plant and animal populations found in forest communities.
5. Minimize the visual impact by designing harvests to blend into the terrain, by restricting clearcut size and/or by using harvest methods, age classes, and judicious placement of harvest units to promote diversity in forest cover.
6. Manage company lands of ecologic, geologic or historic significance in a manner that accounts for their special qualities.
7. Contribute to biodiversity by enhancing landscape diversity and providing an array of habitats.
8. Continue to improve forest utilization to help ensure the most efficient use of forest resources.

9. Continue the prudent use of forest chemicals to improve forest health and growth while protecting employees, neighbors, the public and sensitive areas, including streamcourses and adjacent lands.

10. Broaden the practice of sustainable forestry by further involving non-industrial landowners, loggers, consulting foresters and company employees who are active in wood procurement and landowner assistance programs.

11. Publicly report AF&PA members' progress in fulfilling their commitment to sustainable forestry.

12. Provide opportunities for the public and the forestry community to participate in the AF&PA membership's commitment to sustainable forestry.

Source: http://www.weyerhaeuser.com/environment

Bibliography

Achtemeier, Elizabeth. *New International Biblical Commentary: Minor Prophets I.* Peabody, Massachusetts: Hendrickson Publishers, Inc., 1996.

Aland, Kurt, ed. *Synopsis of the Four Gospels.* (English Edition). Revised edition. United Bible Societies, 1987.

Albom, Mitch. *Tuesdays With Morrie: An Old Man, a Young Man and Life's Greatest Lesson.* New York: Doubleday, 1997.

Alexander, John F. *Your Money or Your Life: A New Look at Jesus' View of Wealth and Power.* San Francisco: Harper & Row, Publishers, 1986.

Amundsen, Darrel W. *Christian Ethics 101, Koinos Program.* Seattle: Pacific Association for Theological Studies, Spring 2000.

Aquinas, Thomas. *Summa Theologica.* New York: Benziger Brothers, Inc., 1947.

Bauer, P.T. "Western Guilt and Third World Poverty," *The Corporation: A Theological Inquiry.* ed. Novak, Michael and Cooper, John W., Washington D.C.: American Enterprise Institute for Public Policy Research, 1981.

Baum, Geoff. "Different.com," *Forbes ASAP.* New York: Forbes, Inc, May 29, 2000.

Beckman, David M. *Where Faith and Economics Meet.* Minneapolis: Augsburg Publishing House, 1981.

Berman, Phyllis. "Throwing away the book," *Forbes.* New York:

Forbes, Inc., November, 2, 1998.

Blomberg, Craig L. *Neither Poverty Nor Riches: A Biblical Theology of Material Possessions.* Grand Rapids: William B. Eerdmans Publishing Co., 1999.

Book of Confessions: The Constitution of the Presbyterian Church (U.S.A.) Part I. New York: The Office of the General Assembly, Presbyterian Church (U.S.A.), 1983.

Book of Order: The Constitution of the Presbyterian Church (U.S.A.) Part II. Louisville, Kentucky: The Office of the General Assembly, Presbyterian Church (U.S.A.), 1998.

Boskin, Michael J. "Capitalism and Its Discontents," *Hoover Digest: Research and Opinion on Public Policy.* Stanford: Hoover Press, Fall, 1999.

Brown, R.E. *An Introduction to the New Testament.* New York: Doubleday, 1997.

Bruce, F. F. *New International Biblical Commentary: Philippians.* Peabody, Massachusetts: Hendrickson Publishers, Inc., 1983.

_____, *The Message of the New Testament.* Grand Rapids: William B. Eerdmans Publishing Co., 1972.

Byker, Gaylen. "Free Market Requires Legal, Moral, and Religious Foundations," *Religion & Liberty.* Grand Rapids: Acton Institute, November and December, 1998.

Cassidy, John. "The Hayek Century," *Hoover Digest: Research and Opinion on Public Policy,* Stanford: Hoover Press, Summer, 2000.

Charette, B. B. *NEW TESTAMENT 1.* Course NS500. Seattle: Fuller Theological Seminary, Fall, 1998.

Chilton, David. *Productive Christians in an Age of Guilt Manipulators.* Tyler, Texas: Institute for Christian Economics, 1985.

Conquest, Robert. "The Spector Haunting Russia," *Hoover Digest: Research and Opinion on Public Policy.* Stanford: Hoover Press, Spring, 2000.

Crosby, Cindy. "Engaging the Community," *The Life@Work Journal.* Fayetteville, Arkansas: The Life@Work Company, January/February, 2000.

Danker, Frederick W. *Luke (Proclamation Commentaries,* Second Edition, ed. Krodel, Gerhard) Philadelphia: Fortress Press, 1987.

Davids, Peter H. *New International Biblical Commentary: James.* Peabody, Massachusetts: Hendrickson Publishers, Inc., 1989.

de Soto, Hernando. *The Mystery of Capital: Why Capitalism Triumphs in the West and Fail Everywhere Else.* New York: Basic Books, 2000.

Diamond, Larry. "Debt for Democracy," *Hoover Digest: Research and Opinion on Public Policy* Stanford: Hoover Press, Winter, 2001.

Doebele, Justin. "Chinese Capitalism Gets a Face," *Forbes.* New York: Forbes, Inc., November 29, 1999.

D'Souza, Dinesh. *The Virtue of Prosperity.* New York: The Free Press, 2000.

_____, "The Virtue of Prosperity," *Hoover Digest: Research and Opinion on Public Policy.* Stanford: Hoover Press, Winter, 2001.

Edwards, James R. *New International Biblical Commentary: Romans.* Peabody, Massachusetts: Hendrickson Publishers, Inc., 1992.

Erisman, Albert E. "20/20 Vision in a Myopic World," *Ethix*, interview of Richard E. Stearns. Bellevue, Washington: Institute for Business, Technology & Ethics, August, 2000.

Fee, Gordon D. *New International Biblical Commentary: 1 and 2 Timothy, Titus.* Peabody, Massachusetts: Hendrickson Publishers, Inc., 1988.

Fukuyama, Francis. Trust: The Social Virtues and the Creation of Prosperity. New York: Free Press, 1995.

Fuller, R.H. and Rice, B.K. *Christianity and the Affluent Society.* Grand Rapids: William B. Eerdmans Publishing Co., 1967.

Gasque, Laurel. *Christianity and the Arts 101, Koinos Program.* Seattle: Pacific Association for Theological Studies, Spring 2000.

Gasque, W. Ward, *Christianity Monday Through Friday.* Mercer Island, Washington: Mercer Island Presbyterian Church lecture series, January, 1999.

_____, *New Testament 101, Koinos Program.* Seattle: Pacific Association for Theological Studies, Fall, 1999.

_____, "Panel #1: Religion, Egalitarianism and Economic Justice," *Theology, Third World Development and Economic Justice,* ed. Walter Block and Donald Shaw. Vancouver, B.C: The Fraser Institute, 1985.

Gibson, William E. "An Order in Crisis, and the Declaration of New Things," in *Reformed Faith and Economics* ed. Stivers,

Robert L. Lanham, Maryland: University Press of America, 1989.

Gilder, George, "The Faith of a Futurist," *The Wall Street Journal.* New York: Dow Jones Publishing Company, January 1,2000.

_____, *Recapturing The Spirit of Enterprise.* San Francisco: ICS Press, 1992.

_____, "The Soul of Silicon," *Forbes ASAP.* New York: Forbes, Inc., June 1, 1998.

_____, *Wealth and Poverty.* San Francisco: ICS Press, 1993.

_____, "Zero-Sum Folly, From Kyoto to Kosovo," *The Wall Street Journal.* New York: Dow Jones Publishing Company, May 6, 1999.

Gill, David W. *Becoming Good: Building Moral Character.* Downers Grove, Illinois: InterVarsity Press, 2000.

_____, "No Integrity, No Trust; No Trust, No Business," *Ethix,* Bellevue, Washington: Institute for Business, Technology & Ethics, October, 2000.

Gillis, Cydney, "High-tech millionaires discuss ways they cope with newfound wealth," *Eastside Journal.* Bellevue, Washington: Horvitz Newspapers, September 23, 2000.

Glasser, Susan B. "Cash-poor Russia lobbies for nuclear waste," *The Seattle Times,* Seattle: Seattle Times Publishing Company, March 18, 2001.

Goldingay, John. *How to Read the Bible.* London: Triangle, 1997.

Gooden, Winston, E. "Confidence Under Pressure," *Faith in Leadership,* ed. Banks, Robert and Powell, Kimberly S., San Francisco: Jossey-Bass Publishers, 2000.

Gorski, Isidore, "Ethical Reflections on the Economic Crisis," *Theology, Third World Development and Economic Justice,* ed. Walter Block and Donald Shaw. Vancouver, B.C: The Fraser Institute, 1985.

Greaves, Richard L. Theology and Revolution in the Scottish Reformation: *Studies in the Thought of John Knox.* Grand Rapids: Christian University Press, 1980.

Green, Joel B. *The Theology of the Gospel of Luke.* Cambridge, England: Cambridge University Press, 1995.

Greenfeld, K. T. "A New Way of Giving," *Time.* New York: Time, Inc., July 24, 2000.

Griffiths, Brian. *The Creation of Wealth.* Donners Grove, Illinois:

InterVarsity Press, 1984.

Gronbacher, Gregory M.A. *Economic Personalism: A New Paradigm for a Humane Economy.* Grand Rapids: Acton Institute, 1998.

Guinness, Os. Lecture, Seattle, Washington: Discovery Institute, February 26, 2001.

_____, "Rediscovering 'Calling' Will Revitalize Church and Society," *Religion & Liberty.* Grand Rapids: Acton Institute, 1998.

_____, *The Call.* Nashville: Word Publishing, 1998.

Guthrie, Shirley C. *Christian Doctrine.* Louisville, Kentucky: Westminster/John Knox Press, 1994.

Hagner, Donald A. *New International Biblical Commentary: Hebrews.* Peabody, Massachusetts: Hendrickson Publishers, Inc., 1990.

Hamilton, Michael S., "We're in the Money!" *Christianity Today*, June 12, 2000.

Hardy, Lee. " My Job Is Not My Calling," *WRF Comment.* Mississauga, Ontario, Canada: Work Research Foundation, Summer, 2000.

Hardy, Quentin. "The Radical Philanthropist," *Forbes.* New York: Forbes, Inc., May 1, 2000.

Havel, Vaclav as quoted in Ericson, E.E., Jr. "Living Responsibly: Vaclav Havel's View," *WRF Comment.* Ontario, Canada: Work Research Foundation, Winter, 1999.

Hawthorne, G.F. and Martin, R.P. ed. *Dictionary of Paul and His Letters.* Downers Grove, Illinois: InterVarsity Press, 1993.

Hay, Donald A. *Economics Today: A Christian Critique.* Grand Rapids: William B. Eerdmans Publishing Company, 1989.

Hayek, F.A. *The Road to Serfdom.* Chicago: University of Chicago Press, 1960.

Hayford, Jack, *Studies In The Book Of Revelation.* Van Nuys, California: Soundword Tape Ministry, 1991, sound cassettes CO438-447.

Henderson, David R. "Capitalist Culture," *Hoover Digest: Research and Opinion on Public Policy.* Stanford: Hoover Press, Fall, 1999.

Heyne, Paul. *"The Catholic Bishops and the Pursuit of Justice.* Washington, D.C.: Cato Institute.

_____, "Controlling Stories: On the Mutual Influence of Religious

Narratives and Economic Explanations" (paper presented at a
session of the Southern Economic Association conference on
"The Influence of Religion on Economics and Vice Versa,"
November, 18, 1990)

_____, *The Economic Way of Thinking, Ninth Edition.* Upper
Saddle River, N.J.: Prentice Hall, 2000.

Hillyer, Norman. *New International Biblical Commentary: 1 and 2
Peter, Jude.* Peabody, Massachusetts: Hendrickson Publishers,
Inc., 1992.

Holland, Jeffrey, various sermons and lectures. Mercer Island,
Washington: Mercer Island Presbyterian Church, 2000,1.

Hood, John M. *The Heroic Enterprise: Business and the Common
Good.* New York: The Free Press, 1996.

Huber, Peter W. "No, the Sky Is *Not* Falling," *Hoover Digest:
Research and Opinion on Public Policy.* Stanford: Hoover Press,
Winter, 2001.

Hurtado, Larry W. *New International Biblical Commentary: Mark.*
Peabody, Massachusetts: Hendrickson Publishers, Inc., 1989.

Interfaith Council for Environmental Stewardship, *The Cornwall
Declaration on Environmental Stewardship.* Grand Rapids:
Acton Institute, February 1, 2000.

Jervis, L. Ann. *New International Biblical Commentary: Galatians.*
Peabody, Massachusetts: Hendrickson Publishers, Inc., 1999.

John Paul II. *Centesimus Annus,* Encyclical Letter. Rome: May 1,
1991

Johnson, Thomas F. *New International Biblical Commentary: 1, 2,
and 3 John.* Peabody, Massachusetts: Hendrickson Publishers,
Inc., 1993.

Johnston, Robert K., ed. *The Use of the Bible in Theology: Evangelical Options.* Atlanta: John Knox Press, 1985.

Jones, Reginald H. "The Transnational Enterprise and World
Economic Development," *The Corporation: A Theological
Inquiry,* ed. Novak, Michael and Cooper, John W., Washington
D.C.: American Enterprise Institute for Public Policy Research,
1981.

Karlgaard, Rich, "Room at the Bottom," *Forbes.* New York: Forbes,
Inc, December 11, 2000.

Keynes, John Maynard. *The General Theory of Employment, Interest and Money.* London: Macmillan, 1936.

Kristol, Irving. *Two Cheers for Capitalism.* New York: Basic Books, Inc., Publishers, 1978.

Kwong, Jo. "Suburban Sprawl and Human Ecology," *Religion & Liberty.* Grand Rapids: Acton Institute, March and April, 1999.

Lacordaire, Henri Dominique. *God: Conference Delivered at Notre Dame in Paris.* London: Scribner, 1870.

LaSor, W.S., Hubbard, D.A., and Bush, F. W. *Old Testament Survey: The Message, Form and Background of the Old Testament,* 2d ed. Grand Rapids, Michigan: William B. Eerdmans Publishing Co., 1996.

Lenzner, Robert and Kellner, Tomas. "Corporate Saboteurs," *Forbes,* New York: Forbes, Inc, November 27, 2000.

Lewis, C.S. *The Abolition of Man.* London: Macmillan, 1953.

Lindblom, Charles E. *The Market System: What It Is, How It Works, and What To Make of It.* New Haven: Yale University Press, 2001.

Lindsel, Harold. *Free Enterprise: A Judeo-Christian Defense.* Wheaton, Illinois: Tyndale House Publishers, Inc., 1982.

Lipset, Seymour Martin. "Still the Exceptional Nation?" *Hoover Digest: Research and Opinion on Public Policy.* Stanford: Hoover Press, Spring, 2000.

Little, David. "Economic Justice and the Grounds for a Theory of Progressive Taxation in Calvin's Thought," in *Reformed Faith and Economics* ed. Stivers, Robert L. Lanham, Maryland: University Press of America, 1989.

Lovejoy, Arthur O. *Reflections on Human Nature.* Baltimore: Johns Hopkins University Press, 1961, as quoted by Murchland, Bernard, "The Socialist Critique of the Corporation," *The Corporation: A Theological Inquiry,* ed. Novak, Michael and Cooper, John W., Washington D.C.: American Enterprise Institute for Public Policy Research, 1981.

Mann, Thomas W. *The Book of the Torah.* Atlanta: John Knox Press, 1988.

Martin, R.P. and Davids, P.H. ed. *Dictionary of the Later New Testament & Its Developments.* Downers Grove, Illinois: Inter-Varsity Press, 1997.

McCracken, Paul W. "The Corporation and the Liberal Order," *The Corporation: A Theological Inquiry* ed. Novak, Michael and Cooper, John W., Washington, D.C: American Enterprise Institute, 1941.

McKim, Donald K. *Westminster Dictionary of Theological Terms.* Louisville: Westminster John Knox Press, 1996.

Meilaender, Gilbert C. "To Be Drawn Out of Ourselves Toward God," *Religion and Liberty.* Grand Rapids: Acton Institute, January and February, 2001.

Michaels, J. Ramsey. *New International Biblical Commentary: John.* Peabody, Massachusetts: Hendrickson Publishers, Inc., 1989.

Milne, Bruce. *Know the Truth, Rev. Ed.* Downers Grove, Illinois: InterVarsity Press, 1998.

Moltmann, Jurgen. *The Trinity and the Kingdom: The Doctrine of God.* Minneapolis: Fortress Press, 1993.

Montgomery, Lori. "After Communism's Fall," *The Seattle Times.* Seattle: Seattle Times Publishing Company, November 8, 1999.

Morais, Richard D. "Bullterrier Banking," *Forbes,* New York: Forbes, Inc, July 24, 2000.

Morse, Jennifer Roback. "Who Puts the Self in Self-Interest?" *Religion and Liberty.* Grand Rapids: Acton Institute, November and December, 1998.

Mounce, Robert H. *New International Biblical Commentary: Matthew.* Peabody, Massachusetts: Hendrickson Publishers, Inc., 1991.

"Movin' On Up," *The Wall Street Journal,* New York: Dow Jones and Company, August 17, 2000.

Moxnes, Halvor. *The Economy of the Kingdom.* Philadelphia: Fortress Press, 1988.

Murchland, Bernard, "The Socialist Critique of the Corporation," *The Corporation: A Theological Inquiry,* ed. Novak, Michael and Cooper, John W., Washington D.C.: American Enterprise Institute for Public Policy Research, 1981.

"Murder rate, serious crime plunge in U.S." *The Seattle Times.* Seattle: The Seattle Times Publishing Company, November 22, 1999.

Murphy, Cait. "The Next Revolution," *Fortune.* New York: Time, Inc., June 12, 2000.

Murphy, R. E. and Huwiler, E. *New International Biblical Commentary: Proverbs, Ecclesiastes, Song of Songs.* Peabody, Massachusetts: Hendrickson Publishers, Inc., 1999.

Murray, John. *Principles of Conduct: Aspects of Biblical Ethics.* Grand Rapids: William B. Eerdmans Publishing Co., 1957.

Nasar, Sylvia and Mitchell, Kirsten B. "Rising tide lifts young black men from joblessness," *The Seattle Times,* Seattle: The Seattle Times Publishing Company, May 23, 1999.

Nash, Ronald H. *Poverty and Wealth: The Christian Debate Over Capitalism.* Westchester, Illinois: Crossway Books, 1986.

Noll, Mark A. *Turning Points: Decisive Moments in the History of Christianity.* Grand Rapids: Baker Book House Company, 1997.

Novak, Michael. "In God We Trust," *Hoover Digest: Research and Opinion on Public Policy.* Stanford: Hoover Press, Spring, 2000.

_____, *The Fire of Invention: Civil Society and the Future of the Corporation.* Lanham, Md.: Rowman & Littlefield Publishers, Inc., 1997.

_____, *The Spirit of Democratic Capitalism.* New York: Simon and Schuster, 1982.

_____, "A Theology of the Corporation," *The Corporation: A Theological Inquiry,* ed. Novak, Michael and Cooper, John W., Washington D.C.: American Enterprise Institute for Public Policy Research, 1981.

Ostrom, Carol M. "Sudden wealth, hard questions" *The Seattle Times,* Seattle: The Seattle Times Publishing Company, November 5, 2000.

Owensby, Walter L. *Economics for Prophets.* Grand Rapids: William B. Eerdmans Publishing Co., 1988.

Patzia, Arthur G. *New International Biblical Commentary: Ephesians, Colossians, Philemon.* Peabody, Massachusetts: Hendrickson Publishers, Inc., 1990.

Paxon, Bud, quoted in Caldwell, Stephen. "Funding the Great Commission," *The Life@Work Journal.* Fayetteville, Arkansas: The Life@Work Company, March/April, 1999.

Pelikan, Jaroslav. *The Illustrated Jesus Through the Centuries.* New Haven: Yale University Press, 1997.

Pentecost, J.D. *The Words and Works of Jesus Christ; A Study of the Life of Christ.* Grand Rapids: Zondervan Publishing House, 1981.

Phillips, Cassie. "Identifying Problems and Challenges Associated with Private Forest Lands," *Washington Private Forest Forum.* Tacoma: Weyerhaeuser Company, March 29, 2000.

Powell, Jim. *The Triumph of Liberty*, New York: The Free Press, 2000.

Quinlivan, Gary M. "Multinational Corporations: Myths and Facts," *Religion & Liberty*. Grand Rapids: Acton Institute, November and December, 2000.

Remenyi, Joe and Taylor, Bill. "Credit-Based Income Generation for the Poor," in Schlossberg, H., Vinay, S. and Sider, R. ed. *Christianity and Economics in the Post-Cold War Era: The Oxford Declaration and Beyond*. Grand Rapids, Michigan: William B. Eerdmans Publishing Co., 1994.

Romer, Paul M. "It's All in Your Head," *Hoover Digest*. Stanford, CA: Hoover Press, 1999.

Rosenberg, Nathan and Birdzell, L. E., Jr. *How the West Grew Rich*. New York: Basic Books, Inc., 1986.

Rowan, Barry. *A Search for Meaning in Work*. Seattle: Barry Rowan, 1996.

Rowland, Randy. *Christian Ministry 101, Koinos Program*. Seattle: Pacific Association for Theological Studies, Spring 2000.

Sadowsky, James, "Panel #1: Religion, Egalitarianism and Economic Justice," *Theology, Third World Development and Economic Justice,* ed. Walter Block and Donald Shaw. Vancouver, B.C: The Fraser Institute, 1985.

Scalise, Pamela. *HEBREW PROPHETS*. Course OT502, Seattle: Fuller Theological Seminary, Winter, 2000.

_____, *PENTATEUCH*. Course OT501, Seattle: Fuller Theological Seminary, Fall, 1999.

_____, *WRITINGS*. Course OT504, Seattle: Fuller Theological Seminary, Winter, 2000.

Schall, James V. *Religion, Wealth and Poverty*. Vancouver, Canada: The Fraser Institute, 1990.

Schlossberg, H., Vinay, S. and Sider, R. ed. *Christianity and Economics in the Post-Cold War Era: The Oxford Declaration and Beyond*. Grand Rapids, Michigan: William B. Eerdmans Publishing Company, 1994.

Schuller, Robert H. *Prayer: My Soul's Adventure With God*. Nashville: Thomas Nelson, Inc., 1995.

Schumpeter, Joseph A. *Capitalism, Socialism, and Democracy*. New York: Harper & Brothers, 1942.

Schwarz, John E. *Word Alive! An Introduction to the Christian*

Faith. Minneapolis: Tabgha Foundation, 1993.

Schweizer, Eduard. *The Good News According to Luke,* trans. Green, D. E. Atlanta: John Knox Press, 1984.

Scott, James M. *New International Biblical Commentary: 2 Corinthians.* Peabody, Massachusetts: Hendrickson Publishers, Inc., 1998.

Sewall, Dale. *A Willingness to Be Known as Christians.* Sermon preached at Mercer Island Presbyterian Church, October 15, 2000.

"Sharing the Wealth," *Forbes.* New York: Forbes, Inc., July 3, 2000.

Shepherd, J.W. *The Christ of the Gospels.* Grand Rapids: William B. Eerdmans Publishing Co., 1946.

Sider, Ronald J. "Concrete Strategies for Implementing the Biblical Vision of Economic Justice." paper presented at the *Christian in the Marketplace* annual conference, Regent College, Vancouver, Canada, February 10, 2001.

_____, "Is There a Biblical Definition of Economic Justice?" paper presented at the *Christian in the Marketplace* annual conference, Regent College, Vancouver, Canada, February 10, 2001.

_____, *Rich Christians in an Age of Hunger.* Dallas: Word Publishing, 1997.

Simon, William E. "Talents and Stewardship," *Religion and Liberty.* Grand Rapids: Action Institute, 2000.

Sirico, Robert A. *Acton Notes.* Grand Rapids: Acton Institute, April, 1997.

_____, *Acton Notes.* Grand Rapids: Acton Institute, February, 1999.

_____, *Acton Notes.* Grand Rapids: Acton Institute, December, 2000.

_____, *Toward a Free and Virtuous Society.* Grand Rapids: Acton Institute, 1997.

Smith, Adam. *An Inquiry into the Nature and Causes of the Wealth of Nations.* (Modern Library Edition) New York: Random House, Inc., 1937 [1776].

Soards, Marion L. *New International Biblical Commentary:1 Corinthians.* Peabody, Massachusetts: Hendrickson Publishers, Inc., 1999.

Sowell, Thomas. *Barbarians Inside the Gates.* Stanford, California: Hoover Institution Press, 1999.

Sparks, John A. ed. *Is Capitalism Morally Bankrupt?* lecture series.

Grove City, Pennsylvania: Grove City College, June, 2000.

Stackhouse, John. "Money and the Church." paper presented at the *Christian in the Marketplace* annual conference, Regent College, Vancouver, Canada, February 10, 2001.

Stanley, T. J. and Danko, W. D., *The Millionaire Next Door.* New York: Simon & Schuster, Inc., 1996.

Stevens, R. Paul. "Mission field or Mission?" *Vocati.* Vancouver, Canada: Regent College Foundation, December, 2000.

Stivers, Robert L., ed. *Reformed Faith and Economics.* Lanham, Maryland: University Press of America, 1989.

Stone, Ronald H. "The Reformed Ethics of John Calvin" in *Reformed Faith and Economics* ed. Stivers, Robert L. Lanham, Maryland: University Press of America, 1989.

Stotts, Jack L. "By What Authority…?" in *Reformed Faith and Economics.* ed. Stivers, Robert L. Lanham, Maryland: University Press of America, 1989.

Strauss, Robert L. "My Road To Nowhere," *Stanford.* Stanford, California: Stanford University Alumni Association, May/June, 2000.

Tawney, R. H. *Religion and the Rise of Capitalism.* New York: Mentor, 1947.

Templeton, Sir John M. interviewed in "Ministries of Service in the Marketplace," *Religion & Liberty.* Grand Rapids: Acton Institute, November and December, 2000.

_____, quoted in Hall, Elizabeth. "Competition Seen As Spur to Expansion of Prosperity, Ethics, and Knowledge," *Progress in Theology.* Radnor, Pennsylvania: John Templeton Foundation, August, 2000.

Thomas, Gary L. *Seeking the Face of God.* Eugene, Oregon: Harvest House Publishers, 1994.

Thurow, Lester C. *The Zero-Sum Society: Distribution and the Possibilities for Economic Change.* New York: Basic Books, 1980.

Tillich, Paul. *Systematic Theology, Volume Two.* Chicago: University of Chicago Press, 1963.

Turner, Dale E. *Different Seasons.* Homewood, Illinois: High Tide Press, Inc., 1997.

_____, "Jesus a great giver, and receiver, also," *The Seattle Times.* Seattle: The Seattle Times Publishing Company, March 7, 1998.

U.S. Census Bureau, *Statistical Abstract of the United States: 1999* (119th edition) Washington D.C., 1999.

U.S. Census Bureau, *The White House Economics Statistics Briefing Room*, Internet, Washington D.C., 2000.

Veblen, Thorstein. *The Theory of the Leisure Class.* London: Macmillan, 1899.

Wall, Robert W. *New International Biblical Commentary: Revelation.* Peabody, Massachusetts: Hendrickson Publishers, Inc., 1991.

Waterman, A. M. C. "Mind Your Own Business: Unintended Consequences in the Body of Christ," *Faith and Economics.* Wenham, Massachusetts: Association of Christian Economists, Spring, 2000.

Weber, Max. *The Protestant Ethic and the Spirit of Capitalism.* New York: Scribner, 1958.

Wesley, John. "The Use of Money" read by Reed, Ronald at the *Christian in the Marketplace* annual conference, Regent College, Vancouver, Canada, February 10, 2001.

West, John G., Jr. *Public Life in the Shadowlands.* Grand Rapids: Acton Institute, 1998.

Weyerhaeuser Company, *1999 Annual Environment, Health and Safety Report.* Federal Way, Washington, 2000.

Weyerhaeuser Company, *1999 Annual Report.* Federal Way, Washington, 2000.

Wheeler, S.E. *Wealth as Peril and Obligation.* Grand Rapids: William. B. Eerdmans Publishing Co., 1995.

Williams, David J. *New International Biblical Commentary: Acts.* Peabody, Massachusetts: Hendrickson Publishers, Inc., 1990.

_____, *New International Biblical Commentary: 1 and 2 Thessalonians.* Peabody, Massachusetts: Hendrickson Publishers, Inc., 1992.

Williams, Preston N. "Calvinism, Racism, and Economic Institutions," in *Reformed Faith and Economics* ed. Stivers, Robert L. Lanham, Maryland: University Press of America, 1989.

Wilson, James Q. "Capitalism Cuts Crime," *The Wall Street Journal.* New York: Dow Jones Publishing Company, August 17, 2000.

Wright, Christopher. *New International Biblical Commentary: Deuteronomy.* Peabody, Massachusetts: Hendrickson Publishers,

Inc., 1996.

Wright, N.T. *Jesus and the Victory of God*. Minneapolis: Fortress Press, 1996.

Zakaria, Fareed. "The American Age," *Hoover Digest: Research and Opinion on Public Policy*. Stanford: Hoover Press, Summer, 2000.

Zelnick, Bob. "Why the New Populism Won't Go Away," *Hoover Digest: Research and Opinion on Public Policy*. Stanford: Hoover Press, Winter, 2001.

Acknowledgments

B ecause many of the thoughts expressed herein have been a life-time in the making, acknowledgments are rightfully due a long list of people who have influenced and directly contributed to my thinking on economic and theological matters.

In terms of this particular book I would like to express special gratitude to biblical scholar W. Ward Gasque, whose imperturbable explanations during lengthy conversations and his thorough reviews of my manuscript contributed considerably to the clarity of my thinking. He has been a marvelous faith-filled inspiring mentor.

Considerable assistance was provided by William Dorsey. His unusual background as both an ordained Baptist minister and head of a large industrial construction company provided him with a rich perspective and insight which he brought to a valuable review of my original manuscript.

Thanks are also due to Dale Sewall, Senior Pastor of Mercer Island Presbyterian Church, in whose Spirit-filled presence it is humbling to be, as well as to Blaine Charette, Associate Professor of New Testament, Northwest College, Kirkland, Washington, and Pamela Scalise, Associate Professor of Old Testament, Fuller Theological Seminary, Seattle, Washington whose insights contributed greatly to my understanding of Scripture.

Also appreciation is expressed to Jane Eagle Cable, whose mastery of English significantly improved the text, and to William

Hargrove who ably reviewed my manuscript for both conceptual and technical inconsistencies and errors.

Finally, to my beloved wife Marilyn I extend my deep gratitude for her patience through three years of my pre-occupation with this project, her diligent review of every thought and word contained in the manuscript and her loving support and encouragement. That we can share in this book means a great deal to me.

About the Author

Robert R. Richards is an economist, entrepreneur, banker and church lay leader.

After graduating with a BA in economics from the University of Washington and an MBA in business economics from the Graduate School of Business of Stanford University, he commenced his career as an economist with the Weyerhaeuser Company, culminating his role as a business economist as vice president and chief economist for the National Bank of Alaska, that state's largest bank.

He and associates founded Alaska Pacific Bank, of which he served as president and which in 1985 became the first acquisition by KeyCorp when that banking organization embarked upon its western United States expansion strategy. He reinvested the proceeds from that sale in founding with an associate The Commerce Bancorporation in Seattle of which he served as president and co-chief executive officer until his retirement in 1998.

Mr. Richards served on the faculty of Whitman College and taught economics at Pacific Lutheran University, the University of Alaska and the University of Washington. He is a member of the Association of Christian Economists and is chairman of the Visiting Committee of the Department of Economics of the University of Washington.

Mr. Richards is former chairman of the board of directors of the YMCA of Greater Seattle and currently serves as Elder for Christian Education of the Mercer Island Presbyterian Church. He is chairman of the board of directors of the Pacific Association for Theological Studies, an organization devoted to research and innovation of programs for theological education, particularly for the laity.

Mr. Richards has studied theology at Fuller Theological Seminary and is a graduate of the KOINOS certificate program in Christian foundations. For the past three years he has been in full time research, study and prayer, seeking answers to the relationship between capitalism and Christianity. This book presents his findings.

ORDERING THE BOOK

God and Business:

Christianity's Case for Capitalism

Price: $30.00

Books can be ordered by telephone directly from the publisher:

1-866-381-BOOK (2665), 24/7 toll-free

or

Books can be ordered by mail from:

Pacific Association for Theological Studies
101 Nickerson Street   Suite 330
Seattle, Washington 98109

_____ books @ $30 (tax included): $_____

Enclose check or charge to VISA or MasterCard

Card number_____

Expiration date_____

Signature_____

Your name:_____

Address:_____

_____

_____

Printed in the United States
3598